TURTLES
TORTOISES
and TERRAPINS

A NATURAL HISTORY

TURTLES
TORTOISES
and TERRAPINS

A NATURAL HISTORY

RONALD ORENSTEIN

FIREFLY BOOKS

A FIREFLY BOOK

Published by Firefly Books Ltd. 2012

Publisher Cataloging-in-Publication Data (U.S.)
Orenstein, Ron.
Turtles, tortoises and terrapins : a natural history / Ron Orenstein.
2nd ed.
[448] p. : col. photos. ; cm.
Includes bibliographical references and index.
Summary: As part of the global movement to protect turtles, this book provides important information about turtles and their ecology.
ISBN-13: 978-1-77085-119-1
1. Turtles. 2. Turtles – Life cycles. I. Title.
597.92 dc23   QL666.C5.O746   2012

Library and Archives Canada Cataloguing in Publication
Orenstein, Ronald I. (Ronald Isaac), 1946-
Turtles, tortoises and terrapins : a natural history / Ron Orenstein. -- 2nd ed.
Includes bibliographical references and index.
ISBN 978-1-77085-119-1
1. Turtles. 2. Turtles--Ecology. I. Title.
QL666.C5O74 2012   597.92   C2012-902278-0

Design: Interrobang Graphic Design Inc.

Cover photo: © Martin Woike / Age Fotostock

Printed in China

Permission to quote from *The Aye-Aye and I* was kindly granted by the Estate of Gerald Durrell.

The publisher gratefully acknowledges the financial support for our publishing program by the Government of Canada through the Canada Book Fund as administered by the Department of Canadian Heritage.

Contents

Acknowledgments

First Edition   Writing this book has been, among other things, a great learning experience. Many of the people who helped me along the way deserve my thanks not only as advisers but as teachers. My only regret is that the book is not—indeed, cannot—be long enough to include everything they taught me.

My first thanks must go to my three consultant editors, Jeanne Mortimer, Peter Pritchard, and George Zug. All three read the manuscript in its entirety, offering much advice and information and making many valuable suggestions. My visits to Peter's home and George's office were both productive and memorable, and I only wish I could have joined Jeanne in the Seychelles and Aldabra! Nonetheless, Jeanne and I worked together at the CITES Meeting in Nairobi in 2000. I count all three of my editors as valued friends. Of course, any mistakes in this book are my responsibility, not theirs.

I must also thank Anders Rhodin and Marydele Donnelly for their encouragement and help in the early stages, and Anders deserves a vote of thanks from all turtle enthusiasts for spearheading the invaluable journal Chelonian Conservation and Biology, which he co-edits with John Behler and Peter Pritchard.

I received help, encouragement and advice on specific portions of the text from a number of turtle biologists and other experts. Once again, the responsibility for any errors is mine, but my thanks must go to Randall Arauz, Brian Bagatto, John Behler, Peter Bennett, Kurt Buhlmann, John Cann, Joanna Durbin, Lee Durrell, Jack Frazier, Terry Graham, Karen Holloway-Adkins, Donald Jackson, Rod Kennett, Ursula Keuper-Bennett, Faith Kostel-Hughes, Colin Limpus, Ron Nussbaum, Gary Packard, Frank Paladino, Charles Peterson, Grahame Webb, and particularly to Robert Reisz, who not only read over the entire chapter on turtle evolution, but took the time to invite me to his office and untangle, slowly and carefully, the almost baroque controversy over turtle origins.

My thanks, also, to the many friends and colleagues (and a few total strangers) who answered my questions, provided reprints, chased down obscure bits of information, or simply cheered me up when the slogging got heavy. They include Sandra Altherr, Solomon Aquilera, Sali Bache, George Balazs, Allen Bolten, Marny Bonner, Carol Britson, Juan Carlos Cantu, Kathryn Craven, Osha Gray Davidson, Claudia Delgado, Karen Eckert, Scott Eckert, Daniela Freyer, Eugene Gaffney, Hedelvy Guada, Marinus Hoogmoed, Douglas Hykle, Frank Ippolito, RC "Hank" Jenkins, Shirley McGreal, Barry Kent Mackay, John Levell, Peter Lutz, Peter Meylan, Ann Michels, Russell Mittermeier, Nicholas Mrosovsky, José Truda Palazzo, Doug Perrine, Nicholas Pilcher, Pamela Plotkin, Damaris Rotich, Anne Roy, Allen Salzberg, Chloe Schauble, Jeanette Schnars,

Diane Scott, Dionysius S.K. Sharma, Jessica Speart, James Spotila, Teresa Telecky, Wayne Van Devender, John Wehr, Blair Witherington, Frank Bambang Yuwono, and many posters to the internet discussion list CTURTLE. I'm sure there are others I have forgotten to mention, and to them I offer both my thanks and my apologies.

In particular, I would like to thank the organizers, speakers, poster presenters, and the many other people who attended the 21st Annual Symposium on Sea Turtle Biology and Conservation in February 2001. For education, enthusiasm, and inspiration, the symposium was hard to beat. This book would be much poorer had I not been able to be there, and my thanks to Dan Morast and the International Wildlife Coalition for making it possible.

To Key Porter Books, and in particular to Susan Renouf and to Janice Zawerbny, my long-suffering editor, my thanks for their patience, their encouragement, and their occasional threats as this seemingly endless project wound down to the wire.

Finally my thanks to my parents, Charles and Mary Orenstein, without whose support I would have accomplished very little, and to my children, Randy and Jenny, for their (more or less) reasonable tolerance as their father disappeared from view, for days on end, into a world of turtles.

Second Edition　 A great deal has happened in the fields of turtle biology and turtle conservation in the last ten years, and preparing this revised edition has proven a daunting task. Fortunately I had help, and the good wishes and support of many people.

Peter Pritchard took on the role of consultant editor for the entire book; I am very grateful to him, and to both Peter and his wife Sibilla for their hospitality at their home in Oviedo, Florida. I must also single out Peter Paul van Dijk, who thoroughly reviewed Chapters 3 and 4, and provided me with a great deal of relevant, up-to-date and (in many cases) highly entertaining information. Chris Shepherd of TRAFFIC Southeast Asia reviewed much of Chapter 9. Robert Reisz provided me with many useful insights on advances in turtle paleontology, including his own first-hand observations of *Odontochelys semitestacea*. Karen and Scott Eckert reviewed portions of the text on sea turtles, and Richard Vogt and Nicole Valenzuela provided invaluable guidance on the intricacies of sex determination in turtles.

In addition, the following people generously provided me with assistance, guidance and information, including review of sections of the text referring to their work: Jérémy Anquetin, Heide Burke, Jérôme Bourjea, Constance Browne, Luis Cardona, Judith Cebra-Thomas, Pelf Nyok Chen, Fung Chen Chung, Jon Costanzo, Ben Creisler, Cajus Diedrich, Michael G. Frick, Christine Griffiths, Graeme Hays, Wen-San Huang, John Iverson, Fredric Janzen, Shigeru Kuratani, Peter Lindeman, Johan Lindgren, Heather Lowe, Luca Luiselli, Katherine Mansfield, Nikolay Natchev, Ryan T. Paitz, Maurizio Percipalle, Kevin J. Peterson, John H. Roe, Michael Salmon, Jeffrey Seminoff, Rick Shine, Juliana Sterli, C. Richard Tracy, Ingmar Werneburg, Matthew Wolak, Xiao-chun Wu, and Judith Zbinden.

I am also grateful for the help and advice I received from members of the IUCN Tortoise and Freshwater Turtle Specialist Group via their listserve, and in particular to the group's former chair Anders G.J. Rhodin.

As a consequence of the closure of the original publisher, it was impossible to re-use all of the illustrations from the first edition. Most of the photographs in this edition are new, and I must thank some of the people who helped me obtain them. I am particularly grateful to John Cann, Indraneil Das, and David Peters, who provided many excellent photographs and art work including some images previous readers will recognize. Chun Li and Xiao-chun Wu kindly gave permission for me to include illustrations of the remarkable fossil turtle *Odontochelys semitestacea*, surely the most astonishing testudine discovery of the last ten years.

For giving me the chance to undertake this revision I must thank Firefly Books, and in particular their senior editor Michael Mouland. Finally (but most importantly), a special thank you—for just about everything—to my wife, Eileen Yen Ee Lee.

A Word about Words

"When we were little," the Mock Turtle went on at last, more calmly,
though still sobbing a little now and then, *"we went to school in the sea.
The master was an old Turtle—we used to call him Tortoise."*
"Why did you call him Tortoise, if he wasn't one?" Alice asked.
"We called him Tortoise because he taught us," said the Mock Turtle
angrily: *"really you are very dull!"*

—LEWIS CARROLL, ALICE'S ADVENTURES IN WONDERLAND

The first problem that faces someone trying to write a popular book about the members of the Order Testudines is what to call them. Different corners of the English-speaking world use the names turtle, tortoise, and terrapin in contradictory ways. Originally, the word turtle meant sea turtles only. Freshwater turtles were terrapins, and their heavy-footed land-based relatives were tortoises. That is still the usage in England (where, of course, there are no turtles, except for the occasional sea turtle). South Africans tend to follow British usage, calling their freshwater turtles terrapins even though most of them belong to a quite different branch of the Testudines order from the terrapins of the Northern Hemisphere. In North America, the name terrapin became restricted to a single species, the Diamondback Terrapin (*Malaclemys terrapin*). All other freshwater turtles, unless they were specifically called something else, like cooter (an African-derived word) or slider, became simply turtles.

Meanwhile, in Australia, where "true" tortoises do not exist, everything that was not a sea turtle, including some animals that almost never leave the water, was called a tortoise. Today, the tendency in Australia is to call them all turtles instead.

I have decided, for the purposes of this book, to adopt, by and large, the North American usage. In this book, then, when I say "turtles" I mean the whole lot, tortoises and terrapins thrown in. For the scientific names of individual species, but not always for English ones, I follow *Turtles of the World, 2011 Update: Annotated Checklist of Taxonomy, Synonymy, Distribution, and Conservation Status*, the most recent list of the turtles of the world adopted by the Turtle Taxonomy Working Group of the IUCN Tortoise and Freshwater Turtle Specialist Group (TFTSG). I have followed the 2011 update in capitalizing English names of species and subspecies. I use the South African name padloper (which means "trailwalker" in Afrikaans) for the pygmy tortoises of the genus *Homopus*, for no better reason than that I like the way it sounds.

Why Turtles Matter

"Turtles," Anders Rhodin of the Chelonian Research Foundation wrote over ten years ago, "are in terrible trouble." I began the preface to the first edition of this book with his words. For the second edition I can do no better than quote him again, this time from a statement he made in 2011: "Turtles are in serious trouble. They are some of the world's most endangered vertebrates, more than mammals, birds, or even highly endangered amphibians."

Few herpetologists—the scientists who study reptiles and amphibians—would disagree with him. His 2011 statement was made upon the release of a multi-authored report, *Turtles in Trouble: The World's 25+ Most Endangered Tortoises and Freshwater Turtles—2011*, detailing just how bad things are. Half of the turtle species in the world are threatened with extinction. There is hardly a place left on earth, land or sea where turtles are safe. In some places, most particularly in southern Asia where forests and rivers are being swept clean of turtles to supply growing and voracious markets for food and pets, their situation is little short of desperate. Some species have probably already disappeared; more will almost certainly do so, or be reduced to an existence in captive colonies, despite efforts we make to save them. Pollution, habitat destruction, overhunting, climate change and disease strike at species after species. During the last five years of the 20th century, populations of the largest turtle in the world, the Leatherback Sea Turtle (*Dermochelys coriacea*), collapsed throughout the Pacific Ocean. Poachers are stealing the beautiful Radiated Tortoise (*Astrochelys radiata*), even from national parks. The unique Central American River Turtle (*Dermatemys mawii*), the only living representative of its family, is being eaten out of existence.

There is more to turtles than most of us know. We think of them as the quintessence of slowness. When Camille Saint-Saëns assigned music to the tortoise in *Carnival of the Animals*, it was Jacques Offenbach's famous cancan—played at a glacial pace. But anyone who lets a careless hand get too close to an angry snapper or softshell will learn just how rapidly a turtle can move. The Big-headed Turtle (*Platysternon megacephalum*) of Southeast Asia can scale a slippery boulder or even climb into a tree. The Pig-nose Turtle (*Carettochelys insculpta*) of Australasia can dart away at four times the speed of a swimming human, and a sea turtle can fly through the water with balletic grace.

Imagine if turtles had vanished long ago, with the dinosaurs, and we knew them only from fossils. Surely we would be amazed that such bizarre creatures, sealed in bone, ribs welded to their shells, had existed; had ranged successfully almost throughout the world, in deserts, rivers, and forests, and far out into the open sea; had dug burrows that became homes for other creatures; had a role to play in the habitats where they lived. We would regret that we had missed the opportunity to see them plodding their way through ancient forests, beneath the feet of monsters.

But turtles, unlike so many other reptiles of past ages, did survive, and for many of us they are a commonplace. Some of us think of them with amusement, as comic-strip characters, plush toys for children, or dancing, top-hatted figures on a box of candy. For others, turtles are a source of food and income, whether from selling a tortoise as a pet or showing tourists a sea turtle laboriously digging its nest in the sand. For some, turtles are even an object of veneration, to be protected and fed on the grounds of a temple. Humankind sees turtles as anything but what they really are: highly evolved, remarkable creatures, necessary components of their shrinking and ever more degraded ecosystems. We in the West have ceased to be amazed by them.

I have written this book because turtles do amaze me. I am not a herpetologist but an ornithologist, a student of birds, and turtles were always on the periphery of my attention. I could not help, though, collecting bits and pieces of information about them, and the more I learned the more astonished I became at the sheer range of adaptation in such superficially humble creatures.

As I have gone on from ornithology to a career in wildlife conservation, lobbying against the excesses of the international wildlife trade, turtles have come more and more into the center of my vision. In recent years, I have supported the ban on international trade in tortoiseshell, the beautiful scutes of the Hawksbill Sea Turtle (*Eretmochelys imbricata*), and joined efforts to regulate the almost uncontrolled turtle markets of eastern Asia. I have tried to become not just an admirer of turtles but one of their advocates.

If you are not one already, I hope that this book will make you, too, their admirer and advocate. Turtles should fill you with a sense of wonder, and our treatment of them should fill you with a sense of concern. I know it is entirely unscientific to ascribe human qualities to the processes of evolution, but it is hard not to admire turtles for their sheer doggedness in having successfully made it this far; that they are here for us to wonder at means that we should wonder at them, and make sure that our children and grandchildren have the chance to do the same.

In 1953, the authors of *Reptiles and Amphibians: A Guide to Familiar American Species* wrote that turtles (and lizards, and snakes) "are interesting and unusual, although of minor importance. If they should all disappear, it would not make much difference one way or the other." Although we know better today, it is our generation that is presiding over their disappearance.

It is up to us to rescue turtles from the terrible trouble in which we have placed them. Turtles matter because of what they are; because of the path they have taken; because of their role in the natural world; because of their impact, over the centuries, on our society, culture and even our religions. They matter because it would be shameful if their long tread through 200 million years of evolutionary history should end through our negligence, our greed and our failure to act.

PART ONE

WHAT TURTLES ARE

CHAPTER ONE

The Essential Turtle

I ONCE ASKED a professor of mine, a noted authority on the anatomy and biology of turtles, why he had devoted his life to their study.

"I have great respect," he replied solemnly, "for any animal that can get its shoulder girdle inside its rib cage."

My professor, Dr. Thomas S. Parsons, was only half joking. He had, in fact, put his finger on one of the things that makes turtles so puzzling and fascinating: the fact that almost everything about them, from their inside out, represents a tremendous evolutionary distortion of what we expect from the body of a land vertebrate. That distortion—including the weird relationship between ribs and shoulder girdle that so fascinated Dr. Parsons—is the product of a marvelous series of evolutionary adjustments that have refitted turtles for life encased in their single most notable and distinctive feature: the shell. The shell does not merely encase a turtle; to a great extent, it defines what a turtle is. It has meant redesigning much of a turtle's internal anatomy simply to allow it to carry out normal, everyday functions—functions as basic as breathing.

How does a turtle, locked inside its shell, take a breath? Other armored vertebrates, such as armadillos, have soft bellies that can move as they inhale or, like the trunkfishes puttering around coral reefs, do not have lungs at all. Only turtles face the challenge of filling their lungs while sealed, above and below, in a case of armor (though admittedly the plastron, the portion of the armor covering the belly, may be flexible, especially in sea turtles). They cannot expand their ribs to breathe, as we do, because their ribs are fused to the shell itself.

OVERLEAF

A Green Sea Turtle (*Chelonia mydas*) swims over the reefs of Sipadan Island, Sabah, Malaysia, beneath a school of Bigeye Jacks (*Caranx sexfasciatus*).

OPPOSITE

The carapace and plastron of these Steindachner's Snake-necked Turtles (*Chelodina steindachneri*) are joined together by a bony bridge.

As we shall see at the end of this chapter, turtles have found not just one way to breathe, but several. As specialized, constrained, and uniform as turtles seem to be, they have shown, in this and other ways, a remarkable ability to adapt and change. This ability has carried them, through 200 million years of evolution, around the world and into almost every conceivable habitat except the polar wastes and the deep sea. In all of these areas, turtles have found ways to thrive. Their shell, far from being a restriction, has been a key to their survival, and to their adaptability.

Therefore, to understand the essential nature of turtles, we must begin with the shell.

Scutes and Plates

The turtle shell is a composite, built of elements from the surface strata of the skin, others from deeper skin layers, and still others from deep within the turtle's body. It is made up of two main sections: one covering the upper side of the body, called the *carapace*, and a second, the *plastron*, protecting its underside. In most turtles, the carapace and plastron are locked together on each side by *bridges*. The bridges are more than simply links; they form a brace. The bridges and plastron form a solid band of bone across the bottom of the carapace, and make the whole shell considerably harder to crush.

Turtle carapaces may be quite flat or steeply domed, almost circular or elongate (or even vaguely rectangular), smooth and polished or rough, sculptured, saw-backed or even spiny. The plastron may be an extensive, thickened breastplate or a cross-shaped remnant. It is usually flat, though in many male turtles—most tortoises, which mate on land, in particular—the middle or rear portion of the plastron is concave, a useful shape for an animal that has to mount a female with an unyielding, rounded carapace (see page 270, Chapter 7).

The outer surface of the shell usually consists of a series of epidermal plates, called scutes, arranged in distinctive patterns. A typical turtle has 54 scutes: 38 on the carapace and 16 on the plastron. The scutes around the margin of the carapace are called *marginals*, while the row running down the center of a turtle's back, over its vertebral column, are the *vertebrals* (except for the very first one, which is called the *cervical* or *nuchal* because it overlies the neck). Running down the sides of the carapace between the vertebrals and marginals are a row of four *pleurals*. The scutes of the plastron have names, too, such as gular, humeral, pectoral, abdominal and so on.

There are variations on this arrangement in some turtles. The number of scutes may differ, even among individuals. Though most turtles have 12 pairs of marginals, the Assam Roofed Turtle (*Pangshura sylhetensis*) has 13, and mud turtles and musk turtles (Kinosterninae) have only 11 (or 9, according to authorities who consider one pair, the *humerals*, to be single split scutes rather than two separate ones). Their Central American relatives in the subfamily Staurotypinae have only 8 pairs. The Alligator Snapping Turtle (*Macrochelys temminckii*), with some fossil turtles, has an extra row of small scutes above the marginals, called *supramarginals*. Softshell turtles (Trionychidae), the Pig-nose Turtle (*Carettochelys insculpta*) and the Leatherback Sea Turtle (*Dermochelys coriacea*) have no scutes at all, though there are vestiges of them in very young leatherbacks. Instead, their shells are covered by leathery skin.

Scutes normally abut against one another, interlocking like tiles in a mosaic. In some turtles, the scutes on the carapace may overlap. The carapacial scutes of a young Hawksbill Sea Turtle (*Eretmochelys imbricata*) are drawn out, as it grows, into backwards-facing points lying over one other like shingles.

Scutes are really giant scales. They are not made of bone, and for good reason. Bone is highly porous, full of passages for blood vessels, and weathers

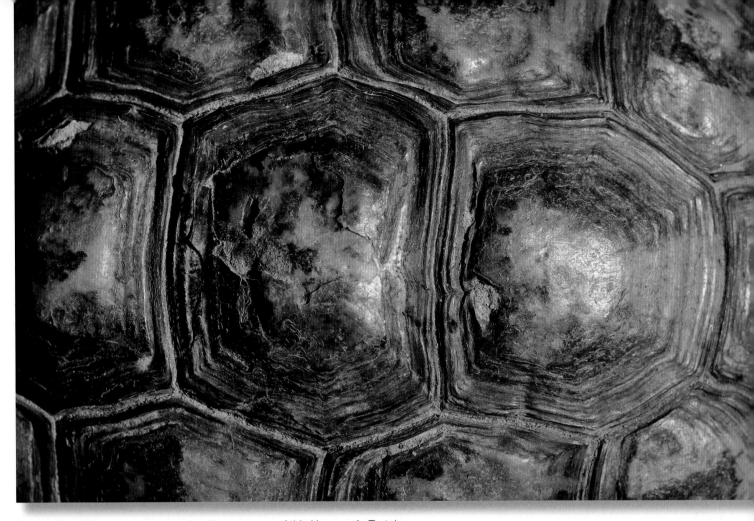

The keratin plates, or scutes, covering the carapace of this Hermann's Tortoise (*Testudo hermanni*) are roughened and ornamented.

rapidly when exposed to the open air. Scutes are made, instead, of a much more durable substance: the protein *keratin*, which is the same material that makes up your hair and fingernails, the feathers of birds, and the rhinoceros's horn.

Like other scales, scutes form in the outer layer of skin, the *epidermis*. Turtle epidermis produces two types of keratin: a flexible material called α-keratin found in almost all vertebrates, including ourselves, and β-keratin, a hard and brittle compound only found in reptiles (including birds). The carapace of softshell, pig-nose, and leatherback turtles is covered by a leathery skin with a surface made entirely of α-keratin; however, β-keratin is the only kind of keratin in the shell of most turtles. Tortoiseshell—the scutes of the hawksbill sea turtle—is β-keratin. Plates of it can even be welded together.

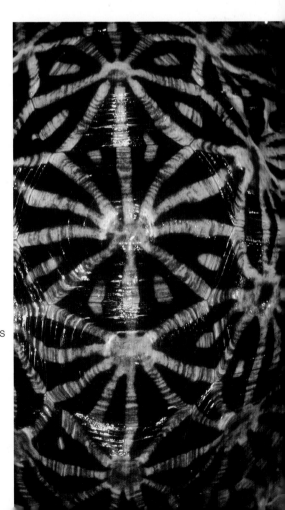

Deposits of color on its growing scutes create sunburst patterns on the carapace of the Geometric Tortoise (*Psammobates geometricus*).

As each scute grows outward (often asymmetrically) from its central nucleus, or *areola*, deposits of color may form rings or eyespots, as on the plastra of young sliders (*Trachemys* spp.), or rays streaming out from the areolae to form the sunburst patterns of tent tortoises (*Psammobates* spp.) or the Indian Star Tortoise (*Geochelone elegans*). Each scute develops its own pattern. Only rarely do the patterns cross from scute to scute; it is as though each scute is a separately designed tile, independently painted but forming part of a greater mosaic.

Bright colors and patterns adorn the plastra of turtles in many families, including the Spiny Turtle (*Heosemys spinosa*, below right), D'Orbigny's Slider (*Trachemys dorbigni*, below left), and the Variable Mud Turtle (*Pelusios rhodesianus*, right).

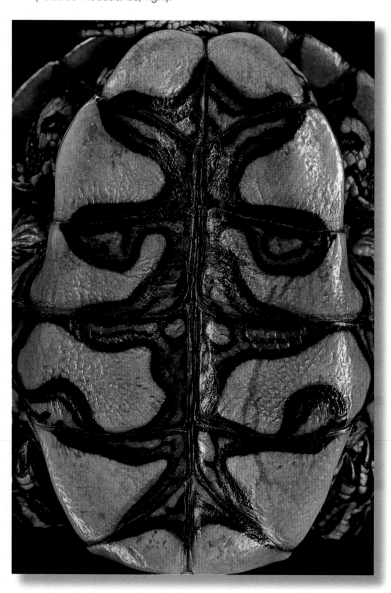

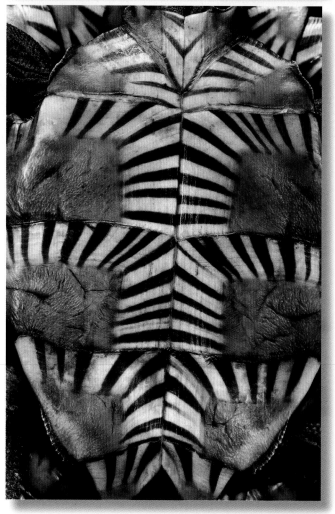

Many turtles grow darker, and their shell patterns grow more obscure (or, sometimes, more complex), as they age. Western Painted Turtles (*Chrysemys picta bellii*), particularly males, tend to develop a network of narrow dark lines on the carapace once they mature. What purpose (if any) this *reticulate melanism* serves remains unclear. The color of a turtle's carapace may match the surrounding environment. African Leopard Tortoises (*Stigmochelys pardalis*) tend to be paler in dry areas, and a richer buff in wetter regions where the soil is darker. Black Spiny Softshells (*Apalone spinifera atra*) tend to be at their blackest in the deeper lagoons within their tiny Mexican range.

Some turtles can even grow darker or lighter, though this hardly makes them shelled chameleons. The process, apparently under hormonal control, can take weeks or months. Eastern Snake-necked Turtles (*Chelodina longicollis*) that researchers switched from black to white backgrounds took 30 days to change color. Not all turtles react to their background in the same way. The carapaces of captive hatchling Midland Painted Turtles (*Chrysemys picta marginata*) grew lighter when the hatchlings were raised on white backgrounds, but did not darken against black backgrounds. Red-eared Sliders (*Trachemys scripta elegans*) in the same experiment darkened on black backgrounds, but remained unchanged against white ones.

Each year, a new scute forms beneath the previous year's. Sliders, map turtles and some others may shed the old scute entirely. Macleay River (*Emydura macquarii*), Eastern Snake-necked, and Painted Turtles (*Chrysemys picta*) shed only the outer layer of their old scutes. The Big-headed Turtle (*Platysternon megacephalum*) loses its old scutes in flakes, while tortoises do not lose theirs at all. Instead, their old and new scutes pile up in layers like the steps of a (more or less) flattened pyramid. As the new scute is larger than its predecessor, its outer edge shows around the perimeter of the older one in the form of a growth ring or band (often called an *annulus*). The bands are arranged in concentric polygons around the areola. In strongly

seasonal climates, turtles alternate periods of activity and rapid growth with months of inactivity and slow growth. The bands trace this annual cycle of feast and famine, and are pronounced in turtles that shed the outer layer of their scutes at more or less regular intervals. Like the growth rings of a tree, the annuli can sometimes give some idea of their bearer's age. Their accuracy, however, may vary from species to species, from area to area, from youth to old age, or even from individual to individual. Multiple rings may occasionally form in a single year. Counting rings is not, in general, a reliable way to age a turtle.

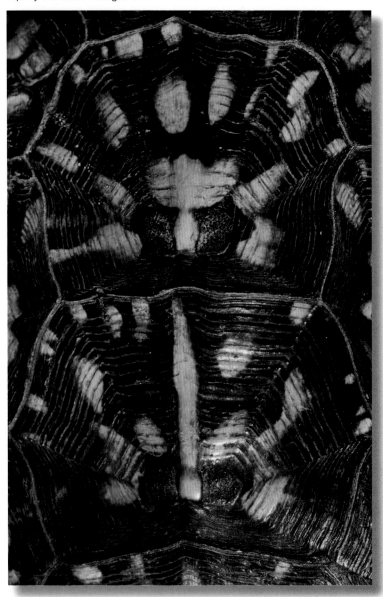

Growth rings, or annuli, on the carapace of an Eastern Box Turtle (*Terrapene carolina*). The wider the annuli, the more rapidly the turtle has grown.

Wide bands show good growth, while narrow bands imply poor growth. A fair-sized Bell's Hinged Tortoise (*Kinixys belliana*) from Africa may only have a few annuli on the scutes of its plastron, suggesting that it has grown very rapidly over a short time. By contrast, a Spider Tortoise (*Pyxis arachnoides*) from Madagascar, a much smaller animal, may have numerous bands closely packed together, a sign that it has taken many years to reach even its diminutive proportions.

The (Very) Old Shell Game

If you could peel the scutes away (or if you can find a long-dead turtle shell), you would uncover another layer of plates, this time made of bone. There are normally 59 of them, though the exact count may vary: 50 in the carapace, and 9 in the plastron. They are arranged in a pattern similar to the arrangement of the scutes, but not, as you might expect, identical. As an embryo turtle develops within its shell, the scutes form before the bony plates beneath them. Each scute is not exactly matched to a bone below. This mismatch adds to the overall strength of the shell, like the different layers in a sheet of plywood.

The bones of the shell have their own names. Those around the margin of the carapace are not called marginals but *peripherals*. The bones underlying the vertebral scutes are called *neurals* because they correspond to the neural spines of the vertebrae, the arches through which the spinal cord passes. These bones are reduced in some side-necked turtles, and in some members of the family Chelidae, including members of the genera *Emydura* and *Platemys*, the neurals are no longer visible. Between the neurals and the peripherals lie the largest carapacial bones, the *costals*, so-called because they overlie the ribs, or costae. A few of the other bones of the carapace have individual names, and the bones of the plastron all have names ending, quite reasonably, in "plastron."

Bone is an invention of the vertebrates. There is nothing particularly unusual about a vertebrate covered with bony armor. There are armored fishes, lizards, crocodiles, and mammals. Turtle armor is unusual because of the kind of bone that goes into its makeup.

We soft-skinned humans tend to think of bone as something that forms deep within our bodies; however, the very earliest bone to evolve actually formed within the underlayer of the skin called the dermis, and so is known as *dermal bone*. Our facial bones are largely dermal, as are the only part of our skeleton we can actually see: the enamel of our teeth.

The first fishes, 450 million years ago, had a skeleton of dermal bone around the outside of their bodies, but no bone at all on the inside. Internal bone did not come along for millions of years. The earliest internal skeletons were formed not of bone but of cartilage, as are the skeletons of sharks today. The first internal bone either formed around this cartilage or within it. Bone that forms within cartilage, like the bones of our vertebral column, shoulder and hip girdles, and arms and legs, is called *endochondral bone*.

All of the armored vertebrates we know of, except turtles, have armor composed entirely of dermal bone. The turtle shell, alone among all the types of armor that vertebrates have developed since the first fishes swam, combines dermal bone with elements from deep within the skeleton, particularly the ribs and the vertebral column.

The question of the true nature of the turtle carapace has vexed anatomists and developmental biologists for more than two centuries. As far back as 1800 the great zoologist Georges Cuvier opined that the carapace was simply an expansion of the ribs and the spines of the vertebrae. The idea that dermal bone might be involved was first proposed in 1834 by the remarkable polymath Carl Gustav Carus, whose accomplishments included painting, anatomy, psychology, and medicine. The debate eventually focused primarily on the origin of the costals, the bones that form the bulk of the carapace's bony structure.

In a turtle embryo, the costals depend for their organization and growth on the way the ribs form as they grow out from the vertebral column. In most other land vertebrates the growing ribs curve around the chest cavity, but not in turtles. Turtle ribs grow outward, like the spokes of a wheel, toward a band of thickened tissue called the *carapacial ridge*, a turtle peculiarity that marks the edge of the still-developing shell. As the tip of the developing rib enters the carapacial ridge, it releases special proteins, called *fibroblast growth factors* (FGFs), that interact with other FGFs from the ridge itself and coordinate the merger that integrates the ribs into the superstructure of the shell.

Meanwhile, the costals begin to take shape. As the ribs stretch toward the carapacial ridge, they move outside the layers that would normally lie above them—layers that form the muscle and connective tissue surrounding the ribs in other animals. Once this happens, these layers degenerate and disappear. The developing ribs end up lying just under the surface of the skin, embedded in a layer of dermal tissue. Plates of bone—the developing costals—begin to assemble both around the ribs and in the dermal spaces between them. From an embryologist's point of view, because they arise by a process called *intramembranous ossification* instead of being pre-formed in cartilage, these plates are dermal bone. However, because their growth is controlled and organized by chemical signals from the ribs, and because, in time, the plates and the ribs fuse together, the final result ends up as a mixture of dermal and endochondral elements.

You can see the result most easily on the inside of an empty turtle carapace. Here, the vertebral column and ribs stand out like roof beams, bracing the shell. The ribs are short, and are fused to the undersurface. So are most of the 10 trunk vertebrae; only the first and last are merely attached to the carapace, rather than fused with it. Buttressing ribs stretch out and over the animal's shoulders. This is the source of Dr. Parsons' paradox: in order for the ribs to become the supporting buttresses of the carapace, they have to lie not inside the shoulder and hip girdles, but above and outside them.

This oddest of anatomical shifts is a consequence of the way the embryo develops into something that is, recognizably, a turtle. As vertebrate embryos grow, their body walls begin to fold inward, and the way the various layers fold determines the shape and position of the organs that develop from them. In turtles, the body wall not only folds but twists; a bit of embryonic origami that brings the developing carapace, rib cage, and shoulder girdle into the peculiar positions they eventually occupy. The turtle shoulder girdle actually develops in front of the rib cage, exactly where it ought to in a non-turtle. It ends up inside the rib cage because the growing second rib (the first rib in turtles is very small), instead of pointing backward, extends forward over the developing shoulder girdle as it reaches out to the front of the carapacial ridge.

As the carapace assumes its final form, more plates of bone, including the future peripherals, form a ring around the edges of the carapace. At this stage, the combination of the vertebral column, ribs and encircling plates resembles a carriage wheel. The enclosed spaces between the ribs and the shell margin—between the spokes of the wheel—are called *fontanelles*. In a few species the fontanelles remain more or less open, but in most turtles they eventually fill in with bone, spreading from rib to rib until the carapace is complete. Hatchling turtles usually have another fontanelle in the center of the plastron. In the Arrau (*Podocnemis expansa*) the plastral fontanelle takes seven months to close. In many side-necked turtles the fontanelle is closed upon hatching, but in some turtles it never closes completely.

There are endochondral bones in the plastron as well, though their identity is less obvious. Two of the plates at the front end of the plastron may be the transformed remnants of the clavicles (the bones that form our collarbone) and portions of the coracoids, bones otherwise attached to the shoulder girdle. The rest of the plastron appears to be purely dermal bone, an entirely new structure with no equivalent in the skeletons of other reptiles. Just possibly, though, it may be partly derived from abdominal ribs, or *gastralia*, dermal elements that float freely in the underside of some reptiles where we have our breastbone.

What Are Turtle Shells Good For?

If there is any question about turtles that might not seem to need answering, surely it is this one. The turtle shell is, as almost anyone would tell you, its "house"—the place to which the turtle retreats for protection from its enemies. Turtle shells certainly do protect their owners against attack by predators (unless the predators are big enough to swallow them whole!). This is probably true even for sea turtles, which are incapable of withdrawing their head and limbs. This obvious answer, though, is not the only one.

A turtle or tortoise on land may spend, or its ancestors may have once spent, much of its life under the feet of herds of bison or troops of wildebeest. They may have had less to fear from being eaten than from being stepped on. The Ornate Box Turtle (*Terrapene ornata*) of central North America has a taste for the insects in dung, and risks being trampled as it roots for them on cattle trails. Its high, domed carapace may be harder to crush than the flattened shells of its more aquatic relatives. In a tortoise, the bony bridge and the plastron combine to lock the sides of the carapace together, making it even more difficult to crush from above. Some tortoises, like the Leopard Tortoise of Africa, further protect themselves by growing rapidly to a size too great for even the most negligent ungulate to miss (though its shell is still vulnerable to the attacks of ground hornbills).

Large turtles have stronger shells than small ones. A 400 g (14 oz) Ornate Box Turtle is only eight times heavier than a 50 g (1.8 oz) youngster, but its shell is 13 times more massive. Box turtles, though, are comparatively small and have lost the

The domed shape of the carapace of this Ornate Box Turtle (*Terrapene ornata*) makes it harder to crush if the animal is stepped on.

bony bridge that adds structural rigidity to a completely braced shell. Possibly to compensate, they have fused the bones of their carapace into a single unit, a process called *ankylosis*. This fusion may make the shell less likely to spread apart and split open if something steps on it; however, it may make it easier to shatter. If a crack starts, it may continue right across the carapace instead of stopping at a suture between separate plates of bone.

Ankylosis comes with a cost. The bones of the shell grow at their edges, so without those edges a turtle can no longer grow. Once the process of ankylosis is completed, an individual box turtle is as big as it will ever get. The trade-off in increased shell strength may make up for its inability to grow large enough for a bison to notice.

Oddly enough, the Central American River Turtle (*Dermatemys mawii*), which almost never comes out of the water, also has a fully ankylosed shell at maturity. So do three highly aquatic (and highly endangered) Asian turtles: the Northern and Southern River Terrapins (*Batagur baska* and *B. affinis*) and the Painted Terrapin (*B. borneensis*). Why, we don't know. The only tortoises to have full ankylosis belonged to an extinct genus, *Cylindraspis*, from the Mascarene Islands in the Indian Ocean. *Cylindraspis* tortoises were medium-large animals, sharing the islands with nothing larger than turkey-sized flightless birds like the dodo. It is hard to imagine what they did with the extra strength, assuming they had it at all; the shells of *Cylindraspis* tortoises were quite thin.

In tortoises, the shell may be as much for offense as for defense. Many male tortoises use the thickened leading edge of the plastron as a butting and ramming weapon, either to drive off a rival or to batter a female into submission. In a few species, including the Angulate Tortoise (*Chersina angulata*) of South Africa and, especially, the rare Ploughshare Tortoise or Angonoka (*Astrochelys yniphora*) of Madagascar, the front of the male's plastron juts forward to form a prominent and highly effective hook. This hook can be a lever to flip a rival over, or even a goring weapon that can cause serious injury. In the African Spurred Tortoise (*Geochelone sulcata*) the paired gulars at the front of the plastron form a double ramming structure. The less aggressive Asian Brown Tortoise (*Manouria emys*) uses its thickened gulars to help it burrow in leaf litter, and the Texas Tortoise (*Gopherus berlandieri*) uses them to help scoop out its resting place, or pallet, in the soil (though this does not explain why they are larger in males).

The shell can provide protection against the elements. Many tortoises live in open country, where desiccation in the hot sun is a real threat. By greatly reducing the area of skin that it exposes to the sun, its shell may keep a tortoise from drying out. Moreover, the shells of many tortoises and box turtles may help them to survive the fires that can sweep their habitats (though Agassiz's Desert Tortoises (*G. agassizii*), shell or no shell, are more likely to survive if they hide in their burrows). In northern Greece, fires caused a 40 percent mortality rate in a population of Hermann's Tortoise (*Testudo hermanni*), but large adults were able to survive even if all their scutes burned away. Eastern Box Turtles (*Terrapene carolina*), which often live among dry leaf litter, are particularly susceptible to fires, though they can recover from severe burns. Pioneering turtle biologist Archie Carr once remarked that box turtles "appear to have no notion of how to escape an advancing blaze." Healing and reconstruction, even in such tough animals as these, has its limits. If an adult box turtle is damaged by fire, when its shell heals it may no longer have separate, identifiable scutes.

Even sea turtles, which surely cannot encounter fire very often, may be able to recover from burning. Some indigenous people used to remove Hawksbill Sea Turtle scutes by roasting the animal alive over a fire, and then return the victim to the sea in the belief that the animal would heal and grow a new set of scutes. How many turtles survived this, though, is unknown.

The shell of this Eastern Box Turtle (*Terrapene carolina*) has been damaged by fire, but the turtle has survived.

There are more subtle uses for a turtle's shell. The shell of the North American Painted Turtle (*Chrysemys picta*) may be crucial to its ability—remarkable for an air-breathing animal—to spend months every winter beneath the ice of a frozen pond. During those long weeks the turtle functions entirely without breathing air and to a very great extent without oxygen at all (see page 209, Chapter 5). The lactic acid that builds up in its tissues as a result of this oxygen deprivation would surely kill it, or drive it to the surface, were it not for the vast storehouse of minerals in the bones of its shell. These minerals act as buffering agents, neutralizing the acid before it can build to harmful levels. Perhaps equally vital reasons for turtles to have shells, especially for the many turtles that we know less well, remain to be discovered.

Variations on a Theme

Turtle shells have changed little in their basic architecture since the earliest days of the dinosaurs. That does not mean that all turtle shells are alike.

Variations on the basic shell theme have had much to do with the adaptability of the turtle body plan, and may reflect quite specific adaptations to a mode of life. The Central Asian Tortoise (*Testudo horsfieldii*), for example, has a relatively low, smooth, rounded shell for a tortoise; this may make it easier for the animal to burrow freely in soft sand.

Most land-dwelling turtles have higher, more domed shells than their water-living relatives. Turtles that spend much of their lives swimming tend to have flat, smooth shells, the better to slice through the water. The shells of aquatic turtles in the Emydidae and Geoemydidae tend to be less variable than those of more terrestrial turtles. The round, flattened shells of many softshell turtles cut through the water like a discus through the air. Their shape makes them unstable in a crosscurrent, and while some softshells enter the ocean, they generally avoid the open sea. Sea turtle shells, on the other hand, are elongate teardrops, a highly efficient shape for reducing drag and ensuring stability. The sea turtle with the most elongate shell, the Leatherback, is also the one that ranges most

This juvenile Spiny Turtle (*Heosemys spinosa*) from Southeast Asia bears a spiked carapace (and a beautifully patterned plastron; see page 18).

One of the "sawbacks," the Black-knobbed Map Turtle (*Graptemys nigrinoda*), of rivers in Alabama and Mississippi, USA.

widely through the open ocean (though the Green Sea Turtle is a better swimmer than the Hawksbill, which has the more elongate shell).

Some turtles have highly sculptured shells. The Spiny Turtle of Southeast Asia (*Heosemys spinosa*) has the scutes of its carapace produced into prickly spikes that may not only make it an unpleasant mouthful for a predator, but a difficult animal to detect in the leaf litter of the forest floor. Among the North American map turtles (*Graptemys*), the so-called sawbacks have a saw-toothed keel running down the midline of the carapace. The scutes of a Wood Turtle (*Glyptemys insculpta*) carapace are heaped up into rough pyramids. This shape does not involve the underlying bone; but in tortoises, including the Tent Tortoise (*Psammobates tentorius*) of southern Africa, the bone itself may be raised into humps. Leopard Tortoises in the Serengeti frequently have humped shells, perhaps because they get more protein than usual by scavenging the carcasses of large mammals or eating the feces of Serengeti carnivores. A combination of a high-protein diet and low humidity—a blend unlikely to occur in the wild, where food is scarce during the dry season—may produce humped shells in captive African Spurred Tortoises. A rare spinal deformity called *kyphosis* can cause the entire carapace of an affected turtle to arch upward; kyphotic turtles appear perfectly healthy, though, and seem none the worse for their condition. *Lordosis*, an inward curvature of the spine, is also known in turtles, including marine turtles and tortoises.

Some tortoises, including the Indian Star Tortoise (mostly large females from Sri Lanka) and the Tent Tortoise, develop humped scutes as a matter of course as they age. These rough growths may save the animal's life. Many turtles, if they find themselves upside down, can turn over again with a push of their muscular necks. High-shelled tortoises, though, cannot do this. A tortoise on its back may die from heatstroke if it cannot get out of the sun, and of course is vulnerable to any predator that happens by. If it becomes overturned accidentally, the humps may tilt its body to one side, making it easier for the tortoise to flip itself back over and continue on its way.

Some Asian river turtles (Geoemydidae), including the closely related river and Painted Terrapins, have paired, internal sheets of bone running like buttresses from carapace to plastron, one pair at the front of the shell and one near the rear. These may allow the shell to withstand the crushing bites of crocodiles. Female river and Painted Terrapins have solid bony shells, but the smaller males retain throughout life a series of fontanelles along each side, like a row of portholes. In a living terrapin these openings are covered by the scutes; the porthole effect is only visible in a skeleton. What these openings are for—assuming that they have any function at all, and are not simply a reflection of the fact that males mature at a smaller size than females—no one knows, though they may, somehow, allow a male terrapin to sense vibrations in the water. Why the male should need to do this and not the female it is hard to imagine, unless it somehow helps him find a mate.

The Central American River Turtle has such thin scutes that they can hardly be called armor at all. The scutes are easily damaged or abraded, and once injured heal very poorly. The leathery skin that replaces the scutes of a softshell turtle may increase its ability to function beneath the surface. Many aquatic turtles can take up oxygen through their skin when they are under water (see page 206, Chapter 5), and the greater the skin area, the more oxygen a softshell may be able to absorb. The shells of softshell turtles, by the way, are not really soft, except at the edges; most of their bony plates are quite thick and solid. They are rubbery around the rim, because softshells, except for the Indian and Burmese Flapshells (*Lissemys* spp.), have lost the peripheral bones around the edge of the carapace (see page 114, Chapter 3). *Lissemys* has a series of *posterior peripheral ossicles* around the back of the carapace that appear to be the equivalent of the peripheral bones in other turtles.

For the ultimate in bone loss, though, we must turn to the Leatherback. This largest of all turtles has almost no identifiable bones in its shell. Even its ribs only lie up against the underside of its carapace, rather than being embedded in it as in all other turtles. Instead, its shell is made of thick, tough connective tissue covered by leathery skin, lying over a layer of thousands of tiny, separate bony plates, arranged like the tiles in a mosaic. These plates consist of dermal bone, but not (except for a single element, the *nuchal*) the same type of dermal bone that makes up the carapace of more typical turtles. Instead, they form within a layer of the dermis closer to the surface of the skin, and are technically referred to as *epithecal*, as opposed to *thecal*, bone. Some are as little as 3 mm (0.12 in) thick; the largest lie along the seven ridges running down the length of the carapace. When a Leatherback dies and rots, its shell simply disintegrates.

Flexible Shells

Hatchling turtles have quite flexible shells; after all, they have to curl enough to fit inside an egg. Normally, however, as the turtle grows, the sutures where the bones of its shell meet become rigid and immovable. Their edges weave back and forth in a complex series of interlocking fingers, like dozens of tiny mortise and tenon joints. The soft tissue between the bones diminishes or, in a few species, even disappears.

In many turtles, though, this seemingly rigid suit of armor is not entirely inflexible, even in adults. Snapping turtles and the Big-headed Turtle (*Platysternon megacephalum*) of Southeast Asia can flex the plastron slightly along the midline, at the bridges. A sea turtle—especially a Leatherback, whose bony plastron is reduced to a ring of splints—can make its whole plastron bulge, aided by boneless sutures along the midline and on the bridges. If you were to turn a sea turtle on its back (something that, of course, you should not do), you could see its chest heave as it breathes.

Turtles from five different families have developed hinges, with associated muscles and ligaments, that allow portions of their shells to move up or down. These hinges are almost always somewhere on the plastron, except in the hinged tortoises of the African genus *Kinixys*, which have theirs across the rear portion of the carapace, between the seventh and eighth marginal scutes. The evolution of hinges has affected the shape of the plastron; its edge must fit neatly against the carapace to seal the animal inside its shell when it closes the hinge. Turtles that sport hinges do not usually have them when they hatch (the Spider Tortoise of Madagascar is an exception), but develop them as they grow. Before a hinge can develop, the scutes and underlying bones

African hinged tortoises, such as this Forest Hinge-back Tortoise (*Kinixys erosa*), are the only turtles with a hinge across the carapace.

An Eastern Box Turtle (*Terrapene carolina*) from the Florida Panhandle seals itself in its shell by raising its plastral lobes.

must line up in the same spot. In hinged tortoises, the scutes and the bones along the hinge lines do not finish lining up until later in their development, and some individuals never develop a hinge at all.

Hinges have evolved over and over again, even within a single family like the Asian river turtles (Geoemydidae). In the Spider Tortoise, the two southern subspecies have a hinge while the third, which lives to the northwest, has none. In some tortoises of the genus *Testudo*, including the Spur-thighed Tortoise (*T. graeca*), females have hinges but males do not.

There is usually only one hinge on the plastron, on one side of the bridge or the other. Of course, that means that only one lobe of the plastron can normally move, because the bridge locks the other one in place. However, a number of American pond turtles (Emydidae) and Asian river turtles have solved this problem by replacing the bony bridge with a flexible, fibrous ligament. That permits animals like the emydid American box turtles (*Terrapene* spp.) and the geoemydid Asian box turtles (*Cuora* spp.) to close both lobes of their plastra around a single hinge. Mud turtles (*Kinosternon* spp.) keep the bony bridge, but have two hinges, one in front of the bridge and one behind it.

A hinge seems an obvious antipredator device, the equivalent of a portcullis or a drawbridge. This, though, may not be its only function. The hinge on a Spider Tortoise, for example, is well developed, but the muscles that control it, and would be needed to raise the "drawbridge," seem quite weak. In Central America, the White-lipped Mud Turtle (*K. leucostomum*) is partly terrestrial, while its larger relative

A Southeast Asian Box Turtle (*Cuora amboinensis*) closes its single plastral hinge, sealing itself from (most) dangers.

(and frequent predator) the Mexican or Northern Giant Musk Turtle (*Staurotypus triporcatus*) is a full time water-dweller. The White-lipped Mud Turtle has a much more extensive plastron than the Giant Musk, with two hinges, one on either side of the bridge, that allow its shell to close completely. This may be an adaptation to avoid drying out during its time on land.

Some turtles may need a hinge, or a flexible shell, to pull the head in at one end or to pass eggs out at the other. Male Spur-thighed Tortoises, like other tortoises such as the Speckled Padloper (*Homopus signatus*), have larger shell openings than females, giving them more freedom to move their legs and tail—important advantages to an animal that must fight off other members of his own sex and jockey itself into position to copulate with its mate.

Though snapping turtles lack a hinge, their slightly flexible plastral joints make it easier for them to retract their very large heads and fold up their long necks, and their reduced, cross-shaped plastra leave "bulging room" around the bases of the limbs. Giant musk turtles have large heads and a powerful bite. When they retract their heads into their shells, they open their mouths widely as a threat to any attacker. If they could not lower the front of the plastron around the hinge, there would not be enough room to fit their gaping heads and enormous necks within the shell. Their relative, the Narrow-bridged Musk Turtle (*Claudius angustatus*), does manage this without a hinge; it pivots the anterior part of its rigid plastron downward instead, tilting it like a see-saw.

The need to lay a fairly large egg may explain why female Spur-thighed Tortoises, but not males,

The shell of the Black Wood Turtle (*Rhinoclemmys funerea*) of Central America may have to flex to allow its enormous egg to be laid.

have a hinge on the rear lobe of the plastron, though their close relative, the Egyptian Tortoise (*Testudo kleinmanni*), has a hinge in both sexes. Some small turtles in the family Chelidae, such as the Twist-necked Turtle (*Platemys platycephala*) of South America, lay large eggs for their size, but do not have a hinge. Like box turtles, their bridges are fibrous, allowing the space between the carapace and the plastron to stretch a bit while laying eggs. The neo-tropical wood turtles of the genus *Rhinoclemmys* lay enormous, hard-shelled eggs; a Guyana Wood Turtle (*R. punctularia*) with a carapace 20 cm (8 in) long may lay an egg nearly 7 cm (2.8 in) long and 4 cm (1.6 in) wide. They can flex the sutures between the bones at the posterior end of the carapace and plastron, possibly to make room for the egg.

Turtles have other ways of getting around the problem of how to lay a large egg. The Yellow-footed Tortoise (*Chelonoidis denticulata*) of South America has a semicircular notch at the rear edge of its plastron, just large enough to allow an egg to fit through. A number of turtles and, particularly, tortoises, have simply changed the shape of their eggs from spherical to long and narrow, making it easier for a large egg to fit through what may be a very small space between the carapace and the plastron.

Though it lacks a hinge, the Indian Flapshell (*Lissemys punctata*), one of the soft-shelled turtles,

The Burmese Flapshell Turtle (*Lissemys scutata*) has fleshy flaps on its plastron that can be drawn up to conceal its hindlimbs.

can close its shell openings by flexing the rear part of its carapace downward, and the front part of its plastron upward, with the help of a pair of fleshy flaps that it pulls up to conceal its hindlimbs. The ultimate in shell flexibility is reached by two remarkable and quite different species, the Malayan Softshell (*Dogania subplana*) in Asia and the Pancake Tortoise (*Malacochersus tornieri*) in Africa.

Though softshell turtles have a fair bit of flexibility between the bones of their plastra, their bony carapaces are usually quite rigid. The exception is the Malayan Softshell, whose anatomical abilities were first described by Peter Pritchard. Its individual shell bones are rigid enough, but every

bone in a Malayan Softshell's carapace is free to move. No other turtle in the world has a shell that can do this—not even a Leatherback, whose shell is bound together by a heavy layer of fibrous tissue into a tough and fairly inflexible unit. The Malayan Softshell may need such a flexible shell because it has a relatively enormous head and long neck. When it draws them back into its body, its whole shell must bulge to let them in. This extreme flexibility may also help it slip into a crevice, or under a boulder in the bed of a forest stream.

The ability to hide in a crevice—though on dry land rather than in the water—is the raison d'etre for one of the most peculiar of all turtle shells, that

The shell of the Malayan Softshell (*Dogania subplana*) must bulge to make room for its enormous head and neck.

The flexible shell of the Pancake Tortoise (*Malacochersus tornieri*) locks the animal in place in its rocky crevice.

of the Pancake Tortoise of Kenya, Tanzania and Zambia. Pancake Tortoises spend much of their lives in deep crevices on rocky outcrops. If disturbed, they wedge themselves so tightly in place that it is difficult to remove them. The tortoise does this by bracing its hind legs, forcing the rear of its carapace against the ceiling of the crevice. If the opening is narrow enough, it pulls in its legs as tightly as it can, forcing its carapace and plastron to bulge outward and lock the tortoise in place.

This locking mechanism requires extreme flexibility, but the Pancake Tortoise does not achieve this by a system of hinges or by loosening the joints between the bones of its shell. Instead, it has reduced the bones themselves to such a remarkable degree that they have become flexible. The peripheral bones that ring its carapace are as solid and rigidly locked together as in any other tortoise, but the neural and pleural bones that form its center are reduced to paper thinness and penetrated by a series of fontanelles. The fontanelle in the middle of its plastron is so large that, when the turtle braces itself, its body bulges through it like a balloon. Far from being a rigid, armored creature, a Pancake Tortoise—though it looks solid enough from the outside—is so soft and pliable that when you hold one in your hand, you can feel its heart beating through its shell.

Turtle Heads, How to Hide Them, and Other Matters

Though the shell is certainly the most distinctive and unique feature turtles have, it is not the only thing that separates them from other living reptiles. Most turtles have a much more solid and rigid skull than, for example, lizards and snakes. The evolution of snakes has led to a skull in which every bone but the braincase can move freely, an adaptation to swallowing prey that is much wider than the snake itself. Turtle evolution has gone in the other direction. In juvenile turtles the bones of the skull can be very loose, but in adults they are sutured together into a rigid, immovable whole (the sutures are still visible, except in the extinct Mascarene tortoise genus *Cylindraspis*). Its form can be remarkably varied; though most turtle skulls would be immediately recognizable even to a non-expert, a few might give a trained zoologist pause.

The elongate skulls of softshell turtles reach an extreme in the narrow-headed softshells (*Chitra* spp.) of southern Asia. Their skulls are ridiculously slender, and carry the eye sockets, or orbits, so far forward that they can be easily mistaken for oversize nostrils. This peculiar placement means that the turtle can bury its enormous body in the sand and

still watch for prey, with only the tip of its snout and two tiny eyes projecting into the open to reveal the presence of the more than 100 kg (220 lbs) of predator concealed beneath.

Even more peculiar-looking is the skull of the Matamata (*Chelus fimbriata*) of northern South America. It looks as though the turtle's nose had been run over by a steamroller. Its front half is so thoroughly flattened that it is less than a centimeter thick, even in an adult weighing some 10 kg (22 lbs). The back half, by contrast, sweeps upward at a steep angle and sports on each side a huge projecting flange like the decorations on a particularly extravagant murex snail. These flanges bear the turtle's ears, spacing them widely apart, a positioning that may help the Matamata home in on its prey in murky river waters. You might be forgiven for overlooking the tiny space, in the midst of this riot of bone, reserved for the animal's brain.

In most living turtles, deep embayments, or *emarginations*, cut into the back of the skull on either side to make room for the jaw muscles (in the Chelidae, the family of turtles that includes the Matamata, the embayment sweeps up instead from the side of the skull in front of the ear). However, in some turtles, including sea turtles and the Big-headed Turtle, the embayments are greatly reduced or even absent, making for a skull with a complete, solid bony roof. It is probably not a coincidence that these are animals that cannot withdraw their heads into their shells, either because (in the case of the Big-headed Turtle) the head is simply too large, or (in the sea turtles) because the requirements of streamlining have meant that the neckline flows smoothly into the shell over the thick neck muscles, leaving no place to tuck the head out of the way.

No living turtle has teeth. Some of the very earliest fossil turtles had teeth in the center of the palate, but these were gradually lost as turtles evolved. As far as we know, only the earliest turtle of all, the remarkable *Odontochelys* (see page 48–49, Chapter 2), had fully developed teeth in what we think of

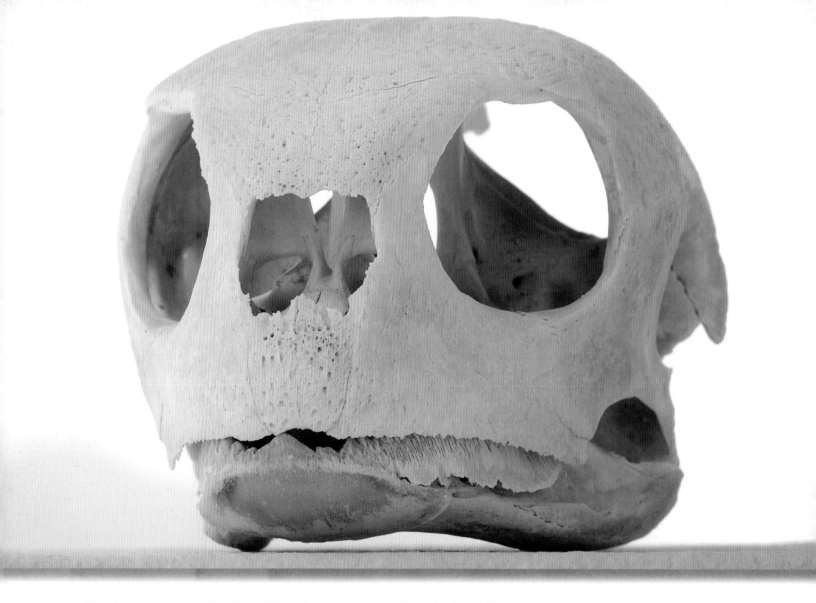

The skull of the Green Sea Turtle (*Chelonia mydas*) has a solid roof, without the emarginations seen in most other turtles.

as the normal place, along the edges of the jaws. Instead of teeth, turtle jaws are lined with sheaths of keratin. Sheaths may be sharpened into cutting edges (for meat eaters), outfitted with serrated ridges (for plant eaters), or broadened into crushing plates (for mollusk eaters), depending on what the turtle does with them. A baby turtle in the egg has another hard, sharp bit of keratin, the *egg tooth* or *egg carbuncle*, on its snout. It uses it to slice its way out of the eggshell; a few days later, its job done, the egg carbuncle is absorbed or falls off.

As anyone who mishandles a snapping turtle or a softshell will learn, some turtles can deliver a powerful bite. Anthony Herrel and his colleagues found that turtles vary considerably in the force they can bring to bear. Of the 28 species they examined, the strongest biter by far was the Guyanan Toad-headed Turtle (*Mesoclemmys nasuta*) with a bite force of 432 Newtons (the average bite force for domestic dogs is roughly 250 Newtons). Snapping turtles, some softshells and the Pacific Coast Giant Musk Turtle (*Staurotypus salvinii*) are also forceful biters. Perhaps surprisingly, the Common Snapping Turtle (*Chelydra serpentina*) can generate a stronger bite than its larger cousin the Alligator Snapper (*Macrochelys temminckii*). At the other end of the scale, the Jardine River Turtle (*Emydura subglobosa*) could manage only 1.9 Newtons and the weird Matamata (*Chelus fimbriata*), which depends on its remarkable suctioning abilities rather than its jaws

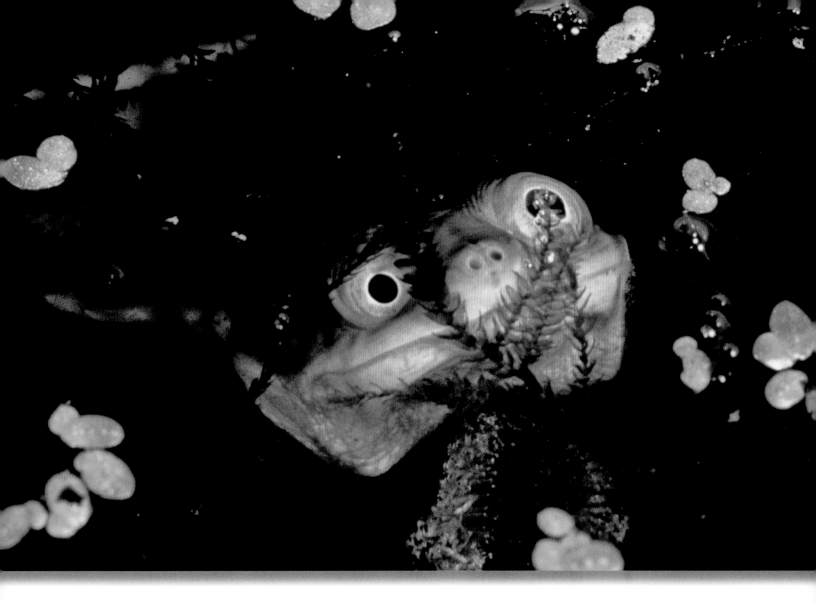

Turtle sight is quite keen. Here, a Broad-shelled Turtle (*Chelodina expansa*) from southeastern Australia peers above the water before emerging to bask.

to catch prey (see page 243, Chapter 6), manages barely more than 5 Newtons.

Turtle sight is quite keen, at least at close range, both above and below the water. We know from experiments that turtles have color vision, particularly at the red end of the spectrum. The eyes of the Red-eared Slider contain seven different types of color-sensitive cone cells, making their color-vision system the most complex known in vertebrates. Desert tortoises can distinguish red, yellow, green and orange. Young captive Leopard Tortoises showed a strong preference for red, light green, olive and yellow objects, an attraction that may lead them in the wild to particularly choice flowers and green plants.

Sea turtle eyes have spherical lenses, which are better able to correct for refraction in seawater, and have shifted their retinal sensitivity toward the short end of the visible spectrum, a trait they share with a number of shallow-water marine fishes. The retina of the Loggerhead Sea Turtle (*Caretta caretta*) is adapted for both sharp vision and light sensitivity. Unlike diving mammals such as whales, however, sea turtles do not appear to have traded their color vision for a better ability to see in poor light.

Turtles have a good sense of smell. Like other reptiles, they have both olfactory receptors and a specialized structure called a *vomeronasal organ* (VNO) that allows them to detect tiny chemical particles; in turtles, the nasal cavity is lined with patches of olfactory and vomeronasal receptors, each transmitting to a different part of the fore-brain. Some turtles, including the Red-headed Amazon River Turtle (*Podocnemis erythrocephala*), apparently use smell to find food, and Richard Vogt has reported that a tribe in the Amazon catches Yellow-footed Tortoises "by tying a dead agouti [a large rodent] over a hole dug in the ground, return-ing after a week or two to collect the turtles that have been attracted to the odor and fallen into the pit."

VNO receptors in particular are sensitive to pher-omones. At least some male turtles may need to be able to smell females to be sure that they have found a potential mate (to avoid putting the moves on aggressive rival males). Male Common Musk Turtles (*Sternotherus odoratus*) are attracted to the scent of females, though females show no interest in the odor of the opposite sex. Hermann's Tortoises (*Testudo hermanni*) of both sexes can recognize the smell of their own species, but only males have a sensitivity that allows them to detect sexually mature females.

How well turtles hear is difficult to judge. Turtles lack an external ear opening. The ear of modern turtles is surrounded by the otic capsule, a bony box found in no other reptile. The ear drum, or tympanum, is covered with scales. Turtles are acutely aware of low-frequency vibrations in the water and, to a lesser extent, on land. It is probably this awareness, rather than hearing as we experience it, which sends a turtle slipping into the water long before you can approach it.

Many turtles produce sounds of their own, par-ticularly while mating; presumably they can hear themselves or their partners. Copulating Galápagos tortoises (*Chelonoidis nigra* complex) bellow and roar, Red-footed Tortoises (*C. carbonaria*) cluck, and Hermann's Tortoises whimper. Arrau use vocal-izations to call to each other and, remarkably, to their young (see page 260, Chapter 7). The Oblong Turtle (*Chelodina oblonga*) of Western Australia has recently been found to possess an extensive underwater vocabulary. Its repertoire, according to Jacqueline Giles and her colleagues, includes "clacks, clicks, squawks, hoots, short chirps, high short chirps, medium chirps, long chirps, high calls, cries or wails, hooos, grunts, growls, blow bursts, stac-catos, a wild howl, and drum rolling," not to men-tion whines, moans and a sustained series of pulses lasting some four minutes, ending in a rhythmic vibrato, that may help an amorous male advertise its whereabouts during the breeding season. Exactly how they make these sounds is unknown. Their unusual vocal range may compensate for the dif-ficulty Oblong Turtles have in seeing each other in the murky or tannin-stained waters where they often live.

Turtles have extremely flexible necks. This flex-ibility perhaps makes up for the rigidity of their shells. Turtle necks range from very short, as in sea turtles, to remarkably long and snake-like, as in the Eastern Snake-necked Turtle (*Chelodina longicollis*). Long or short, all turtle necks have the same number of vertebrae—eight. This kind of consistency is unusual in reptiles, but has a parallel in mammals: all mam-mals, except sloths, have only seven cervical vertebrae, whether you are talking about a giraffe or a whale.

Necks, or the way turtles use them, are a key to their relationships. Living turtles fall into two fun-damental lineages, primarily based on the way they tuck their heads beneath their shells. By far the larger group accomplishes this by bending the neck into a vertical S-curve, pulling the head straight back into a slot in the body cavity. Since this action tucks the neck completely out of sight, the group is known as the Cryptodira or hidden-necks—though some cryp-todires, including sea turtles, cannot tuck their heads in at all. All the turtles of North America and Europe, all but one of the turtles of Asia, all sea turtles, and all "true" tortoises are cryptodires.

The second group is much less well-known to us northerners. It includes an extensive array of turtles from South America, Madagascar and Africa, and all but one of the freshwater turtles of Australia. The

Side-necked turtles or pleurodires such as the West African Mud Turtle (*Pelusios castaneus,* top) tuck their heads to one side, whereas hidden-necked turtles or cryptodires such as the Maranhao Slider (*Trachemys adiutrix,* bottom) bend their necks in a vertical S-curve, pulling the head into the shell.

members of this group cannot pull their necks into an S-curve. Instead, they bend them around to the side, tucking their heads beneath an overhanging lip of the shell. They are the Pleurodira, or side-necked turtles.

There are other, more subtle distinctions between cryptodires and pleurodires. In pleurodires, for example, the pelvic girdle is sutured to the carapace and fused with the plastron. It is free, and movable, in cryptodires. There are also important differences in the jaw-closing mechanism of the two groups.

Skin, Muscles, Limbs and Tails

Most turtles have rather smooth skins, but some sport a variety of tubercles, flaps and bumps, especially on the head and neck. The Alligator Snapper, the Fitzroy River Turtle (*Rheodytes leukops*) of Australia, and especially the Matamata, carry such processes in considerable number and variety. The Twist-necked Turtle, a pleurodire, has a series of blunt tubercles on its neck that may give it some protection when it tucks its head away beneath its carapace. In the Matamata, flaps of skin along the side of its neck are well supplied with nerves, and apparently help the turtle find prey in the murky waters where it lives (see page 243, Chapter 6).

Many freshwater turtles, particularly snapping turtles (Chelydridae), mud and musk turtles (Kinosternidae), and pleurodires, have fingers of skin, called *barbels*, dangling under their chins. Most pleurodires have a single pair; the Big-headed Amazon River Turtle (*Peltocephalus dumerilianus*) and the Yellow-spotted River Turtle (*Podocnemis unifilis*) of South America, as the latter's scientific name implies, only have one. Snapping turtles have four pairs, and the Scorpion Mud Turtle (*Kinosternon scorpioides*) of Central and South America may have two, three, or four pairs, or some irregular number haphazardly arranged. We do not know exactly what these barbels are for, but they appear to be sensitive. Some Australian sidenecks touch each other's barbels as part of their courtship. I have watched Yellow-spotted River Turtles in the Frankfurt Zoo resting and stroking their barbels on the carapaces of other turtles as they swam.

Like other reptiles, turtles lack the facial muscles we mammals have, other than the muscles that open and close their eyelids, swivel, focus and adjust their eyes, or operate their jaws. A turtle's limbs, neck and tail are well muscled, and turtles with hinged shells may have special muscles to operate them. Within the shell, though, there is little need for the trunk musculature that other vertebrates use to flex their spines or expand their ribs. These muscles, accordingly, have been lost.

Turtle limbs vary from the columnar, heavy-footed legs of tortoises to the elongate, blade-like flippers of sea turtles. Their supporting bones and muscles vary with them. Tortoises with high, domed shells have elongate shoulder blades, while those of flatter-shelled turtles are, of necessity, shorter so the bones can move inside the shell. The forelimb muscles of tortoises are robust, with the muscle masses partly fused together, giving them the added stability and strength they need to support their often heavy owners. The muscles in aquatic freshwater turtles are relatively unfused, allowing them the freedom of movement and fine control that a swimming animal needs.

Most turtles have five toes, often webbed, on each limb (a number that, some humans may be disappointed to learn, is the primitive condition in all but the earliest land vertebrates). Some of the smaller tortoises have lost one of the toes on the front foot—always the first digit, the last to appear as the embryo turtle develops. The limbs of softshell turtles have five toes, but only three bear claws. Some American box turtles have only three toes on each limb. The most modified limbs of any turtle, the swimming paddles of sea turtles, retain only one or two claws, and in the Leatherback even these are lost.

The columnar, elephantine front limbs of the Santa Cruz Giant Tortoise (*Chelenoidis porteri*) give it stability and support.

Sea turtle forelimbs have been modified into flippers, their individual digits drawn out to great lengths and fused together to form a flat paddle like a penguin's wing. A sea turtle has the normal complement of separate toe bones, though they are far longer on the forelimbs than in typical turtles, but these bones are bound together into a single stiffened unit by layers of fibrous connective tissue and an overlying scaly skin. The hindlimbs of sea turtles are much smaller than the front limbs, and are stabilizing and steering rudders (and nest-digging tools) rather than propelling paddles. Sea turtle limbs, both fore and aft, have other functions, too: males use the curved claws on their forelimbs to grip the shoulders of the female during mating; females have to be able to haul themselves back up onto the beach with their forelimbs, dig out a nest burrow using both fore- and hindlimbs, and then cover it up again; and hatchlings of both sexes use them to dig their way into the air and scramble down to the sea.

Sea turtles swim in a manner quite different from that any other turtle (except for the Pig-nose Turtle, which also has transformed its limbs into flippers and rudders). In a typical pond turtle, the hindlimbs are larger than the forelimbs; they provide the swimming stroke, thrusting outward alternately, one after the other. Sea turtles, though, have transferred the main propulsive role to the long, flipper-like forelimbs. Instead of pushing outward on one side and then the other, they usually sweep them up and down simultaneously, weaving a figure-eight pattern. This pattern is basically the same as the wing strokes of a flying bird, or of a swimming penguin—the reason both penguins and sea turtles are said to fly under water.

Finally, turtle tails vary considerably in length and thickness. They are particularly long in snapping turtles (see page 100, Chapter 3) and in the Big-headed Turtle, which can actually use its tail as a brace to help it climb. The largest Australian sideneck, the Mary River Turtle (*Elusor macrurus*),

even takes its name from its oversized tail. Male turtles often have longer and heavier tails than females, and for a reason. The *cloacal* opening—the common opening of the digestive and reproductive tract in turtles—is part way down the underside of the tail, so a male with a longer tail has an easier job arranging himself in an appropriate position for mating. Further, the male's penis lies inside the cloacal opening in the base of the tail, and the tail has to be large enough to accommodate it.

In some turtles, including mud turtles (Kinosternidae) and the tortoises of Madagascar, the tip of the tail sports a hard, horny spine in males and, in some cases, in females. The spine may assist the male in bracing himself in position while he accomplishes the acrobatically difficult task of mounting his mate.

The forelimbs of sea turtles, such as this Hawksbill (*Eretmochelys imbricata*) on a reef off Tahiti, have been modified into swimming paddles.

How Do Turtles Breathe?

Turtles have evolved modifications, alterations and workarounds to carry on life in a variety of niches while still remaining essentially turtles. Some of the fundamental changes they have undergone must have happened at the very beginning of their evolution (see page 46, Chapter 2). As the flexibility of their rib cage was sacrificed to the protective architecture of the shell, turtles must have simultaneously developed ways to draw breath into their lungs without it. Their solutions—and there are more than one—to their breathing problems must be very old indeed.

We come back, then, to the challenge turtles faced early in their history. How do turtles breathe? It has taken turtle biologists a long time to find out, and we still do not know the answer for more than a few species (and that answer is unlikely to apply to turtles such as the Asian river terrapins [*Batagur* spp.], which have internal bony buttresses in the shell). Two of them, the Common Snapping Turtle (*Chelydra serpentina*) and the Spur-thighed Tortoise, do not fill their lungs in exactly the same way. Surely other turtles have tricks of their own. A number of turtles, including the Indian Flapshell, have a special sheet of muscle that envelops the lungs. When this muscle contracts it probably helps the turtle exhale, but we still do not understand precisely how.

Turtles have perfectly good, multi-chambered lungs. They lie just under the carapace, with the rest of the internal organs—the viscera—lying below them. Their upper surface is actually attached to the carapace, while their lower surface is tied to the viscera by a sheet of connective tissue. If the viscera move downward, away from the carapace, they will drag the lungs open. That creates a negative pressure, and the air flows into the lungs. When they move upward and inward, they push against the lungs and squeeze the air out again. But how can a turtle move its viscera?

Part of the answer is, by using both special muscles and the movements of its limbs. A Common Snapping Turtle relies on four sets of muscles. Two lie near the front of the shell. Two more, at the rear, attach to a sort of membranous abdominal sling, somewhat equivalent to the human diaphragm. When the snapper contracts one set at each end, particularly the abdominal set which pulls the sling forward, it forces the viscera inward and upward; humans can produce the same effect with the abdominal muscles, as every opera singer knows. The other sets have the reverse effect, including pulling the abdominal sling backward. But the turtle can also force its viscera inward by drawing in its limbs, or let them slump back by extending them again. A freshwater turtle floating at the water's surface is free to use its legs as a sort of piston pump. Even the simple act of walking, which rocks its shoulder girdles back and forth within its shell, may help a turtle pump air in and out of its lungs.

Part of the answer, too, is to let outside forces do some of the work. When a turtle walks on land, gravity alone pulls its viscera downwards. For a snapping turtle, with its slightly flexible plastron, that means their sheer weight will hold the lungs open above them, making inhalation a fairly effortless process. The trick is getting the air out again, and for that the snapping turtle must make a physical effort. A snapping turtle floating in the water faces a different problem. Here, it must deal not with gravity, but with water pressure. Instead of pulling the plastron and viscera outward, water pressure pushes them in. The deeper the turtle holds its body while it stretches its neck upward to take a breath of air, the greater that pressure will be. If it is strong enough, the turtle will have no problem exhaling, because the pressure will do the work. This time, though, it will have to use effort to inhale. If its body rises closer to the surface, it may reach a point where gravity and water pressure cancel each other out, and the turtle must fill and empty its lungs without any outside help. It is one of the remarkable things about turtles that they seem able to adjust to these changes without difficulty, so that they can breathe with the least amount of effort no matter what their circumstances.

The Spur-thighed Tortoise works matters a bit differently. Its plastron is too rigid to allow gravity to help it inhale. Gravity probably helps its viscera return to their normal position after the tortoise exhales, but it cannot drag the viscera down enough to create the negative pressure the tortoise needs to fill its lungs. For that, and to exhale, the tortoise must resort to its muscles and, particularly, to its limbs. It does not have the anterior muscle, the *diaphragmaticus*, that a snapping turtle uses to exhale. Instead, it rocks its shoulder girdle inward and upward, or outward and downward, accomplishing the same thing by different means.

That may take care of normal breathing, but what happens when a turtle pulls in its head and limbs? They have to go somewhere, particularly in cryptodire turtles that draw the whole head and neck back into the body cavity. With the head, the limbs, and the viscera all tucked within its shell, a turtle has no room for air in its lungs. As long as it stays that way, it cannot breathe. Nor can it breathe, or at least breathe air, during a deep dive, or, for the turtles that do so, while it overwinters at the bottom of a pond. Turtles have, therefore, not only developed their own unique ways of breathing air; they have evolved methods for getting along without air, and even, in some circumstances, without oxygen. We shall see how they do this in Chapter 5.

Our story so far, though, should be enough to show that turtles are far more variable and adaptable than their humble appearance suggests. In the next chapter, we will reach back over 200 million years to see, as best we can, how these remarkable creatures came to be.

When a San Cristobal Giant Tortoise (*Chelonoidis chathamensis*) walks, the movement of its shoulder girdles pumps air in and out of its lungs.

CHAPTER TWO

Turtles in Time

IF WE WERE ABLE to take a journey back in time, passing, as we went, generation after generation of turtles evolving steadily in the opposite direction, we would probably see disappointingly little in the way of changes from modern turtles back to their distant ancestors. We could traverse the whole of the Cenozoic period, observing, in reverse, the passage of the Age of Mammals; continue through the great cataclysm that ended the reign of the dinosaurs 65 million years ago; cross the Cretaceous and the Jurassic periods, while dinosaur empires rose and fell and continents split and drifted across the globe; and all through that span of over 200 million years, turtles would still, basically, be turtles.

We would, of course, pass species and even families of turtles that have not survived to our own time. We would pass such oddities as the meiolaniids, great tortoise-like creatures sporting steer-like horns. We would cross the trail of giants, creatures paleontologists have named, with suitable awe, *Colossochelys* and *Stupendemys*. But all these animals would still, very obviously, be turtles, and their individual peculiarities would lead us no closer to the creatures from which, in the distant past, turtles first arose.

Our journey back would lead us to the Late Triassic, some 205–215 million years into the past, and an animal called *Proganochelys quenstedti*. *Proganochelys*, despite a few anatomical peculiarities including a set of teeth, was—no question about it—a turtle. If one crossed the road in front of you today, you probably wouldn't give it a second glance.

OPPOSITE

The earliest known turtle: the remarkable *Odontochelys semitestacea*.

CHART 1: Geologic Time Scale

Eon	Era	Period		Epoch	Dates
Phanerozoic	Cenozoic	Quaternary		Holocene	0–2
				Pleistocene	
		Tertiary	Neogene	Pilocene	2–5
				Miocene	5–24
			Paleogene	Oligocene	24–37
				Eocene	37–58
				Paleocene	58–66
	Mesozoic	Cretaceous			66–144
		Jurassic			144–208
		Triassic			208–245
	Paleozoic	Permian			245–286
		Carboniferous			286–320
					320–360
		Devonian			360–408
		Silurian			408–438
		Ordovician			438–505
		Cambrian			505–570
Proterozoic	Also known as Precambrian				570–2,500
Archean					2,500–3,800
Hadean					3,800–4,600

Proganochelys would tell you very little about the changes that must have taken place to turn an ordinary reptile into the highly specialized, almost distorted armored creature that turtles have become. For that, we must step back even further.

From its discovery in the 1880s until the first decade of the 21st century, *Proganochelys* was the oldest turtle known. Then, in 2008, scientists in China announced the discovery of a still older Triassic turtle, about 40–50 cm (16–20 in) long, dating from roughly 215–220 million years ago. It has been named *Odontochelys semitestacea*, and if you saw one alive you might well be forgiven for wondering just what sort of an animal it was. The name *semitestacea* means "half-shelled," and though *Odontochelys* had a fully formed plastron and oddly broadened ribs that resemble miniature cricket bats, the known specimens show almost no trace of a bony carapace.

Odontochelys represents an earlier stage in turtle evolution than that of any other fossil turtle so far discovered. *Proganochelys* had only *palatal* teeth, situated not where we have our teeth but on the roof its mouth (though there are vestiges of teeth on the premaxillary bone at the front of the jaw). *Odontochelys*, by contrast (*Odontochelys* means "toothed turtle"), still has a reptilian snout lined, like our own jaws, with *marginal* teeth.

Odontochelys' ribs join up with its spinal column in a manner typical of other reptiles rather than later turtles. Though a series of bony neural plates run above its spine, they do not fuse with the vertebrae as they do in almost all other turtles. Instead of radiating forward over the shoulder girdle, the first few ribs appear to point backward as they do in a turtle embryo before its carapace begins to develop. Does *Odontochelys* represent a transitional stage, before turtles had evolved fully formed shells?

Its discoverers thought so, but other paleontologists are not so sure. Robert Reisz, who has examined the specimens, thinks that *Odontochelys* represents an animal, like the modern Leatherback (*Dermochelys coriacea*), in the process of losing a carapace its ancestors once had. He believes that the anterior ribs may point backward because they became damaged and distorted after death. The rest of the ribs splay outward as they do in other turtles, suggesting that the *Odontochelys* embryo had a carapacial ridge (see page 21, Chapter 1)—something that could hardly have been present if there had been no carapace (though other scientists point out that the carapacial ridge may have been present but not, as in modern turtles, complete). Its plastron extends to the sides between the front and hind limbs, as though it was connecting to, or bracing, something—perhaps, Reisz suggests, a leathery carapace that once had been supported by bone.

Based on its limb structure, *Odontochelys* appears to have been an animal that spent most of its time in the water (though its toe bones are rather short, a feature recalling more terrestrial turtles). Did turtles evolve from swimming creatures that did not need extensive bony armor? Or did they develop from armored land dwellers, making *Odontochelys* the first known turtle to return to the sea? For those searching for the ultimate turtle ancestor, these questions may be crucial.

The Case of the Missing Ancestor

The origin of turtles remains one of the great unanswered questions of evolutionary biology. By comparison, the more famous debate over the origin of birds is a comparatively minor disagreement. All the possible choices for the ancestral bird—dinosaurs, crocodile relatives and others—are to be found within one subgroup of advanced reptiles, the archosaurs. By contrast, the candidates for a turtle ancestor have spanned almost the entire range of reptiles, living and extinct.

The potential candidates for a proto-turtle include a menagerie of peculiar creatures that died out either long before the rise of the dinosaurs or just as those most famous of extinct reptiles were coming into prominence. Unlike the dinosaurs, their names are only known to experts and fossil enthusiasts: captorhinids (a once-favored group we can thankfully ignore), pareiasaurs, procolophonoids and sauropterygians. To understand why paleontologists have not yet solved the case of the turtles' lineage, we must first learn something about the way scientists classify reptiles today; secondly, we must learn about these obscure creatures and their cumbersome names. We must go even further back in time, past the great catastrophe that began the Triassic period 250 million years ago and wiped out more than half of all living species—the worst mass extinction in the history of the planet—and enter the Permian period.

One long-shot candidate, a little reptile called *Eunotosaurus* that lived in South Africa during the Permian, had a very peculiar rib cage. Instead of being a thin bow of bone, each rib was a broad, flattened paddle. It did not take much imagination to visualize the paddles growing even broader, fusing together and forming the turtle shell. For years, however, biologists dismissed *Eunotosaurus* on the grounds that turtle ribs are not expanded, but fused to plates of dermal bone. A careful study of *Eunotosaurus* showed that in almost every feature it was nothing like a turtle. *Eunotosaurus* was accordingly dropped from the list of suspects until the discovery of *Odontochelys*, which has expanded ribs of its own, created a brief flurry of renewed interest in it. The ribs of *Eunotosaurus* are, however,

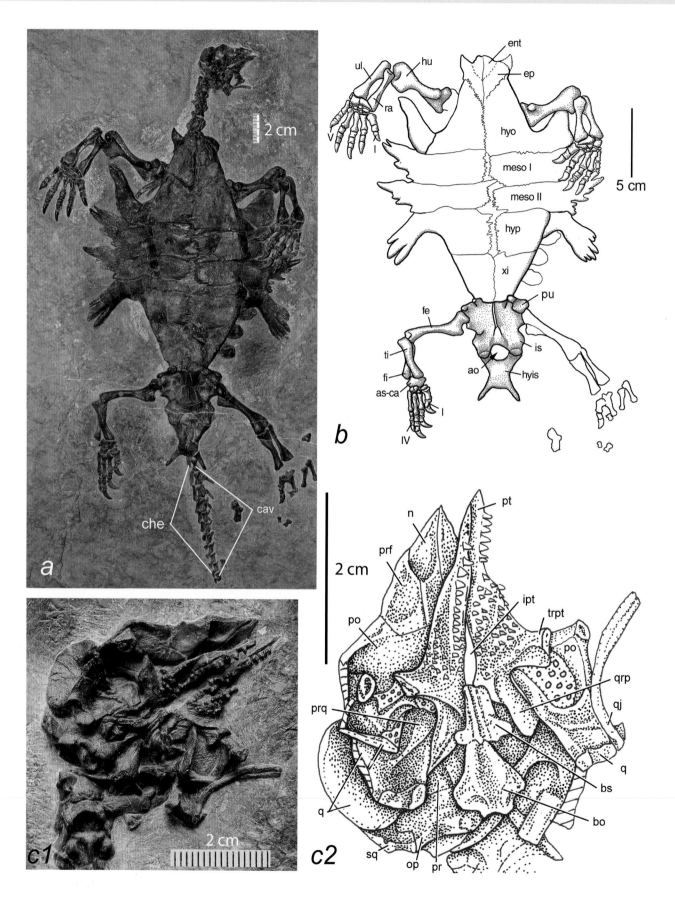

The paratype specimen of *Odontochelys semitestacea* shows us the animal from below; note the well-developed plastron and palatal teeth.

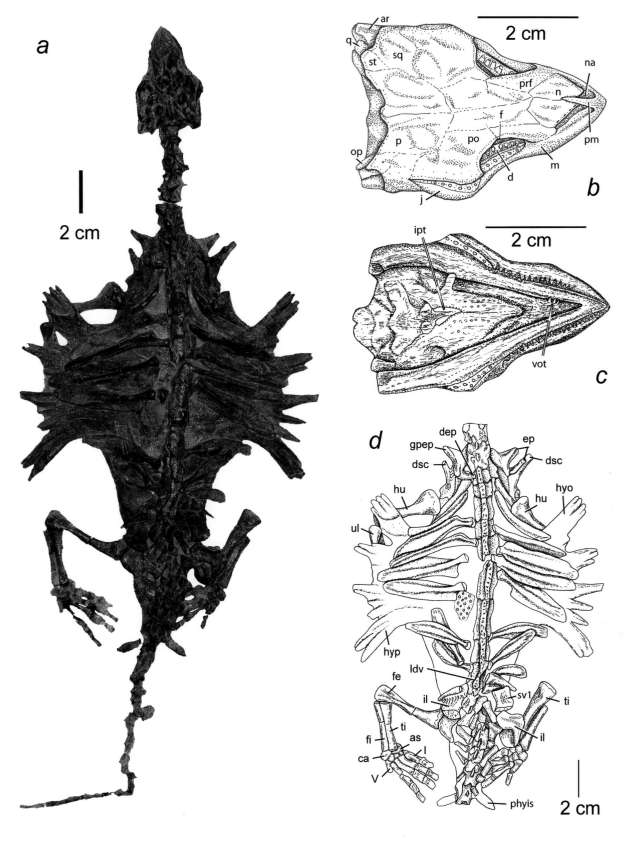

The holotype specimen of *Odontochelys semitestacea* shows its backwards-pointing ribs and the near-complete absence of a carapace (except for a narrow row of neural plates covering the spine).

CHART 2: Amniotes and their relatives
(not all fish groups shown)

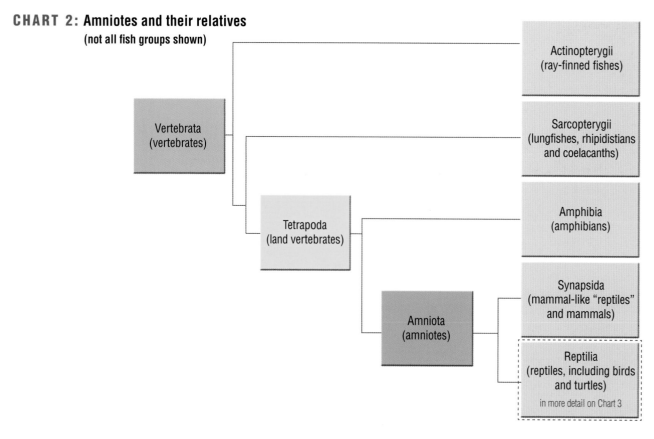

not really like those of *Odontochelys* (their shape is different, and they wrap around the chest cavity in non-turtle fashion). Besides, *Eunotosaurus* lived a very long time ago—some 45 million years before even *Odontochelys*, more than the distance separating turtles from another candidate group, the pareiasaurs (see page 52). Its role in turtle evolution seems, despite superficial similarities, unlikely.

Holes in the Head

At one time, the most important thing to know about turtles for anyone seeking their ancestors was the absence of the right kind of holes in their skulls. The earliest reptiles had a solid, massive skull roof that covered the top of their heads, with major openings only for eyes, ears and nostrils. The skull roof formed separately from the braincase inside it. Early reptiles were, in fact, rather like Darth Vader in his helmet, the helmet being the equivalent of the skull roof.

With time, however, openings, called *temporal fenestrae*, began to develop in the skull roof between the eye and the ear. The temporal fenestrae lightened the skull and gave the jaw muscles, previously sandwiched between the skull roof and the braincase, somewhere to go when they bulged. Some later reptiles had a single opening high on the side of the skull. In others, the opening was lower down, while still others had two openings, one above and one below.

Accordingly, students of fossil reptiles once classified their subjects into four main categories. Reptiles with solid skull roofs were called *anapsids*, meaning "without openings." Those with a single high opening were called *euryapsids*, meaning, as you might expect, "high opening". Those with the lower opening were called *synapsids*, and those with both openings were called *diapsids*. Turtles aside (for the moment), all living reptiles, as well as dinosaurs (and their descendants, the birds), pterosaurs and some other, less well-known animals, are diapsids. The euryapsids included extinct marine reptiles like the plesiosaurs, which we will be discussing later because they have a possible role in the turtle story. Today, though, euryapsids are considered to be diapsids that

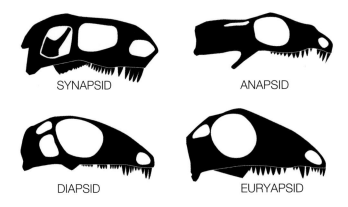

SYNAPSID   ANAPSID

DIAPSID   EURYAPSID

The four traditional categories of amniote skull based on the number and position of the temporal fenestrae.

lost their lower opening, and so the euryapsids as a group have disappeared from the scientific literature.

The synapsids, before dying out in the Triassic, gave rise to mammals, including us. That may surprise you, because you may not think that you have a hole in the side of your head. In fact, you do. Your temporal fenestrae, however, have become so large that almost all of the bone that once framed them is gone. There is practically nothing of your original skull roof left.

Turtles have no temporal fenestrae. Instead, in most modern turtles the jaw muscles bulge out of the emarginations in the skull (see page 33, Chapter 1). Under the system of reptile classification that held until very recently, therefore, turtles are anapsids, and the ancestral turtle had to be sought somewhere among the cluster of primitive reptiles lacking temporal fenestrae.

The New Reptiles

In recent years, the very idea of what constitutes a reptile has changed. Modern biologists no longer define animal groups on the basis of how similar their members look. Instead, they try—usually using computers to analyze their data—to set up categories that reflect the actual branching patterns of evolution. A modern taxonomic category may include animals that seem very different from one another, but are grouped together because they are all on the same branch of their family tree. This approach is known as *cladistics*. Under a cladistic approach, for example, birds are reptiles, because they sit on the same branch of the family tree as lizards, snakes, crocodiles and dinosaurs. In fact, they share a sub-branch of that tree with crocodiles and dinosaurs, but not with lizards and snakes, so that if lizards, snakes and crocodiles are all reptiles then, to be consistent, birds must be reptiles too. By the same logic, all mammals, including we humans, are synapsids.

All land vertebrates, except amphibians (the group that includes the living frogs and salamanders), evolved from animals that laid a *cleidoic* egg—that is, an egg sealed within a shell that allowed it to survive out of water. The embryo that grows within this type of egg is surrounded by a membrane called the *amnion*, so the descendants of those first ancestors are called *amniotes*. The amniotes form a natural group—a single branch of the vertebrate family tree that includes modern reptiles, birds (which are, as we have explained, reptiles) and mammals.

Zoologists used to use the term *reptile* to cover all of the early amniotes. However, when we use cladistics to examine how the amniote branch evolved, we find that the synapsids (including the mammals) are not on the same sub-branch as the one leading to living reptiles (including the birds). In other words, if we define the term *reptile* to include all of the animals that descended from the common ancestor of reptiles that are alive today, the synapsids are amniotes, but not reptiles—not even well-known synapsid "reptiles" such as the sail-backed *Dimetrodon* and the whole range of creatures we have been calling "mammal-like reptiles" for years. Using cladistics, the synapsid mammal-like reptiles are not reptiles.

Turtles, though, are unquestionably reptiles, even in the modern sense of the term. We can therefore ignore the synapsids (barring an occasional glance in the mirror) for the rest of this story, and concentrate on the occupants of the reptile family tree. Aside from a few early side branches, the reptile tree apparently split into two main limbs over 300 million years ago, near the beginning of the Permian.

The first limb contains the lizards, snakes, crocodiles, dinosaurs and birds; indeed, except perhaps for the turtles, it contains every reptile that survived the Triassic. Because it contains most of the animals we traditionally think of as reptilian, its members are called *eureptiles*. This means true or good reptiles. They are called a number of other things as well; scientists have not yet agreed (to put it mildly) on the various choices. We'll continue to call them eureptiles here.

The second limb contains most of the animals with anapsid skulls. These are the *parareptiles*. As Robert Reisz, an expert on the parareptiles, points out, "Just as paramedics are not exactly doctors, and paramilitary forces are not exactly military forces, parareptiles are not exactly true reptiles." That is, they are not eureptiles, but, unlike the synapsids, they are perfectly good reptiles.

The Usual Suspects

Do turtles belong on the parareptile branch or on the eureptile branch? Up until about 20 years ago, the answer would have been obvious. Turtles, with their solid skull roofs, were clearly anapsid. Therefore, they were parareptiles—the only parareptiles to survive to

this day. Which parareptile group, though, would be the best candidate for a turtle ancestor?

Some paleontologists have championed the pareiasaurs, great lumbering armored Permian behemoths, something like a cross between a buffalo and a toad. Others prefer the procolophonoids, much less unusual-looking animals by our standards—rather like large, clumsy lizards. The procolophonoids actually survived into the Triassic,

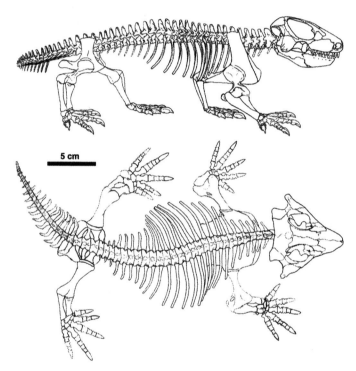

Skeletal reconstruction of *Procolophon*, a 225-million-year-old procolophonid from the early Triassic of South Africa.

Scutosaurus, a 2.5 m (8 ft), 250-million-year-old pareiasaur (and possible turtle ancestor) from the Permian of Russia.

the era of *Odontochelys*. They are the only para-reptile group to have done so, something that may make them a bit more likely to have evolved into turtles than the pareiasaurs.

Supporters of the procolophonoids point to skeletal similarities between turtles and such animals as *Owenetta*, a vaguely lizard-like little creature, less than a foot long, from the Upper Permian and Lower Triassic of the Karoo in South Africa. We have very good fossils of *Owenetta*. Most importantly, we have well-preserved skulls. Fossil skulls are rare, but they provide particularly valuable clues for turtle detectives. Most of a turtle's skeleton has changed so radically, as the shell has evolved, that it provides very few clues as to its origin. Though turtle skulls are highly variable in shape and proportion, their fundamental structure has changed far less from the typical reptilian condition. That makes it easier to compare the skulls of potential ancestors, bone for bone, with modern turtles—providing, of course, that we are lucky enough to find them. We were lucky with *Owenetta*, and its skull seems to share a number of similarities with, and only with, turtles.

However, Michael Lee of the South Australian Museum has made an extended and detailed argument that turtles belong with the pareiasaurs. According to Lee, turtles are not just related to pareiasaurs, they *are* pareiasaurs, descendants of some of the smaller members of that lineage. He points to a number of features that he says turtles and pareiasaurs share. Like turtles, many of the pareiasaurs carried bony dermal armor. Pareiasaurs also share a projection of the shoulder blade called the *acromion process*, a structure found elsewhere only in turtles. Lee has even proposed a series of evolutionary steps by which small pareiasaurs could have developed into turtles. Nour-Eddine Jalil and Philippe Janvier placed turtles closest to the dwarf South African *Pumiliopareia pricei*, smallest of the pareiasaurs, and the Russian paleontologist E.G. Kordikova argued in 2002 that the palatal structure of the Triassic turtle *Proganochelys* "confirmed" its place among the parareptiles.

The last known pareiasaur, however, died out almost 40 million years before *Odontochelys*, the first known turtle. That is a tremendous length of time. Pareiasaur opponents point out that if these large, armored animals really did survive to become the ancestors of turtles, we should have found at least some fossil evidence that they were there. That may seem to be a weak argument; after all, we might still find the missing fossils, or perhaps the animals that would have left them lived somewhere like modern Antarctica, where their fossils are out of reach.

Armor made from dermal bone is not just found in pareiasaurs and turtles, but in a long list of other vertebrates living and extinct (including, for example, armadillos). The fine structure of pareiasaur armor is quite unlike that in turtles. The special thing about turtle armor, as we discussed in the first chapter, is that it combines dermal with endochondral bone—and pareiasaurs don't do that. In fact, nothing else does.

Furthermore, the acromion process in pareiasaurs may be an entirely different structure from the one in turtles. *Odontochelys*, the earliest known turtle, lacks an acromion process altogether—the exact opposite of what you would expect of a supposedly ancestral feature, though it could, like the carapace, represent a secondary loss. The "acromion" in turtles may be a modified version of a bone turtles are otherwise missing, the anterior coracoid. If that is true (and Lee certainly argues that it is not), then it cannot be the same bone as the one in pareiasaurs, because pareiasaurs have both the acromion and the anterior coracoid.

Surprising Developments

That would seem to bring us back to the procolophonoids. However, a number of studies have forced paleontologists to consider the almost disturbing notion that turtles may belong with the eureptiles. Many of the characteristics that supposedly united turtles with procolophonoids, including the structure of the *stapes* (the "stirrup bone" in our middle ear), also turn up in some eureptile groups, leading to the possibility that turtles and procolopholoids, instead of being related, derived their similarities independently.

But how could turtles, with their solid skull roofs, be eureptiles? The fact that turtles are, technically, anapsids may be misleading us about what their true ancestors were. Some eureptiles—members of an extinct group called araeoscelids—may have been losing their temporal fenestrae. Dwarf caimans (*Palaeosuchus* spp.), living relatives of alligators from South America, have actually lost their upper fenestrae. Some parareptiles, conversely, had fenestrae of their own. The solid skull roof of turtles may mean that they lost temporal fenestrae that their ancestors possessed, not that, like other anapsids, they never had them at all. Instead of being the last survivors of an ancient anapsid lineage, turtles may be highly specialized relatives of lizards and crocodiles.

What could have led to such a surprising conclusion? Blair Hedges and Laura Polling have argued that some crocodiles, and an extinct group of vaguely crocodile-like eureptiles called aetiosaurs, had bony armor, but, as we have seen with the pareiasaurs, that alone doesn't mean much. A good deal of the evidence is molecular—computer-generated analyses of similarities among molecules of mitochondrial DNA and other genetic material from a variety of living animals. All of these studies put turtles firmly among the diapsids.

Of course, the parareptiles are all extinct and, contrary to misconceptions stemming from movies such as *Jurassic Park*, we are in no position to analyze the DNA of animals that vanished 180 million years ago. However, a number of molecular studies have placed turtles closer to one of the two main branches of the Sauria—the lineage that contains all living diapsids—than to the other. To use cladistic terms, they nest within one of the two surviving clades, and that makes them eureptiles.

The two living diapsid branches are the Lepidosauromorpha, containing lizards, snakes and the Tuatara (*Sphenodon punctatus*) of New Zealand, and the Archosauromorpha, the lineage that includes crocodilians, dinosaurs and birds. Most molecular analyses have placed turtles among the archosaurs. Unfortunately, other molecular studies have come to the opposite conclusion, placing turtles with, or close to, the lepidosaurs.

Still other studies, in particular a combined meta-analysis by Robert Hill, have subjected old-fashioned morphological characters—bumps, processes and shards of bone from animals both living and extinct—to modern, computer-assisted cladistic analyses. Most have also found turtles ensconced within the eureptiles. They have, however, only added to the confusion as to where among the eureptiles turtles might fit. Though the molecular studies have mostly favored the archosaurs, the morphological analyses lean strongly to the lepidosaurs. There is, nonetheless, a single skull character, the *laterosphenoid*, that the main lineage of archosaurs seemingly shares only with *Proganochelys* (the known skulls of *Odontochelys* are too crushed for the bone in question to be made out). In addition, the β-keratins in turtle scutes more closely resemble those of archosaurs than they do the β-keratins of lepidosaurs.

The problem may be, if turtles really are eureptiles, that they split from the diapsid tree so long ago, and so close in time to the point at which the archosaurs and the lepidosaurs split from each other, that resolving the true shape of their family tree may be next to impossible. It may even be—as Olivier Rieppel and Robert Reisz argued over a decade ago—that clues to the origin of turtles may lie not among the lizards or crocodiles, but with another group of peculiar, extinct diapsids: the sauropterygians. Though they are probably not turtle ancestors (at best, they may be close turtle cousins), the sauropterygians are worth a look. They represent a line of potential turtle relatives that had returned to the sea to live.

Pseudo-turtles

The best-known sauropterygians are the plesiosaurs, creatures like the long-necked *Elasmosaurus*, once aptly described as looking like a snake threaded through the body of a turtle. Their short-necked, crocodile-headed cousins the pliosaurs included immense creatures that must have been the largest and most fearsome predators of the entire Age of Reptiles, *Tyrannosaurus rex* not excepted.

For our purposes, though, the most interesting sauropterygians were the placodonts, a group that never made it out of the Triassic. Placodonts may have lived like reptilian walruses or, just possibly, seacows. Most of them had broad, flat, powerful teeth that were probably used to crush mollusks and crustaceans (though one paleontologist, Cajus Diedrich, has suggested that placodonts ate tough marine algae instead). In appearance, a typical placodont would probably have reminded you of a cross between a manatee and a marine iguana. The last group of placodonts to survive, though, the cyamodontoids, were far stranger.

Some cyamodontoids had extremely flattened bodies and long, whip-like tails. They may have lived something like modern stingrays. Others were the closest any animal group has come to producing the equivalent of a turtle. One, *Placochelys*, was even portrayed as a fossil turtle on a 1969 Hungarian postage stamp. Another, the meter-long *Henodus*, had a broad turtle-like shell splayed out at the sides like the head of a double-bladed ax, complete with carapace and plastron. Like the earliest turtles, *Henodus*, which lived in saltwater lagoons in Europe, had lost most of its teeth. *Henodus* had even shifted its shoulder girdle inside its rib cage, the only animal other than turtles ever to achieve this.

Turtles are not placodonts, though, and *Henodus* was certainly not a turtle. Its shell is actually quite unlike a turtle's carapace. Its ribs are not involved, and its armor is made up of a series of interlocking hexagonal plates of bone laid out like the tiles on a bathroom floor. The body armor of *Henodus* and other cyamodontoid placodonts is entirely dermal, though some of it apparently started out as cartilage (as does our own collarbone, itself a dermal element). The turtle-like characteristics of *Henodus*, which certainly evolved independently from those of real turtles, tell us less about turtle relationships than they do about the sort of conditions that might have led to the evolution of both groups.

One of the chief difficulties in imagining how turtles evolved has been the breathing problem. As turtles became sealed in their bony shells, they had to switch from a breathing system that involved expanding and collapsing the rib cage to one that involved using the legs as a sort of piston pump. Since land animals need their legs for support, it is hard to see how this transition could have occurred. What would the intermediate evolutionary steps have been like? A land animal whose legs were only partly adapted for breathing, but had lost in the process some of their ability to hold up its body, might seem an unlikely candidate for evolutionary success. Tortoises use their legs in breathing, of course, and seem quite able to walk and breathe at the same time; however, as they almost certainly evolved from river turtles, their breathing system would have been quite advanced by the time they took to a terrestrial life.

Rieppell and Reisz pointed out that *Henodus*, which presumably faced the same problem, certainly evolved its shell in the water. An aquatic animal, whatever else it may use its legs for, does not need them to hold itself up. If the ancestor of turtles also lived in the water instead of on land—as *Odontochelys* apparently did—the breathing problem disappears. Rieppell and Reisz came up with a number of other arguments for an aquatic origin for turtles, including the suggestion that armoring one's underside—as both turtles and cyamodontoid placodonts do—only makes sense if you are likely to be attacked from below. This is much more likely to happen to a swimming animal than to one walking about on dry land, and it may be why *Odontochelys* had a fully developed bony plastron.

There are some flaws in this argument. All of the earliest turtles we have found—except for *Odontochelys*, the earliest—appear to have been land dwellers. The plastron could have evolved, not as armor, but as a brace locking the sides of the carapace together (see page 16, Chapter 1). Other armored land vertebrates, like armadillos, may have no belly armor, but unlike turtles they either can roll into a ball to protect their undersides, as armadillos do, or are so huge that they could have protected their bellies by simply squatting on the ground, as the extinct glyptodonts, giant armored relatives of armadillos, may have done.

If turtles did evolve as swimmers, it is unlikely that their ancestors were sturdy landlubbers like the pareiasaurs (though some pareiasaurs, such as *Pareiasaurus serridens* from South Africa and the less heavily armored *Deltavjatia vjatkensis* from Russia, may have lived amphibiously, like reptilian hippos). However, if both turtles and sauropterygians started out as swimming animals, then perhaps the similarities between them have less to do with relationship than with the results of the evolutionary constraints of a watery existence.

After Rieppell and Reisz, using morphological characters, placed turtles among the diapsids with the sauropterygians as their closest kin, they ran their analysis again, leaving the sauropterygians out. To their surprise, the turtles, instead of winding up among the eureptiles, landed back among the parareptiles. In other words, the reason that the turtles had come out among the eureptiles in the first place was because the sauropterygians were there. The characters turtles and sauropterygians share had pulled the turtles into the eureptile camp. When Robert Hill, a few years later, ran another morphological analysis using more characters and a greater range of animal groups (including the sauropterygians), the turtles ended up back among the diapsids but, this time, closer to the lepidosau-

rians—suggesting that the sauropterygians may not have been entirely responsible for the result (unless the sauropterygians are themselves lepidosaurians, which is at least a possibility!).

An Unsolved Mystery

Where does all this leave us? Are turtles, despite all the new evidence, really parareptiles, as scientists have thought for years? Or should we accept what the computer programs conclude, that turtles belong among the eureptiles, even if this seems at the very least counterintuitive?

There are some features of the ankle joint, as well as a unique jaw ligament, that turtles seem to share only with eureptiles. If turtles really evolved from a swimming ancestor, should we look for that ancestor near the sauropterygians? If not, what sort of swimming creature was it? Or is Lee right, is the ancestral turtle to be found among the lumbering pareiasaurs? Or somewhere else altogether? Ingmar Werneburg and Marcelo R. Sánchez-Villagra have recently presented evidence that the timing of the appearance of embryological characters in turtles differs from that in other living reptiles. They conclude from this that turtles represent a separate branch of the reptile tree, but they do not say where.

Part of the debate turns on how the carapace, and particularly the costal bones, evolved (see page 21, Chapter 1). The so-called composite hypothesis states that the costals are the result of fusion of the ribs with dermal plates, called *osteoderms*, that were already there in the turtle ancestor—a view that could point to the armored pareiasaurs (or, of course, anything else with dermal armor). The de novo hypothesis holds that the dermal elements that ossify around the developing ribs are newly evolved structures, with no relation to any armor that might have been present in a presumed proto-turtle (whatever it may have been). *Odontochelys*, which has broadened ribs and lacks any sort of costal armor, may point to the de novo hypothesis,

CHART 3: Four Hypotheses of Turtle Relationships

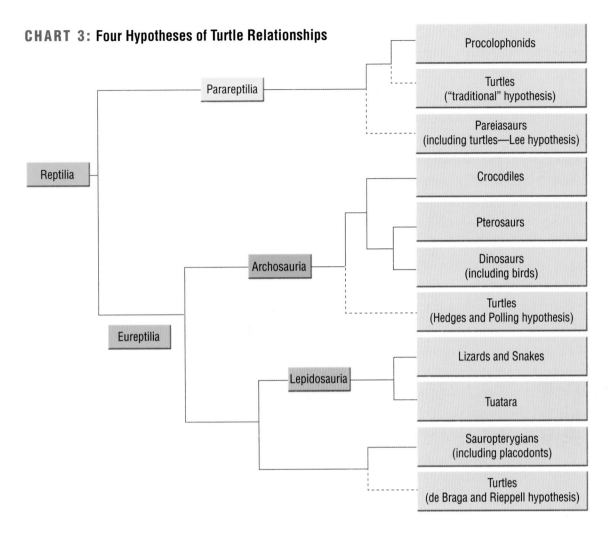

but only if it is evolving, rather than losing, its carapace—and we don't know that yet.

The eureptile argument is certainly gaining ground, but our level of confusion may be best illustrated by two papers, published in 2010 and 2011 respectively. One used morphological characters to place turtles among the parareptiles (though most of these characters are also found in at least some diapsids), and the other relied on molecular data to ally turtles with the lepidosaurs. Both papers had the same primary author.

What we really need is a fossil we have yet to discover, something transitional between a genuine turtle and whatever its ancestor might have been—or, if turtles really are diapsids, an unquestionable early turtle with diapsid temporal fenestrae. Unfortunately the most likely time for such an animal to have existed—unless some telltale splotches on a very young *Odontochelys* specimen currently being carefully examined in China are, in fact, the remains of temporal fenestrae that would have closed later in life—would be the Early Triassic, a period that has left us comparatively poor fossil remains. Since the center of parareptile evolution was probably in the former Southern Hemisphere supercontinent of Gondwanaland, and since one of the biggest chunks of Gondwanaland, Antarctica, is buried beneath tons of ice, some of the fossils we need may be far beyond our current reach. The ancestral turtle, whatever it was, may keep its mystery.

The Second-Oldest Turtles

It is, I confess, with some relief that I lead my readers a short distance forward in time, away from the welter of potential proto-turtles, pseudo-turtles, quasi-turtles and definitely-not-turtles that littered the Permian and the Early Triassic, to the first genuine, unquestionable turtles that we have. They include the animals we met at the beginning of this chapter, *Odontochelys* and *Proganochelys*, and another Triassic turtle, *Chinlechelys tenertesta*, from the famous Chinle fossil formation in New Mexico. *Chinlechelys* lived at the same time as *Proganochelys*, or perhaps even earlier: between 205 and 220 million years ago. All we have of it are fragments of the carapace, plastron and bridge, one costal with ribs, a neck spine and a few other isolated bits. *Chinlechelys* seems to have had a very thin shell, less than 1 mm (0.04 in) thick in places, with the costals and ribs only weakly fused together—possible evidence for the composite hypothesis, in which the dermal armor came first and fused to the ribs later on. The ribs themselves are flattened vertically, a unique condition in turtles but a widespread one in early reptiles in general, suggesting that *Chinlechelys* was a very primitive turtle indeed.

It's too bad we don't have more of it. Interpreting often fragmentary, poorly preserved remains can be fraught with danger. Researchers claiming that a recently discovered fossil turtle from China had some most unusual features in its plastron apparently perceived the fossil the wrong way around. Once it was pointed out that the supposed front end of the fossil was actually its rear, the "unusual features" disappeared!

We know quite a bit, by contrast, about *Proganochelys*. This is largely thanks to Eugene Gaffney's extremely detailed, bone-by-bone description of a number of excellent, near-complete specimens. There are fragments of *Proganochelys*-like turtles known from Greenland and Thailand, but the best specimens, the ones Dr. Gaffney examined, come from Germany. *Proganochelys* looked rather like a modern Common Snapping Turtle (*Chelydra serpentina*). Paleontologists have long assumed that it lived like one, walking along the bottom of shallow swamps with occasional forays onto dry land; however, studies of its limb proportions and the bone microstructure of its shell suggest that *Proganochelys* resembles a land-living turtle more than an aquatic one. Of course many living turtles seem quite able to switch from water to land without difficulty despite their anatomies, but *Proganochelys* and other early turtles (except *Odontochelys*) may have lived more like Triassic tortoises. *Odontochelys* aside, the earliest known aquatic turtle may have been *Eileanchelys waldmani* from the Middle Jurassic of Scotland, a much later animal than *Proganochelys*.

Neither *Odontochelys* nor *Proganochelys* could withdraw their heads beneath their shells (of course, *Odontochelys* may not have had much of a shell in the first place). *Proganochelys* perhaps made up for this with a row of spines protecting the back of its neck. The scutes of its carapace were rough and peaked. Its last few tail vertebrae were fused into a club, though it is not at all clear if *Proganochelys* could have used them as one.

Proganochelys shows that turtles did not acquire all their special features at once. Though Gaffney identified six characteristics that *Proganochelys* shares only with other turtles, he found six more that it shares only with other early reptiles. Most of these involve the skull.

Proganochelys has a fairly advanced shell, its most obvious turtle feature. Its skull, though, is in many ways still the open, unfused, flexible structure of a typical early reptile. *Proganochelys* still has two bones, the *lacrimal* and the *supratemporal*, found in early reptile skulls but missing in more advanced turtles. It has two *vomers*, bones that lie side by side in the roof of the mouth. In later turtles these have been reduced to one or, in some South American river turtles (*Podocnemis* spp.), lost. Most importantly, perhaps, while modern turtles have a solid box of bone hemming in their middle ear, *Proganochelys* has the same open, unossified ear region as other early reptiles.

A clue to how the change from the condition

The skull of *Proganochelys* retains many of the features found in other early reptiles.

in *Proganochelys* to that in modern turtles may have taken place came with the description in 1994 of another early turtle, *Australochelys africanus*. Known only from a skull and a fragment of shell, *Australochelys* lived millions of years after *Proganochelys*, in the Early Jurassic. It is the oldest turtle ever found in Africa, beating its nearest rival by 60 million years. Like *Odontochelys* and *Proganochelys*, *Australochelys* retained many features found in other early reptiles. Its ear region was almost the same as in *Proganochelys*, but not quite. *Australochelys* had made a significant advance, a first step in the transition from an open, flexible skull to a closed, rigid one.

In *Proganochelys*, as in other early reptiles, the braincase attaches to the rest of the skull by a movable joint just in front of the ear. It could, at least in theory, move slightly within the animal's skull. With a movable braincase pushing or pulling against the middle ear, it may have been difficult to form a rigid bony box around it. Things would have been much easier if the braincase could have been locked in place first.

That, in fact, is the change we see in *Australochelys*. Instead of a movable hinge, its braincase is fused to the skull by a solid, sutured immovable joint. This change may have taken place well before *Australochelys*, during the Triassic. In 2007, Juliana Sterli and her colleagues re-examined the anatomy of a much earlier turtle, *Palaeochersis talampayensis* from the Late Triassic of northwestern Argentina, and confirmed that, like *Australochelys*, its braincase was sutured to its skull. *Palaeochersis* and *Australochelys* may be each other's closest relatives among known fossil turtles.

With that important first step taken, the evolution of the modern, rigid turtle skull may have been only a matter of time. The further evolution of a box around the middle ear may have given turtles such an advantage that it happened not once but twice, in pleurodires and in cryptodires.

Of course *Palaeochersis* and *Australochelys* did not evolve their rigid braincases so that their descendants could ossify their ear capsules. Evolution does not plan ahead. These two turtles are widely separated in time, so the state of their skulls must have served them well for millions of years. Perhaps the more rigid skull the fused braincase joint allowed may have affected the way *Palaeochersis* and *Australochelys* fed.

Stem Turtles and the Great Divide

The debates over turtle evolution do not stop once we finally arrive at genuine, unquestionable turtles. Another debate, made possibly more confusing by a number of recent discoveries, is currently raging over the timing of the split that divided living turtles into pleurodires and cryptodires.

Are some of the very earliest turtles true pleurodires or cryptodires, or are they *stem* (or basal) turtles, arising from the stem of the turtle family tree before it split into its two surviving lineages? If even one Triassic turtle can be classified as a cryptodire or a pleurodire, then the evolutionary divide between cryptodires and pleurodires must have already happened. Basal turtles like *Odontochelys*, *Chinlechelys*, *Proganochelys* and the Jurassic *Australochelys* may have been living fossils even in their own far-off day.

The best evidence for an early cryptodire-pleurodire split, the view strongly held by Gaffney

and his collaborators, comes from another Triassic turtle. *Proterochersis robusta*, described as long ago as 1913, was a European turtle known only from its high-domed, tortoise-like shell and seemingly advanced limb girdles. More than two dozen have been found. It lived at almost the same time as—likely earlier than—*Proganochelys*. Like modern pleurodires, but unlike *Proganochelys*, its pelvic girdle is firmly fused to its shell. For Gaffney, that means that *Proterochersis* was a pleurodire, the earliest one known by some 50 million years.

Walter Joyce and his colleagues argue instead that the pleurodire-cryptodire split did not happen until at least the Middle Jurassic. They propose that pleurodires may have evolved from proto-cryptodire-like ancestors. Supporters of this idea can point to *Palaeochersis*, a turtle that provides evidence that *Proterochersis* may not be a pleurodire after all.

Everyone, including Gaffney, agrees that *Palaeochersis* is a stem turtle. Like *Proganochelys*, it could not tuck its head into its shell. It did not have the neck armor that protected *Proganochelys*, but its neck may have been protected instead by a forward extension of its carapace, as in a number of living sidenecks and tortoises. It had an open, largely unfused skull. It was certainly not a pleurodire, but, like *Proterochersis*, its pelvic girdle appears to be sutured to its shell. Though *Palaeochersis* and *Proterochersis* are probably not close relatives, *Palaeochersis* displays a few minor features that are otherwise known only from *Proterochersis*.

The unexpected combination of a primitive skull and a pleurodire-type shell may mean that having a pelvic girdle sutured to the shell is not a pleurodire character after all, but may have been widespread in stem turtles. Though Gaffney has argued that the pelvis of *Palaeochersis* is not really fused to the shell but simply appears that way due to the crushed state of the fossil material, Sterli's 2007 study confirmed the fusion of the pelvis to both carapace and plastron. Sterli noted that the fused elements in the pelvic girdle were not precisely the same as in *Proterochersis* and later pleurodires (to be precise, the connection to the xiphiplastron in *Palaeochersis* is via the medial ischial process rather than the lateral ischial process). *Palaeochersis* and *Proterochersis* may have achieved their pelvic fusion independently. Though her 2007 study found *Proterochersis* to be a basal pleurodire, Sterli's later analyses, using more characters and covering more species, support the view that it too is a stem turtle.

There has been further argument over the earliest known (purported) cryptodire, *Kayentachelys aprix* from the Kayenta formation of northeastern Arizona. *Kayentachelys* lived in the Early Jurassic, 185 million years ago—20 to 30 million years before the next-oldest cryptodire fossils. Joyce and others argue that *Kayentachelys* is yet another stem turtle, but in a 2010 study of its skull Gaffney and Farish Jenkins insist that it was a genuine, if primitive, cryptodire. In part this is because it shows a key feature of the jaw hinge that only cryptodires have.

Reptiles (including birds) close their jaws by means of a powerful muscle, the *adductor mandibulae*; we mammals do not, because the bones that serve as the jaw hinge in reptiles are now part of our middle ear, and our muscles have changed accordingly. In early reptiles, and in *Proganochelys* and *Australochelys*, the adductor mandibulae attached by means of a tendon that met the lower jaw at a more or less shallow angle. In all modern turtles, this tendon passes instead around a bump of bone called the *trochlea*. The trochlea acts as a sort of pulley, forcing the tendon to meet the jaw at a right angle. This not only keeps the tendon out of the way of the enlarged, bony ear capsule; it also results in a much more powerful bite (an excellent reason to keep your fingers out of a turtle's mouth).

Both pleurodires and cryptodires have a trochlea, but Gaffney argues that it must have evolved separately in each group because the bones involved are not the same. In cryptodires the trochlea is part of two bones called the *proötic* and the *quadrate*, while in pleurodires it forms part of a different bone,

the *pterygoid*. According to Gaffney, *Kayentachelys* has its trochlea on the proötic and quadrate, so *Kayentachelys* must have been a cryptodire.

Gaffney's evidence is a bump called the *processus trochlearis oticum*, the only sign in the skeleton (as opposed to non-fossilized soft tissue) of a cryptodire jaw mechanism. In 2007 Sterli and Joyce argued that the bump was not really there. Gaffney and Jenkins, relying in 2010 on a better-quality specimen, replied (in considerable detail) that yes, it certainly was. Joyce has also argued that the pleurodire mechanism could have evolved from the "cryptodire" mechanism, which may have been present in a number of early turtles anyway. Gaffney disagrees, and the debate continues.

Kayentachelys was not a modern turtle. Bone had not yet completely enclosed its middle ear, which was still open from below. In technical terms, *Kayentachelys* lacked the posteromedial process of the pterygoid, the piece of bone that forms the floor of the ear capsule in advanced cryptodires. *Kayentachelys* still had teeth, confined, like those in *Proganochelys*, to its palate. If Gaffney is correct, then the ancestor of pleurodires and cryptodires must have had teeth too. Pleurodires and cryptodires would have had to lose their remaining teeth independently.

Did tooth loss (and a number of other changes from *Kayentachelys* to modern turtles) really occur twice, once in cryptodires and once in pleurodires? If *Palaeochersis*, *Proterochersis* and *Kayentachelys* are stem turtles, the various changes needed to derive a modern turtle, including loss of teeth, need only have occurred once.

By this argument, not only are all of the Triassic and Early Jurassic species stem turtles, but other Middle Jurassic turtles that Gaffney considers to be cryptodires, *Eileanchelys waldmani* from Scotland, *Heckerochelys romani* from Russia and *Condorchelys antiqua* from Argentina (which had already lost its teeth, and may [Gaffney] or may not [Sterli] have had a processus trochlearis oticum), must be stem turtles too. So are the Upper Cretaceous *Mongolochelys efre-movi* from Mongolia and *Kallokibotion bajazidi* from Transylvania, and the horned meiolaniids that we shall meet later in this chapter. For Joyce and his supporters, the stem turtle lineages were far more diverse than we have realized, and had a large geographic range, a lengthy geological history, and a broad range of lifestyles. Whatever their eventual fate, they were an evolutionary success.

Gaffney continues to disagree. In their 2010 study of the skull of *Kayentachelys*, Gaffney and Jenkins assert that only *Proganochelys*, *Palaeochersis* and *Australochelys* fall outside the main pleurodire-cryptodire lineage (the paper does not discuss *Odontochelys* and *Chinlechelys*). They argue that many of the adaptations that would've had to evolve separately in cryptodires and pleurodires are comparatively minor, and could easily have happened a number of times. They also point to molecular evidence dating the cryptodire-pleurodire split to 207–216 million years ago, firmly within the Jurassic and the time of *Proterochersis*.

We need more and better fossils, and particularly skulls; but, for any readers who might be confused by all this, the general shape of the turtle family tree remains roughly the same whichever theory you choose to follow. It really comes down to shifting just a few of the lower branches.

The Rise of Modern Turtles

Once we move forward to the Late Jurassic, we begin to encounter turtles that everyone agrees are either cryptodires or pleurodires—though, once again, not everyone agrees on just where, within these lineages, their relationships lie. On the cryptodire limb of the turtle tree, a number of side branches lead to families now extinct. The Pleurosternidae and the Baenidae are sometimes grouped together (with the recently described, and apparently basal, *Arundelemys dardeni* from the Early Cretaceous of Maryland) as the Paracryptodira, based largely on

the paths that their carotid arteries followed into their skulls. The Baenidae, first known from the Upper Cretaceous, survived into the Eocene; eight distinct baenid lineages, including the common genus *Boremys*, weathered the extinction event that wiped out the dinosaurs 65 million years ago and continued to thrive in the Paleocene (for a short time after the disaster turtles of one sort or another may have been the dominant land vertebrate group). Baenids, which resembled (and probably lived like) modern pond turtles, are known only from North America. There are many described species, though most are based on fragmentary remains.

The Pleurosternidae, whose earliest members date from the Middle Jurassic, may have lived across the whole of the northern hemisphere. They died out at the end of the Cretaceous, but an apparent close relative, *Compsemys victa* of western North America, survived into the Paleocene. *Compsemys* bore a strong superficial resemblance to the modern Big-headed Turtle (*Platysternon megacephalum*) of southeast Asia, and may have lived in a similar manner (see page 123, Chapter 3).

Among the turtles that presumably branched off from the cryptodire line before the common ancestor of the living forms are the Jurassic marine turtles of the Plesiochelyidae, animals we will meet later in this chapter, and a number of Middle Jurassic to Paleocene fossils. Many are known from partial remains and have proven difficult to classify (including the delightfully named *Chelycarapookus arcuatus* from Australia). Some mostly Asian turtles have been grouped under a variety of family names (e.g. Sinemydidae, Macrobaenidae, Xinjianchelyidae, Chengyuchelyidae) without much agreement as to which species belong in each, or on whether these "families" are natural groups at all. North American "macrobaenids" include the Late Cretaceous *Judithemys sukhanovi* from Dinosaur Provincial Park, Alberta. Its anatomy suggests that it was fully aquatic, a strong swimmer with a lifestyle resembling the living snapping turtles (Chelydridae).

CHART 4: Relationships of the Major Turtle Groups
(not all taxa shown. Taxa in dashed boxes shown in more detail in Chart 5)

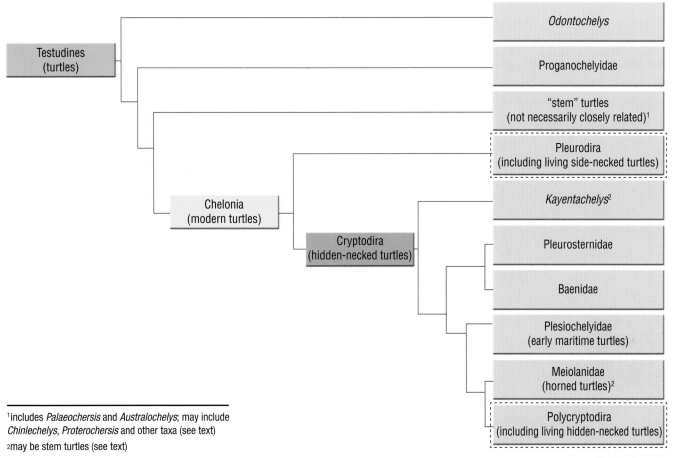

Testudines
(turtles)

Odontochelys

Proganochelyidae

"stem" turtles
(not necessarily closely related)[1]

Pleurodira
(including living side-necked turtles)

Chelonia
(modern turtles)

Kayentachelys[2]

Cryptodira
(hidden-necked turtles)

Pleurosternidae

Baenidae

Plesiochelyidae
(early maritime turtles)

Meiolanidae
(horned turtles)[2]

Polycryptodira
(including living hidden-necked turtles)

[1]includes *Palaeochersis* and *Australochelys*; may include
Chinlechelys, *Proterochersis* and other taxa (see text)

[2]may be stem turtles (see text)

Plesiobaena antiqua, from the Judith
River Formation in Alberta, Canada,
was an Upper Cretaceous member
of the Baenidae. It lived between
80 and 75 million years ago.

Sandownia harrisi was described in 2000 as a peculiar Early Cretaceous relative of the modern softshell turtles (Trionychidae), but Joyce has suggested that it is part of an earlier radiation. Known from a skull and jaw from the Isle of Wight, England, *Sandownia* had an extremely strong skull and an extensive secondary palate forming a bony roof to the mouth, both strengthening adaptations that may have given an unusually powerful crushing bite. Octávio Mateus and his colleagues include *Sandownia* in a separate cryptodire group, the Angolachelonia, with a few other fossil turtles including the Late Cretaceous *Angolachelys mbaxi*, the oldest cryptodire known from Africa.

The living cryptodire families (and some extinct cousins), whose branches cluster together in the end of the limb, form the "crown group" Polycryptodira (that is, all cryptodires, living and extinct, descended from the common ancestor of the living forms). Though we may think of this as a "modern" group, the Polycryptodira has been around for a long time. Its oldest probable member,

Peltochelys duchastelli from the Early Cretaceous of Belgium, may be related to the softshells and pig-nose turtles (Carettochelyidae), and to two extinct families, Adocidae and Nanhsiungchelyidae. *Peltochelys* dates back 120 million years. Only 10 million years later, still in the Early Cretaceous, it seems that the Polycryptodira was not only well established, but had already split into lineages that lead to the turtle families alive today.

Proterochersis aside, pleurodires do not appear in the fossil record until the Late Jurassic, and we have to wait until the Early Cretaceous, 145 million years ago, before we find an unquestionable pleurodire skull. Only three Jurassic pleurodires are known: *Platychelys orbendorferi*, *Caribemys oxfordiensis* and *Notoemys laticentralis*. *Notoemys* must have been a highly successful genus; it is known from Cuba, Argentina and Colombia. The Colombian species, *Notoemys zapatocaensis*, shows that the genus survived into the Early Cretaceous.

Though *Platychelys*, *Caribemys* and *Notoemys* sit on side branches of the pleurodire tree, the next

BELOW

Another turtle from the Upper Cretaceous of Alberta: *Basilemys*, a large terrestrial or freshwater member of the extinct family Nanhsiungchelyidae. Its carapace could have been a meter long.

OPPOSITE

This 49 million-year-old pair of *Allaeochelis crassescultata*, a member of the pig-nose turtle family (Carettochelyidae) found in the Messel open-pit site in Germany, may have died during copulation.

oldest unquestionable pleurodire is much closer to living forms. This is *Araripemys barretoi*, a 110-million-year-old fossil from Brazil with an extremely flattened carapace. Though *Araripemys* has been placed in a now-extinct family, Araripemydidae, it appears to be more closely related to two of the living pleurodire families, the Pelomedusidae and Podocnemididae, than to the other living family, the Chelidae. It may even be an early pelomedusid. If that is true, then the Chelidae must have already split from the other families by the Early Cretaceous.

The discovery of another family of Cretaceous pleurodires, the Bothremydidae, has had a direct effect on the way living pleurodires are classified. The Pelomedusidae and Podocnemididae used to be considered part of the same family. The Bothremydidae, though, were actually closer to the Podocnemididae than to the Pelomedusidae. As a result, the Podocnemididae must be treated as a separate family, one that split from the Pelomedusidae as far back as the Cretaceous.

Bothremydids were a successful and varied lineage, with diverse feeding adaptations and a geological range from the Cretaceous to the Miocene. They showed the greatest variation in skull shape of any turtle family, living or extinct. Some, including the Paleocene *Bothremys maghrebianus*, and one of the earliest, *Cearachelys placidoi* from the Early Cretaceous Santana formation in Brazil, had broad jaws and crushing mouthparts like some modern map turtles (*Graptemys*). Like them, they may have been mollusk eaters. *Labrostochelys galkini* from the Paleocene had a long, narrow snout like some softshells and may have been a fish eater, while the Eocene *Phosphatochelys tedfordi* had a short, broad skull like a sea turtle. *Bothremys*, *Labrostochelys* and *Phosphatochelys* were all found in marine deposits in Morocco.

The Bothremydidae include probable marine species (see page 70) as well as freshwater turtles like *Foxemys mechinorum* from southern France and *Chedghaii hutchisoni* from North America. Recent bothremydid discoveries include the extremely narrow-skulled (and wonderfully named) *Chupacabrachelys complexus* from the Late Cretaceous of Texas and the broad-skulled *Kinkonychelys rogersi* from the Upper Cretaceous of northwestern Madagascar, whose nearest relatives are from India— not surprisingly, as Madagascar and India were connected until about 88 million years ago.

We do not have the space here to follow the living turtle families through the Age of Mammals to the present day. Instead, we will end this chapter by looking at three highlights of turtle history: the rise of the sea turtles, the story of the meiolaniids and the question of what, exactly, was the world's biggest turtle.

Return to the Sea

In the Mesozoic period, the seas were invaded by reptiles from a number of different lineages: sauropterygians, ichthyosaurs (which may have been sauropterygians too), seagoing crocodiles and mosasaurs, which were either seagoing lizards or seagoing snakes. The discovery of *Odontochelys* may mean that turtles either evolved in the sea from marine reptilian ancestors or returned there very early in their evolution, depending on which explanation of *Odontochelys*' peculiar features you prefer.

Though the first fully shelled turtles were probably land (or at least coastal) animals, their descendants, too, repeatedly returned to the sea during the Mesozoic. Turtle paleontologists have not been able to agree on how many families of fossil sea turtles there are, mostly because of disagreements about some of the more primitive forms. They do agree that the modern sea turtles and their immediate fossil kin, even including the highly distinctive Leatherback, are each other's closest relatives and belong in a single group, the Chelonioidea.

Before the rise of the modern sea turtles, during the Jurassic, a group of primitive cryptodires swam in the shallow seas off the coast of what is now Europe. These were members of the Plesiochelyidae, a family that apparently vanished before the end of the Jurassic. Plesiochelyids represented a radiation of marine turtles quite separate from the lineage that survives today. Though they were not particularly modified for an oceangoing life, isotopes in their fossilized shells suggest that plesiochelyids must have spent much of their lives in the sea. Unlike modern sea turtles, their front limbs were no larger than their hind limbs, so they could not have been the graceful, balletic swimmers the living species are (which does not mean they couldn't swim; living softshells, which swim very well, also have limbs of roughly equal size).

The early cryptodire *Neusticemys neuquina* shared nearshore seas off Argentina with other Jurassic marine reptiles including ichthyosaurs, plesiosaurs, seagoing crocodiles and *Notoemys laticentralis*, a pleurodire that appears to have lived along ocean beaches. *Neusticemys* had elongated limbs (though not fully developed into flippers or paddles), including extra bones in the fifth digit of the hind foot, a feature known in no other turtle. We will have to wait for the discovery of its skull to learn whether *Neusticemys* was related to plesiochelyids or later sea turtles.

The sea turtles of today are a pale remnant of the variety that existed in the past. In the first half of the Cretaceous there were five separate lineages of sea turtles. They included the very large European sea turtle *Allopleuron hoffmanni*, seemingly highly evolved for life in the open ocean, with an elongate, streamlined shell and rigid hindlimbs that were more likely rudders than swimming paddles. Quite different were relatively unmodified forms like *Toxochelys* (with four known species), which had a rounded shell, unspecialized, flexible flippers and upward-facing eye sockets. Like modern snapping and softshell turtles, it may have spent much of its time lying on the bottom in shallow water. *Toxochelys* and its relative *Ctenochelys* lie just outside the Chelonoidea, as its "sister group,"

rather than within the lineage leading to modern sea turtles.

Cretaceous sea turtles seemed to stay in their own corners of the ocean. Some Cretaceous sea turtles, for example, are found in European deposits but not in North America, and vice versa. That may explain why there were so many of them; each region had its own sea turtle fauna. Apparently, they did not undertake the great migratory journeys of their living relatives, though perhaps we just haven't found the fossils of Cretaceous wanderers, or perhaps some of the fossil turtles we have found in different regions are not really separate species.

Modern sea turtles first appeared in the Cretaceous, though a fossilized shallow-water Jurassic trackway—from the Jura Mountains of France, the ones that gave rise to the name "Jurassic"—appears to have been made by a giant marine turtle that swam by moving its front limbs simultaneously, as modern sea turtles do. Both of the modern sea turtle families, the Cheloniidae (typical sea turtles) and the Dermochelyidae (leatherbacks), had representatives in the Cretaceous.

The most famous turtle to swim Cretaceous seas, though, belonged to an extinct family, the Protostegidae. This was *Archelon ischyros*, largest of all sea turtles, an inhabitant of the shallow Niobrara Sea that once rolled over what are now the Great Plains of central North America. Just how big *Archelon* really was we will discuss at the end of this chapter, but it must have been an impressive creature. Its head alone may have been a meter (about 3 ft) long, and it culminated in a powerful, hooked beak. *Archelon* and its near relative *Protostega* were the most advanced of the protostegids. *Protostega* appears to have been adapted for life in the open ocean; remains of two specimens show traces of attack by Ginsu Sharks (*Cretoxyrhina mantelli*), rivals to the modern Great White Shark (*Carcharodon carcharias*) in size and the largest sharks of their time. Whether the sharks hunted the turtles or were simply scavenging their remains, however, we cannot say.

The protostegid line started with some fairly small and unspecialized animals. *Santanachelys gaffneyi*, from the 105-million-year-old Santana fossil beds of Brazil, was very small by sea turtle standards: only about 20 cm (8 in) overall. Its front limbs had yet to become fully modified into long, flat, rigid swimming paddles. However, it has one crucial adaptation to life in the ocean: a space in the skull where the living species have large salt-removing glands. These glands are vital for an animal that must drink seawater, even inadvertently (the remains of *Santanachelys* were found in a fossilized lake basin connected to the sea). Sea turtles apparently developed the ability to handle the salt load in seawater before they had fully evolved the elegant structures they use to swim through it.

The Late Cretaceous *Terlinguachelys fischbecki* from Texas, which had long, mobile hind limbs and probably lived close to the seashore, may have been another relatively unspecialized protostegid. It had a relatively elongate plastron, an adaptation to a more streamlined body shape also found in modern sea turtles. The main line of protostegid evolution, however led to larger and larger size, more and more massive heads, huge limbs, and, like the leatherbacks, a tendency to reduce the amount of bone in their carapaces and, eventually, to lose their bony carapace scutes altogether.

Protostegids are usually regarded as close relatives of the modern sea turtles, closer in fact to the leatherbacks than to the cheloniids. Based on some supposedly primitive characters, Joyce has removed *Santanachelys*—and, by inference, the other protostegids—to a more distant lineage outside the Polycryptodira. Others, including Benjamin Kear and Michael Lee, disagree, retaining *Santanachelys* with the chelonioids as the oldest of the Protostegidae.

The protostegids were a diverse and successful group in their day. They (or their close relatives) appear to have been the only Mesozoic sea turtles to have reached Australia. Other Early Cretaceous chelonioids may have been barred from entering Australia by seasonally cold waters and sea ice. Australian protostegids ranged from the smallish *Notochelone costata* (possibly closer to leatherbacks than to protostegids), with a carapace under a meter in length, to the immense *Cratochelone berneyi*, known only from fragmentary remains. *Cratochelone* may have reached 4 m (13 ft) overall.

The protostegids may have been adapting to the pursuit of a specific group of food items. The seas of the Mesozoic were dominated by the ammonites, distant relatives of the living chambered nautilus. Like it, ammonites had spectacular shells (some of them truly immense). Unlike the deep-water nautilus, though, many of them drifted in the upper layers of the ocean. To pursue them, an ammonite hunter needed the ability to swim after them and, once it had captured them, to crush their shells. The protostegids seem to have been well adapted on both counts. *Archelon*'s enormous flippers, or, rather, the shoulder joints that supported them, appear to have been designed more for straight-line distance swimming than for deep diving, and its enormous head would certainly have been capable of dealing with an ammonite shell.

Short of finding a protostegid fossil with an ammonite in its stomach, we cannot prove that *Archelon* and its relatives were actually eating ammonites, but it seems a reasonable enough speculation. It may also explain their eventual extinction well before the end of the Age of Reptiles. Ammonites went into a decline toward the end of the Cretaceous, and the protostegids appear to have done the same thing. By some 75 million years ago, there may have been only one protostegid left, an animal called *Atlantochelys*, pursuing the last of the ammonites.

OPPOSITE

A beautiful specimen of a large fossil softshell, from the Eocene Green River Formation of Wyoming.

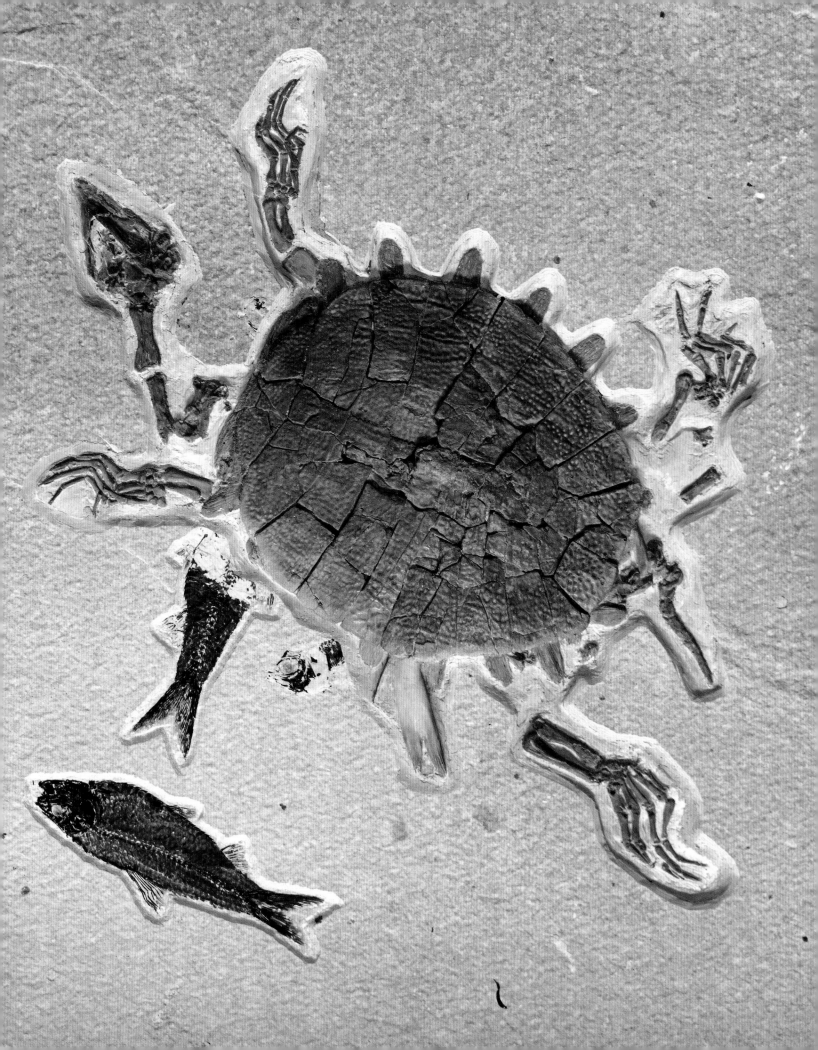

The pleurodires, possibly including the early *Araripemys*, also entered the sea during the Cretaceous. Marine members of the diverse extinct family Bothremydidae included *Taphrosphys*, a genus of Late Cretaceous turtles known from North America, South America, Africa and Europe. This is not as big a range as it may first appear. In Cretaceous times, the Atlantic was a narrow ocean, just beginning to spread. *Taphrosphys* may have been able to move freely among the continents along its shores. Although bothremydids do not seem to have been particularly modified for life in the sea, their fossils are often found in near-shore marine deposits. They may have been as close as the Cretaceous pleurodires ever came to producing a seagoing turtle. Marine, or at least near-shore, podocnemidids were widespread in the Tertiary. The Miocene podocnemidid *Bairdemys*, known from Venezuela and Puerto Rico, apparently nested on coastal beaches and may have lived in marine or brackish waters close to shore.

After the end of the Cretaceous, the open seas were left to the "modern"—that is, surviving—sea turtle lineages and their near relatives. They repeatedly radiated into a variety of forms specializing on different diets. Today, the Loggerhead Sea Turtle (*Caretta caretta*) is "durophagous"—adapted to crush hard-shelled prey using flat jaw surfaces and a muscular head—while the Green Sea Turtle has sharp, shearing jaws able to crop sea grass, its primary food. Cretaceous sea turtles appear not to have developed either specialization (sea grasses did not appear until late in the period), but since then durophagous and shearing jaws appear to have evolved and re-evolved at least four times each, with each new appearance arising independently after the extinction of its predecessor.

There may also have been an array of Eocene softshell turtles living in shallow marine waters off the coast of what is now Pakistan. Softshell remains from the area (only one of which has been given a name, *Drazinderetes tethyensis*) include bones from a possible monster, with a carapace that may have been more than 2 m (6.5 ft) long.

Ninja Turtles

In 1992, Eugene Gaffney had to find a new generic name for *Meiolania oweni*, a fossil turtle from the Pleistocene of Queensland, Australia. He named it *Ninjemys*, "in allusion to that totally rad, fearsome foursome epitomizing shelled success." Let it never be said that turtle paleontologists lack a sense of humor.

If ever there really were ninja turtles, surely they would have belonged to the Meiolaniidae. More bizarre creatures than *Ninjemys* and its kin would be difficult to imagine. Large, tortoise-like animals, most meiolaniids sported startling head ornaments, culminating in steerlike horns that either arched backward (in the members of the genus *Meiolania*) or jutted straight out to the side (as they did in *Ninjemys oweni*). The only hornless meiolaniid, *Warkalania*, bore horizontal corrugated ridges instead, while *Niolamia*, the oldest member of the family and the only one known from South America, supplemented its *Ninjemys*-like horns with a bony frill over the back of its neck. Meiolaniid tails were surrounded by rings of dermal armor and tipped with a bony club.

Aside from the oldest of them, *Niolamia* from the Eocene of Argentina, meiolaniids are known only from eastern and northern Australia, Lord Howe Island in the Tasman Sea, and the archipelagos of Vanuatu, Fiji and New Caledonia in the Southwest Pacific. Recent discoveries have proven that these remarkable animals survived on Efate, in Vanuatu, until only about 2,800 years ago. Between 2004 and 2006, Arthur White and Trevor Worthy excavated hundreds of limb bones and shell fragments of a previously unknown species, tentatively named ?*Meiolania damelipi*, from midden deposits of the Lapita people, the first humans to colonize

Meiolania platyceps from Lord Howe Island near Australia, best-known of the bizarre horned turtle family (Meiolaniidae).

the Southwest Pacific. The remains were only found in the lower midden layers. The colonists seem first to have exterminated the turtles in their immediate area, and then hunted out the remaining populations elsewhere. The animals must have been easy to catch, because the Lapita apparently preferred them to sea turtles as long as they were available. The extinction of *damelipi* could have been hastened by the islanders' pigs, which may have eaten its eggs and young (as they did to the now-extinct giant tortoises of Mauritius). The last of the meiolaniids disappeared about 300 years after the first human colonists arrived on the island.

South America, Australia and New Caledonia were all part of the great southern continent of Gondwanaland during the Mesozoic, so the first meiolaniids could have walked from one to the other (there are fragmentary remains from the Cretaceous of South America that may be meiolaniid). Lord Howe Island, though, did not emerge from the Tasman Sea until the late Miocene, so the ancestors of its horned turtle, *Meiolania platyceps*, must have reached it over water, with possible stops along the way on islands that no longer exist. The same is true for the meiolaniids of Vanuatu and Fiji. Perhaps they drifted there, as the giant tortoises of Aldabra and the Galápagos probably did in their turn.

The name *Meiolania* means "lesser ripper." This may seem like a strange name for even such peculiar animals as these, but it stems from one of the more famous mistakes in paleontology. When George Bennett found the first meiolaniid skull in Queensland, Australia, in 1879 (the skull that Gaffney would later rename *Ninjemys*), he identified it correctly as belonging to a turtle. However, when he sent the specimen to England it came into the hands of Richard Owen, the famous paleontologist who coined the name "dinosaur" and bitterly opposed Charles Darwin's theory of evolution. Owen rejected Bennett's conclusion, and decided instead that the skull belonged with the bones of a giant monitor lizard he had described in 1858 as *Megalania prisca*. *Megalania* means "great ripper," a name the lizard certainly deserved.

When Owen received specimens of the Lord Howe meiolaniid, a smaller animal, he decided that they were lizards, too, and named them *Meiolania*. A few years later, he added to his mistake by mixing in foot bones from *Diprotodon*, a giant wombat-like marsupial. By 1887, Darwin's great champion Thomas Henry Huxley was able to use newly discovered material from Lord Howe Island to show that Owen's "lizard" was, as Bennett had thought, a turtle. Owen grudgingly admitted that perhaps his remains belonged to a group of animals intermediate between lizards and turtles—a peculiar stance for someone who did not believe in evolution. Huxley tried to give the turtles a more appropriate name, *Ceratochelys*, which simply means "horned turtle," but was defeated by the rules of zoological nomenclature, which give priority to older names, however inept. The name *Megalania* is now only associated with the giant lizard named by Owen. Bennett's skull became *Meiolania oweni* (later to be changed to *Ninjemys oweni*), and the Lord Howe horned turtle remains *Meiolania platyceps.*

There has been considerable controversy over where the meiolaniids fit on the turtle family tree. They have been variously called pleurodires, cryptodires, or, more recently, stem turtles—which, if true, would make them the only stem turtle lineage to have survived into historic times. Like *Proganochelys*, but unlike modern turtles, meiolaniids had ribs attached to their neck vertebrae. Certainly meiolaniids were incapable of retracting their necks in either the pleurodire or cryptodire fashion. As Gaffney wrote, "even a cursory examination of the horns on a *Meiolania* skull would show that either form of neck retraction would result in a kind of chelonian 'hara-kiri'." Dr. Gaffney has argued that meiolaniids are, nevertheless, cryptodires—though very peculiar ones only distantly related to modern families—based on a number of characters including the pattern of arterial circulation in the head and the jaw-muscle mechanism.

One of their closest relatives may be *Chubutemys copelloi*, a recently described cryptodire from the Early Cretaceous of Argentina that apparently lies outside the lineage of living cryptodire groups. Like the meiolaniids *Chubutemys* had a fully roofed-over skull, though it probably acquired this independently. *Patagoniaemys gasparinae*, a relatively large Upper Cretaceous turtle from Argentina, *Otwayemys cunicularius* from the Early Cretaceous of Australia and *Mongolochelys efremovi* from the Upper Cretaceous

of Mongolia may have been even closer to the meiolaniids than *Chubutemys* (though Gaffney, who still champions *Chubutemys*, disagrees).

We can only speculate on the uses to which meiolaniids would have put their formidable armament. In South America, Australia and some Pacific islands, they would have faced large and dangerous predators (including crocodiles in the Pacific), but not on Lord Howe where they were probably the largest animals around. Perhaps they fought each other in spectacular battles over mates, but we will never know for sure.

The Lord Howe Island horned turtle, *Meiolania platyceps*, is the only one of its family for which we have reasonably complete skeletons. The others are known from skulls, tail armor, or even more fragmentary remains. At 2 m (6.5 ft) overall length, it was a substantial beast. If skulls and bits of horn are any guide, though, it was actually one of the smaller meiolaniids. Others may have been twice as large, making them among the largest turtles ever to have lived. The larger skulls of *Ninjemys* measure almost 70 cm (2 ft) across from horn tip to horn tip. Without better specimens, though, they cannot—bizarre and wonderful as they may have been—be candidates for consideration in the final section of this chapter, which addresses that very question.

Giants

We started this chapter with one of the most difficult questions one can ask about fossil turtles: how did they evolve? In following our story thus far we have dealt with other equally complex and abstruse issues. Let us end the chapter, though, with a much more straightforward question: what was the biggest turtle that ever lived?

Most people, assuming they stopped to think about such things, would give the crown to *Archelon*, the giant protostegid sea turtle of the Cretaceous. *Archelon ischyros* was the largest sea turtle known to science (but it may have had a near rival in the

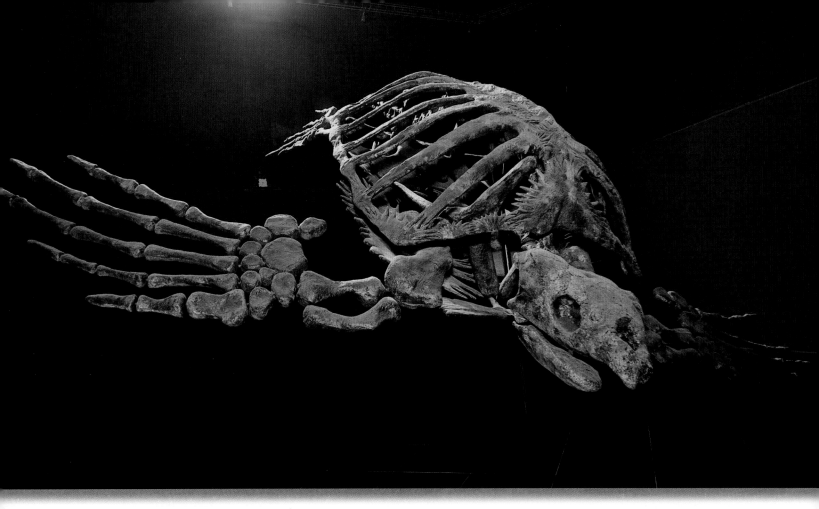

Archelon ischyros from the Cretaceous of North America, largest of the Protostegidae, and the biggest marine turtle known.

Australian *Cratochelone berneyi*). It was certainly an enormous animal, though its exceptionally long skull may give it a greater total length than its actual bulk implies. Turtle biologists tend to think of size in terms, not of total length, but of the length of the carapace (a more useful measurement for fossils anyway, as paleontologists don't always find the whole animal). In that department *Archelon* may not have been much bigger than a modern Leatherback; its carapace, measured in a straight line, is about 1.9 m (6.3 ft) long. The giant Eocene softshells of Pakistan may have been even larger.

How big was *Archelon*? Its average length may have been about 3 m (9–10 ft), though two specimens found in South Dakota in 1996 and 1998 measured roughly 3.6 m (12 ft) from snout to tail. A specimen on exhibit in Vienna, collected in the mid-1970s, measures 4.5 m (15 ft) from snout to tail and 5.25 m (16.5 ft) from tip to tip of its out-stretched flippers. It may have weighed 2,200 kg (4,500 lbs) when alive.

At one time, the most likely candidate for the largest land or freshwater turtle would have been a giant tortoise that roamed India, Thailand and Indonesia about 2 million years ago, during the Pleistocene. Its fossilized remains in India's Siwalik Hills may have contributed to legends of battles between giant heroes, commemorated in the Hindu epic *Mahâbhârata*. From its fragmentary first remains, the naturalists who described it in 1844 calculated that its carapace was a staggering 3.6 m (12 ft) long. They named it *Colossochelys atlas* in consequence (it is sometimes called *Geochelone* or *Testudo atlas*, or *Geochelone sivalensis* today, but it does not seem to belong to either of these living genera and its relationship to other tortoises is not yet clear). Had this first calculation proven to be correct, *Colossochelys* would unquestionably have remained the largest turtle known, even to this day. Unfortunately later workers, with better material, revised the figure downward to 2.3 m (8 ft), and then to about 1.8 m (6 ft). That still makes it one of the largest tortoises ever found (though there is a similar-size fossil giant known from Spain). It was much bigger than any living form, but it is out of contention for the overall world record.

With *Colossochelys atlas* whittled down to size, the world record for the largest turtle that ever lived, based on carapace size—at least as far as we know—passes (despite the Pakistani sofstshells) to another, even more remarkable creature. In 1972, a paleontological expedition from Harvard University unearthed the remains of several huge fossil turtles in northern Venezuela. Roger Conant Wood, who described them in 1976, gave these "gargantuan" turtles, as he called them, the name *Stupendemys geographicus*. The origin of the name *Stupendemys* should be obvious enough—*emys* simply means "turtle." *Geographicus* refers to the National Geographic Society, which funded Wood's research. Gratitude, in science, makes good sense.

The largest *Stupendemys* carapace Wood examined was 2.3 m (8 ft) long. That would have been enough to give it the record right there, now that *Colossochelys* is out of the running, but in 1992 an even larger specimen turned up, 3.3 m (11 ft) long and 2.2 m (7 ft) wide. Unfortunately, we don't have a complete skeleton, so we cannot be certain exactly how this translates into the overall size of the animal. With a shell like that, *Stupendemys* would appear to be well in front of its rivals. The great size of its shell is compensated for by its lightweight construction, a feature also seen in the shells of other very large turtles.

Stupendemys lived about eight million years ago, in the late Miocene. It was a member of the same pleurodire family, Podocnemididae, as the largest living sideneck, the Giant River Turtle or Arrau (*Podocnemis expansa*) of northern South America. The enormous, flattened shell of *Stupendemys* is very like that of other aquatic podocnemidids. Like the Arrau, it probably spent almost all of its life in the water—probably in fresh water, though, like the Cretaceous sideneck *Taphrosphys*, it may have entered the ocean as well. Its peculiarly squat, massive humerus suggests that its limbs, unlike those of other pleurodires, may have been modified into flippers.

Stupendemys may have only been one of a whole group of giant podocnemidid turtles. Remains of very large podocnemidids have been found in several parts of the Amazon basin. One, known only from a single vertebra, may have been even larger than *Stupendemys*. Without skulls clearly associated with fossil shells, it is difficult to tell how many forms are actually involved. One skull may belong to *Stupendemys*, but there is no proof of this and the fossil has been given its own name, *Caninemys tridentata*. The skull, and a lower jaw that seems to match it, are massive, more like those of an Alligator Snapper (*Macrochelys temminckii*) (or, as Peter Meylan and his colleagues put it, a bulldog) than a podocnemidid. The hooked lower jaw seems to fit between two bony "teeth" on the skull, creating what must have been an impressive bite. *Caninemys*—or *Stupendemys*, if that is indeed what it was—must have been a formidable predator, "snapping up," in the words of its describers, "passing fish, caimans, and anacondas."

Stupendemys, in fact, lived in a land of giants. The Urumaco formation of northern Venezuela, where it was first discovered, was a vast complex of fresh- and brackish-water marshes during the Miocene, like the Everglades or the Pantanal today. It has yielded fossils of giant crocodiles, and, surprisingly, giant rodents. One of them, *Phoberomys pattersoni*, was a monster even more surprising that *Stupendemys*: the biggest rodent that ever lived. It was 3 m (10 ft) long, 1.3 m (4 ft) tall, and may have weighed up to 700 kg (1,550 lbs)—fit company, perhaps, for the largest of the turtles.

CHART 5: **Relationships of Living Turtle Families and Their Extinct Relatives**
(not all extinct families shown)

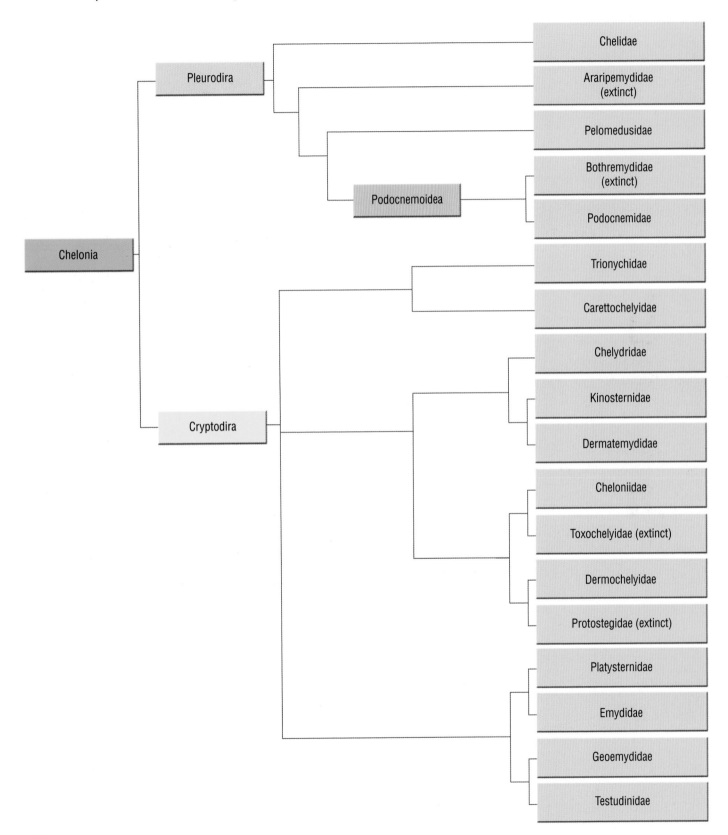

CHAPTER THREE

TURTLES AROUND THE WORLD I:
Side-Necks and Hidden Necks

THERE ARE ONLY 320 species of turtle alive today. A further eight, most of them giant tortoises from oceanic islands, became extinct in historic times. That is a small number, indeed, compared to the numbers of lizards (more than 4,500) or snakes (nearly 3,000). And yet, that small number covers almost as great a span of the globe as either of those larger groups—and, if the sea turtles are included, a much greater one. Turtles live on every continent except Antarctica, roam all but the coldest seas, and have reached a range of isolated oceanic islands from the West Indies to the Galápagos and the islands of the Indian Ocean. The European Pond Turtle (*Emys orbicularis*) reaches latitude 56° N in Europe, and the Pampas Tortoise (*Chelonoidis chilensis*) ranges to latitude 42° S in South America.

Of the 3 families of pleurodires and 11 families of cryptodires, only the tortoises (Testudinidae) come close to having a global reach on land, and even that family is missing from Australia. Cryptodires are mostly northern (except for the sea turtles and the softshells which range throughout Africa and northern Australia, though tortoises have done very well in southern Africa, Madagascar and South America), and one family, the Carettochelyidae, survives today only south of the equator in New Guinea and tropical northern Australia. The earliest freshwater turtle known from Australia, the Cretaceous *Otwayemys cunicularius*, may have

OPPOSITE

The Purvis's or Manning River Sawshelled Turtle (*Elseya purvisi*), a member of the Chelidae, is found only in the Manning River system of central coastal New South Wales, Australia.

been a cryptodire related to the horned meiolaniids (see page 72, Chapter 2). Pleurodires are entirely southern, confined to South America, Sub-Saharan Africa, Madagascar, New Guinea, Roti/Timor and Australia (where they apparently did not arrive until the Tertiary), with a single, tiny toehold in south-western Asia—though, once again, fossils show that they once enjoyed a wider range.

How the Pleurodires Got to Where They Are

The living pleurodires fall naturally into two groups, one containing the more "advanced" Chelidae, and the other the remaining two families: the Pelomedusidae and the Podocnemididae. The Chelidae live in Australia, New Guinea and nearby islands, and South America. The Podocnemididae has all but one of its living members in South America, but that one exception lives, of all places, only on the island of Madagascar. The third family, the Pelomedusidae, is the only pleurodire group in Africa.

This distribution looks extremely peculiar, until you remember that the southern land masses where they live were once united into a single supercontinent. This great vanished block of land, which received the name Gondwanaland long after it had sundered, contained the pieces of the earth's crust that were to become Antarctica, South America, Africa, Madagascar, Australia, New Zealand, Arabia and India. In the Early Jurassic it even included part of the future North America. Gondwanaland did not break up until the Jurassic, probably after the pleurodires and cryptodires had gone their separate evolutionary ways. Pleurodire turtles were free to spread throughout Gondwanaland, perhaps even crossing the narrow stretches of sea that opened as the supercontinent split.

What is odd is that none of the Gondwanaland remnants carries all three living pleurodire families. There are no chelids in Africa, no podocnemidids or pelomedusids in Australia, and no pelomedusids in South America. There are no living pleurodires in India, and no land turtles of any kind in New Zealand.

The explanation for this may be a phenomenon biogeographers call *vicariance*. A vicariant event, like the breakup of Gondwanaland, splits up what was once a continuous ecosystem. It isolates animals and plants into separate areas where they follow their own independent histories. In some of the separate bits, one group may go extinct and another may survive; in other areas, for one reason or another, the opposite may happen. We know that happened to the podocnemidids, because fossils related to the living genus *Podocnemis* have been found in Africa, South Asia, and even in Europe and North America (see page 70, Chapter 2). Extinct relatives of the living Malagasy genus *Erymnochelys* have a long fossil record in Africa, and *Erymnochelys* itself (or a close relative) may have lived in Africa during the Miocene. No fossil chelids, though, have ever been found on the continent. Could it be that they never occurred there? What is their history?

Gondwanaland did not break up all at once. By the mid-Cretaceous, 125 million years ago, Africa had drifted away to the north, but South America remained close to, and, perhaps, joined with a land mass that still included Antarctica and Australia. Antarctica was not a polar wasteland but a rich expanse of territory boasting dense, cool forests, its own special dinosaurs, and turtles. Their presence there is testified to by a single fossil bone, a neural dating from the Miocene. The podocnemidids and pelomedusids probably evolved in the northern part of Gondwanaland, but the chelids, which can tolerate cold better than the other pleurodires, may have evolved in Antarctica. They could have walked into Australia and crossed the narrow ocean gap (if indeed there was one) that may have separated Antarctica from Patagonia. By the Late Cretaceous, though, it was too late for them to walk, or swim, into Africa.

Australasian (e.g. Parker's Snake-necked Turtle, *Chelodina parkeri*, from New Guinea, top) and South American (e.g. the South American Snake-necked Turtle, *Hydromedusa tectifera*, bottom) long-necked chelids probably evolved long necks independently.

Did the chelids make the crossing to South America once or twice? In both Australia and South America, chelids come in two distinct body types: long- and short-necked. For a long time, herpetologists assumed that the Australian longnecks of the genus *Chelodina* were close relatives of the South American longnecks of the genus *Hydromedusa*. If that is true, it would mean that the present distribution of the Chelidae is the result of two separate vicariant events. The first would have split the family into long- and short-necked forms. Each of these lines would have, then, spread on its own to Australia and South America, before another vicariant event split them into Australian and South American groups, and Antarctica lost all of its turtles beneath miles of ice.

It may be, however, that *Chelodina* and *Hydromedusa* are not each other's closest relatives after all. Peter Pritchard pointed out in 1984 that they differ in a number of anatomical features, including details of the skull and forward extension of plastron that shields the head and neck when they are tucked out of the way. Recent molecular studies, though unclear on other details, support the idea that the two longnecks are not closely related. They suggest that *Chelodina* is most closely related to the Australian short-necked chelids, while *Hydromedusa* seems closer to the other South American species. If this is true, we now need only one vicariant event to explain the modern distribution of the Chelidae, the one that separated the Australian and South American branches of the family. It also means that chelids evolved long necks at least twice, once on each continent. Since both genera (and many other turtles) use their necks in the same way—to make a rapid, snake-like strike at their prey—the fact that they have hit upon the same evolutionary solution should not be too surprising. Nonetheless, Paula Bona and Marcelo De La Fuente believe that the long-necked chelids, with a South American Late Cretaceous-Paleocene genus, *Yaminuechelys*, which appears particularly close to *Hydromedusa*, arose as a group in southern South

America, perhaps in the Upper Cretaceous. Torsten Scheyer's 2009 study of bone microstructure supports this view, but, he cautions, "only slightly."

Chelidae: Australo-American Sideneck Turtles

There are roughly 50 species in the family Chelidae, the majority of them—some 30 or so—located in Australia and New Guinea, with the remainder in South America. Chelids are usually flat-headed and often rather flat-shelled animals, often with soft skin or small scales covering their heads instead of the large, plate-like scales that cap the other sidenecks. Chelids spend most of their lives in fresh water. Some, like the Mary River Turtle (*Elusor macrurus*) and the Fitzroy River Turtle (*Rheodytes leukops*) of Australia, almost never leave it. The Northern Long-necked Turtle (*Chelodina rugosa*) even lays its eggs under water—a truly remarkable feat (see page 288, Chapter 7). On the other hand, the South American Twist-necked Turtle (*Platemys platycephala*) is a largely terrestrial animal that rarely enters the water (other than rain puddles) at all, and Zulia Toad-headed Sidenecks (*Mesoclemmys zuliae*) often emerge to hunt for food on the forest floor.

The Australasian chelids first came to the knowledge of Western scientists during Captain James Cook's 1770 expedition to Australia, when Joseph Banks collected an Eastern Snake-necked Turtle (*Chelodina longicollis*) somewhere near Botany Bay,

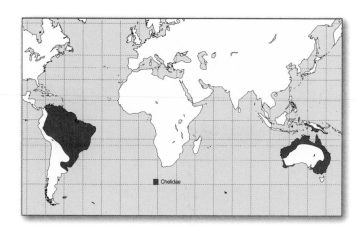

south of the present-day city of Sydney. To a northerner, the *Chelodina* turtles are startling animals, with elongate, seemingly overstretched necks and vaguely eel-like heads. When an Eastern Snake-necked Turtle extends itself, its head and neck add some 60 to 65 percent to its overall length. The distinctive Oblong Turtle (*Chelodina oblonga* or, as some herpetologists prefer, *Chelodina colliei*) of Australia's southwestern corner is even more extreme, with a head and neck stretching to 90 percent of the length of its carapace—an impressive figure for a turtle whose shell may reach 31 cm (12 in).

The Eastern Snake-neck is one of some 14 long-necked turtles from Australia, New Guinea, and the Lesser Sundas where a single, Critically Endangered species, the Roti Island Snake-necked Turtle (*Chelodina mccordi*), lives on two isolated Gondwanan remnants, the islands of Timor and Roti (see page 375, Chapter 9). In the southeast, the Eastern Snake-neck shares much of its range with the Broad-shelled Turtle (*Chelodina expansa*); both

live throughout Australia's largest river system, the Murray-Darling, in lagoons, lakes, and swamps and in the rivers themselves, though Eastern Snake-necks are most abundant in waterholes and temporary pools far from permanent rivers while the Broad-shelled Turtle prefers the river channels.

The genus has been divided into three subgenera: *Chelodina*, including the Eastern Snake-neck, with broad plastra; *Macrochelodina*, a narrow-plastroned group including a number of tropical species and the Broad-shelled Turtle, and a third subgenus (sometimes called *Macrodiremys*, but the name may not be valid for technical reasons), containing only the Oblong Turtle. New *Chelodina*s are still being described: the Arnhem Land Long-necked Turtle (*Chelodina burrungandjii*), a member of the subgenus *Macrochelodina*, was first reported by Peter Pritchard but was only named in 2000, by Scott Thomson, Rod Kennett and Arthur Georges. Another species, from farther west in the Kimberlies, was described as the Kimberley Snake-necked Turtle (*Chelodina wal-*

The Arnhem Land Long-necked Turtle (*Chelodina burrungandjii*) was only recognized as a separate species in 2000.

loyarrina) in 2007, but it may not be distinct from *burrungandjii*. Northeastern Australian populations of the New Guinea Snake-necked Turtle (*Chelodina novaeguinae*) were recognized as a distinct species, Cann's Long-necked Turtle (*Chelodina canni*), in 2002. Cann's Long-necks hybridize occasionally with Eastern Snake-necks where the two meet in east-central Queensland.

Chelodina turtles are active and very efficient predators. Fish, freshwater shrimp, tadpoles and frogs are the chief items on their menu, but the Oblong Turtle will occasionally seize a waterbird. Eastern Snake-necks eat a wide range of animal life, and adults in particular will feed on carrion. The Arnhem Land Long-neck, unusually for its genus, also eats some plant material. When necessary, members of the subgenus *Chelodina* will undertake lengthy overland migrations to reach better feeding sites (*Macrochelodina* turtles do less well out of the water, and await better times buried in the last damp mud at the bottom of a riverbed or billabong). When an Eastern Snake-necked Turtle crawls from one pond to another, it shelters its head and neck from the hot sun beneath the overhanging lip of its carapace. Broad-shelled and Oblong Turtles, though, seem to disdain such measures, and stretch their heads and necks out to their full extent as they march along.

The short-necked Australasian turtles are grouped into six genera, three of them—*Elusor*, *Pseudemydura* and *Rheodytes*— with a single species each. The Mary River Turtle (*Elusor macrurus*) is the largest chelid in Australia, with a carapace 40 cm (16 in) long. Males have a long, heavy tail as thick as a human wrist—the largest tail on any Australian turtle, much bigger than its head and neck. What it uses this immense tail for we have no clear idea, but it probably has something to do with cloacal breathing (see page 208, Chapter 4) and mating. The male's cloacal opening is a long slit more than halfway down the underside of the tail, so possibly the male uses its tail to bring the opening into posi-

tion for inseminating the female. At least, that is the rule for other male turtles boasting less impressive equipment.

Remarkably, the Mary River Turtle remained unknown to science until 1990. Starting in the early 1960s, pet shops in Adelaide, Bristol, Melbourne and Sidney began receiving large shipments of hatchling turtles that no one could identify. Although the shipments continued until around 1984, when it became illegal to sell hatchling turtles in the state of Victoria, no one knew where they were coming from. For 25 years, Australian turtle enthusiast John Cann explored river systems from one end of Australia to the other (and in New Guinea, just in case), searching for the turtle, called, variously, "shortneck alpha" or "petshop 1".

Finally a contact in Maryborough, Queensland, John Greenalgh, sent Cann a note saying "I've got one." Cann dashed to Maryborough—only to find that the turtle swimming in a water-filled metal drum on his host's property was perfectly ordinary. Cann was furious—until Greenalgh said, "Well, if that's not him, let's have a look in this drum." The next drum held a full-grown female of Cann's mystery turtle.

In October 1990, Cann found four specimens himself, in the clear waters of the Mary River, south of Maryborough—an area already well-known to zoologists as one of only two rivers where the Australian Lungfish (*Neoceratodus forsteri*) is found. He described it in 1994, with American biologist John Legler, as *Elusor macrurus*, meaning roughly "the hard-to-find animal with the big tail." It was once thought to live only in deep pools along 100 km (60 m) of the river's middle reaches, but we now know that it occurs throughout the river basin.

The Fitzroy River Turtle or White-eyed River Diver, one of the most thoroughly aquatic of all turtles, is another fairly recent discovery by Legler and Cann. This time only seven years elapsed from 1973, the first time a turtle hobbyist showed Cann a specimen he could not identify, until its official

The recently discovered Mary River Turtle (*Elusor macrurus*) is confined to a single river system in Queensland, Australia.

Mary River Turtles first turned up—as far as scientists were concerned—as unidentified hatchlings in pet stores. Born black, the hatchlings change color after three weeks.

Another recently discovered and highly distinctive Australian chelid, the Fitzroy River Turtle (*Rheodytes leukops*).

description in 1980. Like the Mary River Turtle, *Rheodytes* is confined to a single river system in Queensland, this time the drainage of the much larger Fitzroy River system, named after the captain of Darwin's ship, the *Beagle*. The Fitzroy River itself has become polluted from the tailings of upstream mining operations, but, fortunately, the turtle lives in the other major contributing rivers of its drainage system. Its hatchlings have distinctive shells with serrated edges that look as though they had been trimmed with a pair of pinking shears.

The genus *Pseudemydura* may once have been widespread in Australia; a Miocene *Pseudemydura* has been found in the Riversleigh fossil beds of northwest Queensland. Today its sole representative, the Western Swamp Turtle (*Pseudemydura umbrina*), is not only the rarest turtle in Australia, but one of the rarest in the world. Though described in 1901, it was forgotten until 1953 when a Perth schoolboy named Robert Boyd exhibited one at a pet show. One of the judges, a famous Western Australian naturalist named Vincent Serventy, spotted the animal, had no idea what it was, and passed it on to Ludwig Glauert, curator of the Western Australian Museum. Glauert described it as a new species, but other scientists soon realized that it was the same animal that had been named at the beginning of the century.

The Critically Endangered Western Swamp Turtle (*Pseudemydura umbrina*) lives only in swampland near Perth, Australia.

No one has ever found the Western Swamp Turtle anywhere but in two tiny patches of swampland about 30 km (18.6 mi) north of Perth. Both patches were purchased by the Western Australian government and set aside as nature reserves, Ellen Brook (163 acres) and Twin Swamps (387 acres), but unfortunately the population at Twin Swamps disappeared during the 1980s. That left only 20 or 30 individuals at Ellen Brook and a number of others in captivity. The situation was dire, but a combination of successful captive breeding, publicity and habitat management has brought the species' numbers up to more than 150. In 1994, the turtle was reintroduced to Twin Swamps, and is now protected by an electrified fence to keep out (introduced) European red foxes.

The other Australasian chelids are the river turtles of the genus *Emydura* and the Australian snappers of the genera *Elseya* and *Myuchelys*. The widespread Eastern Short-necked Turtle (*Emydura macquarii*) is fairly typical of the *Emydura*s. It shares the Murray-Darling river system with its long-necked cousins the Eastern Snake-necked Turtle and the Broad-shelled Turtle. Unlike its predatory relations, the Eastern Short-necked Turtle is an omnivore, eating pretty much whatever it can get including plant matter, insects, carrion and fish. Like most of its congeners (members of the same genus), the Eastern Short-neck is a rather plain-looking turtle, with a pale stripe running from the corner of its mouth down the side of its neck. Some of the tropical *Emydura*s, though, like the Jardine River Turtle (*Emydura subglobosa*) of New Guinea and the northern Cape York Peninsula of Australia are quite colorful animals, with stripes and patches of yellow and red. In Australia, this species is restricted to the pristine Jardine River drainage in Cape York, where the few animals found may have been stragglers from New Guinea; none have been seen there for years.

The Victoria River or Northern Australian Snapper (*Elseya dentata*) is one of a number of species—some, like the White-throated or Southern Snapper (*Elseya albagula*), only recently named—

The Jardine River Turtle (*Emydura subglobosa*) of New Guinea and tropical Australia is one of the more colorful chelids.

The saw-toothed edge of its carapace, which smooths away with age, gives the Victoria River Snapper (*Elseya dentata*) its specific name.

living in river systems across the tropical north and northeast of Australia. It may live up to its name if handled carelessly; a large one can deliver a severe bite. In the juvenile, each of the marginal scutes on its shell is tapered into a point, giving the edge of the carapace a saw-toothed look (hence its specific name, *dentata*, which means "toothed"). The Victoria River Snapper is almost entirely a plant eater. *Myuchelys* turtles may be more carnivorous, like the Saw-shelled Turtle (*Myuchelys latisternum*) of northern and eastern Australia, or, like Bell's

Turtle (*Myuchelys bellii*), omnivorous. They are equally effective biters, and the Saw-shelled Turtle, like most chelids, can emit a powerful musky stink.

The rest of the chelids live across the Pacific, in South America. There are five genera of South American short-necked chelids: *Platemys*, containing only one species, the Twist-necked Turtle (*Platemys platycephala*); *Acanthochelys* (four species, formerly included in *Platemys*); *Mesoclemmys* (ten "toad-headed" turtles); *Phrynops* (four species); and *Rhinemys*,

The Twist-necked Turtle (*Platemys platycephala*) lives in shallow water in rainforests of northern South America.

The Black Spiny-necked Swamp Turtle (*Acanthochelys spixii*) is widely distributed in Southern Brazil, Uruguay and northern Argentina.

containing only the Red Side-necked turtle or Red Amazon Sideneck (*Rhinemys rufipes*). The species in *Platemys* and *Acanthochelys* are quite small turtles. Most are less than 20 cm (8 in) in carapace length. The Twist-necked Turtle of northern South America lives in and near shallow water in marshes, ponds and rainforest creeks. It is apparently a poor swimmer, but will leave the water and travel overland at times. Russell Mittermeier of Conservation International has found several in puddles on forest paths in Suriname, and they have been captured while swimming by night among the trees in the flooded rainforest. The Black Spiny-necked Swamp Turtle (*Acanthochelys spixii*), known in Brazil as *cágado-preto* (black turtle), is widely distributed in southern Brazil, Uruguay and northern Argentina, where it lives in temporary ponds and slow-moving waters at the edge of the *cerrado*. In some parts of its range it encounters severe winters, and may respond by going into hibernation.

Though formerly placed in the single genus *Phrynops*, *Mesoclemmys*, *Phrynops* and *Rhinemys* turtles are a quite variable lot. Geoffroy's Side-necked Turtle (*Phrynops geoffroanus*), which ranges from Colombia to northern Argentina, thrives in polluted, sewage-laden urban rivers, and is a common city turtle in some places. The Red Amazon Sideneck of northwestern Brazil and southeastern Colombia seems to be a food specialist, something unusual among turtles. It lives only in closed-canopy rainforest streams, where it feeds on palm fruits that fall into the water. Although once thought to be one of the rarest turtles in the world, a study of the species by William E. Magnusson and his colleagues has suggested that it may be one of the most abundant turtles of the Amazon.

Toad-headed sidenecks have large, broad heads with powerful, bulging jaw muscles. The Common Toad-headed Sideneck or Guyanan Toad-headed

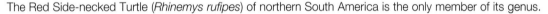

The Red Side-necked Turtle (*Rhinemys rufipes*) of northern South America is the only member of its genus.

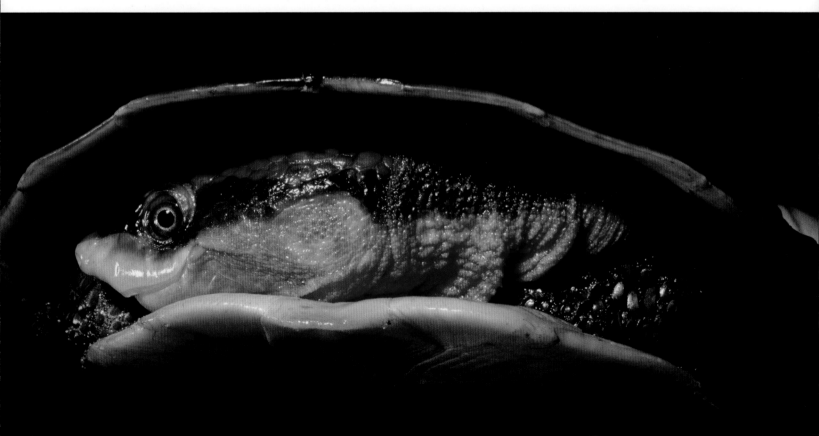

Turtle (*Mesoclemmys nasuta*) of the Guianas and the Amazon basin has a head width equal to one-quarter of the length of its carapace. What it does with this enormous head we are not quite sure. Its jaw surfaces are poorly developed and, perhaps fortunately, it does not bite when handled. The Piaui Side-necked Turtle (*Mesoclemmys perplexa*) was named in 2005 after its discovery in 2000 in the Parque Nacional da Serra das Confusões in Piaui state, Brazil. The park, created in 1998, protects a type of semi-arid, rocky habitat known as *caatinga*,

where the new turtle seems to be dependent on perennial waterholes in deep, forested canyons.

The South American Snake-necked Turtle (*Hydromedusa tectifera*) lives from southeastern Brazil to Paraguay, northeastern Argentina and Uruguay. Maximilian's Snake-necked Turtle (*Hydromedusa maximiliani*) is confined to the coastal Atlantic rainforest of Brazil, one of the most endangered habitats on earth. While most South American freshwater turtles dwell in large, deep, often muddy rivers, Maximilian's Snake-neck lives

The common Toad-headed Sideneck (*Mesoclemmys nasuta*) has an enormous head, with powerful, bulging jaw muscles.

in clear, cool, shallow streams with rocky or sandy bottoms, where it hunts insects, crustaceans and other prey. It is normally found only above 600 m (1,900 ft), but where there are no South American Snake-necks in the lowlands it may descend to 100 m (330 ft). Unlike the South American Snake-neck, which can survive in polluted streams, Maximilian's Snake-neck seems to require unpolluted water flowing through undisturbed montane rainforest. It can be quite common in the right spots, reaching densities of 190 turtles per hectare of river, but its habitat preference may affect its chances of survival in the future. There is little undisturbed montane rainforest left in Brazil.

There is a third South American longneck, farther north in the Amazon and Orinoco drainages: the Matamata Turtle (*Chelus fimbriata*). According to molecular studies, it may be more closely relat-

ed to the other South American chelids than to *Hydromedusa*. Whatever its affinities, it is the best known, and certainly the most bizarre, of South American turtles. Once you have seen a Matamata, you will surely never forget it. It looks more like a pile of dead leaves than a turtle—useful camouflage for an ambush predator that spends most of its time lying in wait for prey at the bottom of murky streams. Its carapace is flattened and rough, each scute raised into a conical boss. Its head is so broad and flat that it looks squashed, and is decorated with fringed, fleshy filaments on the underside and along the sides of its neck. Its snout is drawn out into a long, thin snorkel whose tip only needs to touch the water surface to keep the Matamata supplied with air. It is the largest chelid in South America, though not quite as big as the largest specimens of the biggest Australian species, the Mary River Turtle.

South Americans may avoid eating the Matamata Turtle (*Chelus fimbriata*) because of its bizarre appearance.

The Matamata rarely surfaces; it is a bottom-walker that may only emerge to nest, close to the water's edge. Individuals are occasionally carried out to sea at the mouth of the Orinoco, washing up on the shores of Trinidad seemingly none the worse for wear despite having, sometimes, been at sea long enough to acquire a collection of small barnacles. Despite its seeming sluggishness, it is a very effective hunter, with a highly evolved feeding technique (see page 243, Chapter 6). Its strange appearance has had a paradoxical effect on its relationship with people. It is highly prized in the pet trade, and was apparently esteemed as food over 200 years ago in French Guiana, but along the Rio Negro in Brazil local people told Juarez Pezzuti and his colleagues that the Matamata was "ugly," "horrible," and "disgusting"—not even to be touched, much less eaten. Peter Pritchard and Pedro Trebbau reported in *The Turtles of Venezuela*:

"…[Matamatas] are so peculiar in appearance that they are not eaten even in many areas where turtles of all other types—even mud turtles—are highly favored. In Venezuela, I found no evidence that this species was eaten along the middle Rio Orinoco, even though the more numerous and 'normal-looking' *Podocnemis* were eaten in large numbers… Fiasson (1945) wrote that the flesh of the Matamata was as tasty as that of *P. unifilis*, but that the former was not sought after due to its repulsive appearance."

Podocnemididae: South American River Turtles and Their Malagasy Cousin

The other seven pleurodire turtles of South America—the Big-headed Amazon River Turtle (*Peltocephalus dumerilianus*) and the six species of *Podocnemis*—belong to the Podocnemididae. Most are river turtles, with low, broad, rounded shells streamlined for swimming in a current. Several enter backwaters and ponds, and the Savanna Side-

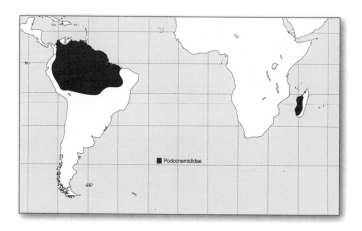

necked Turtle (*Podocnemis vogli*) is confined to the llanos of Venezuela and Colombia, an Everglades-like maze of swamps, streams and pools. The Big-headed Amazon River Turtle of the Amazon and Orinoco river basins is a large animal, weighing up to 15 kg (33 lbs). Its head is indeed massive, covered with plates that give it its generic name, "helmet-headed." The male is the larger sex.

The genus *Podocnemis* includes a species of great scientific interest, ecological significance and former economic importance, the Arrau or Giant South American River Turtle (*Podocnemis expansa*). It is the largest living pleurodire. The carapace of a male Arrau may be 40 to 50 cm (16 to 20 in) long. Females are significantly larger, averaging between 60 and 70 cm (24 and 28 in) in carapace length. An average female Arrau may weigh between 20 and 25 kg (45 and 55 lbs) In earlier times, before the largest specimens had been hunted out of existence, some may have weighed up to 90 kg (200 lbs).

The Arrau lives, or lived, throughout much of the Amazon, Orinoco, and Essequibo basins. It spends most of its life in the large rivers, swimming into the flooded forest during the wet season to feed on fallen fruit. Males almost never leave the water, and the females only do so to nest, or to bask on the edges of sandbanks in the weeks before nesting begins. The nesting season of the Arrau ushers in a great natural spectacle. Legends along the Orinoco tell of a "magical turtle lady" who guards the Arrau and shows them the best places to lay their eggs.

A Big-headed Amazon River turtle (*Peltocephalus dumerilianus*) from French Guiana gapes at the photographer.

Perhaps responding to her call (but more likely, according to recent research by Richard Vogt, coordinating their movements with underwater vocalizations), huge numbers of turtles crawl ashore at night on traditional sandy nesting beaches. In the past, they may have numbered in the hundreds of thousands.

Such a high concentration of easily exploited protein has proved irresistible to humans. For centuries, the meat and eggs of the Arrau were a staple for the river tribes. Some villages kept turtles in pens for year-round use. With the arrival of European settlement, exploitation of the Arrau increased enormously. Oil from its eggs was used as, among other things, fuel for lamps, and even

as insect repellent. By the mid-20th century, Arrau populations had collapsed throughout much of their range (see page 367, Chapter 9). Only in the 1980s did the Brazilian government begin a special effort to protect Arrau nesting beaches—an effort that apparently paid off, resulting in a 1,200 percent increase in egg production in the 13 years prior to 1997. A similar program is also in place in Venezuela, with some modest success. Nonetheless, poaching of adults and juveniles remains a serious problem, and the effects of ongoing commercialization on Arrau populations are not fully known. Although the International Union for Conservation of Nature (IUCN) still classifies the Arrau as Lower Risk/Conservation Dependent, the IUCN Tortoise and Freshwater Turtle Specialist Group (TFTSG) believes that it should be reclassified as Critically Endangered.

The other *Podocnemis* turtles are considerably smaller than the Arrau. Like it, they generally nest on riverbanks and sandbars, though most nests of the Red-headed Amazon River Turtle (*Podocnemis erythrocephala*), smallest of the genus, found along the Lower Tapajós river were dug in savanna vegetation a considerable distance from the water's edge. Most of the other *Podocnemis* have not been the target of such an intense and focused harvest. They are nonetheless heavily hunted in many parts of their range. The TFTSG recommended in 2010 that the extremely attractive Yellow-spotted River Turtle (*Podocnemis unifilis*) should be considered

Endangered, and that the Endangered Magdalena River Turtle (*Podocnemis lewyana*), a species that has been hunted intensively for as long as records exist, be categorized as Critically Endangered.

The Yellow-spotted River Turtle, reported to have the tastiest meat of its genus, has become rare in many areas, especially as the Arrau has become difficult to find and hunters have turned their attention to its smaller cousins. There is evidence that as the species' numbers have fallen some local populations have become inbred, reducing their ability to cope with the stresses of environmental change. As the Yellow-spotted has declined in its turn, hunters have switched to a still smaller species, the Six-tubercled Amazon River Turtle (*Podocnemis sextuberculata*), a species that nests, like the Arrau, on

In Amazonian Peru, Yellow-spotted River Turtles (*Podocnemis unifilis*), and their eggs, are intensely hunted.

exposed sandy beaches where its eggs and females are easy to collect. Russell Mittermeier has compared this downward progression to a similar shift to smaller and smaller species by the whaling industry as whalers decimated the larger animals.

The Magdalena River Turtle of the Magdalena, Sinú and nearby river basins in Colombia, the only member of its genus west of the Andes, has become the victim of a seasonal coincidence. In strongly Catholic Colombia the church forbids chicken and beef during Holy Week, but not turtle or fish. Easter falls in the dry season, when fish are scarce; a supply of turtle meat for the holidays is practically a necessity. It is also, unfortunately, when the turtles emerge from their rivers to breed, making it easy for local people to collect females and eggs on their nesting beaches. As the largest freshwater turtle in northern Colombia, it is an important source of protein and income. Adults fetch the equivalent of $5–14, and eggs go for 40–60 cents each. It continues to be hunted (and collected for sale as a pet) despite having been, at least on paper, totally protected since 1964. To make matters worse, sand and gravel mining are destroying its nesting grounds, pollution is taking its toll in more urban areas, and cattle from widespread ranching operations trample its nests when they come down to the rivers to drink. On the Sinú and Prado Rivers, regular releases of water from hydroelectric dams flood most of the available beaches, probably drowning thousands of eggs per year. Management programs aimed at protecting the species are underway, but they are still in their infancy.

Far away from the other podocnemidids, across the Atlantic and past the continent of Africa, lives the Malagasy Big-headed Turtle (*Erymnochelys madagascariensis*), a large, mostly gray and brown turtle that may weigh up to 15 kg (33 lbs). A Gondwanaland relic, it may be the only living turtle whose ancestors walked into Madagascar instead of floating there from Africa. Today, *Erymnochelys* lives in open water in slow-moving rivers, backwaters and lakes in the lowlands of western Madagascar. We do not know

very much about it, but fishermen in the area report that they usually only find *Erymnochelys* during the rainy season. In May, at the beginning of the cool, dry winter, it disappears, but we do not know exactly where. A popular food item among the local people, *Erymnochelys* is heavily fished, and has been increasingly caught as bycatch as fishermen switch to using nets. It is classified by IUCN as Critically Endangered, though it still occurs—if increasingly thinly—over a wide, and little-studied, area.

Anatomical and fossil evidence suggests that *Erymnochelys* may be most closely related to *Peltocephalus*, though molecular analyses link it more closely to *Podocnemis*. All three genera have been separated evolutionarily for a long time—perhaps, according to the molecular evidence, for as long as 80 million years.

Pelomedusidae: African Mud Terrapins

The Pelomedusidae, the only living sidenecks on the African continent, make up a fairly small family with only two genera and 18 species. Sixteen species of *Pelusios* terrapins live in sub-Saharan Africa. Some live in temporary puddles, but others prefer permanent bodies of water—a risky choice because crocodiles prefer the same places. Perhaps in response, most *Pelusios* species can protect their head and front limbs behind a hinged plastron—the only pleurodires to do so. They operate the hinge

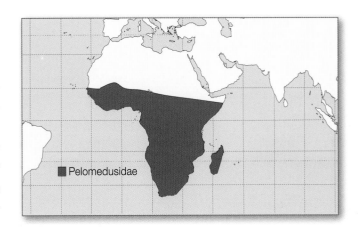

with a powerful muscle derived, it seems, from one of their breathing muscles.

Their habitats range from the tropical rainforest streams where the African Forest Terrapin (*Pelusios gabonensis*) lives to the deep waters of the Okavango Swamp and the upper Zambezi, home to the Okavango Hinged Terrapin (*P. bechuanicus*). Broadley's Mud Terrapin (*P. broadleyi*) is known only from the tributaries feeding into the southeastern shores of Lake Rudolph in northern Kenya, and Adanson's Mud Turtle (*P. adansonii*) inhabits shallow rivers and lakes in the very dry Sahel region, where water temperatures may reach 40°C (104°F). The Pan Hinged Terrapin or East African Black Mud Turtle (*P. subniger*) lives in permanent waters over most of its East African range, but in southeastern Africa it will also live (as its common name implies)

in pans and other temporary water bodies. So will the Yellow-bellied Hinged Terrapin (*P. castanoides*) and the West African Mud Turtle (*Pelusios castaneus*). When their pools dry out, they bury themselves in the mud to await the next rainy season.

The first sideneck I ever saw in the wild was a Helmeted Terrapin (*Pelomedusa subrufa*) determinedly making its way across the dry plains of the Serengeti. This common and widespread species (which may, according to recent molecular evidence, be a complex of several species—perhaps as many as nine) ranges throughout Africa in dry, open country, from south of the Sahara to the Cape, as well as all over Madagascar. It has even crossed the Red Sea to establish a population in Yemen, making it the only pleurodire in Asia (except for the snake-necked chelids on Timor and Roti, islands that are politically

A Serrated Hinged Terrapin (*Pelusios sinuatus*) in South Africa's Kruger National Park.

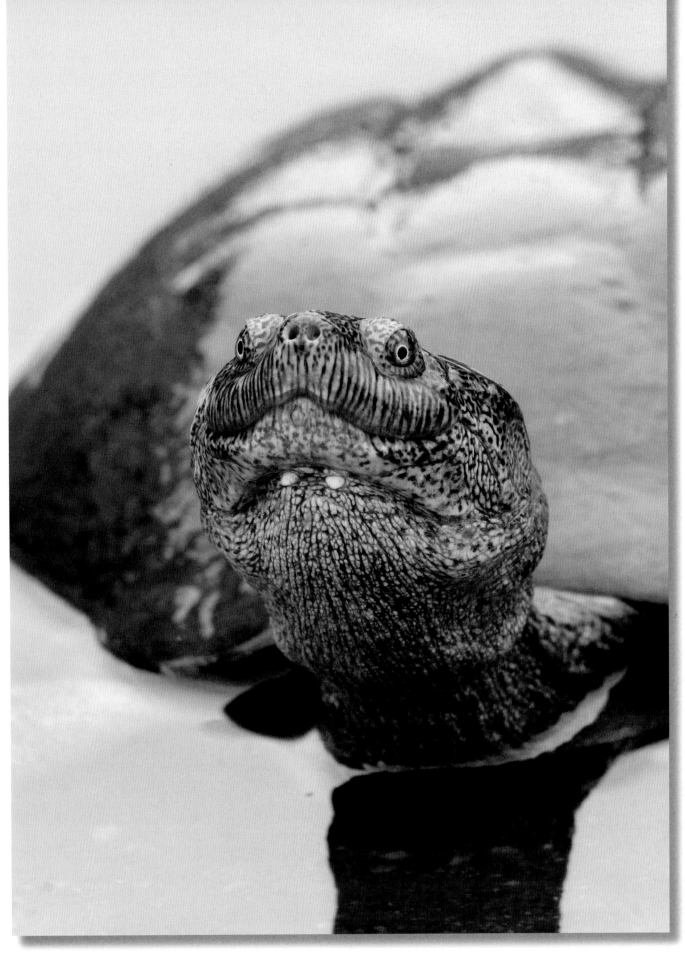

The Helmeted Terrapin (*Pelomedusa subrufa*) ranges widely through Africa, and also lives in Yemen and Madagascar.

A Helmeted Terrapin (*Pelomedusa subrufa*) rides a Hippopotamus (*Hippopotamus amphibius*) in Kruger National Park, South Africa.

part of Asia, but biologically Australasian). It is a thin-shelled turtle, usually missing from permanent bodies of water where crocodiles live. This vulnerability, though, may have served it in good stead. Its preference for temporary, crocodile-free rain pools has probably allowed it to spread to many areas that might seem unsuitable for a semiaquatic turtle. In South Africa, it even reaches the dry Central Karoo. Like the Pan Hinged Terrapin, another thin-shelled species that seems to avoid crocodile country, it buries itself in mud when its ponds dry.

The Helmeted Terrapin is a carnivore and scavenger, and may even pick parasites from the skins of rhinoceroses that enter their water holes. In his *Field Guide to Snakes and Other Reptiles of Southern Africa*, Bill Branch notes that Helmeted Terrapins "are belligerent, long-necked and ever-willing to

bite or to eject their cloacal contents." He concludes, naturally, that "they do not make the best pets."

A few pelomedusids have spread beyond Africa to the surrounding islands. The Helmeted, Pan Hinged and Yellow-bellied Hinged Terrapins have reached Madagascar. The Pan Hinged Terrapin also occurs on Mauritius, where it may have been introduced. With the Yellow-bellied Hinged Terrapin, it has reached the Seychelles, home of the now-extinct Seychelles Mud Terrapin (*Pelusios seychellensis*), once the only pleurodire to be confined to small oceanic islands. Discovered in 1895, when three specimens were reportedly collected from, apparently, a highland marsh on Mahé, it has never been seen again.

The surviving terrapins on the Seychelles are now Critically Endangered, restricted to a few scattered acres of marsh and river habitat. Only 120 adult Seychelles Yellow-bellied Hinged Terrapins and 660 adult Seychelles Pan Hinged Terrapins (or Seychelles Black Mud Turtles) remained in the wild by 2005. Much of what was once prime terrapin habitat has been drained and developed. The Nature Protection Trust of Seychelles has initiated a conservation plan for both species.

It is possible that some, or even all, of the Malagasy and Seychelles pelomedusid turtles reached these islands with human help, though Justin Gerlach believes that the Seychelles species arrived of their own accord (particularly the Seychelles Mud Terrapin, whose nearest relatives may be in West Africa). *Pelusios* was formerly reported to have occurred on Diego Garcia in the Chagos islands, a place it could not have reached by natural means. Humans certainly brought the Pan Hinged Terrapin to the island of Guadeloupe in the West Indies, and a small population of this or a related species has possibly been established around Miami, Florida.

The pelomedusids on Madagascar must be fairly recent arrivals. Most Malagasy reptiles are found nowhere else. While the only other sideneck on the island, the Malagasy Big-headed Turtle, is an ancient relic whose nearest relatives are in South America, the three Madagascar pelomedusids do not even belong to endemic (sub)species (that is, species found nowhere else), and the Yellow-bellied Hinged Terrapins on Madagascar and the Seychelles may not even be distinct subspecies. If they have not displaced their larger and much more ancient cousin (assuming that they could do so), it is probably because they occupy different habitats. *Erymnochelys* prefers open water in permanent rivers and lakes. The Yellow-bellied Hinged Terrapin occupies densely vegetated areas, while the Helmeted Terrapin lives mostly in temporary ponds. The Pan Hinged Terrapin does not even meet *Erymnochelys*; in Madagascar it is only found along part of the east

coast, while the Malagasy Big-headed Turtle is confined to the west.

The Cryptodires

The eleven families of cryptodires include four with only a single living species each—the Dermochelyidae (Leatherback Turtles), Carettochelyidae (Pig-nose Turtles), Dermatemydidae (Central American River Turtles) and Platysternidae (Big-headed Turtles). By contrast, there are between 49 and 58 species of tortoises (Testudinidae), depending on how many species you recognize in the Galápagos, and 70 species of primarily Asian river turtles (Geoemydidae) in 19 genera.

Snapping turtles (Chelydridae) were formerly considered, with their presumed Asian ally, the Big-headed Turtle (Platysternidae), the most basal of the cryptodires. The two sea turtle families, Cheloniidae and Dermochelyidae, occupied a second branch, the Chelonioidea. The remaining limb of the cryptodire tree has usually been split into two main branches. One, the Trionychoidea, has included on one sub-branch the softshell turtles (Trionychidae) and their relative the Pig-nose Turtle (Carettochelyidae), and on the other, the mud and musk turtles (Kinosternidae) and their relative the Central American River Turtle (Dermatemydidae). The other branch, the Testudinoidea, includes the Asian river turtles (Geoemydidae), the tortoises (Testudinidae) and the American pond turtles (Emydidae).

Much of this arrangement, however, has now been called into question. The Big-headed Turtle (Platysternidae), until recently considered closest to snapping turtles, now seems to belong in the Testudinoidea, perhaps closest to the Emydidae. Genetic evidence suggests that the "Trionychoidea" is not a natural group. Trionychids and, presumably, *Carettochelys* share an arrangement of their cranial arteries that appears to be newly derived (but resembles that in sea turtles, though softshells and sea turtles probably evolved the arrangement independently). The arrangement in kinosternids and *Dermatemys* is like that in other living turtles.

The softshells, not the snappers, now seem to be the most basal branch of the cryptodires. One molecular study suggests that the softshells and *Carettochelys* might be basal to all other living turtles, including the pleurodires—a view that has not proven popular among turtle biologists, though it has been called a "lingering possibility."

Snappers may be closer either to sea turtles or to kinosternids and *Dermatemys*—a 2009 molecular study supports both results. In 2010, Anthony Barley and his colleagues, using a complex of 14 genes from the cell nucleus, confirmed a close relationship between snapping turtles and kinosternids (and presumably *Dermatemys*), with sea turtles as their next closest relatives.

The center of cryptodire distribution is the northern hemisphere. Except for the wide-ranging sea turtles and occasional stray giant softshells (*Pelochelys* spp.), only a single cryptodire species, the Pig-nose Turtle (*Carettochelys insculpta*), reaches Australia, and then only in its tropical north. Only 2 of the 11 families, the Trionychidae and Testudinidae, colonized sub-Saharan Africa, though the tortoises have their highest diversity there. Trionychids may not have reached India until the subcontinent, drifting northward after its breakup with Gondwana, collided with the main Asian land mass. By contrast, 7 of the 9 families of land and freshwater cryptodires are represented in North America.

Southeastern North America and tropical and subtropical Asia are particularly rich in cryptodires, with diverse arrays of, respectively, emydids and geoemydids. Both regions are, at their core, geologically, climatically and ecologically stable, largely free from the advancing and retreating sheets of ice that scraped away many of the plants and animals of other northern lands. Today, they are uniquely rich,

not just in turtles, but (mostly north of the richest turtle hotspots) in groups as diverse as magnolias and salamanders.

Chelydridae: Snapping Turtles

There are only two genera in the Chelydridae: *Chelydra*—now divided into three species, the Common Snapping Turtle (*C. serpentina*) of North America, the Central American Snapping Turtle (*C. rossignonii*) and the South American Snapping Turtle (*C. acutirostris*)—and *Macrochelys* (formerly called *Macroclemys*), the Alligator Snapping Turtle (*M. temminckii*). They are distinctive, fearsome-looking animals, with oversize heads and hooked jaws. Their carapaces are ornamented with three keeled ridges, though in an old Common Snapper the ridges may be almost worn away. The chelydrid plastron is very much reduced, shrunk to a blunt cross in the center of the often bloated-looking belly. The arms of the cross still reach out to connect with the carapace by a narrow bridge. Chelydrids cannot fully withdraw into their shells, though this may have less to do with their supposed primitive condition than with the size of their heads. Their plastra are so reduced that "into their shells" may not mean much anyway.

Chelydrid tails are the longest on any living turtle—possibly a holdover from the long tails common in early turtle lineages. A Common Snapper's tail is

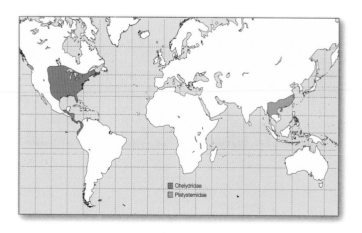

The Common Snapping Turtle (*Chelydra serpentina*) is famous for its aggressive behavior.

The South American Snapping Turtle (*Chelydra acutirostris*) is much less well known than its North American relative.

as long or longer than its carapace. Some people will tell you that the tail is the safest thing to grab should you wish to pick up a snapping turtle—advice you should not take, because picking up a large snapper in this way may injure or even kill it. Picking it up by the sides of its shell is risky too; it has a long neck, and is quite capable of reaching around and biting you if you try. Given its famously pugnacious disposition, you probably should not pick one up at all. Its strike is amazingly fast, the edges of its jaws are sharp cutting tools, and it can also emit a foul-smelling musk from glands along the lower edge of its carapace and bridge. This is not an animal to treat lightly; it is an amazing survivor.

Like many another primitive-looking creature, the Common Snapping Turtle is tough, widespread and successful. It ranges from southern Canada westward to the Rocky Mountains. Its tropical relatives range southward through Central America, even penetrating into South America as far as western Ecuador, though they may be very scarce, or even absent, over much of their geographic range.

Escapees from the pet trade have become established in Europe and in several regions of Japan, where it appears to be spreading. In 2005, the Japanese Ministry of the Environment characterized it as a particularly invasive alien species.

Snappers can live in almost any freshwater habitat they come across, even polluted ones, and they will enter brackish coastal waterways. They have a preference for soft, muddy bottoms in shallow water. Here, they bury themselves, waiting for prey, only their eyes and nostrils showing, occasionally stretching upward for a breath without emerging from their hiding place. A Common Snapper eats water plants, fruits and seeds, and just about any animal it can subdue, from a muskrat to a snail, in addition to carrion and various sorts of water plants. In one study on the upper Mississippi River, snapping turtles took at least 13 of 448 radio-tagged Mallard ducklings (*Anas platyrhynchos*) between 1991 and 1994. On the other hand, humans have developed a taste for snapping turtles, a taste that has taken a severe toll on some populations.

The Common Snapping Turtle (*Chelydra serpentina*) is an aggressive hunter, often attacking ducklings and other young water birds.

Though they are among the most aquatic of turtles, Common Snappers will occasionally climb out of the water to bask, or even make surprisingly long overland journeys in search of hibernation sites, nesting grounds or new ponds; one was found on the top of Big Black Mountain, Kentucky, more than 2 km (1.24 mi) away from the nearest decent-sized stream.

The remaining representative of the Chelydridae, the Alligator Snapping Turtle, is a unique and marvelous creature. The Alligator Snapper is confined to the southeastern United States, from Kansas and Illinois south to north-western Florida, Louisiana and Texas, where it lives in the river systems flowing into the Gulf of Mexico. Habitat destruction and alteration, coupled with overharvesting, has greatly reduced its population in parts of its range. It prefers the deeper water of large rivers, though it will venture into lakes, ponds, oxbows and bayous. Even more aquatic than its smaller cousin, it rarely leaves the water except to nest. The Alligator Snapper is one of the heaviest freshwater turtles in the world. It may reach 113 kg (248 lbs).

The most obvious way to identify an Alligator Snapper, other than sheer size and bulk, is the position of its eyes. In a Common Snapper, the eyes are positioned high and forward, but in the Alligator Snapper, they lie on the sides of its head. The keels on an Alligator Snapper carapace are even more pronounced than on the Common Snapper, and are more likely to persist even in old individuals. But

An Alligator Snapping Turtle (*Macrochelys temmincki*) displays the pink, worm-like lure on its tongue.

to see the Alligator Snapper's most unusual feature, you would have to open its mouth—it is usually glad to oblige.

On the surface of its tongue is a little, whitish forked structure that sits on a rounded, muscular base. At times, it fills with blood, stretches out and comes to look like nothing other than a succulent pink worm. The resemblance is not an accident. What the turtle does with this peculiar object was first described in this account, quoted by Archie Carr in his classic *Handbook of Turtles*:

> Several baby *Macrochelys*, three to four inches in carapace length, were kept in an aquarium and supplied with live fish. The young turtles would hide between rocks in a corner of the aquarium and open their mouths widely. The muscular base of the lure would then pull down, first on one side and then on the other, imparting a wiggling motion to the two portions of the appendage. Sometimes the turtle would "fish" for hours without success, but often a *Molliensia* or a *Gambusia* would swim into the open jaws and bite at the "bait." The turtle's jaws would immediately snap shut on the fish, which was next manipulated into position and then swallowed whole.

Peter Pritchard appears to have settled a long-standing controversy about the fearsomeness of the Alligator Snapper's bite. Although some writers have claimed that an Alligator Snapper is barely capable of biting a pencil in two, Pritchard taunted a 75 kg (165 lb) specimen with the handle of a brand-new household broom. The turtle bit clean through it.

Dermatemyidae: The Central American River Turtle

The Central American River Turtle (*Dermatemys mawii*) is the last survivor of what was once a wide-ranging family, with fossil representatives from North America, Europe and eastern Asia. It is found only in the Atlantic lowlands of southern Mexico, Belize and Northern Guatemala. One of its fossil relatives, *Zangerlia testudinimorpha* from Mongolia, may have been a tortoise-like land animal, but *Dermatemys* is almost helpless on land. Out of the water, it is barely able to lift its head. It probably never emerges except to nest. Even then, it uses the rainy season floods to lift it to its nest sites. The annual rise of the waters carries the turtle to places it could not reach over land.

Dermatemys is a fairly large turtle, with a carapace up to 65 cm (26 in) long. Its feet are webbed; like some softshells, its head appears small for such a big turtle. Its shell is unusual; though its bones are relatively thick, the scutes covering them are thin, delicate and easily injured. In old turtles the boundaries between the scutes are often obliterated.

The Central American River Turtle is almost entirely a herbivore. It lives on water plants, and on fallen leaves and fruits. Captive juveniles will take meat, and perhaps in the wild they are more omnivorous than their parents.

Because this turtle is so helpless out of the water, it is surprising to find that in Guatemala it sometimes occurs in isolated seasonal pools called *aguadas*. How does it get there? The answer may have less to do with its natural history than with its flavor. The Central American River Turtle is highly prized for its meat, and is much in demand in local markets. It is possible that the turtles in the *aguadas* are placed there, as if in a holding pen, until they are ready to be eaten or sold.

Years of overhunting are taking their toll on the Central American River Turtle. Hunting has almost eliminated it from Mexico, and populations elsewhere are declining. Belize has begun a program to protect it, and the Turtle Survival Alliance is training local conservationists to monitor the remaining populations. Even so the Central American River Turtle may be the most endangered turtle in the Americas today. Though efforts have been made to control large-scale commercial hunting, the tradition of eating hicatee, as *Dermatemys* is called in Belize, is deeply entrenched and may, despite the best efforts, be impossible to overcome.

Kinosternidae: Mud and Musk Turtles

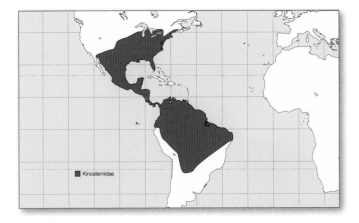

The 25 species of mud and musk turtles are confined to the Americas, where they range from southern Canada to northern Argentina. The center of their distribution, though, is Mexico and northern Central America, home to 17 species. One, the Jalisco Mud Turtle (*Kinosternon chimalhuaca*), was only described in 1996, though Peter Pritchard had found one some years earlier. Even their fossils have only been found in the New World; the oldest known, *Xenochelys formosa*, is from the Oligocene of South Dakota. The most wide-ranging land or freshwater turtle in the New World is the Scorpion or Red-cheeked Mud Turtle (*Kinosternon scorpioides*), found from Mexico to Argentina. Compared to other mud turtles, the Scorpion Mud Turtle lays smaller eggs in more clutches per year, presumably an adaptation to life in the tropics where the chance of a predator destroying any given clutch is high. It

The White-lipped Mud turtle (*Kinosternon leucostomum*) ranges from Mexico to northwestern Peru.

times hatching to the onset of rains, giving its young a better chance of finding a rich food supply. These traits may explain why it has spread so successfully through the South American tropics.

Musk turtles take their name from a series of four glands along the edges of the shell. One pair opens at the posterior end of the bridge; the other, about halfway between the front of the bridge and the front of the carapace. If you pick up a musk turtle (and if it doesn't bite you first), these glands can give off a yellowish fluid with a very unpleasant odor, pungent enough to have given the Common Musk Turtle both the scientific name *Sternotherus odoratus* and the unflattering nickname "stinkpot". The fluid consists of a number of acids, two of which (5-phenylpentanoic acid and 7-phenylalka-noic acid) are responsible for the odor. The smell probably deters predators, but no one has ever been able to establish how well it works.

All members of the family except for the Chopontil or Narrow-bridged Musk Turtle (*Claudius angustatus*) have at least one hinge across the plastron. Apparently this originally evolved as a way to open the front of the shell as the turtle reacts to a threat by pulling its head back into the shell and opening its jaws wide at the same time (see page 27, Chapter 1). In the mud turtles (*Kinosternon*), the mechanism for opening the shell has switched to one that closes it. Some of the more terrestrial mud turtles can raise both the front and back lobes of the plastron, using hinges both in front of and behind the bridge, and effectively seal themselves inside their shells.

The typical mud and musk turtles (subfamily Kinosterninae) are small to medium-sized, rather dull-colored animals. The young of some species have two yellow stripes on the side of the face that tend to break up and fade with age. Although they spend much of their lives in the water, mud and musk turtles are poor swimmers; instead, they walk along the bottom, searching for worms and insects. Some are most active at night, particularly during the warmer months of the year, something that may explain why

they are so seldom seen, even in areas where they may be among the most abundant turtles.

The 18 species of mud turtles (*Kinosternon*) are much more likely to spend extended periods of time on land. The Sonoran Mud Turtle (*K. sonoriense*) of the American southwest and the Scorpion Mud Turtle of Central and South America travel overland from one pond to another, sometimes setting off in groups. Creaser's Mud Turtle (*K. creaseri*), a localized species of the northern central Yucatan Peninsula in Mexico, lives in isolated temporary pools and caves, and must be able to wander over land to reach new homes. Other mud turtles, including the Eastern Mud Turtle (*K. subrubrum*) of eastern North America, the Striped Mud Turtle (*K. baurii*) of the Atlantic seaboard from Virginia to Florida, and the White-lipped Mud Turtle (*K. leucostomum*) of Central America, may wander extensively on land. Yellow Mud Turtles (*K. flavescens*) in Iowa and Illinois nest and burrow in sandy hill country, while Eastern and Striped Mud Turtles may nest up to 180 m (590 ft) from the edges of their ponds.

The Eastern Mud Turtle is particularly terrestrial. Sometimes, especially in the spring and fall, it hunts worms and caterpillars on land. It frequently overwinters there, usually in forested areas, in burrows in the soil, rotten logs, piles of debris or leaf litter. This species, and to a lesser extent the Striped Mud Turtle, can also tolerate brackish or salt water. Eastern Mud Turtles may be abundant in tidal marshes. On the island of San Andrés in the Caribbean, Scorpion Mud Turtles live in mangrove swamps where salinity may reach that of the open sea during the dry season. The turtles burrow in the mud or under mangrove roots to avoid the saltiest conditions.

Musk turtles (*Sternotherus* spp.) are, in general, more tied to the water than are mud turtles; their shells are often covered with algae and they may be infested with leeches. Common Musk Turtles live in a wide range of watery habitats in eastern North America, from southern Ontario to Florida and Texas, though they prefer waters with a slow current and a soft bottom. At times, they can be found far from water, sheltering under leaves or debris. Much more localized is the Flattened Musk Turtle (*S. depressus*), a species restricted to a single river system, the Black Warrior, in west-central Alabama. The same area is also the only known home of at least one species of salamander, three fishes, one mollusk and six caddisflies.

Musk turtles are surprisingly good climbers. Common Musk Turtles and Loggerhead Musk Turtles (*S. minor*), a large-headed species of the American southeast, will occasionally scale cypress knees or small tree trunks to bask. They may climb 2 m (6.6 ft) or more out of the water. The Razorback Musk Turtle (*S. carinatus*), which ranges from Oklahoma and eastern Texas to the lower Mississippi, basks more than the other species. It has a high, arched shell, and may take longer to heat up than its flatter relatives. The flattest-shelled of the lot, the Flattened Musk Turtle, rarely leaves the water. Its flattened shell reflects its preference for hiding in crevices in the surrounding bedrock.

Mud and musk turtles are mostly omnivores, with a preference for items like insects, crayfish, and snails. Female Stinkpots may eat more crayfish than males in certain seasons, probably to gain extra nutrients for their developing eggs. Flattened Musk Turtles and Loggerhead Musk Turtles of the nominate race (*S. minor minor*) shift their diet, as they age, from insects to clams. As they do so, their jaw muscles grow heavy, and their jaws develop expanded crushing surfaces. Flattened Musk Turtles specialize in eating snails and clams, and Sonoran Mud Turtles (*Kinosternon sonoriense*) in Arizona have been recorded eating lizards and snakes. The Mexican Rough-footed Mud Turtle (*K. hirtipes*) is almost entirely carnivorous; one researcher baited them in successfully with canned sardines preserved in soybean oil.

The other subfamily, the Staurotypinae, includes only three species, all restricted to Mexico and northern Central America: the two giant musk turtles of the genus *Staurotypus*, and the Narrow-bridged Musk Turtle. Anyone familiar only with the rather small musk turtles of the United States might be startled to encounter a Northern Giant Musk Turtle (*S. triporcatus*), and might be forgiven for mistaking it for a snapping turtle. It even shares a snapping turtle's reduced, cross-shaped plastron and triple ridges running the length of the carapace. As in an Alligator Snapper, these ridges become more prominent with age.

The Northern Giant Musk Turtle (*Staurotypus triporcatus*) can deliver a severe bite.

The Northern Giant Musk Turtle lives in the Gulf and Caribbean lowlands of southern Mexico south to western Honduras. With a carapace that may reach almost 40 cm (16 in), it is the largest in the family and an impressive turtle by any reckoning. It has a particularly large head; its jaws have powerful crushing surfaces that it uses to devour, among other things, smaller turtles, especially mud turtles that have the misfortune to share its range. As Jonathan Campbell writes in *Amphibians and Reptiles of Northern Guatemala, the Yucatan, and Belize*, "This turtle is capable of delivering a severe bite and readily defends itself. It should never be handled just for the hell of it."

The Pacific Coast Giant Musk Turtle (*S. salvinii*) of the Pacific drainage of southern Mexico, Guatemala and El Salvador is smaller, with a carapace reaching 25 cm (10 in). It seems to share its congener's disposition. Carl Ernst and Roger Barbour report, in *Turtles of the World*, that "[t]his species is well known for its vile temper and sharp jaws!"

By contrast, the Narrow-bridged Musk Turtle is one of the smallest members of the whole family. Its carapace averages only about 12 cm (4.7 in) for males and slightly less for females. Its range is almost the same as that of its larger cousin, the Northern Giant Musk Turtle, though it does not reach as far as Honduras. Its plastron is even more reduced than that of the giant musk turtles, and it is the only member of the family to lack any trace of a plastral hinge. It has a large head and formidably hooked jaws, with a pair of sharp toothlike cusps on the upper jaw below the eye—a feature found in no other turtle. These cusps may help it to hold on to slippery prey, including frogs which gather in great numbers in the shallow marshes it prefers.

During the rainy season, the Narrow-bridged Musk Turtle swims into seasonally flooded fields to forage among the grasslands. What it does in the dry season we are not altogether sure (see page 221); until very recently, this was one of the least known turtles in its family. It was thought to be very rare, but it can be abundant in localized patches of habitat. Biologists simply did not know where to find it. Fishermen do, and in coastal Veracruz, Mexico they have been catching Narrow-bridged Musk Turtles for centuries.

Cheloniidae: Sea Turtles (Except the Leatherback)

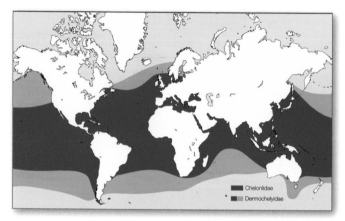

All of the living sea turtles, except the Leatherback, are placed in the family Cheloniidae. Sea turtles are so distinctive, and so well known, that they hardly need describing. Beautifully adapted for life in the sea, they range throughout the warm waters of the world. Four of the six usually recognized species are almost global in range; only the Leatherback, which swims into colder waters, has a broader distribution. The two exceptions are the Flatback (*Natator depressus*) of the coastal waters of northern and northeastern Australia, and Kemp's Ridley (*Lepidochelys kempii*), which is confined to the Atlantic. Kemp's Ridleys nest almost exclusively on the southern portion of the coast of the state of Tamaulipas, Mexico, though some females nest as far east as Louisiana and Florida and as far southeast as Campeche at the base of the Yucatan Peninsula. The other ridley, the Olive (*L. olivacea*), ranges widely in the Indian and Pacific Oceans, but in the Atlantic rarely swims north of the southern Caribbean Sea.

OPPOSITE

A female Flatback Sea Turtle (*Natator depressus*) returns to the ocean after nesting on Crab Island, off the Cape York Peninsula in Queensland, Australia.

The six species of cheloniid sea turtles are the Green (*Chelonia mydas*), the Flatback, the Hawksbill (*Eretmochelys imbricata*), the Loggerhead (*Caretta caretta*), Kemp's Ridley and the Olive Ridley. A recent molecular study suggests that there are two main lineages in the family, one (Chelonini) containing the Green and the Flatback, and the other (Carettini) for the Hawksbill, the Loggerhead and the two ridleys. Some scientists recognize a seventh species, the Black Sea Turtle (usually called *Chelonia agassizii*), though molecular studies have failed to support its uniqueness. Arguments have waxed hot and heavy in recent years about whether this animal, which lives alongside "typical" Green Sea Turtles in the Indian and Pacific Oceans and is frequently recognized as distinct by local peoples, is really a separate species, a well-marked form of the Green Sea Turtle, or merely a localized color phase. There have been accusations that some who recognize the Black Sea Turtle do so only to make it easier to attract attention to it for conservation purposes.

Sea turtles fly through the water, beating their elongate flippers in a forward-tilting figure-eight in a symmetrical manner, unlike the opposite strokes of nearly all freshwater turtles. Unlike a flying bird, a sea turtle can use its neutral buoyancy in the denser medium of water to drive it forward on the upstroke as well as on the downstroke. Underwater flight, with the flippers moving successively up and down, is the normal way that sea turtles swim. It is not the only way; in shallow water, sea turtles will sometimes use their limbs in alternate strokes like other turtles. Newly emerged hatchlings use opposite strokes in their struggles across the beach to the sea, then instantly switch to "flying" when they hit the water.

The transformation of their limbs is far from the only adaptation sea turtles have for life in the ocean. Their bodies have become streamlined for swimming speed and efficiency. In doing so, they have lost the sheltering overhang at the front of the carapace that protects most other turtles when they withdraw their heads into their shells. Without the ridge, water can flow smoothly over the shell as the turtle swims forward, instead of being swept into turbulent eddies that would create friction and drag. As a consequence, sea turtles cannot pull their heads into their shells, though the Hawksbill does retain some slight ability to do so. Perhaps to compensate, they, like the Big-headed Turtle, have solid, roofed-over skulls.

Their reshaping for life in the sea has left sea turtles ungainly on land. A male sea turtle may never touch dry land again after he joins his siblings in digging himself out of his nesting burrow and scampers down to the water's edge. Females usually only return to land to lay their eggs. In a very few places, including the white sand beaches of French Frigate Shoals and the black sand beaches of the Big Island of Hawaii, Green Sea Turtles haul themselves out on the beach to bask in the sun. You can watch them at Punaluu State Park, if you observe the signs and keep a respectful distance.

Sea turtles are mostly omnivores, but the different species have their own dietary preferences. Green Sea Turtles are primarily vegetarians. They will take animal food when they can get it, including sponges and jellyfish, but in most parts of their range they graze on sea grass and other marine plants. They even keep sea-grass gardens (see page 320, Chapter 8). Flatbacks are more omnivorous than Greens. The Hawksbill is a coral reef specialist that eats both animal and plant matter, but seems particularly partial to sponges and other soft invertebrates. Loggerheads are more carnivorous, and the two ridleys almost exclusively so.

Ridley nesting beaches are, or were, scenes for one of the great spectacles of the natural world. While other sea turtles come ashore singly or in small groups to lay their eggs, ridleys may emerge in vast numbers. The greatest of these concentrations, or *arribadas*, occur today on the beaches of the state of Orissa in India, home of a genetically distinct population of ridleys that may be ancestral to populations elsewhere. Tens of thousands of Olive Ridleys may come ashore in a single night. How long this will continue no one knows. Trawlers dragging off the Orissa coast for shrimp and fish drown thousands of turtles every year—one of the heaviest annual kills of any endangered species. More than 90,000 turtles were killed off Orissa in the eight years before 2003. There is no safety in numbers; hunters and egg collectors destroyed at least three major *arribada* assemblages in Mexico before the 1970s. Natural cycles may also affect the size of nesting aggregations. The *arribada* on Nancite Beach on the Pacific coast of Costa Rica was once one of the most important ridley nesting areas. Between 1970 and 2009, despite full protection, it declined in size by 90 percent for reasons we do not

fully understand. It may now have stabilized; 8,320 females were counted nesting at Nancite in 2007.

The Green Sea Turtle's vegetarian preference apparently, and unfortunately, has made it particularly tasty to humans. Hawksbills have been singled out for even greater economic attention, not for food—its flesh can be toxic—but for the beautiful, translucent scutes of its carapace, the only source of genuine commercial tortoiseshell. International commercial trade in tortoiseshell is now banned (see page 413, Chapter 10).

The IUCN Marine Turtle Specialist Group (MTSG) has classified all but the Olive Ridley and the Flatback—whose populations appear to have been stable for some time—as Endangered or

Female Olive Ridleys (*Lepidochelys olivacea*) come ashore at sunset during a mass nesting, or arribada, at Ostional, Costa Rica.

Critically Endangered throughout their global range since at least 1996. Some biologists balk at assigning these categories to such wide-ranging species, especially considering that some populations (for example, Green Sea Turtles breeding on Ascension Island in the Atlantic) appear to be healthy or even increasing (see page 402, Chapter 10). A few, including the famous Green Sea Turtles of Hawaii, have shown a remarkable ability to rebound after successful conservation efforts. Nonetheless, a 2009 status review of the listing of Loggerheads under the U.S. Endangered Species Act, which lists the species as Threatened, recommended maintaining the listing as a whole. All nine Discrete Population Segments (DPS) had the potential to decline in the future, though nesting trends in the southwest Indian and South Atlantic Oceans appeared to be increasing. Three DPSs, in the Northwest Atlantic, South Pacific and North Pacific Oceans, had a "high likelihood" of extinction in the near future.

It is one of the paradoxes of sea turtle biology that while we probably know more about their nesting habits than we do about those of any other turtle, many aspects of their lives—particularly during the years between hatching and sexual maturity, which sea turtles pass in the open ocean—remain a mystery. Today, though sea turtles are flagship species for conservation around the world—certainly more so, in the public eye, than any other reptile—we are a long way from understanding them, or from giving them the protection they need.

Dermochelyidae: The Leatherback

The Leatherback (*Dermochelys coriacea*), largest and strangest of turtles, is the only living member of the Dermochelyidae. So unusual is the Leatherback that scientists once placed it in a group separate from all other turtles. Today we include it in the same

A Leatherback (*Dermochelys coriacea*), largest and strangest of turtles, ashore on a beach in French Guiana.

major group of cryptodires, the Chelonioidea, as the other sea turtles, but as the last survivor of an evolutionary line that went its own way far back in the Cretaceous. Its teardrop-shaped carapace, crossed with parallel ridges, recalls a stringed lyre and has given rise to its French name, *tortue luth*. The 16th-century naturalist Guillaume Rondelet, the first to describe it for science, called it Mercury's turtle after the lyre the god fashioned from a tortoise shell.

An animal whose shell is made of thousands of tiny separate pieces of bone (see page 27, Chapter 1) is not likely to produce very complete fossils, and *Dermochelys* has a poor fossil record. The Dermochelyidae, though, was once more diverse than it is today. There appear to have been at least six dermochelyid species in the Eocene (56–35 million years ago), representing three different lines within the family. Eocene fossil leatherbacks have even been found in Antarctica, and a Miocene species, *Maorichelys wiffeni*, has been described from New Zealand. Why these other lines became extinct we do not know, but by the end of the Pliocene two million years ago, only the modern line seems to have survived.

Its size alone singles out the Leatherback. A Leatherback's carapace may be up to 180 cm (71 in) in length. Its forelimbs, too, are exceptionally long; a Leatherback with its flippers stretched out may measure over 270 cm (9 ft) across, from tip to tip.

Even if it were smaller, the Leatherback would still be an amazing creature. Roger Conant Wood and his colleagues have called it the most remarkably specialized turtle in the world. No other turtle has carried bony shell reduction to such an extreme degree. The Leatherback has no surface β-keratin at all: no claws, no scales, no scutes, not even cutting plates lining its jaws—structures hardly necessary for an animal that lives almost entirely on jellyfish. It is the fastest-growing of all turtles, increasing its body weight by roughly 8,000 times between hatching and sexual maturity, within possibly as few as nine years.

The Leatherback is the most wide-ranging reptile in the world, with at least eight separate breeding stocks scattered throughout the world's oceans. It has traveled north to Alaska and Iceland, and south of the Cape of Good Hope. It can live, and thrive, in seas far colder, and dive far deeper, than any other sea turtle (see page 204, Chapter 5). Atlantic Leatherbacks may spend at least four months of the year in the cold waters off Nova Scotia, where other turtles rarely venture. The Leatherback accomplishes all this with physical and physiological adaptations more like those of a marine mammal than a turtle. An adult can even maintain its body temperature well above that of the surrounding waters, thanks to counter-current heat exchangers in the arteries and veins at the base of its flippers, and possession of heat-generating brown fat tissues.

In the Atlantic, Leatherbacks seem to be doing reasonably well, and may even be on the increase. They still return in numbers to their nesting beaches in the Guianas and Trinidad, to Chiriqui Beach in Panama, and to Tortuguero Beach on the Caribbean coast of Costa Rica. Nesting apparently decreased at Tortuguero, where illegal egg collecting remains an issue, by almost 70 percent between 1995 and 2006. The small nesting population in Florida (perhaps 1,000 individuals) has been steadily increasing by 10.2 percent per year since 1979, as has the population in the Virgin Islands. Leatherbacks dig 30,000 nests per year on the coast of Gabon, their largest nesting ground in the world, and large numbers still nest on Bioko in the Gulf of Guinea, their second most important African breeding ground. A 2007 population assessment estimated that there were 34,000 to 94,000 animals in the North Atlantic, including 20,000 to 56,000 adult females, with nesting almost equally divided between Africa and America.

The Pacific population, however, collapsed during the last five years of the 20th century. Between 1982 and 1986, the world population of adult female Leatherbacks fell from 115,000 to 34,500. The once-famous nesting beaches of Terengganu in Malaysia have been all but deserted since 1994. At the once-huge colony on the Pacific coast of Mexico, numbers fell from 70,000 in 1982 to fewer than 250 in 1998–1999. In Costa Rica, James Spotila's team counted 1,367 nesting females at Playa Grande in 1988–1989, but only 117 a decade later. On the important breeding grounds of Las Baulas Marine Park the estimated number of nesting females fell from 1,504 in 1988–1989 to only 68 in 2002–2003. The causes range from over-harvest of eggs on the nesting beach to accidental capture in fishing gear—especially by long-liners, drift nets and squid nets on the high seas (see page 398, Chapter 10). Tidal flooding, erosion and predation by pigs affect nesting beaches in Indonesian Papua, one of the Pacific Leatherback's last strongholds.

We still do not understand why the Leatherback's fate has been so different in the two great oceans, though Atlantic populations may be benefiting from an increase in their jellyfish prey and the collapse of shark populations in the northwest, and Pacific Leatherbacks may be affected by more limited food supplies and the effect of weather cycles like El Niño. IUCN now classifies the Leatherback as Critically Endangered. Jeffrey Seminoff, Frank Paladino and Anders Rhodin, in the introduction to a special 2007 issue of the journal *Chelonian Conservation and Biology*, called the struggle to save the Leatherback a "conservation arms race:"

The leatherback is an indicator of ocean health and ecological balance; it represents the desperate challenges and threats that sea turtles face throughout the world and also the still-present opportunity that we have to preserve the beauty and health of marine ecosystems and biodiversity.

Trionychidae: Soft-Shelled Turtles

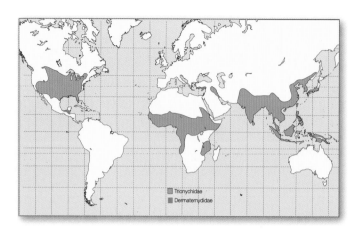

It is hard to mistake a softshell turtle for anything else. Their narrow, elongate heads, tipped with snorkel-snouted nostrils, are unlike those of any other turtle. Their long, broadly webbed, three-clawed feet (*Trionychidae* means, roughly, the "three-clawed ones") emerge from a leather-covered carapace so round and flat that its owners have been compared to animated pancakes. They have no scutes, and no peripheral bones except in a single genus, *Lissemys*. Even in *Lissemys*, these bones (the posterior peripheral ossicles) are small and, rather than forming a continuous ring around the shell, are embedded separately in the leathery skin at the margin of the carapace. They may have a different embryonic origin from the peripheral bones found in other turtles.

Softshells spend much of the time submerged in the water or buried in the mud of the bottom, only the tip of their snorkel poking occasionally above the surface. They are excellent, powerful swimmers and active hunters, agile and often wary. They are also, frequently, scavengers, and some species are omnivores. Softshells have long necks that they can shoot out and twist around with great speed and agility. That, combined with an often aggressive disposition, sharp raking claws, and, in many species, sharp cutting edges to the jaws, makes a softshell an animal that should be definitely handled with care (if at all).

The Florida Softshell Turtle (*Apalone ferox*) is one of only three species in the family Trionychidae found in the New World.

Though softshells are primarily creatures of fresh water, at least two species enter the sea and even nest on ocean beaches. The Asian Giant Softshell has been found nesting on the same sandy beaches in Orissa, India that the Olive Ridley uses for its massive *arribada*s. Its tolerance for salt water has probably helped it colonize much of its range. The African Softshell (*Trionyx triunguis*) has turned up off the coast of West Africa, in Senegal and Gabon, and has been found well out to sea in the Aegean and Mediterranean. Once considered a pest by Turkish fishermen, it is still locally common in some rivers in Turkey and Israel, but is apparently extinct in Egypt.

Today, softshells are primarily an Old World family, concentrated in Africa and, particularly, in Asia. Fossils show that they were once widespread and abundant in Europe, and softshells survived in Australia until only about 500,000 years ago. In the New World, a number of fossil softshells have been found, including a Cretaceous genus from North America, *Aspideretoides*, also known from Central Asia. Only a single genus, with three species, lives in North America today. There are none in South America, though three records from the Miocene and Pliocene of Venezuela show that they once reached at least the northern limits of that continent as well.

The seven flapshells of the subfamily Cyclanorbinae are fairly small to medium-size turtles. When a flapshell withdraws into its shell, it covers its hind limbs with fleshy flaps of skin, called *femoral valves*, attached to the rear of the plastron. Four flapshells live in sub-Saharan Africa, grouped in two genera, *Cycloderma* and *Cyclanorbis*, with two species in each. There are three Asian species,

The Indian Flapshell Turtle (*Lissemys punctata*) is a member of the subfamily Cyclanorbinae.

On its back, a Senegal Flapshell (*Cyclanorbis senegalensis*) reveals the flaps of fleshy skin that cover its hind limbs when it withdraws into its shell.

The Senegal Flapshell Turtle (*Cyclanorbis senegalensis*) of West and Central Africa is the most widespread of the African flapshells.

including the Indian Flapshell (*Lissemys punctata*) and the Burmese Flapshell (*Lissemys scutata*). In 2011, Peter Praschag and his colleagues separated Sri Lankan Flapshells as a third species, *Lissemys ceylonensis*, on molecular grounds, though they admitted that they could not identify Sri Lankan animals on external appearance alone.

None of the flapshells is particularly well known. They are shy animals, and seem to spend much of their time hidden in mud or sand at the bottom of rivers or ponds, waiting for prey. The Indian Flapshell, the best known of the subfamily, is an omnivore. It will come on shore at night to feed on carrion. The fossil softshells of Australia may have been part of the flapshell group, as may another fossil lineage, the plastomenines, which was apparently widespread in North America from the late Cretaceous to the Eocene. The cyclanorbines may have arisen in North America, disappearing there after they spread to the Old World.

The other 24 species of the family, the typical softshells, make up the subfamily Trionychinae. Except for the Asian giants *Chitra* and *Pelochelys*, they were all once included in the genus *Trionyx*, now split into nine separate genera.

In a family of generally large, small-headed animals, the Malayan Softshell (*Dogania subplana*) stands out. It is both fairly small (its carapace reaches just over a foot long) and markedly large headed. Its skull may be over half as long as its carapace, and its unusually flexible shell bulges visibly when the turtle pulls it out of sight (see page 31, Chapter 1). Its diet is fairly unusual for a softshell, including algae and fruits that fall into the forest streams where it lives. The Malayan Softshell ranges from Myanmar and Thailand southward and eastward to Borneo, Java and the Philippines.

The best-known and most thoroughly studied of the softshells are the three American species in the genus *Apalone*. The Smooth Softshell (*A. mutica*) lives primarily in the watersheds of the Ohio, Mississippi and Missouri rivers. The Spiny Softshell (*A. spinifera*), named for the spiny projections along the front edge of its carapace, has a much broader range, from southern Ontario to northern Florida and far northern Mexico, with isolated populations in Lake Champlain, Montana and Wyoming. There is an introduced population in the Colorado River basin. The third American species, the Florida Softshell (*A. ferox*), is found, as its name implies, throughout Florida, north to southern South Carolina, Georgia and Alabama. The Black Spiny Softshell (*A. spinifera atra*), confined to the Cuatro Ciénegas basin of northern Mexico where it is under severe threat of extinction, had been considered a full species but is now regarded as a blackish subspecies of Spiny Softshell. It appears to be adapted to deep, dark-bottomed lagoons. Nearby rivers and shallow playa lakes are homes to lighter, but genetically very similar, individuals of another Spiny Softshell subspecies, *A. spinifera emoryi*.

Smooth and Spiny Softshells are primarily river animals; the Smooth, in particular, prefers large rivers with at least moderate currents. It is primarily an insect eater, feeding in mid-water; insects amounted to 75 percent of the diet of Smooth Softshells in Iowa. It eats a wide range of other animals as well, including frogs, young birds, and small mammals, but will also eat plant material. The Spiny Softshell, by contrast, is a carnivore in both sexes and prefers feeding on the bottom, while the Florida Softshell is an omnivore, though one with definite carnivorous preferences. The Florida Softshell prefers canals, ditches, swamps and similar areas, and is more likely to be seen out of the water than its relatives. It is usually a much easier animal to watch.

Most softshells are medium-sized to fairly large animals, but some are very large indeed. The Indian Narrow-headed Softshell (*Chitra indica*), whose original range stretched from Pakistan across India and southern Nepal to Bangladesh and Assam, reaches 120 kg (265 lbs). The Asian Narrow-headed Softshell (*C. chitra*), which ranges from Thailand and West Malaysia to Sumatra and Java (with its own distinct subspecies), has reached 254 kg (560 lbs). A third species, the Burmese Narrow-headed Softshell

A fully grown Asian Narrow-headed Softshell (*Chitra chitra*) may weigh up to 254 kg (560 lbs).

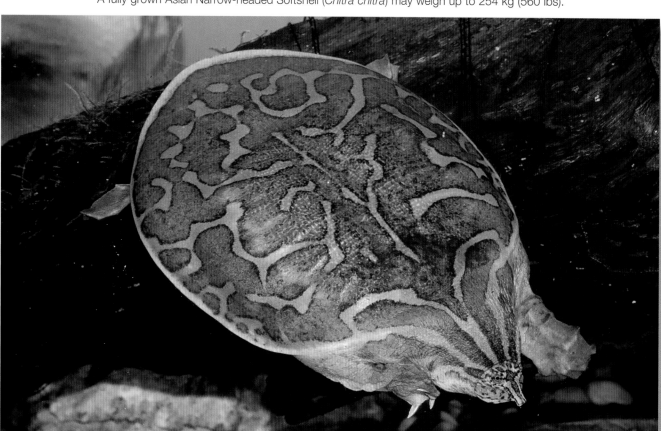

(*C. vandijki*), was described from Myanmar in 2002. All three *Chitras* contrast immense boldly patterned bodies with narrow, truncated-looking heads. They apparently spend much of their lives buried in silt, awaiting their prey (see page 242, Chapter 6).

Indian Narrow-headed Softshells are highly prized as food in Nepal and Bangladesh. In India, hunters snare them with lines bearing hundreds of unbaited hooks. They seek their *calipee*, the fibrous cartilage on the outer rim of the carapace. After boiling and drying, the calipee is shipped, apparently via Bangladesh and Nepal, to China and other countries for use in soups and traditional medicine. The Indian government is now taking steps to protect the species, study its population, and monitor its use.

Hunters in Java search for Asian Narrow-headed Softshells in groups of four, armed with iron-tipped bamboo spears they use to pin the animals to the river bed so they can be hauled up. Even so, one huge turtle managed to tow four hunters who had speared it for 100 m (330 ft) along a stream before breaking off the spear points and escaping. Some commercial hunters in east Java shock the animals into submission with battery-operated probes.

All three species of *Chitra* are at serious risk of extinction. The Indian Narrow-headed Softshell is considered Endangered, and the Asian Critically Endangered—a status that will surely apply to the almost unknown Myanmar species once it is formally evaluated.

The Asian Giant Softshell (*Pelochelys cantorii*), a very large animal with a relatively broad head, ranges from India south and east over a vast area to Sumatra, Borneo and the Philippines. The lowlands of New Guinea are home in the north to the recently recognized Northern New Guinea Giant Softshell (*P. signifera*) and in the south to the New Guinea Giant Softshell (*P. bibroni*). More species may be recognized in the future. Other than sea turtles and the Pig-nose Turtle, giant softshells are New Guinea's only cryptodires.

The only species left in *Trionyx* is the African Softshell. It is the largest member of the Trionychidae after the Asian giants; a big one may weigh 45 kg (100 lbs). Though it probably evolved in southern Europe, it ranges today throughout most of the river systems of the African continent except for the south and northwest. Like the much smaller Malayan Softshell, it is an omnivore, varying its diet of mollusks, frogs, fish and insects with palm nuts and dates. In return, it is eaten by human beings in many parts of its range.

In Asia, the Euphrates Softshell (*Rafetus euphraticus*) lives in warm, shallow, slow-moving waters in the basins of the Tigris and Euphrates, where it has faced the environmental effects of two Gulf Wars. Probably in decline everywhere (though we know little or nothing of its status in Iraq and Syria), it has seemingly disappeared from the rising waters behind the Ataturk Dam in Anatolia. Cold, chemically altered water released from the dam has had a serious effect on the greatly diminished populations below it. In Khuzestan Province, Iran the main threats are habitat loss, including increasing river pollution from industrial development, as well as deliberate killing by fishermen who regard the turtle as an unwelcome competitor.

The only other species of *Rafetus*, the little-known Swinhoe's Softshell (*R. swinhoei*), lives far away to the east in southern China and Vietnam, and is one of the rarest turtles in the world. Only four individuals are known to survive: two in captivity in China; one in the wild that was discovered in 2007 in Dong Mo Lake in Ha Tay province, Vietnam; and another, revered by many as a living god, that has lived for decades in Hoan Kiem Lake in the center of Hanoi, drawing crowds on the rare occasions when it surfaces. The animal was recently removed from the lake for a thorough cleaning and health check before being returned in July 2011. The two Chinese turtles, fortunately of opposite sexes, have been brought together in the Suzhou Zoo in

The giant softshells of New Guinea have recently been recognized as two separate species: the New Guinea Giant Softshell (*Pelochelys bibroni*) at top, of the south, and the Northern New Guinea Giant Softshell (*P. signifera*) at bottom, of the north.

an attempt at captive breeding that has produced many eggs but, so far, no hatchlings. The Cleveland Zoo's Asian Turtle Program established a Rafetus Conservation Project at Dong Mo Lake in 2007, and in 2008 staffers rescued the same individual seen the previous year, an animal weighing 69 kg (152 lbs), from local trade and returned it to the lake.

The other Asian softshells range from India to China and Borneo. The Asiatic Softshell (*Amyda cartilaginea*), a handsome turtle decorated with an attractive pattern of yellow freckles, has a broad range stretching from Myanmar south to Borneo and Java. It even reaches Lombok on the other side of Wallace's Line, the boundary between the Oriental and Australasian zoogeographic regions. The Asiatic Softshell is valued for food and the supposed medicinal qualities of its flesh and cartilage; its meat fetches high prices, and the species may be in decline across much of its range. It rarely leaves the turbid waters where it lives. Asiatic Softshells studied in Loagan Bunut National Park, Sarawak, were omnivores with a high percentage of plant matter in their diet. Karen Jensen and Indraneil Das considered *Amyda* "a keystone species in its contribution to recycling nutrients in the peat swamp ecosystem."

The Wattle-necked Softshell (*Palea steindachneri*) and the four species of *Pelodiscus* are native to China, Laos and Vietnam. The Wattle-necked and Chinese Softshells (*Pelodiscus sinensis*) are now established in Hawaii, and the Chinese Softshell has also been introduced into the Bonin Islands, Timor and, apparently, Japan (though the Japanese turtles, established in the islands for centuries, may be a native population). They were probably brought to Hawaii by Chinese or Japanese immigrants in the late 1800s, though both species were imported for food until the outbreak of the Second World War. The Wattle-necked Softshell may have a better chance of survival in Hawaii than in its native range.

Four of the five species of *Nilssonia*—the species previously included in *Aspideretes*—live in India and adjoining countries, while the Myanmar Peacock Softshell (*Nilssonia formosa*) is confined to Myanmar and, possibly, Thailand. This species and the Indian Peacock Softshell (*N. hurum*) get their names because the carapace of young animals is decorated with four large, striking eyespots like the markings on a peacock's train, dark circular splotches bordered with yellow and ringed with black. The markings, which fade with age, may startle a predator long enough to help the baby turtle escape—or may not; no one is quite sure. The Indian Peacock Softshell is still relatively common, though it is heavily hunted for its meat and calipee. Leith's Softshell Turtle (*N. leithii*) is endemic to southern India, where it is hunted with unbaited hooks, eaten, and sold to local markets. It has been little studied, and appears to be rare.

The Black Softshell or Bostami Turtle (*N. nigricans*) was long thought to survive only for religious reasons. The entire population appeared to consist of some 150–300 animals held in semi-captivity in a single enclosed artificial pond, or tank, about 8 km (5 mi) from Chittagong, Bangladesh, where visitors and pilgrims feed them bread, bananas and offal. The tank is attached to an Islamic shrine devoted to a famous saint, Sultan al-Arefin Hazrat Bayazid Bistami (or Bayazid Bostami, 777–874), who was supposed to have turned the evil spirits haunting the site into turtles. The turtles have been there at least since 1875, and possibly for far longer, nesting on its banks (though the area available for nesting is shrinking, and only the east bank and a raised area near the west are still suitable for the turtles). According to an early report:

> The Mahommedans will neither kill them nor permit them to be killed; they believe they are in some way connected with the saint. The tank is surrounded by steps leading down to a platform a few inches under water, and the turtles are so tame that they come to feed when called, placing their forefeet on the edge of the platform or even

climbing upon it and stretching their necks out of the water … Some even allowed us to touch them, and ate pieces of chicken from wooden skewers held in our hands.

Molecular evidence has recently revealed that the Black Softshell still survives in the wild, in nearby Assam, India. There must be many more than 300 of them, but how common or rare the Black Softshell really is we have yet to learn.

Carettochelyidae: The Pig-Nose Turtle

The Pig-nose Turtle belongs in its own family, and looks it. It is one of the most distinctive of all turtles. At first glance, it looks like an undersized sea turtle; its carapace rarely reaches more than 50 cm (20 in), and is usually only 30–34 cm (12–13 in) at 14 to 16 years of age, when it reaches maturity. Its front limbs have been transformed into soft, flexible flippers and its hindlimbs into paddles. Like a sea turtle, it flies through the water, moving both front limbs at the same time instead of alternately as other freshwater turtles do. Each flipper and paddle retains two free claws on its leading edge. The turtle uses the claws on its flippers for ripping food apart; the only time it appears to use its hind claws is while digging its nest. Males seem to use their front claws while mating: one researcher in Australia found "mating scars" on both sides of the neck in 60 percent of adult females, but never in males or juveniles.

The Pig-nose Turtle (*Carettochelys insculpta*) has sea turtle-like flippers, but is more closely related to the softshells.

The Pig-nose's snout—the source of its rather unattractive Australian common name—is extended into something that looks almost like the beginnings of a trunk. Its shell is covered by a thin, velvety skin, and the bones of its carapace are dotted with tiny pits that may anchor the skin to the bone (another of its common names is "pitted-shelled turtle"). Unlike the softshells, though, *Carettochelys* still has a heavy, complete bony shell. It still retains, for example, a set of 10 pairs of peripherals around the edge of the carapace, bones that the softshells have lost. The bony plates of its carapace are juxtaposed together, but are not sutured to one another.

Fossil carettochelyids have been found in North America, Europe and Asia, in deposits dating from the Cretaceous to the Oligocene. The living Pig-nose Turtle is confined, instead, to the savannas of southern New Guinea and northern Australia, where it dwells in clear, shallow rivers, swamps, water holes and billabongs. Along the shores where the Pig-nose swims grows a dense gallery forest of broad-leafed trees, including figs, whose fruits and leaves fall into the water to become food for the turtles. The turtles also feed on aquatic plants, and on animal food including shrimp, insects, snails and carrion. Like sea turtles, they only come to land when the females haul themselves ashore to dig their nests, usually in a sandbank but sometimes in mud, loam or gravel. In New Guinea, but not in Australia, they sometimes nest on ocean beaches. Groups of up to a dozen females search together for suitable nesting areas. Once they have selected a site they spend several days nesting, with one to three females emerging each night.

For a long time, scientists thought that the Pig-nose Turtle lived only in the Fly River region of southern New Guinea, where they discovered it in the 1880s. It was not until 1970 that Harold Cogger, then of the Australian Museum, published the first report proving that the species lived in the Northern Territory of Australia as well. The Aborigines, of course, had known it was there all along. Rock paintings near Kakadu National Park clearly depict the Pig-nose Turtle—paintings, ironically, that had been photographed and studied by Europeans for over a century, and may date back more than 7,000 years.

There seem to be fairly high densities of Pig-nose Turtles in some rivers in New Guinea, and in the Alligator River of Australia. The Pig-nose is heavily exploited in New Guinea, both for international trade and locally, where their meat is highly prized and their eggs are heavily collected (see page 370, Chapter 9). The World Wildlife Fund (WWF) has named it one of the 10 most wanted species in the global illegal wildlife trade. In 2005, one foiled smuggling attempt in Merauke, Indonesia involved 7,275 Pig-nose Turtles. Jakarta, Bangkok and Singapore act as major entrepots for smuggled turtles destined for China, Japan, North America and Europe. Pig-noses are greatly in demand as unique pets, and may fetch $1,500 to $2,000 per animal on the international market.

Platysternidae: The Big-Headed Turtle

The Big-headed Turtle (*Platysternon megacephalum*), sole member of its family, lives in rocky mountain streams from southern China southward into Thailand. It deserves its name. Its head is so large that it looks out of place on its body—it may be half the width of the carapace.

Since the Big-headed Turtle cannot withdraw its oversized head into its shell, it carries armor instead. The top of its head is entirely covered by a single tough, horny scute, and its skull is completely roofed over with bone, without the emarginations for the jaw muscles found in most other turtles. The horny sheath lining the edges of its jaws extends up over its face, almost reaching the scute on the top of its head, leaving only a narrow band of exposed skin between eye and nostril.

Almost nothing is known about the Big-headed Turtle in the wild. It appears to be nocturnal and carnivorous to omnivorous, hiding under rocks at the sides or bottom of a stream by day and emerging to hunt for small animals in the streambed at night. It rarely swims, preferring instead to navigate the streambed with its strong claws and tail. As befits an animal that has to clamber over slippery boulders, the Big-headed Turtle is a remarkably good climber. It can scale sheer, nearly vertical slopes and even climb trees. Its bridge is flexible, perhaps as an adaptation to allow it to use its limbs more freely as it climbs. It can even use its long, stiff tail as a climbing prop; its tail is strong enough to support the turtle's entire weight.

In 2007, Jian-Wei Shen and his colleagues purchased 16 Big-headed Turtles from a dealer, sexed them, fitted them with transmitters, and released them in streams on protected land in Hebei Province, southern China. They monitored the turtles' movements for eight months, from April to November. The turtles were very sedentary, remaining hidden most of the time and moving only short distances, usually at night. They almost never basked, rarely came out on land, and never traveled farther than 5.8 m (19 ft) from the stream bank. Males tended to move farther than females, but females spent more time on land than males, presumably while searching for suitable nest sites.

There has been a great deal of uncertainty as to where this peculiar animal belongs on the turtle family tree. Based mainly on the anatomy of its skull, Eugene Gaffney placed it in the Chelydridae. Indeed, it has some resemblance to snapping turtles, though it is far smaller, with a carapace length of only 18.4 cm (7.2 in). It has a similar combination of large head, long tail and ridged carapace (though it has only a single, slight median ridge instead of three pronounced ones; the ridge disappears with age). Its shell structure, though, is very different; its plastron, for example, is much broader and more extensive. There are also a number of differences in its skeleton. A 2006 analysis of its complete mitochondrial genome placed the Big-headed Turtle firmly within the Testudinoidea, probably close to the American pond turtles (Emydidae). A 2010 study of nuclear DNA confirmed this result, and found strong support for the Emydidae as the Big-headed Turtle's closest relatives.

Like many other Asian turtles, the Big-headed Turtle is heavily exploited and under threat. It is widely used for food and traditional medicine. Nine percent of all live turtles exported from China between 1998 and 2002 were Big-headed Turtles. It is becoming increasingly scarce and hard to find, even in the remotest parts of its range.

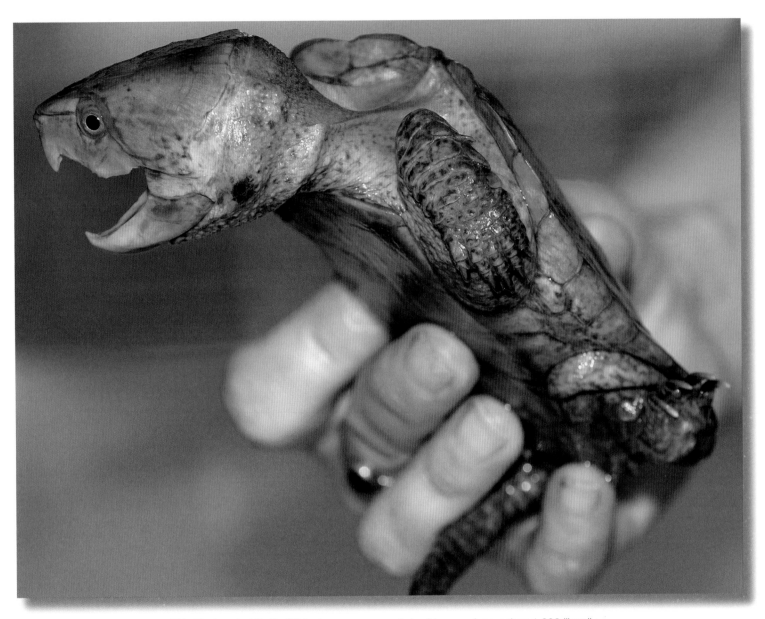

This Big-headed Turtle (*Platysternon megacephalum*) is one of more than 1,000 illegally
imported turtles confiscated from a New York loft in July 2003.

CHAPTER FOUR

TURTLES AROUND THE WORLD II:
Terrapins and Tortoises

CLUSTERED TOGETHER ON a branch of the cryptodire tree are the three largest families of turtles: the Emydidae (American pond turtles), Geoemydidae (Asian river turtles, formerly called Bataguridae) and Testudinidae (tortoises); recently, it appears Big-headed turtles (Platysternidae) also belong on that branch. Exactly how they cluster there, though, has been a matter for some debate. Until 1967, scientists did not realize that the Emydidae and Geoemydidae—the animals Britons call terrapins—represented separate branches of the tree. To make matters more confusing, there are Asian river turtles in Central and South America and American pond turtles in Europe. Asian river and American pond turtles look very much like each other. There are box turtles in both families: *Terrapene* spp. in North America and *Cuora* spp. in Asia. Both have domed shells and hinged plastra, and it was once thought that they were each other's closest relatives. It took deeper analysis—particularly, a comparison of the structure of the bones and cartilages of the lower jaw and palate, plus a few other skeletal details—to show that this was a case of parallel evolution.

The Asian river turtles are actually more closely related to the tortoises than they are to their American near look-alikes. The tortoises may have arisen from within the Geoemydidae. Some Asian pond turtles may be more closely related to tortoises than they are to others within their own family. If so, the tortoise "family," to be consistent, would have to be reduced to a subgroup of the Geoemydidae; however, molecular analyses support maintaining tortoises and Asian pond turtles as separate, but closely related, groups.

OPPOSITE

Perhaps the best-known emydid: a hatchling Painted Turtle (*Chrysemys picta*), in the Okanagan Valley of southern British Columbia, Canada.

Asian box turtles, including the Southeast Asian Box Turtle (*Cuora amboinensis*, top) are members of the Geoemydidae, only distantly related to American box turtles of the Emydidae, like the Eastern Box Turtle (*Terrapene carolina*, bottom).

For our purposes, it is easier to think of these turtles as members of three separate, but closely related, families, and to survey them one at a time. We will start with the turtles most familiar to North Americans: the members of the Emydidae.

Emydidae: American Pond Turtles

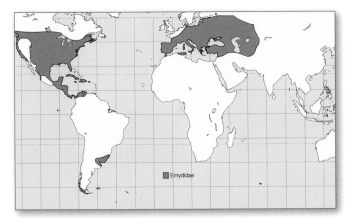

For most North Americans, the Emydidae are the typical turtles. They are familiar not only because they are varied and abundant, but because they are often easy to watch as they bask in the open on floating logs or emergent stones. Many of us—at least those over a certain age—can remember having a baby emydid, most probably a Red-eared Slider (*Trachemys scripta elegans*), as a (usually) short-lived childhood pet. Emydids include aquatic and terrestrial species, generalists and specialists, carnivores, herbivores and omnivores. Dietary specialists may have evolved up to 16 times from generalist ancestors.

Emydids range through the Americas from southern Canada to northern Argentina, including the West Indies. Along much of the Pacific coast there is only one species, the Western Pond Turtle (*Actinemys*, or *Emys*, *marmorata*), a misnamed animal that prefers streams and rivers to ponds. It even extends to the Mojave, an isolated desert river in California, where it is apparently a holdover from wetter times in the Pleistocene. Four species of slider reach South America. The chief emydid stronghold, though, is the eastern United States. Some 35 species live east of the Mississippi River. Some have tiny distributions: the Alabama Red-bellied Turtle (*Pseudemys alabamensis*) only lives in two counties around Mobile Bay, Alabama. By contrast, the Painted

The declining Western Pond Turtle (*Actinemys marmorata*) is the only freshwater turtle along much of the U.S. Pacific coast.

Two Spotted Turtles (*Clemmys guttata*) bask on a log in Indiana, USA.

Turtle (*Chrysemys picta*) ranges clear across the continent, the only North American turtle to do so.

The Western Pond Turtle is a comparatively dull creature that seems to have escaped the pet collectors' furore, probably thanks to timely protection in all three Pacific states; however, it suffered drastically in the 19th century from the terrapin soup trade. The Spotted Turtle (*Clemmys guttata*), Bog Turtle (*Glyptemys muhlenbergii*) and Wood Turtle (*Glyptemys insculpta*) have not been so fortunate; their beauty has made them the most sought-after turtles in North America. All four species suffer from habitat loss—much of the habitat of the Western Pond Turtle, in the fertile San Joaquin Valley of California, has been drained and converted to agriculture, leaving the turtle to survive best in

sewage treatment facilities—and the three eastern species from (mostly illegal) collecting for the pet trade. They have disappeared from a number of parts of their former range.

The Spotted Turtle ranges from southern Ontario south to northern Florida, mostly along the eastern seaboard of the United States. The spots on its carapace that make it so attractive and easy to recognize are actually places where the scutes are transparent, revealing deposits of yellow pigment lying beneath. Some Spotted Turtles lack them, or may lose them with age. The Spotted Turtle prefers bogs, woodland streams and other areas with clear, shallow water, muddy bottoms and lots of vegetation, though island populations in Georgian Bay, Ontario often resort to rock pools devoid of emergent vegetation, perhaps to warm up in the sun without being exposed to the cool air. It has declined throughout its range under a barrage of threats ranging from overcollection, wetland drainage, pollution and habitat fragmentation to predation from increased numbers of raccoons and foxes, road mortality and overgrazing by livestock.

The attractive little Bog Turtle, a bright orange blotch daubing the side of its head, is a habitat specialist. It favors sedge-dominated fens, tamarack and spruce swamps, and marshy meadows, though in some areas individuals will move to streams during drier periods. It is the smallest turtle in North America, with a carapace reaching only 11 cm (4.4 in) or so. Increasingly rare, it survives in scattered and fragmented colonies in the northeastern United States south to northernmost Georgia, with a gap between northern and southern population groups in Maryland and, locally, Virginia. It may have suffered, oddly enough, from the demise of free-range cattle ranching and dairy farming. Grazing livestock eat the young trees and other invasive plants that otherwise fill in bogs that the turtle requires (in earlier days, beavers would have provided the open bogs). Allowing goats, cattle and sheep to graze in wet meadows has become an important part of Bog Turtle conservation.

The Wood Turtle ranges from Virginia north to Sudbury, Ontario. It is mostly brown with bright orange, yellow or red on its throat, neck, tail and the underside of its forelimbs. In contrast to the smooth, almost polished shell of the Spotted Turtle, the scutes of the Wood Turtle's carapace are decorated with radiating, raised ridges crossed by well-marked growth rings. They give the shell the appearance of a cluster of limpets, and justify the scientific name *insculpta*, which means "carved" or "engraved." Though it can be found in other places, the Wood Turtle prefers forested streams with open areas along their banks. During summer, it may spend quite a bit of its time on land, especially in the eastern part of its range.

Actinemys, *Clemmys* and *Glyptemys* lack a hinge across the plastron. Their more advanced relatives, the European Pond Turtle (*Emys orbicularis*), Blanding's Turtle (*Emydoidea*, or *Emys*, *blandingii*) and the American box turtles, have developed hinges, but to varying degrees of effectiveness. Box turtles can seal themselves tightly within their shells, both fore and aft. Some Blanding's Turtles can do the same, but others seem hardly able to raise the plastron at all. Most European Pond Turtles cannot close their shells completely (perhaps they don't need to).

The European Pond Turtle, one of only two members of the Emydidae native to the Old World, is a shy carnivore that prefers still or slow-flowing waters with muddy or sandy bottoms and abundant vegetation overhanging their banks. In Poland, for example, it prefers lakes, and ponds in peat bogs. It has a low, rounded carapace that may be olive brown, brown or black, often heavily dotted and streaked with yellow. It ranges northeast to Latvia and Lithuania, south and east to Iran and the Caspian Sea, and across the Straits of Gibraltar to Morocco, Algeria and Tunisia. North of Spain, Italy and the Balkans, it is the only freshwater turtle of any kind. Its remains have been found as far north as Sweden, and in the British Isles. The only other Old World emydid, the Sicilian Pond Turtle (*Emys trinacris*) of Sicily and the adjacent Italian mainland, was only recognized as a distinct species (primarily on molecular grounds) in 2005. Molecular evidence suggests that the European Pond Turtles are close relatives of the Western Pond Turtle and, especially, Blanding's Turtle. The ancestors of the European forms may have crossed into the Old World via a Bering Sea land bridge some 16 million years ago.

Blanding's Turtle has one of the most northerly ranges of all turtle species. Its range is concentrated around the Great Lakes and the Midwest, reaching no farther south than south-central Indiana and Illinois. There are isolated colonies in New England,

The European Pond Turtle (*Emys orbicularis*) of Europe, Western Asia and
North Africa is one of only two emydids in the Old World.

Blanding's Turtle (*Emydoidea blandingii*) is a northern North American species, able to tolerate low temperatures.

Nova Scotia and southern New York State. It tolerates fairly low temperatures; Blanding's Turtles have even been seen swimming under the ice of a frozen Indiana pond in November. It is a larger animal than the *Glyptemys* and *Clemmys* species, with a higher, more domed carapace and a long neck highlighted by a bright yellow chin and throat. Like its close relative, the European Pond Turtle, Blanding's Turtle is a carnivore, usually catching its food underwater, though it may make extensive journeys on land in search of temporary ponds or nesting sites. Females in Minnesota may travel overland as far as 7.5 km (4.6 mi) before they nest. Blanding's Turtles mature very slowly, and are threatened by collecting for the pet trade, mortality on roadways, and loss and destruction of their habitat.

American box turtles recall miniature tortoises, with high, domed shells, heavy-set limbs and a preference, at least among the more northern forms, for a land-based life. The Eastern Box Turtle (*Terrapene carolina*) of the eastern United States (and south-western Ontario and southern Québec, where it may be introduced) usually lives in open deciduous or mixed woodlands, though it sometimes can be found in marshy meadows or, in Florida, in palmetto thickets. Though primarily a land animal, it needs access to water, where it may spend time sitting and soaking around the edge of a pond. It may be particularly active after rain. The Gulf Coast (*T. carolina major*) and the Florida (*T. carolina bauri*) subspecies, in particular, spend considerable time in the water. Eastern Box Turtles eat a wide variety of plant and animal foods; a turtle may stay within a ripening raspberry or blackberry patch until it has eaten every berry it can reach. The Ornate Box Turtle (*T. ornata*) of the American midwest south to Texas and northern Mexico, as befits an animal of the prairies, is more likely to be found in sandy plains or open grassland country, while the very poorly known, and possibly rare, Spotted Box Turtle (*T. nelsoni*) is restricted to hilly savanna or dry woodland in scattered localities in northwestern Mexico.

The little-known Northern Spotted Box Turtle (*Terrapene nelsoni klauberi*) lives in scattered localities in the states of Chihuahua, Sinaloa and Sonora, Mexico. Another subspecies ranges south to Jalisco.

The Coahuilan Box Turtle (*Terrapene coahuila*), the most aquatic of the American box turtles, is confined to the Cuatro Ciénegas wetlands of Coahuila, Mexico.

The fourth species, the Coahuilan Box Turtle (*T. coahuila*), is, however, not terrestrial but semi-aquatic. It is confined to a single isolated wetland basin, no more than 800 sq km (320 sq mi) in extent, the Cuatro Ciénegas (Four Pools) in the otherwise arid state of Coahuila, Mexico. It shares the pools with two other endemic and endangered turtles, the Cuatro Ciénegas Slider (*Trachemys taylori*) and the Black Spiny Softshell (*Apalone spinifera atra*). Herpetologists think that it is the descendant of an isolated population of Eastern Box Turtles that retreated to small, spring-fed pools as the surrounding country became too dry even for their terrestrial lifestyles. Today, the Coahuilan Box Turtle is effectively trapped within its wetland refuge, and risks further isolation and inbreeding should populations in different parts of the basin be cut off from each other. The pools continue to shrink as canals drain the water away for irrigation, though, ironically, abandoned irrigation canals connecting the pools may be the turtles' best protection against inbreeding. The species is considered Endangered both by IUCN and under the U.S. Endangered Species Act. In 2007, a reserve established to protect the area in 1994 was expanded tenfold.

Clemmys, *Glyptemys*, *Terrapene* and *Emys* (with its close relatives *Actinemys* and *Emydoidea*) form the subfamily Emydinae, the smaller (in terms of species numbers) of two major evolutionary lines within the Emydidae. The other subfamily, the Deirochelyinae, includes the "typical" log-basking pond and river turtles: painted turtles (*Chrysemys*), sliders (*Trachemys*), cooters (*Pseudemys*), the Chicken Turtle (*Deirochelys reticularia*) and the map turtles (*Graptemys*). It also includes the only turtle to be entirely confined to brackish water, the Diamondback Terrapin (*Malaclemys terrapin*).

Groups of Painted Turtles clustering on a log, lying on top of each other, pushing each other out of the way in an attempt to reach the sun, are a common sight at many a northern pond.

The Painted Turtle is one of the most thoroughly studied species of freshwater turtle in the world. It occupies an extremely broad range, from Nova Scotia to Vancouver Island, southward through the eastern and midwestern United States to the Gulf of Mexico, and in scattered localities in the southwest. Its four races differ in details of color pattern, but all have attractively marked carapaces with varying amounts of red on the edge. The form in the south-central United States is sometimes treated as a separate species (*Chrysemys dorsalis*, the Southern Painted Turtle). It has a bright red or yellow stripe running down the midline. The Painted Turtle is an omnivore, foraging along the bottom or skimming fine particles of food from the water's surface. Like Blanding's Turtle, it tolerates cold temperatures; it will swim in ice-covered ponds, or even emerge to bask before the ice on the water surface has quite melted.

There are now 15 recognized sliders, following the split of the Common Slider (*Trachemys scripta*) into a number of distinct species. Only two live north of the Mexican border: the widespread Common Slider and the Big Bend Slider (*T. gaigeae*) of central New Mexico and the U.S.-Mexican border country along the upper Rio Grande, with two isolated subspecies that may prove not to be each other's closest relatives. Three species are endemic to Mexico, including the highly localized Cuatro Ciénegas Slider. The Nicaraguan slider (*T. emolli*) lives in Nicaragua and Costa Rica, while the Meso-American Slider (*T. venusta*) ranges from Mexico to Colombia. Gray's Slider (*T. venusta grayi*), a subspecies with scattered populations—some highly endangered—along the Pacific coast from Oaxaca to Guatemala, can reach a carapace length of 60 cm (24 in), making it one of the largest freshwater turtles in the Americas. Three sliders are found only in South America. The Colombian Slider (*T. callirostris*), of Colombia and northwestern Venezuela, is heavily overhunted throughout its range despite legal protection. Separated from it by a gap covering most of the Amazon basin are D'Orbigny's Slider (*T. dorbigni*) of southeastern Brazil, Uruguay and Argentina and the recently described Maranhao Slider (*T. adiutrix*) from the Amazon delta region of eastern Brazil. Four slider species are confined to Cuba and the Caymans, Jamaica, Hispaniola, Puerto Rico and the Bahamas.

One form of Common Slider has been taken up by our own species and turned, willy-nilly, into perhaps the best-known, most widespread, and least endangered turtle in the world. The tiny brilliant patch of red on the side of the head of *Trachemys scripta elegans*, the Red-eared Slider, once singled it out as the quintessential dime-store turtle. Bred for the pet trade and for food, and exported around the world in huge numbers, accidental populations of Red-eared Sliders soon began to appear in all sorts of unlikely places, often deliberately released by pet owners tired of their growing charges. Today, there are wild Red-eared Sliders on every continent except Antarctica and on a wide range of oceanic islands, including nearly 60 countries and a number of island territories throughout the world.

The impact of this massive, human-assisted range expansion is not yet fully understood, but the IUCN Global Invasive Species Database named it one of the 100 World's Worst Invasive Alien Species, the only turtle on the list. In Bermuda, Red-eared Sliders may be competing with the small population of native Diamondback Terrapins (*Malaclemys terrapin*) for nesting sites. In Europe, sliders, which are more fecund, mature earlier and take a wider range of foods, may be out-competing native turtles for food and basking sites.

Introductions have made the Red-eared Slider (*Trachemys scripta elegans*) the world's most widespread freshwater turtle.

A probable pair of Peninsula Cooters (*Pseudemys peninsularis*); note the long foreclaws of the much smaller male.

The United States exported more than 52,000,000 baby sliders between 1989 and 1997. In December 1997 the European Parliament banned the importation of Red-eared Sliders on the grounds that they pose a serious and lasting threat to native species, including the European Pond Turtle. It is still legal to keep and distribute Red-eared Sliders in many European countries. Dealers tried to get around the import ban by switching to different races of slider or to other turtle species. Though the numbers involved are considerably lower, some of the replacement species—such as the Common Snapping Turtle (*Chelydra serpentina*)—are more carnivorous and cold-tolerant than the Red-eared Slider and risk becoming a problem in themselves. Though Red-eared Sliders no longer appear in numbers in North American pet shops and department stores, they are still being exported to China (see page 374, Chapter 9).

The six or seven species of cooter, including the Red-bellied Turtle (*Pseudemys rubriventris*) and the Florida Red-bellied Turtle (*P. nelsoni*), resemble the Painted Turtle and the sliders. Adult males, though, have a distinctive feature (also present in some sliders): extremely long, straight foreclaws that they vibrate along the sides of a female's face during courtship. Though cooters start life as omnivores, the adults are almost entirely herbivorous. In 1990, Alabama named the local and Endangered Alabama Red-bellied Turtle or Red-bellied Cooter (*P. alabamensis*) as its Official State Reptile.

The Chicken Turtle of the southeastern United States, though superficially similar to the cooters and often sharing the same bodies of water, is a quite different animal, a long-necked, narrow-headed hunter specializing in aquatic insects and crustaceans. It is named for its particularly succulent flesh. While most other North American turtles nest in the spring and summer, the Chicken Turtle nests in the autumn, and even into the winter months, as does the Peninsula Cooter (*Pseudemys peninsularis*). Eggs laid late in the year may remain dormant for months, until conditions are right for the hatchlings to emerge.

Map turtles are river dwellers, shy animals that rarely leave their homes for the land, though juvenile Mississippi Map Turtles (*Graptemys pseudogeo-graphica kohnii*) may leave the water to feed on plants growing on the bank. They get their name from the intricate series of yellowish lines on the carapace of several species, lines that may recall the contours on a map. The so-called sawbacks, including the Ringed Map Turtle, have a series of black, spine-like projections running down the middle of the carapace. Some map turtles show a remarkable difference in size and head shape between males and females, paralleling a difference in their diets (see page 234, Chapter 6).

OPPOSITE

Map turtles like this Texas Map Turtle (*Graptemys versa*) may depend on floating logs for basking.

The Chicken Turtle (*Deirochelys reticularia*), unlike the cooters, is mostly carnivorous, feeding on aquatic insects and crustaceans.

The Northern Map Turtle (*G. geographica*) is broad-ranging, from southern Ontario and Québec south to Arkansas and Alabama. The preference of map turtles for rivers, though, has meant that a number of map turtle populations have become isolated in different drainage basins along the Gulf Coast, where they have evolved into localized species with highly restricted distributions. Several are confined to single river systems draining into the Gulf of Mexico, or even to portions of those systems. The Ringed Map Turtle (*G. oculifera*) and the recently described Pearl River Map Turtle (*G. pearlensis*), only recognized as distinct in 2010, share the Pearl River system of Mississippi and Louisiana. The Pascagoula Map Turtle (*G. gibbonsi*) is confined, with the Ringed Map Turtle's closest relative, the Yellow-blotched Map Turtle (*G. flavimaculata*), to the Pascagoula River system of Mississippi, east of the Pearl. Yellow-blotched Map Turtles in the lower Pascagoula River took a hit from Hurricane Katrina in 2005, possibly because salt water was driven into the river from the Gulf of Mexico by the force of the storm. They had not rebounded three years later. The Pascagoula, one of the least disturbed river systems in the United States, has been threatened by a plan—currently on hold after much opposition—to double the amount of water currently taken from it to construct a massive petroleum storage facility.

Map turtles make extensive use of, and even seem to require, logs and other deadwood as basking sites. At night, they roost clinging to their perches below the water line. Removal of deadwood from their home rivers has been held partly to blame, in a study by Peter V. Lindeman, for the decline of both the Ringed Map Turtle and the Yellow-blotched Map Turtle.

The Diamondback Terrapin is a habitat specialist, restricted to salt marshes, mangroves, estuaries and tidal creeks along the whole of the eastern and Gulf coasts of the United States from Cape Cod to the Florida Keys and Texas, with a tiny outlier population on Bermuda. It is the only emydid turtle with a salt-excreting gland (see page 199, Chapter 5). It is a dietary specialist too, eating mostly mollusks and crustaceans, and concentrating in some areas on hard-shelled snails. In Virginia, it prefers Mud Snails (*Nassarius obsoletus*), though it also takes periwinkles, worms, crabs and other shellfish. Saltmarsh Periwinkles (*Littoraria irrorata*) and Blue Crabs (*Callinectes sapidus*) are preferred items in South Carolina. Farther north, terrapins in Connecticut take Marsh and Mud Snails (*Melampus bidentatus* and *Ilyanassa obsoleta*), Marsh Mussels (*Geukensia demissa*) and fiddler crabs (*Uca* spp.). In turn, a Diamondback can become so encrusted with barnacles that its shell may erode.

The Diamondback was once a food staple so cheap that 18th-century slaves actually went on strike to protest the amount of terrapin in their diet. In the late 19th century, though, the Diamondback made an unfortunate transition from despised staple to gourmet delicacy. It remained one until the 1930s, subjected to an intense commercial hunt: between 1880 and 1936, an estimated 200,000 Diamondbacks were processed into meat in Maryland alone. Even though the commercial fisheries have largely collapsed or been closed, turtles continue to drown in large numbers in pot traps designed for crabs. The remaining populations face coastal development, disturbance and increased predation on their nesting beaches, boat injuries and pollution. Terrapins are still being hunted, mostly for sale to Chinese restaurants in New York City. The Diamondback Terrapin continues to decline. A Diamondback Terrapin Working Group was formed in 2004 "to promote the conservation of the Diamondback Terrapin, the preservation of intact, wild terrapin populations and their associated ecosystems throughout their range."

The Diamondback Terrapin (*Malaclemys terrapin*) is a habitat and dietary specialist from the eastern and Gulf coasts of the United States.

Geoemydidae: Asian River Turtles

The Geoemydidae is the largest and most diverse of turtle families. It contains some 70 species, including some of the most handsome and spectacular turtles. They are divided up among 19 genera, though their exact classification has been a matter for some debate. In recent years traditional genera (e.g. *Kachuga*) have been broken up or eliminated, others expanded (e.g. *Batagur*), and a number of species shifted from one genus to another, mainly on molecular evidence. Some formerly well-known Asian genera are no longer recognized. The Chinese Stripe-necked Turtle, an aquatic plant-eating species formerly called *Ocadia sinensis*, has been transferred, on mitochondrial DNA evidence, to *Mauremys*, as have the turtles formerly included in *Chinemys*, though there are skeletal differences between them and the other turtles in

their "new" genus. The Keeled Box Turtle, formerly *Pyxidea mouhotii*, is now included in *Cuora*. This confusing state of affairs has not been helped by the description of a number of "new" species, based on purchased specimens—obtained, in a number of cases, from a single Hong Kong pet dealer—that have turned out to be hybrids. Some may have been deliberately bred in captivity to lure buyers into purchasing supposed novelties.

New geoemydids are still being discovered. The Sulawesi Forest Turtle (*Leucocephalon yuwonoi*) was described in 1995 from seven specimens purchased on the island of Sulawesi in Indonesia by a Jakarta animal dealer, Frank Bambang Yuwono (animals were being kept in Japan as early as 1991–1992). Sulawesi is east of Wallace's Line, making its forest turtle the only geoemydid confined to Australasia. Only one other, the Southeast Asian Box Turtle

(*Cuora amboinensis*), crosses the line, reaching Sulawesi and beyond, to the Moluccas. The Sulawesi Forest Turtle is known from the northern and central regions of the island. Local turtle collectors say it spends the night in forest streams, emerging by day to search for food in the forest. Fallen fruits, especially figs, seem to be an important part of its diet. Under pressure from overcollecting and deforestation, including clearing of forests for oil palm, it remains one of the most endangered turtles in the world.

There have been rediscoveries, too: in May 1994, colleagues of Oscar Shiu bought a pair of live Arakan Forest Turtles (*Heosemys depressa*) from a villager in western Yunnan province, China. They were the first of their species seen by western scientists since 1908; the species was described, based on a specimen from nearby Rakhine (formerly Arakan) State in Myanmar, in 1875. Arakan forest turtles still turn up with some regularity in markets in China and Taiwan, but we still do not know if the market animals represent a Chinese population or, more likely, if they are smuggled over the border. In 2003 and 2009 Steven Platt and his colleagues, assisted by local turtle hunters, found wild turtles in bamboo thickets in the Rakhine Yoma Elephant Range, a remote and extensive protected area. Their local name is *pyant chee zar leik* ("the turtle that eats rhinoceros feces"), but whether Arakan Forest Turtles ever dined on rhino droppings we may never know.

The Sulawesi Forest Turtle (*Leucocephalon yuwonoi*) was described in 1995; it is already extremely rare in the wild.

The Sumatran Rhinoceros (*Dicerorhinus sumatrensis*) became extinct in the region over 50 years ago.

While new turtles are being discovered and described, old ones are disappearing. Most of the geoemydids live in tropical Asia. No other region of the world is being so rapidly stripped of its turtles, both to supply food markets in China and the pet trade in Europe, North America, Japan and elsewhere. Of the 32 full species of turtle listed as Critically Endangered in the 2011 IUCN Red List of Threatened Species, fourteen—nearly half—are geoemydids.

There are so many geoemydids in Asia that it will probably be less confusing to start our survey on the other side of the world, with *Rhinoclemmys*, the neotropical wood turtles. *Rhinoclemmys* is an anomaly, the only living geoemydid genus in the New World, though a fossil genus, *Echmatemys*, is known from the Eocene of Wyoming. There are nine species in the genus, ranging from Mexico south to Ecuador and Brazil. They are attractive turtles, with low rounded shells mostly colored in warm brownish tones. They have no hinge on the plastron, but when a *Rhinoclemmys* withdraws its head two folds of skin close over it like curtains, hiding the head completely from view. What protection this provides (a similar feature can be found in some emydids and tortoises) is hard to say.

Neotropical wood turtles like the Black Wood Turtle (*Rhinoclemmys funerea*) of Central America are the only geoemydids in the New World.

Some *Rhinoclemmys* species, like the Black Wood Turtle (*R. funerea*) of Central America, are more or less aquatic, though the Black Wood Turtle may emerge at night to feed on land. The Furrowed Wood Turtle (*R. areolata*) of Mexico and Central America is largely aquatic, courting and mating under water, but may resort for up to 48 hours to the burrows of Nine-banded Armadillos (*Dasypus novemcinctus*). The most aquatic species in the genus, reputedly a fast swimmer, may be the Large-nosed Wood Turtle (*R. nasuta*) of Colombia and Ecuador. It will even enter brackish water. Other species, including the Mexican Spotted Wood Turtle (*R. rubida*) of the coastal lowlands of western Mexico, spend much of their time on dry land. This difference in habitat preference is mirrored in the texture of their shells. The aquatic species (though not the largely aquatic Furrowed Wood Turtle) have low, smooth shells. The shells of the terrestrial species, free from the need to be streamlined for swimming, are often rough and sculptured.

The only other geoemydids found outside Asia, including Indonesia and other Asian island states, are the ordinary-looking turtles in the genus *Mauremys*. Three of its nine species live in Europe, with one extending to Africa. The Mediterranean Turtle (*M. leprosa*) ranges across North Africa from Morocco to Libya as well as in Spain and Portugal, areas it probably colonized across the Straits of Gibraltar after the last ice age. The Caspian Turtle

The Western Caspian or Balkan Turtle (*Mauremys rivulata*) ranges from Israel to the Balkans.

(*M. caspica*) extends from the Middle East to the countries around the Caspian Sea, and the Western Caspian or Balkan Turtle (*Mauremys rivulata*) lives in coastal regions from Israel to the Balkans, including Cyprus, Crete and Greece. Caspian and Balkan Turtles are active hunters, and in Iran they have been recorded eating fish and frogs in addition to invertebrates, fruit and leaves.

A huge gap separates these turtles from their nearest relatives: the Japanese Turtle (*M. japonica*); the extremely rare Vietnamese Leaf Turtle (*M. annamensis*) of central Vietnam, another victim of overcollecting despite legal protection; the Asian Yellow Pond Turtle (*Mauremys mutica*) of southeastern China, Vietnam and Taiwan, one of the most commonly reared and highly traded turtles in Asia; and the former members of *Chinemys* and *Ocadia*. Thousands of kilometers of *Mauremys*-free territory lie in between, much of it barren desert today, where the genus must once have existed but has now disappeared.

A vast area of perfectly good geoemydid turtle habitat does lie between Iran and China, on the Indian subcontinent. Five genera—*Geoclemys*, *Hardella* and *Vijayachelys* with one species each, *Melanochelys* with two, and *Pangshura* with four—are largely confined to the territory extending from Pakistan to Myanmar.

The Spotted Pond Turtle (*Geoclemys hamiltonii*) is a scarce inhabitant of the Indus and Ganges river drainages, where it lives in quiet, shallow oxbows and sloughs, occasionally entering the rivers themselves. A relatively large and striking animal, it is heavily marked on its head, neck and carapace with prominent orange, yellow or white spots that may fade with age. It is a thoroughgoing carnivore. In the wild it seems to dine principally on snails. By contrast, the Crowned River Turtle (*Hardella thurjii*), a highly aquatic species that lives in slow-moving waters in the same river basins as well as in the lower Brahmaputra drainage, is usually a vegetarian, though a small captive was once seen polishing off a frog. In some areas turtles may eat fish or shrimp, perhaps as carrion. Female Crowned River Turtles are more than three times the length of males, up to 61 cm (24 in) in carapace length, a difference matched only by some of the American map turtles (see page 232, Chapter 6). Once one of the commonest turtles in its range, it has declined in response to overcollecting, pollution and wetland drainage.

The Endangered Cochin Forest Cane Turtle (*Vijayachelys silvatica*), confined to scattered local-

The Spotted Pond Turtle (*Geoclemys hamiltonii*) is a scarce, carnivorous inhabitant of the Indus and Ganges river drainages.

ities in the Western Ghats of southwestern India, is an isolated species not closely related to any other genus in the family. Secretive, largely nocturnal and very local, spending its days sheltering under thick leaf litter in dense evergreen forest, it went unseen by scientists for over 70 years from its discovery in 1911 until the late Indian herpetologist Jaganath Vijaya found it again in 1982. Since then more specimens have been found, and a few have even entered the pet trade. Recent investigations have revealed that this shy little turtle may be more numerous in its limited forest habitat than we had thought. It is an attractive animal; the face of the male sports a blaze of bright red during the breeding season.

The little-known Tricarinate or Keeled Hill Turtle (*Melanochelys tricarinata*) of Assam and Bangladesh is an entirely terrestrial species of hill forests and riverine grasslands. Much better known is the Indian Black Turtle (*M. trijuga*), a widespread and variable species that even reaches the Maldives, though the population there may be introduced. It may spend considerable time on dry land, even living in burrows on Sri Lanka. Groups of more than 100 turtles have been seen scavenging the carcasses of elephants. In the Royal Chitwan National Park, Nepal, Indian Black Turtles not only live in the same terai grasslands as the Great One-Horned Rhinoceros (*Rhinoceros unicornis*); they even incubate their eggs by burying them in rhinoceros latrines.

The high carapace of the Indian Roofed Turtle (*Pangshura tecta*), with its strong median ridge and steeply sloping sides, does look vaguely like the roof of a house. This is another species that lives in quiet streams and ponds in the Ganges, Indus and Brahmaputra drainages, though in Bangladesh it also lives in brackish coastal waters. The rare Assam Roofed Turtle (*P. sylhetensis*) lives along fast-flowing rivers and small streams in eastern Bangladesh and Assam, where it uses its claws to keep a purchase on rocks, logs or roots in the streambed. It is a small species whose carapace only reaches 18.5 cm (7 in) in females and 9.7 cm (3.8 in) in males. The other species are the Indian Tent Turtle (*P. tentoria*) of eastern India, Bangladesh and Nepal, and the Brown Roofed Turtle (*P. smithii*) of the Ganges and Brahmaputra basins, whose female may be more than twice the size of the male.

The high, arched carapace of the Indian Roofed Turtle (*Pangshura tecta*) vaguely recalls the roof of a house.

The Burmese Eyed Turtle (*Morenia ocellata*) is named for the eyespot markings on its carapace.

Only four geoemydid genera—including *Cuora*, the Asian box turtles—are shared by the Indian subcontinent and Southeast Asia. The Burmese Eyed Turtle (*Morenia ocellata*) of southern Myanmar may just barely make it into the northwestern part of the Malay Peninsula, while the Indian Eyed Turtle (*M. petersi*) lives in the floodplain lowlands of the Ganges and Brahmaputra systems of northern and northeastern India and Bangladesh. They get their name from eyespot markings on their carapaces. Eyed turtles are strictly aquatic. William Theobald, who studied them late in the 19th century, reported that during the rainy season Burmese Eyed Turtles ventured out into flooded plains where they became trapped when the waters receded. Local people took advantage of the situation, gathering up the stranded turtles for the pot.

The confusing genus *Cyclemys*, ranging from the Himalayan foothills to Java, has been split in a variety of ways. Seven species are currently recognized, three with yellow plastra and four with their plastra mostly dark brown or black. The Asian Leaf Turtle (*C. dentata*), a semiaquatic denizen of shallow streams from southern Thailand to Borneo and the Philippines, looks rather like one of the more sculptured members of the New World genus *Rhinoclemmys*—or, if you prefer, they both look like a pile of dead leaves on the forest floor, and probably for the same reason: camouflage. Older individuals develop a hinge across the plastron, but though the hinge allows the anterior lobe of the plastron to move a bit, the animal cannot completely close its shell.

The genus *Batagur* now includes three species formerly placed in *Kachuga*, a genus whose other, smaller members have been transferred to *Pangshura*. Only about 500 adult female Red-crowned Roofed Turtles (*B. kachuga*) are estimated to remain in the wild. The Burmese Roofed Turtle (*B. trivittata*), once an inhabitant of large, deep rivers in the Irrawaddy and Salween drainages of Myanmar, went unseen by scientists from 1930 to 2002. Only five to seven nesting females remain in the wild. There are more than 400 individuals in a captive breeding program that it is hoped can be used to rebuild the wild population.

Among the largest and handsomest of the geoemydids are the Northern River or Mangrove Terrapin (*B. baska*), which ranges from eastern India to Myanmar and possibly southwestern Thailand; the Southern River Terrapin or Tuntung (*B. affinis*), which is, or used to be, found from Thailand to Cambodia, Vietnam, Malaysia and Sumatra; and their close relative the Painted Terrapin (*Batagur borneensis*), found from southern Thailand to Sumatra and Borneo. A Painted Terrapin may have a carapace length of 60 cm (24 in) and a weight of 25 kg (55 lbs). All three terrapins live in tidal river estuaries and mangrove forests, and can tolerate brackish water (the Painted Terrapin can tolerate full salt water for hours or even days). They eat the fruits and leaves of mangroves as well as some shellfish. The river terrapins are more carnivorous than the Painted, consuming mollusks, crusta-

ceans and fish; they follow the high tide upstream into the rivers to forage, returning to the estuaries as the tide falls. Some river terrapin populations migrate upstream to nest on sandbanks, while others, including the Painted Terrapin, lay their eggs on sea beaches. The Northern River Terrapin shares (or shared) its nesting grounds with Olive Ridley Sea Turtles (*Lepidochelys olivacea*) in West Bengal and the Irrawaddy delta. In Terengganu, Malaysia, Painted Terrapins nest on beaches used by Olive Ridleys and Green Sea Turtles (*Chelonia mydas*), starting their nesting as the Green Sea Turtle young hatch. Adults of all three species have a pronounced, upturned snout that allows them to breathe while keeping their bodies below the surface of the water.

A number of turtles develop heightened colors during the breeding season. Most *Batagur* males, particularly those of the Painted and river terrapins, go through an extraordinary change.

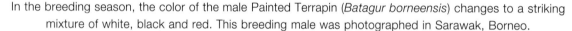

In the breeding season, the color of the male Painted Terrapin (*Batagur borneensis*) changes to a striking mixture of white, black and red. This breeding male was photographed in Sarawak, Borneo.

River terrapins are normally a dull olive-brown above and cream-colored below, but as males come into the breeding season their heads turn a deep, glistening jet black, set off in the Northern River Terrapin by carmine-pink on the neck and front limbs. Southern River Terrapins turn black on their heads, necks, legs and sometimes their whole bodies. Their irises change from yellowish to pure white. The heads of breeding male Painted Terrapins turn almost entirely pure white, with a daub of bright red, outlined with black, running from the tip of the snout to the top of the forehead. Their carapaces turn pale olive-gray, almost white, with three broad black streaks running the length of the shell and black blotches decorating the marginals.

Both river terrapins and the Painted Terrapin have suffered from intense egg collecting, overharvesting, destruction of nesting areas and the clearing of mangrove forests. The overharvest of eggs has been the most important cause of population crashes in West Malaysia. All are hunted; living Painted Terrapins are particularly in demand as good luck charms. All three are categorized as Critically Endangered. The once-abundant Northern River Terrapin has been almost exterminated. Only scattered remnants survive in India and Bangladesh. In Myanmar, it survives only in a few localities, particularly in Mon State where the government is battling insurgent groups and egg collectors dare not go. Along the Dawei River fishermen regard the terrapin as a *nat leik* or spirit turtle, capable of transforming itself into another animal or a human. If one is caught, villagers propitiate it by pouring a mixture of jewels and water over its head before returning it unharmed to the river.

The remaining genera in the family are confined, or nearly confined, to tropical Southeast Asia. They include the Black-breasted Leaf Turtle (*Geoemyda spengleri*) and Ryukyu Black-breasted Leaf Turtle (*G. japonica*), the Malayan Flat-shelled Turtle (*Notochelys platynota*), and the Black Marsh Turtle (*Siebenrockiella crassicollis*) and Philippine Forest Turtle (*S. leytensis*). The Black-breasted Leaf Turtle of southern China and northern Vietnam is almost completely terrestrial, spending much of its time hiding among leaf litter in the forest. It is a very small turtle, with a carapace length of no more than 11 cm (4.3 in).

The Philippine Forest Turtle, unseen by scientists for many decades, is found only along forested streams in northern and central Palawan and the nearby small island of Dumaran. It has suffered from habitat loss and overcollecting, especially since its rediscovery was announced in 2004. Pierre Fidenci and Jérôme Maran found it on sale (clandestinely) in "all major pet markets in Manila" between 2005 and 2009, fetching up to $75, despite national protection under the Philippine Wildlife Act. Illegally collected specimens have been offered in Japanese pet shops for over $1,600, and can reportedly be had in Malaysia on two days' notice. The species is classified as Critically Endangered.

The unusual and handsome Spiny Turtle (*Heosemys spinosa*), one of four species currently placed in *Heosemys*, lives among the leaf litter on forest floors almost throughout the Malayan region. In juveniles, the plastron is covered with beautiful patterns of radiating lines. Almost every scute on the carapace ends in a small spine. The marginal scutes extend outward to form a ring of spikes circling the shell. The spines may increase the turtle's resemblance to a pile of dead leaves, and put off predators such as snakes, though they attract other predators such as collectors for the pet trade. As the turtle ages the spines wear down, until adults are left with only a few serrations at the back of the carapace. The pattern on the plastron blurs, smears and largely disappears with age.

At the other end of the scale of geoemydid appearance is the huge Malaysian Giant Turtle (*Orlitia borneensis*) of the Malay Peninsula, Borneo and Sumatra. With a carapace that may be 80 cm (32 in) long, this is one of the largest turtles in the

Portrait of a Black Marsh Turtle (*Siebenrockiella crassicollis*) from Southeast Asia.

The spines on the carapace and the beautiful patterns on the plastron that make juvenile Spiny Turtles
•   (*Heosemys spinosa*) like this one so attractive to the pet trade wear away in old adults.

family. It has a large, blunt head and a dark carapace that is as smoothly rounded as the Spiny Turtle's is prickly. Like the Arrau of South America, it nests on river banks and river islands; like many large river turtles, it is taken by humans for food. The Malaysian Giant Turtle is an omnivore, but it prefers fish and will even catch the occasional snake.

It is always difficult to know why some animals have the color patterns they do. The attractive little Chinese eyed turtles of the genus *Sacalia* have startling circular eyespots—two in Beale's Turtle (*Sacalia bealei*) and four in the Four-eyed Turtle (*Sacalia quadriocellata*)—on the top of their heads, behind their real eyes. At least, they look startling to us, and we usually assume that eyespots may have the same effect on potential predators. We don't know if they serve that purpose for *Sacalia*, or have some other role, or no role at all. Both species live in southern China, with one, the Four-eyed Turtle,

extending into northern Vietnam and Laos.

The Malayan and Mekong Snail-eating Turtles (*Malayemys macrocephala* and *M. subtrijuga*) are not quite the gastropod specialists that their names imply, but freshwater snails do appear to be the juveniles' primary food. Adults vary their diet with other types of shellfish such as clams. Small turtles of the lowlands of Thailand, Indochina and, for *macrocephala*, West Malaysia and Java, they have a distinct preference for rice fields; in southern Thailand, their local name means "rice-field turtle." Unlike most other turtles, they may have benefited, at least in Thailand, from the conversion of natural wetlands to agriculture (as may the otherwise-declining Asiatic Softshell [*Amyda cartilaginea*]).

Although large numbers of Malayan Snail-eating Turtles are sold for food in Thailand, the species may also be the beneficiary, or victim (depending on how you look at it), of religious

The Malayan Snail-eating Turtle (*Malayemys macrocephala*) has a preference for rice paddies.

Devout Buddhists in Asia release Giant Asian Pond Turtles (*Heosemys grandis*, top) and Yellow-headed Temple Turtles (*H. annandalii*, bottom) into temple ponds.

beliefs. It is one of a number of turtles, including the Giant Asian Pond Turtle or Orange-headed Temple Turtle (*Heosemys grandis*) and the Yellow-headed Temple Turtle (*H. annandalii*), that devout Buddhists release into temple ponds. As Malcolm Smith reported in 1931, "According to the tenets of Buddhism, a live gift offered to the temple gains merit for the donor in his next life. Unfortunately, the obligation ceases after the turtle's life has been saved, and as a result, hundreds of turtles are left to survive on tidbits offered by worshipers." However, most Thai temples with turtle ponds have a monk assigned to care for their turtles, and in the words of the Ven. Lama Tenzin Kalsang, Spiritual Director of the Tengye Ling Tibetan Buddhist Temple in Toronto, Canada, "Saving the life of turtles (or any being for that matter) creates virtuous karma and, further, the person would create still more virtuous karma by feeding and caring for them."

Asian box turtles (*Cuora* spp.) make up the largest genus in the Geoemydidae, with 13 currently recognized species. Many of them are extremely beautiful animals, and consequently highly valued in the pet trade. The Flowerback or Indochinese Box Turtle (*C. galbinifrons*) has a carapace colored like inlaid wood, with contrasting patterns of mahogany, tan and cream. The Southeast Asian Box Turtle has a dark gray head and neck patterned with bright yellow stripes, while the entire head of the Yellow-headed Box Turtle (*C. aurocapitata*), a Chinese species first described in 1988 but not found in the wild until 2004, is rich golden yellow.

They share the ability of American box turtles to seal off their shells by raising their plastral lobes, but the mechanism that permits them to do so was independently evolved, using different muscles and ligaments. Asian and American box turtles are not even that similar in lifestyle. While American box turtles are almost entirely diurnal (though most active at dusk and after rain), some Asian box turtles are often active at night (perhaps because any foolhardy enough to venture out by day have been snapped up for centuries by the human population). The Flowerback, Bourret's (*C. bourreti*), Southern Vietnam (*C. picturata*) and Yellow-margined Box Turtles (*C. flavomarginata*) are highly terrestrial, with the high, domed shells you would expect in land turtles (they are sometimes placed in their own genus, *Cistoclemmys*, though they may not be each other's closest relatives). Most of the others, however, are at least semiaquatic, with lower, flatter carapaces. The most widespread and common species, the Southeast Asian Box Turtle (*C. amboinensis*), lives in wetlands ranging from mangrove swamps to rice fields, but may range far from water into forest habitat. It has webbed toes and is a good swimmer. It feeds, sleeps, migrates and possibly mates in the water, though it will hunt for plants, fungi and worms on land.

Cuora has become a flagship for concern about the trade in Asian turtles. Illegal trade still goes on, and populations continue to decline. Between 2006 and 2009, Taiwanese authorities confiscated more than 2,300 Yellow-margined Box Turtles being smuggled to mainland China. Altogether, seven species of *Cuora*, including the Flowerback and Yellow-headed Box Turtles, are currently listed as Critically Endangered, and more are likely to earn that dubious honor. In April 2000, all species of *Cuora* were listed under the Convention on International Trade in Endangered Species of Wild Fauna and Flora (CITES). Even the Southeast Asian Box Turtle continues to decline in many areas. It is exported by the thousands from Indonesia, both legally and illegally. The legal trade is based on annual quotas, but these quotas are reportedly based—despite the requirements of CITES (see page 389, Chapter 9)—not on the abundance or health of the species, but on how many animals dealers want.

The Yellow-headed Box Turtle appears headed for extinction in the wild. Heavy hunting pressure has almost eliminated the Three-striped or Golden Box Turtle (*C. trifasciata*), of southeastern coastal China, Hainan Island, northern Vietnam and Laos; it is still trapped illegally in its last stronghold,

A wild-caught Three-Striped Box Turtle (*Cuora trifasciata*), valued for its supposed medicinal properties, can fetch $5,000 in Hong Kong.

Hong Kong, where a wild-caught male can fetch $5,000. The Yunnan Box Turtle (*C. yunnanensis*) was known from only a few old museum specimens until it reappeared in trade in 2004. It was finally found in the wild in 2008. McCord's Box Turtle (*C. mccordi*), originally described from market animals, was discovered in the wild in Guanxi Province in 2002, where its total range was less than 50 sq km (19 sq mi). In the 1980s, a single Hong Kong dealer started paying villagers for the animals, once regarded as so worthless that they were used instead of stones to throw at buffaloes. Prices rose as the animals became rare, and in 2008 one turtle sold for $20,000. A survey in 2010 failed to find a single one. About 150 survive in captivity. Zhou's Box Turtle (*C. zhoui*) is also known from markets in Yunnan, where it has not been seen for some years, and there are fears that it may be extinct in the wild. In July 2010, on southern Vietnam's Langbian Plateau, herpetologist Tri Ly found wild specimens of the Southern Vietnam Box Turtle, another species first discovered in Chinese markets where it has become increasingly rare since 2007. His field team included local villagers, but most of the turtles were found by three dogs.

Testudinidae: Tortoises

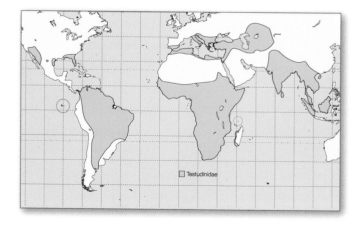

The appearance of tortoises, like that of sea turtles, is so well known as to hardly need description. It too represents a series of adaptations to an extreme habitat—in this case not the sea, but dry land. There are rainforest tortoises in Southeast Asia and South

America, but most tortoises live in places that, if they are not actual deserts, at least go through seasons where water is scarce and the vegetation sere. They are beautifully adapted to survive there.

The high, domed shells of many tortoises decrease their surface to volume ratio, helping them to resist dry conditions. Their heavy, elephantine limbs, flattened in the front but rotund and columnar in the rear, are designed for walking (and, in some species, digging), not swimming. Their limbs are also designed for protection. When a tortoise retracts its head, its front limbs completely close over it, elbow to elbow. Large, shieldlike scales on the outer surface of its front legs protect both the tortoise's limbs and the head hidden behind it. At the rear, only the hardened soles of the feet are exposed for a predator to scrabble at.

Tortoises are, of course, not designed for speed (though they may be more agile than their popular image implies). With all that armor, they usually don't have to be. Perhaps as a consequence, the family contains a higher proportion of vegetarians than any other turtle group. Another consequence, as Peter Pritchard points out in his *Encyclopedia of Turtles*, is that a tortoise "is about the only vertebrate that one can walk up to in the wild and pick up without difficulty." That, of course, has not served them well with people, who have found them, over the centuries, not only easy to pick up but easy to store (they can live, and thus stay fresh, for a long time without being fed) and highly satisfying to eat.

Tortoises, to their detriment, make such attractive pets that tens of thousands of them, of many species, have been taken from the wild for sale into the international pet trade. Overcollecting has decimated, eliminated or nearly eliminated many a tortoise population. For some species, like the Egyptian Tortoise (*Testudo kleinmanni*), overcollection represents the chief threat to their survival. Today, international bans are in place barring legal commercial trade in a number of tortoises. The once-

huge imports of *Testudo* tortoises into the European Union have been brought under control by import bans passed during the 1980s, though importers responded not by cutting back on the tortoise trade but by switching to other species including hinge-backed tortoises (*Kinixys*) and American box turtles (*Terrapene*). However, collecting, both legal and illegal, goes on. So does the increasing use of tortoises for food and medicine in various parts of the world, and the destruction of tortoise habitat through overgrazing, fire and other causes. The world's tortoises remain under severe threat.

Southern Africa is the tortoise capital of the world. Five genera and 14 species of tortoise live there. Of these, three genera, *Psammobates*, *Chersina* and *Homopus*, are found nowhere else. Representatives of all three live at, or within a day's drive of, the Cape of Good Hope.

The Cape is southern Africa's Mediterranean zone. Its native vegetation is *fynbos*, a bewildering and magnificent variety of proteas, heaths, bulbous plants and others. Fynbos is a threatened habitat. In the far southwestern Cape a dry, inland variety of fynbos called *renosterveld* (rhinoceros veld), restricted to acidic, sandy soils, has been particularly hard hit by frequent wildfires and by clearing for agriculture and development. This is the only home of the rarest and most beautiful tortoise in continental Africa, the Geometric Tortoise (*Psammobates geometricus*). Ninety-six percent of its habitat has been destroyed. Today, wild tortoises survive in only 13 tiny patches ranging from less than 10 to no more than 30 ha (25–74 ac), over a total area of approximately 22 sq km (8.5 sq mi). Renosterveld is fire-adapted habitat that needs to be burned regularly to stay open and diverse, but burning risks killing up to 80 percent of the tortoises in the area. The safest time to burn is when the tortoises' eggs are incubating underground.

Psammobates means "sand-loving." The Geometric Tortoise's two more widespread relatives,

The Geometric Tortoise (*Psammobates tentorius*) is the rarest member of a genus of three species entirely confined to southern Africa.

the highly variable Tent Tortoise (*P. tentorius*) and the somewhat more northerly Serrated or Kalahari Tent Tortoise (*P. oculifer*), are arid-country animals, absent from South Africa's more humid east. The Serrated Tortoise lives among the dunes and dry, rocky bushveld of the Kalahari Desert.

All three species are fairly small, with a maximum carapace length of 20 cm (8 in) or less. Males are even smaller than females. In the Geometric and Kalahari Tent Tortoises, each scute on their domed shells, except the marginals, is mounded into a peak. They are beautiful animals, their scutes marked with radiating sunbursts of yellow or even pinkish lines against a blackish background. This pattern is also found on some other tortoises, including the Radiated Tortoise (*Astrochelys radiata*) of Madagascar and the star tortoises of India and Burma. Its function is not beauty but camouflage. The contrasting pattern of black and yellow mimics the dappled sunlight under a desert bush, and may hide the tortoise sheltering there.

The Angulate, or Bowsprit, Tortoise (*Chersina angulata*) is entirely restricted to the lowlands of the southwestern Cape and the nearby Karoo, where it is scarce. It has fared much better there than the Geometric Tortoise, probably because it has adapted to a much wider range of habitats. Angulate Tortoises range from semi-desert to areas of high rainfall, though they prefer sandy coastal regions. Jutting out beneath the Angulate Tortoise's neck is a blunt, upcurved appendage that resembles, particularly in males, the bowsprit of a ship. The bowsprit is formed by the fused gular scutes and underlying bone of the plastron, extended forward into a ramming, pushing and heaving weapon. Particularly in spring and early summer, rival males use it to beat back and, with luck, overturn their opponents. As might be expected in a species featuring contests of strength between males, females are the smaller sex—the opposite of the situation in *Psammobates*. Larger size—and in particular greater width across the rear of the carapace—may be a better guide to predicting a winner than the length of the bowsprit. Fighting tortoises often end up with their front legs clear of the ground as they ram against each other. A wider rear carapace may allow males to use their hind legs to brace themselves more securely, and push forward more forcefully, during their shoving matches.

I once found one of these attractive tortoises making its way across a road in the Karoo, a few hours' drive north of Cape Town. Fortunately, I was not treated to the defensive response Bill Branch describes in his *Field Guide to Snakes and Other Reptiles of Southern Africa*: "… it readily ejects the liquid contents of its bowels when handled, often spraying them up to one metre, and this with surprising accuracy." This defense does not always work; Liz McMahon and Michael Fraser, illustrator and author of *A Fynbos Year*, watched a Verreaux's eagle (*Aquila verreauxii*), a large and spectacular predator, drop an Angulate Tortoise from a height of 30 m (100 ft) onto the rocks below "before gliding down to eat the shattered remains." Kelp Gulls (*Larus dominicanus*) do the same on Dassen Island.

The padlopers or pygmy tortoises (*Homopus*) are the smallest tortoises in the world. Their Cape representative is the Parrot-beaked Tortoise or Common Padloper (*H. areolatus*), a medium-sized (but still very small) member of the genus with a carapace rarely more than 10–11 cm (4–4.3 in). It lives beneath dense cover in a variety of habitats from deciduous woodland to coastal fynbos thickets, where it hides under rocks or in abandoned animal burrows. Its carapace is flattened and colorful, each scute sculptured with concentric ridges and marked with warm reddish-brown splotches in the center, ringed with bright olive or yellow and bordered in turn with black. In the breeding season, the heads of males turn a deep bright orange red, remaining that way for several weeks before the color gradually fades.

The other four padlopers include the recently described Nama Padloper (*Homopus solus*) from southern Namibia. They range from the Greater Padloper (*Homopus femoralis*) of the eastern Cape and the Free State, which tips the scales at 200–300 g (7–11 oz), to the tiny Speckled Padloper (*Homopus signatus*) of Little Namaqualand in the northwestern Cape, which may weigh as little as 85 g (3 oz) even as an adult. Less broad in their selection of habitats than the Common Padloper, they prefer rocky areas. The Karoo or Boulenger's Padloper (*Homopus boulengeri*) is so active on cool, cloud-threatened summer days that it is known in Afrikaans as *donderweerskilpad*, the "thunderstorm tortoise." The Speckled Padloper is entirely confined to boulder-strewn outcrops, or *kopjes*. Several individuals may shelter under a single slab of rock. They emerge in the early morning to feed on small succulent plants growing among the rocks. In their restricted habitat Speckled Padlopers may be quite common, though the species suffers from habitat loss and overgrazing and is classified as Vulnerable in South Africa. Under drier conditions females lay fewer eggs, and climate change may threaten at least the northern subspecies in the future.

The most extreme rockpile specialist of them all, and the most unusual tortoise in the world, is the Pancake Tortoise (*Malacochersus tornieri*) of semi-desert and grassland areas of Kenya, Tanzania and northeastern Zambia, where its presence was first confirmed in 2003. The pancake is a small animal, about 17 cm (7 in) in carapace length, with a shell so varied in color and pattern, from pale yellow to black, that it is hard to find two alike. Its soft, thin shell gives it little protection, and a disturbed Pancake Tortoise, rather than pulling in its head and limbs as other tortoises do, runs for shelter instead. Pancake Tortoises are agile climbers, easily able to right themselves if they fall on their backs. We have already discussed the peculiarities of the Pancake Tortoise's shell (see page 32, Chapter 1), that flattened, flexible construct that allows the animal to wedge itself into a crevice among the rocks. The tortoise spends most of its time hiding there,

The rare Pancake Tortoise (*Malacochersus tornieri*) lives in Kenya, Tanzania and Zambia, where it shelters in rocky crevices.

rarely straying far away. It may spend the whole of the dry season wedged in its crevice.

Just any crevice will not do; a suitable one must provide protection from overheating, be a safe haven from predators, and protect the animal against drying out. The crevice may be horizontal, diagonal or vertical, but whatever its orientation it must be deep, easily accessible from the ground below, and it must narrow, as it penetrates the rocks, to a height of 5 cm (2 in) or less. The surrounding rocks must be weathered and eroded enough for plants to take root, sheltering the crevice and probably providing the tortoise with food close at hand. Such ideal locations, preferably in areas of Precambrian granite below 1,000 m (3,280 ft) elevation, are few and far between. Even where they occur, typically only 1 or 2 tortoises live in each, though sometimes larger groups—generally up to 6, but rarely as many as 10—will share a crevice, particularly in the dry season. A male and a female

may share a crevice—unusual behavior for animals that normally do not pair up. Even under the right sort of conditions, Pancake Tortoises are likely to be thin on the ground, clustered in scattered colonies separated by the flat, unsuitable plains that stretch from *kopje* to *kopje*. Increasingly, habitat alteration by humans has meant that the right sort of conditions are hard to find. Combine that with poaching for the pet trade and a natural breeding cycle that produces only a single egg two or three times a year, and it should not be surprising that the Pancake Tortoise is a species in decline.

Hinged or hinge-back tortoises (*Kinixys*) are rather elongate, medium-sized, omnivorous tortoises with almost rectangular shells. Some individuals never develop the hinge across the carapace that gives the group its name. The six currently recognized species range throughout most of sub-Saharan Africa. They cover a broad ecological range: the Natal Hinged Tortoise (*K. natalensis*) is a dry-country

The attractive Lobatse Hinge-back Tortoise (*Kinixys lobatsiana*) is restricted to northern South Africa and southeastern Botswana.

animal; the wide-ranging Bell's Hinged Tortoise (*K. belliana*) lives in savanna and grassland but favors humid conditions; while the Serrated Hinged Tortoise or Forest Hinge-back Tortoise (*K. erosa*) of West Africa prefers moist forests. At least 90 percent of the swamp forest in Nigeria suitable for Home's Hinge-back Tortoise (*K. homeana*) has disappeared in the last 45 years. The species is heavily hunted for food, traditional medicine and sale to the pet trade. The Serrated Hinged Tortoise—somewhat unusually for the family—is often found in water, where it is a fair swimmer, and is the only *Kinixys* in which the males are larger than the females.

Bell's Hinged Tortoise is one of five surviving tortoises on Madagascar, the only one not confined to that island. It must be a comparatively recent arrival, so recent that herpetologists think human immigrants brought it there from Africa between 1,000 and 1,500 years ago.

Of the other four Malagasy tortoises, two are included in the endemic genus *Pyxis*: the Spider Tortoise (*P. arachnoides*) and the much rarer Flat-tailed Tortoise or Kapidolo (*P. planicauda*). These are very small tortoises, almost as small as the padlopers, restricted to Madagascar's dry west and south. The three subspecies of Spider Tortoise, named for a pattern of yellow lines on its carapace that recalls a spider's web, live only in a narrow belt along the southwest coast no more than 50 km (30 mi) wide.

The Flat-tailed Tortoise, which does indeed have a flattened tail ending in a large nail-like scale, is confined to an area of some 500 sq km (190 sq mi) in

The forest habitat of the Flat-tailed Tortoise (*Pyxis planicauda*) of western Madagascar is being rapidly destroyed.

the Morondava region of western Madagascar. Here, it lives in a type of deciduous forest that is being rapidly destroyed. Even in those few areas where the forest is intact, is an uncommon animal. Rather little is known about its natural history. It spends the dry season buried in leaf litter, emerging to feed (probably on fallen fruits) and to mate only from January to March, when the rains come. Both *Pyxis* tortoises lay but a single egg at a time, and cannot recover quickly, if at all, from a fall in numbers.

Madagascar's other two endemic tortoises are now placed in a genus of their own: *Astrochelys*. A DNA study published in 1999 suggests that all four of Madagascar's endemic tortoises are the descendants of one species, and possibly of a single pregnant female that rafted to the island from Africa between 14 and 22 million years ago.

Like South Africa's Geometric Tortoise, the carapace of the Radiated Tortoise is patterned with starbursts of yellow lines. The Radiated Tortoise, though, grows much larger, reaching a carapace length of 40 cm (16 in). It lives in dry woodlands, including the unique spiny forests where pot-bellied baobabs crouch and thorn-studded *Didieria* trees tower over the sand like enormous flexible candelabras. Until recently the Radiated Tortoise was common in many parts of southern Madagascar, but the spiny forest is being rapidly destroyed, and hunting for food and for the pet trade has increased on a massive scale. The Radiated Tortoise is now in serious trouble (see page 352, Chapter 9).

A male Radiated Tortoise has an extension at the front of its plastron, like a smaller version of the Angulate Tortoise's bowsprit. It seems to use

A male Radiated Tortoise (*Astrochelys radiata*) tries to overturn his rival. Once common, the Radiated Tortoise is now at serious risk of extinction in the wild.

this to attempt to subdue or even overturn the female during mating. The Radiated Tortoise's ram pales in significance, though, beside the enormous upcurved hook, or *ampondo*, jutting out from the plastron of the Ploughshare Tortoise or Angonoka (*Astrochelys yniphora*), a fairly hefty creature with a carapace length of almost 45 cm (18 in). The male's ploughshare is so long that the animal has to tilt its head to one side to see around it, or to feed.

The Angonoka possesses the dubious distinction of being one of the rarest tortoises in the world. Its total wild population is estimated to be fewer than 200, broken up into five isolated subpopulations within the boundaries of Baly Bay National Park in northwestern Madagascar. It is entirely confined to a few small patches of decidu-

ous coastal and bamboo scrub, totaling no more than 40 to, at most, 80 sq km (15.5 to 31 sq mi).

The remaining Angonoka habitat is threatened by brushfires set by local people to stimulate growth of grasses for their cattle, to drive cattle from the forest and to keep bush pigs away from cultivated lands. Natural fires occur there occasionally, but the fires set by people are much more frequent. Even if the tortoises survive them, their habitat, which cannot recover from too frequent burning, may not. Poaching has increased considerably. Numbers of Ploughshare Tortoises have appeared on Asian markets, and black-market prices have reached $10,000. The Ploughshare Tortoise is now the subject of an intensive conservation program, Project Angonoka, coordinated by the Durrell Wildlife Preservation Trust in cooperation with the Malagasy Water and

The world's rarest tortoise may be the Angonoka or Ploughshare Tortoise (*Geochelone yniphora*) of Madagascar.

Forests Authority at the Ampijoroa Forestry Station, within the Ankarafantsika Strict Nature Reserve in Northwestern Madagascar. A reintroduction project is under way at Baly Bay.

Back on the African continent, two very large tortoises live south of the Sahara. The Spurred Tortoise (*Geochelone* or *Centrochelys sulcata*) ranges along the southern edge of the Sahara, from Senegal to Ethiopia, among plant-covered desert dunes, bush country and acacia woodland. It appears well-adapted to near-desert conditions; a study in Mali found that neither high temperatures nor intense sunshine restricted the Spurred Tortoise's range. Other than the giants of Aldabra and the Galápagos, this is the largest tortoise in the world. Captive specimens have reached a carapace

length of 83 cm (33.5 in) and a weight of 105.5 kg (233 lbs), though in the wild a Spurred Tortoise that size would be quite unusual.

The Leopard Tortoise (*Stigmochelys pardalis*) is also one of the largest of the world's mainland tortoises. It varies considerably in size, shell shape and color in different parts of its range. Animals from Kenya are generally smaller than those in southern Africa or farther north, where old animals from northwestern Somalia approach the size of the giant island tortoises. Females are generally larger than males, but the largest recorded specimen in South Africa was a 40 kg (88 lb) presumed male that lived in the Addo Elephant National Park. The local rangers named him "Domkrag" ("auto-jack") because of his habit of crawling underneath

The Spurred Tortoise (*Geochelone sulcata*) of the southern edge of the Sahara is the world's largest continental tortoise.

vehicles and attempting to hoist them up (not to mention his tendency to ram visitors from behind).

The Leopard Tortoise occurs from Djibouti and the southern Sudan through eastern and southern Africa to Angola, Namibia and South Africa. Over this broad area it is a common animal, occurring in a wide range of country from fynbos in the south to dry scrub in the northeast, and from savannah forests to the deserts of Namibia. It can even tolerate South Africa's mountains, where it may face freezing winters and occasional snow. It gets its name not from its habits—it is a vegetarian, though it will nibble on animal droppings and scavenge from carcasses—but from its pattern of black spots on a pale ground. Like the patterns of many turtles, the spots may fade and even disappear with age.

If we cross the Sahara to the north, we enter the range of the Mediterranean tortoises of the genus *Testudo*. These are the animals the Romans first called *testudo*, tortoise. There are three to choose from in Greece, though strangely the Spur-thighed Tortoise—*Testudo graeca*, meaning "Greek"—is probably an introduction from Turkey. Aesop's hare almost certainly raced against a species of *Testudo*. Like Aesop's tale, Zeno's paradox also entertains the idea of a tortoise race (the famous mathematical "proof" that, if the tortoise has enough of a head start, Achilles will never overtake it). The shell of a *Testudo* became, so told the Greeks, the first lyre, fashioned by the young god Hermes; the Latin word *testudo* also means "lyre." Five to seven species are currently included in the genus, though two of them,

The Spur-thighed or Greek Tortoise (*Testudo graeca*) was once traded in huge numbers for the pet market.

Hermann's Tortoise (*Testudo hermanni*) and, particularly, the Central Asian or Steppe Tortoise (*Testudo horsfieldi*) are sometimes separated as *Chersine* and *Agrionemys* respectively. The genus ranges from Spain, the Balkans and North Africa eastward to Pakistan, Afghanistan and northwestern China.

All *Testudo* tortoises but one, the Central Asian Tortoise, may have a weak hinge across the plastron, particularly in gravid females. As its name implies, the Central Asian Tortoise is the most easterly of the lot, a creature of steppes and rocky deserts from the Caspian Sea to the eastern edge of the genus' range in far western China. The most westerly, reaching into Spain, are Hermann's Tortoise and the Spur-thighed Tortoise (the latter an introduction from North Africa), named for a large conical scale on

its hind leg. The Spur-thighed Tortoise ranges eastward to Iran. The Critically Endangered Egyptian Tortoise (*Testudo kleinmanni*) of northeast Libya, coastal Egypt, the Sinai and Israel, which is heavily collected for the pet trade despite legal protection, is as small as the *Pyxis* tortoises of Madagascar or the larger padlopers. Tortoises east of the Nile were separated as *Testudo werneri* in 2001, but the separation has not won acceptance. *Testudo* tortoises are almost entirely vegetarian, although Hermann's Tortoise will sometimes consume a variety of invertebrates.

Traveling eastward and southward into Asia, we reach the range of two more species of *Geochelone*: the Indian Star Tortoise (*G. elegans*) of India and Sri Lanka, a major target for wildlife smugglers, and the Burmese Star Tortoise (*G. platynota*). As their names imply, these tortoises are decorated with the same sort of sunburst patterns that ornament Geometric and Radiated Tortoises. The Burmese Star Tortoise, a beautifully marked, little-known species from Myanmar, has been so heavily exploited for the Chinese medicine and pet trades—despite local beliefs that harvesting the tortoises risks supernatural retribution—that there are essentially no viable populations left in the wild. In two sanctuaries that once protected wild tortoises only captive populations are left, kept under lock and key.

There are three species of *Indotestudo*: the Elongated Tortoise (*I. elongata*), which ranges from Nepal to Vietnam and the Malay Peninsula; the Travancore Tortoise (*I. travancorica*) of southwestern India; and the Sulawesi Tortoise (*I. forsteni*) of central Indonesia. These are forest tortoises that avoid the rocky wastelands favored by the species of *Testudo*. The little-known Travancore Tortoise appears to prefer the vicinity of forested streams,

and it may require open grassy patches in the woods (*vayals*) for grazing. In Thailand and Malaysia, the Elongated Tortoise lives in hill forests where it feeds on everything from slugs and carrion to leaves and fruit. It seems particularly fond of mushrooms. During the breeding season both sexes, but particularly the males, turn pink around their nostrils and eyes. The Elongated Tortoise has suffered from human-caused fires that destroy its forest habitat (and the habitat of other south Asian tortoises), and populations of this once-common species have crashed in western Thailand since the mid-1980s. The Endangered Sulawesi Tortoise is found only on Sulawesi and nearby Halmahera. On Sulawesi, some populations are missing the nuchal scute at the front of the carapace, but tortoises with and without the scute seem to be very similar genetically.

The largest tortoise in Asia is the Asian Brown or Asian Giant Tortoise (*Manouria emys*), which can reach a carapace length of up to 60 cm (24 in). *Manouria* may be, morphologically, the most

The beautiful shell patterns of the Indian Star Tortoise (*Geochelone elegans*) have made it a major target for wildlife smugglers.

The yellow head and pinkish nostrils of this male Elongated Tortoise (*Indotestudo elongata*) are signs that he is in breeding condition.

The largest tortoise in Asia, and possibly one of the most primitive of tortoises, is the
Asian Brown Tortoise (*Manouria emys*), photographed here in Sabah in Malaysian Borneo.

primitive of tortoise genera. With its humid forest habitat, broad, flattened shell and other features, it resembles the geoemydids from which tortoises probably arose. The Asian Brown Tortoise lives in lowland and low-elevation evergreen and rainforests up to 1,000 m (3,280 ft) in elevation, from Assam and Bangladesh to Sumatra and Borneo. The other species of *Manouria*, the Impressed Tortoise (*M. impressa*), is a highly localized and little-known animal of middle-altitude primary evergreen and bamboo forests, found in scattered regions of Myanmar, West Malaysia, Cambodia, Laos, Vietnam and portions of China.

The Asian Brown Tortoise spends much of its time hidden in undergrowth near streams. It is an omnivore, but prefers plant food including bamboo shoots, mushrooms and fallen fruits. This species has religious significance for Buddhists. It is often kept in temple gardens, and sometimes individuals are found with Buddhist inscriptions carved in their shells.

Nonetheless, both *Manouria* tortoises are widely sought after for food, and the Asian Brown Tortoise may end up as the main course at a wedding or religious festival. It has been a trade item for centuries; its remains have been found in 3,000-year-old archaeological deposits in China, far north of their normal range. Even its empty shell may be put to use: in Bangladesh its carapace is occasionally used as a feeding trough for chickens, pigs and dogs. The flesh of both species is considered to have medicinal properties, and the Impressed Tortoise is a prized rarity in the pet trade. Their habitats, too, have been seriously degraded, and both tortoises have become so rare that even professional tortoise hunters have difficulty finding them.

Although North America is rich in turtles, except in eastern Panama it has only a single genus of tortoise, *Gopherus*. The Desert Tortoise (*G. agassizii*) lives in deserts from southern Nevada and southwestern California southward into northwestern Mexico.

A Morafka's Desert Tortoise (*Gopherus morafkai*) emerges from the water in the Santa Catalina Mountains, Arizona.

In 2011, Robert Murphy and his colleagues split the Desert Tortoise into two species separated by the Colorado River, based on morphological characters, genetics and behavioral and ecological differences. Tortoises on valley bottoms in the Mojave Desert north and west of the river—occupying only 30 percent of the former species' range—remain as *G. agassizii*, the Mojave or Agassiz's Desert Tortoise. South and east of the Colorado, living on steep rocky slopes in upland desert scrub, is the Sonoran or Morafka's Desert Tortoise (*G. morafkai*)—which may have to be split, in its turn, into two further forms. The two species may have been separated by the river for more than five million years.

Both desert tortoises have declined substantially in recent decades in the face of pressures ranging from overcollecting and habitat destruction to collisions with automobiles and off-road vehicles, vandalism and disease. Agassiz's Desert Tortoise, whose populations have declined drastically in the last 30 years, may be an endangered species.

The Texas Tortoise (*G. berlandieri*) lives from southern Texas southward to northeastern Mexico, and the southeastern coastal plain, from Louisiana through Florida to South Carolina, is the home of the Gopher Tortoise (*G. polyphemus*). The remaining species, the largest, is the Bolson Tortoise (*Gopherus flavomarginatus*) (considerably larger species are known as fossils). The Bolson Tortoise was much more widespread long ago, during the Pliocene and Pleistocene; remains from the Big Bend region in Texas date to the end of the last ice age, about 11,000 years ago. Early human immigrants in North America may have been responsible for its disappearance. Today it lives only in the Bolsón de Mapimí, an isolated basin in north-central Mexico where it went undiscovered until, so the story goes, scientists visiting the area in 1959 found its shells in a trash dump.

Gopher and Agassiz's Desert Tortoises are consummate burrowers. Their front limbs are highly effective spades, even flatter and more rigid at the wrist than in other tortoises. Desert tortoises spend up to 95 percent of their lives sheltering from the harsh conditions of their environment. Agassiz's Desert Tortoises usually hide in burrows in the soil. An individual tortoise may use from 1 to 20 burrows, varying with location, season, year and sex (males occupy larger areas, and use more burrows, than females). Morafka's Desert Tortoises are more likely to seek shelter under rocks, in woodrat middens, under fallen wood and brush, or in small caves in *caliche*, hardened layers of calcium carbonate-rich soil exposed along a dry wash. Their preference seems to be for deeply incised washes on east-facing slopes, with numbers of caliche caves. The Texas Tortoise does not normally dig a burrow, but uses its front limbs and the edge of its shell to scoop out a shallow resting place, called a *pallet*, under a bush or a cactus.

The Gopher Tortoise is almost entirely restricted to deep sandy soils, suitable for digging its extensive burrow systems. Though a Gopher Tortoise can dig surprisingly fast, its burrow is a life's work that the animal usually starts soon after it hatches. A finished burrow may be 9 m (30 ft) long and 3.6 m (12 ft) deep. The burrow provides refuge from heat, cold, predators and the brush fires that regularly sweep its fire-adapted pineland habitat. Gopher Tortoise numbers are actually higher in habitat that is burned every one to five years, either naturally or as part of human management. If an unburned area becomes too overgrown, tortoises will migrate elsewhere.

Desert Tortoises, and Gopher Tortoises in Mississippi, Louisiana and Alabama, have been listed as Threatened under the U.S. Endangered Species Act. The Texas Tortoise is rather more secure, though its semidesert scrub habitat—now mostly on privately owned rangeland—has been reduced by 90 percent in the Rio Grande valley since the 1930s. The specialized habitat of the Gopher Tortoise, open pine forest over sandy soils, has been severely reduced due to mining, agriculture, urban development and other human uses, and its populations dropped by 80 percent during the 20th century.

Gopher Tortoises are declining in Florida even in protected areas, possibly because these areas are too small to support viable populations. The number of active Gopher Tortoise burrows at Cape Sable, Florida, the southern end of their range, declined by 76 percent between 1979 and 2001, possibly as a result of tropical storms in the area as well as reduction in the quality of their habitat.

The Bolson Tortoise is listed as Endangered. It is still eaten by local people, and during the 1980s its habitat was cut into fragments by roads driven through its range for oil and gas exploration. The remaining tortoises may now be restricted to an area of not much more than 1,000 sq km (400 sq mi), cut into six separate areas, threatened by cattle ranching and corn farming for ethanol production. The Mexican government has declared the area a Biosphere Reserve, and efforts are under way to reduce grazing and educate local people about conserving the tortoise.

In 2006, after two years of planning and discussion, the Turner Endangered Species Fund (TESF) released 26 disease-free Bolson Tortoises from a private facility in Arizona, where they had lived for three decades, into small fenced lots on the Turner-owned Armendaris Ranch in New Mexico. The aim was to see if the Bolson Tortoise could be restored to the wild ("rewilded") in the United States after 11,000 years. The project managers supplied water and dug "starter" burrows, but otherwise left the tortoises to their own devices. The tortoises have bred successfully (with some eggs transferred to an incubator). If the U.S. Fish and Wildlife Service agrees, in a few years the tortoises or their offspring could be released, perhaps into Big Bend National Park, Texas, where we know they once lived.

The four South American tortoises are placed today in the genus *Chelonoidis*, with their giant relatives from the Galápagos. The Red-footed Tortoise (*C. carbonaria*) ranges through much of the continent, mostly east of the Andes, from Colombia to northern Argentina. It has a North, or at least Central, American toehold in eastern Panama. The Yellow-footed Tortoise (*C. denticulata*), which may be a considerably larger animal with a carapace up to 82 cm (32 in) long, is a species of northern and central South America centering on the Amazon basin, though it occurred as far south as northeastern Argentina during the late Pleistocene. Both are also found on Trinidad, and humans have introduced the Red-footed onto a number of other islands in the Caribbean.

The Red-footed may be the most brilliantly colored of tortoises. Its carapace is deep, shiny black, each of its vertebral and costal scutes tipped with a splotch of yellow. Its head is marked with yellow and orange, and, depending on the subspecies, there are bright scarlet spots on its limbs and tail. Not surprisingly, it is a popular pet. In the wild, the Red-footed Tortoise lives in forests and woodlands with nearby grassland, or in moist savannas. In eastern Brazil it may live in rainforest, sometimes alongside Yellow-footed Tortoises. It spends most of its time in "food patches" such as clearings left by fallen trees in the forest, where it eats plants, carrion and living insects such as termites.

The Yellow-footed Tortoise is a strict rainforest dweller, never found in any other habitat. It is even more of an omnivore than its cousin, eating pretty much anything it can get. Both species are widely eaten by humans, and in Venezuela the Red-footed Tortoise is esteemed as a traditional Holy Week delicacy.

In contrast to the other South American tortoises, the Pampas Tortoise (*C. chilensis*), and the Chaco Tortoise (*C. petersi*), often included with it, are species of dry lowlands, the Pampas Tortoise in central Argentina and the Chaco Tortoise in northwestern Argentina, southwestern Bolivia and Paraguay. They are smallest of the genus, with a carapace length of 20 cm (8 in), rarely reaching 43 cm (17 in) in the Chaco Tortoise. Their ecology and lifestyle recall the desert tortoises. Like Agassiz's Desert Tortoise, the Chaco Tortoise is a burrower,

Red-footed Tortoises (*Chelenoidis carbonaria*), particularly young animals, are the most colorful of their family.

The Chaco Tortoise (*Chelonoidis chilensis*), photographed here in the gran chaco of Paraguay,
is probably the closest living relative of the giant Galápagos tortoises.

excavating winter dens that may penetrate several meters into the soil. It may face some of the same threats. In Argentina, much of the range of the Pampas Tortoise is heavily grazed by goats, sheep, cattle and horses. Overgrazing has had a severe impact on the desert tortoises, and the same problem may be harming the tortoises that live at the other end of the Americas.

Island Giants

Tortoises may appear to be landlubbers, but they have a remarkable ability to reach oceanic islands. There were once tortoises, related to the living South American species, on at least nine West Indian islands. In 2000, a single specimen of a large fossil tortoise from Bermuda, thought to be some 300,000 years old, was described as *Hesperotestudo bermudae* (a description confirmed by a fragmentary second specimen described in 2009). Today, the largest tortoises in the world are island animals: the giants of Aldabra in the Indian Ocean and, famously, the Galápagos Islands in the eastern Pacific.

The giant tortoises most people see in zoos come not from the Galápagos, but from Aldabra, a remote and virtually uninhabited atoll within the Republic of Seychelles in the Indian Ocean north of Madagascar. The proper scientific name of the Aldabra Giant Tortoise has been a source of considerable argument among specialists: you can find it labeled as *Geochelone gigantea*, *Aldabrachelys gigantea*, *Aldabrachelys elephantina*, *Dipsochelys elephantina* or *Dipsochelys dussumieri*. As of July 2011, the question of what the proper name for the Aldabra Giant Tortoise should be has been under consideration, under the arcane rules of the International Commission for Zoological Nomenclature, for over two years, and the Commission has yet to vote. Part of the problem is that what appears to be the original, or "type," specimen to which the name "*gigantea*" was attached in 1812 is a misidentified Yellow-footed Tortoise from South America! The Commission can decide to "conserve" the name—in effect validating the mistake on the basis of long usage—or to discard it, leaving us with *dussumieri* (and *Dipsochelys*). For now I will use *Aldabrachelys gigantea*, and keep my fingers crossed.

The Aldabra Giant Tortoise is the last certain survivor of a whole complex of giants. Close cousins of the Aldabra Giant Tortoise once lived on Madagascar and the Comoros. A vanished genus of medium-sized to giant tortoises, *Cylindraspis*, was restricted to the Mascarenes. There were five species: two on Mauritius, home of that most famous of lost Mascarene animals, the dodo; two farther east on Rodrigues; and one to the southwest, on Réunion. The last Mascarene tortoise probably died between 1804 and 1850.

Justin Gerlach and Laura Canning have argued that a number of venerable and odd-looking captives in the granitic Seychelles are not Aldabra Giant Tortoises, but the aged survivors of otherwise-extinct populations native to the Seychelles themselves. They have assigned them to two separate species, *Aldabrachelys hololissa* and *A. arnoldi* (Gerlach generally uses the name *Dipsochelys* for both). Their conclusion remains, though, highly controversial. Although most islands in the granitic Seychelles, located some 970 km (600 mi) northeast of Aldabra, once hosted substantial populations of giant tortoises, there is no unequivocal evidence that they were a distinct species. Prior to 1900, only two specimens of "*A. hololissa*" were collected from the granitic islands, and these were destroyed by fire during the Second World War. Only four specimens of "*A. arnoldi*" were collected around 1840 from an unknown locality in the central Seychelles, and one female lived on St. Helena from 1776 to 1874.

Two 2003 studies failed to find enough difference among the Indian Ocean giants to justify recognizing more than one species. Part of the problem is that visiting mariners were carrying tortoises from Aldabra to other islands, including the Seychelles, by as early as 1823. It is possible that the "true" tortoises of the Seychelles (whether they were separate species or not) were already extinct by then. The old museum specimens of supposed Seychelles tortoises, and Gerlach's Seychelles survivors, may really be transplanted tortoises from Aldabra.

Many authorities believe that the unusual features of the captive tortoises in the Seychelles could have been the result of improper feeding when the animals were young; we know that a diet too high in protein can cause a captive Aldabra Giant Tortoise to grow up with a distorted shell (though this does not affect the plastron, or the relationships of carapace scutes to each other). Even under natural conditions, diet can influence the shape of a tortoise's shell. In the drier realms of eastern Aldabra, adult tortoises are significantly smaller, more rounded, and smoother than are their conspecifics living in the more heavily vegetated northern and western regions of the same atoll.

Captive-bred *hololissa* and *arnoldi* tortoises produce distinctive hatchlings, so diet cannot be the sole explanation for their differences. Hatchlings of Seychelles and Aldabra Giant Tortoises raised under identical conditions tend to grow to resemble their parental types—implying that the differences among them are, as Gerlach has long argued, genetically based. The Turtle Taxonomy Working Group (TTWG) currently recognizes only one species, but with four subspecies: *gigantea* (or *dussumieri*, or whatever), *arnoldi*, *hololissa* and an extinct Seychelles form, *daudinii*—implying that Gerlach's tortoises may be, in fact, what he says they are, relics of the Seychelles' past.

The tortoise population of Aldabra was nearly exterminated by 1900. Fortunately, the government implemented protective measures, and by the late 1960s to early 1970s a census showed the population to number some 150,000 animals. Since then, however, the vegetation on which the tortoises depend for both food and for shelter from the hot midday sun has suffered from, among other things, overgrazing by tortoises, a significant increase in the feral goat population on Aldabra, and persistent drought during the 1980s and 1990s. In 1997, a new census by David Bourn (who also did the census in

The Aldabra Giant Tortoise (*Aldabrachelys gigantea*) is a last survivor of the giant tortoises of the Indian Ocean islands.

the early 1970s) showed that the tortoise population had dropped to some 100,000 animals. Most of the mortality occurred among the dense tortoise populations of the eastern part of the atoll, and had, in fact, been predicted based on data collected in the earlier census. Meanwhile, the population has been increasing elsewhere on the atoll, where tortoise density is lower.

How did tortoises get to Aldabra, or to the other islands in the Indian Ocean that were home to giant tortoises until humans exterminated them? Did the Aldabra giants and their relatives start out as smaller animals that rafted on floating debris to their eventual destinations? It is not at all unusual for a small island immigrant to become a giant. There have been giant island insects, flightless birds and lizards. Giant tortoises, then, should be no surprise.

The Indian Ocean tortoises, though, most likely started out as giants that floated to their ultimate homes. The fossil record shows that within the last 100,000 years—far too short a time for small tortoises to evolve into giants—Aldabra was completely inundated during periods of sea-level rise, and subsequently recolonized by tortoises that must have been giants already. This cycle of flooding and recolonization probably happened at least three times in the course of Aldabra's history.

Giant tortoises once existed on the mainland in many parts of the world. The oldest fossil tortoise known from Africa, from the Eocene of the Fayoum fossil beds in Egypt, was a large animal, appropriately named *Gigantochersina ammon*. An undescribed Miocene tortoise from Colombia had a carapace 95 cm (37 in) in length. If there are no giants on the continents now, we may have ourselves to blame: one of the best specimens of *Hesperotestudo crassiscutata*, a monster tortoise from Florida and Central America with a carapace 1.2 m (4 ft) long, is the shell of an animal that was killed with a wooden spear and roasted over a fire. There are still some pretty big tortoises wandering around the continents today. A Spurred Tortoise may be every bit as

large, or larger, then the two extinct tortoises from the island of Rodrigues; their carapaces measured only 85 cm (33 in) and 42 cm (17 in) respectively. It is not that much smaller than even the Aldabra Giant Tortoise, whose record carapace length in the wild is 106 cm (40 in) though it may grow considerably larger in captivity.

The Aldabra Giant Tortoise, with the tortoises that once lived on the Seychelles, is probably the direct descendant of an even bigger species that swam or drifted from Madagascar, where there were two giant tortoises, *Aldabrachelys abrupta* and *Aldabrachelys grandidieri*, until roughly 750 and 1,000 years ago respectively. The occasional Aldabra Giant Tortoise will even put to sea today, where it bobs in the waves like a cork (a consequence of turtles having large lungs near the top of the shell). If the Aldabra Giant Tortoise and its extinct cousins could float from island to island, their ultimate African ancestor may have floated from the continent. In December 2004, a female Aldabra tortoise completed the journey in reverse. She walked out of the sea onto the shores of Tanzania, emaciated and encrusted with barnacles, after a journey of some 740 km (460 mi) from Aldabra (if, as seems likely, that is where she started). She has since been retired to a breeding center in Dar es Salaam, where at last report she was doing well.

What about the other surviving giants, the tortoises of the Galápagos? A 1999 study by Adalgisa Caccone of Yale University and her colleagues, using mitochondrial DNA sequences, has shown that their closest living relative is actually the smallest species on South America, the Chaco Tortoise. This is not really a surprising result. The Chaco Tortoise, like the Galápagos tortoises, is an animal of dry scrub, while the other two South American tortoises live in humid forests and savannas. Did the Galápagos tortoises, then, become giants only after they arrived on the islands?

Probably not. The Chaco Tortoise once had giant fossil relatives on the South American main-

Aldabra Giant Tortoises (*Aldabrachelys gigantea*) swim surpisingly well, and occasionally even take to the sea.

land. The molecular evidence suggests that the Galápagos tortoises arose as a separate evolutionary line between 6 and 12 million years ago. That probably happened on the continent; until 5 million years ago, the present Galápagos Islands did not exist (though other islands, now submerged, probably did). It appears that for a tortoise to survive the crossing to an oceanic island, it may be better to be a giant to start with.

The most famous encounter between man and tortoise took place on San Cristóbal (Chatham) Island in the Galápagos, on September 17, 1835. What the tortoises thought of it we have no idea, but the man involved wrote the following:

> As I was walking along I met two large tortoises, each of which must have weighed at least two hundred pounds: one was eating a piece of cactus, and as I approached, it stared at me and slowly walked away; the other gave a deep hiss, and drew in its head. These huge reptiles, surrounded by the black lava, the leafless shrubs, and large cacti, seemed to my fancy like some antediluvian animals.

The writer, of course, was Charles Darwin (from *The Voyage of the Beagle*). Contrary to popular myth, he did not see the tortoises, shout "Eureka!" and immediately develop the theory of evolution. Though Darwin found the tortoises fascinating and recorded quite a bit about their natural history, he was not even aware of the most significant fact about them until he was almost ready to leave the islands. He records that the vice-governor, Mr. Lawson, told him:

> ...[T]hat the tortoises differed from the different islands, and that he could with

certainty tell from which island any one was brought. I did not for some time pay sufficient attention to this statement, and I had already partially mingled together the collections from two of the islands. I never dreamed that islands, about 50 or 60 miles apart, and most of them in sight of each other, formed of precisely the same rocks, placed under a quite similar climate, rising to a nearly equal height, would have been differently tenanted; but we shall soon see that this is the case. It is the fate of most voyagers, no sooner to discover what is most interesting in any locality, than they are hurried from it; but I ought, perhaps, to be thankful that I obtained sufficient materials to establish this most remarkable fact in the distribution of organic beings.

The inhabitants, as I have said, state that they can distinguish the tortoises from the different islands; and that they differ not only in size, but in other characters. Captain Porter has described those from Charles and from the nearest island to it, namely, Hood Island [now called Española], as having their shells in front thick and turned up like a Spanish saddle, whilst the tortoises from James Island are rounder, blacker, and have a better taste when cooked. M. Bibron, moreover, informs me that he has seen what he considers two distinct species of tortoise from the Galápagos, but he does not know from which islands. The specimens that I brought from three islands were young ones: and probably owing to this cause neither Mr. Gray nor myself could find in them any specific differences.

How much Darwin actually took from this it is difficult to say. In *The Origin of Species* he does not even mention the tortoises, though he discusses the differences among Galápagos birds at considerable length.

Fifteen distinct forms of tortoise have been described from the Galápagos (only 11 still survive). They have been divided into as many as 14 species. The TTWG recognizes 10 living and recently extinct species as components of a "*Chelonoidis nigra* species complex": one each on Floreana (*C. nigra*, extinct), Pinta (*C. abingdonii*, extinct in the wild), San Cristóbal (*C. chathamensis*), San Salvador (*C. darwini*), Pinzón (*C. duncanensis*), Española (*C. hoodensis*), Fernandina (*C. phantastica*, extinct), and Santa Cruz (*C. porteri*), and two, *C. becki* and *C. vicina*, on the largest island, Isabela.

The Duncan Island Giant Tortoise (*C. duncanensis*) of Pinzón (the English name and scientific names reflect the British designations for the islands used in Darwin's time) is a "saddleback", with the front of its carapace, in Darwin's phrase, "turned up like a Spanish saddle." A saddleback shell—something that could only evolve on a predator-free island because it exposes the entire front of the tortoise to attack—may help its owners stretch up to reach higher browse. It certainly assists in the struggle for dominance among rival males, who determine contests by how high they can reach. The Duncan tortoise was almost wiped out by introduced rats that ate the hatchlings. Today, the rats are being eliminated and captive-bred tortoises have been released on the island to join the few aging originals, all over 100 years old.

Isabela appears to have been colonized at least twice. The Volcan Wolf Giant Tortoise (*C. becki*) from northern Isabela turns out to be less closely related to the Isabela Island Giant Tortoise (*C. vicina*) than to the James Island Giant Tortoise (*C. darwini*). Santa Cruz (Indefatigable) may have been invaded three times. The Indefatigable Island Giant Tortoise (*C. porteri*) seems to consist of two deeply separated genetic lineages, both with rounded shells, plus a small "saddle-backed" outlier population very similar to the Duncan Island Giant Tortoise of

The giant tortoises of the Galapagos (*Chelonoidis nigra* complex) differ from island to island. This one is from Santa Cruz.

nearby Pinzón. One of the rounded-shelled lineages seems closest to the Chatham Island Giant Tortoise (*C. chathamensis*) from San Cristóbal. Apparently, the tortoises have been able to travel between the islands more frequently than we had thought. Their multiple crossings have produced, to put it mildly, a tangled genetic history, made even more complicated by the fact that humans have almost certainly moved tortoises from island to island for their own reasons.

The Abingdon or Pinta Island Giant Tortoise (*Chelonoidis abingdonii*) from the island of Pinta had not been seen since 1906 and was thought to be extinct. In 1971, national park wardens trying to eliminate goats from the island came across a

OPPOSITE

The last of his line: "Lonesome George", the only Abingdon Island Giant Tortoise (*Chelonoidis abingdonii*) in the world.

single male. The last of his kind, he was taken from his island in 1972 and now lives at the Charles Darwin Research Station on Santa Cruz. His name is Lonesome George, and he remains the most famous individual tortoise in the Galápagos, if not in the world.

At the station, scientists have been trying for years to do something about Lonesome George's love life. Short of cloning (something that has actually been considered), a single male cannot produce offspring; but if Lonesome George could be mated with a close relative, then at least some of his genes could be preserved. Attempts to interest Lonesome George in females from islands near Pinta, though, have met with indifference. A molecular study by Adalgisa Caccone may show why. It turns out that Lonesome George's closest relatives are not from close at hand, but from the more distant islands of Española and San Cristóbal. Pinta may have been originally colonized from one of these islands, perhaps by tortoises drifting on the strong current running from San Cristóbal. Like them, Lonesome George is a saddleback. The scientists, it seems, may have been fixing Lonesome George up with the wrong dates.

The right ones, or the closest thing we can get to them, may have been found. Some of the tortoises around the base of Volcan Wolf on Isabela share up to 50 percent of Lonesome George's genotype. They appear to be hybrid descendants of tortoises from Pinta dropped off years ago by sailors, or perhaps dumped overboard by whalers or pirates. Perhaps they can be backcrossed with Lonesome George, though the chances, at this late date, appear slim indeed.

The fate of the other Galápagos tortoises remains uncertain. The scientists at the Charles Darwin Research Station have done a heroic job. Using captive breeding techniques, they have brought the Española or Hood Island Giant Tortoise (*C. hoodensis*) back from the brink of extinction, raising its numbers from 14 to more than 1,400. The goats that had destroyed much of Española's vegetation were eradicated in the 1970s, and the reintroduced tortoises appear to be helping (we are not sure quite how) in the restoration of an endangered island cactus.

The Galápagos is no longer an isolated paradise. Some 30,000 people now live on the islands. In 1995 and again in 2004, fishermen fighting for unlimited rights to take sea cucumbers and, in 2004, shark fins in the waters around the islands held station scientists hostage, threatening to kill the tortoises as a protest if they did not get their way. The politics of wildlife conservation have reared an ugly head in Darwin's living laboratory.

In this way, the Galápagos is a microcosm of the world, and its tortoises of our planet's whole complement of turtles. Lonesome George, living out his life in captivity on an island not his own, is the only turtle that we can honestly call the last of his kind. In years to come, I fear, he may have many others for company.

Postscript:

On the morning of June 24, 2012, as this book was going to press, Lonesome George was found dead in his enclosure at the Charles Darwin Research Station. He was estimated to be about 100 years old. The death of the world's most famous tortoise — and with it, the end of his species — made headlines around the world.

PART TWO

HOW TURTLES LIVE

CHAPTER FIVE

Under the Hood

MUCH OF THE SECRET of not only turtle success, but turtle variety, lies in their physiology.

Turtles have had to cope with just about every kind of environmental stress that nature can throw at them: heat, cold, drought, salt, even lack of oxygen. To survive, they have evolved a range of internal mechanisms that you might not suspect from the seeming uniformity of their body plan.

Much of turtle behavior, too, is a response to physiological stresses. That includes dormancy—not "behaving" at all when it is simply too cold, or too hot, or too dry to carry on safely with normal activities (see page 220, Chapter 6). The key to many things that turtles do, from basking on a log to burying themselves in the mud, is temperature.

Turtles need heat to fuel body processes like growth, digestion, egg production, and muscular activity. In cooler climates, body temperature may limit a turtle's ability to feed itself more than the amount of food available. But, with one remarkable exception that we will consider at the end of this chapter, they cannot generate that heat themselves, or regulate their body temperatures by internal means as mammals do. They must absorb the warmth they need from outside, from the sun or from the surrounding air, earth or water. At the same time, they must avoid, as best they can, dangerous extremes of heat or cold.

Temperature Inside and Out

Active turtles function at their best within a range of optimum body temperatures. Within the range that a turtle can tolerate, how warm it is can have a direct effect on its metabolic rate, including the rate of such basic processes as the uptake of oxygen and the production of carbon dioxide. That range can vary, depending on the species, and may not be the same for every activity. In Northern Map Turtles (*Graptemys geographica*), the optimal temperature for swimming may be lower than for activities on land, where the temperature is often higher. Along one stretch of the Murray River, Australia, herpetologist Bruce Chessman found that while Broad-shelled Turtles (*Chelodina expansa*) stopped taking bait in his traps when the temperature dropped below 18.4°C (65°F), implying that below that temperature the turtles were much less active, he caught Eastern Short-necked Turtles (*Emydura macquarii*) down to a temperature of 16.3°C (61°F), and Eastern Snake-necked Turtles (*Chelodina longicollis*) entered his traps even at 11.9 °C (53.4°F).

North American turtles are generally most active at a temperature range roughly between 20 and 30°C (68 to 86°F). In Minnesota, however, Blanding's Turtle (*Emydoidea blandingii*), which has a more northerly distribution than most other North American turtles, is more active at lower outdoor temperatures than are Painted Turtles (*Chrysemys picta*) or Common Snapping Turtles (*Chelydra serpentina*) living in the same wetlands. Blanding's Turtles can be active several weeks earlier in the spring and later in the fall. On the other hand, many tortoises are adapted to high body temperatures. The normal internal temperature for an active Gopher Tortoise (*Gopherus polyphemus*) is close to 35°C (95°F).

The Spotted Turtle (*Clemmys guttata*), like Blanding's Turtle, prefers cool temperatures, particularly at the northern end of its range. Its activity peaks when the mean monthly air temperature is 15.5°C (60°F), and it will mate in water at only 8.5°C (47.3°F). A male Spotted Turtle was once found crawling slowly beneath the ice in shallow water; its body temperature (or at least the temperature of its cloaca, the most convenient place herpetologists can find to stick a thermometer) was 3°C (37.4°F), the lowest temperature known for any active turtle.

Optimum temperatures may change with the seasons. Turtles in a laboratory can be acclimated to prefer the higher or lower ends of their normal temperature range, and something very like acclimation may happen in nature as winter gives way to spring. In Chesapeake Bay, juvenile Loggerhead (*Caretta caretta*) and Kemp's Ridley Sea Turtles (*Lepidochelys kempii*) prefer warmer water in summer than in winter, even when cooler waters are available. Temperature preference can even change over the life of an individual. Very young turtles may need to seek out higher temperatures to speed up their growth; the sooner they grow, the less likely many predators are to eat them. In a laboratory experiment, hatchling and yearling Florida Red-bellied Turtles (*Pseudemys nelsoni*) preferred water temperatures over 30°C (86°F). Young Common Sliders (*Trachemys scripta*) and Common Snapping Turtles also prefer warmer water if they can get it, and captive hatchling Spiny Softshells (*Apalone spinifera*), given a choice of temperatures from 15 to 30°C, chose the warmest areas they could as long as they had sand to bury themselves.

Behavior can help an active turtle fine-tune its body temperature. Achieving this can be as simple as moving to a warmer spot when the turtle gets too cold, or back again when it gets too hot. At the northern limit of their range in Québec, Wood Turtles (*Glyptemys insculpta*) raise their body temperatures by shuttling back and forth between sun and shade, particularly in the morning as they seek to warm up. At night they usually resort to streams, where they are less likely to lose heat than on land. This behaviour probably requires them to remain in habitats with the right mixtures of sun, shade and available water, but it raises their metabolic rate by 20 to 26 percent above what they would have been able to achieve without adjusting their body temperatures.

Common Musk Turtles (*Sternotherus odoratus*), whose internal temperatures may remain close to that of the water where they swim, migrate into warmer water during cool weather. Freshwater turtles in warmer latitudes may need to do very little; as long as the water temperature remains within a reasonable range, there is no reason for turtles to devote a great deal of effort either to warm up or to cool down.

Even sea turtles may seek out warm water at the extremes of their ranges. Green Sea Turtles in San Diego Bay congregate in the late morning and afternoon in waters warmed by effluent from a local power plant. They shift to cooler waters by late evening. Loggerhead Sea Turtles from the Mediterranean colony at Zakynthos, Greece, seem to seek out patches of warm water, especially early in the season. By doing so they may be able to advance the date when they can lay their first clutch by as much as five days.

Over the course of a day, turtles may switch between periods of activity and periods of rest, either basking in the sun or cooling off in the shade, or in the water, depending on the temperature. Many turtles are more active during the middle of the day on cooler days, but on hotter days switch to early morning and late afternoon activity, interrupted by a midday siesta. In temperate regions, this sort of switch happens over the course of the seasons. Midday activity is commonest in spring and fall, and morning and evening sessions (a *bimodal* pattern of activity) are the rule during the summer. Angulate Tortoises (*Chersina angulata*) on Dassen Island, South Africa, where the summers are hot and dry, are bimodal on warm spring and summer days; in winter and on occasional cool, wet summer days, they are most active at midday (a *unimodal* pattern). In the more temperate Eastern Cape, Angulate Tortoises are unimodal

year round. Temperature-related activity patterns can depend on habitat, too: during long, hot summers in Greece, Hermann's Tortoise (*Testudo hermanni*) has a bimodal activity pattern in open country, but in woodland, where there is more shade, it is active in the middle of the day. Hermann's Tortoises are able to keep their body temperatures above air temperature, particularly on cooler days. Adult females in the mountains of central Italy maintained a greater difference between their body temperatures and the outside air than either males or juveniles.

A Place in the Sun

After a chilly night, the easiest way for a turtle to restore optimum body temperature is to bask in the sun. A log crowded with turtles, often of several different species, is a familiar sight in many parts of North America at least. The turtles certainly look as though they are doing their best to warm up, often positioning themselves for maximum exposure, their legs and webbed feet outstretched to soak up the sun.

Some turtles will put up with considerable discomfort to continue basking. Australian herpetologist Grahame Webb watched captive Eastern Short-necked, Jardine River (*Emydura subglobosa*), and Saw-shelled Turtles (*Elseya latisternum*) that appeared to be undergoing heat stress, at least on their heads, but continued to bask anyway. The turtles gave off a watery discharge from their eyes, panted and frothed at the mouth. They dipped their front feet into the water and wiped them over their heads in an apparent attempt to cool off. They did everything, in fact, except go back into their pool. Did they have to wait until the interior of their bodies reached the proper temperature, no matter how uncomfortable their extremities?

What are basking turtles doing? Warming themselves up, certainly; Northern Map Turtles must bask to warm up to their optimal temperatures, or as close as they can come to them, and

A Florida Red-bellied Turtle (*Pseudemys nelsoni*) basking in the Everglades stretches
its neck and limbs and spreads its toes for maximum exposure.

still have time enough to find food, reproduce or do the other things turtles have to do. However, sliders will "bask" in the dark, or in the rain, so warming in the sun cannot always be the purpose of basking. Once a turtle goes back into the water, it may lose heat more rapidly than it gained it in the sun. Australian zoologists Ben Manning and Gordon Grigg found to their surprise that although Brisbane River Turtles (*Emydura signata*) spend considerable time basking, once in the river their body temperature scarcely differs from that of the water around them. Manning and Grigg wondered if basking had to do with body temperature at all.

However, in a study of Blanding's Turtles in central Minnesota, herpetologists Todd D. Sajwaj and

Jeffrey W. Lang found that basking turtles warmed up quickly to a high body temperature, sometimes greater than 28°C (82.4°F), and kept that temperature for hours each day. Basking time varied from season to season, from individual to individual, and from day to day depending on the weather. On cool, overcast days, the turtles kept to the water, and their bodies stayed close to the water temperature. In spring, more than 90 percent of the turtles crawled out of the water to bask in the morning, usually on sedge mats and in protected areas where they could be very hard to find; by July, that figure had dropped to 40 percent.

Even on sunny spring days, some turtles stayed in the water, perhaps because they needed to feed more than they needed to bask. Northern Map

Turtles and Common Sliders may cut their basking short before their temperatures reach optimum levels, probably for the same reason. The basking turtles that Sajwaj and Lang examined all had food and their stomachs. A hungry turtle may need to spend more time in the water, but for one that has fed, climbing out to bask may be a good idea even if it loses that heat when its sunbath is over. Basking after a meal can speed digestion, especially in herbivores; digestive enzymes work better at higher temperatures (though Common Snapping Turtles in Algonquin Provincial Park, Ontario, did not bask after feeding; instead, they buried themselves in sediment under logs and organic debris). Better digestion can mean faster growth; growth rates in hatchling Painted Turtles (*Chrysemys picta*) had more to do with how much they basked than with how much they ate.

In September and October, female Blanding's Turtles basked, but males did not. This sexual difference is known in other turtles, too: female Common Sliders bask longer than males during the spring and summer, but not during autumn and winter. Perhaps female turtles need extra energy for egg production earlier in the season, while the males need to concentrate on finding mates. In the autumn, males produce sperm for the following spring, and they need higher body temperatures (above 20°C [68°F]) to generate testosterone and begin testis growth and spermatogenesis. Female Painted Turtles in Algonquin Provincial Park, Ontario, tend to bask longer than males during August, when they are developing their ovarian follicles for the next year's eggs. They may need long basking bouts to keep their body temperatures within the best range for follicular growth. Males may simply bask until they reach an optimum temperature, and then return to the water to feed and pursue mating opportunities.

This balance between temperature and a turtle's other needs may be a delicate one. In the former Yugoslavia, at the north of their range, summers are cool and Hermann's Tortoises must spend longer basking in the morning to reach their optimum temperature of around 34°C (93°F). This presents females with a problem. Female Hermann's Tortoises may be twice the size of males, and so take longer to warm up; however, if they take too long to

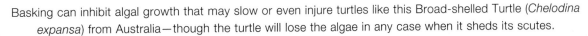

Basking can inhibit algal growth that may slow or even injure turtles like this Broad-shelled Turtle (*Chelodina expansa*) from Australia—though the turtle will lose the algae in any case when it sheds its scutes.

Reducing algal growth can be a reason to bask for European Pond Turtles (*Emys orbicularis*).

Julia Butterflies (*Dryas iulia*) take salts from the head of a basking Yellow-spotted
River Turtle (*Podocnemis unifilis*) in Manu National Park, Peru.

bask, they may not have the time to get the amount of food they need to produce a full clutch of eggs. In the end, they must give up basking time in favor of feeding time, especially on cool days, and operate at a lower temperature—trading off the ability to heat up quickly for a large body capable of producing, and holding, as many eggs as possible.

There are other reasons for basking. Soaking in the sun may help turtles synthesize vitamin D. Basking makes a turtle not only warmer, but drier. This may help it get rid of leeches and other parasites, and inhibit the growth of algae on its shell. A thick growth of algae may make a turtle a less efficient swimmer, may cause the shell to deteriorate, or even spread disease that can kill the turtle. Keeping algal growth down may be an important reason to bask for, among others, the European Pond Turtle (*Emys orbicularis*).

Some turtles bask much more than others. In North America, emydid turtles bask regularly and extensively. Map turtles (*Graptemys* spp.) even have traditional basking sites that have been used for generations. Some absolutely require suitable places to bask as a component of their habitats, usually exposed snags in deep water where the turtles are safe from predators such as foxes and raccoons. In a 13-year study of three species of cooter (*Pseudemys* spp.) at Rainbow Run in Marion County, Florida, Diana Heustis and Peter Meylan found that the availability of basking sites had more to do with how rapidly the turtles grew than the availability of food. Ultimately, this means that basking may affect the demographics, and even the survival, of a whole population. The faster a turtle grows the sooner it becomes too large for some of its predators to eat, and, especially for female cooters that mature at a larger size than males, the sooner it becomes big enough to reproduce.

In Africa, Helmeted Terrapins (*Pelomedusa subrufa*) and Serrated Hinged Terrapins (*Pelusios sinuatus*) are also frequent baskers. So are many Australian turtles, including the Mary River Turtle (*Elusor macrurus*) and the Victoria River Snapper (*Elseya dentata*). On the other hand, North American mud and musk turtles and Australian longnecks (*Chelodina* spp.) bask comparatively seldom. Though American softshells bask frequently, the Chinese Softshell (*Pelodiscus sinensis*) does so only occasionally, and, at least in Hawaii, the Wattle-necked Softshell (*Palea steindachneri*) rarely basks.

Many turtles, including softshells, bask by floating on the surface, or just below it, rather than by crawling out of the water. The Central American River Turtle (*Dermatemys mawii*) only basks in this way; it is sometimes found floating on the surface during the day, apparently asleep. Common Sliders in Florida preferred to bask out of the water when water temperatures average 28.5°C (83.3°F), but switched in their preference to basking while afloat when the water temperature rose to 31.5°C (88.7°F). Sliders living around a nuclear reactor cooling reservoir in South Carolina, where the water temperature was as much as 9°C (16°F) higher than usual, preferred to bask in the water even though perfectly good basking sites were available out of it. Even then, they were being warmed, to some extent at least, by the sun; their body temperatures ended up between 1–3°C (3.8–5.4°F) higher than the water in which they swam.

Sea turtles, to the extent they bask at all (and how much they do is not known), will normally do it afloat. In a very few places in the world, including Hawaii and Australia, Green Sea Turtles (*Chelonia mydas*), particularly females, bask on shore. Perhaps surprisingly, they prefer cooler beaches to warmer ones. Too warm a beach might overheat a basking sea turtle. Green turtles studied by Causey Whittow and George Balazs on the beaches of French Frigate Shoals in the northwestern Hawaiian Islands had carapace temperatures as high as 40–42.8°C (104–109°F). To prevent their surface layers from becoming overheated while their interior rose to an appropriate temperature, the turtles flipped sand onto

Female Green Sea Turtles (*Chelonia mydas*) on Fernandina Island in the Galapagos crawl onto the beach to bask, or to escape over-attentive males.

their flippers and carapace, a behavior that lowered their surface temperature by as much as 10°C (18°F). It is possible that Green Sea Turtles only bask when they are ill; J. Yonat Swimmer found that all of the basking turtles she studied in Hawaii were afflicted with fibropapillomatosis (also known as FP; see page 405, Chapter 10). However, in the breeding grounds on the northwestern Hawaiian Islands where basking is most frequent, FP is far less common than on the feeding grounds off the main islands where Swimmer made her observations.

For many dry-country tortoises, the problem may be too much heat rather than too little. Their basking sessions may be comparatively short. Even then, a tortoise may have to tuck its head and neck out of the way to avoid overheating them while the rest of its body warms up. Gopher Tortoises bask at the entrance to their burrows on cool days. The Texas Tortoise (*Gopherus berlandieri*) warms up in its pallet instead, and will not emerge until its body temperature rises above 28°C (82.4°F).

Shape has a good deal to do with how well a turtle absorbs and retains heat. A tortoise's domed, rounded shell gives it a low surface-to-volume ratio, which is better for retaining heat than for absorbing it. In general, tortoises are able to maintain their body temperatures above 30°C (86°F) for a long time. Size matters, of course: giant tortoises, whose size gives them an even lower surface-to-volume ratio than their smaller cousins, are particularly good at maintaining a stable body temperature. Color also matters: emydid turtles are not only flatter-shelled than tortoises, but usually have darker shells. The closer to black any object is, the faster it will soak up radiant heat.

A basking turtle does not simply have to wait for the sun's heat to penetrate its body. Blood flowing near its skin, or just under its shell, can carry heat into the turtle's interior. When a basking turtle starts to warm up, the blood vessels near its surface dilate and its heart rate increases, shunting more blood to its skin. When it begins to cool (for instance, when it goes back in the water), the vessels constrict again, conserving heat within its body. The results of this sort of adjustment can be dramatic: small Spiny Softshells (*Apalone spinifera*) are so efficient at it that they can warm up twice as fast as they cool down. The heating rate in wild Desert Tortoises (*Gopherus agassizii*) may be as much as 10 times faster than their cooling rate.

This increase, or decrease, in cardiovascular activity is triggered by feedback from temperature sensors in the nervous system. Experiments on Common Snapping Turtles and Coastal Plain Cooters (*Pseudemys concinna floridana*) have shown that blood flow increases as soon as radiant heat is applied to their carapaces, even if the interior of their bodies was already fairly warm. However, studies on Painted Turtles, box turtles (*Terrapene* spp.), and others have shown that not just surface sensors, but the central nervous system, particularly the area of the brain stem called the hypothalamus, is involved in helping the turtles set their internal thermostat.

Too Darn Hot

Overheating can kill a turtle, sometimes in a few minutes. At high body temperatures, turtles lose some of their ability to function, including a righting reflex that is a normal response to being turned on their backs (and may be critical to their survival, particularly for young animals that may easily dry out or be snapped up by predators). Few turtles can survive body temperatures much higher than roughly 40°C (104°F). Blanding's Turtle has a somewhat lower tolerance level (39.5°C or 103°F) than most other North American turtles. By contrast, Gopher Tortoises have survived at body temperatures up to 43.9°C (111°F), the highest figure known for any turtle. The Angulate Tortoise (*Chersina angulata*) of South Africa can also withstand body temperatures over 40°C (104°F).

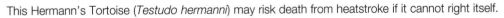

This Hermann's Tortoise (*Testudo hermanni*) may risk death from heatstroke if it cannot right itself.

An African Spurred Tortoise (*Geochelone sulcata*) shelters from the sun at the entry of its burrow in Senegal.

The obvious way to avoid overheating is to get out of the sun, or into the water. Desert Box Turtles (*Terrapene carolina luteola*) in New Mexico may resort to the burrows of kangaroo rats (*Dipodomys* spp.). Shade from shrubby vegetation may be crucial for Ornate Box Turtles (*Terrapene ornata*) in the sandhills of Nebraska. Eastern Box Turtles (*Terrapene carolina*) avoid overheating by sheltering under rotting logs, in mud, or among decaying leaves. If this is not enough, they may find a shady puddle and sit in it for anywhere from a few hours to a few days until conditions become more comfortable.

The desert-dwelling Spurred Tortoise (*Geochelone sulcata*) digs extensive burrow systems where it spends the hotter part of the day. Leopard Tortoises (*Stigmatochelys pardalis*) do not dig burrows, but may use existing ones, or seek shelter among rocks or vegetation. To compensate for a less than suitable shelter (or none at all), tortoises and American box turtles can adjust their blood flow so that they heat up slowly and cool down rapidly, the reverse of the effect during basking. Leopard Tortoises can change the amount of sun they receive by shifting the way they orient their bodies to the sun.

A turtle can cool off by evaporation if it can somehow get its skin wet, as Grahame Webb observed with his basking turtles in Australia. If there is no water available, the turtle will have to provide the liquid itself. When its body temperature rises over 40°C (104°F), an African Spurred Tortoise (*Geochelone sulcata*) begins to salivate. It uses the saliva to wet its head, neck, and front legs. As the

A Leopard Tortoise (*Stigmatochelys senegalensis*) takes to the water in the Okavango Delta, Botswana, perhaps seeking refuge from the heat.

Ornate Box Turtles (*Terrapene ornata*) survive dangerously high temperatures by urinating on their legs and plastra.

saliva evaporates, it cools the tortoise quite effectively. An Agassiz's Desert Tortoise that cannot get into its burrow will do this too, and the Elongated Tortoise (*Indotestudo elongata*) can reportedly withstand outside temperatures of up to 48°C (118°F) by using the same technique.

An Ornate Box Turtle (*Terrapene ornata*) can compound the cooling effect by urinating on its legs and plastron. This works surprisingly well. An Ornate Box Turtle kept at 51°C (124°F), a temperature that would surely kill it in minutes otherwise, managed to keep its body temperature at a dangerous, but not lethal, 40.5°C (105°F) for an hour and a half by both salivating and urinating on itself. Obviously these techniques, even for the turtles that can use them, are last-ditch solutions; too much of them, and the animal will end up trading overheating for dehydration.

Turtles on Ice

Cold can stop a turtle in its tracks as surely as heat. A temperature that is too low can force a turtle to slow its activity rate, stop it altogether, or, if too extreme, kill it. No animal can survive extensive freezing within its cells because the expanding ice crystals rupture the cell membranes. A number of animals, including at least some turtles, can withstand limited freezing of body fluids outside their cells (blood plasma, for instance, or the liquid in their eyes). Eastern Box Turtles can remain active well after the first autumn frost, and may be able to tolerate some degree of freezing within their body tissues; however, this can only go so far. As ice crystals continue to form, the concentration of dissolved substances in the turtle's remaining body fluids goes up. As that concentration becomes higher outside the cells than inside them, the cells will lose water through osmosis. If they lose enough water, they will collapse.

Turtles may go to considerable lengths to avoid freezing temperatures. Ornate Box Turtles in Nebraska and Iowa winter below the frost line, in burrows some half a meter deep (1.5 ft). The communal burrows Agassiz's Desert Tortoises retreat into to escape the winter cold of southwestern Utah, at the northern edge of their range, may be 10 m (33 ft) long. Such structures are hardly the work of a season. This far north, a burrow needs to be at least 4 m (13.2 ft) long to protect a tortoise from freezing—which may mean that those first four metres had to have been excavated before Utah winters grew as cold as they are today. That could, possibly, make those first excavations at least 5,000 years old.

The risk of freezing is a particular problem for hatchling turtles. Most North American turtles hatch in the fall, and some, including Painted and box turtles, spend their first winter underground (box turtles continue to winter underground as adults). If the soil chills too deeply, the hatchlings may die. Some turtles cope with this threat by getting out of the danger zone. When Ornate Box Turtles and Yellow Mud Turtles (*Kinosternon flavescens*) hatch, they dig down through the bottom of their nest and spend the winter deep enough in the soil, if they are lucky, to stay below the frost line. Other hatchlings, such as those of Blanding's Turtles and Common Snapping Turtles, leave their nest and spend the winter at the bottom of a lake, stream or marsh where the water does not freeze.

Painted Turtles, though some broods emerge in the autumn, usually stay in their shallow nest all winter, no more than 8–14 cm (3–5.5 in) below the surface. For them freezing is a real threat, at least in the northern part of their range—one that they face not by behavioral but by physiological means.

We used to think that Painted Turtles got through the winter by relying entirely on an unusual ability to survive freezing. Hatchling Painted Turtles have, indeed, survived for several days with

OPPOSITE

To survive the winter, Painted Turtle hatchlings (*Chrysemys picta*) must keep ice crystals from forming in their bodies.

more than half of their body water frozen, and their ability to tolerate freezing appears to improve with conditioning to colder temperatures.

Even Painted Turtles, though, have their limits. Turtles, as far as we know, do not possess the natural antifreezes of some Antarctic fishes. Some temperate species—including Painted Turtles—can tolerate *supercooling* (cooling below the freezing point without becoming frozen), at least for a short time. The smaller the animal, the greater the tolerance to supercooling, and as a result this ability is pretty much confined to hatchlings.

If their temperature drops much below –10°C (14°F), hatchlings may die even if they do not actually freeze. At such low temperatures their hearts, already beating extremely slowly, may no longer be able to deliver oxygen to their tissues, and the hatchlings are apparently killed by lactic acid buildup. The ability to tolerate supercooling varies among species, and may not always be matched to their ability to tolerate lactic acid. Overwintering adults, hibernating in ponds at warmer temperatures, can get around lactic acid problems by buffering with calcium and magnesium carbonate. Even that, though, requires some blood flow to deliver the buffering agents to their tissues—flow that extremely supercooled hatchlings are unable to provide.

The temperature in a Painted Turtle nest may not always drop below the freezing point, especially if there is snow cover to provide insulation. Nonetheless, if hatchling Painted Turtles are to have a real chance of surviving through the worst spells of a northern winter, tolerance to freezing will not be enough; they must prevent ice crystals from forming in the first place. Ice does not form simply because the temperature drops below freezing; it usually needs a nucleus to solidify around, and the most common nucleus is another ice crystal. If a crystal of ice in its nest can penetrate a baby turtle's skin, the hatchling will freeze quite rapidly.

The skin of hatchling Painted Turtles has a dense layer of lipids lying at the base of the epidermis, a layer that is lacking in turtles that either do not face the same threat of ice penetration or, like Blanding's and Common Snapping Turtles, are less able to resist it. This layer is particularly well marked on the head and forelimbs, the parts of a hatchling that are most likely to come into contact with ice crystals. Hatchlings in the nest normally withdraw their heads into their shells during very cold periods, so that the skin of their necks and other thinner-skinned areas, which are not as well protected, are hidden within their bodies. Is this lipid barrier a hatchling Painted Turtle's chief line of defense against invading crystals of ice?

The question remains open, in part, because examining the physiology of wintering hatchlings in the wild is very difficult. In a thorough review of the problem, Jon Costanzo and his colleagues have pointed out that freezing studies have almost always been carried out in a laboratory. This may give us a poor idea of what wild hatchling turtles are up against—sharp objects in the nest that could penetrate the skin, wet soil following winter rains (a wet hatchling freezes much more readily than a dry one), and so on. Lipids may give some protection to hatchling Painted Turtles, but denser lipid concentrations do not necessarily mean a greater resistance to penetrating ice.

Other mechanisms may be involved—perhaps, in part, something as simple as the number of hatchlings in the nest. The center of a large ball of hatchlings seems to be a safer place to be than the edge, not because the turtles keep each other warm—they don't—but because there is less chance of some foreign object getting through a hatchling's skin. Northern turtle populations tend to lay larger clutches than do southerly ones, and nests with at least nine hatchlings have a higher survival rate than do those with smaller broods.

There seems to be a genuine difference between hatchlings that can tolerate some degree of freezing but have no special mechanisms to resist ice crystal formation (such as Ornate Box Turtles, Diamondback Terrapins [*Malaclemys terrapin*], and, probably, Blanding's Turtles), and those with a high resistance to ice formation but a limited ability to survive freezing once it happens (such as the Northern Map Turtle, an expert at avoiding areas where it is likely to freeze up). Painted Turtles, perhaps uniquely, seem to have the abilities to tolerate supercooling, to prevent ice crystals from forming in their bodies, and to tolerate them if they should form.

Nor Any Drop to Drink

Turtles, especially in dry country, risk not only heatstroke but desiccation. Eastern Box Turtles in mountain wetlands of North Carolina minimize water loss by keeping to the more humid portions of their habitats, particularly during hot and dry spells. A thick, tough skin is some protection against the loss of water, the shell does provide armor against drying, and a turtle with a hinged shell can close itself in still farther, shutting away its head, limbs, or tail. But none of these can entirely protect a turtle from losing water through the lining of its mouth or cloaca, or when it voids its bodily wastes. A dehydrated turtle not only risks dying of thirst; if dehydration affects its ability to function, it may be more vulnerable to predators.

Of course, the easiest way to avoid desiccation is to drink regularly or, failing that, to eat succulent plants or other foods that contain stored water. Tortoises can be adept at finding water in unlikely places. In South Africa, Angulate Tortoises and Tent Tortoises (*Psammobates tentorius*) raise their hind legs, extend their necks, and push their snouts into

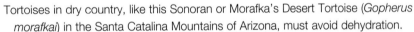

Tortoises in dry country, like this Sonoran or Morafka's Desert Tortoise (*Gopherus morafkai*) in the Santa Catalina Mountains of Arizona, must avoid dehydration.

A hatchling Sonoran Mud Turtle (*Kinosternon sonoriense*), the most desert-adapted
of its family, swims for deeper water in Sycamore Creek, Santa Cruz County, Arizona.

damp sandy soil, filtering and drinking the water that puddles around the edges of their shell, head, or front limbs. Desert tortoises sometimes dig small basins to catch water during showers and thunderstorms; the basins can hold water for up to six hours. Young Agassiz's Desert Tortoises in the Mojave Desert of California were so efficient at finding succulent food during the spring that they took in twice as much water as the scientists studying them had predicted. During the summer, if rainwater was available they drank it and stayed active. If not, they simply retreated into their burrows and remained inactive until the hot, dry weather passed.

Beating a retreat may be the safest thing for a desert turtle to do during a dry spell. Agassiz's Desert Tortoises spend much of their lives in their burrows. The Yellow Mud Turtle reportedly can spend as long as two years in a state of dormancy during an extended drought. Sonoran Mud Turtles (*Kinosternon sonoriense*), the most desert-distributed of their family, are normally highly aquatic, and concentrate in available pools of water during a drought. In some years, though, the ponds or streams where they live may dry completely. Some individuals may travel as far as 1.5 km (0.93 mi) in search of another pond, but most simply burrow into the soil a few meters away and wait for the rains. They seem well equipped to survive an overland trek: under laboratory conditions, the turtles survived at least 80 days without food or water. Whether they migrate or simply burrow out of sight, Sonoran Mud Turtles seem remarkably able to withstand harsh dry periods. After major droughts in the Peloncillo Mountains of New Mexico in 1996 and 1999, their population seemed to be completely unaffected.

Their tenacity appears partly based on a physiological trick first found in tortoises: the ability to store water in their urinary bladder and draw on it when necessary, particularly to top up the fluid levels in their blood plasma. This technique will only work as long as the water in the turtle's bladder is more dilute than its body fluids. As the turtle uses up its bladder storage and more waste products accumulate in its urine, it finally reaches a point at which the concentration of dissolved substances in its bladder becomes the same as in its blood. At that point, its ability to use the bladder as a physiological "canteen" ends. Nonetheless, this can be a long time in coming: with a full bladder, the turtle's canteen amounts to over 15 percent of its body mass. Charles Peterson and Paul Stone found that Sonoran Mud Turtles can draw on their bladders for at least 28 days after taking a drink.

Desert tortoises, which are larger animals with relatively larger bladders, can supply themselves with water in this way for perhaps as long as six months. When water becomes scarce, they can switch from producing liquid urine to excreting a semi-solid sludge, or not urinating at all for months on end. The water they save, in the form of dilute urine, is stored in their bladder canteen.

Water problems seem quite obvious for desert animals, but for an animal in need of a drink, the ocean is as much of a desert as the Kalahari. Reptiles, or for that matter birds and mammals, that take in any amount of sea water—if only in the course of swallowing another marine creature—are taking in a fluid whose concentration of salt is almost three times greater than that in their own body tissues. Even if they do not drink sea water, if their skins are at all permeable they will lose water through osmosis into the saline bath surrounding them. Some softshells can tolerate brackish water, and Chinese Softshells (*Pelodiscus sinensis*) can cope with saline conditions (in a laboratory, and to a limited degree) by building up their bodily concentrations of urea, free amino acids, and water-soluble proteins. This comes at a metabolic cost, and it is probably not a good long-term strategy.

One of the simplest ways to cope with this problem is to grow. The bigger a turtle is, the lower its surface-volume ratio. That means that there is simply less opportunity, proportionately speaking, for water loss through its skin. All adult sea turtles are large. So are most other turtles that enter salt water. The Pignose Turtle (*Carettochelys insculpta*) is a good-sized animal. The two river terrapins (*Batagur affinis* and *B. baska*) and the Painted Terrapin (*B. borneensis*) are among the largest geoemydids, and the seagoing softshell turtles, the Nile softshell (*Trionyx triunguis*) and Asian Giant Softshell (*Pelochelys cantorii*), rank with the largest of their family. The fairly small Diamondback Terrapin (*Malaclemys terrapin*) does not fit this pattern, but it lives in brackish water that is considerably less salty than the open ocean. Placed in 100 percent sea water, a Diamondback may dehydrate. Hatchlings of both Diamondback and Painted Terrapins, which are of course much smaller than adults, do not seem able to tolerate any level of salt water for long and must locate fresh water to drink. Young Painted Terrapins may have to cross 3 km (1.8 mi) of salty water to find it. Hatchling Diamondbacks will feed on land (something hatchling Common Snapping Turtles, for example, seem unable to do), and this behavior may allow them to get away from the high salt levels of their water habitat when the stress becomes too great.

Tolerance to seawater has also been suggested as an explanation for the giant size of some Meso-American Sliders (*Trachemys venusta*). The biggest known sliders live on the Caribbean slope of Costa

The Diamondback Terrapin (*Malaclemys terrapin*) is the only turtle that spends its entire life in brackish water.

Rica, where they make long journeys along the coast to nest on sea beaches. Perhaps they, and other sea-going turtles, became large because larger animals were better able to avoid predators and survive ocean waves and currents. Increased salt tolerance may be a serendipitous side effect.

Sea turtles have developed a mechanism to cut down on their salt water intake while they eat. Feeding Hawksbill (*Eretmochelys imbricata*), Loggerhead, and Green Sea Turtles (*Chelonia mydas*) have all been seen spitting sea water out of their nostrils. What is happening is this: when the turtle swallows, its meal does not go straight to its stomach. The passage from a sea turtle's esophagus into its stomach is guarded by a powerful sphincter muscle, which the turtle

closes as it swallows. It then constricts its esophagus, forcing water back out through its mouth or nostrils. It does not lose its food, because its esophagus is lined with long, stiff projections, or *papillae*, that point backward toward its stomach. The papillae catch the turtle's meal as the water rushes out. Then the turtle relaxes its sphincter, and its meal continues on its way through the digestive tract accompanied by the least amount of sea water possible.

Some does get in all the same. Even if it did not, much of the food that a sea turtle eats has the same high salt concentration as the ocean. Sea turtles still have to have some way to get rid of that excess salt. We mammals have specialized kidneys that can produce urine with a higher salt concentration than our body tissues. Reptiles and birds, including turtles, normally cannot do that.

Instead, they have repeatedly evolved salt-excreting glands, usually by modifying one or the other of the various pairs of glands in their heads. In turtles, salt glands appear to have evolved independently at least four times, not just in the true sea turtles, but in other seagoing turtles such as the Diamondback Terrapin (though the Diamondback's salt glands may not be particularly efficient). The salt glands in turtles are modifications of the lachrymal gland, the one that supplies the tear ducts. This is why a sea turtle on its nesting beach often appears to be crying. Its "tears" are actually droplets of salt solution, which can be either highly concentrated (to get rid of excess salt) or dilute (presumably to lubricate the turtle's eyes) as the animal requires.

The salt glands of a sea turtle can take up quite a bit of space. A Leatherback Sea Turtle (*Dermochelys coriacea*) has glands that are, together, almost twice as massive as its brain (a statistic that would admittedly be more impressive in a brainier creature). Though adult sea turtles probably do not drink sea water deliberately, hatchlings may need to do so during their initial growth spurt. They have proportionately much larger salt glands than adults, presumably because they require a higher desalination capacity. The salt glands of hatchling Leatherbacks, and presumably other sea turtles as well, are ready to start work as soon as the newly emerged turtles take to the ocean.

When a sea turtle's glands are working, they turn out a solution that is impressively salty—more than twice as salty as sea water, and more than six

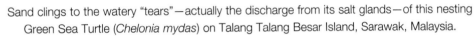

Sand clings to the watery "tears"—actually the discharge from its salt glands—of this nesting Green Sea Turtle (*Chelonia mydas*) on Talang Talang Besar Island, Sarawak, Malaysia.

times as salty as the rest of the turtle's bodily fluids. That means that the salt glands can remove all the salt from a gallon of sea water using less than half a gallon of secretion, leaving the rest for the turtle to use. In most sea turtles, the glands only work intermittently, presumably when the animal's salt load gets too high. Leatherbacks eat jellyfish, which have a higher concentration of salt than the food of other sea turtles, and their glands seem to work almost continuously (Leatherbacks get extra help from structures in the esophagus and stomach that squeeze excess water, with its salt, from their catches and expel it through the mouth and nose). Perhaps, too, the tunic of the Leatherback is not as effective as the armor of its relatives in preventing water loss through its skin.

Taking a Dive

Whether a turtle is in salt water or fresh, its most immediate physiological problem may not be temperature regulation or water balance, but respiration. While a turtle is at the surface, it can breathe air. The long necks and snorkel nostrils of a softshell turtle or a Matamata (*Chelus fimbriata*) may allow their owner to breathe from as far below the water as possible, but there are still likely to be lengthy periods in any aquatic turtle's life when it will be cut off from the surface. Turtles that winter at the bottom of ponds may be submerged, in a state of dormancy, for months at a time. They must rely on physiological mechanisms that free them, to a greater or lesser degree, from having to come to the surface at all.

If our body cells cannot get oxygen, they will continue to respire anaerobically, building up lactic acid as a by-product of their metabolism. Lactic acid is a toxin. When it escapes into the blood it can be carried to the brain, which has an extremely low tolerance for it. At the surface, or on land, the fresh supply of oxygen we take in with each breath breaks down the lactic acid in our blood. Under water, though, this cannot happen. It is the buildup of lactic acid in

the brain that drives us back to the surface. In almost all vertebrates, the brain will die in a few minutes if it is not regularly supplied with oxygen. The brains of at least some turtles have a remarkable ability to survive without oxygen for many hours, but only if the turtle is dormant and its brain activity is very low.

Diving or bottom-walking may take a turtle away from the surface for only a few minutes, but during that time it must be active; its muscles must operate, its brain must function, and the rest of its body must get along with only the oxygen that it has been able to gulp before beginning its descent. Whales and seals, which can stay under far longer than we can, do so not by carrying more oxygen with them, but through a series of adaptations to keep lactic acid away from their brains, including the ability to close off the major blood vessels that would carry it there so that it builds up in their muscle tissues instead.

All sea turtles are accomplished divers. A Flatback Sea Turtle (*Natator depressus*) can dive to over 8 m (26 ft) and remain under for more than five minutes before it is 3 weeks old, though most of its dives will be shallower and shorter. Hawksbill Sea Turtles in the Caymans have been recorded diving to 91 m (300 ft). Most sea turtles spend as little as 3 to 6 percent of their time at the surface. The different species vary in the depth of their dives and the amount of time they spend under water. Juvenile Green Sea Turtles off Florida usually do not descend more than 5 m (16 ft), while juvenile Leatherbacks dive to 18 m (59 ft) (see page 315, Chapter 8). Sea turtle dives usually range from a few minutes to almost an hour, though Clive McMahon and his colleagues have recorded Olive Ridleys off northern Australia diving up to 200 m (650 ft) and remaining under for over two hours, presumably foraging on the sea bottom. A subadult Kemp's Ridley is reported to have stayed under for five hours.

The average dive length for Hawksbill Sea Turtles at D'Arros Island in the Seychelles was over 27 minutes, with larger turtles, capable of carrying

Softshell turtles (e.g. the Spiny Softshell Turtle, *Apalone spinifera*, top) and the Matamata (*Chelus fimbriatus*, bottom) have independently evolved long necks and snorkel nostrils that allow them to take a breath while remaining almost completely submerged.

When a Hawksbill Sea Turtle
(*Eretmochelys imbricata*) dives,
its heart rate almost doubles.

A Green Sea Turtle (*Chelonia mydas*), breathing at the surface of the Red Sea in Egypt, can change all the air in its lungs in a few breaths.

more oxygen in their lungs, staying under longer (up to 62 minutes). Sea turtles, especially small animals, may surface before lack of oxygen actually forces them to do so; it may be better to keep some oxygen in reserve in case there is a need to flee from a predator. Loggerheads in the Mediterranean make their longest dives, up to two hours underwater, in winter; presumably they are able to stay under longer because their bodies, cooled by winter temperatures, are metabolizing at a slower rate.

Like marine mammals, a Green Sea Turtle can shut off blood vessels coming from its limbs to prevent lactic acid from reaching the brain. Sea turtles, though, normally deal with the stresses of diving through physiological adaptations that increase the efficiency of the system that delivers oxygen to their tissues. These adaptations begin in the lungs.

The amount of fresh oxygen that an animal can take into its lungs depends not just on lung capacity, but on how thoroughly it can empty its lungs of the air that is already there before it draws a fresh breath. The volume of air that an animal can actually exchange with each breath is called its *tidal volume*. Sea turtles have a much higher tidal volume—anywhere from 27 percent to more than 80 percent of the total volume of the lungs—than other reptiles, including other turtles. For comparison, human beings can only manage about 10 percent. A sea turtle can completely change the air in its lungs in only a few breaths, so it has to spend less time breathing at the surface before a dive.

All but the smallest passageways in a Green Sea Turtle's lungs, and presumably in other sea turtle lungs as well, are reinforced with cartilage, protecting them against collapse under the pressures of a dive, at least down to depths of 80 m (260 ft) or so. Keeping these passageways open helps prevent excess nitrogen from being forced into the turtle's tissues—the cause of the terrible diving ailment known as the "bends".

Getting oxygen into the lungs, however, is only the beginning. Now, it must be carried to the tissues.

That is determined by the rate at which oxygen can be taken up through the lung wall, and sea turtles are better at doing that than any other reptile. The tissues of a sea turtle's lungs are extensively subdivided, greatly increasing their surface area: the greater the surface area, the faster the uptake. Also, when a sea turtle dives its heart rate nearly doubles, so more blood can be pumped to the lungs to pick up oxygen and deliver it to the tissues.

Typical sea turtles store most of the oxygen they carry for a dive in their lungs, transferring it to their blood supply as needed. A Loggerhead stores some 72 percent of its oxygen in its lungs. This is a perfectly good strategy for turtle that does not dive particularly deeply, but storing air in the lungs is not really an option for the deep-diving Leatherback. A Leatherback may descend to over 1,000 m (3,300 ft), more than three times the depths its relatives reach. At those depths, even reinforced lungs will collapse. Instead, the Leatherback transfers as much oxygen as possible out of its lungs, and carries it in its tissues.

A vertebrate stores oxygen by binding it with hemoglobin (in the blood) or myoglobin (in the muscles). The higher the concentration of hemoglobin and myoglobin, the more oxygen it can store. The Leatherback has among the highest concentrations recorded for any reptile, enough to carry twice as much oxygen in its blood as other sea turtles.

An analysis of 26,146 dives by satellite-tagged Leatherbacks in the North Atlantic Ocean showed that over 99 percent went less than 300 m (984 ft). Occasionally, particularly while on transit to their regular feeding grounds, the turtles made long, slow descents to much greater, colder depths, as deep as 1,250 m (4,100 ft). These deep dives, usually undertaken at midday, may have been survey expeditions in search of concentrations of the gelatinous ocean animals—jellyfish, salps, siphonophores, and the like—that make up their diet. If they found what they were looking for, the turtles could halt their journey and feed at night, when their prey rose out of the depths into shallower water.

A diving Loggerhead Sea Turtle (*Caretta caretta*) stores some 72% of its oxygen in its lungs, transferring it to its blood supply as needed.

Strangely enough, though it descends to greater depths, the Leatherback's dives are usually the shortest of any sea turtle. A typical Leatherback dive may last as little as 4 minutes, and (except for its occasional deep dives, when the turtle may be forced to depend on anaerobic respiration) is rarely longer than 40 minutes—a short time when compared to routine dives over 50 minutes by Hawksbills and female Olive Ridleys. That may be, in part, because, the Leatherback's oxygen storage system faces a heavy demand from another, and quite different, set of adaptations—ones we will consider at the end of this chapter.

Turtles with Gills

There are three ways for a turtle to avoid coming to the surface. It can carry air in its lungs, as cheloniid sea turtles do during a dive; this solution is, at best, a short-term one. Freshwater species like the Caspian Turtle (*Mauremys caspica*) can carry an increased amount of oxygen both by having large lungs and an increased blood oxygen affinity, the capacity to bind oxygen to the hemoglobin in its blood. At best, though, these adaptations stretch a turtle's time under water by minutes, not hours, days or weeks. For a long stay beneath the surface, a turtle must either be able to take up oxygen directly from the water, like a fish, or to do without oxygen altogether. These may seem to be highly unlikely solutions for any reptile, but freshwater turtles do both.

Not all freshwater turtles, however, do both equally well. The tendency has been to opt, primarily, for one solution or the other. Kinosternids and, particularly, softshell turtles, take oxygen directly from the water (though some kinosternids, such as the Mexican Giant Musk Turtle [*Staurotypus triporcatus*] and the White-lipped Mud Turtle [*Kinosternon leucostomum*], are only moderately good at it). Painted Turtles and sliders have mastered surviving without oxygen for long periods.

Thus, while a softshell turtle is better than a Painted Turtle at picking up oxygen from the water, it has a lower tolerance for anoxia (doing without oxygen altogether). The Spiny Softshell (*Apalone spinifera*), in fact, has the lowest anoxia tolerance for any turtle yet studied.

This choice of strategies may depend, at least partly, on where turtles spend the winter (or, perhaps, where a turtle can spend the winter may be dictated by the mechanisms it has evolved for taking up, or doing without, oxygen). A turtle that winters where the water is high in oxygen would be at an advantage to make use of it. Carlos Crocker, Scott Reese, and their colleagues found that Northern Map Turtles (*Graptemys geographica*) in the lower Lamoille River of Vermont assemble for the winter in areas where the water is cold and high in oxygen, and seem able to pass the winter successfully taking up the gas through their skins. The turtles showed hardly a trace of lactic acid buildup in their tissues after five months under water. They can even remain somewhat active, and will swim away from a diver. On the other hand, Painted Turtles and Common Snapping Turtles often winter in stagnant water with little or no oxygen, and must be able to get along without it for long periods of time. Musk turtles can winter in stagnant ponds in the south of their range, where freezing is unlikely and there is a ready supply of oxygen at the surface, but farther north they winter mostly in oxygen-rich lakes and rivers.

We have known for almost 150 years that turtles can take up oxygen from water, since this remarkable ability was first discovered by the famous 19th-century scientist Louis Agassiz. We are just beginning to understand how they manage it.

All a vertebrate needs to breathe under water is a thin, permeable skin well supplied with blood, so that oxygen can diffuse across it into the bloodstream and carbon dioxide can diffuse out again. Maximizing surface area is very important; the concentration of oxygen under water may be less than one-twentieth of its level in the air. The more of the right kind of skin an animal has for its size, therefore, the better. The gills of fishes are simply places where the skin has been drawn out into hundreds of tiny filaments, well supplied with capillaries. This greatly increases the available surface area for breathing, allowing a fish to take up enough oxygen to carry on an active life. If the sheer volume of oxygen is not an issue, though, any bit of suitable skin can be a gill, or, at least, act like one.

Every turtle that has been studied can breathe under water, though not always at a high enough rate to be of much use. Gas exchange, though, is a two-way process: as oxygen goes in, carbon dioxide goes out. Carbon dioxide dissolves much more readily than oxygen in water, so getting carbon dioxide out is much easier than getting oxygen in. Common snapping turtles are rather poor at taking up oxygen from the water, but are much more successful at getting rid of carbon dioxide. Brian Bagatto and his colleagues found that the White-lipped Mud Turtle, when underwater, gave off carbon dioxide through its skin five times more effectively than it took up oxygen.

The advantage of underwater breathing seems obvious enough for wintering turtles. An active turtle may benefit, too, if it can cut down the number of times it has to come to the surface to breathe. It can save energy, spend more time gathering food, and avoid movements that might attract predators or startle prey. These advantages, though, disappear as soon as the turtle comes on land. Skin thin and permeable enough to breathe through in water is more likely to dry out in air. Depending on how much time it spends out of the water, a turtle may be better off with thick, or scaly, impervious skin.

There are, however, other options. A number of turtles breathe through the linings of their mouth and pharynx, or throat cavity, a technique called *buccopharyngeal breathing*. Since these areas are not on the outside, it matters far less if their lining is thin. A turtle that breathes in this way may enhance the process by pumping water in and out of its mouth. Hibernating Red-bellied Turtles

(*Pseudemys rubriventris*) open and close their jaws slightly about five or six times a minute, drawing water in through their mouths and pumping it out again through their nostrils.

Some turtles have even developed filamentous structures, rather like the gills of a fish, to increase the surface area they have available for underwater breathing. A number of softshells have them on the inside of the pharynx, a fact noted long ago by Louis Agassiz. The Common Musk Turtle (*Sternotherus odoratus*) has small lobes, or *papillae*, covering the tongue and much of the lining of the mouth and pharynx. These are well supplied with blood vessels, and probably serve to take up oxygen under water.

Buccopharyngeal breathing can be an important component of a turtle's underwater breathing apparatus. It can provide 30 percent of the oxygen a Nile Softshell takes up below the surface, and about 35 percent for a Common Musk Turtle. In a series of experiments, Spiny Softshells took up almost 22 percent of their oxygen from water, Florida Softshells (*Apalone ferox*) almost 12 percent, but Common Sliders, which lack the modifications of the mouth lining seen in softshells, only slightly over 5 percent. Both softshells, but not the slider, could double their rate of oxygen uptake when necessary. Possibly they pump water in and out of the pharynx more frequently, or supply it, and the skin, with more blood.

Sliders spent longer at the surface than the softshells, taking several breaths before diving again. The softshells took only a single breath. The number of breaths a surfacing turtle takes seems to be genetically programmed. Taking a single breath, as opposed to several, reduced the time softshells had to spend at the surface (though the Florida Softshell, which is not as good at water breathing as the Spiny Softshell, broke the surface more frequently). One-stroke breathing is also characteristic of some other highly aquatic turtles, including sea turtles (which, apparently, do not breathe underwater); it is also the way lungfishes breathe air.

Sliders, such as this Meso-American Slider (*Trachemys venusta*) in Cenote Tulum on Mexico's Yucatan Peninsula, can do without oxygen for a considerable time while swimming under water.

A smaller number of turtles exchange gas through the lining of the cloaca, the common exit of the digestive and respiratory tracts. Cloacal breathing is known in softshell turtles, and is particularly important in some pleurodires. A number of Australian chelids take up oxygen through pouches, or *bursae*, running off the cloaca, lined with with finger-like projections, or *villi*. In *Emydura* turtles and the Mary River Turtle (*Elusor macrurus*) villi only line parts of the bursae, and Eastern Short-necked Turtles (*Emydura macquarii*) rely on them for only 10 percent of their oxygen supply. The White-throated Snapping Turtle (*Elseya albagula*) of central Queensland derives an average of 30 percent of its oxygen from bursae completely lined with flattened, branching villi. It has been recorded diving for over three hours. The most thorough-going cloacal breather, the Fitzroy River Turtle (*Rheodytes leukops*), takes an average of 40 percent, and at times up to 70 percent, of its oxygen through unusually large bursae lined with multi-branching, heavily vascularized villi. It has the highest blood oxygen affinity of any Australian freshwater turtle studied. It swims with its cloaca wide open, pumping water in and out of its bursae at a rate of 15 to 60 times a minute. The Fitzroy River Turtle lives in fast-running waters presumably high in oxygen, where it can, and at times does, remain submerged for days, or even weeks, at a time.

No North American turtle is as thorough-going a gill-breather as the Fitzroy River Turtle, but Spiny Softshells and Common Musk Turtles seem to be able to survive indefinitely under water as long as they are not active. The Common Musk Turtle can respire for long periods without oxygen, but depends on underwater breathing to survive its winter hibernation. The same is probably true for the Northern Map Turtle.

The Fitzroy River Turtle (*Rheodytes leukops*) swims with its cloaca wide open, pumping water into its cloacal bursae.

Breathless

Though it can and does take up oxygen through its skin, the Painted Turtle can survive without oxygen longer than any other air-breathing vertebrate we know. Perhaps it is no better at this than some of its cousins—the Common Snapping Turtle is also highly tolerant of oxygen-poor conditions, and turtles in general, even those least able to get along without oxygen, are still better at doing so than most other vertebrates—but this is the species that has been studied in the most detail, thanks to the work of Donald Jackson and his colleagues. Dr. Jackson's experiments have shown that a Painted Turtle has the capacity to survive under water without oxygen, at a temperature of 3°C (37.4°F), for as long as five months—far longer than it normally has to do in the wild. To accomplish this remarkable feat, it must avoid allowing lactic acid to build up in its tissues to toxic levels. It does so in two separate ways: by lowering the rate at which lactic acid is produced in the first place, and by neutralizing the acid as much as possible once it is released into its body.

Since lactic acid is a by-product of cellular metabolism, the only way a turtle can slow its production is to dial down its metabolic rate. A Painted Turtle denied access to oxygen can lower its metabolism to about 10 to 15 percent of its normal rate. Even for a dormant, cold-blooded animal at a low body temperature, getting cellular activity down to this level is no easy task. A metabolic rate of 10 percent of normal for a Painted Turtle is equivalent to less than 0.01 percent for a rat, even if the rat is resting comfortably at normal temperatures. To achieve a rate this low, a turtle has to shut down so many metabolic pathways that it may have to switch on a few special

ones held in reserve just keep it alive. The heart of a turtle in this state may beat only once every five or ten minutes. This may be the reason why map turtles, which remain more active than Painted Turtles in winter, cannot tolerate long submergence in oxygen-poor water: they may be unable to get their metabolic rates low enough to keep lactic acid buildup at safe levels. Painted Turtles may seek out shallower, cooler wintering sites as way to reduce their metabolic rates; turtles in an oxygen-poor pond in Algonquin Park, Ontario, tended to be colder than animals in a pond with higher oxygen levels, where they could take up at least some oxygen through their skins.

Even at 10 percent of normal activity, the amount of lactic acid an overwintering Painted Turtle produces, even over a few days, would cause serious problems if it could not be neutralized. To do this, the lactic acid has to be buffered (in other words, the pH in the turtle's body tissues must be restored

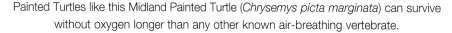

Painted Turtles like this Midland Painted Turtle (*Chrysemys picta marginata*) can survive without oxygen longer than any other known air-breathing vertebrate.

to neutral levels). Buffering requires mineral compounds, particularly calcium and magnesium carbonates, which combine with lactic acid to form pH-neutral salts such as calcium lactate. Though a turtle's body fluids have some built-in buffering capacity, the greatest source of buffering compounds is bone, and the greatest amount of bone by far in a Painted Turtle is in its shell. Its skeleton, including the shell, holds 99 percent of its calcium, magnesium, and phosphorus, 95 percent of its carbon dioxide, and more than 60 percent of its sodium supply.

Many vertebrates can release mineral ions from their bones into their bloodstream to buffer lactic acid in plasma and other extra-cellular fluids. Turtles have the additional ability, also known in frogs and crocodilians, to take up, buffer, and store lactate directly in the bone itself. Experiments by Donald Jackson and his colleagues have shown that as much as 75 percent of the lactic acid buffering that goes on in a submerged Painted Turtle (over three months, at 3°C [37.4°F]) is the result of these two mechanisms; 47 percent of the resulting buffered lactate ends up stored in the turtle's skeleton, all but 3 percent of that in its shell. The Common Snapping Turtle is even better at accumulating lactate in its shell than is the Painted Turtle. Once a turtle regains access to oxygen and begins breathing again, the lactate in its skeleton is slowly released back into the bloodstream where it can be eliminated, as it is in our own bodies, in the course of normal respiration.

The more bone a turtle has in its shell, then, and the higher the mineral content of that bone, the better it should be able to handle lactic acid buildup. It is the sheer mass of bone in its shell that makes the key difference for the Painted Turtle. About 35 to 40 percent of its body mass is bone, all but about 5 percent of it in the shell. For comparison, in a Spiny Softshell (*Apalone spinifera*), which has a less mineral-rich shell (with only 20 to 25 percent of the calcium and phosphorus in the Painted Turtle), the figure is only 12 percent. This is not much more than for a snake or mammal of the same size. The

two turtles seem equally good at storing lactate in their shells, but studies suggest that softshell bone does not release as much buffer into its system as does Painted Turtle bone. The difference may explain why the softshell, though better at taking oxygen from the surrounding water, is far less able to get along without it.

A Warm-Blooded Turtle?

When it comes to physiology, the Leatherback is, in some ways, more like a reptilian whale than a turtle. It swims farther into the cold of the northern and southern oceans than any other sea turtle, and it does so in search of prey—mostly jellyfish—that are extremely low in the kinds of nutrients animals normally need to keep up their energy levels. One Leatherback, tagged and monitored by satellite off Nova Scotia in 2005, dived repeatedly, over a period of 44 days, into waters at less than 2.5 °C (36.5 °F). On two occasions it encountered temperatures as low as 0.4 °C (32.8 °F), only slightly above the freezing point. Other sea turtles can barely tolerate water below 8 °C (46.4 °F). Loggerhead sea turtles off North Carolina appear to avoid waters colder than 13.3 °C (56 °F). The Leatherback alone ventures farther, and it deals with the chilly waters it encounters in a way unique among reptiles. Leatherbacks may have been tolerating cold for a long time; a fossil Leatherback is known from the Eocene of Antarctica.

A warm-blooded turtle may seem to be a contradiction in terms, and Leatherback metabolic rates seem to be no higher than those of other reptiles—unsurprisingly, considering their low-energy diet of jellyfish and other gelatinous marine animals. Nonetheless, an adult Leatherback in captivity reportedly maintained a body temperature of between 25 and 26°C (77 and 79°F) in sea water that was only 8°C (46.4°F). It may not always do this well in nature; four Leatherbacks captured off Nova Scotia had core body temperatures only 8.2°C (14.8°F) above that of the surrounding

Its adaptations for life in the open sea make the Leatherback (*Dermochelys coriacea*) more like a reptilian whale than a turtle.

waters. The animals may have been diving into deeper and colder waters, so the figures may have underestimated their abilities. Accomplishing even this feat, though, may require adaptations both to generate heat, and to keep it from escaping. Leatherbacks apparently do not generate internal heat the way we do, or the way birds do, as a by-product of cellular metabolism. A Leatherback may be able to pick up some body heat by basking at the surface; its dark, almost black body color may help it to absorb solar radiation, though a floating Leatherback sits relatively low in the water and its carapace may rarely dry out enough to absorb much heat. Most of its internal heat comes from the action of its muscles.

Leatherbacks keep their body heat in three different ways. The first, and simplest, is size. The bigger an animal is, the lower its surface-to-volume ratio; for every ounce of body mass, there is proportionately less surface through which heat can

escape. An adult Leatherback is twice the size of the biggest cheloniid sea turtles, and will therefore take longer to cool off. Maintaining a high body temperature through sheer bulk is called *gigantothermy*. It works for elephants, for whales, and, perhaps, it worked for many of the larger dinosaurs. It apparently works, in a smaller way, for some other sea turtles. Large Loggerhead and Green Sea Turtles can maintain their body temperature at a degree or two above that of the surrounding water, and gigantothermy is probably the way they do it. Muscular activity helps, too, and an actively swimming Green Sea Turtle may be 7°C (12.6°F) warmer than the waters it swims through, an accomplishment that may be on a par with the Nova Scotia Leatherbacks.

Gigantothermy, though, would not be enough to keep a Leatherback warm in cold northern waters. It isn't enough for whales, which supplement it with a thick layer of insulating blubber. Leatherbacks don't have blubber, but they do have a reptilian equivalent: thick, oil-saturated skin, with a layer of fibrous, fatty tissue just beneath it. Insulation protects the Leatherback everywhere but on its head and flippers. Because the flippers are comparatively thin and blade-like, they are the one part of the Leatherback that is likely to become chilled. There is not much that the turtle can do about this without compromising the aerodynamic shape of the flipper. The problem is that as blood flows through the turtle's flippers, it risks losing enough heat to lower the animal's central body temperature when it returns. The solution is to allow the flippers to cool down without drawing heat from the rest of the turtle's body. The Leatherback accomplishes this by arranging the blood vessels in the base of its flipper into a countercurrent exchange system.

In a countercurrent exchange system, the blood vessels carrying cooled blood from the flippers run close enough to the blood vessels carrying warm blood from the body to pick up some body heat and raise their blood temperature as they pass. Thus, the heat is transferred from the outgoing to the ingo-ing vessels before it reaches the flipper itself. This is the same arrangement found in an old-fashioned steam radiator, in which the coiled pipes pass heat back and forth as water courses through them. The Leatherback is certainly not the only animal with such an arrangement; gulls have a countercurrent exchange system in their legs. That is why a gull can stand on an ice floe without freezing.

All this applies, of course, only to an adult Leatherback. Hatchlings are simply too small to conserve body heat, even with insulation and countercurrent exchange systems. Young Leatherbacks, with carapace lengths of only a metre (39 in) or less, cannot tolerate the cold an adult can handle and appear to be restricted to waters over 26°C (79°F). We do not know how old, or how large, a Leatherback has to be before it can switch from a cold- to a warm-blooded mode of life. Leatherbacks reach their immense size in a much shorter time that it takes other sea turtles to grow. Perhaps their rush to adulthood is driven by a simple need to keep warm.

These hatchling Leatherbacks (*Dermochelys coriacea*) in French Guiana are still too small to control their body temperature.

CHAPTER SIX

Life as a Turtle

WE ARE A long way from knowing the full range of behaviors and life-styles of land and freshwater turtles. Studying turtles in the wild can be fraught with difficulty. It may be almost impossible to see what goes on in the Amazon's often dark and murky waters, and little is known about the lives of the heavily harvested *Podocnemis* river turtles away from their nesting beaches. We know little of the lives of the rich variety of turtles in tropical Asia, and considering the plight of most Asian turtles, that is a gap we may never fill. That we do not have that information is not merely unfortunate; it is tragic. Much of what we are learning about the better-known turtles of North America is information we need if we are to make intelligent plans for their conservation. If we do not know how much geographic space a turtle needs, how much territory it requires, what types of habitat it uses, or the range of food it needs at different points in its life cycle, we may fail to protect the very elements of its environment that are required if it is to survive.

How Long a Life?

The lifespan of a tortoise can exceed our own. An Aldabra Giant Tortoise (*Aldabrachelys gigantea*), or, just possibly, a native tortoise from the Seychelles, lived on the island of Mauritius for 152 years before its accidental death in 1918. Some Seychellois families living in the granitic islands have kept herds of giant tortoises in captivity in their families for generations. After interviewing the present (now elderly) owners of some of these tortoise herds, Jeanne Mortimer is convinced that certain of the older animals easily exceed 150 years in age.

Harriet, a Galápagos Tortoise (*Chelenoidis nigra*, or perhaps *Chelenoidis darwini*) living in the late Steve Irwin's Australia Zoo, was once believed to have belonged to no less a person than Charles Darwin, who supposedly collected her on San Salvador (James) Island and brought her to England in 1837. Allowing for the voyage home, that would have made Harriet at least 175 years old on her death in 2006. Unfortunately it turns out that Darwin's tortoise, far from surviving into the 21st century, ended up as a stuffed specimen in the British Museum within a few months of its arrival in England where it still exists. Mind you, Harriet was certainly an old tortoise—but perhaps not as old as the zoo liked to claim.

The oldest turtle ever known may have been the famous Tui Malila (or Tu Imalalia), the tortoise Captain James Cook supposedly presented to the Queen of Tonga in either 1773 or 1777. For many years, Tui Malila was thought to be either an Aldabra or a Galápagos Tortoise. To everyone's surprise, in 1958 he was identified as a Radiated Tortoise (*Astrochelys radiata*) from Madagascar. His characteristic star patterns had been burned away at some point during his long and adventurous life; he had the habit of burrowing into piles of dead leaves, which were sometimes set alight by inattentive gardeners.

Tui Malila lived until May 19, 1966. So celebrated was he that, according to Tony Beamish in *Aldabra Alone*:

> ...[H]e was in later life accorded chieftain's rank and given his own apartments in the royal palace. Not only was he old, but he was tough too. Tu Imalalia [Tui Malila] had survived the loss of an eye ... being run over and being kicked by a horse which fractured his shell.

If the tortoise that died in 1966 was indeed the one Captain Cook delivered in the 18th century, he may have been over 200 years old when he died. Unfortunately, there is some doubt as to whether Tui Malila was ever in Captain Cook's hands at all. Even if Tui Malila was not as old as he seemed, the Radiated Tortoise can reach a venerable age; one well-documented animal apparently lived more than 137 years.

Eastern Box Turtles (*Terrapene carolina*) occasionally turn up with initials and dates that seem to be over a century old carved into their shells. An adult male found in Rockingham County, Virginia, in 1985, bore the date 1874 carved into its plastron. To authenticate records like this can be tricky. However, there is good evidence that box turtles can live at least 80 or so, although probably in the wild very few survive past 30 or 40.

Blanding's Turtles (*Emydoidea blandingii*) have been reported surviving to at least 75, and Common Snapping Turtles (*Chelydra serpentina*), like box turtles, may reach the century mark. Data on body size and growth rate suggest the largest individuals in a study of Maximilian's Snake-necked Turtle (*Hydromedusa maximiliani*) may have been 100 years old. Life span may depend on gender; a 24-year study of Spotted Turtles (*Clemmys guttata*) in Ontario suggests that while males may live to be 65, females may reach 110.

Captive animals can be aged more precisely. A Common Snapping Turtle and a Common Musk Turtle (*Sternotherus odoratus*), both in the Philadelphia Zoo, lived over 70 and 54 years respectively, and there is a record of 77 years for a Blanding's Turtle. African Softshells (*Trionyx triunguis*) have lived over 42 years in captivity, a desert tortoise (*Gopherus agassizii* or *G. morafkai*) over 55, and Leopard Tortoises (*Stigmochelys pardalis*) have possibly lived as long as 75 years.

Turtles may no longer be the record holders for vertebrate venerability; a mammal, the Bowhead Whale (*Balaena mysticetus*), may live to be over 200,

Eastern Box Turtles (*Terrapene carolina*) can live at least 80 years, and perhaps more than a century.

and a number of large ocean fishes may be potential centenarians. Nonetheless, if they can escape the perils of their youth it seems that most turtles can look forward to a quite respectable lifespan.

Are Turtles Intelligent?

No one who loves turtles will dispute that they have charm and personality. You may not find the personality of, say, a large snapping turtle particularly attractive, but then you should probably have left it alone in the first place. How much intelligence turtles have, though, is another matter. The late Archie Carr dismissed the issue scathingly in his *Handbook of Turtles*:

Tinklepaugh (1932) averred that the Wood Turtle equaled the "expected accomplishment of a rat" in learning the intricacies of an experimental maze, but one must conclude that Tinklepaugh had known only feeble-minded rats.

Carr may have been doing his beloved turtles an injustice. As far back as 1901, famed psychobiologist Robert M. Yerkes put a Spotted Turtle through a maze that offered it five choices, only one of which led to a nest of moist grass. At first the turtle took 35 minutes to find the nest, but by its 20th try it made the trip in only 45 seconds. By its 5th trial, even O.L. Tinklepaugh's Wood Turtle (*Glyptemys insculpta*), faced with a fairly complex maze, reduced its running time from 15 minutes to less than 6.

Wood Turtles have something of a reputation for intelligence, as turtles go, though their skill in Tinklepaugh's maze may not reflect true problem-solving abilities. Spotted and Wood Turtles, which travel back and forth between freshwater areas and woodlands, may simply be better navigators than more sedentary turtles.

Turtles are also reasonably good at tests that require them to make choices based on color (see page 35, Chapter 1). Japanese Turtles (*Mauremys japonica*), for example, have been trained to tell the difference between red and blue. Similar experiments have shown that turtles not only have color vision, but that they can learn to choose the right color, or pattern, to get a reward. Whatever this says about their intelligence, turtles can engage in quite complicated behavior.

Patterns of Life

Outside of the bustle of the mating season, an active turtle's daily round may amount to little more than a cycle of basking, feeding, and resting in the shade. The details of the cycle shift with season and weather. Big-headed Amazon River Turtles (*Peltocephalus dumerilianus*) spend more time feeding when the weather is warmer. In South Africa's West Coast National Park, the first autumn rains are a stimulus for activity among Angulate Tortoises (*Chersina angulata*). On Egmont Key, Florida, Eastern Box Turtles (*Terrapene carolina bauri*) are only active when the temperature rises above 17°C (63°F) and the humidity is above 24 percent (particularly after rainfall). In the spring, that may mean a whole day of activity; in summer, only a few hours in the morning. For the rest of the summer day, the turtles burrow beneath the leaf litter or bury themselves in shallow, scooped-out depressions, or *forms*, in the cool organic soil.

Many turtles are diurnal, whether they are abroad at midday or only at earlier and later hours (see page 183, Chapter 5). Painted Turtles (*Chrysemys picta*) on a northern Indiana lake stayed active throughout the day, while Common Musk Turtles on the same lake were hard to find except at mid-morning and late evening. Diamondback Terrapins (*Malaclemys terrapin*) spend the night buried in the mud, perhaps to hide from nocturnal predators. Some turtles, though, are active at night, particularly mud and musk turtles (Kinosternidae). Common Musk Turtles seem to be more nocturnal in the southern portion of their range. Stripe-necked Musk Turtles (*Sternotherus minor peltifer*) studied in Tennessee were most active from evening to midnight, particularly during the warmer months of the year. In Northern Guatemala, White-lipped Mud Turtles (*Kinosternon leucostomum*) are almost entirely nocturnal; the same may be true of their distant relative, the Central American River Turtle (*Dermatemys mawii*). Euphrates Softshells (*Rafetus euphraticus*), though mostly diurnal, are often active after dark. About 30 percent of the observations of these turtles by Ertan Taska Yak and Mehmet K. Atatur in southeastern Anatolia, Turkey, were made at night.

How a turtle lives its life may have a great deal to do with its size. There are advantages to being large and different advantages to being small, even for animals living in the same type of country. One of the smallest tortoises in Africa, the Egyptian Tortoise (*Testudo kleinmanni*), lives on the northern edge of the Sahara, and the largest, the Spurred Tortoise (*Geochelone sulcata*), on the southern. In South Africa, the large Leopard Tortoise often lives side by side with the tiny padlopers (*Homopus* spp.).

A large tortoise has fewer potential predators, and may be more likely to survive a fire. A small tortoise, however, can seek shade where a larger animal risks overheating in the sun. It may burrow out of sight or hide in leaf litter, something a large tortoise may find difficult to do. Even large tortoises start off small, but there may be an advantage for them to grow as rapidly as possible. Leopard Tortoises in the Serengeti grow more rapidly than in other areas, possibly because faster-growing tortoises are less likely to be eaten by predators or burned in a fire. The faster the young Leopard Tortoises grow, the more likely they are to escape the risk they run by being small.

The geographic space where an animal spends its life is called its home range. This is not the same thing as a territory, the area an animal defends. Turtles do not normally defend territories, though male Central Asian Tortoises (*Testudo horsfieldii*) are territorial during the breeding season. In southwestern Cameroon, aggressive male Forest Hinge-back (*Kinixys erosa*) and Home's Hinge-back Tortoises (*Kinixys homeana*), may exclude others from the choicest patches in their home range. Spurred Tortoises viciously attack intruders. By contrast, Leopard Tortoises in the Nama-Karoo of South Africa do not defend territories; their home ranges overlap broadly. Painted Turtle home ranges in Michigan averaged 1.2 ha (3 ac) in size, a figure similar to that for a number of other freshwater turtles. Home range shape depends on habitat choice; the home ranges of turtles living along streams or rivers may follow the course of the streambed. Though Eastern Box Turtles are largely terrestrial, home ranges of 10 individuals around a pond in eastern Tennessee all included part of the pond edge.

Turtle home ranges (even if we leave out the vast areas covered by sea turtles) vary tremendously in size, from season to season, and from year to year, even within the same population. The home ranges of juvenile Gopher Tortoises (*Gopherus polyphemus*) studied in northern Florida were, on average, smaller than those of adults. Home ranges of Wood Turtles along a single 42 km (26 mi) stretch of river in the Huron National Forest, Northern Michigan, ranged from 0.04 to 354 ha (1 to 875 ac). Size usually depends on resources; in richer areas, there is less need to wander. Tropical tortoises may have large home ranges because they have no need to stay close to a burrow or other refuge in case of inclement weather. Leopard Tortoise home ranges in the Nama-Karoo are larger than in more humid, and presumably richer, areas, but may shrink in winter when colder temperatures lower activity rates and restrict a tortoise's ability to get around.

If a smaller area can satisfy a turtle's needs, there may be no reason to have a large home range. Red Amazon Sidenecks (*Rhinemys rufipes*) feed on palm fruits that are available all year and grow commonly along the banks of the streams where they live. Their home ranges stretch only a kilometer or two, along a stream that may be only 2.5 m (8 ft) wide. Geoffroy's Sideneck Turtles (*Phrynops geoffroanus*) along an urban stream in Campo Grande, Brazil, are so well supplied with food from domestic waste that they can get along in home ranges as small as 0.04 ha, or 400 sq m (0.01 ac, or 436 sq ft). Bog Turtle (*Glyptemys muhlenbergii*) home ranges in Maryland were as small as 0.003 ha, or 300 sq m (0.007 ac, or 322 sq ft)—about half the size of a small studio apartment. The largest Bog Turtle home ranges, up to 3.12 ha (7.7 ac), were in areas where invasive multiflora rose had choked off the best feeding areas, and the turtles presumably had to travel farther to find food.

Female freshwater turtles often have larger home ranges than males. Female Northern Map Turtles (*Graptemys geographica*) in eastern Ontario had larger home ranges than males along the St. Lawrence River, but not in a nearby lake. The home ranges of female Spiny Softshells (*Apalone spinifera*) in Vermont were more than 10 times the size of males'. Male home ranges may be larger among tortoises, including Gopher (*Gopherus polyphemus*), Texas (*Gopherus berlandieri*) and at least some Angulate Tortoises, and among hinge-back tortoises in Cameroon. Central Asian Tortoise males have smaller home ranges than females, presumably because they have to defend them during the breeding season. Gender appeared to make no difference to the size of Blanding's Turtle home ranges in Algonquin Provincial Park, Ontario.

Within its home range, a Blanding's Turtle (*Emydoidea blandingii*) may have widely separated "activity centers."

Within its home range, a turtle may have core areas where it spends the bulk of its time, or activity centers that may be some distance from the places where it hibernates or nests. David Ross and Raymond Anderson studied Blanding's Turtles in central Wisconsin that had, according to their report in the *Journal of Herpetology*, "well-defined activity centers which were separated by long distances and whose locations changed over time." Like the home ranges themselves, these activity centers may vary in size. The activity centers of Wood Turtles studied by Norman Quinn and Douglas Tate at the northern edge of their range, in Algonquin Provincial Park, Ontario, range from less than a hectare to over 100 ha (250 ac), usually along streams. Individual turtles tend to use the same centers, large or small, year after year. In mid- to late summer, females leave them and travel into the upland portion of their home ranges, presumably on their way to their nesting sites.

The Inactive Life

One of the advantages of ectothermy ("cold-bloodedness") is that when food is not available, or the climate is not right, a turtle can simply hole up somewhere and wait for matters to improve. In cool, temperate regions, turtles pass the winter in, more or less, a state of dormancy. Many herpetologists call this winter dormancy hibernation, but it is difficult to tell if turtles really hibernate in the way some mammals and a very few birds do. Some herpetologists do not use the term *hibernation* at all, or use it only when the overwintering turtle seeks out a refuge, or *hibernaculum*, for the winter.

Dormancy at other times of year—for instance, during periods of drought—is usually called *aestivation* instead. It is probably best, for our purposes, to ignore the debate over what these terms (and others, such as *brumation*, a sort of reptilian hibernation) mean and simply say that at various times of the year, for one reason or another, turtles may find a sheltered spot, dig a burrow, or dive to the bottom of a pond, and simply stop in their tracks for anywhere from a few days to several months. During extreme dry conditions Galápagos Tortoises may select a cactus or small tree and stay beside it for months, presumably awaiting better times.

A turtle seems to spend much of its life doing nothing at all. Central Asian Tortoises spend less than 15 minutes a day searching for food in spring, even though they have to build up enough resources to last through nine and a half months of aestivation during the hot, dry summers and bitterly cold winters of their steppe homeland. Quentin Joshua and his colleagues reported that "The most frequent behavior of Angulate Tortoises [on Dassen Island] during all seasons, except during spring ... was to be withdrawn into their shells. Being immobile was the second most frequent behavior, and during spring, more than 50 percent of the tortoises ... were immobile."

Ornate Box Turtles in Arizona may be active for only a few weeks a year. From November through June, the turtles shelter in the burrows of Kangaroo Rats (*Dipodomys spectabilis*) or other burrowing mammals, remaining inactive (or nearly so) through the cold winter and hot, dry spring. The Narrow-bridged Musk Turtle (*Claudius angustatus*) is active only from June to October, an interval when river waters rise and flood the neighboring grassy marshes. The turtles invade the marshes; as

the dry season approaches and the waters recede, they nest and disappear. For the rest of the year they probably bury themselves in the mud and simply wait until the rains come again; Jonathan Campbell reported seeing one dug out from beneath about a foot of dried mud at the edge of a temporary pool, or *aguada*.

In East Africa, Pancake Tortoises (*Malacochersus tornieri*) spend most of their lives in rock crevices, usually only emerging to feed during the early morning hours. Agassiz's Desert Tortoises spend most of their lives in their burrows, driven there both by winter cold and dry summer heat. In October or November (the timing varies greatly among individuals), the tortoises retire for the winter, emerging anywhere from February through April; in summer, they are active only from dawn until about 10 in the morning, or again after 7 in the evening. Even in midsummer, though, the arrival of a thundershower brings the tortoises out to feed and drink.

Spiny Softshells spend the winter buried in sediment at the bottom of a stream, just deeply enough to be able to reach the water by extending their necks. This is probably so they can pump water in and out of their throats occasionally for buccopharyngeal respiration (see page 207, Chapter 5). If the winter temperature rises above 12°C (53.6°F), the softshells emerge and switch to another burial spot.

There is evidence, strangely enough, that under some circumstances even sea turtles may become dormant. Green Sea Turtles (*Chelonia mydas*) in the Gulf of California have been found buried in the sandy bottom, where they—at least according to the local fishermen—have stayed for up to three months. Loggerhead Sea Turtles (*Caretta caretta*) off the coast of central Florida have also been caught in circumstances that suggest that they were lying dormant in the mud of the bottom, though they may have only been there for a few hours, not weeks or months. The longest dive ever measured for a sea turtle—a Loggerhead in deep waters off Cyprus—was only 10.2 hours. It appears that even in cool

Savanna Side-necked Turtles (*Podocnemis vogli*) bury themselves by the thousands in the mud of the Venezuelan llanos.

winter waters in the Mediterranean Loggerheads may only slow down the pace of their lives, becoming dormant only briefly, if at all. They continue to feed and move about even at temperatures of 12–15°C (54–59°F).

In Australia, short-necked members of the family Chelidae rarely become dormant, but some longnecks (*Chelodina* spp.) do quite regularly. If the water holes they inhabit dry up, New Guinea Long-necked Turtles (*Chelodina novaeguinae*) may try to go elsewhere. If they cannot, they may bury themselves in the mud, their presence revealed only by a slender tunnel to the surface air. They remain there as the mud dries and hardens around them, trapping them in place. Bruce Chessman attached a radio transmitter to the carapace of an Eastern Snake-necked Turtle (*Chelodina longicollis*) and released it into a warm Victorian billabong. The next day, he found it 100 m (328 ft) away from the water, buried 1 cm (0.4 in) below loose soil and leaf litter. Chessman recorded Eastern Snake-necked Turtles remaining in such refuges for up to two and a half months. In colder weather, Eastern Snake-necked Turtles will also enter dormancy underwater; one investigator in northern Victoria found 10 in the end of a hollow log.

The only short-necked Australian chelid known to become dormant is the rare Western Swamp Turtle (*Pseudemydura umbrina*). As summer temperatures rise to 30–40°C (86–104°F) and the swamps where they spend the winter dry out, the turtles find natural tunnels or burrow under leaf litter in the nearby woodlands. Sometimes they bury themselves so that only the top of the carapace and the tip of the snout are showing. There they remain until the rains return in April and May.

The shallow, turbid ponds preferred by the Savanna Side-necked Turtle (*Podocnemis vogli*) of Colombia and Venezuela may disappear completely during the dry season, forcing the turtles to burrow into the mud, sometimes by the thousands. According to Peter Pritchard and Pedro Trebbau in *The Turtles of Venezuela*, the dormant animals "may be buried at almost any angle, head up or down, plastron up or carapace up, as if they had been thrown into the drying mud rather than settled into it voluntarily."

Tortoises of several species aestivate during summer droughts, when temperatures soar and food plants wither. *Gopherus* tortoises in North America, the Egyptian Tortoise in North Africa, Spurred Tortoises south of the Sahara, and the Speckled Padloper (*Homopus signatus*) in the deserts of Namaqualand all enter dormancy during the hottest and driest times of the year. Sometimes it is to no avail; severe or long-term droughts have killed off Agassiz's Desert Tortoises in the Mojave Desert, apparently by starvation when their food crops failed to appear.

The choice of a hibernaculum may depend on the temperature. Ornate Box Turtles (*Terrapene ornata*) usually experience more severe winters than Eastern Box Turtles, and tend to burrow more deeply into the soil in consequence. The underwater hibernacula chosen by many North American and Eurasian turtles often remain above freezing. Because water is most dense at 4°C (39°F), unless a pond or river freezes solid there will be a layer of water above the freezing point near the bottom. Even if that freezes, the turtles may bury themselves safely in the unfrozen mud below. In the Caucasus, European Pond Turtles (*Emys orbicularis*) bury themselves at least 10 to 15 cm (4 to 6 in) deep, and Caspian Turtles (*Mauremys caspica*) from 8 to 30 cm (3 to 12 in).

Blanding's Turtles overwinter underwater, partially buried at the bottom of a marsh, pond or creek. They make no effort to find oxygen-rich water; wintering Blanding's Turtles in Wisconsin survived oxygen-free conditions for 100 days, and in Algonquin Provincial Park, Ontario, Chris Edge and his colleagues found Blanding's Turtles overwintering in oxygen-poor bogs and fens rather than

in a nearby river or lake where dissolved oxygen was abundant. They may either do the same, or aestivate on land, during the heat of the summer. Turtles that winter on land may shift deeper into the soil as the frost line approaches. Eastern Box Turtles can reach nearly 0.5 m (1.6 ft) in the coldest months then dig their way slowly toward the surface again as the frost line recedes.

Many North American turtles spend the winter underwater. Ironically, some of the more aquatic turtles winter on land, even though their watery habitats remain available. Eastern, Yellow and Striped Mud Turtles (*Kinosternon subrubrum, flavescens, and baurii*) winter either on land or in the water. Subadult Eastern Mud Turtles studied in Georgia traveled up to 198 m (650 ft) from the water's edge before burying themselves in the soil. Yellow Mud Turtles studied by Michael Tuma in Illinois burrow into dry sandhills surrounding their ponds both for winter hibernation and summer aestivation, usually choosing a site more than 5 m (16 ft) above the pond level. Chicken Turtles (*Deirochelys reticularia*), in the northern part of their range, leave their ponds and travel, sometimes for some distance, to bury themselves in mud or moist sand. They may do the same in summer, when the temporary ponds they prefer reach their lowest levels; in Virginia, Chicken Turtles have been recorded burying themselves in wooded areas for as long as two weeks.

In some turtles, the refuges, or hibernacula, chosen for the winter may be quite traditional. Eastern Box Turtles in southwestern Ohio traveled as much as 1.5 km (1 mi) to reach their hibernaculum site. Snapping turtles may return to the same general area year after year. One used the same site four years in a row. Twelve Bog Turtles used the same hibernacula two years running.

Some turtles occasionally winter in groups. Timothy L. Lewis and John Ritzenthaler investigated nine Spotted Turtle hibernacula buried beneath the ice and mud of a swamp in Ohio. Seven were simple vertical holes in the mat of vegetation, dug and used only for a single season. Five had one turtle each, and two had two. Of the other two hibernacula, though, one contained eight turtles, and the other, at least at the peak of its winter use, held 34. In both group hibernacula, the vertical entrance led to a horizontal passage. Both were used each winter during the three years of the study.

Up to 70 Wood Turtles have been found wintering together in a beaver pond. They could not have been keeping each other warm because they cannot generate sufficient internal heat and lack effective insulation. Wood turtles at the cold northern end of their range, near Sudbury, Ontario, apparently winter on their own. Possibly there is something about group hibernacula that attracts numbers of turtles; the wintering sites of Northern Map Turtles in the lower Lamoille River of Vermont may be areas where the water is especially high in oxygen (see page 206, Chapter 5). Another possible advantage of wintering in a group is that it makes finding a mate in the spring considerably easier. Carl Ernst reported finding 16 Spotted Turtles in a mating aggregation in a pool in mid-March, and speculated that they may have spent the winter together.

Shifting with the Seasons

Freshwater turtles appear to be sedentary creatures, tied to the ponds, lakes, or rivers where they live. At least some species, though, can and do travel considerable distances. Suwanee Cooters (*Pseudemys concinna suwanniensis*) on the Santa Fe River in north-central Florida may travel more than 2 km (1.2 mi), either upstream or down, within a few days. Male Blanding's and Eastern Box Turtles (and undoubtedly others) may travel to find mates, and females may walk considerable distances in search of nesting sites. Adult Western Caspian Turtles (*Mauremys rivulata*) along the Strymon River in northern Greece shifted from ponds on one bank to a more permanent marsh on the other when it came time to aestivate or overwinter. Many turtles have more or less regular

migration cycles in and out of their activity centers. Mud turtles (*Kinosternon* spp.) are confirmed wanderers. Striped Mud Turtles may bury themselves in the mud when their pond dries, but, like Sonoran Mud Turtles (*Kinosternon sonoriense*; see page 196, Chapter 5), are equally likely to strike off cross-country in search of another one.

Eastern Snake-necked Turtles seem particularly well adapted to overland crossings. They can survive out of the water for 13 to 16 months even though they seem never to feed on land—a useful ability in a country where water can be hard to come by. John Roe and his colleagues followed the movements of more than 2,500 Eastern Snake-necked Turtles in Booderee National Park, New South Wales. The turtles traveled more or less regularly between temporary and permanent wetland areas, returning to the temporary pools with the coming of the rain. In dry conditions their choice of whether to aestivate or to strike off overland was influenced, in part, by how far they had to travel. If permanent water was less than 100 m (328 ft) away, turtles invariably set out to reach it, but if the distances were on the order of 1,400 to 1,500 m (4,600 to 4,900 ft), 67 percent of the turtles chose, instead, to wait for the rains near their temporary ponds. Occasionally a turtle would embark on a surprisingly lengthy trek, up to 2 km (1.3 mi). One individual, captured first in 1985, was found again 22 years later in another wetland 5.2 km (3.2 mi) away.

Helmeted Terrapins (*Pelomedusa subrufa*) are such voracious consumers of tadpoles that a single hatchling in a temporary savanna pond can eliminate its entire tadpole community in a few days. The terrapins then may switch to other foods, or migrate overland to another pond. Mark-Oliver Rödel found that Helmeted Terrapins in the Comoe National Park, Côte d'Ivoire, moved regularly from pond to pond even when their ponds were filled with water; so did two other turtles that shared the ponds, the West African Mud Terrapin (*Pelusios castaneus*) and the Senegal Flapshell (*Cyclanorbis senegalensis*).

Wandering may help turtles find mates, as well as the best sources of food and shelter in a patchwork of localized, diverse ecological situations, or microhabitats. Local shifts in temperature and humidity may drive Eastern Box Turtles from one area to another as they seek the most comfortable spots over the course of a day. Hermann's Tortoises (*Testudo hermanni*) in the outskirts of Rome seek out small patches of desirable habitat (made so by the presence of a number of plant species), crossing through less suitable country within their home ranges to reach them.

Bodies of fresh water, like similar areas on land, can have periods of feast or famine. In some cases they may actually disappear, annually during seasonal droughts or occasionally during unusual dry periods. Even Bog Turtles in North Carolina, not a particularly arid region, abandoned their bog for a nearby streambed when conditions became too dry. There are times when it may be advisable for even the most sedentary turtle to move on.

For some turtles, the cycle of the seasons brings travel to and from feeding areas, winter shelters, and summer resting places. Blanding's Turtles in southern Maine used forested wetlands in spring; sunny wetlands with masses of Wood Frog (*Lithobates sylvaticus*) eggs—a potential source of food—in summer; and deep-water wetlands in late summer and fall. At Cedar Swamp in central Massachusetts, Spotted Turtles spend their winters, from November through March, in permanent red maple–sphagnum swamps. Here, they lie dormant in underwater passageways between the roots of the maples, or crawl slowly through the thick mats of sphagnum that cluster at the bases of the trees.

In late March, melting snows and spring showers fill upland hollows and basins with water, creating temporary pools where invertebrates like caddisfly and damselfly larvae emerge for a frenzy of feeding. The Spotted Turtles emerge from their winter retreat and strike out for the newly filled pools, traveling an average of 120 m (400 ft) to reach them (not an

The annual cycle of the Spotted Turtle (*Clemmys guttata*) takes it from permanent swamps to temporary upland ponds.

unusual distance; in South Carolina a Spotted Turtle on its spring trek traveled 423 m [0.25 mi] in 24 hours). They stay in and around these pools until their waters begin to dry in July and August.

By early August, the turtles begin their journey back into the permanent swamps where they spend the winter. Sometimes—we don't know why—they pause along the way to lie dormant on dry land, resting in shallow forms in grassland or under leaf litter for anywhere from four days to two weeks (there is a Connecticut record of nine weeks) before completing their journey.

As temperature rises in the summer, Wood Turtles in many parts of their range start to spend more and more time on land, and during late spring and summer they may be almost entirely terrestrial. In Virginia, Wood Turtles emerge from the deep pools where they spend the winter in late March early April, and return to the pools in October. Apparently a change in temperature is the chief stimulus that sends them to and from their winter refuges.

Spur-thighed Tortoises (*Testudo graeca*) in the western Caucasus live in areas covered by a patchwork of forests, meadows, open glades, and boulder-strewn screes. In the spring, the tortoises prefer open areas, where they dine on dandelions, clover, and other plants; this is the mating season, and glades are favored places for the tortoises to dig their nests. As temperatures rise in the summer, most tortoises move into the cooler woodlands, often shifting back and forth between sunlight and shade depending on the time of day; on really hot days, they may cluster around forest streams or the few lakes and ponds scattered in the woods. By autumn, they scatter through the woodlands looking for winter shelter.

In Madagascar, the highly localized and endangered Angonoka (*Astrochelys yniphora*) shifts seasonally between microhabitats within its tiny range. In the wet season, when food and water are plentiful, Angonokas may spend more time in open areas, feeding or searching for nesting sites. In the cool, but sunny, dry season, their home ranges shrink, and they spend more time sheltering under savanna grasses or among thickets of bamboo. Understanding how the Angonoka uses different types of vegetation from season to season is crucial to our efforts to conserve it; the variety within its habitat may be essential to its annual cycle.

Finding Their Way

For river turtles, shifting habitat may simply involve moving up or down stream, but for turtles in lakes or ponds an overland trek may be the only way to leave home. This presents wandering turtles with a serious challenge above and beyond the need to survive in a less familiar, dry land environment: how are they to find their way?

American herpetologist Terry Graham found some of the answers in a study of the Eastern Snake-necked Turtle in coastal New South Wales—the same population later studied by John Roe (see page 224). Here, the turtles spend most of their time in lakes among sand dunes. These lakes have the advantage of being relatively permanent, but they lack an abundant food supply. However, in some years, at times as rarely as every seven years or so but usually more often, heavy rains fill the dry beds of nearby swamps and temporary ponds. These newly filled pools quickly become hotbeds of invertebrate life, full of rich food. The turtles set off overland to find them. Graham (who has also studied the rather similar, but annual, journeys of Spotted Turtles at Cedar Swamp, Massachusetts, where the cycle of the seasons is far more regular) followed the turtles by the low-tech (but popular among turtle biologists) method of attaching spools of thread to their carapaces. As the turtles set off, the spools unrolled, leaving a trail of thread for Graham to follow.

Graham's turtles made their way to their bountiful new feeding ground in a remarkably straight line, over hill and dale for almost 0.5 km (0.3 mi). Clearly, they were using some sort of cue to orient

Australian Snake-necked Turtles (*Chelodina longicollis*) can navigate overland, using the sun as a compass.

themselves. Aboriginal workers suggested to Graham that the turtles used smell to find their way, and indeed Graham found that the animals could find piles of swamp debris by odor alone. However, their ability to orient themselves proved to be much greater on sunny days than on cloudy ones. On cloudy days the turtles interrupted their journeys, burrowed into the leaf litter and stayed there until the sun came out again (the opposite of the behavior seen in North American Chicken Turtles, which tend to wander on rainy days and bury themselves on sunny ones). The animals were obviously using the sun as a compass.

Furthermore, the turtles appeared to have some sort of internal biological clock that allowed them to take the time of day into account while they determined the sun's position. Graham proved this by keeping some turtles under artificial conditions in which "dawn" and "dusk" were shifted ahead by six hours. When the turtles were released, they set off at a right angle to the direction they should have followed, showing that their internal clocks were giving them the wrong information. The turtles seem to rely primarily on their view of the sun for the cues they need, followed by their sense of smell and, where possible, their ability to recognize landmarks on the way. By combining these three sets of clues, they are able to make a highly accurate beeline for the rich swamps awaiting them.

Of course that isn't the whole story; Graham's study tells us how the turtles steer themselves toward the ponds, but how do the turtles know where the ponds are in the first place? Do they remember from the last rains? If so, how do they make their very first trip? Do they follow other, more-experienced turtles? We simply don't know. The turtles are not traveling together, though sometimes that does happen; Eastern Snake-necked Turtles have been seen crossing roads by the hundreds.

Some turtles are capable of remarkable feats of orientation. Sea turtles, of course, are master navigators (see page 310, Chapter 8). Leopard Tortoises are among the many turtle species—including Common Musk Turtles, box turtles, and Red-eared Sliders (*Trachemys scripta elegans*)—that appear to have a well-developed homing instinct. Richard Boycott and Ortwin Bourquin write, in *The Southern African Tortoise Book*:

Many farmers have mentioned that tortoises taken to remote areas soon find their way home. One report is of several individuals which were marked and taken 8–13 km [5–9 mi] from the area in which they were found, and returned within two weeks, climbing through, under or over 1.2 m [4 ft] wire-mesh fences to achieve this. They were reported as being able to climb such fences, and having reached the top they simply toppled over to the other side.

Boycott and Bourquin report that a Leopard Tortoise in the Serengeti National Park in Tanzania, taken some 8 km (5 mi) from where it was captured, waited about three and a half months for the rainy season before starting homeward. It took two months to get there, following a roundabout route of about 12 km (7.5 mi).

Hatchling turtles face their own navigational challenges as they make their way from their nests to the water, or search for a safe place to spend their first

This Leopard Tortoise (*Stigmatochelys senegalensis*), on the move in the Kruger National Park, South Africa, is capable of returning home over a considerable distance if necessary—but it may take some time to get there.

winter. As no hatchling receives any care or training from its parents (with one exception; see page 260), newly hatched turtles have no opportunity to learn where they must go. Their orienting skills, which they certainly have, must be entirely innate. Hatchling Wood and Blanding's Turtles apparently follow the trails of other hatchlings, perhaps using scent to find their way—hatchling Blanding's have a distinctive musky odor. Other than that, the cues hatchling turtles appear to use include smell, sight, sound (for example, the noise of rushing water in brooks), and a general tendency to head downhill, usually the best direction to follow to find water.

The longest recorded turtle travels are not on land, but in water. Sea turtles make journeys that no land or freshwater turtle can match, some traveling more than 5,000 km (3,000 mi) (see page 305, Chapter 8). In the Orinoco River, female Arrau (*Podocnemis expansa*) leaving their nesting beaches have been captured months later a few hundred kilometers downstream, or 100 km (60 mi) upstream. In the Rio Trombetas in Brazil, females tagged with radio transmitters by Richard Vogt traveled up to 45 km (27 mi) in two days. Six-tubercled Amazon River Turtles (*Podocnemis sextuberculata*) in Brazil have been found up to 85 km (53 mi) from their capture point (though the average distance they travel is far less), and a Southern River Terrapin (*Batagur affinis*) in Malaysia's Perak River was recovered 80 km (50 mi) upstream from where it was first tagged. Some softshell turtles (*Apalone* spp.) may travel 5–10 km (3–6 mi) to reach their nesting grounds. Not all river turtles are as energetic: a female Alligator Snapper (*Macrochelys temminckii*) traveled only 6.5 km (4 mi) over an entire year.

Omnivores

Most turtles are, more or less, opportunistic, omnivorous generalists. That is a zoologist's way of saying that most turtles will eat whatever they can get, whenever and wherever they can get it. Generalists may lack the evolutionary sophistication of food specialists, but if food becomes scarce or hard to find, or if conditions change, they can switch to other kinds of foods and carry on. Thus, Blanding's Turtles in some populations eat mostly snails, while elsewhere they dine heavily on crayfish. European Pond Turtles (*Emys orbicularis*) in the Louro River valley of northwestern Spain apparently switch from carnivory to a diet of water lilies (*Nymphaea alba*) in summer. César Ayres and his colleagues recovered more than 2,000 water lily seeds from the feces of a single immature turtle. Local populations of Painted Turtle (*Chrysemys picta*) may be either entirely carnivorous, entirely herbivorous or something in between.

Turtle food preferences may take time to develop. In a laboratory study, newly hatched Diamondback Terrapins ate almost anything they were offered. By the end of their first year, though, they began to refuse items they had accepted only a few months before. Preferences may vary with gender: male Mexican Mud Turtles (*Kinosternon integrum*) are primarily carnivorous year round, but females, though more carnivorous than males in the rainy season when they may be building up reserves for nesting, switch to a largely vegetarian diet in the dry season.

A really aggressive and flexible generalist should be able to shift easily from food to food, from feeding technique to feeding technique, and from habitat to habitat, even if environmental conditions decline. Painted Turtles appear better able to find food in increasingly turbid waters than the more specialized map turtles. An opportunistic generalist will be able to turn a wide range of circumstances to its own best advantage. In a changing world, it may have the best shot at survival.

Australia is a land of frequent droughts, with drastic shifts in the kind and amount of food a hungry turtle can find. In this harsh country, it may be better not to have a dietary preference, but to be able to eat whatever comes along. Australian freshwater turtles do include strict carnivores (e.g., the Fitzroy

River Turtle [*Rheodytes leukops*], the Western Swamp Turtle and most of the long-necked turtles [*Chelodina* spp.]) as well as a few herbivores (e.g., the Northern Snapping Turtle [*Elseya dentata*]), but the *Emydura* turtles, the Mary River Turtle (*Elusor macrurus*) and the Pig-nose Turtle (*Carettochelys insculpta*) are omnivorous generalists.

The Pig-nose Turtle eats a wide range of animal food, but it prefers plants. The plants it eats, though, differ from place to place. In Papua New Guinea, it eats the unripe fruits of crabapple mangrove (*Sonneratia* spp.). In Australia, *Sonneratia* grows mostly along the coast. Farther inland, the turtle feeds mostly on the leaves, flowers, and fruits of riverside trees like Fig (*Ficus racemosa*), Bush Apple (*Syzigium forte*) and Screw Pine (*Pandanus aquaticus*). This change probably has little to do with what the turtle prefers; instead, it dines on what is available.

In some billabongs in Kakadu National Park in northern Australia, "what is available" to Pig-nose Turtles includes flying foxes (*Pteropus* spp.). Roosts of these giant fruit bats overhang the waters where the turtles live, and the bats occasionally end up inside the turtles. How they get there we are not sure. Will a turtle actually drown a bat that falls into the water, or will it only scavenge from a carcass? It is hard to say, but perfectly formed hairballs composed entirely of bat fur have been recovered from pig-nose stomachs.

Pig-nose Turtles (*Carettochelys insculpta*) prefer plants, but will take animal food, including flying foxes.

Adults of Purvis's Turtle (*Myuchelys purvisi*) and Georges' Turtle (*Elseya georgesi*), both confined to isolated river drainages in New South Wales, eat a wide range of animals and plants apparently without being, in any measurable way, selective. This sort of indiscriminate behavior may allow the turtles to thrive in a variety of streams, each with a different supply of foods (or, at least, the same foods in different proportions).

Opportunism may be a good strategy for another turtle that faces a wide range of changing circumstances, the Helmeted Terrapin of Africa. This is a species of temporary ponds, places that may offer a variety of foods at different times or in different circumstances. Helmeted terrapins will eat almost anything, animal or plant, though they are carnivores by preference. They are able to switch from a diet of aquatic animals in the wet season to one of terrestrial animals, including mice, lizards, snakes and small birds, in the dry (though they reportedly eat all their meals underwater).

Helmeted Terrapins will scavenge from a rotting carcass, or pull ticks from animals like rhinoceroses that wallow in their pools—a habit they share with the Serrated Hinged Terrapin (*Pelusios sinuatus*). Like North American Common Snapping Turtles, they seize and devour ducklings and other waterbirds. In the Etosha Pan of Namibia, a great flat expense that only occasionally, after exceptional rains, becomes a shallow lake, Helmeted Terrapins may act like miniature crocodiles, seizing doves and sandgrouse that come to the pan to drink and holding them under the water until they drown.

Perhaps the ultimate chelonian omnivore is the Alligator Snapping Turtle. Alligator Snappers will eat just about anything. Their stomachs have yielded fish such as pickerel, gar, and carp; salamanders, including the large, eel-like sirens and amphiumas; snakes; turtles, including its cousin the Common Snapping Turtle and even young members of its own species; small alligators; crayfish; freshwater mussels; snails; Wood Ducks (*Aix sponsa*) and other birds; and mammals, including opossums, armadillos, raccoons, nutria, and muskrats. As if that weren't enough, the Alligator Snapper also eats persimmons, wild grapes, acorns (in a study by Kevin Sloan, Kurt Buhlmann, and Jeffrey Lovich, perhaps at the right season, acorns were the most abundant food item by weight recovered from snapper stomachs), and miscellaneous items including rocks, fishhooks, wood, cardboard and aluminum foil.

The powerful jaws of the Alligator Snapping Turtle (*Macrochelys temmincki*) can crush mussel shells—and other turtles.

These extremely various tastes may seem surprising in an animal that appears, on first examination, to be a highly specialized fish trapper; however, even the fish it eats are not necessarily baited in by the wormlike pink lure on the snapper's tongue. Some may be taken as carrion.

Fishing by lure seems to be used mostly by the juveniles. As the turtles grow and their jaws increase in strength, they rely more and more on other foods. The Alligator Snapper's exceedingly powerful jaws are quite capable of cracking the shells of smaller turtles like the Common Musk Turtle, a dietary staple in some areas. They may actually have evolved, though, for crushing freshwater mussels. Today the huge and diverse fauna of freshwater mussels that once lived in the eastern United States has become, after years of pollution, siltation, and habitat destruction, primarily a catalog of endangered species. Over much of its range, the Alligator Snapper's first dietary choice may no longer be on the menu.

Mollusk Eaters

The Alligator Snapper is not the only turtle with mollusk-crushing jaws. The massive crushing surfaces on the upper jaws of the Mexican Giant Musk Turtle (*Staurotypus triporcatus*) allow it to deal with shells of snails and smaller turtles. In Africa, the Zambezi Flapshell (*Cyclanorbis frenatum*) apparently specializes in freshwater mollusks. According to Richard Boycott and Ortwin Bourquin's *The Southern African Tortoise Book*, "There are reports from Malawi of this species digging up buried mussels using their forelimbs, which requires considerable effort as the mussels are buried vertically in the mud and sand of the lake bottom. The shells of the mussels are apparently crushed first before the mussels are swallowed."

Not every turtle seeking to penetrate a mollusk shell uses brute force. The Mary River Turtle of eastern Australia has no special modifications of the head for crushing shells. Instead, it takes a clam in its mouth, maneuvers it about until it is in line with its neck, and rakes its foreclaws along the edge of the shell until it manages to slip a claw between the valves and scrape away at the soft body inside. Once it does enough damage, the clam is no longer able to hold its valves together and opens. The turtle breaks up the opened shell as it eats, swallowing some bits and ejecting others.

In Australia, some female turtles of the genus *Emydura* develop, as they age, greatly enlarged heads with bulging, solid jaw muscles—a condition called *megacephaly*. At the same time, the horny sheath covering the upper jaw grows backwards over the roof of the mouth. In northwestern Australian species like the Victoria River and Northwest Red-faced Turtles (*Emydura victoriae* and *E. australis*), it may reach back far enough to cover the internal openings of the nostrils and form a secondary palate. This extreme development apparently converts the turtle's head into a powerful and effective crushing instrument, but in old females it may proceed to such a degree that the animal is no longer able to tuck its head under its shell and may even have difficulty eating some kinds of foods.

Why does megacephaly occur in female *Emydura*s, but not males? One suggestion is that females, which must produce shells for their eggs, may need the calcium that mollusk shells provide. In all map turtles (*Graptemys*) the females are the larger sex. In several species, this difference in size is accompanied by striking female megacephaly. In some, the size difference is extreme, the greatest difference in male and female size (sexual size dimorphism) in any land vertebrate.

This seems to be mostly the result of an evolutionary reduction in the size of the males—a

reduction which, in its turn, seems to be brought about by a change in maturation time. Males in the most strongly dimorphic map turtles take only 2 or 3 years to reach sexual maturity, while their females can take 7 to 15. The relatively tiny size of map turtle males may have some as yet undiscovered mating advantage.

Megacephaly and size dimorphism reach their greatest extreme in Barbour's Map Turtle (*Graptemys barbouri*), a species confined to the Apalachicola River and its tributaries in Alabama, Georgia, and Florida. A female Barbour's is more than twice the size of a male, with a carapace up to 33 cm (13 in) long and an enormous, broad head. Not surprisingly, the sexes have different diets, and even different habitat preferences. The small, narrow-headed males eat mostly insects, while the megacephalic females prefer deeper water where they crush the shells of aquatic snails and introduced mussels.

This difference shows up at the species level. All of the narrow-headed, insect-eating map turtles share their rivers with either a moderately broad-headed or an extremely broad-headed, mollusk-eating species. In the Pascagoula River system, the Yellow-blotched Map Turtle (*Graptemys flavimaculata*), a narrow-headed species, lives alongside the megacephalic Pascagoula Map Turtle (*Graptemys gibbonsi*). This division of resources, and the morphological changes that have accompanied it, may reflect not a need for calcium (which presumably affects all turtles, not just the ones that eat mollusks), but the need for the sexes, or the species, to coexist during an evolutionary shift to a strictly carnivorous diet.

In a reversal of what may have happened to the Alligator Snapping Turtle, human activities have shifted the diet of at least some map turtles toward, rather than away from, freshwater clams and mussels. In the 1950s exotic Asian clams of the genus *Corbicula* began an invasion of North American river systems. European Zebra and Quagga Mussels (*D. polymorpha* and *D. bugensis*), presumably introduced in the ballast water of oceangoing ships using the St. Lawrence

The female Barbour's Map Turtle (*Graptemys barbouri*) is more than twice the size of a male like this one.

Seaway, began an economic and ecological reign of terror in the Great Lakes in 1988. As the invaders grew abundant and widespread, map turtles began to eat them. Female Texas Map Turtles (*Graptemys versa*) in the Colorado River drainage had changed from a diverse diet of native clams, insect larvae, sponges, algae, and other items to an almost exclusive reliance on *Corbicula* by 1999. Other map turtles in different river systems have shown similar shifts. In Lake Erie, female Northern Map Turtles, in particular large individuals, are now feeding almost entirely on exotic mussels. Map turtle males, with their more insect-oriented dietary preferences, have been less affected.

Filterers and Drinkers

The Painted Turtle and a number of South American pleurodires, especially the Yellow-spotted River Turtle (*Podocnemis unifilis*) and the Savanna Side-necked Turtle, have a special technique for skimming fine particles of food from the water's surface. The skimming turtle drops its jaw, opens its throat, and slowly adjusts its head until its jaw is just below the waterline. When the cutting edge of the jaw breaks the surface, water, with any bits of food floating on it, pours into the turtle's mouth. After the turtle closes its mouth, it constricts its pharynx and forces the excess water out through its nostrils or its almost-closed jaws.

Yellow-spotted River Turtles (*Podocnemis unifilis*) skim food from the water's surface, a technique called *neustophagia*.

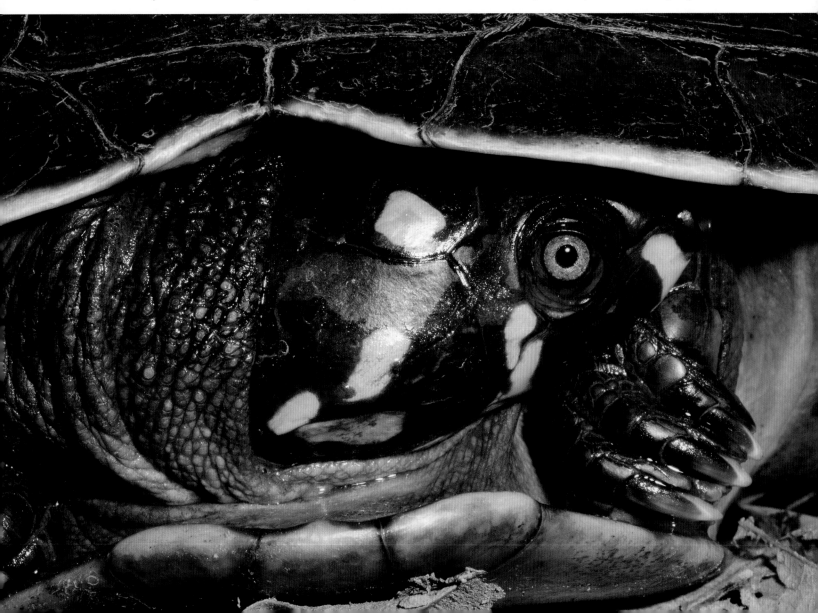

A Leopard Tortoise (*Stigmatochelys senegalensis*) drinks from a puddle in a road through Kruger National Park, South Africa.

This rather crude version of the filter-feeding of flamingos and baleen whales is called *neustophagia*, after the neuston, the technical collective name for the bits of stuff that float on the surface of the water. Neustophagia only works if the surface of the water is calm and still. This may be why turtles like the Magdalena River Turtle (*Podocnemis lewyana*), which lives mostly in fast-flowing rivers, do not practice it.

For terrestrial turtles, finding water may be as important as locating food. Box turtles (*Terrapene* spp.) may get much of their liquid requirements from fruit, at least in season. Drinking may be critically important for tortoises (see page 195, Chapter 5). Summer thundershowers bring Agassiz's Desert Tortoises above ground to drink what they can. Central Asian Tortoises have been observed licking water from leaves after a spring thunderstorm. Radiated Tortoises seem to be able to anticipate

rainfall, and gather in places where it is likely to collect. In November 2009, Sean Doody and his colleagues found almost 100 Radiated Tortoises apparently waiting for rain by a dry creekbed in southwestern Madagascar. Once the rain fell, the tortoises immediately began drinking from pools that collected in crevices on flat rocks. Aldabra Giant, Radiated and Angulate Tortoises (*Chersina angulata*) drink through their noses, allowing them access to very shallow puddles. Standing water may not always be available, and some South African tortoises, including the Tent Tortoise (*Psammobates tentorius*), have developed a way to drink from desert mists. During a mist or light rain, droplets of water condense on the tortoise's carapace. To get at them, the tortoise straightens its hindlimbs. This tilts the shell forward, and the droplets run forward along gutters in the sides of the carapace until the turtle can use its forelimbs and head to direct the water into its mouth.

Vegetarians

Even the least likely turtles can have a streak of vegetarianism. Along the banks of the Tigris near Diyarbakir in Turkey, Euphrates Softshells are accused of raiding the local farmers' watermelon crops. A number of turtles, from a variety of families, are more or less committed vegetarians. This is particularly true of tortoises—Central Asian Tortoises are strict herbivores—though some tortoises can be carnivores at times. The South American Red-footed Tortoise (*Chelonoidis carbonaria*) is an opportunistic omnivore, and the feces of the endangered Geometric Tortoise (*Psammobates geometricus*) have revealed snails and even the remains of young Common Padlopers (*Homopus areolatus*). *Kinixys* tortoises are particularly prone to omnivory. Less than half (47 percent) of the diet of Speke's Hinge-backed Tortoise (*Kinixys spekii*) consists of vascular plants. Speke's Hinge-back is heavily dependent on fungi (41 percent of its diet), but for the remaining 12 percent it turns to invertebrates, and especially to millipedes (despite the toxic chemicals some millipedes exude as defences) and beetles.

A number of turtles, including many species of tortoise, pick up extra nutrients by feeding on dung, animal carcasses, bones, or eggshells. Females may be especially prone to do this, perhaps to build up calcium stores to produce the shells of their own eggs. Eleven percent of the diet of Radiated Tortoises in southwestern Madagascar consists of bones, hair, feces and other items ranging from dried lizard carcasses to charcoal. Angulate Tortoises on Dassen Island, South Africa, eat large quantities of European Rabbit (*Oryctolagus cuniculus*) feces, which are high in protein when fresh. In summer and autumn rabbit droppings amount to more than a quarter of the tortoises' diet.

A Radiated Tortoise (*Astrochelys radiata*) in the Berenty Reserve, Madagascar, dines on (introduced) prickly pear cactus (*Opuntia* sp.).

American box turtles rarely eat feces, but will devour shed snake skins. Agassiz's Desert Tortoises in the Mojave Desert and Florida Box Turtles (*Terrapene carolina bauri*) on Big Pine Key, Florida, have been observed eating the carapace bones of their own kind. These bones are normally from the carcasses of adults, but scats from one box turtle contained the costal bones of a hatchling or very young turtle—suggesting that box turtles may be occasional cannibals.

Does a tortoise simply work its way through its local plant community, eating different species pretty much as it finds them, or is it selective? Studies of Gopher Tortoise and Angonoka have shown that the commonest plants in their diet were also the commonest plants in their environment, implying that the tortoises were not being selective. Other studies, however, suggest that at least some tortoises may be choosy about the plants they eat.

In some species, including Agassiz's Desert Tortoise, selection may amount to little more than preferring soft, nutrient- and mineral-rich herbaceous plants over tough, dry grasses. Central Asian Tortoises on the steppes of Uzbekistan generally ate the most abundant herbaceous plants available, but avoided grasses. Other species seem more selective. The most frequent plants in the diet of Leopard Tortoises in the Eastern Cape of South Africa were fairly uncommon in the tortoise's habitats. The tortoises seemed to be selecting them. If desirable plants are easy to come by, a tortoise may concentrate on them, but if its favorites are not available it may eat anything else it can find. This may also be true for Yellow-footed (*Chelonoidis denticulata*) and Red-footed Tortoises in South America.

In northern Tanzania Leopard Tortoises have a preference for succulents, plants often avoided by mammals because they contain toxic compounds. Jonathan Kabigumila suggested that eating them may help the tortoise avoid competition with grazing herds of antelope. Many of the plants eaten by Central Asian Tortoises are also toxic to mammals.

In Morocco and Algeria, Spur-thighed Tortoises apparently select plants laced with toxins, including Scarlet Pimpernel (*Anagala arvensis*). It has been suggested that they may act as deworming agents. In one experiment, captive Hermann's Tortoises shifted their diet to less toxic plants after being treated with a deworming compound.

The tiny Speckled Padloper prefers spring flowers in general and, possibly, a few species in particular. One of them, *Leysera tenella*, is even known locally as *kleinskilpadteebossie* (literally, "small tortoise tea bush"). The Asian Impressed Tortoise (*Manouria impressa*) appears to be a true botanical specialist, eating almost nothing but several species of forest mushrooms. Texas River Cooters (*Pseudemys texana*) in a lake near Austin, Texas where 18 species of aquatic plants were available confined themselves almost entirely to 4, including Carolina Fanwort (*Cabomba caroliniana*), a plant high in nutrients but low in hard-to-digest fiber.

According to Dionysius S.K. Sharma, the Painted Terrapin (*Batagur borneensis*) "is herbivorous in the wild, feeding mainly on leaves, fruit, flowers, stems and roots of selected riparian plants." In the tropical rain forests of South America, where annual floods may send the rivers out among the trees, fallen fruits are food for many aquatic animals. Fruits and seeds are important items in the diet of a number of South American sidenecks, from the Yellow-spotted River Turtle, which may eat almost entirely plant material (though it will take small numbers of insects and other animals, possibly sweeping the smaller ones up along with the plants it eats), to the more omnivorous Big-headed Amazon River Turtle (*Peltocephalus dumerilianus*). Palm fruits and seeds are particularly important to the Big-headed Amazon River Turtle, possibly because their high caloric content makes them a rich source of energy. It supplements them with fish, insects, freshwater mollusks, and crustaceans.

Adult Arrau keep to the main river channels during the dry season, but when the rains come they invade the flooded forests and feed on fallen fruit and other foods. As waters recede, young turtles may stay in the forest pools, but the adults must return to the rivers to nest. The great 19th-century naturalist Henry Walter Bates joined a hunt for turtles that had become stranded in a forest pool about 1.6–2 ha (4–5 ac) in size; in *The Naturalist on the River Amazons*, he noted that:

> … [Y]ounger turtles never migrate with their elders on the sinking of the waters, but remain in the tepid pools, fattening on fallen fruits, and, according to the natives, on the fine nutritious mud. We captured a few full-grown mother turtles, which were known at once by the horny skin of their breast-plates being worn, telling of their having crawled on the sands to lay eggs the previous year. They had evidently made a mistake in not leaving the pool at the proper time, for they were full of eggs, which, we were told, they would, before the season was over, scatter in despair over the swamp.

Bates also commented that the younger turtles "… were very fat. Cardozo and I lived almost exclusively on them for several months afterwards. Roasted in the shell they form a most appetising dish."

Since animals cannot digest the cellulose in plants, many plant eaters enlist the help of cellulose-digesting bacteria. Herbivores from termites to cattle carry colonies of such bacteria in their guts; so do Green Sea Turtles (see page 319, Chapter 8), and so do some tortoises. The advantages of carrying a bacteria-powered fermentation chamber are considerable. Captive juvenile Galápagos Tortoises can digest a high-fiber diet of 77 percent hay as efficiently as a horse. The Aldabra Giant Tortoise, which does not have cellulose-digesting bacteria in its gut, digests only about 30 percent of the plant matter (mostly tough grasses) it eats. The Red-footed Tortoise, which does, manages about 65 percent (but it eats more fruit). One of the reasons

tortoises prefer high temperatures (see page 183, Chapter 5) may be to keep their microflora operating at top efficiency.

Tortoise meals may take weeks to macerate and digest, particularly at cooler temperatures. Peter Holt used barium meals to show that food can take up to a month to pass through the gut of the Spur-thighed Tortoise. Slow digestion may help desert tortoises deal with periods of feast and famine. They commonly fast for a month even during their active periods. Overall, they may spend only 0.3 percent of their time feeding—a figure amounting to less than 48 hours per year.

Gopher Tortoises face a special problem over the winter. Before entering winter dormancy, they empty their digestive systems, and, of course, they may not eat again for some time. This is enough to starve their complement of microflora. To restart their fermentation chambers, the tortoises recycle a starter sample. They do this by defecating in their burrows in the fall, and eating a sample of their dried feces in the spring.

Vegetarianism is a habit most turtles acquire with age. Even strictly vegetarian turtles may be more or less carnivorous as hatchlings or juveniles, though juvenile Common Sliders can digest (and, with microfloral assistance, ferment) plant material as thoroughly as their elders. Young Yellow-spotted River Turtles studied in Rondonia, Brazil, catch and eat small fishes, but the amount of fish in their diet shrinks as the turtles grow. By the time they reach adulthood, they are almost entirely plant eaters; plant material amounts to over 89 percent of their stomach contents.

Growing young turtles generally need to take up nutrients at higher rates than adults, and may require different diets. Food passes through the digestive system of young desert tortoises more quickly than in adults. Lower-fiber food can be digested more rapidly because there is no need to ferment large amounts of fiber in the gut. This may explain why young desert tortoises prefer lower-fiber plants. The time needed to ferment a high-cellulose diet may be just too great for them.

In Australia, Krefft's River Turtle (*Emydura macquarii kreffti*) undergoes the same shift from omnivory to vegetarianism. The Red-bellied Turtle (*Pseudemys rubriventris*) provides a peculiar exception: hatchlings start out as herbivores, then switch to a diet of crayfish.

A few turtles are lifelong vegetarians. Florida Red-bellied Turtles (*Pseudemys nelsoni*), Coastal Plain Cooters (*Pseudemys concinna floridana*) and Central American River Turtles, supported by colonies of microflora in their small intestines, live on plants from the day they hatch, though juvenile cooters do take some animal food. River turtle hatchlings, at least in captivity, will eat their mother's feces to pick up their microflora.

Hunters and Suckers

Though the turtle body hardly seems designed for active hunting, it is surprising how many turtles are good at it. Turtles can be more agile than they look; creatures as unlikely, and different, as the Nile softshell (*Trionyx triunguis*) and Leopard Tortoise have scaled wire-mesh fences a meter or more high. Sonoran Mud Turtles have been reported capturing and eating live snakes and other animals. A Smooth Softshell (*Apalone mutica*) has been seen chasing down and capturing a brook trout, one of the fastest freshwater fish in North America. African Helmeted Terrapins may even hunt in concert. In ponds where their numbers are high, several terrapins may attack a small water bird, drag it under, and tear it apart, though perhaps such behavior is more of a free-for-all than an organized group hunt.

Some Wood Turtle populations in central Pennsylvania and Michigan draw earthworms to the surface by "stomping," apparently to imitate rain. Carl Ernst, Jeffrey Lovitch, and Roger Barbour describe "worm stomping" in *Turtles of the United States and Canada*:

A stomping turtle typically takes a few steps forward and then stomps several times with one front foot and then the other at a rate of about one stomp per second. Any worm brought to the surface is eaten. The whole sequence usually lasts 15 minutes or more and may include 2–19 stomps (mean 8.1) from the time stomping begins until a worm is eaten. Sequences start with light stomping with the force of each successive stomp increasing, and some stomps are audible for several meters. The plastron may also be banged against the ground in the process.

The fact that only certain Wood Turtle populations do this suggests the remarkable possibility that worm stomping is a learned behavior, evidence of a sort of turtle culture. How such things could develop in animals with no parental care, even leaving aside the question of the Wood Turtle's reputed intelligence, we have no idea.

Freshwater turtles like the Common Musk Turtle explore the bottom actively, a method Ernst called a "peer and probe method of food detection." Carnivorous turtles seeking larger prey may depend primarily on stealth, camouflage, and surprise attacks. The Alligator Snapper, as we have seen, uses its "lure" to bait fish into its jaws.

One of the chief marks of a carnivorous turtle is a long neck, often ending in a streamlined head. With their heads and necks alone, Common Snapping Turtles, most soft-shelled turtles, and the snake-necked turtles of the family Chelidae (*Chelodina* spp. in Australia, *Hydromedusa* spp. in South America) can make a slow, stealthy approach to an unsuspecting fish or small invertebrate, followed by a rapid, snake-like strike and a gulp.

OPPOSITE

Earthworms are a common item in the diet of box turtles, including this Ornate Box Turtle (*Terrapene ornata*).

Many softshells, including the American *Apalone* spp., bury themselves in the sand, the better to ambush their prey. Softshells have particularly long necks and narrow heads, culminating in the weirdly proportioned skull of the Asian narrow-headed softshells (*Chitra* spp.; see page 33, Chapter 1). The Indian Narrow-headed Softshell (*Chitra indica*) is, according to an old account, able to "suddenly shoot out its long neck with inconceivable rapidity." The late Jaganath Vijaya of the Madras Snake Park Trust sent Peter Pritchard the following account of a captive:

> *Chitra indica* seems very much a fish eater. We have a juvenile at the Crocodile Bank who keeps himself buried in sand most of the time. Just the tip of his snout and his eyes are exposed so it is almost impossible to find him. Just as a fish passes overhead he very quietly puts out his head and gulps it. Dr. Moll once observing it said that while grabbing a particularly large fish it almost leapt out of its hiding place, throwing a fountain of sand while grabbing the fish.

Snappers, softshells, African pelomedusids such as the West African Mud Turtle (*Pelusios castaneus*), Eastern Snake-necks, and at least one of the South American species, the South American Snake-necked Turtle (*Hydromedusa tectifera*), have added a further refinement to the final strike—a gape-and-suck technique, usually referred to as *suction feeding*. In effect, they have turned their necks into vacuum cleaners. By using their neck muscles and the *hyoid apparatus* in their throats (the bony and cartilaginous structure that supports the base of the tongue) these turtles can drop the floor of their mouths and expand their necks in a sudden, rapid movement that sucks water, fish, small invertebrates, and anything else in the vicinity into their open jaws. Afterward, they close their mouths loosely and collapse their necks again, forcing out the excess water but retaining their prey.

Maximilian's Snake-necked Turtle (*Hydromedusa maximiliani*) apparently does not eat fish, but concentrates on invertebrates, including insects, that fall into the rivers where it lives; we do not know whether it uses the same technique is its relatives. Franco Leandro Souza and Augusto Shinya Abe saw crickets and cockroaches enter a river where the turtles lived to escape swarms of army ants, fleeing from one predator only to, possibly, fall into the maw of another.

An Indian Softshell (*Nillsonia gangenticus*) gapes and expands its neck, sucking in water and prey.

Suction feeding is an extreme development of the ability many aquatic turtles have to draw food into their mouths and throats, or to manipulate it within the gullet, using some degree of hydrodynamic suction. Turtles that feed on land cannot do this, usually have a comparatively weak hyoid apparatus, and are more likely to manipulate food into their gullets with their tongues. A large, muscular tongue, though, would only get in the way of a suction feeder, and turtles that feed entirely in the water tend to have small, weak tongues and large hyoids. The Loggerhead Musk Turtle (*Sternotherus minor*) is an exception. Its hyoid apparatus is comparatively poorly developed. Adults feed mostly on snails, and apparently manipulate them with large, well-developed tongues. The tongues of Common Musk Turtles, on the other hand, are small and weak. Although Common Musk Turtles have only a limited ability to suck food into their mouths, they position it, once there, using hydrodynamics alone. Turtles that feed on both land and water may have both well-developed hyoids and large, muscular tongues. The Indochinese Box Turtle (*Cuora galbinifrons*), though usually a land dweller, can feed in water. When it does, it sucks in small pieces of food, but positions larger items with its tongue as most land turtles do, using the tongue to hold them in place against its palate. Even in water, its tongue serves a purpose: when the turtle expels any water it has sucked in, the tongue blocks the food item from being tossed out with it.

Softshells (and, to some extent, the Common Snapping Turtle) aside, the Chicken Turtle may be North America's closest ecological approach to the snake-necked suction feeders of the Southern Hemisphere. It has all the requisite anatomical features: a long neck, narrow jaws, a greatly expanded hyoid apparatus with associated neck-expanding muscles, and eyes placed relatively far forward on its head, the better to draw a binocular bead on its prey. Like Maximilian's Snake-neck, though, it does not eat fish. Instead, its diet consists almost entirely of arthropods, mostly aquatic insects and freshwa-

ter crustaceans like crayfish. Its eating habits are, in fact, most like those of Blanding's Turtle, its distant northern relative.

The most extreme suction-feeding predator is the largest chelid in South America, the Matamata (*Chelus fimbriata*). The Matamata lives in murky "black-river" waters where the visibility is very low. It has a weak bite and extremely small eyes, and apparently does not detect its prey by sight; instead, it relies on the various fringes and flaps of skin on its head. These flaps almost certainly provide the Matamata with camouflage, increasing its resemblance to a pile of dead leaves, but that is not all they do. The flaps are extensively supplied with nerve endings, sensitive to even slight movements, that apparently allow the turtle to detect vibrations in water.

While its relatives the *Hydromedusa* turtles, which live in much clearer streams, can make an extremely accurate, direct strike at a victim, the Matamata is more likely to make a blind, sidewise swipe, guided by its built-in vibration detectors and, perhaps, by sound. Its vacuuming abilities, though, more than make up for its near-blindness and relative inaccuracy. Its hyoid bones are enormous, their four branches comparable in size and shape to the bones that make up its lower jaw, and the development of its neck musculature is equally spectacular. Its greatly flattened skull allows it to make a streamlined strike with minimal water resistance. The suction force a Matamata can generate is matched only by the Indian Narrow-headed Softshell, a much larger animal.

When the Matamata detects potential prey, it slowly stretches its long neck out toward its victim, moving at less than half a centimeter (0.2 in) per second. When it is close enough, with the tip of its nose about 2 cm (0.8 in) away, it closes off its nostrils, opens its cavernous mouth (either by raising its skull or lowering its jaw, depending on how close the fish is to the bottom), shoots its head forward, and contracts its hyoid musculature, expanding its throat to four times its original volume. The result

The Matamata Turtle (*Chelus fimbriatus*) of South America is the most extreme "gape-and-suck" predator among turtles.

is a sudden rush of water that, if the turtle's positioning and timing are right, sweeps its prey into its mouth. All this takes place at lightning speed, literally too fast for the eye to follow. Patrick Lemell and his colleagues have clocked the strike, from the start of the gape to final capture, at less than a 10th of a second, with only 4 milliseconds required for the victim to disappear into the turtle's maw. It takes another few seconds for the turtle to expel the excess water and move the fish to the back of its throat to be swallowed.

The Matamata may do more than simply wait for fish to come along. Matamatas in the Bronx Zoo, New York, watched by William F. Holmstrom Jr. developed the habit of herding goldfish in their pool by walking toward them, waving one or the other of their front legs. Driving the fish into shallow water made them easier to catch. Matamatas at the Beardsley Zoological Gardens in Connecticut accomplished the same thing by advancing toward the fish with the front part of their bodies pressed against the bottom and the rear part of the shell angled upward. In the wild, Matamatas feed close to reeds and other vegetation near shore, and may herd prey toward them, though this has never been recorded. If they do, they may not be alone. Turtle enthusiast John Levell has told me that his captive Common Snapping Turtles herd fish by walking toward them with the rear ends of their shells raised, rather like the Matamatas at the Beardsley Zoo. Perhaps this sort of hunting is commoner than we thought.

Getting Along

Turtle communities can be, in some areas, surprisingly rich. Three to five species live together at many North American localities. Ten species of turtle share Round Pond, a single 30 ha (74 ac) floodplain lake in southeastern Illinois. In Australia eight species share the Daly River system in north Queensland, the richest turtle locality on the continent. Nineteen species live in the lower Ganges-Bhramaputra Basin in Asia, where the Indian and Southeast Asian faunas overlap to create the richest turtle diversity in the world, and eighteen in the Mobile Basin, Alabama, USA, the runner-up. Though the species and families involved may vary from continent to continent, freshwater turtle communities have a remarkably similar cast of characters:

- long-necked carnivore/omnivores: Common Snappers, softshells (*Apalone* spp.), Blanding's and Chicken Turtles in North America, other softshells in Africa and Asia, Eastern Snake-necked Turtles and other long-necks in Australia, and *Hydromedusa* long-necks and Matamatas in South America;

- large-headed, strong-jawed mollusk (and, in some cases, turtle) predators: Alligator Snappers, Loggerhead Musk Turtles, and megacephalic map turtles such as the female of Barbour's Map Turtle in North America, giant musk turtles (*Staurotypus* spp.) in Mexico and Central America, and the Colombian Toad-headed Sideneck (*Mesoclemmys raniceps*) in South America;

Red-eared Sliders (*Trachemys scripta elegans*) and River Cooters (*Pseudemys concinna*) can both be found at Aransas National Wildlife Refuge, Texas.

- herbivores: cooters (*Pseudemys* spp.) in North America, the Central American River Turtle in Central America, the Arrau in South America, and the Victoria River Snapper in Australia;

- agile omnivores in rapidly flowing rivers, with a preference for aquatic insects and other invertebrates: Northern Map Turtles and related species in North America, Geoffroy's Sideneck (*Phrynops geoffroanus*) in South America, and the Fitzroy River Turtle (a freshwater sponge eater) in Australia; and a whole range of opportunistic omnivores.

The parallel members of these varying casts are called *trophic equivalents*. Their similarities, for the most part, have evolved independently under selective forces that have driven evolution along parallel paths in different regions of the world. Family after turtle family has produced candidates to fill the various trophic roles. Not all the equivalencies are exact: the giant narrow-headed softshells (*Chitra* spp.) of Asia, like the Alligator Snapper, are oversized, bottom-hiding fish ambushers, but lack the snapper's lure and mollusk- and turtle-crushing equipment.

On land, American box turtles partly fill the role of smaller tortoises like the South African padlopers (*Homopus* spp.), though they are not rockpile specialists. In many of the world's forests there are small, more or less land-dwelling turtles that burrow into, and often resemble, piles of leaves on the forest floor: Wood Turtles in North America, some neotropical wood turtles (*Rhinoclemmys* spp.) in the New World tropics, the Flat-tailed Tortoise (*Pyxis planicauda*) in Madagascar, and the Spiny Turtle (*Heosemys spinosa*), Keeled Box Turtle (*Cuora mouhotii*) and Black-breasted Leaf Turtle (*Geoemyda spengleri*) in tropical Asia.

Similar species of animals that live in the same place and eat the same sorts of food normally must find some way to separate their lifestyles if they are to coexist. This division of living space and resources is called *habitat partitioning*. Sometimes this includes direct competition: larger turtles, for example, may drive smaller ones from favored basking sites. Habitat partitioning may not be absolute. Eastern Snake-necked Turtles and Eastern Short-necked Turtles (*Emydura macquarii*) prefer shallow temporary ponds and main river channels respectively in the Murray Valley of Australia, but share the same waters in urbanized and degraded sections of the upper Paramatta River in Sydney.

Luca Luiselli has proposed that competition for resources may be less important, at least for terrestrial turtles and tortoises, than for other land vertebrates. Fewer species are likely to be found together than, for example, snakes or lizards, and their population densities are often lower as well (as Luiselli notes, tortoise densities can be very high in some areas, though often when only a single species is present; the biomass of tortoises in some African game parks may exceed that of large mammals). Forest and Home's Hinge-back Tortoises coexist across a broad range in West and Central Africa despite being very similar in body size, behavior and habitat choice (Home's is more of a dietary generalist, and tends to feed more in leaf litter and rotting wood). Forest Hinge-backs are rarer than Home's in some areas (e.g., Ghana), and Home's Hinge-backs are rarer than Forest Hinge-backs in others (e.g., western Nigeria), probably because there is some competition between them—particularly in poorer forests—and because they have slight microhabitat differences, and their microhabitats are not distributed equally throughout their joint range.

Map turtles that share the same rivers may have different diets. Conversely, map turtles with similar diets may select different habitats. Northern (*Graptemys geographica*), False (*Graptemys pseudogeographica*) and Ouachita Map Turtles (*Graptemys ouachitensis*) have similar diets, at least among males. In eastern Kansas, where the three species occur together, Northern Map Turtles studied by Linda Fuselier and David Edds preferred shady

Forest Hinge-back Tortoises (*Kinixys erosa*, top) and Home's Hinge-back Tortoises
(*K. homeana*, bottom) coexist across a broad range in West and Central Africa.

streams flowing over rocks and gravel, while False and Ouachita Maps were more likely to live in wider, sunnier rivers with more basking sites. False maps were more likely to live over muddy river bottoms, while the Ouachita Map preferred sandy areas and warmer water. These differences, though, are neither exact nor universal: farther east, where the other two species do not occur, Northern Map Turtles live in the open, sunny areas.

Dietary overlap shifts with the seasons for turtles living in a sluggish stream in Belize, studied by Don Moll. During the rainy season, both White-lipped and Scorpion (*Kinosternon scorpioides*) Mud Turtles eat aquatic insects and small snails. As the dry season progresses, White-lipped Mud Turtles concentrate more on snails, while Scorpion Mud Turtles focus on insects. Why this happens we do not know. It may have something to do with an increase in density; as their rainy-season homes dry up, animals living in nearby temporary ponds migrate to the permanent stream, swelling its turtle ranks.

While the mud turtles become more selective, Mexican Giant Musk Turtles in the same permanent stream broaden their food preferences. Unfortunately for their smaller relatives, they do this by shifting from a diet of giant apple snails (*Pomacea*) to one based more on the increasing numbers of mud turtle refugees fleeing the temporary ponds.

Even within the same species, turtles of different sizes, ages, and sexes often take different foods, either because certain items are easier for a large animal to catch than for a small one, or because smaller items may not be worth a larger turtle's efforts. Male and female Common Musk Turtles may take food items in differing proportions over the course of the year, probably a reflection of differences in their reproductive cycles and activity levels. The sexes may have differing habitat preferences. In ponds in the *cerrado* of central Brazil, male Black Spiny-necked Turtles (*Acanthochelys spixii*) preferred the margins while the generally larger

females tended to stay in the pond center. Their diets were broadly similar, with dragonfly and damselfly nymphs the most important items.

Turtles, as we have seen, may change their diet, or even their habitat, as they grow. Even omnivorous turtles like the Painted Turtle tend to be more carnivorous as hatchlings. Mud and musk turtles tend to take larger prey as they themselves grow bigger. So does Krefft's River Turtle in Australia. Juvenile Indian Black Turtles (*Melanochelys trijuga*) are semiterrestrial animals of hillside streambeds, while the adults are aquatic animals that prefer slow-flowing backwaters and oxbow lakes. In southeastern Brazil, juvenile Maximilian's Snake-necked Turtles stay in shallow water near the riverbank, where they feed heavily on a tiny amphipod crustacean (*Hyalella pernix*). As they grow, the turtles shift to faster and deeper water, and gradually switch to larger prey, including mayfly larvae.

Mature females of the Chinese Stripe-necked Turtle (*Mauremys sinensis*), like the females of many other geoemydid and emydid turtles, are larger than the males (with an average carapace length of 16 cm [6.3 in] as opposed to 12.6 cm [5 in]). In northern Taiwan, adult females tend to be herbivores, feeding chiefly on Marsh Dewflower (*Murdannia keisak*). Males, though, are primarily carnivorous, eating mostly the larvae and pupae of simuliid flies. So are young females; but, unlike the males, they shift to vegetarianism as they grow.

The males of all three American softshells (*Apalone* spp.) are little more than half the size of the females. Smooth Softshell preferences are the reverse of the Stripe-necked Turtle: in Kansas, females concentrated on aquatic insect larvae while males ate large amounts of such things as mulberries and cottonwood seeds. Smooth and Spiny Softshells share the Middle Mississippi River, where Smooth Softshells are commonest in deep, strong-flowing river channels and Spiny Softshells in slower-flowing tributaries and side channels with limited flow.

Some turtles show little difference between the sexes in size, habitat or diet. Luca Luiselli found no such differences in the West African Mud Terrapin in southeastern Nigeria. Augusto Fachin Teran and his colleagues, in a study of five species of turtles in the Guapore river system in Rondonia, Brazil, found differences between the foods eaten by male and female Yellow-spotted River Turtles, but none between the sexes of Geoffroy's Sideneck.

Turtles may not need to divide up resources if there is enough to go around. In northern Florida, omnivorous Yellow-bellied Sliders (*Trachemys scripta scripta*) and herbivorous Coastal Plain Cooters are unlikely to compete unless animal food becomes scarce enough to force the sliders into a vegetarian diet. Food resources in Florida, however, are often abundant, and in constant, year-round supply. Three quite similar turtles, the Suwanee Cooter (*Pseudemys concinna suwanniensis*), the Peninsula Cooter (*Pseudemys peninsularis*) and the Florida Red-bellied Turtle, may live comfortably together in the same Florida ponds, although all three are herbivores, eating plants like Eelgrass (*Vallisneria americana*) and Coontail (*Ceratophyllum demersum*). Karen Bjorndal, Alan Bolten and their colleagues found the level of overlap in their diet to be very high: from 56 percent between the two cooters to as high as 94 percent between the Coastal Plain Cooter and the Florida Red-bellied Turtle. They differ in nesting habits, but with respect to diet the three have found, in one of the most turtle-rich areas of the world, a chelonian Eden.

Enemies

Human beings are certainly the greatest devourers of adult turtles on the planet today, but they are not the only enemies turtles have. Alligator Snappers and Mexican Giant Musk Turtles are major predators on some of the smaller mud and musk turtles. The Alligator Snapper poses such a serious threat to other turtles that several have evolved special means of keeping out of its way. Loggerhead Musk Turtles can detect, and avoid, an Alligator Snapper in murky river waters using chemical cues alone. Even large frogs will eat baby turtles: one radio-tagged Spotted Turtle hatchling was relocated in the stomach of a Green Frog (*Rana clamitans*).

Crocodilians are serious predators of even the largest freshwater turtles. Pan Hinged Terrapins (*Pelusios subniger*) fall prey to Nile Crocodiles (*Crocoodylus niloticus*), and usually live in ponds where no crocodiles can be found. Alligators (*Alligator mississippiensis*) take a number of different species of turtles in the southeastern United States. It has been suggested that the relatively high-domed, thick shells of some populations of River Cooter may have evolved to withstand the force of an alligator's jaws. There is no proof of this, however, and Western Pond Turtle populations (*Actinemys marmorata*) show similar differences though there are no alligators in their range. Variations in cooter shell shape are more likely to be hydrodynamic responses to the flow speeds of various river and lake systems.

Meso-American Sliders (*Trachemys venusta*) in Guatemala may fall prey to Morelet's Crocodile (*Crocodylus moreletii*). Mugger Crocodiles (*Crocodylus palustris*) have been seen eating Indian Softshell Turtles (*Nilssonia gangenticus*) in Chitwan National Park, Nepal. The largest of the crocodiles, the Saltwater or Estuarine Crocodile (*Crocodylus porosus*) of Australasia, will even attack adults of the enormous Asian and New Guinea giant softshells (*Pelochelys* spp.); a crocodile captured by villagers in New Guinea in 1981 had an adult *Pelochelys* in its stomach.

Otters prey on turtles in a number of parts of the world. In Africa, otters will take Zambezi Flapshells, though turtles do not bulk large in their diet. In southern Brazil, a Giant Otter (*Pteronura brasiliensis*) has been seen eating a South American Snake-necked Turtle. Neotropical Otters (*Lontra*

An American Alligator (*Alligator mississippiensis*) makes a meal of a Red-eared Slider (*Trachemys scripta elegans*).

longicaudis) are apparently among the few animals other than humans that regularly eat the Central American River Turtle. Otters are now so rare in its range that they may be more endangered than the turtle. Juvenile Alligator Snapping Turtle carcasses have been found showing traces of predation by Northern River Otters (*Lontra canadensis*). If otters were indeed responsible, that makes them the only animal known to feed on young Alligator Snappers—with the exception of adult Alligator Snappers.

In North America, birds and mammals, from Bald Eagles (*Haliaeetus leucocephalus*) to Black Bears (*Ursus americanus*), will take adults of smaller turtles like the Spotted Turtle. Pumas (*Puma concolor*) prey on Morafka's Desert Tortoises (*Gopherus morafkai*) in the Sonoran desert, and a puma kitten has been seen attacking, and partly devouring, a Texas Tortoise (*Gopherus berlandieri*) in southern

Texas. The most thoroughgoing predator American turtles face, though, is probably the Northern Raccoon (*Procyon lotor*). Besides being adept nest robbers and hunters of juvenile turtles, raccoons will kill and eat adult Spotted, Bog, and Wood Turtles, attack nesting Diamondback Terrapins, and are the number one predator on all life stages of Painted Turtles. Raccoons are adept at digging hatchling Gopher Tortoises out of their burrows, and their depredations can devastate local tortoise populations. The impact raccoons have on turtles in general is probably greater now than it used to be because raccoons themselves have benefited from human activities, and have become much more numerous and widespread.

Smaller tortoises in Africa and Eurasia face predators including jackals, mongooses, monitor lizards, and birds ranging from crows and ravens to eagles and the unique African Secretary Bird (*Sagittarius*

A Jaguar (*Panthera onca*) devours a Red-footed Tortoise (*Chelonoidis carbonaria*) in French Guiana.

serpentarius). Even Ostriches (*Struthio camelus*) have been known to attack Tent Tortoises. Carcasses of Speke's Hinge-back Tortoise (*Kinixys spekii*) in the Sengwa Reserve, Zimbabwe, showed signs of attack by Southern Ground Hornbills (*Bucorvus cafer*). The birds use their bills to hammer through the shell. A ground hornbill has been filmed attacking a Leopard Tortoise in much the same way. Crows and birds of prey break open small tortoises such as the Karoo Padloper (*Homopus boulengeri*) by dropping them on rocks. Legend has it that the ancient Greek dramatist Aeschylus was killed by an eagle that mistook his bald pate for a rock and dropped a tortoise on it.

Turtles, like other animals, attract their share of parasites, both internal (including a variety of worms) and external. The African Tortoise Tick (*Amblyomma marmoreum*) has been accidentally introduced to North America, presumably on tortoises intended for the pet trade. A Madagascar species, *Amblyomma cha-*baudi, entered the United States attached to imported Spider Tortoises (*Pyxis arachnoides*). Invasions like these are a serious matter, as some *Amblyomma* ticks carry human diseases.

In Southeast Asia, *Amblyomma geoemydae* is a turtle specialist. It is most likely to be found attached Asian Brown Tortoises (*Manouria emys*) or to land-living geoemydids like the Spiny Turtle. *Amblyomma geochelone*, known only from the Ploughshare Tortoise of Madagascar (*Astrochelys yniphora*), is probably as endangered as its host.

Freshwater turtles are often heavily infested with leeches, particularly species like Common Snapping Turtles that walk along the bottom where leeches tend to live. Loggerhead Sea Turtles may carry the Marine Turtle Leech (*Ozobranchus margoi*). Wood Turtles and Northern Map Turtles may carry their leeches through the winter. More than half of the Wood Turtles in a West Virginia study

A Common Snapping Turtle (*Chelydra serpentina*) responds to a threat by opening its mouth widely and hissing.

carried leeches of the species *Placobdella parasitica*, usually attached along the front edge of the plastron or the base of the tail near the cloaca.

One of the functions of basking may be to help turtles rid themselves of leeches; however, leeches can survive considerable drying. They have been found on turtles that had been out of the water for four days, so basking may not be a very effective way of getting rid of them. Some turtles look to other animals for help: Common Grackles (*Quiscalus quiscula*) will pick leeches off several species of basking map turtles, and Blacknose Dace (*Rhinichthys atratulus*), a species of minnow, have been seen apparently cleaning leeches from Wood Turtles. Snapping turtles have been found buried in mounds of Carpenter Ants (*Formica obscuriventris*); we do not know if the ants cleaned the turtles of leeches, but one turtle found by Vincent Burke and his colleagues in an ant mound on the George Reserve in Michigan was the only female, of 39 examined in the area, to be free of them. Dean McCurdy and Thomas Herman recorded Wood Turtles in Nova Scotia visiting ant mounds. Whether this was helping them get rid of leeches the investigators could not tell.

Turtles have a number of ways of defending themselves against predators. The most obvious is escape: either getting out of the predator's way in a hurry, or avoiding being noticed in the first place. Though freshwater turtles usually slip into the water if startled, some, including Sonoran Mud Turtles, are more likely to seek refuge on dry land. Possibly it is easier for predators to catch the mud turtles in the shallow temporary ponds where they live than in their terrestrial hiding places. If an Ornate Box Turtle sees a predator, its first reaction is to freeze; only if the predator approaches will it either scuttle away (which it can do surprisingly quickly) or seal itself in its shell. The ability of turtles to sense low-level vibrations can give them advance warning of an enemy approach, and an ample opportunity to flee or hide—anyone who has ever tried to get close to basking turtles will know how difficult it can be to catch them unawares, though unfortunately turtles seem far less aware of passing vehicles. Many turtles can be remarkably cryptic, especially when they are inactive, even if they are not buried beneath mud or leaf litter. The smaller tortoise species, in particular, can be extremely difficult to find.

If withdrawing into their shells is not enough to discourage attackers, many turtles will bite or discharge the contents of the cloaca. Common Snapping Turtles, musk turtles (Kinosternidae), Helmeted Terrapins, the South American Gibba Turtle (*Mesoclemmys gibbus*), and others can release foul-smelling chemicals from their musk glands.

Some turtles have distinct threat displays, including the gaping threats of giant and Narrow-bridged Musk Turtles (see page 29, Chapter 1). If you corner a Common Snapping Turtle on land, it will raise the posterior part of its body as it opens its mouth and hisses at you; if you move, the turtle spins around, sometimes using the tail to help pivot, to keep its head facing its attacker. At closer range, it will strike, and if its bite connects will hang on doggedly. Bell's Hinged Tortoise (*Kinixys belliana*) has a less aggressive technique; if threatened, it may play dead.

Despite the range of predators they face, many turtles, particularly the larger species, may be relatively immune to predation once they reach adulthood. Even in predator-rich Africa, a full-grown Leopard Tortoise may have little to fear. The problem is to reach adulthood in the first place. Nests, eggs, and hatchling turtles are vulnerable to a far greater range of predators than are adults (see page 260, Chapter 7).

A Place in the System

In the Galápagos Islands, a giant tortoise may carry a tiny, brilliantly colored passenger. The Vermilion Flycatcher (*Pyrocephalus rubinus*) uses the tortoise's carapace as a mobile perch, and the tortoise itself as a beater. As the tortoise plods through the underbrush, it startles insects into the air, where the flycatcher, sallying from its perch, snatches them up.

On Frigate Island in the granitic Seychelles, introduced Aldabra Giant Tortoises perform the same function for one of the rarest birds in the world, the Seychelles Magpie Robin (*Copsychus seychellarum*). Elsewhere, the interactions between turtles and the other animals and plants in their ecosystems may be equally close, even more crucial, and far more subtle.

In Bangladesh, the Indian Roofed Turtle (*Pangshura tecta*) feeds on introduced plant pests like water hyacinth, scavenges dead animals, and sometimes devours human waste. In doing so, it helps to reduce environmental pollution, and may slow the spread of infectious human diseases. Juvenile sliders can eat 500 mosquito larvae per day. In the early 1990s, after all other attempts had failed to control mosquitoes breeding in domestic water-storage tanks, a dengue control project in Honduras tried adding young sliders (presumably Meso-American Sliders). Local families were delighted with their new pets, and in two years not a single mosquito was seen emerging from a tank with a turtle in it.

The composition of oak forests in the flood plains of the lower Mississippi may depend, surprisingly enough, on Alligator Snapping Turtles. The turtles eat a wide range of seeds, from acorns to

On Santa Cruz in the Galápagos, a Vermilion Flycatcher (*Pyrocephalus rubinus*) hitches a ride on the back of a Giant Tortoise.

pecans. The trees that bear them depend on the river to carry their seeds downstream, but they may need the turtles if their seeds are to go upstream as well.

Kevin Sloan, Kurt Buhlmann, and Jeffrey Lovich concluded, after a study of the stomach contents of Alligator Snappers caught by commercial fishermen, that "little attention has been focused on the overall role of the species as a scavenger, predator, and possible plant disperser. Our data suggest that [*Macrochelys*] has an important function in the trophic structure and dispersal mechanisms of riparian systems."

Painted Terrapins in Malaysia have been tracked swimming upstream, and seeds of crabapple man-

grove (*Sonneratia*) and madang (Family Lauraceae) from terrapin droppings germinate well. Though tidal movements may carry seeds some distance upstream in low-lying rivers, the terrapins may be important in dispersing them farther, past the point of tidal influence.

In South America, the herbivorous Arrau may be an important agent for dispersing the seeds of rainforest plants. Other turtles may be seed dispersal agents, too; such a role has been suggested for Victoria River Snappers, Big-headed Amazon River Turtles, Mexican Giant Musk Turtles, Eastern Box Turtles (which may also be important dispersers of fungal spores), Black and Brown Wood Turtles (*Rhinoclemmys funerea* and *R. annulata*), and a number of tortoises. Some turtles can carry seeds in their guts for 2 days or more (up to 19 to 20 days for Eastern Box Turtles and Chaco Tortoises [*Chelonoidis petersi*]) before defecating them, unharmed or even with an enhanced ability to germinate. That is enough time for all but the most sedentary to carry them some distance from the parent plant. Painted Turtles may help to distribute Yellow Pond-Lilies (*Nuphar americanum*), and European Pond Turtles may carry the seeds of Water Lilies (*Nymphaea alba*) hundreds of meters before depositing them. Red-footed and Yellow-footed Tortoises may spend days in gaps in the forest, hiding in piles of debris. Seeds they defecate there may have a distinct growth advantage. Even swallowing the seeds may not be necessary for a turtle to be a dispersal agent. Eastern Snake-necked Turtles have been found with the seeds of 10 species of water plants embedded in the algae growing on their carapaces.

Galápagos Giant Tortoises influence the growth and distribution of *Opuntia* cactuses by trampling and disturbing the soil, clearing away plants that might compete for space, and distributing their seeds. As the Gopher Tortoise grazes, it affects the distribution of plants in its pineland ecosystem, and its droppings may help disperse the seeds of understory plants. But it is in its role as a burrower that the Gopher Tortoise may have the greatest impact on its community.

More than 360 animal species, both vertebrate and invertebrate, may make use of Gopher Tortoise burrows. The Florida Mouse (*Podomys floridanus*), an increasingly rare species restricted to the longleaf pine woodlands favored by the tortoise, is particularly dependent on them. The mice build their dens in little side tunnels off the main burrow. They may fall prey there to another declining species, the Eastern Indigo Snake (*Drymarchon corais couperi*). The snake, though, is more likely to prey upon frogs and other snakes—perhaps including yet another threatened animal, the Gopher Frog (*Rana capito*), that finds refuge in the cool, moist tortoise burrows. In the heat of the Mojave Desert, burrows of Agassiz's Desert Tortoise provide a similar refuge for Horned Larks (*Eremophila alpestris*).

An active tortoise burrow is the basis for a whole community of animals, partly because tortoises keep active burrows open and accessible. Probably more important, though, is their habit of defecating in their burrows to recycle their gut microflora. For other burrow animals, tortoise feces form the basis of a food web. An active burrow hosts a constant supply of insects that eat the feces. The insects are food for frogs, lizards, and mice that are preyed on, in their turn, by snakes, Spotted Skunks (*Spilogale putorius*), and Long-tailed Weasels (*Mustela frenata*).

We are only beginning to understand how ecologically vital turtles are, or were. The extinction of the once-abundant tortoises (*Cylindraspis* spp.) of the Mascarene Islands has apparently had a knock-on effect on the islands' ecosystems. Many Mascarene plants, including native grasses, appear to have adapted to being grazed or browsed by tortoises. With the tortoises gone, invasive grasses that do not tolerate being grazed have invaded the few remaining grasslands, crowding out the native species. Tortoises were almost certainly important seed dispersers, too, and many native Mascarene plants regenerate very poorly in their absence.

In 2007, Christine Griffiths, working with the Mauritian Wildlife Foundation and the government of Mauritius (the main island in the Mascarenes), introduced 12 young Aldabran Giant Tortoises and 12 adult Radiated Tortoises to nearby Round Island, where invasive weeds threaten the native plant communities. Further introductions followed, bringing the number of Aldabran tortoises to 104 by April 2011. The hope is the tortoises will fill in for their extinct cousins, disperse seeds, and keep down the exotic weeds. On another small Mascarene island, Ile aux Aigrettes, Aldabran Giant Tortoises introduced through a program that began in 2000

are already acting as successful seed dispersers for the Critically Endangered native ebony *Diospyros egrettarum*. The tortoises eat the ebony fruits and disperse their seeds, and the seeds' passage through the turtles' guts improves their germination. New plants are now sprouting all over the island. A number of scientists are now proposing that large tortoises should be "rewilded"—returned, or introduced, to many areas where they or other large tortoises once lived (see page 169, Chapter 4)—as a way to restore the balance of ecosystems that have become dysfunctional in their absence.

OPPOSITE

More than 360 species of animals make use of the burrows of the Gopher Tortoise (*Gopherus polyphemus*).

This Radiated Tortoise (*Astrochelys radiata*) is one of those released on Round Island, Mauritus, to keep down exotic weeds.

CHAPTER SEVEN

'Twixt Plated Decks

The turtle lives 'twixt plated decks
Which practically conceal its sex.
I think it clever of the turtle
In such a fix to be so fertile.
—Ogden Nash, The Turtle

The ultimate goal of any living creature is to reproduce its kind. Turtles have extracted themselves from Ogden Nash's "fix" not by cleverness, but through a range of life history strategies. These strategies raise the chances that turtles will not only mate, but produce young that will survive to reproduce in their turn.

No turtle gives birth to living young. Males have nothing to do with the reproductive process after they have finished mating except in the Asian Brown Tortoise (*Manouria emys*), which guards its nest mound. Most females pay not the slightest attention to their eggs or young after laying, though C.M. Gienger and C. Richard Tracy have observed Agassiz's Desert Tortoises (*Gopherus agassizi*) near Lake Mead, Nevada, chasing Gila Monsters (*Heloderma suspectum*) out of their nesting burrows (which the lizards sometimes share despite being major egg predators) or blocking their entry with their bodies (not always successfully). There is an old report of a captive Inaguan Turtle (*Trachemys stejnegeri malonei*) that supposedly helped release her newly hatched young by digging away the hard soil over her nest. Otherwise, everything that a turtle contributes to help her offspring survive she must provide before her eggs begin to incubate—with a single remarkable exception.

OPPOSITE

The ultimate product of turtle reproduction: a Hermann's Tortoise (*Testudo hermanni*) struggles out of its shell.

Camila Ferrara and Richard Vogt have recently discovered that Arrau (*Podocnemis expansa*) hatchlings call as they emerge from their nests. They believe that they use these calls to synchronize hatching, digging their way out of the sand and emerging from the nests, and, amazingly, to exchange low-frequency calls with adults waiting for them in the river. The hatchlings join the migrating adults, who lead them to feeding grounds in the flooded forest. Nothing remotely like this is known from any other turtle, including other species of *Podocnemis*.

Animals that lack parental care must compensate for its absence. Their eggs must be well suited to survive their incubation period unaided. They may construct carefully concealed and optimally situated nests, hidden from predators and parasites and placed to provide the best available environment for embryological development (though a good number of rainforest turtles simply deposit their eggs on the ground). To increase the likelihood that at least some young may survive and reproduce, they may lay a large number of eggs over their reproductive lifetimes. Turtles, to greater or lesser degrees, have done all of these; indeed, sea turtles (see page 306, Chapter 8) lay the largest clutches of eggs of any reptile.

Cycles and Seasons

The reproductive life of land and freshwater turtles is governed by the seasons, whether they are the four seasons of the temperate zone or the wet and dry seasons of the tropics. Males and females go through annual cycles of sperm and egg production that do not necessarily peak at the same time. In temperate-zone turtles, males produce sperm over the summer that they will need for mating the following spring. Male Spotted Turtles (*Clemmys guttata*) in southeastern Pennsylvania produce most of their sperm in June and July, concluding in August; their peak mating season is from March through May. This pattern may ensure that the male has viable sperm available when the female ovulates. Most female turtles ovulate in spring, so sperm formation ought, ideally, to take place during the winter; however, the cold prevents this from happening, so males must have their sperm supply ready by the end of the previous fall. They store the sperm in their genital tract until they need it. Painted Turtles (*Chrysemys picta*) produce sperm over the summer, but males carry viable sperm in the epididymis throughout the year.

Female turtles, too, may store sperm, in tubules in their oviducts. Desert and Gopher (*Gopherus polyphemus*) tortoises do most of their mating in the fall when male sperm production is at its peak, but the females store sperm, and delay laying their eggs, until they emerge from their burrows the following spring. Sperm storage lets the female time fertilization and egg-laying so that her hatchlings develop and emerge under the best possible conditions. It also allows her to lay multiple clutches of eggs from a single mating—a useful insurance strategy for many turtles. Female Chinese Softshells (*Pelodiscus sinensis*) can store viable sperm in their oviducts for almost a year, and Painted Turtles for three years. Eastern Box Turtles (*Terrapene carolina*) and Diamondback Terrapins (*Malaclemys terrapin*) have produced fertile eggs four years after their last mating. Captive female Indian Softshell Turtles (*Aspideretes gangenticus*) studied by Nikhil Whitaker laid fully viable eggs fertilized by sperm they had stored in their reproductive tracts for 15 years.

Sperm storage allows a female to collect sperm from several males, and lay clutches of eggs sired by more than one father. Though multiple paternity increases a male's chances of mating, its benefits, and possible costs, to females are not fully understood. Turtle promiscuity has nonetheless been found in podocnemidids, snapping turtles, sea turtles including the Leatherback (*Dermochelys coriacea*), emydid pond turtles and tortoises, including Gopher and Spur-thighed Tortoises (*Testudo graeca*). In one population of Blanding's Turtles (*Emydoidea blandingii*)

Where baby tortoises come from: a mating pair of Marginated Tortoises (*Testudo marginata*).

81 percent of broods were fathered by two or more males, though multiple paternity seems to be rare in the closely related European Pond Turtle (*Emys orbicularis*). Cleiton Fantin and his colleagues found evidence of multiple fathers in six of six Yellow-spotted River Turtle nests (*Podocnemis unifilis*) and in five of six Red-headed Amazon River Turtle nests (*Podocnemis erythrocephala*). Almost all the clutches of Arrau studied on the Rio Caquetá in Colombia were fathered by more than one male, though monogamous matings seem to be the rule among Arrau on the Orinoco in Venezuela where only 10.3 to 25.8 percent of nests showed evidence of multiple paternity.

In North America, most temperate-zone turtles lay their eggs in the spring. In Florida, Striped Mud Turtles (*Kinosternon baurii*) reach their nesting peak, unusually, from September to November, but may nest in any month of the year. Gopher Tortoises in southeastern Florida (though not farther north, e.g. in the Florida panhandle) nest throughout the year. Chicken Turtles (*Deirochelys reticularia*) in South Carolina also nest in the fall, from August to November, but females attempting to nest late in the season may be caught by falling temperatures and have to abandon the attempt. Chicken Turtles can retain fully formed, shelled eggs in their oviducts for up to eight months. A female can wait for a warm spell and try again, leading to a second round of nesting that peaks from mid-February to March. In Mexico, the nesting of the Mexican Mud Turtle (*Kinosternon integrum*) and the Mexican Rough-footed Mud Turtle (*Kinosternon hirtipes*)

Santa Cruz Giant Tortoises (*Chelonoidis porteri*) mate in the El Chato Tortoise Reserve, Santa Cruz, Galápagos.

may be timed so the hatchlings emerge during the summer rainy season.

The mating season of Galápagos tortoises (*Chelenoidis* spp.) may happen at any time, but peaks from January to June, the hottest time of the year. Nesting begins in May and ends in October, when temperatures are cooler; the young emerge between November and April, once again during the rainy season.

In Southern Africa, most temperate-zone terrapins and tortoises tend to nest in the southern spring, but Angulate Tortoises (*Chersina angulata*) can lay eggs at almost any time of year except midsummer (January). Though the Angulate Tortoise's nesting pattern is more like that of a tropical turtle—the Leopard Tortoise (*Stigmochelys pardalis*) can also lay eggs all year—it may be an advantage even in the Cape region to be able to nest whenever conditions are favorable. Farther north, turtle nesting usually starts, or peaks, in summer after the first rains. In tropical Asia, the Indian Roofed Turtle (*Pangshura tecta*) has two distinct nesting periods: one from the beginning of December to the middle of January, and another from mid-February to the end of March. Painted Terrapins (*Batagur borneensis*) nest from June to August on the east coast of Peninsular

Malaysia, and from October to January on the west coast; the difference may reflect rainfall patterns.

Most chelid turtles in Australia lay their eggs in spring, or late in the dry season in the tropical north. In the southwest, the Western Swamp Turtle (*Pseudemydura umbrina*) nests before the summer drought. Broad-shelled Turtles (*Chelodina expansa*) lay their eggs in late fall, with hatching following about a year later. This timing corresponds to the dry-season nesting of tropical Australian turtles. Perhaps the Broad-shelled Turtle is a recent arrival in temperate Australia, its reproductive cycle still tuned to the tropics.

The nesting of Amazonian river turtles may be governed by cycles of flooding. Six-Tubercled Amazon River Turtles (*Podocnemis sextuberculata*) probably start nesting as soon as the water levels fall enough to expose the highest beaches, while the Arrau, which needs vast expanses of beach for its communal nesting grounds, waits until the river reaches its lowest ebb. The Yellow-spotted River Turtle, a solitary nester, breeds on river banks and lake shores before the start of the flood season. In Malaysia, another large riverine turtle that lays its eggs on sand islands and sandbars, the Southern River Terrapin (*Batagur affinis*), also times its nesting to begin as the storms and floods of the northeast monsoons abate and water levels fall. So does the Pig-nose Turtle (*Carettochelys insculpta*), which nests late in the Australian dry season, when low water exposes the river sandbanks.

We are still not certain for more than a few species what environmental cue sets turtle reproductive, and hormonal, cycles in motion. Temperature appears to be a key factor. In some turtles, possibly including the Angulate Tortoise, changes in day length trigger various points in the reproductive cycle. Such changes appear to be major cues for female Painted Turtles and male Common Sliders (*Trachemys scripta*). Blanding's Turtles begin nesting earlier in years with more warm days in early spring; in this case, temperature is apparently more impor-

tant than day length. Common Snapping Turtles (*Chelydra serpentina*) and female Common Musk Turtles (*Sternotherus odoratus*) begin their reproductive cycles in spring as water temperatures rise. They do not seem to be affected by the lengthening days, but decreasing day length is an important trigger for sexual activity in the male Common Musk Turtle.

Courtship

The first step in turtle mating is for the males and females to find one another, or, more specifically, for the males to find the females, as that appears to be the way these things usually happen. Turtles that hibernate in groups, like some Spotted Turtles, may already be in each other's company when spring comes (see page 224, Chapter 6). Most turtles appear to find each other by sight, though female tortoises, musk turtles, and pleurodires release scents that may attract males. Male Common Musk Turtles show a definite preference for the odor of females (see page 36, Chapter 1).

Before a male succeeds in impregnating a female, he may need to deal with his rivals. As many as six male Loggerhead Musk Turtles (*Sternotherus minor*) may attempt to mate with a single female, pushing each other aside in a struggle to mount her. Male Common and Alligator Snapping Turtles (*Macrochelys temmincki*) may behave aggressively toward other males when a female is present. Male Geoffroy's Turtles (*Phrynops geoffroanus*) have been seen attacking other males that tried to horn in during mating; the victims did not fight back, suggesting that these turtles have a dominance hierarchy, with the attacking turtle being higher in the pecking order. Wood Turtles (*Glyptemys insculpta*) also appear to have dominance relationships; one male was seen to open his mouth and pursue another that moved away without contesting the issue.

In Common Padlopers (*Homopus areolatus*), battles between males, and the pursuit of females, can result in bleeding wounds. Males watched in

Two male Hermann's Tortoises (*Testudo hermanni*) battle for the right to court a female.

captivity used their powerful beaks to bite and hold onto the front edge of each other's carapace, and engaged in pushing matches that could go on for an hour. Even after one of the tortoises surrendered and beat a retreat, the victor usually pursued him, biting at his hind legs and shell until his victim could retreat to safety. Jack Hailman and Rosemary Knapp watched an intermittent half-hour battle between two male Gopher Tortoises that involved shoving, attempting to overturn each other with the gular extensions of their plastra, and kicking sand in each other's faces with their hind feet. At times, tortoises seem remarkably human.

An Angonoka or Ploughshare Tortoise (*Astrochelys yniphora*) apparently needs to engage a rival male as a stimulus to mating. The inimitable

Gerald Durrell, in *The Aye-Aye and I*, described the joust that ensues as the males deploy their immense ploughshares (*ampondo* in Malagasy):

The two males, rotund as Tweedledum and Tweedledee dressed for battle, approach each other at what, for a tortoise, is a smart trot. The shells clash together and then the Ploughshare's *ampondo* comes into use. Each male struggles to get this projection beneath his opponent and overturn him to win a victory in this bloodless duel. They stagger to and fro like scaly Sumo wrestlers, the dust kicked into little clouds around them, while the subject of their adoration gazes at their passionate endeavors, showing about as much excitement and enthusiasm as a plum pudding. Finally one or other of the suitors gets his weapon in the right position and skidding along and heaving madly he at last overturns his opponent. Then, he turns and lumbers over to gain his just reward from the female, while the vanquished tortoise, with much leg-waving and effort, rights himself and wanders dispiritedly away.

Competition among males may have affected the evolution of turtle growth. Many freshwater turtle females are larger than males, but in species in which males fight over prospective mates, the males may be the larger sex. The Mary River Turtle (*Elusor macrurus*) is one of only two Australian chelids in which the males are larger than the females, and is the only one in which the males have been seen to fight.

Struggles for dominance may have driven the evolution of shell shape in the saddle-backed species of the Galápagos tortoise complex. Though the peculiar raised front of a saddleback's carapace may have originally evolved to assist in high browsing, it soon provided opportunities for dominance contests among rival males, determined by which male could reach the highest. Once such contests developed, they might have driven, in part, more and more extreme saddleback modifications, permitting an even higher reach, and with it greater social, and sexual, success.

After the prospective partners come within range of each other, and after (or while) any rivals have been dealt with, the next step is courtship. As in humans,

The beginning of courtship: a male Purvis's Turtle (*Elseya purvisi*) sniffs at the female's cloaca.

turtle courtship is not a calm or reasoned process. Captive male Namaqualand Speckled Padlopers (*Homopus signatus signatus*) pursued females constantly until, according to Nicolas Bayoff, both sexes seemingly became so stressed that their feeding rates declined and they broke out in infestations of nematodes.

Tortoises are particularly aggressive fighters, and equally aggressive in pursuing their prospective mates. Convincing an unwilling female to allow them to mount can involve repeated ramming and biting. Leopard Tortoises do not so much court as batter their prospective mates into submission, barging continuously into their backs and sides. In Spur-thighed, Marginated (*Testudo marginata*) and Hermann's Tortoises (*T. hermanni*) a male's success in mounting is directly related to the number of times he rams or bites his prospective mate (plus, once he mounts, the number of calls he makes while mating). Apparently this sort of behavior signals to the female that her suitor is a healthy, high-quality male (or perhaps he simply batters her until she is too exhausted to refuse). Male Hermann's Tortoises can be, quite literally, ladykillers. According to Adrian Haley and Ronald Willemsen, "*Testudo hermanni* has a sharp spur at the tip of the tail, and courtship consists of the male mounting the female and making repeated thrusts around her tail, which may damage the female and lead to mortality from infection or maggot infestation." Perhaps as a result, male tortoises at some sites in Greece outnumber females by more than six to one.

When a male Jardine River Turtle (*Emydura subglobosa*), a chelid from New Guinea and northern Australia, spots a prospective mate, he stretches his neck to its full extent and swims after her, inspecting and sometimes touching her cloacal region. She may twitch her tail in response to his attentions. He tries to swim around in front of her, bringing them face-to-face. If she stops, or slows down, the male escalates his attentions, stroking her face with his forelimb, blinking his nictitating membranes, and bobbing his head so rapidly that even a slow-motion video camera cannot measure the rate. If all is still well, the female rises to the surface and the male follows; the couple float nose to nose, touching briefly. He backs off and blows a stream of water droplets through his nostrils into her face. He may repeat this as many as four times, sinking and resurfacing each time. What happens next, alas, we do not know, but we can assume that, at some point, at least some of the time, copulation will follow.

When a Jardine River Turtle strokes his female's face with his forelimb, or bobs his head up-and-down in front of her, he is using wooing techniques common to a wide range of turtle families. Some of his postures show up in so many different lines of turtles—including both pleurodires and cryptodires—that it seems at least possible that they go back to the earliest days of turtle evolution.

Head-bobbing is a common maneuver in tortoises, though tortoises court on land instead of in the water. A male Impressed Tortoise (*Manouria impressa*) approaches the female from the front and bobs his head up and down while simultaneously opening and closing his mouth. If the female approves, she raises her body high, making it easier for him to mount her. Sometimes, though, she lowers herself again before the male can scuttle around behind her and get into position, and her poor suitor must shift back to the front and start all over again. Unlike most tortoises, the male Impressed Tortoise (who is about the same size as his mate) does not seem to press his suit by butting or biting.

In many animals females are the arbiters of the courtship ritual. They do the selecting, while males outdo each other with brilliant colors and extravagant displays. Some turtles appear to do the same. Male Wood Turtles have "posing" displays during which the male extends his head fully, holds this position for 30 seconds to a minute, and then turns it to one side or the other, exposing the bright orange skin on his neck.

Male European Pond Turtles display themselves to females by rising to the surface of the water every three to four minutes before retreating once more to deeper waters. Scent may also play a role for some species; secretions from the chin gland of a male Texas Tortoise (*Gopherus berlandieri*) seem to stimulate both courtship and combat.

Male Northern and Southern River (*Batagur baska* and *B. affinis*) and Painted Terrapins (*B. borneoensis*), unusually in turtles, don bright colors in the breeding season. Few scientists have watched these rare turtles in the wild, but Faith Kostel-Hughes was able to observe their courtship rituals in the Bronx Zoo's Jungle World. Kostel-Hughes found that each species had special displays that seem designed to show off their particular breeding colors. A courting river terrapin faces his female, touches her nose to nose, raises his head, opens his mouth and pulsates his throat and lower jaw toward her, displaying white throat stripes that stand out sharply against the black of his head. A Painted Terrapin, on the other hand, sways his head rhythmically back and forth, showing off the brilliant red band on his crown. Males of all three species use the same displays while facing down other males; perhaps their colors are intended to intimidate as well as to attract.

In addition to displaying their bright colors, Wood Turtles pursue females aggressively and grab at their

This male Painted Terrapin (*Batagur borneoensis*) is coming into breeding color.

Male Wood Turtles (*Glyptemys insculpta*) use "posing" displays to show off the bright orange skin on their necks and forelimbs.

shells with all four feet. In many turtles, indeed—particularly in mud, musk, and snapping turtles—courtship may appear, to our eyes at least, to amount to little better than rape. Sometimes the females fight back; basking female Smooth Softshells (*Apalone mutica*) often snap at males trying to mount them, and it is not uncommon, during the spring mating season, to find a male suffering from semicircular bleeding wounds on the posterior edge of his carapace.

Some earlier authors doubted that turtles such as the Alligator Snapper courted at all, beyond males simply overpowering females by brute force.

Alligator snapper males, in fact, do court their mates, though their method of doing so may appear, to us, unsubtle. It seems to involve little more than the male pursuing the female and sniffing her, starting at her nose and working his way down, paying special attention to her bridge and cloaca. This behavior may help the male make sure he is dealing with a female. During mating itself, which lasts about six minutes, the male forces bubbles of air out his nose. Whether or not this is part of courtship it is difficult to say, but in Common Snappers both sexes gulp air and bubble it out their nostrils while facing each other.

Tactile stimulation—turtle foreplay, if you will—is apparently part of the courtship of some pleurodires, who touch each other with the sensitive barbels on their chins. Male and female Eastern Short-necked Turtles (*Emydura macquarii*) tilt their heads upward, and press their barbels together. A male Helmeted Terrapin (*Pelomedusa subrufa*) seeking to mate will pursue the female, touching her hindquarters with his snout; if she does not cooperate, he may snap at her tail and hindlimbs. If she is receptive, though, he mounts her, gripping the edges of her shell with all four feet, and rubs his chin barbels on the back of her head. As he mates, he stretches out his neck, sways his head from side to side, and expels a stream of water from his nostrils over his ladylove's face.

Face stroking is widespread in turtles, but only male American emydid turtles enhance the effect by growing elongated front claws. A male Painted Turtle uses the backs of his long, curved foreclaws to stroke the female's head and neck; if she is receptive, she responds by stroking his forelimbs with her own claws. Common Sliders, False Map Turtles (*Graptemys pseudogeographica*), and Chicken Turtles do not stroke the female, or even touch her. Instead, they vibrate their foreclaws along the side of her head. Male cooters (*Pseudemys* spp.), which sport extremely long, straight foreclaws like a handful of knitting needles, are also vibrators rather than strokers. A courting River Cooter (*Pseudemys concinna*) swims above the female, positions his foreclaws beside her face, and uses a quite uniform pattern of vibratory titillation, each burst lasting an average of 506 milliseconds. Perhaps, for the female, the sensation is somewhat akin to the pulsations of a whirlpool bath.

A basking male Florida Red-bellied Turtle (*Pseudemys nelsoni*) at Wakodahatchee Wetlands, Florida, shows the long foreclaws he uses to titillate a female.

Adult males are not the only ones to use their foreclaws in what has usually been called "titillation." Females and juveniles may titillate, too, but their behavior may have nothing to do with courtship. Brent Thomas and Robert Altig found that captive female sliders were more likely to direct their stroking activities at other females than to prospective mates. Even male titillation is not always directed at females, and older males tend to rely more on the tried-and-true techniques of biting and chasing.

Turtle fertilization, like our own, is internal. Males have a penis of spongy connective tissue. It normally lies on the floor of the cloaca, in the base of the tail, but at the right moment, it uses blood hydraulics to enlarge and grow erect, and emerges from the cloacal opening. The opening itself is conveniently located some way down the tail, so that the male has at least some flexibility as he brings it into position. Tortoise copulation can be a particularly noisy affair. A mating male may give vent to sounds ranging from the clucking noises made by the Red-footed Tortoise (*Chelonoidis carbonaria*) to what Peter Pritchard, in his *Encyclopedia of Turtles*, describes as the "deep bellowing groans which can be heard a great distance" emitted by the giants of the Galápagos.

Simply achieving the physical act is fraught with difficulty. Turtles are not built to intertwine. Males, who must mount their females, have the more difficult task. Many male turtles have concave plastra, the better to fit against the female's carapace. That is not true of the Central Asian Tortoise (*Testudo horsfieldii*), whose body shape may be constrained by the species' propensity for burrowing, but males are lighter shelled, longer legged and presumably more acrobatic than females. As the partner on top, they may need to be.

A male turtle may have to use his claws to grip the female shell if he is to stay in position, particularly if the female is larger than he is. A female Steindachner's Turtle (*Chelodina steindachneri*) often carries permanent gouges in her carapace left by the claws of her smaller mates. Many turtles make matters somewhat easier by mating in water, where at least the male does not have to contend, to the same degree, with gravity.

American box turtles, which mate on land and have particularly high, rounded shells, seem to find copulation particularly challenging. A male Eastern Box Turtle must actually lean over backwards to get himself into position. To avoid tumbling over on his back, he hooks his toes behind the rear edge of the female's plastron; she helps by clamping her plastral valve on his claws, locking him in place. Once he has anchored himself as firmly as possible, he rocks backward until his shell rests on the ground, shifts his hind feet slightly to improve his purchase, and tilts forward to the vertical before achieving insertion. This maneuver is not only tricky, but dangerous. Male box turtles sometimes fall onto their backs after copulating, and, if they cannot right themselves, may die.

Investing in Motherhood

Unlike other long-lived reptiles such as crocodiles, turtles may take many years before they are ready to begin their reproductive lives. Even without parental care, the investment reproduction requires can be costly. Painted Turtles in Michigan devote approximately 14 percent of their annual energy budget to reproduction. Mexican Rough-footed Mud Turtles may lay only 12 eggs a year, in four separate clutches, but these equal about 28.4 percent of the female's rather small body mass.

The physical, and physiological, task of developing sperm and, particularly, eggs takes up much of a turtle's energy and resources. This may explain why turtle growth rates slow drastically, or even stop, once the animals become sexually mature. The physiological cost to males, though, may be considerably less than to females, and male turtles often mature at an earlier age.

To get into mating position a male Eastern Box Turtle (*Terrapene carolina*) must lean over backwards, anchoring himself in place by hooking his toes behind the rear edge of the female's plastron.

Even after a female reaches maturity, she may not nest every year if the resources she needs are not available in sufficient quantity. Pig-nose Turtles in the Daly River of northern Australia nest twice every other year, and in alternate years do not nest at all. Eastern Box Turtles studied near Lynchburg, Virginia, may nest for several years in a row, then stop breeding for several more. In some areas Painted Turtles nest almost every year, while in others a female may take two years to build up resources for a breeding season. Blanding's Turtles in western Nebraska apparently breed every year, but only an average of 58 percent of mature female Spotted Turtles do in Georgian Bay, Ontario, and only 37 percent did so three years in a row. In nearby Algonquin Provincial Park, other northern species—Common Snappers, Painted Turtles, and Wood Turtles—are somewhat more likely to nest every year, but it is not unusual for a female, particularly a smaller animal in her early reproductive years, to take an occasional sabbatical.

The reproductive life of a female Spotted Turtle may stretch out for decades. For such a long-lived creature, the importance of any one breeding season to her lifetime production of young may be small indeed. It may be more important to survive to nest again, or, especially early in life, to invest in her own growth and future nesting abilities, than to risk everything for any one season's brood. Female Painted Turtles above 12 years of age lay larger eggs, and produce second clutches more frequently, than younger animals; younger females seem to put fewer resources into breeding than their elders. Eggs from younger females contain higher levels of testosterone, a hormone that may limit yolk formation and, thereby, reduce the resources committed to each egg.

Spur-thighed Tortoises in southwestern Spain apparently lay fewer eggs each year than they are capable of producing, especially in wet years when conditions for success may be poor. Carmen Diaz-Paniagua and her colleagues have suggested that the tortoises, by saving their greatest efforts for favorable years, are maximizing their output over the term of their long lives. An animal that faces unpredictable and difficult conditions from year to year, such as Agassiz's Desert Tortoise, may hedge her bets by holding her resources in reserve for her own needs rather than committing them to her young. This includes reabsorbing ovarian follicles that fail to ovulate and reclaiming the nutrients they contain, a process called *atresia*.

Unlike mammals such as ourselves, turtles do not have a preset maturation time. Maturity seems to have more to do with size than with age. For sea turtles, reaching sexual maturity may take many decades (see page 306, Chapter 8). Land and freshwater turtles mature more rapidly—usually in three to six years for Common Musk Turtles and Painted Turtles. How long maturation takes can vary from place to place. Female Common Snapping Turtles from Cootes Paradise in southern Ontario, Canada, grew almost four times faster, and produced clutches roughly 30 percent larger, than snappers 300 km (186 mi) farther north in Algonquin Provincial Park, near the northern limit of the species' range—even for hatchlings incubated and reared under identical conditions in the laboratory.

Even among individuals in a single population, time to maturity can range from 9 to 15 years for Yellow Mud Turtles (*Kinosternon flavescens*), from 11 to 16 years for Common Snapping Turtles, 12 to 21 years for Blanding's Turtles, and 10 to 21 years for female Gopher Tortoises. This variation probably has something to do with how fast individual turtles grow, and that, in turn, may be governed by such things as the amount and quality of food they can find and eat. In northern Australia, the carnivorous Northern Long-necked Turtle (*Chelodina rugosa*) matures relatively quickly, in less than 4 years for males and just over 6 years for females, but the Victoria River Snapper (*Elseya dentata*), a herbivore with a relatively protein-poor diet, may take more than twice as long to reach maturity.

Eggs

In general, the bigger a female turtle is the more space there is for eggs within her body, the more eggs she can lay, and the larger those eggs may be. Larger females have been documented laying larger clutches in several emydids, including Painted, Spotted and Blanding's Turtles. Colombian Sliders (*Trachemys callirostris*) increase clutch size as they grow, but only up to a point. After reaching a plastron length of 20 cm (8 in), increasing size seems to result in bigger, not more, eggs. Smaller female Agassiz's Desert Tortoises not only lay smaller clutches than larger females, but they lay them later in the spring—perhaps because they have fewer reserves in store. First, they feast on early-spring annual plants to get the nutrients they need to produce the yolks for their eggs.

The larger a mother Painted Turtle or Chicken Turtle, the more massive, roughly speaking, are her eggs and the bigger her hatchlings. The relationship, though, is not exact, and often is not true for every population or species. In other turtles, including the Florida Softshell (*Apalone ferox*), larger females do not lay bigger eggs. Though one might expect a trade-off between laying larger eggs and having more eggs per clutch, there seems to be no such general rule. Nonetheless, a Giant Asian Pond Turtle (*Heosemys grandis*) that lived for over 20 years in the Columbus Zoo in Ohio occasionally laid two clutches per year, the first with a small number of larger eggs and the second with a larger number of smaller eggs.

There may be a minimum size for the egg of even the smallest turtle, or the hatchling it produces will not survive. Small turtles, like the Bog Turtle (*Glyptemys muhlenbergii*) and some of the smaller musk turtles, lay only one, or a few, eggs. Small tortoises like the smaller padlopers (*Homopus* spp.), the Flat-tailed Tortoise (*Pyxis planicauda*), and the Pancake Tortoise (*Malacochersus tornieri*) typically lay only a single egg at a time. Malagasy Big-headed Turtles (*Erymnochelys madagascariensis*) with a carapace length of less than 32 cm (12.6 in) produce a small clutch of eggs, but once they reach 40 cm (15.7 in) or more they commonly lay more than 60 eggs a season, in up to three separate nestings.

At the other end of the scale, a captive Asian Narrow-headed Softshell (*Chitra chitra*) weighing 108 kilograms (238 lbs) laid a clutch of 107 eggs, each one 34 mm (1.3 in) across and 20 grams (0.7 oz) in weight. The turtle died soon after, and its body was found to contain a further 450 developing eggs and ovarian follicles. In the Araguaia National Park in central-eastern Brazil Yellow-spotted River Turtles deposit an average of 10 to 15 eggs per clutch, but the much larger Arrau often lays well over 100. Arrau nests containing 150 eggs have been recorded on the Orinoco.

Tortoises tend to lay fewer and larger eggs than freshwater turtles; even the giants of the Galápagos and Aldabra rarely lay more than 20 eggs to a clutch. The world's smallest tortoise, the Namaqualand Speckled Padloper, lays only one egg at a time, and larger individuals lay larger eggs. Larger Gopher Tortoises usually lay more eggs, but in Palm Beach County, Florida, the largest clutches are laid by intermediate-sized animals. Kyle Ashton and his colleagues suggested that this might be evidence of senescence; the biggest tortoises were simply showing their age.

Female size explains less than half the variation in the egg sizes and clutch sizes of Painted Turtles in Algonquin Provincial Park. Other factors, including genetic makeup and physical condition, may amount for the rest. If they are in better physical condition, Spotted Turtles may lay bigger eggs, and bigger clutches, regardless of their size. Among the geoemydids, the large river and Painted Terrapins lay clutches averaging about 20 eggs each, while the smaller Three-striped Roofed Turtle (*Batagur dhongoka*) lays from 30 to 35. Alligator Snappers grow much larger than Common Snappers, but do not lay as many more eggs as their size difference might suggest (20 to 30 per clutch is normal for the Common Snapper, 20 to 50 for the Alligator Snapper).

In Guatemala, the White-lipped Mud Turtle (*Kinosternon leucostomum*) may lay from 1 to 5 relatively large eggs in a clutch, while its larger relative and sometime predator the Mexican Giant Musk Turtle (*Staurotypus triporcatus*) lays from 4 to 18. The Scorpion Mud Turtle (*Kinosternon scorpioides*) also lays only a few eggs at a time—8 is the probable maximum—but its eggs are relatively small for its body size.

Broadly speaking, the bigger the egg, the bigger the hatchling—though within a species, many other factors, like incubation temperature and the availability of moisture, can affect development. Bigger hatchlings often (but not always) have a better chance of surviving. In a field experiment, Fredric Janzen and his colleagues found that smaller Red-eared Slider hatchlings (*Trachemys scripta elegans*) were more likely than larger ones to be killed by birds such as Red-winged Blackbirds (*Agelaius phoeniceus*) and Common Grackles (*Quiscalis quiscula*). Larger hatchlings are faster, and need spend less time crossing open country where the birds can find them.

Turtle eggs may be hard- or soft-shelled, spherical, oval or elongate. All turtle eggshells consist of a shell membrane—thick and tough in the flexible-shelled eggs of sea turtles, quite thin in hard-shelled eggs—under a layer of hard shell units made of, usually, crystals of aragonite, a form of calcium carbonate. Hard-shelled eggs are hard because their crystalline shell units are larger and are packed closely together, except for occasional pores to allow for the exchange of water and gases. Developing Common Snapping Turtles draw almost 50 percent of their calcium and 40 percent of their magnesium from the eggshell, particularly from the side and bottom (in contrast to Eastern Short-necked Turtles and Spiny Softshells [*Apalone spinifera*], which derive all their magnesium from the yolk). Drawing on these minerals has the added

advantage of thinning and weakening the side of the shell, presumably making it easier for the young turtle to break free.

Soft, leathery shells are frequent in turtles, but chelids, some pelomedusids and podocnemidids, kinosternids, softshells, the Pig-nose Turtle, the Central American River Turtle, neotropical wood turtles (*Rhinoclemmys* spp.) and many tortoises lay hard-shelled eggs. Eggs with flexible shells are more likely to take up water from their environment that hard-shelled eggs; the amount of water they absorb critically affects the size of the hatchling.

Closely related turtles can lay very different eggs. While the eggs of the Yellow-spotted River Turtle are hard-shelled and elongate, those of the Arrau are soft-shelled and spherical. Egg shape may even change as a turtle grows; though the eggs laid by larger, older Common Snapping Turtles are spherical, younger and smaller animals lay oblong eggs, possibly because the passage through the pelvic girdle is too small to pass a sphere of the appropriate size. The Texas Tortoise lays a hard-shelled spherical egg far larger than the opening between its carapace and plastron. When the female lays her eggs, the bones of her shell apparently bend out of their way, the carapace moving slightly upward as the plastron flexes downward.

Since a female turtle does not help her newly hatched offspring find food, the only way she can give them a nutritional head start is by laying a well stocked egg. The yolks of Common Snapping Turtle and Painted Turtle eggs contain more than half again as much food, in the form of stored lipids, as the embryo needs to develop, hatch, and emerge from its nest.

When turtle eggs are laid, their yolk is surrounded by a thick layer of albumin. This is the substance we call "egg white," but that name is a misnomer for turtle eggs. I remember, as a child in Jamaica, being greatly amused by the story of an acquaintance who spent about 45 minutes attempting to fry a sea turtle egg without realizing that

A Scorpion Mud Turtle (*Kinosternon scorpioides*) hatches from a hard-shelled egg (below), while a hatchling Painted Turtle (*Chrysemys picta*) breaks through its leathery shell (top).

turtle albumin, unlike that of a bird, does not coagulate. The albumin carries most of the water supply for the newly laid egg. Within the first week or two, most of that water flows inward to the yolk, through the vitelline membrane. As the embryo develops it is this expanded yolk that supplies it with both food and water.

Multiple Clutches

One of the best ways for a female to increase the selective odds in her favor is to, literally, avoid placing all her eggs in one basket. The more nesting seasons she survives, and the more clutches she can lay per season, the greater her chance of winning through against the very high levels of predation and loss her nests and hatchlings face.

Laying multiple clutches may be a particularly good strategy for turtles that live in uncertain environments. In tropical Australia, Northern Long-necked Turtles face unpredictable monsoons that may vary considerably from year to year; they lay several clutches at different times during the season, increasing the chances that at least some will emerge when the rains come again. By contrast, Victoria River Snappers, which live in permanent rivers, lay only one clutch per year, as do Common Snapping Turtles, Blanding's Turtles and the Arrau.

Other turtles may lay only two clutches. Agassiz's Desert Tortoises in the Mojave Desert of California lay one clutch in late April or early May, and, about 70 percent of the time, a second clutch in late May or early June (Morafka's Desert Tortoise [*G. morafkai*], by contrast, lays only one clutch per year, and may not nest at all in some years). The Mary River Turtle of eastern Australia nests in late October and again about a month later. Central American River Turtles may lay anywhere from one to four clutches in a season, though two or three are more likely.

Some turtles lay several clutches per season, probably using sperm they have stored up from the

spring's (or even an earlier year's) mating. Several North American turtles, including the Escambia Map Turtle (*Graptemys ernsti*), the Peninsula Cooter and the Florida Red-bellied Turtle, lay as many as six clutches a year. Florida Softshells may also lay six clutches annually (three to five is more likely), but some females appear not to nest every year. Western Pond Turtles in the Los Angeles basin may nest only every other year, but may lay double clutches in the years they do nest. Multiple clutching is not universal for all populations of sliders, nor even for all individual females within a population.

Spotted Turtles in Ontario nest only once a year, if that, but may nest two or even three times a year in South Carolina where the warm season is much longer. Laying more clutches does not seem to mean laying more eggs. Instead, southern Spotted Turtles divide their annual output into separate packages. The driving force may be predator pressure. If a female can split up her annual brood, the chance that a single predator will get them all is considerably reduced.

Eastern Box Turtles in southeastern New York lay only one clutch per year, but more southerly animals may turn out up to five. Florida Box Turtles on Egmont Key have the capacity to nest up to three times a year, but only a small percentage of the females on the island actually do so. Not every female nests every year, and not every female that does nest lays multiple clutches; perhaps it is better to lay several clutches in a good year, and none the next, rather than laying every year no matter what the conditions.

Pancake Tortoises lay only 1 egg at a time, but do so two or three times a year. Even larger tortoises, which can produce more eggs per clutch, may nest several times a year if they can. Leopard Tortoises usually lay from 10 to 12 eggs per clutch. Over the course of the nesting season, a Leopard Tortoise may lay four to five clutches, with 22 to 31 days elapsing between each nesting. Galápagos Giant Tortoises may lay five clutches a year. The earlier eggs take much longer than the later ones to hatch, allowing all the hatchlings to emerge at the best possible time, at the onset of the rainy season.

Multiple clutches may be particularly important for small turtles like the Striped Mud Turtle. A small turtle simply cannot carry within her body as many fully developed eggs at one time as a large one; mud turtle clutches normally contain only two or three eggs. The only way for a female mud turtle to increase her annual reproductive output is to lay several clutches over the course of the season. Some tropical mud turtles may lay clutches throughout the year; the Mexican Giant Musk Turtle, which is capable of producing a much larger clutch, may still nest as many as nine times a season. Though the Scorpion Mud Turtle invests less in its small eggs than its cousin the White-lipped Mud Turtle does in its larger ones, it has a long breeding season, and may nest a number of times over the course of a year. By spreading out its egg-laying efforts it increases the chance that at least one clutch will escape the attention of predators or the vagaries of the weather.

The All-Important Nest

Some turtles seemingly pay little attention to where they deposit their eggs. Neotropical wood turtles (*Rhinoclemmys* spp.) drop their enormous eggs (see page 30, Chapter 1) in crevices or among the leaf litter in the forest, as may the Gibba Turtle (*Mesoclemmys gibbus*). Narrow-bridged Musk Turtles (*Claudius angustatus*) lay their eggs among tangles of vegetation. Yellow-footed Tortoises (*Chelonoidis denticulata*) may bury their eggs: completely, cover them with a thin layer of soil or dead leaves, or simply drop them in the leaf litter on the forest floor. Kinosternids seem particularly haphazard about where they leave their eggs: Eastern Mud Turtles (*Kinosternon subrubrum*) may bury their eggs in the soil or rotting logs, hide them under boards, deposit them in beaver, muskrat or even alligator nests, or simply drop them in the leaf litter if the ground is too hard. The White-lipped Mud Turtle scrapes out a shallow depression in the ground and covers her eggs with a thin layer of leaf litter or soil. Loggerhead Musk Turtles leave their eggs in a barely concealed scratch in the ground, often against a tree stump or rock, and Yellow Mud Turtles may leave their eggs in burrows they dig in the sandy soil for their own use. Karoo (*Homopus boulengeri*) and Speckled Padlopers (*Homopus signatus*), tiny tortoises that live in stony places where digging a nest may be impossible, apparently hide their single egg under an overhanging rock.

Most turtles lay their eggs in a specially prepared nest, and have been doing so since at least the Cretaceous. A fossilized clutch found in China, containing at least 27 eggs, was apparently buried in the manner many turtles use today. In some species, the labor involved in preparing the nest seems minimal. The Impressed Tortoise apparently digs only a very shallow nest, and covers the eggs with leaves that she scrapes into place with her hind legs. A more typical nest is usually a flask-shaped chamber in the soil, excavated by the female with alternating strokes of her hind legs. The claws of female Red-eared Sliders are longer than the males', presumably because longer claws make better digging implements. The shape and depth of the nest depend on how far she can reach from the surface. Many land and freshwater turtles use their hind feet to arrange the eggs as they are laid, sometimes into two or three layers separated by thin partitions of dirt.

Some turtles, including the Alligator Snapper, dig a body pit first, clearing away vegetation and loose soil that might otherwise fall into the nest chamber. A female Eastern Mud Turtle starts excavating with her front feet, throwing the dirt aside until she is almost out of sight, before she turns around and uses her hind feet to finish digging the nest chamber.

Gopher Tortoises start their nests by swinging their bodies in a circle and scraping out a shallow bowl with their front feet. Peculiarly, these tortoises,

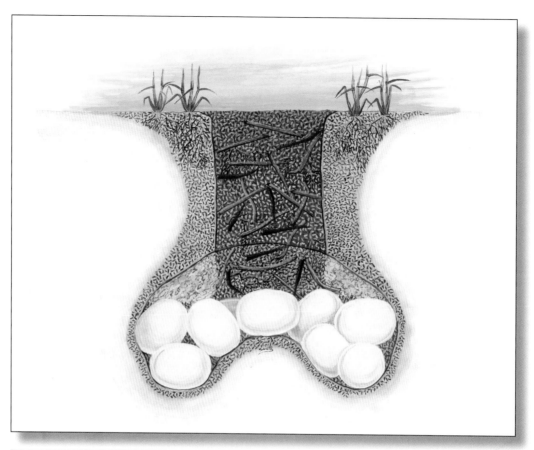

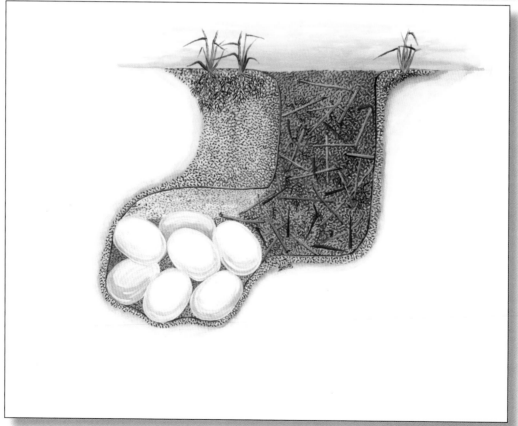

Two cross-sectional views of the nest of an Australian Broad-shelled Turtle (*Chelodina expansa*).

which have specially modified front limbs capable of digging deep and extensive burrow systems, use their hind feet to dig out the nest cavity. Digging a nest hole, though, is physically quite a different task from excavating a burrow.

Many turtles, even diurnal ones, dig their nests at night, though they sometimes start before dusk. On cloudy days, Blanding's Turtles and False Map Turtles may nest in daylight hours as well. In Guatemala, sliders will only nest on particularly dark, often moonless nights. Common Snapping Turtles lay their eggs during the day, usually in the early morning or late afternoon. In some places heavily exploited turtles like the Arrau, which normally nests in large numbers by day, have switched to nighttime nesting, presumably to avoid human hunters.

Softshells generally nest during the day, but their cousin the Pig-nose Turtle nests by night. Numbers of Pig-noses leave the water together, occasionally colliding as they scramble onto the nesting beach. They dig with their hind flippers, holding themselves up with one while the other hauls out two or three flipperfuls of sand, then switching flippers and carrying on. As soon as the chamber is completed they lay their eggs, cover the result with sand, and head back to the water. The whole process usually takes less than 30 minutes.

For some turtles, though, excavation can take a long time. The columnar hind feet of tortoises make digging especially slow. Captive Bell's Hinged Tortoises (*Kinixys belliana*) in Tanzania usually took up to six hours to dig their nests, starting just before dusk. The whole process, from digging, through laying, to covering the finished nest, can take more than 2 1/2 hours for river terrapins, and up to 8 hours for Spotted Turtles in Ontario. This last is exceptional: other turtles in the same area usually take less than 90 minutes, and even Spotted Turtles farther south in Pennsylvania took no more than 2 hours. At the western limit of their range, and in Illinois, however, Spotted Turtle females needed up to 12 hours to complete their task.

The Right Spot

Turtles may devote considerable time and effort to selecting a suitable place to nest. Spotted Turtles in Georgian Bay, Ontario, dug their nests in soil and lichen that collected in crevices in the outcrops of Precambrian stone, probably the sunniest and warmest places available so far north. Females often spent days wandering around among the rocks before digging their nest, presumably searching for just the right spot.

Mary River Turtles drift around on the surface for a week or so before coming ashore to nest, possibly deciding on the best place to emerge. An Eastern Mud Turtle may try several sites before she finds one that satisfies her. Some Blanding's Turtles on the E.S. George Reserve in Michigan start digging the evening they leave their marshes, but others may stay on land for several days first.

Diamondback Terrapins appear to select their nest sites using such physical features as the slope and height of sand dunes and the extent of plant cover, and choose their timing on the basis of the tidal phase and the weather. Black-knobbed Map Turtles (*Graptemys nigrinoda*) sniff the sand on their chosen river beach, make test scratches with their front feet or, occasionally, dig a test nest. Apparently they are gathering information that helps them find the best place to dig when they nest in earnest.

Pig-nose Turtles have been observed "sniffing" the sand before leaving the water to lay their eggs; a number of turtles, including Painted Turtles (and sea turtles), "ground-nuzzle" or "sand-smell" as they search for a site, repeatedly pressing their heads and the underside of their necks against the ground. Why they do this we are not quite sure, but they seem to be checking for cues—perhaps chemical cues—to guide them in making their decision.

A properly constructed and situated turtle nest is an incubator that must expose the eggs to the proper range of temperature and humidity. The humidity of nest soil may affect water loss from the eggs, and

A female Common Snapping Turtle (*Chelydra serpentina*) lays her clutch of eggs.

that in turn may affect the size of hatchling turtles. As for temperature, too little heat, and the eggs do not develop; too much, and the embryos die. Wood Turtles nesting on sandy beaches near Sudbury, Ontario, at the northern end of their range, chose sites where the soil tended to be warmer than expected if the turtles had been digging at random. The right spot may depend on the female's size. In the temperate zone, medium to large turtles often nest in open sunny areas, placing their eggs deep enough in the soil to avoid overheating. Striped Mud Turtles are too small to dig a deep nest, and avoid sunny nest sites in central Florida. Instead, they place their nests near clumps of grass or other vegetation. Because their eggs incubate fairly close to the surface, they apparently need the shade that the plants provide.

Colombian Sliders in the Pijiño wetland of Colombia also preferred shaded spots, often under Water Hyacinth (*Eichhornia crassipes*). Nesting in shade may not only reduce the chance of overheating but may provide some concealment from predators. On the other hand, Eastern Box Turtles in central Illinois are more likely to nest in bare ground in the open, perhaps because digging is easier or the ground warmer. The risks they face, though, are considerable. Beth Flitz and Stephen Mullin found that 87.5 percent of the nests they studied were destroyed by predators in the first 72 hours after the eggs were laid.

Tradition may be important for selecting nest sites. Texas Tortoises may use the same sites for years. Arrau on the Rio Trombetas in Brazil nested in large numbers on the same beach in 1978, 1979,

An Eastern Box Turtle (*Terrapene carolina*)
deposits an egg in her nest.

The soil or sand where a female proposes to nest must be the right consistency for digging. Gopher Tortoises may excavate their nests in the apron of sand at the mouth of their burrow. Sometimes, the best spot may be where another animal has already done some of the work. Nests of the New Guinea Giant Softshell (*Pelochelys bibroni*) have been found buried in the nest mound of a New Guinea Crocodile (*Crocodylus novaeguinae*), and Florida Red-bellied Turtles (*Pseudemys nelsoni*) may carry out their excavations in the nest of an American Alligator (*Alligator mississippiensis*). Since crocodilians, unlike turtles, guard their nests, a turtle nest in an alligator or crocodile mound may gain an extra measure of protection.

Several Australian freshwater turtles, including the Eastern Snake-necked Turtle (*Chelodina longicollis*) and Eastern Short-necked Turtle, prefer to nest after heavy rains. Rain may wash away scent trails that could attract predators. Water-soaked soil is softer, easier to dig, and less likely than dry soil to break up and fall into the nesting hole. That may also be why many turtles, including Painted Turtles whose nesting behavior appears to be cued by temperature rather than rain, void copious amounts of highly dilute urine into the nesting cavity. The water that a Painted Turtle carries in her bladder may weigh more than the eggs themselves.

Depositing water may be an essential part of the nesting process. At the E.S. George Reserve in Michigan, Owen Kinney and his colleagues found that if they interrupted a female Painted, Common Snapping, or Blanding's Turtle on her way to nest, and she urinated in response (as turtles often do when handled), on release she headed back to the water to take on another supply before setting off once more to lay her eggs. John Cann watched an Eastern Snake-necked Turtle that made several trips to a nearby lagoon, over an hour and a half, to take on water, returning each time to release it into the nest cavity.

and 1980, completely ignoring three apparently similar, and equally suitable, beaches a short distance away. Yellow-spotted River Turtles may select their nest sites by following other nesting females, rather than by responding to environmental cues on their own. Midland Painted Turtles (*Chrysemys picta marginata*) on Beaver Island, Michigan, often nest within 25 m (80 ft) of sites from previous years, suggesting a preference for familiar areas; Painted Turtles in other populations may be more random in their choices. At least some female Diamondback Terrapins favor familiar nesting sites. Most Blanding's Turtles return to nesting areas they have used before, and individual Striped Mud Turtles in Florida repeatedly returned to the same general area to nest, year after year.

Turtles may spend some time finishing off their nests. Instead of simply burying their clutches, Painted and other turtles will, if possible, work the moistened soil into a plug that seals the opening, leaving an air space between the roof of the nest and the eggs. Many turtles drag their plastra over the completed nest, smoothing the soil above it. In Galápagos Giant Tortoises this can go on for days. A female Red-bellied Turtle (*Pseudemys rubriventris*) flattens the soil over her eggs by raising herself as high as possible and dropping heavily on top of her nest. A Leopard Tortoise or Angulate Tortoise may do the same by lifting and dropping her shell repeatedly on the spot.

Some female cooters, including the Suwannee Cooter (*Pseudemys concinna suwanniensis*) and the Peninsula Cooter (*Pseudemys peninsularis*), have a unique trick to fool nest robbers. Instead of building one nest, the female digs three: a principal nest where she lays most of her eggs, and two satellite nests, one on each side, with only a few eggs in each. After she lays her eggs, the female covers the principal nest as thoroughly and carefully as possible, doing her best to obscure all traces of its existence. The satellite nests, though, she covers only haphazardly, if at all. A predator like a raccoon may have no trouble finding the satellite nests, but may miss the principal nest altogether. The satellite nests, in short, are decoys, and

Her egg-laying finished, a female Common Snapping Turtle (*Chelydra serpentina*) covers her nest.

the eggs laid in them sacrifices—but not always successful ones—to the safety of the rest of her brood.

On the Beach

Turtles have been laying eggs in the sand for a long time. A 75-million-year-old clutch, recently excavated from what was once in a sandy riverbank in Alberta, was apparently laid by *Adocus*, a Cretaceous relative of the softshells. The fossil of another *Adocus*, one that apparently died before she could nest, had eggs of the same type in her body.

Sandbars and sandy beaches are the preferred nesting places of a number of river-haunting turtles in different parts of the world, including Amazon River turtles, many softshells, river and Painted Terrapins, map turtles, and the Pig-nose Turtle. Nesting on a sandbar has its advantages: less distance to travel from the water, and, if the sandbar is on an island, possibly some protection from predators. However, open sand can get very hot and dry in the sun; it may not be a coincidence that many of the turtles that nest on it are large, and can dig relatively deep, well-insulated nests.

On sandbars in Brazil's Araguaia National Park, Arrau tend to dig their nests high on the sandbars, often over 3m (10 ft) above river level, while Yellow-spotted River Turtles nest closer to the water. Part of the difference may have to do with their eggs. Arrau lay flexible-shelled eggs that can take on, or lose, water fairly easily through their shells. Yellow-spotted River Turtles lay rigid-shelled, largely impermeable eggs. By laying higher up, the Arrau not only reduces the risk of its vulnerable eggs being flooded, but can dig a deeper nest less likely to overheat (though on some nesting beaches the egg chamber may be warmer in its depths than higher up), or dry out. The egg chambers in Arrau nests are more humid than the surrounding sand, possibly because the female expels water or mucus while laying.

A hatchling Arrau (*Podocnemis expansa*) emerges from its nesting burrow in the Trombetas region of eastern Brazil, where turtle nesting grounds are threatened by damming and bauxite mining.

Sea turtles are not the only turtles to nest on ocean beaches. In North America, Diamondback Terrapins nest on barrier beaches and dunes. In Asia, Southern River Terrapins nest en masse (or used to) on beaches on the Perak and other rivers in Malaysia, and Northern River Terrapins nest in the Irriwady River delta of Myanmar, or on islands in the Sunderbans of India and Bangladesh. Their relative, the Painted Terrapin, nests on sea beaches in West Malaysia and, on the west coast, on river sandbanks. The Asian Giant Softshell (*Pelochelys cantorii*) and the Mediterranean population of the Nile Softshell (*Trionyx triunguis*), may nest on sea beaches, and in southern New Guinea Pig-nose Turtles do the same.

Turtles that use open sand may have physiological adaptations to nesting there. Eggs of most sandbar-nesting turtles can tolerate remarkably high incubation temperatures. Smooth Softshells require relatively higher incubation temperatures than many other North American freshwater turtles—no less than 25°C (77°F), and preferably higher; 30°C (86°F) may be optimal. Even though their deep nests protect them from the intense heat of the sun, temperatures in an Arrau egg chamber may climb to over 36°C (96.8°F) for more than half of the incubation period, a temperature that kills even Smooth Softshell eggs if maintained for too long. Eggs of Diamondback Terrapins and Pig-nose Turtles can briefly tolerate temperatures of 40°C (104°F) or more.

Perhaps the most unexpected beach nesters are a population of oversized Meso-American Sliders (*Trachemys venusta*) in Tortuguero National Park on the Caribbean coast of Costa Rica, a place much more famous for its Green Sea Turtles (*Chelonia mydas*). Females emerge from the rainforest and actually swim some considerable distance along the seacoast to reach their nesting beaches. The journey is a risky one. Sliders are not particularly tolerant of salt water, and not every female survives her passage through the sea. The risk may be worth it; if the turtles traveled directly through the forest to the beach, they might be tracked, or leave a scent trail that predators could follow.

Before human beings began to demolish the rainforests, these beaches may have been the only place the sliders could go to lay their eggs in a reasonably open area exposed to the right amount of sun. The turtles do not nest entirely in the open, where temperatures of the surface of the sand may approach 73°C (163.4°F); here, it would take a much larger turtle, like a Green, to dig to a safe depth. Instead, they prefer the shade of Cocoplums (*Chrysobalanus icaco*) growing on the upper beach. The trees provide not just shade, but camouflage, both for females as they nest and for the young as they eventually emerge.

Off the Beach

How far should a freshwater turtle's nest be from the water? The answer can vary, even for species sharing the same area. In the Taim Ecological Reserve in southern Brazil, D'Orbigny's Sliders (*Trachemys dorbigni*) and Hilaire's Side-necked Turtles (*Phrynops hilarii*) travel some 50m (164 ft) before nesting, but South American Snake-necked Turtles (*Hydromedusa tectifera*) prefer slopes closer to the water's edge (12.6 m [41.3 ft] on average).

Some species travel a considerable distance, possibly because the farther a nest is from an obvious marker like a shoreline, the harder it may be for a predator to find. Eastern Short-necked Turtles in the upper Murray River tend to nest farther from the river edge, even though open areas closer to the bank may provide better nesting sites. Nests farther from the bank may be less vulnerable to introduced foxes. The females are putting themselves at some risk: foxes are more likely to attack them the farther they wander from the water.

Though Blanding's Turtles may nest only a short distance from the water's edge, others travel more than a kilometer before laying their eggs—an unusually long distance for a North American freshwater turtle. Even Yellow-spotted River Turtles,

A Spot-legged Turtle (*Rhinoclemmys punctularia*) crosses a sandbar at the mouth of the Maroni River, French Guiana.

which nest on sandbanks, may travel more than 100 m (328 ft) from the river to find a suitable patch of sand. Savanna Side-necked Turtles (*Podocnemis vogli*) walk for kilometers, but Magdalena River Turtles (*Podocnemis lewyana*) in the Mompos Depression of northern Colombia ranged no more than 39 m (128 ft) and usually nested less than 10 m (33 ft) from the nearest water.

Painted Turtles usually nest no more than 50 m (164 ft) from the water, though Painted Turtles in southern New Hampshire, where development has reduced available nesting habitat, have been recorded traveling 115 m (377 ft) before nesting. Common Sliders normally travel more than 10 times farther away. John Tucker has suggested that the difference has to do with the dangers emerging hatchlings face on the journey back. Painted Turtle

hatchlings are smaller, and have more permeable skins, than hatchling sliders. They may need to make the shortest, and fastest, dash possible to the water's edge to avoid drying out on their journey.

Female Striped Mud Turtles in central Florida may journey more than 240 m (787 ft) to their nest site; however, a trip of 60 to 180 m (197 to 262 ft) is more usual. Dawn Wilson found that the turtles did not head back to the water after the exertions of their overland trek and egg-laying activities but buried themselves nearby, below the soil and leaf litter, for anywhere from 1 to 35 days. This type of behavior, which is typical of a number of other mud turtles and is also known in the Western Swamp Turtle, may not simply be the result of exhaustion. The females may be waiting for rain, either to avoid dehydration themselves, or so that, when they do head back to the water, they will not leave a scent trail that could guide a predator to their nest. Yellow Mud Turtles bury themselves directly on top of their eggs, possibly to protect them from predators.

If the best nesting grounds are far from their feeding grounds, turtles may need to migrate to reach them. Such migration is common for turtles that nest on sandy beaches; the journeys of the Arrau are famous (see page 229, Chapter 6), and of course the sea turtles make the longest migratory journeys of any reptile (see page 305, Chapter 8). Painted Terrapins migrate, usually down-river, to find nesting sites unlikely to be flooded by river and sea tides. Even land turtles may migrate. On Santa Cruz (Indefatigable) Island in the Galápagos, nesting sites are particularly hard to come by. Santa Cruz Giant Tortoises (*Chelonoidis porteri*) must travel from their upland feeding grounds to the southwestern lowlands, where the silty soil of special nesting areas called "campos" is suitable for digging. To reach them, the tortoises follow a system of trails they have trodden for generations.

Putting Development on Hold

In the temperate zone, the number of eggs a female turtle can develop, and the number of clutches she can lay, may be restricted by the number of warm days available. Her ability to nest over and over again through the year may be cut off by the approach of winter. A hatchling that emerges in, say, mid-December might not have a very long life expectancy.

Many turtles in the warmer parts of the temperate zone, however, have developmental tricks that may allow them to extend the nesting season. A female Chicken Turtle can carry eggs in her oviduct over the winter (see page 261). In other turtles, or in autumn Chicken Turtle nests, clutches laid late in the year simply stop developing when winter comes.

The embryos overwinter in the eggs, and development is completed in the spring. Sonoran Mud Turtles (*Kinosternon sonoriense*) are active during a brief period of summer rain, and eggs laid one summer may not deliver their hatchlings to the surface until the following summer, more than 11 months later. Apparently they pass the winter as embryos.

If development is put on hold early in incubation, but after the eggs are laid, it is called *embryonic diapause*. An egg in diapause will not continue its development even if the temperatures are right. Many of the eggs of Broad-shelled Turtles, which nest in late fall, are laid in a state of diapause, and will not develop for several weeks, no matter how high the temperature. In some turtles such as the Pig-nose Turtle, the pause occurs late in development, with the embryo, almost ready to hatch, dialing down its metabolism, rather like an adult turtle entering dormancy; this is usually called either delayed hatching or *embryonic aestivation*.

Diapause usually occurs among certain turtles with a number of things in common: they tend, for example, to lay hard-shelled eggs, though the Chicken Turtle is an exception. Turtles with diapause, including a number of mud turtles such as the Striped Mud Turtle, tend to live in the warmer parts of the temperate zone. No turtle living above latitude 35° north is known to exhibit diapause. This makes some sense if the advantage of diapause is to permit turtle embryos to overwinter in the egg; north of a certain point, the risk of freezing may be too great for any overwintering egg to survive. The Painted Turtle, a northern species that overwinters in its nest, does so not as an egg but as a hatchling (see page 192, Chapter 5). Some tropical turtles exhibit embryonic diapause too, including some chelids, kinosternids, the Indian Softshell (*Nilssonia gangenticus*), at least two geoemydids, and the Pancake Tortoise.

Though Scorpion Mud Turtles lay clutches at different times of the year, all of the young hatch at the start of the rainy season when conditions for rapid growth are at their best. The embryos achieve this by a combination of diapause during development and dormancy once they reach full term. Depending on how long before the rains their eggs were laid, embryos may incubate for anywhere from two and a half to seven and a half months. This species' unusual reproductive strategy, combining a scattergun egg-laying pattern with synchronized hatching at the optimal time of year, may be responsible for its successful spread across a broad range of the American tropics.

Once diapause is underway, how does the embryo in the egg know when to start developing again? Clearly it needs some sort of environmental cue. A fall in temperature appears to do the trick for Geoffroy's Turtle, at least in the laboratory. Chicken Turtle eggs begin developing when ground temperatures rise in April. The embryos seem to require extended exposure to low temperatures, either in their mother's oviduct (presumably) or in the nest, to develop properly; Eggs incubated in a warm lab shortly after being laid in autumn showed poor hatching success. Broad-shelled Turtles may also fail to break diapause if they are incubated at constant high temperatures. The cue for the Pig-nose Turtle, which nests on land but whose hatchlings must reach water to survive, is a cutoff of the egg's oxygen supply—something that presumably happens in the wild when the eggs are flooded by the first heavy rains of the season, or by the rising waters where the hatchlings will spend their lives.

Taken at the Flood

A nest that is too close to the water risks being flooded. Flooding can have serious consequences. If the eggs of Smooth Softshells are flooded for even a few days during the early stages of development, their chance of survival is slim; six days underwater is enough to kill the whole brood. In some years, Six-tubercled Amazon River Turtles in the Samiria River in Peru may lose all their nests when the river floods. Yellow-spotted River Turtle nesting beaches are often washed away. Perhaps as an evolutionary response, their eggs develop more rapidly than is usual in turtles, increasing the chances that the young will hatch, emerge, and be safely in the river before the floods arrive.

Central American River Turtles (*Dermatemys mawi*) are so helpless on land that they must nest very near the water, usually less than 1.5 m (5 ft) from the water line. Nest flooding is regular. Their eggs show a remarkable ability to tolerate a prolonged spell underwater, at least during early development. *Dermatemys* eggs have survived 28 continuous days beneath the surface. Flooding, as long as it does not last too long, may even be an advantage for these turtles if it hides the nest from predators.

We do not know if Central American River Turtles deliberately lay their eggs where they are likely to be flooded, or even if they occasionally nest in shallow water. Mekong Snail-eating Turtles (*Malayemys subtrijuga*) in the Tonle Sap Biosphere reserve, Cambodia, nest in partially flooded, water-logged soil at the end of the wet season, when suitable dry nesting sites are hard to come by, and possibly nest underwater at times.

A tropical Australian turtle, though, lays its eggs under water as a matter of course—the only reptile in the world known for certain to do so. Rod Kennett discovered the remarkable nesting habits of the Northern Long-necked Turtle almost by accident. These turtles are commonest on tropical flood plains in Australia's Northern Territory. Here, from December through April, monsoonal rains inundate thousands of square kilometers, creating great shallow marshlands that dry almost completely in the near-rainless months outside the monsoon. As the waters recede, turtles retreat, if they can, to the few permanent water sources, or bury themselves in the drying mud to await the next coming of the rains.

Kennett could not understand why, no matter how common these turtles were in the billabongs he was studying, he was unable to find a single

Northern Long-necked Turtles (*Chelodina rugosa*) build their nests in shallow lagoons; the eggs do not develop until the lagoon dries.

nest despite two years of searching. The Aboriginal people knew the answer: they said that the turtles buried their eggs in the mud beneath the shallows as the rainy season came to an end, before the waters themselves dried.

In 1991, Kennett and his co-workers tried an ingenious test of the Aboriginal story. They implanted tiny egg-shaped radio transmitters in the oviducts of gravid turtles at a lagoon near Darwin. When the turtles laid their eggs, the transmitters became part of the clutch, broadcasting the nests' locations. The trick worked twice. The transmitters' signals proved that the Aboriginals were right: both nests were under water, buried beneath clumps of aquatic vegetation 17 m (56 ft) and 14.5 m (47.5 ft), respectively, from shore.

The transmitters solved one mystery, but left the scientists with even greater ones. How do the eggs survive such treatment? And why do the turtles nest under water in the first place?

Flooding kills most reptile eggs because it denies them the oxygen they need to develop, and because water entering by osmosis may cause the egg to swell and the shell to crack. In some turtles, water entry is not necessarily a problem, and may even be a normal part of development, as long as the underlying membranes surrounding the embryo remain intact. If these rupture, though, the embryo will likely die.

Northern Long-necked Turtle embryos solve these problems by having a particularly water-resistant vitelline membrane surrounding the yolk and the embryo, and by simply not developing until the waters above them recede and air can reach the eggs. Some eggs can survive under water for up to six months, in a state of diapause—a remarkable feat, considering that embryos of their relative the Eastern Snake-necked Turtle, will die after only about two weeks under water. Eggs kept under water for six weeks in a laboratory not only survived better than eggs submerged for 25 weeks, but better than eggs not submerged at all. The embryos entered diapause whether they were flooded or not, and a short period of inundation speeded up their eventual development by up to nine weeks. The longer they were kept under water, the longer they remained in diapause, but at seven weeks of submergence—close to the six-week optimum inundation time—their incubation period equalled that for eggs incubated out of the water.

Why do these turtles have such a bizarre adaptation? The answer probably has to do with the temporary and unpredictable nature of their watery habitat. Other tropical Australian turtles live in more or less permanent waters, and nest on land in the traditional manner, even, apparently, including the Arnhem Land Long-necked Turtle (*Chelodina burrungandjii*), which may be the Northern Long-necked Turtle's closest relative. Turtles that live in temporary floodwaters may not be able to find a safe dry-land site at the right time of year.

If the turtles lay on land during the rainy season, or toward the end of the dry season, their eggs may be flooded when the waters rise again, and flooding during the later stages of development, as opposed to immediately after laying, will kill even their embryos. Waiting until the waters recede at the end of the rainy season could delay nesting by several months, and cost them the chance to lay more than one clutch. Jardine River Turtles get around this problem by nesting on floating mats of vegetation, and Branderhorst's Snapping Turtles (*Elseya branderhorsti*) in southern Papua New Guinea seek out whatever higher ground is available, but the Northern Long-neck's strategy—which bears a closer resemblance to the breeding strategies of some species of fish than it does to that of a reptile—arguably gives it a much greater range of nesting choices.

By nesting under water, Northern Long-necked Turtles can lay their eggs anytime from March or, preferably, April until the ponds dry up and the adults are forced to aestivate, and still put their young in the best position to survive to hatching. In exceptionally dry years their reproductive efforts may fail, but in normal years having their eggs develop during the dry season ensures that their young will only emerge when times are right. If the rains may come too early the embryos may not have completed their development, but if the hatchling turtles finish development before the rains arrive the hard-baked ground over their heads may be impossible to break through. When the rains come at the right time the hatchlings can leave the nest, and only then will there be safe habitat for them to prosper in.

Heat, Sex, and Turtle Eggs

In the mid-1960s, scientists made the bizarre discovery that, for many reptiles, incubation temperature not only determines an embryo's development rate, but its sex. In reptiles with *temperature-dependent sex determination* (TSD or TDSD), eggs incubated at either low or high temperatures produce females, while those incubated at a range of middle temperatures produce males. A clutch of eggs incubated at or near the temperatures at which the changeovers occur (the *threshold* or *pivotal* temperatures) will produce a mixture of males and females; at threshold temperatures, males and females should, in theory, be produced in equal numbers.

In practice, there are three different types of TSD. In one type, TSDIb, eggs incubated at higher temperatures develop into males while those at lower temperatures hatch out as females (as in some crocodilians). There are two types in turtles: TSDIa, in which eggs produce females only at higher temperatures (podocnemidids, sea turtles, most emydids, tortoises, and some geoemydids); and TSDII, in which females are produced at both lower and higher temperatures (pelomedusids [the few we know about], snapping turtles, some kinosternids, and at least one geoemydid, the Indian Black Turtle [*Melanochelys trijuga*]).

What the threshold temperatures are varies widely. For some reptiles, the lower, or higher, temperatures needed to produce females are either rarely encountered in the wild, or are lethal if they are. We now know, though, that even so-called TSDIb species like alligators produce females again if the incubation temperatures are high enough, and some biologists believe that there is only one type of TSD, TSDII, with the difference being whether, in nature, the eggs of a turtle with TSD are likely to encounter, or survive, the upper or lower thresholds. However, recent molecular studies suggest that the genetic pathways involved are not the same in all TSD species. Eggs of Painted Turtles, a

TSDIa species, failed to produce females even when incubated at a comparatively cool 21.5°C (70.7°F).

The sex of a number of turtles has nothing to do with incubation temperature. So far as we know, all chelids, softshell turtles (though one study found that incubation temperature did affect the sex ratio of hatchlings in Chinese Softshells), and Giant and Narrow-bridged Musk Turtles (Staurotypinae), have *genotypically-based sex determination* (GSD). So do one emydid, the Wood Turtle, and two geoemydids, the Brown Roofed Turtle (*Pangshura smithi*) and the Black Marsh Turtle (*Siebenrockiella crassicollis*), In chelids, staurotypines and a few others, gender may be determined by the presence or absence of a sex chromosome, as our own gender is. Sex chromosomes have been detected in Eastern Short-necked Turtles and in the Eastern Long-necked Turtle, which has a system involving microchromosomes (very small chromosomes present in birds and reptiles but, apparently, not in mammals). Turtles with TSD do not have sex chromosomes, at least as far as we can tell.

The sex of this juvenile Mississippi Map Turtle (*Graptemys pseudogeographica kohnii*) was determined by its incubation temperature.

The distinctions between TSD and GSD are not always clear-cut. Mud and musk turtles include apparent TSDIa species such as the Mexican Mud Turtle, TSDII species such as the Loggerhead Musk Turtle, and a number of others that seem to be intermediate including one, the Striped Mud Turtle, which may have both TSD and GSD. In the Alligator Snapping Turtle there appears to be no temperature that will cause all the eggs in a clutch to develop as males. This suggests the possibility that at least some of its eggs—perhaps as many as a third—may be destined to be female no matter what their incubation temperature.

Threshold temperatures appear to be under genetic control. The upper threshold temperature (the only important one in TSDIa turtles) varies from species to species. In Red-eared Sliders it may vary from clutch to clutch. It ranges from as low as 27.5°C (81.5°F) in the Painted Turtle to as high as 33.4°C (92.1°F) in the Magdalena River Turtle and 32.5–34°C (90.5–93.2°F) in the Arrau. The upper threshhold is highest in podocnemidids and tortoises. For the Gopher Tortoise, it lies somewhere between 29°C (84.2°F) and 32°C (89.6°F), while in Hermann's Tortoise (*Testudo hermanni*) it is 31.5°C (88.7°F). In the Japanese Pond Turtle (*Mauremys japonica*) it is 28.8°C (83.8°F), and in most emydid turtles, it ranges from 28–30°C (82.4–86.0°F). In TSDII turtles the lower threshold is usually less than 26°C (78.8°F). It reaches below 22°C (71.6°F) in northern populations of Common Snapping Turtle. In the Helmeted Terrapin the lower threshold may be as high as 29°C (84.2°F), while the upper reaches a reported 32.1°C (89.8°F).

Threshold temperatures may have a great deal to do with where female turtles choose to nest. Conversely, the kinds of nesting sites available may have affected the way threshold temperatures have evolved. In North America, northern turtles tend to have lower threshold temperatures. In the hotter southeast, some species deliberately choose nest sites in the shade. In the dry southwest, where cool nest sites may be hard to find, turtles with TSD tend to have higher threshold temperatures. The South American Arrau, which has the highest known threshold temperature, selects sites on river sandbars where the incubation temperature may be very high indeed. This increases the chances that its young will develop quickly enough to escape rising floodwaters, and its threshold temperature appears to have shifted upward in consequence. Gender may even depend on where an egg lies in its nest. The nests of Common Snapping Turtles may be warmer at the top, near the surface, and cooler at the bottom. Eggs from the upper reaches of the nest chamber are more likely to hatch as females, while hatchlings emerging from its depths tend to be males. In Pig-nose Turtles and Agassiz's Desert Tortoises, later clutches, laid when the climate is hotter, produce more females than those laid earlier under cooler conditions.

In TSD turtles, gender depends less on the average temperature in the nest than on exposure to a specific range of temperatures at the right stage in development and for the right amount of time. Only the temperature during the middle third of the incubation period—the temperature-sensitive period or TSP—seems to be important. Laboratory experiments have shown that, during the TSP, eggs have to be exposed to temperatures above the threshold level for several days, for at least four hours a day, to turn out females.

Scientists have come up with models that look at just how much development actually takes place when the temperature is above threshold. The latest, developed for Painted Turtles by Jennifer Neuwald and Nicole Valenzuela, requires five mathematical equations to account for the complex interactions involved, and even its authors admit it falls short of explaining all the variations.

What are the chances that, during the TSP, nest temperatures will be close enough to threshhold to produce both males and females? Often the answer seems to be "not very good," though most of 19 Magdalena River Turtle nests monitored by Vivian

Páez and her colleagues in the Mompos Depression, Colombia, did produce young of both sexes. Studies on nests of map turtles (*Graptemys* spp.) and Painted Turtles have found that most of the young that came out of any given nest were of the same sex. Colin Limpus and his colleagues found the same for sea turtle nests in Australia. A female may need to ensure, not that each nest produces a gender mix, but that at least some of her nests produce males and others females. According to Dionysius S.K. Sharma and his colleagues, Painted Terrapins at Rhu Kudung, Malaysia, "lay their eggs at different sites on the beach platform, exposing their eggs to different temperature regimes. This will produce a natural male-female hatchling sex ratio."

We are not exactly sure how TSD works. It appears to be related to the effect temperature has on the activity of certain enzyme and hormone precursors involved in the development of the embryonic gonads (including aromatase, an enzyme involved in the synthesis of estrogen). Without the action of these precursors gonads become ovaries, possibly by default, but within the range of temperatures favorable to their activity the gonads develop into testes instead.

In Painted Turtles, a TSD species, temperature affects the operation of a genetic complex associated with gonadal development (including the gene associated with aromatase). In Smooth Softshells, a GSD species that apparently evolved from TSD ancestors, it does not. Some genes associated with TSD may still be sensitive to temperature even in softshells (Nicole Valenzuela has identified one such gene, the Wilm's tumor-associated gene (*Wt1*), which is involved with testis development in mammals), but their sensitivity is effectively "overruled" by genes (such as Steroidogenic factor 1 or *Sf1*, a major regulatory gene involved in estrogen synthesis) that operate farther down the chain of protein synthesis leading to the development of the gonads. In Painted Turtles both *Wt1* and *Sf1* are temperature-sensitive. Either or both may act as a thermal "master switch" that allows temperature to determine the gender of the hatchling.

TSD seems to expose turtle reproductive success to the mercy of the environment. Why does it exist? GSD has apparently evolved at least five times in different turtle families, so an adaptive alternative is available. TSD must have its advantages—or, at least, it may not load turtles down with severe disadvantages – but scientists are not yet sure what these advantages, if any, are.

Reptiles with TSD may have a "buffering" capacity that resists, under normal circumstances, the effects of too great a fluctuation in temperature on the sexual development of their embryos. TSD may do no harm as long as the sex ratios it produces are not too wildly skewed. In many wild turtle populations one sex may outnumber the other without any apparent ill effects. Having more females than males may be a better outcome, as each male can fertilize several females. One population of Mexican Mud Turtles in the state of Mexico had more than half as many females as males. Nonetheless, males outnumbered females in a Common Musk Turtle population in an Indiana lake, and male Leopard Tortoises in northern Tanzania may outnumber females by better than two to one.

Shifting from TSD to GSD may only give turtles an advantage under extraordinary circumstances. Nicole Valenzuela and Dean Adams have found that when one sex determination mechanism has evolved into the other—in turtles, normally when TSD has given way to GSD—the change has been accompanied by a shift in chromosome number. They have proposed that these changes not only occurred together—signifying a marked evolutionary development—but that they happened at the same time as extreme shifts in global temperature.

Does the tendency of TSD nests to produce same-sex hatchlings somehow prevent interbreeding years later, when the turtles mature? It is difficult to see how, especially if the same female lays several clutches in different places, some producing males and others females. Some turtle biologists have suggested that TSD may maintain size differences between the sexes, on the assumption that temperatures producing one gender, but not the other, promote faster growth. Male Common Snapping Turtles are larger than females, and tend to grow faster at the intermediate temperatures that produce males. However, growth after hatching may be more important than growth in the egg. Incubation temperature has nothing to do with how fast snapper hatchlings grow in their first six months. Female False Map Turtles may start out smaller than male hatchlings, but they end up the larger sex because the males stop growing after four years of age.

Too high a temperature can result in a smaller hatchling. Alligator Snapper eggs incubated at 30.5°C (86.9°F) produce smaller hatchlings than eggs at cooler temperatures. Wei-Guo Du and his colleagues found that Reeves's Turtle (*Mauremys reevesi*) hatchlings incubated at a constant 24°C (75.2°F) and 27°C (80.6°F) weighed more, and had larger carapaces and longer limbs, than hatchlings incubated at 30°C (86°F) and 33°C (91.4°F). Hatchlings incubated at 27°C (80.6 °F) and 30°C (86°F) crawled and swam faster than hatchlings incubated at higher and lower temperatures.

However, in nature turtle eggs rarely, if ever, face constant temperatures. Daily fluctuations in temperature have been found to affect such things as carapace growth in embryos of Smooth Softshells, a GSD species, but the effects were not consistent. Fluctuations affect hatchling sex ratios in Painted Turtles, but not other traits such as growth, behavior and immune response. In a study by Ryan Paitz and his colleagues, eggs incubated at a constant 27°C produced all males; eggs kept at an average 27°C (80.6°F) with a 4°C (7.2 °F) fluctuation in either direction over a 24-hour period produced 30 percent females, and an 8°C (14.4 °F) fluctuation produced all females (presumably because this took the eggs above the threshhold temperature for long enough each day to make a critical difference). At

least in Paitz's turtles, TSD does not match size, or other traits, with sex.

Some of the sex ratios we see today may be our fault. Clearing of forests by humans has left fewer cool, shady, male-producing nest sites than there used to be. The sex ratio of Yellow-spotted River Turtles in the Guapore River in Rondonia, Brazil, is strongly skewed toward males, with six males to each female. Perhaps there are fewer females because nests that produce females are laid out in the open, where they may be easier for predators, including humans, to find; or humans may be catching more adult females at open nesting sites.

Whatever the evolutionary advantages of TSD in the past, global climate change could turn it into a serious liability. Fredric Janzen suggested, in 1994, that a rise of about 4°C (7.2°F) in the mean July temperature could "effectively eliminate the production of male offspring" in the population of Painted Turtles he was studying in central Illinois. Janzen may have overstated the case. Turtles, by and large, are flexible and resilient creatures, quite capable of dealing with rising temperatures by finding cooler nesting sites or nesting earlier in the season; however, some turtles, particularly rare or local species, may not be so adaptable. By compensating for rising temperature, a nesting female could expose her eggs to other risks including potentially lethal temperatures.

John Tucker and his colleagues, who trapped and marked almost 10,000 Red-eared Sliders in west-central Illinois between 2001 and 2005, found an increasingly greater proportion of males over the course of their study. You might expect that climate change would result in more females, but one probable result of temperature rise is that in 2006 turtles started nesting 21 days earlier than in 1995. That meant more nests when the weather was still cool and nest temperatures were more likely to produce males. An extra early-season clutch was likely to be a male clutch. This does not prove that climate change was responsible for the increase in males, or that Tucker's results are part of an inexorable trend, or even that this shift will harm the population. They do suggest, though, that Janzen's concerns (at the very least) bear watching.

Hatching and Emergence

The amount of time it takes for turtle eggs to incubate varies tremendously, both among different species and within a single species. Some of this variation is simply a matter of temperature; all things being equal, eggs at cooler temperatures take longer to develop. In a laboratory experiment, eggs of the Narrow-bridged Musk Turtle incubated at a range of temperatures took anywhere from 95 to 229 days to hatch. The shortest incubation time known for any turtle, 28 days, was recorded for a Chinese Softshell, though 40 to 80 days is more normal for that species.

By the time a turtle is ready to hatch, its eggshell has been greatly weakened. The eggshell is a major source of calcium for the embryo. By hatching time much of its calcium has been used up, and what remains may not be a serious barrier to escape. Late in incubation, the brittle outer layer of the Furrowed Wood Turtle's eggshell (*Rhinoclemmys areolata*) expands and cracks. When the hatchling finally emerges, its carapace is less than 40 mm (1.6 in) wide. Within a day or two, though, the shell expands to almost 50 mm (2 in)—considerably wider than the egg from which it emerged.

Escape can still be a slow process. The hatchling's first breach of its shell wall is called *pipping*, and it can happen well before the turtle finally hatches. Archie Carr described the hatching of a Common Musk Turtle that took almost three days to break out of its shell. A hatchling turtle slices its way out with a sharp little bump of keratin on the tip of its snout, the *egg-tooth* or egg-carbuncle, which falls off or is absorbed within a few weeks. Sometimes it makes a number of holes and cracks that join together until a piece of the eggshell falls

away. Red-eared Slider hatchlings use their long front claws to open the eggshell, and, the following spring, to dig their way to the surface; by the time they emerge, their front and hind claws are significantly shorter than they were on hatching, presumably worn down by their exertions.

Hatchling turtles are good diggers. Yellow Mud Turtles and Ornate Box Turtles (*Terrapene ornata*) are quite capable of digging their way through the bottom of the nest to escape the advancing frost line, to depths of 60 cm (24 in) or more (see page 192, Chapter 5). If the ground above them is frozen, or baked hard by the sun, digging out may, nonetheless, be impossible; but under such conditions, emergence is something that it may be well to delay. Common Snapping Turtles, though they hatch in fall, may stay in the nest for up to two months. Hatchling Spur-thighed Tortoises in the Caucasus normally take only about 80 days to develop, and may appear on the surface as early as late July. However, some hatchlings, presumably those resulting from late nestings, may winter underground and emerge in late May the following year. There is no point in hatchlings digging out into a world that is too cold, too hot, or too dry to sustain them. It is better to wait until conditions are right. Extra yolk, which is often not fully absorbed on hatching, provides the food reserve they need to wait it out.

Turtles whose hatchlings remain in the nest have a proportionately greater supply of lipids in their egg yolks than those whose young emerge at once or, like Speckled Padlopers, are on the surface already. Newly hatched padlopers have already absorbed their yolk sac, and begin to feed almost immediately. Agassiz's Desert Tortoises typically stay in their burrows for the first 24 hours after hatching until the last of the yolk sac, which can otherwise interfere with their getting around, is absorbed. Hatchling Gopher Tortoises still have enough yolk, even after they hatch, to sustain them for some time. They move little during their first winter, and are not interested in food, but instead

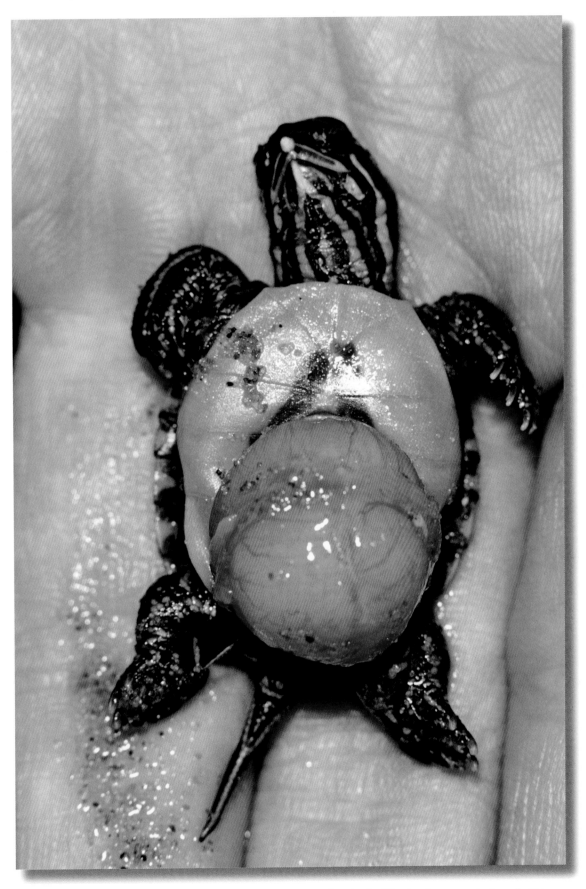

This hatchling Painted Turtle (*Chrysemys picta*) has yet to absorb all of the food reserves in its yolk sac.

soon turn their attention to the activity that will occupy them through much of their adult life—burrowing. They may dig their first burrow within a week of emerging from the nest.

In many turtles, the rate at which the embryos grow and metabolize drops off just before hatching, and may remain relatively low until the hatchlings are able to feed themselves. Even if the yolk is no longer visible, its concentrated energy remains in the body cavity and fuels the hatchling until it reaches suitable feeding grounds and learns how to find food. Smooth softshell embryos grow particularly rapidly during a short incubation period and emerge into an environment, the shallow waters around stream sandbars, with little to eat. Even if the hatchlings are able to hunt, doing so may make it more likely that they themselves will be spotted and caught. With yolk reserves to rely on, the hatchlings can spend much of their time buried in the sand, keeping their own foraging activities to a minimum and increasing their survival chances during their first winter.

When hatchlings do emerge, it may take the efforts of the entire brood to breach the plug of soil over their heads and escape into the open air. It has been suggested that the large broods of Common Snapping Turtles, some 30 to a clutch, must work together to break out of their nest before winter sets in. Even for turtles that can dig their way free one by one, emerging together may increase the chances that at least some will escape waiting predators. It may lessen the chance that the exit burrow left by early-emerging hatchlings will lead predators to the rest of the brood. However, though all the eggs in a nest are normally laid at the same time, temperature and humidity differences within the egg chamber may prevent them from developing at the same rate. Hatching together requires coordination, and a signal.

Pig-nose Turtle broods appear to hatch together in response to water levels in the nest, or possibly to vibrations picked up from nearby eggs. This appears to be because the embryos enter diapause when they are almost ready to hatch, so that by the time, usually some 20 days later, that rising water cuts off their oxygen supply—the direct cue for hatching—all the eggs are fully developed, and they hatch together within minutes.

For other turtles, there may be timing mechanisms that allow them to synchronize both hatching and emergence; Arrau may cue each other with vocalizations that begin between 8 and 32 hours before hatching. Less fully developed Eastern Short-necked Turtle embryos somehow speed up their development—by as much as five days in controlled experiments—in the presence of more-developed eggs, ensuring that the whole brood hatches together. Eastern Long-necked Turtles appear unable to do this. Painted Turtles, rather than speeding up their development, pip their shells prematurely in the company of hatching nestmates, at some neuro-muscular cost to themselves; premature hatchlings may take longer to break free of the egg, and they are slower to right themselves if turned over, than fully developed young. What signal hatching Painted, or Eastern Short-necked, turtles receive from their more advanced siblings we do not, as yet, know.

Hatchling turtles do not always emerge together. Though all hatchlings emerged on the same day, in 70 percent of 59 Blanding's Turtle nests monitored on the E.S. George Reserve in Michigan, individual turtles from other nests took up to four days to make their escape. Hatchlings from the same Gopher Tortoise nests in Florida emerged as much as 16 days apart. Though Painted Turtles may emerge together, broods in northern Indiana have been recorded taking well over a month before the last hatchling emerged. Painted Turtles hatch, and sometimes emerge, in autumn (see page 192, Chapter 5). In New Hampshire, only a few hatchlings may do so, presumably months ahead of their broodmates. Why, then, do Painted Turtles synchronize their hatching if they are not going to emerge as a group? Paul Colbert and his colleagues have speculated that early hatching may give premature hatchlings an opportunity to jockey with their nestmates for a better position in the egg chamber—one less likely to expose them to freezing, for example.

Hatchling Helmeted Terrapins and Leopard Tortoises do not emerge until the ground above their heads has been softened by rain. In the Mediterranean climate near the Cape of Good Hope, it is the first winter rains that trigger the emergence of young Geometric Tortoises (*Psammobates geometricus*). Hatchling turtles that migrate to water, like Common Snapping Turtles, risk dehydration in the course of their journey, and emerging in rainy weather may reduce that risk. Rain not only acts as a "hatching releaser" for the Indian Softshell; it may help the hatchlings make their first journey. If the nest is a long way from the water's edge, hatchling softshells hide under bushes or in cracks in the soil. It takes the next heavy rain to sweep them into the river.

Red-eared Sliders, which overwinter in the nest, are apparently cued to emerge by changes in temperature. As the sun warms the surface, the soil over their heads becomes warmer than the soil at the bottom of the nest, and emergence may simply be the result of the hatchlings trying to find the warmest spot possible.

Once the hatchlings emerge from their nest, they have to find their way to suitable habitat (assuming they are not there already). John Iverson and his colleagues have found that hatchling Yellow Mud Turtles are able to orient toward water. Perhaps, like hatchling sea turtles, they respond to polarized light (see page 308, Chapter 8). By their second year, they have added an internal compass, possibly one sensitive to the angle of the sun or to the earth's magnetic field. However, Justin Congdon and his colleagues, who released 76 hatchling Painted Turtles and 746 Common Snappers from experimental nests to study their orientation, concluded that the turtles were relying solely on visual cues other than polarized light. The hatchlings appeared to head toward open, brightly lit near horizons despite any other kind of information that might be available. Hatchling Blanding's Turtles orient instead toward distant dark horizons, a difference that may reflect the fact that Blanding's often nest far from the water, away from any direct visual cue that might lead hatchlings to their mother's home wetland.

For freshwater turtles, travel to water may involve a substantial, and dangerous, journey. Wood Turtle hatchlings may spend days or even weeks on land, sheltering under vegetation, feeding and growing, before taking to their overwintering sites under water. Some of the hatchling Blanding's Turtles studied by Brian Butler and Terry Graham in Massachusetts made the trip—an average straight line distance of just under 35 m (115 ft)—in slightly less than 12 hours, but others took up to nine days. On the way, they kept under cover when they could, burrowing under sphagnum moss and rotted logs, spending the night in the burrows of Short-tailed Shrews (*Blarina brevicauda*) or among the roots of Royal Ferns (*Osmunda regalis*). Both Blanding's and Wood Turtle hatchlings will follow the trails of others. Sheila Tuttle and David Carroll used fluorescent powder to track hatchling Wood Turtles at night, and found that they often tracked each other's trails exactly even when far from the nest, and even on separate nights. Tuttle and Carroll suggested that they were picking up their nestmate's scent.

Though hatchling Blanding's Turtles normally spend their first winter under water, a few may overwinter on land if the circumstances are right. Their earliest instincts may not be to head for water at all. Though Massachusetts hatchlings traveled more or less directly to water, newly emerged hatchlings studied by Natalie McMaster and Thomas Herman in Nova Scotia generally did not. Some avoided it altogether, even if the investigators released them right next to the water's edge. They seemed to prefer to seek cover instead. Newly hatched Diamondback Terrapins, perhaps also seeking cover, may head for the nearest clump of vegetation, regardless of whether it is uphill, downhill, or in the same direction as the water they will eventually reach.

Staying Alive

Turtles stand only a modest chance of hatching at all, and an even smaller one of surviving to the end of their first year. Matthew Aresco recorded near-total losses of Florida Cooter and Common Slider nests in northwestern Florida. Gopher Tortoises may only be able to bring off a successful clutch, with hatchlings living long enough to emerge from the nest, once every 9 or 10 years. During a 7-year study of Common Snapping Turtles in Michigan, nest losses averaged 70 percent (with a range of 30 to 100 percent). Environmental stresses account for some losses; winter kill may be substantial for northern Painted Turtle hatchlings overwintering in the nest, despite their ability to withstand freezing (see page 192, Chapter 5).

Predators dispose of a high proportion of turtle nests—often well over 90 percent. Often they are raided within 24 hours of laying, either because disturbed soil around the nest acts as a marker or because the female's scent still hangs about the nest site. In North America, Northern Raccoons (*Procyon lotor*) are probably the number one mammalian nest predator. On Ruler's Bar, a small island in the Jamaica Bay Wildlife Refuge, New York, raccoons destroy more than 92 percent of Diamondback Terrapin nests. Oddly, in the first half of the nesting season raccoons eat only the contents of the Diamondback eggs, leaving the shells, but from July onward they eat the eggs shell and all. In northeastern Florida, where raccoons are also major predators, Fish Crows (*Corvus ossifragus*) and Boat-tailed Grackles (*Quiscalus major*) watch for Diamondback females as they make their way to their nesting sites. Birds may begin digging at the nests as soon as the females leave.

Predators destroyed 272 of 285 Painted Turtle nests monitored in 2005 by Jeramie Strickland and his colleagues near Thompson, Illinois, 57 percent of them on the first night after laying. Nests dug on rainy days (when tell-tale odors can presumably be washed away) had a better chance of surviving. All 20 unprotected nests of Striped Mud Turtles monitored in Florida by Dawn Wilson and her colleagues were destroyed by predators, including raccoons and snakes. Nests protected by the researchers did much better, with 23 out of 26 nests producing at least one young.

Of the unprotected Blanding's Turtle nests studied by Butler and Graham in 1990, 33 of 35 were robbed by predators. Predators, primarily raccoons, destroyed 78.2 percent of 182 Blanding's Turtle nests monitored over the 23 years of the George Reserve study in Michigan. In 9 out of the 10 years between 1985 and 1994, they destroyed every one. Raccoons patrol the nesting grounds, probably watching for female turtles at work. Most nests were raided the night they were dug. Sometimes raccoons stole eggs from the nest chamber while the female was still laying.

Mongooses raid many nests of the Angulate Tortoise in South Africa. In Australia, introduced foxes find and destroy almost 90 percent of Eastern Snake-necked, Broad-shelled, and Eastern Short-necked Turtle nests along the lower Murray River. Jackals and monitor lizards are the chief predators on the nests of the Indian softshell. Water Monitors (*Varanus salvator*), wild pigs, feral dogs, crabs, and ants attack the nests of Painted Terrapins in Malaysia. Tegu lizards (*Tupinambis* spp.) destroyed nests of Six-tubercled Amazon River Turtles in Rio Trombetas Biological Reserve in Pará, Brazil. The lizards were the most important predators of the nests of Arrau, Yellow-spotted River Turtles and Six-tubercled Amazon River Turtles in the Pacaya-Samfria National Reserve, Peru. The Crested Caracara (*Caracara cheriway*, a carrion-eating relative of falcons) and the Common Tegu (*Tupinambis teguixin*) are the chief raiders (other than human

The nest of this Australian Broad-shelled Turtle (*Chelodina expansa*) has been raided, perhaps by an introduced fox.

beings) of the nests of Yellow-spotted River Turtles on the Capanaparo River in Venezuela. The eggs of Big-headed Amazon River Turtles (*Peltocephalus dumerilianus*) face another enemy: their own kind. Adults have been found with eggs of their own species in their stomachs.

Ghost Crabs (*Ocypode quadrata*) and Norway Rats (*Rattus norvegicus*) attack hatchling Diamondback Terrapins, and ants can be a serious problem for many nesting turtles. Fire ants have attacked the nests of Chicken Turtles and Gopher Tortoises. Red Imported Fire Ants (*Solenopsis invicta*), an introduced predator, are a serious problem for turtles in the southeastern United States. Fire ants are quite capable of boring through the shells of turtles that lay soft-shelled eggs, including Diamondback Terrapins, Common Sliders and Painted Turtles, but are stopped by the hard shells of Florida Softshell (*Apalone ferox*) and Common Musk Turtles.

Once they emerge, hatchlings run a gauntlet of predators from alligators to crabs and from bullfrogs to eagles (see page 249, Chapter 6). In South Africa, Fiscal Shrikes (*Lanius collaris*) may skewer hatchling Angulate Tortoises on thorns. According to a review by Deborah Epperson and Colleen Heise, Gopher Tortoise eggs, hatchlings and juveniles are preyed upon by raccoons, Gray Foxes (*Urocyon cinereoargenteus*), Striped Skunks (*Mephitis mephitis*), Virginia Opossums (*Didelphis virginiana*), Nine-banded Armadillos (*Dasypus novemcinctus*), Red-tailed Hawks (*Buteo jamaicensis*), Cottonmouths (*Agkistrodon piscivorus*), Eastern Diamondback Rattlesnakes (*Crotalus adamanteus*), Coachwhips

(*Masticophis flagellum*), Eastern Indigo Snakes (*Drymarchon corais*), and fire ants. Gopher Tortoises stand a 94 percent chance of being killed before they are a year old, with the largest proportion succumbing in their first month of life. In their early years, over 50 percent of young Gopher Tortoises, Agassiz's Desert Tortoises and Bolson Tortoises (*Gopherus flavomarginatus*) die each year.

Hatchling turtles are food for so many animals that you might not expect them to draw attention to themselves. The hatchlings of a surprising number of freshwater turtles from several different families (e.g. Painted, Eastern Mud, Eastern Snake-necked and Chinese Soft-shelled Turtles), are nonetheless brilliantly colored. Many bear startling patterns of red, yellow, or orange, particularly on their undersides. Usually, when otherwise defenseless (or tasty) creatures are decked out in this way, it is as a warning to predators that their prospective prey is toxic, venomous or in some other way an item to avoid. No hatchling turtles, though, carry dangerous poisons. What, if anything, are the turtles warning of, and what kind of predator is the target of the warning?

Carol Britson and William Gutzke suggested a possible answer in 1993. One of North America's most voracious aquatic predators, the Largemouth Bass (*Micropterus salmoides*), avoids hatchling turtles. Britson and Gutzke tried a number of experiments to see why. They found that bass had no problem eating hatchling meat, or whole hatchlings, of Painted Turtles as long as the prey were dead or anesthetized. Taste, then, was not the problem. Nonetheless, if a bass attacked a live hatchling, it usually spat it out after three to five seconds. It appears that the hatchlings put up such a struggle, clawing and biting at the inside of the fish's mouth,

that they were not worth eating. The bright colors may warn fish that have had a bad experience with a hatchling turtle to pass on the next opportunity.

In Australia, C. Dorrian and H. Ehmann have tested hatchlings of the Eastern Snake-necked Turtle on predatory fishes like the Murray Cod (*Maccullochella peeli*) and Long-finned Eel (*Anguilla reinhardtii*). One hatchling faced down an eel by flipping on its back, exposing the brilliant orange-red blotches on its plastron to its pursuer. After being denied food for nine days, an eel did try to swallow a hatchling, but spat it out at once. Dorrian and Ehmann were only able to persuade a Murray Cod to eat a dead hatchling after they blackened out its patches of color. The problem, for the fishes, may not be the hatchling's claws but its stink; Eastern Snake-necked Turtles, both young and old, can emit a particularly pungent liquid containing six different acids, and few predators will attack them.

The idea that hatchling colors are there to warn off fishes gets some support from the behavior of the turtles themselves. Hatchlings with bright colors—at least in North America—tend to be active swimmers; those without, like the young of Common Snapping Turtles, usually burrow in the mud. Keeping the colorful areas largely on the underside may alert fishes, which are likely to attack from below, without signaling the hatchling's presence to other predators, such as birds, that strike from above. Sea turtle hatchlings are active swimmers that lack bright colors, but they also lack the equipment to rake the inside of a fish's mouth. They are devoured by a host of fishes.

Hatchlings of the Big-headed Turtle (*Platysternon megacephalum*) may have another way to use their colorful undersides. Hatchlings, but not adults, can make a squealing noise. The combination of the squeal with a flash of bright color, suddenly revealed, might just startle a predator enough to give the hatchling a chance to escape.

The best defense young turtles have, though, is simply to reach adult size. By the time Gopher and Bolson Tortoises reach adulthood, their annual mortality has fallen from 50 percent to about 2 percent. Other adult turtles may not do as well—annual survivorship for Common Snapping Turtles, Painted Turtles and Common Sliders in eastern North America runs at about 81 to 85 percent—but nonetheless, if a hatchling can escape the gauntlet it runs in its early years, its chance of living to a ripe old age is vastly improved.

Since turtles suffer their greatest mortality as small animals, it usually makes adaptive sense for them to grow as quickly as possible. Most turtles grow rapidly in their first years of life. Though other Madagascar tortoises grow extremely slowly, juvenile Angonoka grow at a rate of approximately 16 percent per year. Their growth slows drastically when they reach adulthood. Rapid growth may be essential to weather not just predation, but environmental stresses like drought. If Western Swamp Turtles do not reach a minimum size in their first year, they are unlikely to survive their first period of aestivation.

For large tortoises, reaching adult size can involve an enormous change of magnitude: by the end of its journey from egg to adulthood, an adult male Spurred Tortoise (*Geochelone sulcata*) with a carapace length of 83 cm (33 in) and a weight of 105.5 kg (233 lbs) has increased its length by 18 times, mostly during its first twenty years of life, and its weight by 3,822 times.

OPPOSITE

Some Australian turtle hatchlings, like this *Chelodina* sp., may also warn fish away with their bright plastral colors.

CHAPTER EIGHT

The Endless Journey

THE CYCLE OF LIFE that sends freshwater turtles out onto the land to nest becomes, in the sea turtles, a grand sweeping arc carrying them across thousands of kilometers of open ocean. It may return them, decades later, to the general area, if not the precise spot, of their birth. It is a cycle that, for some sea turtles, follows the circular paths of the great current systems (or gyres) that swirl about whole ocean basins.

The life cycle of a sea turtle is much the same for all seven living species. It begins when a hatchling, aided by its nestmates, struggles out of the sand and scrambles down the beach to the sea. If it escapes the predators that wait for it on the beach, in the surf, or in the sky overhead, the hatchling will leave the coast behind and become a denizen of the upper layers of the open sea (except for the Flatback [*Natator depressus*], which apparently spends its whole life on the Australian continental shelf).

ABOVE

A mature Green Sea Turtle (*Chelonia mydas*) spends much of its life migrating to and from its nesting grounds.

OPPOSITE

A hatchling Leatherback (*Dermochelys coriacea*) scrambles to the sea to begin its lifelong journey.

Here the turtle floats, perhaps carried vast distances by the currents, feeding on tiny creatures that share the surface waters, and growing, probably quite rapidly.

Once it reaches a certain size, its habits, and its diet, change. The Leatherback (*Dermochelys coriacea*) remains, by and large, a creature of the high seas (though what Leatherbacks do before reaching a meter or so in length is pretty much a mystery). Perhaps thousands of kilometers away from the waters where the hatchling first entered the sea, it takes up residence on a small patch of the continental shelf, hunting or grazing near the bottom. Here it may live for years, even, as we are now beginning to learn, for decades, until it reaches sexual maturity; or, perhaps, it settles in a series of such habitats one after the other, as it grows and develops; or even spends some of those years wandering the ocean or roaming the coasts. We do not know for sure.

When sea turtles mature, they enter a more predictable cycle of migration, to and from their nesting grounds, alternating reproduction with a return to the feeding grounds to build up their resources for another breeding season. That journey is not always a long one—Green Sea Turtles (*Chelonia mydas*) nesting in the Red Sea may spend their whole lives within its waters—but for others, it extends for thousands of kilometers.

Female sea turtles do not make their nesting journey every year, except for the two ridley species. Kemp's Ridley (*Lepidochelys kempii*), and two-thirds of the females in a Surinam population of Olive Ridleys (*Lepidochelys olivacea*), nest annually. For the others, it may take from two to five years, or even more, before a female is ready to commit to another round of migration and nesting. This period, from nesting year to nesting year, is called the *remigration interval.*

In the years she does nest, a female sea turtle commonly lays multiple clutches, two to eight per season depending on the species. Between nestings, she returns to the sea while her next clutch ripens in her ovaries. This interesting interval takes anywhere from 9 to 30 days. Only after she lays her final clutch of the season will she return to her feeding grounds, perhaps by a different route from the one she followed to her nesting beaches.

We once believed that male sea turtles remained on the feeding grounds, or only traveled occasionally to the breeding areas. We thought that females stored their sperm for years, as some land turtles do (see page 260, Chapter 7). We now know that males may migrate, too (though often in smaller numbers), and may hover in the seas off the nesting beaches, fertilizing the eggs a female carries roughly a month before she digs her first nest. There may be a good reason for males to follow their mates across the ocean. Over the huge range of most sea turtles, nesting seasons vary with climate and latitude. The same species of sea turtle may nest in December in one area, and in June in another.

The lifelong journeys of sea turtles are governed and regulated by the physical parameters of their ocean environment, the richness and availability of their food supply (which may in turn be driven by changing patterns of climate and ocean temperature), and the cycling of hormones and apportionment of resources within their own bodies. Their ability to traverse the seas depends on their internal mechanisms for finding their way out of their nest, down to the sea, across it and, eventually, back again.

In some ways, we know far more about sea turtles than we do about their land-bound relatives; in others, we know far less, though increasingly sophisticated research is giving us a better, and more detailed, idea of their lives. New methods of paternity analysis, combining genetic studies with advanced statistics, are telling us more about the elusive adult males, far harder to study directly because they rarely come ashore. Nonetheless, important questions—many of vital importance for sea turtle conservation—remain unanswered. A 2010 survey of 35 sea turtle researchers from 15 countries identified more than 200 of them.

Grouped into 20 "metaquestions," some as basic as "What are the past and present roles of sea turtles in the ecosystem?" and "What constitutes a healthy turtle?", they form both a picture of our ignorance and a manifesto for future research. Though nesting sea turtles have been minutely studied, prodded and examined, as have their eggs and their newly hatched babies, when sea turtles return to the sea, they vanish, and the mystery of what they do with most of their lives is only beginning, over the last few decades, to yield to science.

Down to the Sea

A sea turtle begins its life buried about 60 cm (24 in) deep in its nesting beach (deeper for Leatherbacks, and less so for the two ridleys). Though sea turtles have been hatched for years in incubators, we know little of what goes on when they hatch in the wild. Some observations have been made with artificial nests, mostly on Greens and Loggerheads (*Caretta caretta*), and they give us an idea of what must take place under the sand.

A fully developed hatchling lies curled in its egg around the remnants of its yolk sac. It uses its egg-tooth to cut its way through its parchment-like shell, but before it fully escapes it may rest for anywhere from one to three days while its plastron straightens and the remainder of its yolk is absorbed into its body. The liquid left in the eggshells drains into the sand, and the shells themselves collapse, leaving room for the hatchlings to struggle free.

Normally, the eggs in a clutch hatch within a few hours of each other, and emergence is a project for the whole group. Over several hours, the brood alternates rest periods with bouts of seemingly coordinated digging, each hatchling stimulated into activity by the struggles of those around it. The hatchlings at the top of the writhing mass of newborn turtles scrape away at the sand over their heads. As the sand falls into the nest cavity, their siblings at the bottom of the heap trample it into the

floor beneath them. The hatchlings are not really coordinating their efforts, but these individual struggles slowly carry the whole brood upward.

Sometimes, instead of emerging together, hatchlings may leave the nest in small groups over 24 to 74 hours. Emergence may take 11 days for Loggerheads, 8 days for Greens, 4 for Hawksbills, and 9 for Flatbacks (in shallow nests in a hatchery; deeper, and naturally dug, nests emptied in much less time). On Fethiye Beach, Turkey, some Loggerhead nests took as long as 17 days to empty. At this site the sand is coarse and pebbly, and eggs in the upper levels of the nest were frequently destroyed by tenebrionid beetles. Dead eggs may have blocked the passage for smaller hatchlings in the lower part of the egg chamber trying to fight their way free.

The process of hatching and escape can take from 3 to 7 days—long enough for a hatchling to use up its reserves of yolk. Loggerheads studied by Elaine Christens in a turtle hatchery in Georgia averaged 5.4 days from the first pip of the shell to final emergence. Most of this time was spent resting; the hatchlings did not start to climb in earnest for the surface until the last day or two. By the time the hatchlings do break through to the surface, they will have lost weight. They will gain it again by drinking seawater once they enter the ocean (see page 197, Chapter 5) Olive Ridleys gain 0.2 g (0.07 oz) per day once they begin drinking, according to research by Susan Clusella Trullas and Frank Paladino.

If the nest temperature, and particularly that of the sand over their heads, becomes too warm, the hatchlings will stop—a response that makes it more likely that they will break through to the surface at night, when the sands are relatively cool. Emerging by day can be very dangerous; the heat of the surface sand on a sunny day can kill an emerging hatchling, and many a (staged) natural history film has shown hatchling sea turtles scrambling down to the sea by day, only to be snapped up by hovering flocks of

A hatchling Leatherback (*Dermochelys coriacea*) struggles to the surface—an effort that may have taken several days.

predatory frigatebirds (*Fregata* spp.). On Europa Island in the Mozambique Channel, where a small percentage of Green Sea Turtles emerge during the day, every one of 1,828 hatchlings seen to emerge before dark by Frédéric Lagarde and his team was immediately snatched up by a Great Frigatebird (*Fregata minor*). Lesser Frigatebirds (*Fregata ariel*), which also breed on the island, did not hunt the hatchlings, possibly because they were too large for the smaller bird to manage.

Once they are exposed to the dangers of the surface, it is vital for the hatchlings to find, and get to, the sea as soon as possible. Even at night, predators await them. Leatherbacks emerging at night at Playa Grande, Las Baulas, Costa Rica, face Ghost Crabs (*Ocypode occidentalis*), Great Blue Herons (*Ardea herodias*), and Yellow-crowned Night Herons (*Nycticorax violaceus*). The hatchlings wait for some 20 minutes on top of the nest before scrambling, in groups, across some 46 m (150 ft) of beach to the sea, making for an average of 34 minutes spent on the surface. 83 percent of them make it.

Hatchling sea turtles use a number of cues to tell them where the sea is. The most important seems to be light. The sky is usually brightest over the sea. Cover a hatchling's eyes, and it cannot find the sea even if there is other information available, such as a downward slope of the sand toward the water's edge. The hatchlings respond to light cues

OPPOSITE

Loggerhead (*Caretta caretta*) hatchlings may be drawn to the sea by light on the horizon.

in a "cone of acceptance" that takes in a horizontal sweep of roughly 180 degrees, but covers a vertical range of only about 30 degrees above the horizon or, depending on the species, even less. Because hatchlings only react to lights that are close to the horizon, they are less likely to be confused by moonlight. They seem less attracted to yellow light than to other colors—Loggerheads show an aversion to yellow light—and this preference may keep them from becoming disoriented by the rising sun.

It is usually safest to have more than one internal compass, and hatchlings seem to be guided by more than light alone. They will steer away from the high, dark silhouettes of sand dunes and vegetation. This may merely be because they block out the light, but sensitivity to shapes around them does apparently help hatchlings find the sea on a bright moonlight night, when the strongest light might not be coming from the horizon above it.

All these reinforcing cues, however, are not enough to guide hatchlings away from the artificial lights that now burn on many a beach environment. Artificial lighting is often strong enough to completely overcome the signals a hatchling sea turtle is programmed to recognize. Artificial light, if it is bright enough, becomes a stimulus so powerful that the hatchlings respond to nothing else, crawling toward it from hundreds of meters away (even once they enter the sea, hatchlings may head straight for well-illuminated ships). The result, on land, is often fatal. Lured away from the sea, the stranded hatchlings fall to predators, desiccate in the hot sun the following day, or simply starve. In highly developed areas like the Florida coast, artificial light may be the greatest threat hatchlings face.

If all goes well, and the hatchlings scramble over the sand in the right direction, avoid their enemies, and reach the surf, a new set of orienting mechanisms takes over. As soon as they are afloat, the hatchlings begin to swim at more than 1.5 km/hr (0.9 mph); Osamu Abe and his co-workers measured hatchling Green Sea Turtles that swam away from their nesting beaches in southwestern Japan at 1.62 km/hr (1 mph). They dive into the path of the wave undertow, where the receding waters sweep them outward, away from the beach. When they surface again, they head for open sea.

This time, they are guided not by sight but, apparently exclusively, by the direction of the incoming waves. Experiments with Loggerheads, Greens, and Leatherbacks have shown that hatchlings swim toward approaching waves, but if the sea is calm they swim randomly or in circles. Hatchlings will swim into the waves even if, under experimental conditions, doing so sends them back to the beach again.

The farther a hatchling gets from shore, the less-reliable wave direction becomes as a pointer to the open sea. Nicolas Pilcher and his colleagues have shown that hatchling Green Sea Turtles released from a hatchery in Sabah, Borneo (East Malaysia), are able to navigate around small islands, and keep swimming offshore, even when there are few waves to guide them. They may be relying on yet another internal compass, this time oriented to the earth's magnetic field.

Experiments by Jeanette Schnars and her colleagues suggest that Leatherback and Olive Ridley hatchlings "switch on" their geomagnetic compasses almost as soon as they are out of the nest. Though the hatchlings get a geomagnetic "fix" as soon as they leave the nest, and appear to be able to use it as a reference point, they will not follow it blindly if other cues, such as light and sound, are available.

Their geomagnetic compass will only be of use if hatchlings can determine their heading in the first place. A simple directional compass—one that always sent the turtles westward, for instance—would be useless if the open sea lay in some other direction. Therefore, a magnetic compass does not so much tell a hatchling turtle which way to go as keep it on course once it has determined its heading from some other cue.

A hatchling Hawksbill (*Eretmochelys imbricata*) swims through the dark waters off Sipadan Island, Sabah, Malaysia.

Hatchling Loggerheads and Leatherbacks tested in an experiment, once they had established a heading toward a distant light, successfully used the magnetic field of the earth to keep them on course even in total darkness. Another set of experiments, using a wave tank instead of a distant light, showed that once the hatchlings had set themselves on course by heading into the waves, their magnetic compass was able to keep them on track after the wave action was turned off. If the hatchlings did not have the chance to see the light first, or sense the wave direction, their magnetic compass was useless to them.

Once in the open sea, as they enter the gyres that will carry them to the habitats where they will develop into subadults, their geomagnetic compass is probably their most important navigational guide. Kenneth Lohmann and his colleagues tested Loggerhead hatchlings by exposing them to magnetic fields imitating what they would encounter at various points in the gyre. The hatchlings swam in what would have been, had they been at sea, the appropriate direction for each point. Their ability to tell apart magnetic field conditions at widely scattered positions in the gyre, should help them stay in its waters as they are swept across the ocean.

This still leaves a problem. As they are swept around the gyres, hatchlings cross lines of latitude twice—once on their northward journey, and again, hundreds of kilometers to the east or west (depending on the gyre), as they pass southward. To get a fix on where they really are, the turtles need to be able to judge not just latitude but longitude. Until a recent study by Nathan Putman and his colleagues, no one knew how they, or any other migratory animal, managed to do that.

The researchers exposed Loggerhead hatchlings to magnetic fields similar to those they might meet near Puerto Rico on the western side of the Atlantic and near Cape Verde, at the same parallel of latitude on the east. In each case the hatchlings swam in the appropriate direction, northeast and southwest respectively, something they could only do if the magnetic field was giving them information about longitude as well as latitude. Their magnetic compass provides hatchlings with two kinds of information: one, called the *magnetic inclination angle*, and another, the *magnetic field intensity*. The combination of the two differs at almost every point on a hatchling's migration route. In much the same way as a human cartographer combines latitude and longitude, though not consciously and probably without forming any sort of geographic image in their brains, hatchlings may be using these magnetic coordinates to determine their position within the gyre.

Lost and (Partially) Found

The hatchlings struggling seaward from their natal beaches are about to enter a period Archie Carr termed the "lost year". This mysterious interval stretches from the moment they disappear into the surf until the day they return, as much larger juveniles, to coastal waters. Today we know that the lost year is often far longer than a year; it may last one to three years for Atlantic Hawksbills (*Eretmochelys imbricata*), or a decade or more for Loggerheads. The hatchlings, thanks to a number of recent discoveries, are no longer quite so lost to turtle biologists.

Sea turtle biologists call the instinctive rush that hatchlings make, first for the surf and then for the open sea, the *frenzy*. Like most frenzies, it doesn't last long—about 24 hours in Loggerheads, Greens, and Leatherbacks leaving the nesting beaches of eastern Florida. Hawksbills may not have a frenzy at all. Chung Fung Chen and her colleagues recorded the swimming behavior of newly emerged Green and Hawksbill hatchlings from the Turtle Islands Park, Sabah, Malaysia. Whereas the Green Sea Turtle hatchlings swam nearly continuously in their observation tanks for about 17 hours a day over their first two days, Hawksbills swam for only a few hours a day and were less active in their first few days than later on. When they do swim, newly emerged Hawksbills use an inconspicuous "rear-flipper kicking" stroke involving their hind limbs, or a "dog-paddle" stroke when they surface to breathe, rather than "power stroking" with their front flippers, a gait they adopt gradually over the next few days. Instead of sprinting through nearshore waters full of predators to reach the open sea, as other sea turtles do, Hawksbills may avoid detection by remaining inactive and either hiding among, or seeking to be taken for, floating leaves or mats of algae. Perhaps they depend on tidal currents to, eventually, carry them out to sea.

According to Jeannette Wyneken and Michael Salmon, by their second night on the water hatchlings have begun to enter a more relaxed phase, the *postfrenzy*. They still swim seaward by day, but rest during at least part of the night. Loggerheads swim mostly by day. Greens spend about 10 percent of each night swimming as well, while Leatherbacks swim as much as 30 percent of the night.

The frenzy is not a rush to get to their pelagic feeding grounds, a journey that, after all, may take months. It is an adaptation to avoid predators. The longer a hatchling turtle stays in inshore waters, the greater its chance of ending up inside a predator's stomach. Predators took 40–60 percent of Green Sea Turtle hatchlings leaving hatcheries in Sabah, Borneo, during their first two hours at sea. This may be partly because the hatchery caretakers released the hatchlings en masse, usually at the same time and place each day, thus creating "feeding stations" for the local fish. Farther out at sea the hatchlings are likely safer.

Not every hatchling faces an equal risk of predation on its first swim; Emma Gyuris found that larger Green Sea Turtle hatchlings had a better chance of surviving their passage over the outer reef surrounding Heron Island, Australia, than smaller ones. Just as on land (see page 302, Chapter 7), size provides a measure of protection. This selective advantage is probably why the Flatback, which stays in predator-rich inshore waters, produces hatchlings twice as large as those of other sea turtles.

Florida hatchlings do not have to swim far offshore before they encounter the brown, knotted mats of the alga *Sargassum*. Hatchling Leatherbacks, already searching for the gelatinous creatures that are their only food, avoid any kind of floating debris. Greens hover around its edge, hunting free-floating prey in open water. For Loggerheads, though, floating debris, especially *Sargassum*, is home. Their brown and tan colors match the *Sargassum* itself, concealing the young turtles among the fronds. When researchers led by R.G. Mellgren added clumps of *Sargassum* to tanks holding captive Loggerhead hatchlings still in their frenzy, the turtles climbed into, or on top of, the floating weed, and stopped swimming.

In the waters around the Azores, 4,000 km (2,500 mi) eastward from Florida, rich upwellings of plankton from the Mid-Atlantic Ridge support a floating ecosystem. Hosts of jellyfish and other marine organisms float here among clumps of *Sargassum*. Here, too, are young Loggerhead

A hatchling Atlantic Loggerhead (*Caretta caretta*) conceals itself in a clump of floating *Sargassum* weed.

turtles, ranging from tiny animals not much bigger than hatchlings to medium-sized juveniles weighing some 23–27 kg (50–60 lbs). Thanks to tagging and DNA-fingerprinting studies by Alan Bolten and his colleagues, we now know that these are turtles that hatched on the southeastern coasts of the United States and in the Caribbean, about 80 percent of them on the beaches of Florida. They are carried to the Azores by the clockwise current of the North Atlantic gyre. After 10 or 12 years, they follow its southward loop back to the Caribbean.

Though we are far from having all the details, it appears that an eastward passage around the circuit of a gyre is typical for hatchling Loggerheads, whether they hatch in Florida, eastern Australia, Japan, or on the east coast of South Africa. George

Hughes has tracked South African Loggerheads into the Indian Ocean gyre. Mitochondrial DNA markers and, as we shall see, satellite tracking have proven that Loggerheads from Japan and, probably, Australia aggregate off the coast of Baja California, where biologists have recorded a concentration of some 10,000 juvenile turtles. Wherever they are, they spend their early years feeding on floating animals in the upper layers of the sea, concentrating on the stinging jellyfish *Pelagia noctiluca* in the Atlantic and on the delicate violet snails (*Janthina* spp.) and a colonial polyp, the By-the-wind Sailor (*Velella velella*), in the Pacific.

We still have very little idea of what other sea turtles do during their lost year. The one thing we can say for certain is that, if they survive, they

A Green Sea Turtle (*Chelonia mydas*) feeds on a Moon Jellyfish (*Aurelia aurita*) in the seas off Hawaii.

grow, but we are not even precisely sure how that happens. Milani Chaloupka and George Zug have suggested that the growth of at least one species, Kemp's Ridley, happens in two spurts. The first peaks at about 12 months of age, and second at around seven years.

The fate of hatchling Leatherbacks in particular is, according to John Musick and Colin Limpus, "one of the great mysteries of sea turtle biology." Once they leave their nesting beaches, young Leatherbacks simply disappear. It probably takes about four years for growing juveniles to reach over 1 m (3.2 ft) in carapace length, the size of the smallest subadults researchers see. Where they go during that time we have no idea. All we can say is that by the time they are adults, Leatherbacks have increased their length about thirtyfold and weigh some 6,000 times more than they did when they first emerged from the egg.

Following juvenile sea turtles to see what they do in the open ocean is no easy task. Michael Salmon and his colleagues got around this difficulty by releasing laboratory-raised Greens and Leatherbacks, tethered to tracking devices, into the Florida Current at roughly two-week intervals and observing them during their brief newfound freedom. Each species explored its patch of ocean in its own way. Most Leatherbacks and all of the Greens made dives, but the Leatherbacks generally dove deeper (up to 17.1 m [56 ft]) and stayed down longer (see page 200, Chapter 5). The Leatherbacks fed on *Aurelia* jellyfish, ctenophores (comb jellies)

It may be years before hatchling Leatherbacks like this one at Playa Ventanas, Costa Rica are seen again.

and other gelatinous animals that they may have had to dive some distance to find, while the Greens preferred surface or near-surface items like floating seaweed, a ctenophore (once), and a few gelatinous eggs. Leatherbacks tended to increase their dive depth as they grew older. Greens did not, though the duration of their dives increased with age. It appears that the diving abilities of Leatherbacks improve rapidly as they grow, and that juveniles of both species soon adopt the behaviors, peculiar to their own kind, that will serve them through their lost years.

Miners and Gardeners

At the end of its lost year, only the Leatherback remains a pelagic animal; the projecting, tooth-like cusps on its upper jaw may help it hold on when it bites into the huge, gelatinous bells of open-ocean jellyfish such as the Lion's Mane (*Cyanea capillata*). The Flatback never leaves the continental shelf in the first place. The other sea turtles leave the open ocean for feeding grounds on the continental shelf, often far from the beaches where they were born. Mitochondrial DNA evidence collected by Anna Bass and Wayne Witzell shows that Green Sea Turtles hatched in Costa Rica, Mexico, Venezuela, and Surinam may assemble on feeding grounds on the east coast of Florida, while juveniles in the nearby Bahamas may even include a few individuals hatched as far away as Ascension Island or Guinea Bissau.

By the time they arrive in their new homes, young sea turtles are big enough to ignore most of the predators that threatened them on their first journey through continental waters. Once a sea turtle reaches more than about 20–30 cm (8–12 in) in carapace length, it has little to fear from anything but a large shark or a Killer Whale (*Orcinus orca*); it is simply too big and too hard-shelled for most other predators.

Sharks, including Great White (*Carcharodon carcharias*), Bull (*Carcharhinus leucas*), and Tiger Sharks (*Galeocerdo cuvier*), are the primary marine predators on both adult and large juvenile sea turtles. In the aptly named Shark Bay, Western Australia, Tiger Sharks regularly attack Greens and Loggerheads. Loggerheads, slower and less agile than Greens, seem particularly vulnerable. Male Loggerheads are attacked more than females. We do not know why, beyond a suggestion that males, which may require extra resources to compete for females, may be more likely to seek food in areas sharks prefer. In other words, males take more risks.

Leatherback turtles have actually been seen harassing sharks. One full-grown Leatherback that successfully chased off a large reef shark (*Carcharinus* sp.) then turned its attention to the observers' boat, ramming it half a dozen times with the leading edge of its carapace before swimming off, only to return to the attack after two members of the crew decided to swim after it.

Immature sea turtles may resort to places that adults rarely visit. Kemp's Ridleys, which nest almost exclusively in Mexico, may wander throughout the Gulf of Mexico as adults; juveniles and subadults range farther, north along the Atlantic Coast as far as maritime Canada or, in small numbers, to northwestern Europe. Long Island Sound appears to be an important feeding ground for Kemp's Ridleys at roughly three to six years of age. Of the 5,000 to 10,000 Loggerheads, and perhaps more than a thousand Kemp's Ridleys, that spend the summer in Chesapeake Bay off the eastern coast of United States, some 95 percent of the Loggerheads and probably all of the ridleys are juveniles. Large numbers forage in the sounds off North Carolina as long as the water remains warm. From September onward, the turtles move south to waters off Georgia and the Carolinas, returning again the following May and June.

In the Pacific, Green Sea Turtles may be less likely to wander, though turtles in a feeding aggregation around the Yaeyema Islands, Japan, come from as far away as the eastern Pacific, Southeast

A Tiger Shark (*Galeocerdo cuvier*) scavenges the carcass of a Green Sea Turtle
(*Chelonia mydas*) killed by native Torres Strait hunters off Mabuiag Island, Queensland, Australia.

Asia, and Papua New Guinea. Turtles from Hawaii and the Galápagos tend to stay around their island reefs, though tagged Galápagos females have been recovered from Costa Rica to Peru. Immatures monitored since 2001 along the Pacific coast of Baja California del Sur, Mexico, tend to select a specific foraging ground and stay there, though a few move from one area to another. In the southern Great Barrier Reef, some juvenile turtles have been under observation in the same localized feeding areas for over 20 years. Immature Green Sea Turtles arriving on foraging grounds off Mantanani Island, Sabah, Malaysia apparently remain there for 6 or 7 years.

Once they reach about 30–50 cm (12–20 in) or so in carapace length (in the western Atlantic), or 70 cm (28 in) or more (in Australia), Loggerhead Sea Turtles move to the continental shelf and shift their foraging attentions from the surface to the bottom, though juveniles off North Carolina may shift back to oceanic waters, either seasonally or for periods of several years, switching from bottom feeding to surface feeding again as they go. Larger juvenile and adult Loggerheads have two distinct choices of lifestyle. Some remain primarily deep-water foragers, while others, even turtles from the same breeding population, spend their adult lives near shore. Loggerheads in the Northwest Atlantic are a conglomeration of several different nesting stocks. Some travel north and south along the continental shelf, while others follow the Gulf Stream to the North Atlantic where surface temperature limits their northward movement. Some return to

A Loggerhead (*Caretta caretta*) dines on a Spiny Lobster (*Paniluris argus*) in the Bahamas.

the foraging ground each year, while others remain at sea for one to three years.

In the Gulf of Mexico, these immature Loggerheads dine on animals like Sea Pen (*Virgularia presbytes*) that live on, or beneath, the sea floor. The diet of Loggerheads feeding on the continental shelf may shift with the seasons; off the coast of Texas, the turtles switch from sea pens to crabs in the summer and fall, when crab numbers go up. Off the coast of Virginia, Horsehoe Crabs (*Limulus polyphemus*) were the most common Loggerhead prey item during the early to mid-1980s, but as fishing pressure reduced their numbers the turtles switched to Common Blue Crabs (*Callinectes sapidus*). When heavy fishing, in turn, reduced blue crab numbers in the early 1990s, fish became the chief items in the Loggerhead diet. As the turtles are not agile enough to catch many fish by themselves, today they appear to get most of their food from discarded bycatch or fishing nets. In North Carolina, however, Loggerheads continue to eat a diet heavy in blue crab, and rarely take fish.

Loggerheads in Moreton Bay, Queensland, trench mine the bottom sediments for prey, particularly clams and polychaete worms. According to Anthony Preen, the turtles "dug body pits in the sediments, and used their foreflippers to erode the sand wall in front of their faces. The turtles fed from this eroding wall, picking at individual organisms as they were exposed." The turtles' mining activities leave hundreds of trenches 40 cm (16 in) deep scarring the floor of the bay.

Hatchling Green Sea Turtles may take a variety of invertebrates (Roy Caldwell observed a captive hatchling trying to attack a small octopus), and during their time in the open sea, juvenile Greens tend to be omnivores. Older juveniles and adults are, usually, vegetarians, though the populations in the eastern Pacific and in the Arabian Sea are somewhat more carnivorous. During El Niño episodes, when the sea is particularly warm, Green Sea Turtles from the eastern tropical Pacific appear in large numbers off the coast of Peru where they feed heavily on the abundant scyphozoan jellyfish *Chrysaora plocamia*.

The switch to a vegetarian diet obliges Greens to move into shallow waters (such as along the Turkish coast in the eastern Mediterranean) where they can reach growing plants on the sea bottom. Although juvenile Greens in the eastern Mediterranean begin eating sea grasses as soon as they arrive in shallow waters, it takes some time before they begin to derive most of their nourishment from them. Until they reach a carapace length of 60 cm (24 in) or so, most of their nutrients come from animal food; the commonest items in the stomach of a juvenile Green found dead in the western Adriatic were Parchment Worms (*Chaetopterus variopedatus*), animals that burrow in the sea-bottom sand in seagrasses beds. This may be because the ability of smaller sea turtles to digest plant material is poor at cooler temperatures, and for a good part of the year the waters of the eastern Mediterranean are below 20°C (68°F). In warmer climates young turtles may be able to make an earlier switch to a more exclusively vegetarian diet.

The plants Green Sea Turtles feed on may vary from place to place. Their preferred foods, when they can get them, are various sorts of seagrass (Zosteraceae), one of the few flowering plant families to grow on the ocean floor. In Hawaii and on some parts of the Great Barrier Reef, where there are few seagrasses beds (e.g., in Kane'ohe Bay, Oahu, where turtles eat the sea grasses *Halophila decipiens* and *Halophila hawaiiana*) the turtles graze on algae, especially red algae, growing on the rocks, often within a few feet of shore. In Hawaii, turtles in different areas may prefer specific species of algae. Some populations have shifted their diet in recent years to include accidentally introduced algae such as *Acanthophora spicifera*, a red alga that spread rapidly in the islands after its arrival in the 1950s. The gut microflora seagrasses eaters rely on to digest their meals cannot break down algae, and vice versa. Most turtles carry only one or the other. In some areas, though, including parts of Australia, Green Sea Turtles eat both seagrass and algae, apparently digesting both with equal ease. Stomachs of Green Sea Turtles stranded in the Ra's Al Hadd area of Oman contained brown, red, and green algae of various sorts, animal matter including a number of mollusks, and sea grasses, as well as bits of assorted debris.

In the Gulf of California, East Pacific Green Sea Turtles feed primarily on marine algae, particularly the abundant red alga *Gracilariopsis lemaneiformis* as well as sponges, tube worms, soft corals, and sea hares and other mollusks. Sea grasses are sporadic and uncommon in the Gulf, but the turtles do eat them where they grow. They may lack the appropriate gut flora to deal with certain types of brown algae, and appear to avoid them.

In northern Australia, Green Sea Turtles eat the leaves and shoots of mangrove trees, even reaching out of the water to snip off a tasty shoot; sea grass, though, remains their food of choice. The turtles can be picky about precisely which seagrasses shoots they will graze, and may travel long distances to find the plants they prefer. Green Sea Turtles along the Queensland coast tend to prefer the sea grasses *Halodule uninervis* and *Halophila ovata* over a third species, *Zostera capricorni*. *Zostera* has lower nitrogen levels and higher fiber content than the others, and is therefore less nutritious. The only other large seagrasses grazer in the area, the Dugong (*Dugong dugon*), a mammal related to manatees (and elephants), has the same preference.

A Green Sea Turtle (*Chelonia mydas*) grazes on a seagrass bed off Mayotte in the western Indian Ocean.

Young shoots of seagrass are more nutritious than older plants. Green sea turtles in the Caribbean take advantage of this by continuously re-grazing the same beds. This regular pruning ensures a continuous crop of nutritious new shoots; in effect, the turtles are gardeners, tending their plots to produce the highest quality yield.

Olive Ridleys apparently do most of their foraging on the sea floor, often in deep water (see page 200, Chapter 5). Some adults remain over the continental shelf, while others follow oceanic currents far out to sea. Stomach contents from different parts of its range give wildly different pictures of what an Olive Ridley eats. A stomach from Papua New Guinea was almost entirely filled with snail shells. Stomachs from Sri Lanka were often full of algae. One from Surinam contained, among other things, two fresh catfish, while another taken off Japan was full of what appeared to be the liquefied remains of either jellyfish or the floating, gelatinous, colonial sea squirts known as salps. Salps were also key items in the stomach contents of eight Olive Ridleys caught in the Hawaii-based longline fishery.

A large-scale study of the Olive Ridley's diet examined the stomachs of 24 males and 115 females taken off Oaxaca on the Pacific coast of Mexico. The Mexican ridleys seemed to be dining largely on fish and salps, but although these items accounted for the bulk of the material, they all came from a small proportion of the turtle stomachs: 14 percent for salps, and 5 percent for fish. The rest of the stomachs may have been largely empty. These turtles were on their nesting grounds, and many breeding female sea turtles eat little or nothing during the nesting period.

Juvenile Hawksbill Sea Turtles floating in the open sea are apparently herbivores, reportedly living mostly on algae like *Sargassum*. Before they become

A Hawksbill (*Eretmochelys imbricata*) digs through coral rubble off Sipadan Island, Sabah, Malaysia, while reef fish wait for scraps.

adults and sponge specialists, juvenile Hawksbills may pass through an intermediate, omnivorous stage, foraging on the sea bottom for a variety of invertebrates and algae. Hawksbills resort to coral reefs when they reach between 20 and 35 cm carapace length (8-14 in), usually close to the areas where they first hatched and sometimes after a relatively brief period in the open sea. Here they become not just carnivores, but, in some cases, extreme specialists. Over most of their range, Hawksbills live primarily on sponges, either biting at them or scraping encrusting sponges from the coral surface. In the Caribbean, they eat little else, though they have been recorded eating Thimble Jellyfish (*Linuche unguiculata*) in the Cayman Islands.

Hawksbills are particular about the sponges they eat. They avoid sponges (such as the once-ubiquitous bath sponge) with a skeleton of tough, organic fibers or *spongin*. They have no problem, though, eating sponges whose bodies are studded with sharp spicules—tiny, often ornate spikes of calcium carbonate or silica—and, in many species, laced with a variety of toxic compounds. The turtles store the toxins in their own bodies. Hawksbill meat is occasionally poisonous. Records of sea turtle poisoning go back to at least 1697, many involving multiple deaths. The medical literature has documented hundreds of cases of human mortality from eating Hawksbills, especially in Madagascar and the Indo-Pacific. Between 1930 and 1996, 571 poisoning cases, involving 81 deaths, were reported in coastal Madagascar villages.

Hawksbills and Greens have been implicated as the source of chelonitoxism, a severe form of food poisoning with a high mortality rate. Other species, including Leatherbacks and Loggerheads, may be toxic on occasion. Greens in Japan have been found to contain lyngbyatoxin, a poison from the cyanobacterium *Lyngbya*.

In 2002, 19 members of one family from Rangiroa in the Tuamotu Islands became ill after eating a traditional meal of what they thought was a Green, but turned out to be a Hawksbill. One, a 26-year-old pregnant woman, lapsed into a coma and died.

Fellow Travelers

A sea turtle, like many a large fish, may provide shelter for pilot fish and other small fry, or a hitching post for a Remora *(Remora remora)* or its close cousin, the Sharksucker *(Echeneis naucrates)*. Generations of turtle hunters from East Africa to the West Indies have taken advantage of the remora's predilection for clamping itself, by its suckerlike dorsal fin, to the shell of a sea turtle. In 1494, on his second voyage, Christopher Columbus watched the Taino Indians of Cuba fish for turtles by tying a rope to a remora's tail, lowering it into the water near a turtle, waiting for the fish to attach itself, and slowly reeling in their catch.

On coral reefs, Hawksbills may be accompanied by angelfishes (Pomacanthidae) nibbling at exposed soft sponge tissue or eating the crumbs turtles drop. Reef-dwelling Hawksbills and Greens may take advantage of the local cleanup crew. Alice Grossman and her colleagues recorded Hawksbills being cleaned by Sergeant-Majors *(Abudefduf saxatilis)* and Rocas Damselfish *(Stegastes rocasensis)* off Fernando de Noronha in the southwest Atlantic. The turtles regularly sought out cleaning stations, either conspicuous rocky outcrops staffed by juvenile Sergeant-Majors or algal gardens tended by the damselfish. Here they hovered in the water, stretching their limbs and elevating their bodies to allow the fish access to their undersides. Julie Booth, who made some of the first regular underwater observations of Green Sea Turtles on the Great Barrier Reef in Australia, watched a large female being cleaned by two species of fish:

> About a dozen [sergeant-majors] *Abudefduf sexfasciatus...* were plucking algal growths from her head and plastron, while several moon wrasses, *Thalassoma lunare...* were

picking at small barnacles attached to the skin of her neck. The female would arch her neck first to the right, then to the left, apparently to stretch and tighten the skin and provide access to the barnacles for the fish.

Besides camp followers, cleaners and hangers-on, some sea turtles carry their own miniature ecosystems around with them. At least 100 different species of animals and plants have been found attached to Loggerhead turtles, though the greatest variety seems to be on sick animals. These range from the algae and barnacles that you might expect (and that also attach to other turtles like the Diamondback Terrapin) to colonies of star coral, snails, sea anemones, and crabs. Hawksbills and ridleys tend to carry a

Mats of Gooseneck Barnacles (*Lepas* sp.) cover the shells of juvenile Loggerhead Sea Turtles (*Caretta caretta*) in the Azores.

A Hawaiian Green Sea Turtle
(*Chelonia mydas*) gets cleaned by
surgeonfish (*Ctenochaetus strigosus*
and *Zebrasoma flavescens*).

very small number of large barnacles. Leatherbacks may carry hundreds of barnacles in the Pacific but, oddly, not in the Atlantic. A number of *chelono-philic* ("turtle-loving") barnacles are known only from sea turtles, including species reportedly found on 15-million-year-old turtle fossils. Some attach themselves to the carapace or plastron, but others are embedded into the skin of the flippers or the leathery shells of Leatherbacks, anchoring themselves in place with short spines or, possibly, releasing chemicals that induce the turtle's skin to surround them with a web of connective tissue.

Organisms that live on others are called *epibionts*. All sea turtles may have them, but Loggerheads, for some reason, have the largest and most diverse epibiont communities; a Kemp's Ridley may have no more than a few barnacles. Hawksbill epibionts found off Puerto Rico include larvae of the midges *Clunio* and *Pontomyia*, among the very few truly marine insects. The turtles may be agents in the midges' dispersal. Loggerheads may be assisting the future spread of the Veined Rapa Whelk (*Rapana venosa*), an invasive Asian shellfish predator that has wreaked havoc among oyster and mussel populations in the Black Sea, along the eastern seaboard of North America. The whelks, currently known only from Chesapeake Bay, have been found as epibionts on a juvenile Loggerhead stranded near Norfolk, Virginia, and on eight nesting adults on Wassaw Island, Georgia.

Some Loggerhead epibionts grow on other epibionts; all the known examples of Star Coral (*Astrangia danae*) on Loggerheads were actually growing on a variety of barnacles. Others need a protected place to attach themselves to avoid being swept off as the turtle swims; one Loggerhead sported some 200 sea anemones of the species *Diadumene leucolena*, all growing in a series of deep scars left from a collision with a boat propeller.

Supporting this little community can be, quite literally, a drag. A load of epibionts on a turtle's shell may cut down considerably on its streamlining, making swimming much harder work. This drain on energy may be particularly serious for younger turtles, which will have to work harder to compensate for the added drag on their shells. At least some turtles, though, may carry around their own cleanup crew.

Loggerheads, Green Sea Turtles and Hawksbills in the central Atlantic have all been found carrying specimens of the Columbus Crab (*Planes minutus*), usually clinging to the tail, hindlimbs, or around the cloaca. It appears that the Columbus crabs feed on the other epibionts, both plant and animal (including juveniles of their own species), as well as tiny organisms floating nearby and, probably, scraps dropped from the turtle's mouth. They may be quite important in keeping the turtles clean. The turtle, in return, may provide the crab with both an opportunity to find a wide range of food and an important breeding ground. Pairs of adult crabs, and females bearing eggs, are much commoner on turtles near Madeira than on the floating mats of *Sargassum* weed surrounding them, though breeding crabs on surrounding flotsam carry as many eggs as those living on a turtle. Juvenile crabs are commoner in the weed, which may mean that the *Sargassum* weed, by providing a nursery for the crabs, is essential to the health of young sea turtles.

Turtles in Space!

An enormous span of years may elapse between the time a female sea turtle hatches to the day when she drags herself ponderously out of the ocean to dig

Crabs, possibly Columbus Crabs (*Planes minutus*), cling to the cloacal area of a Loggerhead Sea Turtle (*Caretta caretta*).

her first nest. Not all turtles mature at the same age, or at the same size. Female Loggerheads hatching in Japan and maturing in the North Pacific gyre vary in their growth rates, which presumably depend on their luck in finding food. Rapidly growing turtles remain in the open sea and apparently reach sexual maturity at a smaller size and earlier age, while slower-growing animals shift to coastal waters and mature more slowly there; estimates for time to maturity for Loggerhead Sea Turtles off the coast of Georgia range from 20 to 63 years.

Young Leatherbacks grow surprisingly rapidly (see page 113, Chapter 3), and may continue to grow for a time after reaching sexual maturity. Young Green Sea Turtles may grow fairly quickly, but slow once they take up life in coastal waters and shift to a diet of plants. They may have the longest time to maturity of any vertebrate. Colin Limpus has found that Greens on the coast of Queensland may take from 30 to the astonishing age of 70 years to reach their first breeding season. Maturity may take even longer in the Galápagos; by one calculation, it could take 92 years for a turtle to reach even the size of the smallest nesting females seen in the islands. An alternate calculation suggests that Galápagos Greens may *only* need 63 years to reach this size. More recently, Jeffrey Seminoff and his colleagues have estimated that Greens in the Gulf of California grow to nesting

size in only 9 to 21.9 years, but may not be sexually mature for decades more. Growth rates in the Gulf are much higher than in the Galápagos, though it is not clear why; they may reflect food quality, environmental or genetic differences, or even a population rebound after decades of exploitation.

Once a sea turtle reaches maturity, however long that takes (or perhaps even later), it begins a migratory cycle to and from its breeding grounds that will last for the rest of its life. The simplest way to follow a sea turtle travels on its migratory journeys involves attaching a metal or plastic tag to its flipper. If the turtle is found again, the information on the tag can tell us where and how long ago it was last seen. In 2000, newspapers in Hawaii carried the story of Green Sea Turtle 5690, tagged as a juvenile by George Balazs near Hilo on the Big Island in 1981 and next seen nesting on Maui 19 years later. Tagging can give us information on a great many animals. A recent study of Cuban Green Sea Turtles drew on data from 742 animals tagged in Cuba over a 23-year period, (from 1989 to 2002) and 391 others tagged elsewhere, but recovered in Cuban waters.

Flipper tags are cheap and (providing the tags stay on and the turtles reappear) effective, and readable by anyone without a scanner or other special equipment. Sea turtle biologists have used them for many years. For Leatherbacks in particular, they

A research assistant attaches a flipper tag to a nesting Green Sea Turtle (*Chelonia mydas*) on Talang Talang Besar Island, Sarawak, Malaysia.

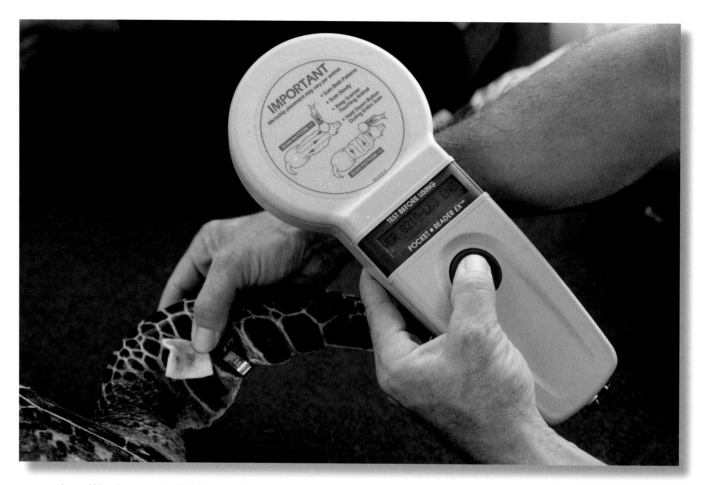

Larry Wood, sea turtle biologist and Curator of the Loggerhead Marinelife Center of Juno Beach, Florida uses a PIT (passive integrated transponder) scanner to read a microchip embedded in a Hawksbill Sea Turtle's muscle tissue.

are now replaced by the more sophisticated passive integrated transponder (PIT) tags, glass microchips about the size of a grain of rice injected into a turtle's shoulder muscle and read with a hand-held scanner. Richard Reina and his colleagues have used PIT tags to mark and identify nesting female Pacific Leatherbacks at Las Baulas Marine Park, Costa Rica, and to find out how frequently they return to the nesting grounds (every 3.7 years on average).

Tagging was not enough to satisfy pioneer sea turtle biologist and conservationist Archie Carr. In the 1960s, he fitted a number of Green Sea Turtles in Tortuguero National Park, Costa Rica, with radio transmitters carried above the waves by bright yellow helium balloons on 15–18 m (50–60 ft) cords. As the turtles put out to sea, Carr and his co-workers were able to follow them a little way with binoculars and directional antennas.

Balloon tagging, though, would hardly do to track turtles over thousands of miles of ocean. In his book *The Sea Turtle: So Excellent a Fishe*, Carr told how he had dreamed of tracking his turtles with orbiting satellites, but initially dismissed the notion as an impractical fantasy:

The ideal way to maintain contact with the island-seeking turtles cruising in the open sea would be by satellite. This thought occurred to me a long time ago, when Telstar was put into orbit; but I dismissed it as grandiose daydreaming, bound to lead only to discontent. Then, lo, a letter came asking me to submit a plan to use tracking facilities of one of the experimental satellites of the Apollo program. My brother, Tom, who is a physicist and radio astronomer, and David Ehrenfeld and I quickly put together a proposal to be submitted to NASA for tracking turtles by earth-orbiting satellites.

The first attempt to use satellites to track sea turtles (and one of the first for any animal) was made with Loggerheads in the early 1980s. Satellite tracking did not come into widespread use until the 1990s—too late for Carr, who died in 1987. In the mid-1980s Richard Byles began the first consistent satellite telemetry program, on Loggerheads and Kemp's Ridleys in Chesapeake Bay. George Balazs began satellite tracking Green Sea Turtles on the French Frigate Shoals in the Leeward Islands of Hawaii in 1992. On June 7, 1995, he fitted a satellite transmitter to a male Green Sea Turtle first flipper-tagged in 1982 and seen again, with no clue as to where it had been, in 1984. 12 days later, tag number 6038 set off for the open sea. For 30 days, he traveled southeast, swimming for 1,200 km (746 mi), far out of sight of land, over water thousands of meters deep, till he reached the feeding and resting grounds of Kahului Bay on the northern coast of Maui. Biologists were able to follow him, by satellite and computer, all the way.

In 1994, Barbara Schroeder, Llewelyn Ehrhart, and George Balasz attached satellite transmitters to three Greens, named Honu, Fairly, and Keya, nesting in the Archie Carr National Wildlife Refuge in eastern Florida. To the scientists' surprise Honu, Fairly, and Keya did not travel far in the few months their transmitters operated. Their feeding grounds seemed to be in Florida waters, and the results helped explain why no long-distance tag recoveries had been reported for Greens tagged on Florida beaches.

In the Atlantic, Steve Morreale and, later, Scott Eckert began satellite tracking Leatherbacks nesting in Trinidad, giving us the first inkling that turtles from the same population may differ in their migratory path. Though they both started from the same point, one of two tracked Leatherbacks traveled north along the Gulf Stream to the North Atlantic, while the other headed almost due east, straight across the ocean, and spent the next few months wandering up and down

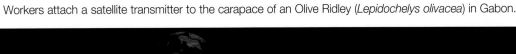

Workers attach a satellite transmitter to the carapace of an Olive Ridley (*Lepidochelys olivacea*) in Gabon.

the Atlantic coasts of Europe and North Africa.

In 2000, two satellite-tagged Leatherbacks set out across the Pacific from their foraging grounds off Monterey Bay, California, heading almost directly toward their probable nesting grounds in Papua New Guinea. They covered some 40 km (24 mi) a day. Because they made only shallow dives on the way, they were probably not feeding, relying instead on the fat stored up from their gelatinous feast in Monterey Bay. We know that female Greens eat little or nothing during the nesting period, and this may be true of Leatherbacks as well.

Early satellite-tracking efforts thus revealed a great deal about turtle migrations, telling us (as tagging data could not) whether the turtles follow paths that allow them to take advantage of ocean currents or prevailing winds, or whether they stop to feed during long-distance migrations. Paladino's satellite tracks reinforce the conclusion, derived from mitochondrial DNA studies by Peter Dutton and his colleagues, that the Leatherbacks off the West Coast

of North America come from the breeding population of the western Pacific, which nests in Malaysia, Indonesia and Solomon Islands. The Leatherbacks nesting in the eastern Pacific, on the shores of Mexico and Costa Rica, are genetically distinct and range, instead, southward along the coast of South America.

Tag and satellite data can complement one another. In the North Pacific, Loggerhead turtles nest in Japanese waters and feed in the ocean off Baja California in Mexico, thousands of kilometers away. Until 1996, when Wallace Nichols satellite tagged a fully grown female Baja Loggerhead named Adelita, nobody knew for certain if these were turtles from the same population. Nichols tracked Adelita for 11 months as she swam 10,000 km (6200 mi) across the Pacific to Japan. But did turtles from Japan swim to Baja California? The answer came from a flipper tag recovered from a Mexican fisherman who had kept it on his key chain for five years. It, in turn, came from a turtle hatched on Yakushima Island, where a third of Japan's Loggerheads nest. The hatchling had spent

After seven months at the Centre for Study and Care for Marine Turtles (Cestmir) in the Aquarium La Rochelle, France, a Loggerhead Turtle (*Caretta caretta*), fitted with a satellite transmitter, is returned to the sea.

This Kemp's Ridley (*Lepidochelys kempi*) has been fitted with a satellite transmitter.

its first year at the Okinawa Aquarium, where it was tagged and released in 1988.

In 2008, Brendan Godley and his colleagues were able to review more than 130 scientific papers based on satellite telemetry of sea turtles, the vast majority published since the turn of the new century. 82 percent of the studies involved Loggerheads, Greens or Leatherbacks. The first Flatbacks to be tagged were only fitted out in 2004. There has also been an understandable bias toward tagging nesting females, which are far easier to come by than adult males or juveniles.

Advanced satellite telemetry has revealed the foraging grounds of Leatherbacks in the open sea, the division among Loggerheads between coastal and pelagic adults, the varying migratory patterns of turtles from different nesting populations, and much more. By pinpointing areas where adult turtles concentrate when away from their nesting beaches, and by drawing our attention to potential danger zones, they have provided us with essential information for conservation. Richard Byles' early study showed that Kemp's Ridleys do not migrate through the relatively

safe open waters of the Gulf of Mexico, but along the coast in shallow water less than 46 m (150 ft) deep, where they may fall foul of fishing nets. Scott Eckert and his colleagues found that Leatherbacks from Florida nesting grounds, thought to spend the bulk of their time in the open sea, traveled between March to November to coastal shrimp-fishing grounds near the Georgia-Florida border where, in 2001, 17 Leatherbacks were found dead on nearby beaches, presumed accidental victims of the shrimping fleet.

Satellite-tagging programs, many of which can be tracked online, have brought the issue of turtle conservation to the public's attention and have been used to call for action from governments. I-Jiun Cheng used data showing that turtles nesting on China's Nansha (Spratly) Archipelago traveled to nearby Malaysia and the Philippines to advertise the need for cooperation within the region. Jeanne Mortimer's data from the Seychelles showed that Hawksbills breeding in the islands may spend their entire adult lives within the confines of the Seychelles Bank—providing a convincing argu-

Satellite transmitters have traditionally been attached to Leatherbacks (*Dermochelys coriacea*) using harnesses, as here in French Guiana, but these are now known to affect the turtle's swimming abilities.

Transmitters are now usually mounted on baseplates attached directly by drilling holes in the Leatherback's carapace, as here (also in French Guiana).

ment to counter those Seychellois who objected to protecting turtles that would only be slaughtered elsewhere (see page 420, Chapter 10).

Satellite tracking is expensive and difficult. Its cost (roughly $2,000–$4,000 per transmitter, plus a further charge per turtle per year for satellite time) has limited the animals bearing transmitters to a select few. On the Turtle Islands in the Philippines, the Pawikan Conservation Project (*pawikan* is Filipino for "sea turtle") fitted 8,071 turtles with flipper tags between 1984 and 1998, but was only able to attach satellite transmitters to 12 turtles between 1998 and 2002 (Jack Frazier and his co-workers fitted out the first two in October 1998).

Between 1999 and 2003, Michael James and his colleagues attached transmitters to 38 Leatherbacks captured at sea off Nova Scotia, creating the largest data set thus far for the species in the Atlantic. Over the next months they tracked the turtles south-east, to the mid-Atlantic, the Caribbean, and the north-

ern coast of South America. The data showed that the turtles spent much more time than expected in heavily fished coastal waters, where they risked boat strikes and entanglement with gear. The authors called for greater efforts to reduce the likelihood of accidental Leatherback deaths while the Atlantic population was still relatively healthy.

The devices themselves, known as platform terminal transmitters (PTTs), are attached to the carapace with epoxy, or fiberglass cloth and resin. For Leatherbacks, they have traditionally been strapped on with harnesses or tethers, but this has been shown to affect the turtles' swimming and diving abilities. PTTs are now usually mounted on baseplates attached directly by drilling holes in the Leatherback's carapace (this does not seem to harm the turtle). PTTs must withstand the rigors of several months on a turtle's back. Their most fragile and exposed element, the antenna, is especially liable to be broken off as the turtle rubs itself against rocks, coral or debris—or it may be knocked off by an amorous male attempting to mount.

The PTT carries a microprocessor that continually gathers data (providing its batteries keep working—usually less than a year). Its signal is sent to satellites circling the earth in a polar orbit, gathering weather information for the U.S. National Oceanographic and Atmospheric Administration (NOAA). At least five carry instruments, manufactured by the French company CLS-Argos, capable of receiving the ultra-high-frequency (UHF) signals the transmitters send.

Standard satellite-tracking methods, though, have two major drawbacks. First, the transmitter must be above water to send a signal, and the satellites must be "in view" above the horizon when the turtle is at the surface. Each satellite is likely to be in the proper position for only about two 12-minute passes per day, or less if the satellite passes low over the horizon. To get an accurate fix on the turtle's position, the satellite needs to receive at least four signals on each pass. It may take 30 seconds to several minutes for the satellite to lock on to the transmitter signal, and if the turtle submerges quickly the opportunity may be lost. Second, the Argos system can place a turtle no closer than within 100 m (330 ft), and at times no better than within 4 km (2.5 mi). This is good enough if you are trying to track a turtle across an entire ocean, but useless for fine-scale information about its daily movements.

Tracking technology, however, has taken major steps forward. Satellite relay data loggers (SRDLs) send data to Argos in the same manner as a standard transmitter. They can also record a wide array of data while the turtle is beneath the surface, including the depth and duration of dives, ocean temperatures, and water pressure. The data are compressed and transmitted when the turtle resurfaces. In a 2010 study, Sabrina Fossette and her colleagues used SRDLs to track movements and diving behavior of 16 Leatherbacks from different parts of the Atlantic. They found that the turtles visited 22 Temporary Residence Areas (TRAs), presumably

productive foraging areas in various regions of the open ocean or the continental shelf, where they paused to dive and feed. Turtles from different nesting populations tended to make for specific TRAs. Turtles from Suriname migrated to the North Atlantic while those from Gabon traveled into the South Atlantic.

SDRLs do not provide pinpoint location data. For that, in 2005 Tohya Yasuda and Nobuaki Arai developed GPS-Argos PTTs, which can send conventional Argos data but can also make use of the Global Positioning System (GPS), which is much more accurate (to within 10 m [33 ft] under the right circumstances), and relies on many more satellites. Recent improvements to GPS receivers have meant that satellite signals can now be picked up within milliseconds of a turtle's appearance above water; however, compared to older models, the new PTTs are expensive and power hungry. In 2006, off Zakynthos, Greece, Gail Schofield and her colleagues bypassed the satellites (and their associated fees) by fitting Loggerheads with non-transmitting GPS data loggers and time-depth recorders (TDRs). The data were retrieved later when the turtles were recaptured, either at sea or on the nesting beach.

For short-term nearshore tracking, satellite transmission can be combined with other methods. Jesse Senko and his colleagues studied daily movements of Green Sea Turtles in a coastal lagoon in Baja California by fitting them with 10 m (32 ft) monofilament tethers leading to floating buoys fitted with both GPS data logger/receivers and VHF transmitters. The researchers picked up their signals from shore or from a boat using a handheld directional antenna. Louise Brooks and her colleagues, who first used this technique, called it a "high-tech, low-cost tool" for tracking marine animals.

At the other end of the scale is the global location sensor (GLS), a technology that has been around for some time but has only fairly recently been applied to sea turtles. The device in this case (another that must be retrieved manually from the turtle carrying it) determines position by taking a fix, twice every 24 hours, on ambient light intensity and relating it to the season and time of day. GLS has the advantage of being relatively light and inexpensive, and can last for up to 220 days, but it is even less accurate than standard satellite telemetry, has a margin for error of up to 150 km (93 mi), and is only useful for tracking large-scale movements. Wayne Fuller and his colleagues used GLS loggers to track Greens and Loggerheads at sea in the Mediterranean.

Satellite and tag data are being increasingly combined with molecular tracing, oceanographic current modeling, and other high-tech sources of information to gain insight into the movement of turtles coming from the same nesting colony. In a 2010 study, Brendan Godley and his colleagues used this combined approach to analyze the dispersal patterns of Green Sea Turtles from the largest breeding aggregation in the eastern Atlantic, at Poilão Island, Guinea-Bissau. They were able to demonstrate that turtles of all age classes from the island beaches remain in largely coastal waters off West Africa, rather than crossing the Atlantic. This sort of information can be extremely important for conservationists seeking to protect particular turtle stocks.

Recently, satellites tracked nine Leatherback Sea Turtle from New Guinea to the west coast of North America, the first record of a trans-Pacific migration by a Leatherback. The study was led by Scott Benson, who has now synthesized results from 126 Leatherbacks tagged between 2000 and 2007. Leatherbacks nesting during the boreal summer migrated to Large Marine Ecosystems (LMEs) of the temperate North Pacific Ocean or into tropical waters of the South China Sea, while turtles nesting during the boreal winter transferred instead to temperate and tropical LMEs of the southern hemisphere. Turtles from different subpopulations headed to different regions. Like Atlantic Leatherbacks, they sought out areas of the ocean where their prey was concentrated, traveling great distances to reach

them. Animals resorting to the remote, temperate California Current ecosystem took 10 to 12 months to cross the Pacific, forcing them to stretch their breeding intervals into multiple years, while others heading for tropical foraging grounds needed only half the time and, potentially, may nest more frequently.

Pamela Plotkin, in one of the first extensive satellite studies of Olive Ridleys, has found that in the eastern tropical Pacific these turtles do not have a regular migration at all. They seem to be ocean nomads wandering aimlessly over the sea, perhaps responding to the unpredictable conditions of an ocean realm governed by the vagaries of El Niño.

There seem to be no limits on what you can record with the right kind of sensor. Inter-mandibular angle sensors (IMASEN) can track the movement of a turtle's jaws as it eats. I have not even mentioned critter cams. Perhaps Jürg Blumenthal and his colleagues were being ironic when they described snorkeling to watch what turtles (in this case, Hawksbills) actually do as "a complementary and substantially under-utilized method in marine turtle research"!

Homeward Bound

Now that we have some idea, based on tagging, genetic analysis, and satellite tracking, where and when sea turtles go on their breeding migrations, we can consider the more difficult questions of how and why. What sends sea turtles to one breeding area and not another? How do they find their way? And given that most sea turtles do not nest every year, what distinguishes a promising nesting year from a bad one?

No matter how much sea turtles from different rookeries may mix together on their feeding grounds (and the extent to which they do so can be considerable), they go their separate ways, to their own natal beaches, when it comes time to nest. No Leatherback tagged in South Africa, for example, has been found nesting anywhere else in the world, though South African Leatherbacks are genetically indistinguishable from those nesting in Florida, Costa Rica, or Surinam. This attachment to the land of one's birth is termed *philopatry*, and modern genetic profiling techniques, particularly involving analyses of mitochondrial DNA (mtDNA), has revealed a great deal more about it in recent years. Nonetheless, mtDNA can tell only part of the story. Because sperm lack mitochondria, mtDNA tells us nothing about the genetic dispersal of males, and the patterns of male and female gene flow are known to differ in some Green Sea Turtle populations.

We have known for some time that female turtles exhibit philopatry. Nancy Fitzsimmons and her colleagues demonstrated in 1997, using mtDNA analysis, that male Australian Greens return to their native waters to mate. This pattern may not hold for all sea turtles. Male Olive Ridleys, in particular, may mate with any females they come across over a wide geographic area. But, for Australian Greens at least, male philopatry may ensure, as I suggested early in this chapter, that their own breeding cycles coincide with those of the females. Even within Australia, some Green Sea Turtle populations breed in summer and others in winter. Arriving among the right batch of females at the right time of year may be critical.

More recently, Kiki Dethmers and her colleagues analysed mtDNA variation among nesting females from 27 Green Sea Turtle rookeries in Australasia, from Malaysia to Australia, Micronesia, and New Caledonia. The results show that philopatry operates on a fine scale. Turtles tend to return to specific areas within the region, and have apparently been

The breeding cycle of Green Sea Turtles (*Chelonia mydas*) in the southwestern Pacific is affected by El Nino events.

doing so long enough to have developed distinctive and identifiable combinations of genetic markers, or *haplotypes*. Dethmers was able to distinguish 17 different breeding stocks (termed Management Units or MUs), some confined to single rookeries and others spread among rookeries separated by as much as 500 km (310 mi). Population data and tagging returns prove that turtles with specific genetic profiles return to nesting beaches within their MU. Tagging data shows that 6 percent of returning females change rookeries within their MU between one breeding season and the next. In general turtles head back to their natal areas, but should circumstances change they can shift elsewhere, a flexibility important over the long evolutionary term, as some key nesting areas were well inland during the last ice age when sea levels were considerably lower. When the waters returned between 10,000 and 6,000 years ago, females wandering from their nesting grounds presumably colonized the new beaches.

In some areas this ability to colonize has traversed oceans. The southernmost tip Africa extends into cold south temperate waters, and would seem to be a barrier separating Green Sea Turtles in the western Indian Ocean from their cousins in the South Atlantic. Jérôme Bourjea and his colleagues nonetheless found an Atlantic mtDNA haplotype in turtles nesting in the southern Mozambique Channel. There must have been some recent gene flow from the Atlantic to the Indian Ocean. Other Atlantic haplotypes are missing and there is no evidence of Indian Ocean haplotypes in the Atlantic. Perhaps only a few females (hatchlings, juveniles or breeding adults) carried their genes around the Cape of Good Hope.

In the South Atlantic, one of the most important nesting areas for the Green Sea Turtle is the remote volcanic island of Ascension (the site of the annual sea turtle mating bash in the comic strip "Sherman's Lagoon"). The turtles that nest on Ascension travel there from feeding grounds off the coast of Brazil, 2,300 km (1,430 mi) or more to the west. What drives Brazilian turtles to Ascension,

and how do they find this tiny spot, only 248 sq km (96 sq mi) in area? The magnetic and solar compasses hatchlings use to find their way through the open sea are not enough to do the job. Kenneth Lohmann and his colleagues have pointed out that:

> [S]ystematic error in directional steering as small as a few degrees will cause a turtle migrating from the Brazilian coast to Ascension Island to miss its 11 km wide target after the 2,200 km-long oceanic trip. Given that animal compasses are generally thought to have limited accuracy (e.g., some estimates of compass accuracy are about ±40° [Wiltschko and Wiltschko, 1995]), reaching the island with a compass alone appears impossible.

Combine this with drifting currents that can carry even the strongest-swimming turtle off course, and the task Ascension-bound females face seems daunting indeed.

Archie Carr and others suggested some years ago that sea turtles navigate across the open ocean by taking a heading from the direction of the rising sun. Once they get close to their nesting areas, the turtles would home in on chemical cues carried over the water from their final destination, much as migrating salmon find the rivers of their birth by the chemical taste of the water. The existence of these supposed chemical signatures, however, has yet to be demonstrated.

C. W. Brown proposed, in 1990, that for Ascension at least this complex mechanism may not be necessary. Ascension lies in the middle of the South Atlantic Equatorial Countercurrent, a river of seawater that flows eastward through the surface layers of the ocean during the austral summer. During the austral winter, the surface waters between Ascension and Brazil are driven westward, this time by the southeast trades. Turtles nest on Ascension from December through June, with a peak between late February and April. For adults headed for their nesting grounds in the austral summer, the waters of the current provide a corridor through the ocean leading them to Ascension. Their flow eases the turtles' eastward swim, reducing the energetic cost of migration. In 51 to 57 days, turtles leaving the eastern bulge of Brazil could be at their island destination. Since their eggs take roughly 60 days to incubate, most hatchlings emerge in the austral autumn, just as the southeast trades intensify. The westward-flowing waters probably sweep the bulk of them to Brazil. Their parents, heading back to their feeding grounds at roughly the same time, of course swim on their own, but could certainly take advantage of the boost the trades provide.

Brown's mechanism requires no chemical cue. In fact, as he points out, an eastward-flowing current would sweep any chemicals from Ascension to the east, toward Africa, rather than westward, toward Brazil. Furthermore, satellite tracking has shown that turtles often follow more or less straight paths to their transoceanic goals, something they would be unlikely to do if they were following a chemical trail drifting on the surface of the sea. The current provides both a direction for the turtles to swim, and a good reason—energy efficiency—for the turtles to follow it. However, current flow does not explain how Green Sea Turtles find the tiny dot that is Ascension. Nor does their geomagnetic sense; even if that sense is disabled by attaching magnets to a female's head, she still seems able to find, with enough time, her breeding island (possibly using a solar compass). Further, the earth's magnetic field fluctuates, and even minor changes may be enough to lead her astray. For an Ascension-bound female, following the same magnetic heading she relied on three years earlier could cause her to miss the island by 45–60 km (28–37 mi).

A Green Sea Turtle (*Chelonia mydas*) leaves her nesting site on Ascension Island in the South Atlantic.

Turtles heading for Ascension, or other remote breeding islands, probably rely on a combination of sensory inputs. The information that leads them in the right general direction as they start their journey may be supplanted by other cues as they near their goal and fine-tuning becomes necessary. These could be chemical signals, visual landmarks, patterns of wave interference as the ocean swirls around a protruding landmass, or even encounters with other turtles. Perhaps, at the end of the journey, even some trial-and-error searching may be involved.

Ocean temperatures may be responsible for the breeding patterns of Indo-Pacific Greens on the Great Barrier Reef of Australia. In 1974, Colin Limpus arrived for his first season of turtle tagging on Heron Island, in the Capricorn Group near the southern end of the reef. He was prepared to tag no more than 200 to 600 turtles, the numbers an earlier researcher Robert Bustard, had suggested were typical for a Heron Island nesting season. But, as he reported in a paper co-authored with Neville Nicholls:

> To our surprise, we tagged ~1200 nesting females in the 1974–1975 breeding season and the local residents spoke of the greatest number of nesting turtles in their memory. We returned the following summer equipped to tag thousands of nesting green turtles only to be met by a total of 21 females breeding on Heron Island for the entire summer. Understandably we were puzzled. Some locals suggested that "Limpus has scared the turtles away."

Heron Island did not see another peak breeding year for a decade, and then not again until 1996 and 1999. The clue tying these years together proved to be the fluctuation in ocean temperatures known as the El Niño Southern Oscillation (ENSO). Each season followed two years after a major El Niño event, and each crash, when breeding numbers plummeted, followed two years after its opposite, La Niña. Following the 1998 El Niño event in the Western Indian Ocean,

Jeanne Mortimer reported similar cyclic fluctuations in the nesting density of Green Sea Turtles.

What is going on here, and why the two-year delay? Individual female Greens in eastern Australia breed only once every five or six years. It takes over a year for a Green Sea Turtle to build up the resources she needs to travel to the breeding grounds and generate the yolk for her enormous store of eggs. Therefore the conditions for a successful nesting season—in particular, a good food supply—must be set well before a female commits to migration and breeding.

The key, then, appears to be not how ENSO affects the turtles, but how it may affect their food supply. A bumper crop of turtle food plants supplies the resources that can go toward a successful breeding season in a later year. A bad year on the seagrasses beds, or the algal mats, may deny the turtles the food they need to prepare for nesting two years later. So far, Limpus has not been able to tell exactly how ENSO affects turtle food supplies, but he has shown that failures of seagrasses crops from other causes, such as storms, floods and algal blooms, have led directly to poor nesting years for the turtle populations of Moreton Bay and other sites on the Australian coast.

Sea surface temperatures may have a significant effect, often well before the actual nesting year arrives, on the nesting behavior of a number of sea turtle species including Greens, Loggerheads and Leatherbacks. In 2008 Milani Chaloupka, Naoki Kamezaki, and Colin Limpus reported that higher sea surface temperatures in core Loggerhead foraging areas in the western Pacific were followed by lower nesting rates the following summer. Here, too, the key may be food supply: the animals Loggerheads eat may be more abundant in cooler waters. Rising ocean temperatures may make it harder for a female Loggerhead to build up fat reserves for a successful nesting season. Warmer waters may also raise the turtle's own metabolism, requiring her to devote more energy to her own maintenance than to reproduction. Ocean temperatures seem to be rising as climate change progresses, and unless sea turtles can shift their foraging to cooler waters the consequences for them could be considerable.

Courtship at Sea

Sea turtle courtship and mating seems every bit as chaotic and brutal as it is for their cousins on land or in fresh water (see page 264, Chapter 7). Males bite the females on the head, neck and flippers, and scratch the females' shells with their claws. A female, even in the act of mating, may be accompanied by several attendant males. Other males trying to horn in on the mating will often bite the male in position, sometimes causing serious injuries to his flippers or tail. In fact, one of the best indications we have that female sea turtles only mate before they lay their first clutch is that, over the rest of the nesting period, the open sores their mates inflict on them progressively heal.

Michael Frick and his co-workers observed Loggerhead courtship while conducting aerial surveys of Loggerheads off the coast of Georgia and northeastern Florida. A male makes his first, slow approach to the female as she floats on the surface with her flippers and hindlimbs tucked against her body. He circles for two to three minutes, while she pivots about, facing him. The male then dives under her, and begins sniffing and nuzzling at the scent glands near her bridge (this may help him make sure that the turtle he is courting is actually a female). After a minute or so, his nuzzling gives way to vigorous biting at her hindlimbs. Sometimes that is all that is necessary before she allows him to mount. If it is not, he resorts to gentler means, facing her and stroking her head and neck with the upper surfaces of his forelimbs. Three to five minutes of this may do the trick, but one male, even after all this effort, "was chased away by wild splashing and snapping from the female."

MATING

Olive Ridleys (*Lepidochelys olivacea*) mate at sea off Puerto Vallarta, Mexico.

Julie Booth observed similar postures in courting Green Sea Turtles, but argued that some of the positions taken up by the female are not part of a courtship ritual, but attempts to keep males at bay. Tucking in her hindlimbs may prevent males from getting access to her cloacal opening. Female Greens regularly take up this position just after egg laying. A really unreceptive female adopts a refusal position, holding her body vertically in water with her limbs spread wide. A male confronted with this posture usually gives up and swims off.

Mature males of cheloniid sea turtles develop a soft, leathery spot in the center of their plastra that may provide them with improved traction as they cling to their females, or even an extra bit of tactile sensation as they mate. Jeffrey Miller describes the details in *The Biology of Sea Turtles*:

> The male mounts the female quickly, usually at the surface with a lot of splashing, and hooks onto her carapace using the enlarged claws on his front flippers and the large claws on his hind flippers to hold himself in place. The male curls his long tail to bring their cloacae into contact. His penis is erected into her cloaca. The shape of the penis with the bifurcation of the sperm duct at the tip allows for the transfer of semen into each oviduct without passing through the environment of the female's cloaca. In captive situations the pair may remain coupled for 10 or more hours.

There is evidence that the longer the male remains in place, the better chance he has to fertilize the female (this was evident among captive turtles at the Cayman Turtle Farm). Two male Green Sea Turtles in Cyprus were so persistent that each remained clinging to his female even after she dragged herself out of the water and crawled some 5–10 m (15–30 ft) up the beach.

Males may leave after the mating period, sometimes weeks before the females, or hover off the nesting beaches throughout the season, making repeated (but usually unsuccessful) efforts to mount females after they have begun laying. Male Olive Ridleys off Orissa, India, concentrate in aggregations at sea; during mating, these aggregation areas may hold 26 mating pairs per square kilometer (68 per square mile).

During their receptive period, females may mate with several males, and males with several females. Multiple matings in both directions have been identified in Leatherbacks. The sperm the females collect will be stored in their oviducts, available to fertilize each clutch as it develops through the season. In Loggerheads, Kemp's and Olive Ridleys, and Greens, scientists have found clutches with eggs fertilized by more than one male. Multiple paternity may be a regular, though not universal, feature among sea turtles in general.

There may be striking paternity differences among colonies of a single species. On the Pacific slope of Costa Rica, where some Olive Ridleys nest in *arribada*s while others nest more or less alone, M.P. Jensen and his colleagues found that the proportion of nests sired by more than one male was only 30 percent among solitary nesters at Playa Hermosa, but rose to 92 percent on the mass nesting beaches at Ostional where some nests contained eggs fathered by three or four males. Judith Zbinden and her colleagues found an equally high level of multiple paternity (14 out of 15 clutches, with two clutches sired by at least five males) among Loggerheads nesting at Zakynthos, Greece. This is a far higher proportion of multiple parenthood than at Melbourne Beach, Florida, where 48 out of 70 clutches had only a single father.

The Zakynthos rookery is the largest in the Mediterranean. A concentration of males may increase the chances of multiple paternity, but at only 500 or so breeding females Zakynthos is still (in Zbinden's words) "at the very low end of the spectrum of sea turtle rookeries for which multiple paternity data is available." High population density at Zakynthos and Ostional may be more influential than absolute numbers. At Zakynthos, the bigger the female, the more males were likely to have fathered her brood. The males, it seems, are being selective, and size—a possible indicator of fecundity in a nesting female—seems to matter.

The sex ratio in adult and juvenile sea turtles is frequently highly biased toward females. Among juvenile Hawksbills on foraging grounds in the U.S. Virgin Islands, the proportion of females is reportedly as high as 80 percent, and among juvenile Kemp's Ridleys at one Florida site females outnumbered males by an estimated 3.7 to 1. A female's opportunity to mate with more than one male, coupled with her ability to store sperm for long periods, may give these turtles a considerable amount of evolutionary flexibility even in the face of climate change, should higher temperatures in the nest reduce the relative number of males still further.

Male Loggerheads return to the nesting beaches at Zakynthos at least twice as frequently as do females. Though they arrive first, males leave the breeding area many weeks before the females and presumably invest less in the process. Females outnumber males at Zakynthos by better than two to one, but do not return every year and sometimes stay away for 3 to 4 years. The operational sex ratio from a smaller number of males that visit every year and a larger number of females that nest occasionally is probably close to 50:50.

The Mating Cycle

The cycle of mating and nesting in sea turtles, as in other vertebrates, is regulated by the ebb and flow of hormones. It begins with a surge of testosterone, which may stimulate the onset of mating and nesting behavior. This happens in both males and females, but the male peak comes first, and is already on the decline before female levels reach their highest point. In captive Loggerheads, the act of mating itself has been shown to stimulate ovulation. In the females, a rise in the hormone estradiol kicks the ovary into

high gear. The follicles in the ovary begin to mature into yolk-filled eggs, a process called *vitellogenesis*. As the eggs mature, the calcium that will form the superstructure of their shells peaks in the female's blood plasma. Once the eggs are complete and ripe, another hormone, vasotocin, stimulates the female to deposit them in the nest.

Internesting intervals in both Loggerheads and Greens have been found to shorten with a rise in surface temperature. The onset of vitellogenesis, and the speed with which the eggs mature, may be affected by the temperature of the ocean. Loggerheads in the Atlantic and Mediterranean nest earlier in years when the spring and summer temperature of the sea surface near their breeding grounds is higher. Individual females seek out warm patches of water once they arrive, presumably speeding their egg development still further. In 2010, John Weishampel and his colleagues examined 20 years of data for Loggerheads and Greens nesting on the same barrier island in east-central Florida. Though both species began nesting earlier in years when the spring surface temperature of the ocean was warm, the nesting seasons grew shorter for Loggerheads but became longer in Greens. This may be due to differences between the species. At nearby Canaveral National Seashore David Pike found that sea surface temperature had no effect on when Greens started to nest, though again Loggerheads nested earlier and had shorter seasons at warmer temperatures. It may also be the result of a recent expansion of Green Sea Turtle nesting on the island, with more older, experienced females that tend to lay more clutches.

Twenty-four to 48 hours after she returns to the sea, soon after the beginning of her internesting interval, a surge in progesterone and luteinizing hormone (LH) resets her ovarian clock for the next nesting cycle. How many times this happens, and how long the internesting interval lasts, depends on the species. It is usually anywhere from 10 to 18 days. Some Loggerheads nesting in Oman spend the internesting interval close to shore, while others make looping journeys of hundreds of kilometers into the open ocean. Many sea turtles do not feed during their internesting intervals, relying instead on the fat reserves they have built up during previous years. They will lose about a fifth of their body weight (16–22 percent in Loggerheads, Greens, Hawksbills, and particularly Kemp's Ridleys). Others, even others of the same species, may use the internesting interval as an opportunity to take on food. Sea temperature may determine whether an individual turtle's internesting interval is at the longer or the shorter end of its species' range. The two ridleys have the longest internesting intervals, 20 to 28 days for Kemp's Ridley and 17 to 30 days for the Olive Ridley. Ridley nesting, especially in *arribadas*, is very much influenced by wind, rain and other weather conditions, and their internesting intervals may be highly unpredictable.

Kemp's Ridleys nest only three times a season, each nesting supplied from ovaries successively depleted of their follicles until none are left by the end of the third nesting. Hawksbills average four to five clutches per season, though as few as one and as many as eight nestings have been recorded (possibly turtles recorded nesting only once shifted elsewhere for their other clutches). Leatherbacks may nest up to 10 times, or even more, and ovulate every 9 or 10 days throughout the season—the shortest internesting interval for a sea turtle (though recorded intervals of 11 to 13 days for Green Sea Turtles on Colola Beach in Michoacán, Mexico, are not much more). Leatherbacks at Las Baulas Marine Park on the Pacific coast of Costa Rica averaged between 4 and 8 clutches per season, but one female laid 13 clutches during 1998–99. Leatherbacks are able to lay so many clutches because at each nesting they deplete only 10 percent of the follicles in the ovary, compared to 50 percent for Kemp's Ridley. A female that lays more clutches may not deposit fewer eggs per clutch; Javier Alvarado-Diaz and his colleagues found no relationship between clutch size and number of clutches among the Greens at Colola Beach, and other researchers have found similar results elsewhere.

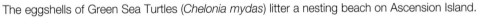

The eggshells of Green Sea Turtles (*Chelonia mydas*) litter a nesting beach on Ascension Island.

Multiple clutches may not be as universal among sea turtles as we once thought. William David Webster and Kelly Cook found that, of 127 nesting female Loggerheads they tagged on Bald Head Island, North Carolina, 55.9 percent laid only a single clutch per season. Possibly these were younger females; other, perhaps more experienced animals, nested anywhere from two to six times.

All sea turtles except the Leatherback and the Flatback commonly lay more than 100 eggs per clutch. The Leatherback averages more than 80 in the Atlantic (fewer in the Eastern Pacific), though at 10 clutches per season that still amounts to a breeding-year output of more than 800 eggs, each one weighing 90 g (3.2 oz)—the largest of any sea turtle. Flatback clutches average more than 50 eggs each. Their eggs are almost as large as those of the much bigger Leatherback. This is probably related to the unusually large size of Flatback hatchlings, which in its turn may be a response to a high level of hatchling predation (see page 313). However, much of what makes up the size difference between Flatback eggs and those of other sea turtles may be water. Water makes up 78.8 percent of a Flatback's egg, compared to 67.5 percent for Leatherbacks, 66.7 percent for Greens and 59.4 percent for Hawksbills. Yolk lipid levels are also high, at least compared to freshwater turtles (there is little comparative data for other sea turtles). A mother Flatback apparently invests considerable resources in each egg.

Nonetheless, the huge clutches of eggs sea turtles are capable of laying probably reflect the very small chances that any one of their offspring will survive. Archie Carr suggested in additional reason: since sea turtle nests are deep and hatchlings are small, below a certain clutch size their may simply not be enough turtles in a brood to make the group effort necessary to dig their way out of the egg chamber. Whatever their significance, large clutches require that each individual egg represent a proportionately small investment of energy by its parents.

A Place in the Sand

With her eggs fertilized, fully developed, and ready to lay, a female is finally ready to return to the land. She now faces a critical choice: where and when to emerge, dig her nest, and deposit her eggs. Daniel Wood and Karen Bjorndal have argued that when a female sea turtle selects a nest site, she is making an adaptive trade-off between the cost of her search (in terms of both in the energy she may use up and the risk that she may be attacked by a predator while she is on the beach and relatively helpless) and the benefits of picking a site that is suitable for the successful incubation of her clutch.

The risk of predation on both adults and hatchlings probably drove the evolution of mass nesting in ridleys. On Playa Nancite, Costa Rica, American Crocodiles (Crocodylus acutus) sometimes attack isolated Olive Ridleys on the beach; possibly the *arribada*, with its masses of turtles, may provide safety in numbers. Kemp's Ridley *arribadas* tend to occur on windy days; possibly the sound of the surf stimulates the turtles to head for the beach (Peter Pritchard has suggested that the sound of breakers may be an important nesting cue for sea turtles in general).

Though philopatry may guide a turtle back to the general area of its birth, it has little or nothing to do with where, in that area, she chooses to lay. Sea turtles often show nest site fidelity — a tendency to dig their successive nests, over the course of the season, in the same general area where they deposit their first clutch. Amy Chaves and her co-workers reported that Leatherbacks nesting on Playa Langosta generally dug each nest within 100–300 m (330–990 ft) their previous one.

Do females return to the nesting beach where they themselves were hatched (natal philopatry)? As it is pretty much impossible to track a single hatchling through the decades it takes to mature and to reach its first nesting season, the only way

Female Olive Ridleys (*Lepidochelys olivacea*), taking part in an arribada at Ostional, Costa Rica, crawl ashore at sunset.

to get at this question is by fine-scale genetic analysis (assuming that each nesting beach has its own specific genetic fingerprint). Patricia Lee and her colleagues tried to do that with nesting Green Sea Turtles on Ascension Island. Applying sophisticated molecular techniques and statistical probability analyses involving both male and female turtles, they were able to suggest that at least some females were, indeed, probably returning to their natal beaches. Males, however, were not quite so faithful to their birthplaces. Much of the gene flow among Green Sea Turtles at Ascension may be the result of wandering, highly promiscuous males.

It is not at all unusual for a female to spread the nests she lays during a single breeding year across several beaches even if she remains within the same general area. Some females are very conservative, always returning to the same short stretch of beach. Others in the same population may wander more widely. Over the long term, the conservative females maintain the existing rookery, while the more adventurous ones found new colonies—essential if the original beach is degraded or destroyed as may often happen on the constantly shifting shores of offshore barrier islands where sea turtles frequently nest. For an individual female, spreading out her nests may well avoid the risk that a single, localized catastrophe could wipe out an entire season's output. Loggerheads in North Carolina, Japan, and South Africa all tend to space their successive nestings an average of roughly 4 km (2.5 mi) apart. In the Guianas, home of the largest Leatherback nesting colonies left in the world, females may shift back and forth between nesting beaches in Surinam and French Guiana—a necessity at times, as the coastline in this area is constantly shifting. In 2000, 18 percent of the Leatherbacks that dug 11,925 nests on three Surinam beaches had been tagged in the neighboring country.

A female sea turtle preparing to nest has a number of choices to make. Some she must make while

The trails of nesting Green Sea Turtles (*Chelonia mydas*) mark the previous night's nesting activities on Talang Talang Besar Island, Sarawak, Malaysia.

still at sea: what beach she should select, and where on that beach she should emerge from the water. Once she hauls herself out on land, she faces a third decision: how far up the beach should she crawl before selecting the right spot to begin her excavation——or even if she should nest at all, or abandon the attempt and return to the sea, leaving behind only a curving track called, rather misleadingly, a "false crawl."

Exactly how she makes the first two decisions we do not know. Obviously a female cannot tell, while she is still in the water, whether any beach she picks will be ideal for digging —unless she has nested there before, or is emerging en masse, like the two ridleys, with a host of other turtles. She can decide, however, whether the beach is easy to reach. This is an important consideration for an animal so ungainly on land. Jeanne Mortimer found that Green Sea Turtles prefer unlit beaches with wide sandy offshore approaches free of clutter.

For some populations at least, the slope of the beach seems to be a primary consideration. Wood and Bjorndal showed this for Loggerheads nesting on the Archie Carr National Wildlife Refuge in Florida, as did E. Balasingam for Leatherbacks in Malaysia. It is vital that the eggs in the eventual nest be above the high-tide line or the seawater table to avoid being flooded with salt water. The beach platform must be high enough in the first place, and the steeper the slope, the shorter the distance a female will have to crawl to reach a safe level above the sea and the easier will be her return—clearly a consideration for a 270 kg (600 lb) Leatherback. The farther from the water's edge, though, the less likely a nest is to be destroyed by flooding or sea storms, so a wide beach may be a better choice than a narrow one, especially for smaller turtles such as the Olive Ridley. The importance of beach slope may vary from species to species. On El Cuyo

Beach, Yucatán, Greens seem to prefer steeper slopes than do Hawksbills.

The nature of the beach sand itself may be important. It must be easy to excavate, loose enough to allow air to get to the developing eggs and for the hatchlings, eventually, to escape, and yet firm enough for the nest to hold its shape as the female digs. At Ra's Al-Hadd Reserve in Oman, peak nesting by Green Sea Turtles coincides with the southwest monsoon season, when the moisture the monsoons bring makes the beach sand more compact and less likely to collapse as the female excavates her nest. Too much moisture, however, may harm the developing brood; Sükran Yalçin-Özdilek and her colleagues found that hatching on Samanda Beach in Turkey was poor, or even failed altogether, if sand humidity levels were above 8 percent. These characteristics are hard, if not impossible, to judge before the female actually crawls from the water, though Ahjond Garmestani and his co-workers found that Loggerhead Sea Turtles in Florida's 10,000 Islands preferred to emerge on beaches with fewer shells. A shelly beach is probably more difficult to dig in, and may well be uncomfortable for a sea turtle to cross (though the eminently suitable nesting beaches of Guyana are composed entirely of shell).

Ho-Chang Chen and his colleagues found that a moderate amount of vegetation cover, between 10 and 30 percent, made for an improved site for Green Sea Turtles on Wan-An Island, Taiwan. The dune grasses held the sand, together with any moisture, together, particularly at depths below 30 cm (12 in) where the egg chamber would come to lie. If the vegetation was too dense, however, digging became much more difficult. The line of vegetation provided turtles with a way to tell that they had climbed far enough up the beach to avoid flooding. On beaches where the grass zone was too far from the water's edge, the size of the sand grains became important; without vegetation, finer-grained sand was more likely to hold together than sand made up of coarser particles.

Beach topography may also be a consideration; according to Michael Salmon and his colleagues, Loggerheads nesting on the oceanfront off Boca Raton, Florida, preferred to dig in front of tall objects, perhaps because they blocked light coming from the city beyond. In Oman, beaches surrounded and framed by rocky hills have a higher density of nesting turtles than adjacent beaches in more level country, perhaps because there may be less chance that the nesting female or her eventual hatchlings will become confused about the direction of the sea.

Flatbacks at Fog Bay, Australia, nest at the base of rocky dunes; the dunes may provide some necessary shade for the sand over the nest. Flatback eggs can withstand higher incubation temperatures and soil moisture levels than other sea turtles; they have tolerated prolonged exposure to temperatures as high as 36.5°C (97.7°F), well above the 33°C (91.4°F) previously recorded as an upper tolerance limit. Nest temperature affects both survival and sex. Sea turtles exhibit TSDIb (see page 289, Chapter 7). Their threshhold temperature is high, reaching 30.5–31°C (86.9–87.8°F) in Olive Ridleys. Sex ratios among hatchling sea turtles, like those in adults, may be highly skewed, but not always in predictable directions: in Leatherbacks alone, reported hatchling sex ratios have ranged from all female in Malaysia and 53.6 percent female in Suriname to only 7.7 percent female on the Huon Coast of northern Papua New Guinea.

Nonetheless, despite many studies of nest site selection among sea turtles, scientists have yet to come up with a list of specific features that always signify, to a turtle, the best available nesting site. Some things sea turtle eggs need to develop properly—high humidity and low salinity in the nest chamber, for example—may be out of the female's power to control. Further, turtles can and will accept a wide range of conditions. Loggerheads on Florida's Ten Thousand Islands have nested more or less successfully on low and high beaches, even where nests risk (or even experience) flooding with salt water. One researcher, perhaps in despair, suggested that once females pass the high tide line, they simply crawl a random distance inland, stop, and dig where they are.

Full Circle

At last, having grown, traveled the high seas, matured, navigated her way back to her native waters, mated and selected her nesting beach, the female is ready to make what may be (except for those few Green Sea Turtles that bask on Hawaiian beaches) her first journey on land since the night she hatched—or, if she is older, only one of many such journeys over a long reproductive lifetime.

She usually prefers to emerge either at, or just after, high tide. Not only does this shorten the distance she has to travel on land, it lowers the risk that an incoming tide will overtake her before she finishes her labors. At Cape San Blas, Florida, 98 percent of females left the water on a rising tide. Most sea turtles choose, to nest at night; daytime temperatures on a hot beach can be lethal. Almost 97 percent of the Green Sea Turtles nesting at Ras Baridi, Saudi Arabia, emerged from the sea between 7:00 p.m and 2:00 a.m. The exceptions are the Flatback, which regularly nests during the day; the two ridleys, whose mass *arribadas* may (and, in Kemp's Ridley, usually do) take place during daylight hours; and Hawksbills in the Western Indian Ocean and, to a lesser extent, in the Persian Gulf.

After she ascends the beach—moving her forelimbs alternately if she is a Loggerhead, Hawksbill or ridley, or by "humping" along with her limbs moving together if she is a Green or Leatherback (Flatbacks do both)—the female selects her digging spot. First, she prepares a body pit, sweeping debris out of the way with her flippers and excavating down to a level where the sand is firm enough to hold its shape as she digs the egg chamber. Like other turtles, she digs her nest with her hindlimbs, using them alternatively, like cupped hands, to scoop clumps of sand from the deepening pit and place them to one side and then the other. Through the entire process, a female Green Sea Turtle only breathes when she stops now and then to rest. The shape and depth of her finished labor depends on the length and extent of her hindlimbs: shallow and rounded in Hawksbills, deeper and more flask-shaped in Greens. Her digging behavior is purely instinctive. A female with a missing hindlimb will still swing her stump in alternation with her functional flipper, as though it, too, were removing loads of sand.

Sand flies as a Green Sea Turtle (*Chelonia mydas*) prepares to dig her nest on Mayotte in the Western Indian Ocean.

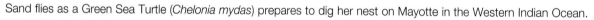

The chamber finished, she releases her clutch of eggs into the hole, usually singly or in groups of two, three or four. As the female Leatherback lays, the strange yolkless eggs—little sacks of albumin, surrounded by a shell, that are a feature of almost every Leatherback clutch—emerge last from each of her two oviducts. As many as 233 yolkless eggs have been found in a single clutch in Surinam. Yolkless eggs are laid late in the laying process, and Peter Pritchard has suggested that they may fill spaces among the large fertile eggs that could otherwise become packed with sand, hampering the flow of oxygen to the developing embryos. Since the oviducts do not empty at the same time, though, the yolkless eggs may not be the last eggs she actually lays. When her clutch has been laid, she scrapes the moist sand she has excavated back over her eggs, piling it in and compacting it in place with her hindlimbs. Then she crawls forward, throwing sand backwards over the nest site with her front flippers, possibly to conceal the site, but more likely to add a layer of insulation on top of the nest. Only then does she return to the sea.

A Green Sea Turtle (*Chelonia mydas*) deposits eggs in its nest on Mayotte, in the western Indian Ocean.

The eggs she leaves behind will incubate in their chamber for anywhere from 6 to 13 weeks, depending on the temperature, providing, of course, they are allowed to do so. Sea turtle eggs in an undisturbed nest have a naturally high success rate, typically 80 percent or more. Undisturbed nests, though, may be hard to come by. Their greatest enemy, on many sea turtle nesting beaches around the world, is our own species. In some places, poachers and collectors take every egg from every clutch (see Chapter 10). Even on protected beaches, though, nest failure may be very high.

Up to 60 percent of Leatherback nests may be destroyed by tides, storms, and beach erosion alone, though this varies from place to place. Fungal contamination may destroy entire clutches. Fly and beetle larvae may infect sea turtle eggs, though a study of Flatback nests in central Queensland, Australia, suggests that fly larvae are not attacking viable eggs or living hatchlings, but instead are scavenging eggs and hatchlings that died from other causes. They may actually be doing the survivors a service by acting as a cleanup crew.

Mole crickets of the genus *Scapteriscus* destroy some 15 percent of Leatherback and 7 percent of Green Sea Turtle eggs on nesting beaches in French Guiana. Ants may attack emerging hatchlings. On Sanibel Island, Florida, Red Imported Fire Ants (*Solenopsis invicta*) invading their nests are probably the worst enemy Loggerhead hatchlings face. The same species has recently spread to the West Indies, where it may pose a long-term threat to nesting sea turtles. Another introduced species in the West Indies, the Small Indian Mongoose (*Herpestes javanicus*), is already such a threat. Mongooses tend to avoid the open beach, and Hawksbill nests in Barbados are particularly likely to fall victim to them if they are dug near vegetation.

Feral dogs take large numbers of Leatherback hatchlings in French Guiana, South Africa, and in Tortuguero National Park in Costa Rica. Half the Green Sea Turtle nests at Tortuguero are destroyed

Black Vultures (*Coragyps atratus*) wait while an Olive Ridley (*Lepidochelys olivacea*) lays her eggs at Ostional, Costa Rica.

by dogs, Coatis (*Nasua narica*), Black and Turkey Vultures (*Coragyps atratus* and *Cathartes aura*) and Ghost Crabs (*Ocypode quadratus*). At Chiriqui Beach on the Caribbean slope of Panama, an awareness campaign in 2004 convinced many local dog owners to tie up their animals, leading to a drop in nest predation.

In the Mediterranean, foxes are the chief threat to Loggerheads nesting on beaches in Turkey. Rueppell's Fox (*Vulpes rueppellii*) digs up Green Sea Turtle nests and hatchlings in Saudi Arabia and raids Hawksbill nests in Qatar. At Ra's Baridi in Saudi Arabia, according to Nicolas Pilcher and Mustafa al-Merghani:

Foxes waited for the hatchlings to emerge, and then decapitated as many hatchlings as possible before they reached the sea. The foxes then returned to consume those they had killed. In this manner it was believed that they were able to consume more hatchlings that if they had consumed one at a time after emergence.

Yellow-spotted Monitor Lizards (*Varanus panoptes*) raid Flatback nests in Fog Bay, Western Australia. Gray Foxes (*Urocyon cinereoargenteus*), feral pigs, and particularly Northern Raccoons (*Procyon lotor*) raid Loggerhead nests on the Gulf

A Horned Ghost Crab (*Ocypode ceratophthalma*) scavenges a dead Flatback
Sea Turtle (*Natator depressus*) hatchling on the Cape York Peninsula, Australia.

Coast of Florida. A 1995–1996 raccoon removal program in Florida's Ten Thousand Islands National Wildlife Refuge brought nest loss on Panther Key from as high as 100 percent down to zero. In earlier days, Black Bears (*Ursus americanus*) visited the beaches around Naples, Florida, to feed on Loggerhead eggs. Charles LeBuff, author of *The Loggerhead Turtle in the Eastern Gulf Of Mexico*, was present when one of the last of them was shot, in the spring of 1958. Many other animals, including crows, herons, frigatebirds, and others that may be ill-equipped to dig out eggs in their nests, will snap up hatchlings on their way to the sea.

The most remarkable predator on sea turtle nests may be the Taiwanese Kukrisnake (*Oligodon formosanus*). Kukrisnakes are specialized feeders on reptile eggs, which they split open with specially enlarged teeth. Wen-San Huang recently discovered that female kukrisnakes on Orchid (Lanyu) Island off southeastern Taiwan not only eat Green Sea Turtle eggs, but actively defend their nests against other kukrisnakes trying to muscle in on their food supply. The snakes hunt for turtle nests at dawn and dusk. The males always seem to be the first to arrive, and a number of males may enter the same nest and dine on the eggs—until the female snakes show up.

Once that happens, the females drive out the adult males, often wounding them in the process (though the expelled males usually try to make their way back in if they can). This aggressive behavior makes the female kukrisnake—the smaller sex, by the way—the only snake in the world known to defend a territory.

Despite this array of predators, some eggs do hatch and some hatchlings do survive, grow, and embark on the path sea turtles have followed for millions of years into the gyres of the sea. The paths the hatchlings follow may depend, as they leave their natal beaches, on the currents that carry them as they drift out to sea. Recently Graeme Hays and his colleagues combined satellite-tracking of adults with a particle-tracking model that simulated the paths drifting hatchlings would likely follow from the Loggerhead nesting beaches at Zakynthos, Greece at different times of year. Their results suggested that the paths adults follow when they return from their breeding grounds to their foraging areas may be influenced by the journey, at the mercy of wind and water, that they took when they first crawled down the sand and became true creatures of the ocean.

I have called this chapter, the last in this book to deal with turtle biology, "The Endless Journey." Of course no journey, least of all of a species, is truly endless; but whether the travels of sea turtles continue for millenia, or end in the next few decades, is up to us. In our last two chapters, we will turn from the biology of turtles to the most crucial of the issues that surround them: their conservation.

PART THREE

WILL TURTLES SURVIVE?

CHAPTER NINE

Peril on Land

IN 1684, FOUR years after the last dodo is thought to have died on Mauritius, the explorer and some-time pirate William Dampier (1652–1715) visited the Galápagos Islands.

His description of its tortoises is not only the first detailed account of them we have, but gives us an idea of what was in store for them at our hands:

> The land-turtle are here so numerous, that five or six hundred men might subsist on them alone for several months, without any other sort of provision: They are extraordinarily large and fat, and so sweet, that no pullet eats more pleasantly. One of the largest of these creatures will weigh one hundred and fifty or two hundred weight, and some of them are two feet, or two feet six inches over the callapee or belly. I never saw any but at this place, that will weigh above thirty pounds weight. I have heard that at the island of St. Lawrence or Madagascar, and at the English forest, an island near it, called also Don Mascarenha or Bourbon, and now possessed by the French; there are very large ones, but whether so big, fat and sweet as these, I know not.

The tortoises from Madagascar, the Mascarenes, and the West Indies that Dampier refers to are now extinct; Madagascar's giant tortoises had already vanished by Dampier's time. The first Western settlers cut their island forests, introduced alien species and diseases, and killed them relentlessly for food. Mariners provisioned their ships with living tortoises

17th-century Mariners provisioned their ships with giant tortoises, like this one from Santa Cruz in the Galápagos.

to provide fresh meat for long journeys at sea. Sailors on six early voyages to the Mascarenes took almost 21,000 tortoises from the islands. We did not know, then, and probably would not have cared if we did know, that these were creatures of slow growth, long lifespan, and a limited ability to regenerate their numbers, ill-equipped to handle the drastic short-term changes that we humans can inflict. They could not withstand us, or the pigs, rats, and other interlopers we brought with us, and they disappeared.

Today, we are doing to the whole planet what we once did to the islands of the giant tortoises. Our actions are taking a tremendous toll on turtles the world over. Of the higher vertebrate groups, only primates, our own taxon, has a higher proportion of endangered species. Turtles are victims of almost the entire catalog of abuses we heap on our environment. We cut their forests, dam their rivers, drain their wetlands, and mine and develop their nesting beaches. By creating urban and suburban habitats for animals like raccoons and skunks in North America (not to mention domestic cats), we stimulate huge increases in the populations of turtles' natural predators. It is ironic, and disastrous, that the richest areas in the world for turtle diversity, South and Southeast Asia—the places where we have the most to lose—are also the places where we seem likely, through a combination of overexploitation and habitat destruction, to lose the most.

We compound the situation by introducing exotic alien species. Some exotics hunt turtles or destroy their nests, as foxes do in Australia (see page 298, Chapter 7). Some ruin their habitat. In the Alligator River region of northern Australia, introduced Water Buffalo (*Bubalus bubalis*) trampled sandbanks that were nesting grounds for the Pig-nose Turtle (*Carettochelys insculpta*), ate the young waterside plants that turtles depend on for food during

Introduced Red-eared Sliders (*Trachemys scripta elegans*) are a potential threat to native turtles in many countries. This one is swimming in the Vidourle River in southern France, far from its native range.

the dry season, and destroyed the edges of billabongs where new food plants must grow. It took a massive (and controversial) shooting campaign in the 1980s and 1990s, undertaken to avoid the spread of livestock disease, to reduce their numbers. Today water plants have returned in many areas. Other exotics compete for food or space, and may risk bringing diseases or parasites with them. This has certainly happened the other way round; exotic Red-eared Sliders (*Trachemys scripta elegans*) in Spain have been found with parasites they probably acquired from native turtles. In the West Indies, introduced Red-eared Sliders have hybridized with their native cousins, threatening the genetic integrity of the island species.

Even plants, exotic or otherwise, can affect turtle populations. In Malaysia, flood-borne silt deposits have allowed the native Lalang Grass (*Imperata cylindrica*), a serious invasive in many other parts of the world, to take over ancestral nesting beaches of the Southern River Terrapin (*Batagur affinis*). The terrapins now depend on clearing efforts by egg collectors and Wildlife Department officials. An invasive strain of Common Reed (*Phragmites australis*) now dominates wetland plant communities in many parts of North America. At Long Point, Ontario, it spreads rapidly through nesting grounds of the Spiny Softshell (*Apalone spinifera*), eliminating the areas of sandy, unshaded soil that the turtle seems to require.

Pollution has been implicated in the spread of bacterial shell disease in freshwater turtles in the Rappahannock River, Virginia. Turtles accumulate dieldrin, polychlorinated biphenyls (PCBs), and other contaminants in their tissues, reducing their resistance to infections. Chemical pollution from the first Gulf War threatened the Euphrates Softshell (*Rafetus euphraticus*), a threat compounded in Anatolia, in the words of Ertan Taskavak and Mehmet K. Atatür, by "the ongoing trend of dumping waste of every kind, domestic or otherwise, directly into the Euphrates and Tigris systems" (see page 119, Chapter 3). Light pollution has been called the greatest threat to hatchling Loggerhead

Sea Turtles (*Caretta caretta*) on the Florida coast (see page 310, Chapter 8). It also misdirects hatchling Painted Terrapins (*Batagur borneensis*) in those areas of Malaysia where this Critically Endangered species still manages to survive.

Greenhouse gas pollution contributes to global climate change, which in turn could lead to destabilizing shifts in the sex ratios of turtles with temperature-dependent sex determination (see page 289, Chapter 7). Climate change brings not just high temperatures but increasing aridity. Drought may be the biggest climate-related threat to a number of turtle species. Winter rainfall is key to the survival of juveniles in a reintroduced population of Hermann's Tortoises (*Testudo hermanni*) in the Ebro delta of northeastern Spain. Increasing dryness in the Mediterranean could threaten this Vulnerable species, particularly at the edges of its range.

On the Seychelles, climate change may reduce available habitat for the Yellow-bellied Hinged Terrapin (*Pelusios castanoides*), but increase it for the Pan Hinged Terrapin (*Pelusios subniger*), which is expected to gain territory in the interior of Mahé. Earl McCoy and his colleagues found that body condition is strongly correlated, in the short term, with rainfall in Agassiz's Desert Tortoise (*Gopherus agassizi*) but not in the Gopher Tortoise (*Gopherus polyphemus*). Gopher Tortoises do not normally face droughts. Their burrows provide some refuge on the rare occasions when they do, but we do not know how they would deal with the much drier Florida we may face over the next 50 years.

We hunt land and freshwater turtles, and their eggs, almost everywhere they occur. Those we do not eat directly we sell to seemingly insatiable food markets, or deliver into the wasteful and often illegal international traffic in reptilian pets. Our vehicles kill turtles on roads in increasing numbers. In Europe road mortality may pose a threat to European Pond Turtles (*Emys orbicularis*). It may be high enough in busy areas of North America to threaten the survival of local pond turtle populations. Matthew Aresco,

Turtles and tortoises are increasingly the victims of road mortality. This Hermann's Tortoise (*Testudo hermanni*) was crushed on a road in Corsica.

A Three-toed Box Turtle (*Terrapene carolina triunguis*) scrambles across the middle of a county road in central Missouri, USA.

who analyzed turtle mortality along a stretch of highway crossing Lake Jackson, Florida, concluded that "the estimated probability of a turtle successfully crossing U.S. Highway 27 decreased from 32 percent in 1977 to only 2 percent in 2001."

In Maine, road mortality is an especial risk for Blanding's Turtles (*Emydoidea blandingii*) at the height of the nesting season in June when females are on the move, and early July when males are more likely to make long journeys between wetland areas. In many places death by automobile singles out breeding females crossing to their nesting sites. Roadkill is a likely cause of shifts in the sex ratio of Diamondback Terrapins (*Malaclemys terrapin*) in southern New Jersey. Populations of Painted Turtles (*Chrysemys picta*) and Common Snapping Turtles (*Chelydra serpentina*) near Syracuse, New York, have higher proportions of males in areas with high road density.

James Gibbs and David Steen found a correlation between the expansion of surface road in the United States since 1930 and an increasing proportion of males in turtle populations. A 2006 review by 19 turtle biologists concluded that females are indeed more likely to be highway victims than males. The authors warned that this is probably responsible for increasingly skewed sex ratios now, and may lead to population declines in future as females are progressively removed. The problem may be easy to deal with; barrier fences, deployed where turtles are likely to cross roads, have already made a difference in a number of areas.

Our agricultural equipment plows up turtle nests, kills their hatchlings, and maims adults. Painted Terrapins, Diamondback Terrapins, Spiny Softshells and other estuarine and riverine turtles collide with boats and drown in fishing gear. Passive fishing traps such as hoop and fyke nets, which may remain in the water for hours or days, are a particular problem for turtles in river systems such as the Mississippi in North America and the Murray-Darling in Australia. Design changes, including fitting fyke nets with bycatch-reduction devices (BRDs), have been developed that allow turtles to escape without affecting the quality of the catch.

Today, 71 species of tortoises and freshwater turtles are listed as either Endangered or Critically Endangered in IUCN's 2011 Red List of Threatened Species. A further 57 are listed as Vulnerable. Direct human exploitation has been partly or entirely responsible for the current perilous condition of 18 of the 28 species classified as Critically Endangered. The difference between William Dampier's contemporaries and ourselves, I hope, is that today we have a better understanding of the damage we do to wild species, and the potential harm that that damage can do to our own lives. But can we apply that understanding in time to save the world's turtles?

Habitat Loss, Pollution, and Disease

Turtle habitat is disappearing everywhere, whether through outright loss or severe degradation, as we convert it to our uses. Some common and adaptable species, including the Painted Turtle, may appear to thrive for a time, in man-made habitats, including urban rivers and suburban ponds that provide them with food and nesting sites. Michael Marchand and John Litvaitis, who have studied Painted Turtle populations in increasingly urbanized parts of New Hampshire, warn that other changes we make to their environment, including road construction and our inadvertent support for increasing raccoon populations, may reduce the numbers of juveniles entering the population and, in the long term, eliminate turtles from their urban settings.

On the coastal plain of South Carolina, over 90 percent of bay wetlands, the favored habitat of the Chicken Turtle (*Deirochelys reticularia*), has been altered or eliminated. Southeastern longleaf pine forest, a favored habitat of the Gopher Tortoise, has been reduced by 97 percent. River Cooters (*Pseudemys concinna*) have become endangered in

Illinois, according to Michael Dreslik, as swamps and oxbows have been drained, rivers channeled, and vegetation lost. Bog Turtles (*Glyptemys muhlenbergii*) disappear with their bogs, and Wood Turtles (*Glyptemys insculpta*) with their woods.

On the Great Lakes coastline of Ontario, turtles have diminished in numbers and variety almost everywhere human settlement has altered their habitat. Common Musk Turtles (*Sternotherus odoratus*) appear to have disappeared from historic localities along the lower Great Lakes; they remain abundant only in relatively undisturbed marshes on Georgian Bay. Even protected areas are losing their turtles. Point Pelee National Park in southwestern Ontario once held healthy populations of 10 species of turtles, the highest diversity in Canada. Even though the park is fully protected, four of the ten disappeared between 1972-73 and 2001-02, and today only one, the Painted Turtle, still has a thriving population. Blanding's and Spotted Turtles (*Clemmys guttata*) were once abundant, but today the Spotted is gone and Blanding's persists only in very low numbers. Large adult Blanding's still roam the park, but there are fewer and fewer juveniles to replace them. There may be a variety of causes: long-ago drainage of swamp forest habitat, a population of nest-raiding raccoons four times the provincial average, heavy use of the park by human visitors or long-term shifts in forest succession following the suppression of fires.

The rising waters behind the Ataturk Dam in southeastern Anatolia have completely submerged the natural sandbanks where the Euphrates Softshell once nested. Australian freshwater turtles face increasingly turbid rivers, banks devoid of waterside vegetation, the presence of introduced competitors such as European Carp (*Cyprinus carpio*), and a list of other threats, current and potential, to the integrity of their habitat.

Pampas Tortoises (*Geochelone chilensis*) have lost habitat to agriculture in Argentina, and Central Asian Tortoises (*Testudo horsfieldii*) to irrigation in

Turkmenistan. Drought and desertification, which have been linked both to climate change and to poor agricultural practices, may threaten the Spurred Tortoise (*Geochelone sulcata*) in countries like Mali along the southern edge of the Sahara. Agricultural practices, including the planting of large stands of single crops, plowing of virgin land, destruction of hedgerows, burning of stubble, spread of chemical fertilizers, and use of heavy agricultural machinery, have been implicated in the decline of Spur-thighed Tortoises (*Testudo graeca*) in the Balkans. The destruction of the native renosterveld in the Cape region of South Africa, for urban development and agriculture, is the chief threat facing the Endangered Geometric Tortoise (*Psammobates geometricus*).

In eastern Asia, loss of primary evergreen forest endangers Travancore Tortoises (*Indotestudo forsteni*), Cochin Forest Cane Turtles (*Vijayachelys sylvatica*), Keeled Box Turtles (*Cuora mouhotii*), and Spiny Turtles (*Heosemys spinosa*). Sand mining, much of it illegal, threatens the nesting beaches of Southern River Terrapins, Painted Terrapins, narrow-headed softshells (*Chitra* spp.), Asian Giant Softshells (*Pelochelys cantorii*), and a number of species of roofed turtle (*Batagur* spp.).

In sections of the Perak river system, and in the Setiu River in Terengganu, home of the largest nesting population of Painted Terrapin in Malaysia, dams and watergates prevent both Painted and Southern River Terrapins from migrating to productive areas upstream. On the Perak, unseasonal flooding of nesting banks, caused by the untimely opening of sluice gates and the deforestation of surrounding watersheds, has had "disastrous effects on the river terrapin population," according to Dionysius S. K. Sharma and his colleagues. Increasing contamination has polluted nesting beaches along the coast and degraded several important terrapin rivers, including the Perak and Setiu. In 1996 Sharma reported that a rubber processing factory on the Perak was releasing effluent directly into the river opposite Painted Terrapin nesting banks in the Bota

Kanan Terrapin Sanctuary. Most of the terrapins had been driven away. Currently Bota Kanan is the site of an incubation facility, operated by the Department of Wildlife and National Parks, which has reportedly released some 40,000 hatchlings into the Perak River since 1975.

Turtles at forest edges risk injury or even mutilation beneath the wheels of our vehicles, in the blades of agricultural mowing machines or under the hooves of our cattle. Turtles are highly vulnerable to habitat fragmentation as their forest habitat is cut into smaller and smaller pieces and they are forced to venture, more and more, into the open. Eastern Box Turtle (*Terrapene carolina*) numbers in an isolated 18.5 ha (45.7 acre) woodlot owned by the University of Delaware fell from 91 adults in 1968 to only 22 in 2002 even though the woodlot remained intact. Mowing machines, which the turtles encountered when they ventured from the woodlot, were the chief human cause of mortality. By 2002 there were no juveniles left in the woodlot, the sex ratio was biased toward males, the survival rate was low and the remaining population did not appear to be viable.

For Wood Turtles, the reasons why fragmentation creates problems are not immediately obvious. Fragmentation creates more edge situations, and Wood Turtles actively seek out forest edges—so why do they not benefit as we chop up their territories? Raymond Saumure and J. Roger Bider suggested some reasons in a 1998 study of the effect of agricultural development on a population of Wood Turtles in southern Québec. Agricultural areas carry increased numbers of the Wood Turtles' most persistent predator, the Northern Raccoon (*Procyon lotor*), which hunts turtles along the woodland borders. More than 70 percent of the turtles sampled by Saumure and Bider were mutilated to some degree, either through accidents or encounters with predators; several had lost a limb or a tail. Though these sorts of injuries happened in forest areas as well, Saumure and Bider found that at their agri-

In North America, the Wood Turtle (*Glyptemys insculpta*) suffers from poaching and habitat fragmentation.

cultural site where they encountered humans and machinery, turtles had 2.7 times more mutilations than in their forest sites. Since then Claude Daigle and Jacques Jutras have found that the population of adult Wood Turtles in their study area along the Sutton River, Québec, had declined by 50 percent between 1995 and 2002.

Turtles may suffer from multiple effects as we take over their habitats. Seekers for waterfront recreation on the eastern seaboard of the United States leave little safe room for the Diamondback Terrapin (*Malaclemys terrapin*). PCBs may be affecting the health and growth of juveniles. Mercury accumulates in terrapin tissues and is deposited in their scutes. Increasing human use leads to bulkheading and other stabilizing techniques that make the shoreline better for people but eliminate terrapin habitat. Efforts to check local development in the name of terrapin conservation, however, can falter because, thanks to another effect of beachfront recreation, there may be no terrapins left to protect. More people hunting for seafood along the coast has meant more use of inshore crab traps. Terrapins enter crab pots and drown; Willem Roosenburg once found a single trap that had killed 49 terrapins.

Death by crab pot has been identified as the greatest threat to the species' survival in six American states, and is among the top three threats in five others. New Jersey and Maryland laws now require terrapin excluders (a sort of turtle escape hatch) on all recreational crab pots, and other states are considering introducing similar requirements. Nonetheless, in 2007 investigators found 133 dead terrapins in just two abandoned crab pots near St. Simons Island, Georgia—more than double the estimated number of live terrapins left in the area. Georgia does not have a crab pot clean-up program, something that has been established in North Carolina and the states along the Gulf of Mexico.

Female terrapins are the larger sex, and a full-grown female is too big to enter a crab trap. Males rarely reach that size, but small juvenile males can escape from a trap, once in it (though there is no certain evidence that they actually do). One odd result of this, uncovered by Matthew Wolak and his colleagues, is that after 60 years of large-scale commercial crab trapping in Chesapeake Bay adult females now grow faster, and reach a larger size (by about 15 percent), than either females from Long Island Sound where there is no commercial crab fishery or among Chesapeake Bay terrapins collected before the onset of commercial crabbing. The male population is almost entirely composed of younger animals; Wolak's study found no males in Chesapeake Bay older than 8 years of age.

Agassiz's Desert Tortoises in the American Southwest, Texas Tortoises (*Gopherus berlandieri*) in Texas, and Gopher Tortoises in the Southeast have become victims of a highly contagious upper respiratory tract disease (URTD). (Morafka's Desert Tortoises [*Gopherus morafkai*] contract the disease, but at a much lower frequency than Agassiz's.) It is primarily caused by *Mycoplasma agassizii*, one of a category of organisms that have been implicated in human diseases from pneumonia to Gulf War syndrome, though a number of related pathogens also appear be involved. The disease was first discovered in 1988, in the Desert Tortoise Natural Area (DTNA) of Kern County, California, when it was already well established. Its effect on some tortoise populations has been catastrophic. In a single 2.6 sq km (1.04 sq mi) plot in the DTNA, tortoise numbers fell from 204 counted in 1982 to only 13 ten years later. Gopher Tortoises can apparently be infected with *Mycoplasma agassizi*, and even develop some URTD-like symptoms, without actually contracting the full-blown disease. Not all Gopher Tortoises that contract the disease die immediately, and some infected populations show no increase in mortality that seems related to the disease. The tortoises develop a chronic form of URTD, with an effect in the long term that is difficult to measure.

The disease spreads easily among captive tortoises in the same pen, and the epidemic probably started in captivity. There may be more than 40,000 Agassiz's Desert Tortoises in captivity in Las Vegas Valley, Nevada, and over 200,000 in California.

An epidemic of upper respiratory tract disease has infected populations of the Mojave or Agassiz's Desert Tortoise (*Gopherus agassizii*).

Owners of sick tortoises commonly release them into the desert, where they infect their wild cousins. Besides its direct effect on the animals, URTD hampers our efforts to conserve the Desert Tortoise. Relocating tortoises to areas where they have disappeared is an important part of managing species, but the stress of relocation may itself make the animals more susceptible to disease. Transferring animals in the early stages of URTD, before their symptoms become obvious, may inadvertently spread the disease to healthy wild populations. However, the risk posed by *Mycoplasma* may not always be as great as first thought. There is some evidence that mycoplasmal infections of one sort or another may have been present in *Gopherus* tortoises for millions of years. Not every infection amounts to a URTD epidemic, and conservation strategies for Gopher Tortoises may need to focus on ways to avoid the spread of the more virulent forms of the disease in addition to simply trying to reduce spread of the infection.

Turtles as Food

People have been eating turtles for a long time. Remains of Hermann's Tortoises (*Testudo hermanni*) and a European Pond Turtle (*Emys orbicularis*) have recently been found among 1.2 million year old human leavings in the Sima del Elefante archaeological site in northern Spain, the earliest evidence of turtles in our diet to date. The bones of Angulate Tortoises (*Chersina angulata*) litter Die Kelders Cave in South Africa, the remains of Middle Stone Age meals dating back at least 57,000 years. Today, almost everywhere turtles occur, people eat them or gather their eggs. Turtles are easy to catch, easy to keep alive—at least, until they are ready for the pot—and are a ready source of protein. Their shells even provide built-in cooking vessels. Aboriginal women and children in northern Australia collect aestivating turtles, particularly Northern Long-necked Turtles (*Chelodina rugosa*), by feeling for them in mud or

A 2,000-year-old ochre rock painting in La Mauricie National Park, Québec, Canada, testifies to the importance of turtles in the lives of nomadic Algonquian peoples. Today, the park holds a population of Wood Turtles (*Glyptemys insculpta*), a Threatened Species in Canada.

An Australian Aboriginal hunter poses with his catch, a Northern Long-necked Turtle (*Chelodina rugosa*).

shallow water, using their hands, their feet, or a stick (today, steel rods are a frequent substitute). They dig pits where they store their catches, covered with layers of bark and earth, until they are ready to be eaten. The turtles, killed, gutted and washed, are roasted on hot coals in the shell, which will provide a serving plate when the cooking is done.

In the United States, Diamondback Terrapins, Chicken Turtles, Common Snapping Turtles and Alligator Snappers (*Macrochelys temmincki*) have been part of local cuisine for generations. In Sarawak, Malaysia, Asiatic Softshell Turtles (*Amyda cartilaginea*) are prized food items among indigenous peoples. Traditionally they have been caught with baited hooks or by searching for them in the mud during the dry season, but today (despite legal protection since 1998) it is easier to buy them in a market. The market price of softshell meat rose from RM (Malaysian Ringgit) 14–15/kg in the mid-1990s to RM24–25/kg a decade later, a change

of 36–41 percent, possibly reflecting the turtles' increasing rarity and protected status under law.

Not every turtle makes a worthwhile meal. Few people can get past the musky smell of a Helmeted Terrapin (*Pelomedusa subrufa*). Though some inhabitants of the Petén region of Guatemala will cook White-lipped Mud Turtles (*Kinosternon leucostomum*) in their shells while the turtle is still alive, recent immigrants to the area find the practice repugnant. Most other turtles, though, seem to be eaten by at least some people, and many are in high demand.

Today, in many parts of the world, the combined effect of environmental stresses, the growth of human populations, the shift in settlement patterns, and the introduction of new technology has upset whatever balance existed between turtle hunters and their prey. The shift from traditional local use to commercial trade has increased the pressure on turtle populations as more and more people demand their meat and eggs. Tradition alone is no longer enough to protect turtles; without a scientific knowledge base and a management plan that is backed by government and supported by local peoples, animals that have provided food and traditional medicine for generations may be eaten out of existence.

The remains of a Central American River Turtle (*Dermatemys mawii*) have been unearthed from a Mayan burial ground in Uaxactún, in the Petén. The Mayans who brought it there (there is no suitable habitat for the species in the immediate area) undoubtedly valued its white flesh, and their descendants still prize it as the most delicious turtle meat in the Petén. The chief difference from Mayan times may be that today, *Dermatemys* is Critically Endangered.

Though protected, at least on paper, by a number of local and international laws, Central American River Turtles are under pressure throughout their range. Their meat is still highly prized, and they are harpooned, netted, and captured by divers. John Polisar has reported that in Belize, although some hunters and villages are interested in conserving the river turtle:

Low-income rural people who share riverine habitats with *Dermatemys* view it as a commodity roughly equivalent to a common catfish. Though disappointed if it disappears, their concern is solely economic. They are unaware of its endemism, its antiquity, or its ecological uniqueness.

Efforts are being made on its behalf by a number of organizations, including the Turtle Survival Alliance, the Wildlife Conservation Society, and Conservation International. Nonetheless, unfortunately, there is a good chance that the Dermatemydidae may soon be the first full family of turtles to disappear from the wild since the death of the last of the meiolaniids (see page 71, Chapter 2).

In the Dominican Republic, the endemic Hispaniolan Slider (*Trachemys decorata*) fetches a high price as a gourmet food or a source of traditional medicine. Poachers concentrate on the larger females, especially as they come ashore to lay their eggs, and all known populations of the species have declined substantially in recent years.

Antandroy and Mahafaly peoples in the far southwest of Madagascar regard the Radiated Tortoise (*Astrochelys radiata*) as *fady*, or taboo, though poverty has eroded many of the traditional Malagasy taboos against eating this increasingly rare species. Neighbouring tribes, however, and less traditional Antandroy, consider it a delicacy. Other Malagasy peoples consume large specimens of the Malagasy Big-headed Turtle (*Erymnochelys madagascariensis*), and overexploitation for food by a rapidly growing population may be the main threat facing this unique species. In the large lakes and backwaters that were once its chief stronghold, populations of *Erymnochelys* have been hunted to near or total extinction. There has been an increase in the use of fishing nets in its range, and more turtles are being caught as bycatch. Today *Erymnochelys* probably thrives only in small, hard-to-reach lakes and swamps—if this turtle, now listed as one of the world's most endangered, can

be said to thrive anywhere. The Durrell Wildlife Conservation Trust, Conservation International, and Madagascar National Parks are cooperating on programs to protect it, including close cooperation with local communities. The species' status is improving in one area, Ankarafantsika National Park in Madagascar's northwest.

African Softshells (*Trionyx triunguis*) are eaten in many parts of Africa, softshells of various species are illegally trapped for sale in markets in northeastern India, Bangladesh and Myanmar, and giant softshells of the genus *Pelochelys* are avidly sought from India to New Guinea for their meat and cartilaginous shells, valued in traditional Chinese medicine. Most populations of Asian Giant Softshell have already been extirpated. Villagers along the Sepik River in Papua New Guinea use the bony carapaces of *Pelochelys* and the much commoner, and smaller, New Guinea Snapping Turtle (*Elseya novaeguinae*) to make elaborate ceremonial masks. The masks are subsequently sold to tourists, often at high prices.

Local peoples in both New Guinea and Australia prize the flesh of the Pig-nose Turtle. In New Guinea, where Pig-nose eggs are a delicacy, the arrival of outboard motors, the decline of clan warfare, and the migration of hill peoples to coastal regions have turned what was once a strictly localized harvest into a commercial enterprise. The eggs are collected in huge and growing numbers for local markets. During a two-month survey in August–September 1998, investigators in West Papua, in the Indonesian sector of New Guinea, recorded the collection of some 84,000 eggs. In one district alone, the regency of Merauke, collectors took an estimated 1.5–2 million eggs each year, despite the fact that this species is legally protected in Indonesia.

These intense harvests are taking their toll. In the Kikori region of southern Papua New Guinea, surveys in 2007–09 found that the number of eggs passing through local markets had declined by 57.2 percent since 1981. On Turovio, one of the most remote nesting islands in the region, collectors destroyed

97 percent of the more than 100 nests dug each year in 2007–08 and 2008–09. Nesting females were significantly smaller than in the 1980–82 nesting seasons. The Kikori region has not, as yet, become part of the global trade networks that are thought to be fuelling massive declines in Pig-nose populations in Indonesian New Guinea, but even in this remote area the population has declined markedly. Carla Eisemberg and Arthur Georges have noted that "A conservation ethic has yet to penetrate [local Papuan] community perspectives, and many villagers believe that the turtles are abundant, have always been abundant and will continue to be so."

Overharvesting of eggs has been the chief threat facing the Critically Endangered Painted, Northern River and Southern River Terrapins. In Peninsular Malaysia, for example, where eating the meat of terrapins is forbidden by Islam, terrapin eggs may fetch at least 10 times the price of chicken eggs. In some areas they are valued as aphrodisiacs. In the 1930s, half a million eggs could be collected in a single year. During the Japanese occupation of Malaya in World War II, large numbers of adults and eggs were eaten, and the terrapin population fell catastrophically. The Malaysian government has established hatcheries and licenced egg collectors, who are allowed to take a quota of terrapin and sea turtle eggs from designated sections of beach and are required to turn over 70 percent of the eggs they collect to the hatcheries. There has often, however, been little enforcement. Poaching, has been intense the past 20 years, particularly along the west coast of the peninsula where the number of wild clutches of Southern River Terrapin eggs has fallen from a few thousand to less than 40.

Though eggs are still collected and sold as a local delicacy, the situation is slightly better on the east coast. Conservation efforts by the Department of Wildlife have helped maintain a small nesting population along the Terengganu River, home of the largest population in Malaysia (and perhaps anywhere) of the eastern subspecies *Batagur affinis edwardmolli*. On the Setiu River, where collectors had been taking 100 percent of the eggs for decades and none of the nesting beaches are officially protected, Eng Heng Chan and Pelf Nyok Chen of the Malaysia-based Turtle Conservation Centre began a Setiu River Terrapin Recovery

Turtles are offered for sale in a Papua New Guinea market.

Wildlife Conservation Society Field Veterinarian Martin Gilbert holds a Southern River Terrapin (*Batagur affinis edwardmolli*), once treasured in Cambodia as a "royal" turtle, at his house in Phnom Penh in 2005, after its rescue from a soup pot thanks to a microchip in its leg. WCS is working with fishermen to conserve this rare turtle in Cambodia.

Project in 2004. It aims to rebuild the Southern River Terrapin population by purchasing eggs from local collectors, incubating them and releasing the hatchlings, a technique called *headstarting*, on Terrapin Independence Day. The project has had considerable success working with egg collectors and local fishermen, but sand mining and a recently approved shrimp culture project threaten the nesting grounds. In 2010, Chan and Chen discovered another significant population of Southern River Terrapins in the Kemaman River in Terengganu. They are now working with local fishermen on a long-term basis to incubate eggs (a total of 650 eggs have been protected in 2011) and to headstart hatchlings for release.

Turtles and People in Amazonia

For centuries, riverside communities throughout the Amazon and Orinoco basins have depended on turtle eggs and meat, especially of the river turtles of the genera *Podocnemis* and *Peltocephalus*. In the basin of the Rio Negro, turtles, including river turtles, remain a significant source of food, though the Arrau (*Podocnemis expansa*) is now a high-priced luxury item and poor people have had to shift to smaller species. Despite local taboos and cultural restrictions, particularly on the Amazon Toad-headed Turtle (*Mesoclemmys raniceps*) and Red Side-necked Turtle (*Rhinemys rufipes*), whose meat is said to cause allergic reactions, and the Matamata (*Chelus fimbriata*), shunned on the basis of its appearance (see page 92, Chapter 3), turtles feature in 7 percent of all meals during the wet season and more than 20 percent in the dry. In addition to prizing them as food, locals value Red-footed and Yellow-footed Tortoises (*Chelonoidis carbonaria* and *C. denticulata*) for the supposed medicinal value of their fat and carapace scutes. Tortoise fat is used for rheumatism, toothache, hemorrhages, and other ailments. Arrau are still widely used in Amazonian folk medicine. In Pará State, Brazil, people use Arrau egg shells and, particularly, fat (often made into medicinal soap for commercial sale in Belém) to treat 16 different diseases including acne, arthritis and rheumatism.

As long ago as 1541, Father Gaspar de Carvajal, who crossed the Andes and journeyed down the

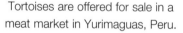

Tortoises are offered for sale in a meat market in Yurimaguas, Peru.

Amazon with Francisco de Orellana, noted that turtles were the most common food item in villages along the river. He found more than 1,000 turtles in enclosures in a single village. By the middle of the 19th century, some 2 million turtles were being taken for food every year in the state of Amazonas alone. The great 19th-century naturalist Henry Walter Bates (1825–1892) found stocks of Arrau in every backyard pond. In his classic book *The Naturalist on the River Amazons* (1863), he described the many ways turtle meat was prepared:

> The entrails are chopped up and made into a delicious soup called sarapatel, which is generally boiled in the concave upper shell of the animal used as a kettle. The tender flesh of the breast is partially minced with farinha, and the breast shell then roasted over the fire, making a very pleasant dish. Steaks cut from the breast and cooked with the fat form another palatable dish. Large sausages are made of the thick-coated stomach, which is filled with minced meat and boiled. The quarters cooked in a kettle of Tucupi sauce form another variety of food. When surfeited with turtle in all other shapes, pieces of the lean part roasted on a spit and moistened only with vinegar make an agreeable change.

In Bates's time, Arrau eggs were a major cash crop. With unusual insight for a naturalist of his time, he wondered how long the bonanza could continue:

> The destruction of turtle eggs every year by these proceedings [the immense egg harvest] is enormous. At least 6,000 jars, holding each three gallons of the oil, are exported annually from the Upper Amazons and the Madeira to Para, where it is used for lighting, frying fish, and other purposes. It may be fairly estimated that 2,000 more jars full are consumed by the inhabitants of the

villages on the river. Now, it takes at least twelve basketsful of eggs, or about 6,000 by the wasteful process followed, to make one jar of oil. The total number of eggs annually destroyed amounts, therefore, to 48,000,000. As each turtle lays about 120, it follows that the yearly offspring of 400,000 turtles is thus annihilated... [The Indians] say that formerly the waters teemed as thickly with turtles as the air now does with mosquitoes. The universal opinion of the settlers on the Upper Amazons is that the turtle has very greatly decreased in numbers, and is still annually decreasing.

There were some limited attempts to control the harvest. State authorities nominated judges to oversee the collection of eggs on the nesting beaches; Bates reported that in the Tefé region the council appointed a yearly commandante to keep an eye on things, and sentries were posted on each beach to make sure that only authorized collectors were allowed to dig up the eggs. Nonetheless, by the 1890s even this system seems to have broken down.

Arrau populations continued to dwindle through much of the 20th century. Sale of Arrau and Yellow-spotted River Turtle (*Podocnemis unifilis*) meat continues near Noel Kempff Mercado National Park in eastern Bolivia. In Venezuela, according to government figures, Arrau numbers on the middle Orinoco fell from 123,622 in 1945 to between 700 and 1,300 by 2002. Poaching still goes on, particularly of juveniles. A program to relocate and reintroduce nests, started in 1993 as a way to maintain the population, was felt to be necessary even though translocated hatchlings appear to have health problems and increased mortality.

A number of South American governments have set up management plans for various Amazonian river turtles. Bolivia, Brazil, Colombia, Ecuador, Peru, and Venezuela operate management projects for Yellow-spotted River Turtles. The Brazilian

Hatchling Yellow-spotted River Turtles (*Podocnemis unifilis*) are readied for release in Peru.

government began managing the Arrau in the mid-1970s (see page 93, Chapter 3), after warnings that river turtles might become extinct in 10 years at then-current levels of exploitation. In 1990 it set up a National Center for Amazonian Turtles (Centro Nacional dos Quelônios da Amazônia [CENAQUA], renamed RAN [Centro de Conservação e Manejo de Répteis e Anfíbios] in 2001) to oversee its national management program. Ten percent of the hatchlings produced by the management program in each Amazonian state go to approve commercial turtle breeders who raise the animals for meat. According to a report by Jack Sites and his colleagues:

> … [E]fforts from 1979–92 have resulted in the release of over 18,000,000 young turtles back into rivers after they hatched from nests on protected beaches. CENAQUA fields a crew of over 70 people during the nesting seasons, and teams monitor nesting activity on about 115 beaches in 15 regions on 12 rivers flowing through 9 Brazilian states.

Unfortunately a 2008 bureaucratic division split RAN's administrative agency in two, an action that has left the project in limbo as the respective successor agencies jostle for control.

Protecting nesting beaches alone, though, will not be enough to conserve Amazonian river turtles. Richard Vogt, who works in Brazil's Mamirauá Sustainable Development Reserve, believes that involving local villagers in the conservation of their turtles is absolutely essential if populations are to recover. In the Mamirauá Project, villagers themselves help monitor nesting populations and guard beaches from poachers. Fundacion Natura has been doing similar work with five indigenous communities on the borders of Cahuinari National Park in the Amazon region of Colombia. Claudia Nuñez and her colleagues counted about 5,000 nesting Arrau females there between 1994 and 1997. They enlisted residents to recover and incubate eggs in nests they considered to be at risk, and release the hatchlings in neighboring lakes. A conservation and monitoring project for Arrau and Yellow-spotted River Turtle, begun in 1990 and operated since by the Cofán Indians in Ecuador, has not only raised local awareness about and led to a ban on the killing of adults, but has influenced the Ecuadorian government to grant the Cofán rights to manage their territorial lands within the Cuyabeno Wildlife Reserve.

Despite these and similar projects in other parts of the Amazon basin, river turtles continue to be exploited at unsustainable rates throughout most of their range. Nesting beaches are subject to flooding from upstream hydroelectric dams, and in many areas lack protection of any kind. Around the town of Barcelos on the Rio Negro, the only species still frequent enough to be hunted is the Big-headed Amazon River Turtle (*Peltocephalus dumerilianus*). Local fishermen sell Arrau to river ferry operators, who can resell them (illegally) in Manaus for a handsome profit (in addition to numbers of legal, hatchery-raised turtles also shipped downriver to Manaus). Local people in the Rio Trombetas Biological Reserve in Pará, Brazil, take large numbers of the Six-tubercled Amazon River Turtle (*Podocnemis sextuberculata*), and in some Peruvian nesting colonies of this species, collectors converging from local and surrounding areas take over 90 percent of the nests. On unprotected sand beaches in Colombia and Peru, the take reaches 100 percent. Even in the Mamirauá Reserve itself, poachers have eliminated the Arrau and driven the Yellow-spotted River Turtle and the Six-tubercled Amazon River Turtle to historic low numbers.

The human population is growing in Amazonian Brazil (including cities like Manaus, with a population of more than two million), catered to by a lucrative black market that the government has been unable to control. Turtles remain in demand, not simply as staple items but as special attractions for private parties and celebrations. "As a result," say Larissa Schneider and her colleagues in a 2011 review, "there is illegal turtle hunting, continued exploitation of stocks, intensified black markets for eggs and turtles in cities, and increased black market prices. The situation in the Brazilian Amazon is critical: the commercialization of turtles and the illegal catch drive many river people to a permanent life of crime in trafficking in turtles and other wildlife."

What is to be done? Schneider, and her colleagues urge the Brazilian government to act on a number of measures: a massive education program aimed at both adults and children; a review to ensure that relevant laws are effective and appropriate to Amazonian society; improved enforcement aimed at providing effective deterrents for middlemen (no easy task in this often violent and lawless region: in 2008 a government boat was attacked by poachers in broad daylight—a volunteer was killed and an inspector wounded); provision of alternatives for local poachers; and constant monitoring to ensure that Amazonian turtles are not swept into the global market for turtles that has already decimated so many species in Asia (see page 386).

Can We Use Turtles Sustainably?

Involving local communities in the conservation of the turtles they consume, as is being done in the Amazon, is both valuable and important. Does that

Thousands of young Arrau (*Podocnemis expansa*) wait before being freed into the Orinoco River at Santa Maria del Orinoco, Venezuela, in 2004 as part of a government program.

These hatchling Arrau (*Podocnemis expansa*) have been bred for release in the Rio Trombetas Biological Reserve, Brazil.

mean that the key to the conservation of turtles, and everything else, is "sustainable use"—harvesting animals, for local use, commerce, or even international trade? In the Kikori region of Papua New Guinea, where Pig-nose Turtle eggs are an important source of protein for local people, cultural tradition may mean that they will continue to be so even if other sources become more available. Simply cutting people off from an unsustainable harvest may be as impossible as it would be unpopular. An attempt to make the harvest more sustainable may be the only option.

Nonetheless, Larissa Schneider and her colleagues noted in their 2011 review of conservation along the Rio Negro in Amazonia:

> Although some kind of sustainable hunting can be implemented in the Amazon, it will almost certainly have to exclude the most common forms of market or commercial hunting... As with most forms of commercial hunting, subsistence hunting makes it difficult to sustain animal populations. Not only are indigenous peoples capable of hunting at rates too high for wildlife populations to sustain, they are also tempted to shift to even heavier levels of commercial hunting as markets become available.

Its proponents argue that sustainable use, by providing an economic incentive to conserve wild species, is the way forward for wildlife conservation in a more and more overpopulated and developed world. Sustainable use requires that take levels be maintained at a low enough level for populations to be able to make good their losses. If turtle populations are capable of rebounding from a harvest in short order, surplus individuals can then be collected or consumed without affecting their underlying stability. Turtle populations have been found with high rates of growth; Adrian Haley found a growth rate of 14.7 percent in a population of Spur-thighed Tortoise on the Greek island of Paros, and argued

that such a population could be used sustainably under tightly regulated controls. Unfortunately, trade in *Testudo* tortoises like the spur-thighed has been anything but tightly regulated (see Chapter 10).

Many turtle populations have been hunted for generations, using traditional methods and at traditional levels of demand. In some cases even this sort of use has wiped out populations or even species—the extinction of the meiolaniids (see page 71, Chapter 2) may be the best example, and the Central American River Turtle seems poised to provide us with an even better (or worse) one. In many others, turtle populations seem to have adapted to human predators and survived—perhaps because of a dynamic ability, only recently recognized by

Thousands of juvenile turtles, like these Spur-thighed Tortoises (*Testudo graeca*), have ended up in the pet trade.

turtle biologists, to compensate for losses with shifts in their patterns of reproduction and growth.

In Northern Australia, the traditional aboriginal hunt for Northern Long-necked Turtles has been disrupted by feral pigs. The pigs damage turtle habitat, and often find and eat most of the aestivating turtles before human hunters can reach them. However, if the pigs can be fenced out the turtles have a remarkable ability to recover, sometimes in as little as a year or two (a phenomenon referred to as *density-dependent compensation*). Increasing numbers of hatchlings are apparently produced, and survive, when adult numbers fall. Damien Fordham and his colleagues have calculated that if the pigs are controlled a 20 percent annual subsistence take of

Australian aboriginal children hold their mother's catch of turtles.

adults and subadults, or a 30 percent harvest every second year, would be sustainable over the long term. Eastern Short-necked Turtles (*Emydura macquarii*) and Painted Turtles also seem able to compensate for a drop in population density, not because adults produce more hatchlings but because juvenile turtles speed up their growth and become sexually mature and capable of reproducing at an earlier age.

Some herpetologists nonetheless argue that whatever its merits as a conservation philosophy, turtles are either not suitable for sustainable use, at least at commercial levels, or unlikely to be hunted in any kind of sustainable way even if they are. Despite density-dependent compensation, most depleted turtle populations may take decades to recover, if they do at all. In many turtle populations there may be no such thing as a surplus, at least not of adults. Justin Congdon and his colleagues have shown that harvesting as few as 10 percent per year of a population of adult Common Snapping Turtles could result in a 50 percent decline of adults within 15 years.

Turtles that lay large clutches of eggs and experience high hatchling mortality may well have surplus eggs or young, animals that will probably never reach maturity. For turtles that lay only one or a very few eggs at a time, such as the Pancake Tortoise (*Malacochersus tornieri*), even that surplus may not exist. We have no idea if species like the Pancake Tortoise are able to compensate for losses as Painted Turtles and Northern Long-necks apparently do. Without evidence it is safest, and most precautionary, to assume that they cannot, and may not be able to withstand even moderate levels of harvest.

Today, traditional-level hunts, whether for subsistence or to provide local markets, have been largely supplanted by intense, demand-driven commercial exploitation on an unprecedented scale. Even turtles adapted to survive considerable falls in their numbers may not be able to keep up. In the opinion of the IUCN Tortoise and Freshwater Turtle Specialist Group (TFTSG):

It is not evident that any [country] has conclusively demonstrated that substantial offtake of tortoises and freshwater turtles from its wild populations is sustainable over the long term... Due to their life history characteristics of late maturity, low fecundity, high juvenile mortality, and long reproductive lifespans, wild turtle populations are highly susceptible to overexploitation, and sustainable harvest from wild populations is exceedingly difficult if not impossible to achieve.

Even a supposedly adaptable species may suffer from overharvesting. Colombian Sliders (*Trachemys callirostris*) had lower numbers of nesting females, and a smaller body size among the females that remained, in heavily hunted areas of northern Colombia than in other parts of their range. Painted Turtles have been heavily hunted in a number of American states, usually with hoop traps or a basking trap, a floating platform with a suspended net in the center. The turtles climb up the sloping sides of the platform to bask, but if they fall into the center they cannot climb out. In Minnesota they were taken in their thousands, particularly since the 1980s, for the pet and biological supply trades (in 1994 one harvester captured 35,000 turtles). In a two-year study reported in 1994, Tony Gamble and Andrew Simons trapped less than half the number of turtles in harvested than in unharvested lakes. This may not directly relate to the hunt (environmental differences between lakes could have played a role), and Gamble and Simon were unclear on whether the hunt was sustainable.

The exploitation of Alligator Snappers has apparently contributed (in combination with destruction and degradation of habitat) to a drastic decline throughout much of their range. Commercial trappers stepped up their harvests of Alligator Snapping Turtle from the 1960s through the 1980s. Dealers preferred large (and, presumably, sexually mature)

animals because they had greater amounts of meat; meat with bones sold for up to $13/kg ($6/lb) in parts of the state. In 1995 Kevin Sloan and Jeffrey Lovich published a case study of exploitation of Alligator Snappers in Louisiana, where they had long been hunted for their meat. Between 1984 and 1986, a single dealer in south-central Louisiana purchased 17,111 kg (37,737 lbs) of Alligator Snapper meat, representing approximately 1,223 individuals. The Louisiana Department of Wildlife and Fisheries had estimated that there were at least 35 large-scale dealers in Alligator Snapper meat. After 1995 only one butchering operation remained, and in 2004 the state banned all commercial hunting of

Decades of overexploitation have depleted populations of the Alligator Snapper (*Macrochelys temmincki*).

Alligator Snappers. The species is now legally protected in most of the states within its range.

Commercial harvest of all turtles is now banned in 10 eastern states. Others have banned the commercial sale of all native turtles except the Common Snapper. In 2009 the Florida Fish and Game Commission limited turtle collectors to one animal a day for "non-commercial use." In 2010 California banned the import of non-native turtles from other states (but not from overseas) for the meat market.

The apparently insatiable demand for turtle meat in China has nonetheless created a worldwide market, especially now that populations of many Asian species have collapsed (see Chapter 10). In parts of the United States this has led to massive and intense commercial hunts, especially for Spiny Softshells and Red-eared Sliders. Despite limited protection, the harvest in Texas is particularly intense. Donald Brown and his colleagues concluded in 2011 that without season and bag limits (already enacted in 14 eastern states) the hunt for turtles is unlikely to be sustainable in the long term. However, the demand for American turtles in China is now being met, to a great extent, from another source: turtle farms in China itself.

Farming

Turtle farming, or turtle ranching—the terms are often used interchangeably—is a booming business. Does it, perhaps, provide a way to produce and sell large numbers of animals without depleting wild populations?

Turtle farming has spread rapidly in East and Southeast Asia; in 1997 farms in Taiwan reportedly produced more than 2 million kg (4.4 million lbs) of softshell meat. Farming has reached particularly massive proportions in China, the largest consumer of turtle products in the world. The first large-scale turtle farms in China were established in the 1980s. New operations followed throughout the 1990s, and by 2002 there were 1,499 officially recognized large turtle farms in China, plus an unknown number of smaller ones, mostly in the southeastern provinces. By 2008 known turtle farms in China covered an estimated 10,000 ha (24,700 ac), with individual farms up to 33.3 ha (82.3 ac) in size.

The most commonly farmed species, and the subject of most early farming efforts, is the Chinese Softshell (*Pelodiscus sinensis*), which has the advantage of being relatively prolific and quick to mature. However, the supply of Chinese Softshells seems now to have met the demand. Newer operations have diversified into a number of "hard-shell" turtles. Reeves's Turtle (*Mauremys reevesi*) is the most commonly farmed hard-shell species, followed by the Red-eared Slider. Others include the Chinese Three-striped Box Turtle (*Cuora trifasciata*), Yellow Pond Turtle (*Mauremys mutica*), Chinese Stripe-necked Turtle (*Mauremys sinensis*), and, increasingly, Common and Alligator Snapping Turtles. As of June 2008, 22 species of hard-shelled turtles were being farmed in China, only seven of which were native. The large aquatic species are farmed for food and medicine, while smaller terrestrial animals such as Keeled Box Turtles (*Cuora mouhotii*) and Black-breasted Leaf Turtles (*Geoemyda spengleri*) are raised for sale to the pet trade.

The total number of animals farmed in China is staggering. According to its owner, one farm on the Chinese island of Hainan held more than 50,000 individuals of 50 species, including 30,000 Chinese Softshells. His stock included at least 1,000 Three-striped Box Turtles, and between 7,000 and 8,000 Asian Yellow Pond Turtles. In 2008 the breeding stock of Red-eared Sliders alone was estimated at 2.5 million. Shi Haitao and his colleagues estimated that the 684 Chinese farms they surveyed in 2002 offered 127,932,800 turtles for sale each year (including 124,849,800 Chinese Softshells), with a total value of $749,308,300. Extrapolating these figures, the total value for farmed turtles in China was more than $1.3 billion per year.

Though hatchling Red-eared Sliders, once the standard dime-store turtle, have been banned from sale in the United States since 1975, huge numbers have been farmed there for export. In the 1980s, up to 100,000 Red-eared Sliders were being taken from the wild each year to supply farming operations in United States, with a further 765,000 adults taken for direct export as food. At least 182,000 were imported into Taiwan for the pet trade alone between 1994 and 1998; Taiwan now bans the import of reptiles as pets. Between November 2002 and November 2005 the United States exported 31,783,380 turtles, more than half of them (17,783,380) sliders, mostly to Asian aquaculture facilities where they were raised to adulthood before being sold. Most of the sliders shipped to Asia were farmed, but the figure includes 732,949 animals taken from the wild.

Trade in wild sliders raised problems of its own. In 1990 and 1991, Lisa Close and Richard Siegel compared harvested and undisturbed populations of Red-eared Sliders in southern Louisiana and Western Mississippi. They found that "the most conspicuous difference among the populations was the virtual absence of turtles greater than 22 cm [8.7 in] carapace length from harvested sites; in essence, the entire upper end of the size distribution had been eliminated." However, as China has built up its own stock of farmed sliders and other North American species, the bottom may have fallen out for both the turtle farming industry and the wild harvest (at least for these species) in the United States. More than half of the farms in Louisiana and Mississippi have gone out of business in the past seven years. The price of adult wild-collected sliders has fallen to 50 cents a pound—not enough to cover the cost, in boat fuel and other items, of collecting them. Red-eared Slider farming in China does seem to have taken pressure off the wild population as its breeding stock has grown large enough to take over the market.

It may also have done so for the Chinese Softshell. Ting Zhou and her colleagues expressed the hope that "[c]aptive breeding will hopefully satisfy the desire for turtles as food, medicine, pets, or research animals, and will reduce the demands on wild turtle populations." However, as Zhou recognized, most turtle farms rely heavily, at least in their early years, on adults collected from the wild to replenish their breeding stock. The Chinese farms, far from supplanting the trade in wild turtles, are now its biggest customers. Because the stocks of farmed turtles lose their reproductive potential over time, there is a constant demand for "fresh blood." To Haitao Shi and his colleagues, that means that farming, far from being a conservation solution, is not sustainable:

> Established turtle farmers with enough capital are continuing to purchase turtles whenever possible, opting to earn profits while they can, apparently with little regard for the future. In the short term there may be some benefits in terms of deflecting pressure from imported species... but these gains can only be considered temporary, with a permanent cost to wild Chinese turtles. In the long term turtle farms serve no function beyond generating profit for a few entrepreneurs.

There seems to be no clear evidence that farmed animals really do cut into the demand for wild-caught Asian turtles. Demand is so enormous that all the farmed and imported turtles available, plus the wild turtles in the markets, cannot fill it. Wild turtles are still cheaply available, may cost less than farmed animals, and are widely believed, particularly in China, to be of superior quality and potency, and therefore fetch a much higher price. Traders who deal in protected turtles face a low risk of prosecution, and their profit margins remain high.

True closed-cycle farming may have been achieved in China for Chinese Softshells and Reeves' turtles, and may be on the way for snapping turtles, Red-eared Sliders and perhaps American softshells. Even if turtle farms are true "closed" breeding operations, however, they still raise concerns associated with all types of wildlife farming: the increased risk of disease, and the chance that farmed turtles could escape, as Red-eared Sliders have done, and establish themselves outside their normal range to the detriment of native turtle populations. That is a problem farming shares with a much more unequivocal threat to wild turtles: the pet trade.

The Pet Trade

For many people, their first love for turtles came from owning a pet. Before the United States banned the domestic sale of turtle hatchlings in 1975—not as a conservation measure, but over fears that hatchlings spread diseases such as salmonella, which is known to be carried by both captive and free-ranging turtles—vast numbers of baby Red-eared Sliders became what Ted Williams, in a 1999 article in *Audubon Magazine*, called "disposable pets." Today, owning reptiles is a popular hobby in many countries; there may be somewhere between 2.5 million to 15 million pet turtles in United States alone. A 2004 survey in Texas found 58 native and exotic turtle species offered for sale as pets in shops or at reptile expositions, with prices ranging to $300 for a Pig-nose Turtle or a Matamata. The United States imports at least 30,000 turtles a year, the vast majority caught in the wild. Certainly many hobbyists cherish their animals, buy them only from reputable breeders, know what they are doing, and take an active interest in their conservation. Unfortunately, these reputable hobbyists are but a tiny part of a vast and wasteful international traffic in turtles. The most unscrupulous practitioners of the trade defy national and international laws, often with impunity.

The international trade in wild-caught pet turtles condemns many animals to slow and miserable deaths. Many die long before reaching a retail store, during capture or shipment. Some species suffer particularly high mortality in transport, reaching over 30 percent for Florida Softshells (*Apalone ferox*) and map turtles (*Graptemys* spp.). Veterinarian Barbara Bonner, director of the Turtle Hospital of New England, told Ted Williams that:

> Virtually all turtles from pet stores are desperately sick when purchased. "It takes about six months just to clean them up and rid them of parasites," she says. "Some are half the body weight they ought to be. It's estimated that 95 percent of the wild turtles that enter the pet trade are dead within a year. Pet stores don't make their money selling the turtle; they make their money selling the $250 setup that goes with it. So if your pet dies, it doesn't matter to them, because with that kind of investment, you're going to buy another.

The trade in pet turtles does more than threaten its immediate victims. Imported turtles can be hosts for parasites and diseases that could spread to native species. Out of 585 Spur-thighed Tortoises smuggled from North Africa into Italy in 2008, 221 were infested with exotic tortoise ticks (*Hyalomma aegyptium*). Eighty-one out of 220 tortoises from the same shipment tested positive for salmonella.

Between 1975 and 2005, a total of 2,062,289 tortoises of the genus *Testudo* alone were recorded in an international trade involving 58 importing counties and 112 exporting countries. For all five species in the genus the trend in numbers, especially between 1975 and 1985, was drastically downward. International commercial trade in wild-caught specimens of Egyptian Tortoise (*Testudo kleinmanni*), has been banned under CITES (see page 379). Wild-caught tortoises of three species were banned from commercial import into the European Union in 1984 out of fears that the trade was unsustainable, and four species were banned under revised EU regulations in 1997. Since then the legal trade in wild specimens of these species has shifted to markets in Japan and the United States. Large numbers of captive-bred tortoises continue to be sold in Europe, both animals bred within the EU and, for Spur-thighed Tortoises, imported specimens, mostly from Jordan, Turkey, and Lebanon (until 2004, when

Lebanon banned all exports after concerns were raised about the authenticity of supposed "breeding" facilities in the country). Illegal trade remains a problem. Tourists visiting Morocco frequently bring cheaply bought tortoises to Europe via the border crossing at Gibraltar. Tortoises are being smuggled from North Africa to Europe in increasing numbers, with the animals involved often being offered for sale on the Internet—an increasing source worldwide for the sale of turtles of both legitimate and, all too often, questionable origin.

Wild-caught Central Asian Tortoises can still be legally imported into the EU. The Central Asian Tortoise remains one of the most popular, and heavily-exported, turtles in the world. It represents almost half of all recorded trade in *Testudo* since 1975 (and probably a much greater proportion since the 1990s), and is the only *Testudo* species to

The Central Asian Tortoise (*Testudo horsfieldi*), at home on the steppes of Kazakhstan, is the victim of massive unregulated collecting for the pet trade.

show a rise in numbers traded after 1990—though David Lee and Katrina Smith have noted that "Of all the wild-caught reptiles currently in the pet trade, from both husbandry and conservation perspectives, it is hard to think of a less ideal candidate for a pet or for mass commercial exploitation." It is slow-growing, it has a low reproductive output, and collecting is largely unregulated (with only about 15 percent taken with official permission as of 2002).

Despite this nearly a million animals, if not more, were exported between 1975 and 2007, primarily from Uzbekistan and Tajikistan. Most of the exports go to Great Britain, Germany, the United States and Japan, though the European Union banned their import from 2005 to 2007. A ranching operation in Uzbekistan rears hatchlings from eggs that are either collected in the wild or laid by gravid females that are released after laying, but though some 72,000 ranched tortoises were exported from Uzbekistan between 2001 and 2008 the bulk of the trade still depends on wild-caught animals. Uzbekistan reported legal exports of a quarter of a million wild-caught tortoises between 1999 and 2008. Exports have often exceeded government-set quotas. Illegal trade is a serious problem, with some 20,000 tortoises reportedly exported illegally every year from Tajikistan and Uzbekistan to the Russian Federation and the Ukraine. Despite some legislative improvements, the government of Uzbekistan seems unable, or perhaps unwilling, to control the trade.

Between 5 and 25 percent of the exported tortoises die during shipment. Most of the tortoises imported into the United States are in poor health, and many die within a year. Numbers in the wild are already starting to fall as collecting intensifies and tortoise habitat is converted for agriculture. Sharp declines have been recorded in local populations in Uzbekistan's Kyzil Kum Desert, probably as a direct result of intense overcollecting for the trade.

The demand for novelties has even led to the deliberate "manufacture" of new turtle species, later revealed to be not discoveries but deliberately concocted hybrids for sale to unsuspecting collec-

A taste for novelty among pet collectors has threatened the existence of the Roti Island Snake-necked Turtle (*Chelodina mccordi*).

tors. "Species" such as *"Ocadia glyphistoma"* and *"Sacalia pseudocellata"* have since been consigned to the taxonomic scrapheap.

The eagerness to fill the demand for the latest rarity can have drastic effects. The Roti Island Snake-necked Turtle (*Chelodina mccordi*) was only described as a separate species in 1994, though it was first collected in 1891. It is confined to Roti, an island south of Timor, where two isolated subspecies occur, and to extreme eastern Timor-Leste. There is nothing particularly extraordinary about it, as snake-necked turtles go, except its rarity and novelty. That, though, has been enough.

Before 1994, when it was regarded as simply a form of the New Guinea Snake-necked Turtle (*Chelodina novaeguinae*), no one paid much attention to it. Turtles were exported from Roti to Europe (in fact most "New Guinea Snake-necks" in Europe turned out to be *mccordi*), but local people who caught them in their fishing nets considered them too poor-tasting and snake-like to be worth keeping, and usually threw them back. All that changed after the

Roti Island Snake-neck was recognized as a separate species. Suddenly it was in demand. Its price in the trade rose to $2,000 and more. Collectors, descending on Roti from Java and beyond, trapped the turtles into commercial extinction within five years. Today the species is listed as Critically Endangered, a situation that—despite destruction of the turtle's habitat and pollution from chemicals used in rice fields— can be blamed squarely on the pet trade. The Timor-Leste subspecies may be in better shape, but its status is not well known.

Indonesia has banned its export since 2002, but enforcement has been pretty much non-existent and poaching of the few remaining animals continues. Indonesia has been urged to establish a wildlife preserve for the species on Roti, but its best chance for survival may be, ironically, in captive-bred insurance colonies far from its natural range. Indonesia, with TRAFFIC SE Asia, conducted a conservation workshop for the species on Roti in 2005, and recently released 50 captive-bred animals (from illegally acquired parents, of uncertain subspecies) into the wild.

History may be repeating itself with Pritchard's Snake-necked Turtle (*Chelodina pritchardi*). Another recently described species, it is confined to a tiny area east of Port Moresby, the capital of Papua New Guinea. It, too, has become an expensive novelty and is already classified as Endangered.

Though rarities often fetch high prices when they first appear in international markets, their prices may soon fall. Traders and dealers often respond to the bonanza a rarity may bring by flooding the market. If breeders are successful with the new arrival, they may soon be able to undercut the price of imports with captive-bred animals. Unfortunately, this price fall does not necessarily take pressure off wild populations. As the price drops more and more, less affluent buyers can afford the animals, and demand may rise again. If the price drops far enough, cheap wild imports may undercut the prices offered by breeders, making it more economical to deal in wild-caught animals greater than to breed them in captivity. Michael Klemens and Don Moll described such a trade pattern for the Pancake Tortoise in the early 1990s, when legal exports of the species from the wild still occurred:

> This recent flooding of the U.S. market with pancake tortoises has saturated the market far beyond the limited number of serious collectors and institutions willing to pay hundreds of dollars for a single tortoise, causing a subsequent reduction in price. Under these conditions the demand for pancake tortoises will continue unabated as the price is now within the range of many casual pet owners. This devalued market will consume as many pancake tortoises as can be supplied, while providing no financial incentive to breed the species in captivity. A previous example of a "bottomless tortoise market" was the insatiable post–World War II demand for inexpensive Mediterranean tortoises (*Testudo graeca* and *T. hermanni*)

Pancake Tortoises (*Malacochersus tornieri*) flooded the U.S. pet market in the early 1990s.

which continued until 1988 throughout Western Europe. Although many populations of *Testudo* were severely damaged by collecting activities, the wide geographic range of these species prevented their extinction. However, the pancake tortoise is much more vulnerable to this "bottomless market" type of exploitation because of its comparatively small geographic range, narrow habitat requirements, and localized populations.

The United States is one of the few countries to have issued meaningful penalties against turtle smugglers. A violation of the Lacey Act, which makes it illegal to import animals in violation of the laws of their home country, carries a maximum penalty of five years in prison and a $250,000 fine. In recent years, there have been a number of well-publicized Lacey Act indictments that involved turtle smuggling.

In 1998, Michael Van Nostrand, owner of Strictly Reptiles in Hollywood, Florida, pled guilty to charges of illegally importing reptiles includ-

A customs officer in Düsseldorf, Germany, demonstrates a cigarette box, used to hide smuggled turtles, at an airport information stall in 2008.

ing Pig-nose Turtles, Chaco Tortoises, Red-footed Tortoises and Yellow-spotted River Turtles. He was sentenced to 8 months imprisonment, 8 months home detention, and a fine of almost $250,000 to be paid to the Indonesian chapter of the World Wildlife Fund. In December 2000 Keng Liang "Anson" Wong, an alleged kingpin in the illegal wildlife trade in Malaysia, after spending nearly two years in a Mexican prison fighting extradition to the United States, pled guilty to 40 felony charges ranging from money-laundering to smuggling the world's most endangered tortoise, the Ploughshare Tortoise or Angonoka (*Astrochelys yniphora*). On June 7, 2001, Wong was sentenced to 71 months in prison—the maximum term under federal guidelines—and a fine of $600,000. In 2010 he was arrested again, this

time on a Malaysian airlines flight, with 95 illegal boa constrictors in his possession. He was eventually sentenced to 5 more years in jail. In August 2011 a Malagasy woman, one of two arrested for smuggling Malagasy tortoises into Malaysia the previous year, alleged that she, too, had been working for Wong. Yet Wong was released in February 2012 after a Malaysian Appeals Court reduced his sentence.

In July 2010 U.S. Fish and Wildlife Service agents, in an undercover action dubbed "Operation Flying Turtle," purchased 10 smuggled turtles and tortoises from a wildlife smuggling ring apparently run by Atsushi Yamagami, a Japanese citizen. In August the agents arrested Hiroki Uetsuki, a Japanese from Osaka, as he arrived in Honolulu with 42 turtles. Uetsuki told agents he had been paid by Yamagami. In January 2011 Yamagami and an accomplice, Norihido Ushirozako, were arrested at Los Angeles International Airport with 55 turtles, including Big-headed Turtles (*Platysternon megacephalum*) and Indian Star Tortoises (*Geochelone elegans*), packed into snack-food boxes in their luggage. All three men pleaded guilty to smuggling charges. Uetsuki and Ushirozako were sentenced to time served and have been released, but Yamagami was sentenced April 30, 2012, to 21 months in federal prison, and fined $19,403.

Unfortunately, felony indictments and a scattered number of relatively stiff sentences do not seem able to stop the excesses of reptile smugglers. Even within the United States, poachers continue to strip entire watersheds of their populations of Wood Turtles. Part of the problem is the sheer size of the task of enforcement: even in the United States, which probably has more wildlife inspectors at its border crossings than any other country, no more than 10 percent of incoming shipments are inspected.

Imports do not have to be illegal to be appallingly wasteful. Ted Williams also interviewed Joe Ventura, a Fish and Wildlife inspector who works at the Port of Los Angeles:

"We've seen turtles stacked on their sides like dinner plates so they couldn't extend their limbs," [Ventura] says. Turtles destined for the pet trade are often shipped in cardboard boxes that get crushed when cargo shifts, and it's not unusual to see these boxes soaked with blood. In one shipment from Tanzania, 511 pancake tortoises and 307 leopard tortoises had been packed on top of one another. Fifty animals were dead, 400 appeared near death, and almost all were grievously dehydrated. There was much blood, many broken carapaces, and dozens of missing legs. About 50 females carried broken eggs.

This should not happen. The International Air Transport Association (IATA) issues regulations for the humane transport of live animals, and these regulations are a requirement for the parties to the CITES Convention. That CITES cannot entirely stop the excesses that Williams describes is one of the frustrations for those of us who have spent much of our lives dealing with, and trying to support, this powerful, often valuable, and yet at times painfully impotent international instrument.

Turtles and CITES

The Convention on International Trade in Endangered Species of Wild Fauna and Flora (CITES) was signed in 1973, and came into force in 1975. Today, it has 175 signatories. CITES is not an international endangered species list. Instead, it deals with a single issue: the need, as it states in its Preamble, to provide "international protection... for certain species of wild fauna and flora against overexploitation through international trade." How well it succeeds, though, depends on the will and resources of its signatory nations, and both may fall short of the mark where turtles are concerned. The species that CITES protects, or seeks to protect, are listed on one of three Appendices.

Species listed in Appendix I are considered to be "threatened with extinction," and are, or may be, affected by international trade. Appendix I species may not be taken from the wild and traded internationally for "primarily commercial purposes." Species listed in Appendix II are "not necessarily threatened with extinction," and may be traded commercially, but their trade requires regulation to ensure that they do not become threatened. Species may also be listed in Appendix II as a control measure because they look so much like another listed species that customs officials would be unlikely to be able to tell them apart. Only the Parties voting as an assembly (the *Conference of the Parties*) can add a species to Appendix I or Appendix II, remove it, or transfer it from one Appendix to the other. However, any Party can add its own population of a species to a third list, Appendix III, as a way of getting international help in controlling its trade.

As of December 2011, there are 139 tortoise and freshwater turtle species on the CITES Appendices, including 20 on Appendix I, 89 on Appendix II, and 30 on Appendix III. In 2000, all species of Asian box turtle (*Cuora*) were added to Appendix II, and in 2002 a long list of Asian freshwater turtles was added including narrow-headed and giant softshells (*Chitra* and *Pelochelys* spp.), the Big-headed Turtle, and a number of geoemydids. In 2004 the Spider Tortoise (*Pyxis arachnoides*) was transferred to Appendix I (see page 384), and more Asian and Australasian turtles were listed on Appendix II, including the Pignose Turtle and the Roti Island Snake-neck. There were no new or changed listings in 2007 or 2010, but at the time of this writing some are being discussed informally in preparation for the 16th meeting of the Conference of the Parties in March 2013.

Listing a species on a CITES Appendix can help bring it to the attention of conservationists, and can provide country governments with the framework to create and enforce national laws to control trade in turtles. Increasingly sophisticated forensic techniques, including recently developed DNA analyses to identify medicinal preparations made with turtle shell, are available to assist in enforcing CITES listings. Some have argued that listing species, especially those in demand for the pet trade, simply flags them for the attention of smugglers. There is little evidence that this has actually happened.

CITES can protect turtles, but only if it is properly implemented and enforced, and if there is the will and the wherewithal to make it work. All too often this fails to happen. Smugglers have ways, including well-organized laundering techniques, of getting around rules if the incentive is high enough.

Laundering is one of the most serious problems facing CITES' attempts to regulate the trade in pet reptiles, turtles included. To get around requirements in their countries of origin, animals are frequently claimed to have originated in countries where they do not, in fact, exist. The Egyptian Tortoise was transferred from Appendix II to Appendix I—at the request of Egypt—at the 1994 CITES meeting in Fort Lauderdale, Florida (where, ironically, substantial numbers were being offered for sale in local shops). Egyptian Tortoises are still offered, illegally, for sale in Egypt, although the species is now extinct there after years of heavy collecting. In 2002 Sherif Baha El Din found that Egyptian Tortoises captured in Libya, particularly in the eastern part of the country, were being sold to Egyptian traders who took them back across the border. Hundreds were exported after 1994 as "Egyptian Greek tortoises": in other words, as Spur-thighed (not Egyptian) Tortoises from Egypt. The problem is, as far as we can tell, that there are no wild Spur-thighed Tortoises in Egypt.

The Pancake Tortoise is listed on Appendix II. Kenya bans their export, and Tanzanian exports are ostensibly restricted to animals raised in ranching facilities. In the late 1990s, Pancake Tortoises began appearing in international markets labeled as animals from Mozambique and Zambia. The species almost certainly does not occur in Mozambique, but despite some skepticism it turned out that there

A ranger poses with an injured Indian Narrow-headed Softshell Turtle (*Chitra indica*), confiscated from poachers and placed in Chitwan National Park, Nepal, where a Turtle Conservation Breeding Centre has been established.

was, indeed, a small population in Zambia (though whether it was really the source of animals claimed to be coming from that country remains unclear). As a result, countries accepted the tortoises even though those labeled "Mozambique" were surely smuggled out of Kenya or Tanzania in the first place. At the 2000 CITES meeting in Nairobi, Kenya proposed that the whole species be transferred to Appendix

Egyptian Tortoises (*Testudo kleinmanni*) are still being sold illegally in Egypt, though the species is almost extinct there.

I, but withdrew the proposal after Tanzania refused to support it. Tanzania did, however, agree not to allow the export of wild-caught tortoises (which have in any case been under a zero quota since 1992). Despite this, in 2001, the Uganda Wildlife Authority confiscated 209 Pancake Tortoises packed in an animal trafficker's hand luggage at Entebbe airport, and numbers of Pancake Tortoises were found on sale at the Chatuchak animal market in Bangkok, Thailand in 2006 and 2007. Between 1999 and 2007, 700 Pancake Tortoises were imported into Thailand from the Democratic Republic of Congo (where the species does not occur), as well as 130 allegedly captive-bred animals from Lebanon.

CITES provisions make it easier to trade in captive-bred animals, and false claims of captive breeding are regularly used to slip wild-caught animals under the rules. Hundreds of Indian Star Tortoises have been confiscated by customs authorities in a number of countries, many of them claimed by their exporters to have been captive bred in Jordan, Lebanon, Ukraine, the United Arab Emirates, or Slovenia. It is highly unlikely that these claims are true. There are no records that these countries ever imported breeding stock, no large captive breeding facilities are known to exist, and there is no evidence that breeding has gone on long enough to produce the numbers of tortoises

they claim to export. The same is almost certainly true for Afghanistan, which recorded exports of 2,100 animals between 2002 and 2004, all of which were supposedly collected in the wild although the species does not occur in that country.

A listing of North American box turtles (*Terrapene* spp.) on Appendix II in 1994 (the Coahuilan Box Turtle [*T. coahuila*] was already on Appendix I) gave the U.S. federal government leverage to deal with exports of Eastern Box Turtles from Louisiana, the only state with a legal export trade. Trade in Appendix II species is only supposed to take place if the Office of Scientific Authority (OSA), one of the administrative bodies each Party must set up, finds that the export will not harm the wild population—in technical terms, it must make a *non-detriment finding*. Because there was no valid information on how Louisiana's trade, which exported thousands of animals annually, was affecting the turtles, the OSA reduced its export quota to zero in 1996 and 1997. Louisiana filed, and lost, an appeal. A campaign launched by two Louisiana residents, Martha Ann Messinger and George Patton, finally convinced the state government to ban the commercial harvest, sale and trade of wild-caught box turtles in 1999.

The powers of CITES are not limited to trade bans. A dozen species are, or have been, subject to a Significant Trade Review, designed to help Parties to improve their non-detriment findings and put

Louisiana has now banned exports of box turtles like this Three-toed Box Turtle (*Terrapene carolina triunguis*).

trade on as sustainable a basis as possible. Through the review, it has tried to persuade the government of Madagascar to bring the trade in its unique reptiles, including its tortoises, under control. CITES has coordinated cooperative international efforts to control unsustainable trade in broad categories of wild species. It is partly in that role that it has turned its attention—whether effectively or not it may be difficult to say—to the most immediate, and probably the most serious, of all issues facing turtle conservation: the immense and devastating trade in the turtles of South-East Asia.

Madagascar: Tortoises on the Edge

The unique fauna of Madagascar is one of the most beleaguered in the world, and its turtles, sadly, are no exception. Ron Nussbaum and Chris Raxworthy's commentary on the state of the once-common, but now Critically Endangered, Radiated Tortoise (*sokake* or *sokatra* in Malagasy) could well serve

An adult Angonoka (*Geochelone yniphora*) at the Jersey Wildlife Trust's Project Angonoka in northwestern Madagascar.

for most of them: "Their habitat is being degraded and destroyed at an increasing rate, they are being harvested by the thousands every year, and local law-enforcement does little to mitigate the situation or stop such activities. The laws protecting *sokatra* are well-known to the Malagasy, but they have learned that these laws have been completely ignored."

Madagascar's capital, Antananarivo, lies in the deforested and degraded center of the island. It is far from the Malagasy coasts, where smugglers' boats put in to take on shipments of endemic, and supposedly protected, tortoises. The animals are frequently transshipped eastward to the island of Réunion. Pet tortoises are highly popular on Réunion, where they are often given as wedding presents or to promote good luck. The chief advantage of Réunion to a smuggler, though, is that it is politically a part of France. Once the tortoises reach the island, they are, for customs purposes, in Europe, and they may be shipped throughout the EU without a shred of customs documentation.

Poachers have threatened the integrity of one of the best-known tortoise conservation programs in Madagascar. By 1996, Project Angonoka, the captive breeding program for the Critically Endangered Angonoka operated by the Durrell Wildlife Conservation Trust (formerly Jersey Wildlife Preservation Trust), had produced well over 150 babies. Then, in May 1996, someone—it has never been established who—broke into the breeding compound at Ampijoroa and stole 73 hatchling tortoises and two adults.

Months later, young Angonoka, surely from the breeding station, began appearing in European pet markets. In 1998, the Netherlands government confiscated 35 animals and sent them to the Bronx Zoo in New York for veterinary care. The Madagascar government filed a court action for their return (the tortoises were legally its property) and won. To avoid potential health risks, an arrangement was made to have the Angonoka housed by a commercial dealer. Before the United States returned the tortoises, the animals were marked indelibly on their carapaces. That way, they could never be sold again.

Project Angonoka has recovered. When I visited the station in 1997, the project managers had already installed an improved security system, and at least 30 new baby tortoises had been hatched. Meanwhile, the project has conducted in-depth studies of the tiny wild population, and developed plans to protect its habitat and to help the people that live there to care for their local environment. It has established good relations with the people of Baly Bay, who, according to Lee Durrell, "are proud to be involved in the safeguarding of 'their' tortoise." Since 2006, a reintroduction program at Baly Bay has been releasing captive-bred animals into their natural habitat (see page 162, Chapter 4). In 2009 it, too, was the victim of thieves, who stole four tortoises waiting to be released into the wild.

In 2000, the Madagascar government suddenly raised its CITES export quota for the rarest and most localized of its tortoises after the Angonoka, the Flat-tailed Tortoise or Kapidolo (*Pyxis planicauda*), from 25 to 800. At the same time, it raised the export quota for the Flat-tailed's more widespread relative, the Spider Tortoise, from 25 to 1,000. Considering that the entire population of the Flat-tailed Tortoise must be small, there is no way that such a quota could be biologically justified. Nonetheless, hundreds of Flat-tailed Tortoises, certainly caught in the wild, began appearing in U.S. markets. According to U.S. government figures, imports for 2000 of Flat-tailed Tortoises, Spider Tortoises, and Malagasy Big-headed Turtles into the United States alone, all bearing export permits issued by the government of Madagascar, exceeded even the new global quotas by 179 percent. After protests from conservationists, Madagascar reset the quota to zero early in 2001, but the animals continued to appear, even though initial high prices tumbled.

Though the Flat-tailed Tortoise is poorly known in the wild, there seemed little doubt that, if its trade was not brought under real control, the species would suffer serious harm. In May 2001, members of the IUCN Captive Breeding Specialist Group facilitated a meeting of Malagasy and expatriate field workers in Madagascar to assess the status of many species, including the Flat-tailed Tortoise, and con-

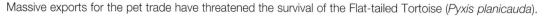

Massive exports for the pet trade have threatened the survival of the Flat-tailed Tortoise (*Pyxis planicauda*).

Southeast Asia was being drained of its turtles at a rapid and growing rate. The alarm was sounded at a December 1999 workshop in Phnom Penh, Cambodia, where 45 delegates from 15 countries met to assess the impact of the rapidly expanding trade. The facts it uncovered were startling:

> Based on the most recent available data, a minimum of 13,000 metric tons of live turtles are exported from South and Southeast Asia to East Asia each year. At least 5,000 tons of wild-collected turtles are exported from Indonesia annually and 1,500 tons from Bangladesh, as well as 4,000 tons of farm-produced softshells from Thailand and 2,500 tons of turtles from wild and farm sources in Malaysia. The actual amounts may be substantially higher and these numbers do not include amounts exported from Cambodia, Laos, Myanmar, or Vietnam.

More than nine million live turtles of many species were imported to Hong Kong in 1998 alone—an increase of 28 times since 1992. The majority of them (81.5 percent) originated in Indonesia and Thailand. Most were probably destined for sale as food in Chinese markets. Though these figures included farmed Red-eared Sliders and Chinese Softshells, they undoubtedly represented a huge number of wild-caught animals.

Bangladesh exported an estimated 10,000 tonnes (11,023 tons) per year of Indian Peacock Softshells (*Nilssonia hurum*) between 1985 and 1992, before the species was listed on CITES' Appendix I. Chris Shepherd of TRAFFIC Southeast Asia reported that two exporting companies in the provinces of North Sumatra and Riau, Indonesia, shipped more than 22.7 tonnes (25 tons) of wild-caught live turtles each week to China, Hong Kong, and Singapore. Ten of Sumatra's 13 freshwater turtle and tortoise species were sold, including large quantities of Malaysian Giant Turtle (*Orlitia borneensis*), one of the two most heavily exported species despite the fact that all trade in Malaysian Giant Turtles is illegal in Indonesia.

The vast majority of turtles in Chinese markets, mostly softshells and the larger "hard-shell" turtles, are sold as food or for use in traditional medicine (softshell turtle powder has been shown to alleviate

Though protected by law in Indonesia, the Malaysian Giant Turtle (*Orlitia borneensis*) has been exported in huge numbers.

fatigue in mice). Others are sold as pets or turned into curios. Some are used for religious rituals in which celebrants release turtles into the wild, often far from their natural habitats. Turtle imports into China increased tenfold between 1977 and the turn of the century, partly because, in 1989, the Chinese government allowed its currency to be exchangeable with that of other countries. The fashion for turtle meat and other turtle products is growing in China, and is spreading to the north where turtles were, traditionally, not very popular.

The demand for turtle meat in China is intimately tied to the demand for ground shell, bone and other turtle products for traditional Chinese medicine (TCM). Historically, softshells have been considered to be a delicacy in China, while other species, the so-called hard-shelled turtles, were reserved for medicinal use. Today, however, both softshells and hardshells are eaten, and their meat is valued not only for its flavor but for its reputed medicinal properties. Plastra, broken shell bones, and dried pieces of cartilage from soft-shelled turtles are traded for their apparent medicinal value. In June 2011, for example, border guards in Bangladesh seized more than 120 kg (265 lbs) of dried turtles, valued at around $140/kg. Between 1999 and 2008, Taiwan imported an average of 228 tonnes (251 tons) per year of such items, representing roughly two million turtles, although almost none of this trade shows up in CITES records. Tien-Hsi Chen and his colleagues have described the trade as "highly unsustainable" and have accused TCM traders of a "blatant disregard ... for laws and authority."

Few turtles have carried a higher price than the Chinese Three-striped Box Turtle. Even its common trade name, "golden coin turtle," conveys the image of a rare treasure. The reason is its medical reputation. Its meat and, particularly, its ground plastron, mixed with medicinal herbs and marketed as *guilinggao* or "turtle jelly," are believed to have cancer-reducing and detoxifying properties. Priced at only $50-$100 in the mid-1980s, by the late 1990s

a Three-striped Box Turtle could fetch $1,000 or more in Hong Kong—if one could be found. Today they are being farmed by the thousands, but wild turtles are still in demand both for medicine (supposedly more potent from wild animals) and as breeding stock. The farms incubate their eggs at too high a temperature to produce males, and recently a wild-caught male changed hands for $20,000. Over most of their range, Three-striped Box Turtles have become almost, if not entirely, impossible to locate in the wild. In Laos, where hunters once avidly sought them to sell to Vietnamese traders, the numbers of turtles passing through the market towns of Ban Guner and Ban Maka-Nua fell from some 300 per year in the early 1990s to 10 or less by 1998.

Turtle plastra have been shown to contain traces of selenium, an element which apparently does have cancer-reducing properties. The amounts present are so slight, however, that it is highly unlikely that turtle jelly really has the properties touted for it. Meiling Hong and her colleagues analyzed a number of geoemydid turtles, including the Chinese Three-striped Box Turtle, and were unable to determine anything special about their supposed medicinal properties. Their selenium levels were considerably lower than in softshell turtles or, for that matter, in oyster shells. Hong's study concluded that "where

The Chinese Three-striped Box Turtle (*Cuora trifasciata*) has fetched high prices for its purported medicinal properties.

Asian box turtles such as the Southeast Asian Box Turtle (*Cuora amboinensis*) are in heavy demand for food, for medicine or as pets. All *Cuora* turtles are listed on Appendix II of CITES.

nutritional composition and content are concerned, the human consumption of turtles could be completely substituted by cheaper domestic animals, aquatic animals, or mineral supplements." Today, *guilinggao* (unless it is very expensive) is more likely to be made with cheaper substitutes, including the Asian Yellow Pond Turtle or the Malayan Flat-shelled Turtle (*Notochelys platynota*), if it contains any turtle at all. Much of the *guilinggao* now sold commercially is purely herbal.

A 35-month survey of turtle markets in Hong Kong, Shenzhen, and Guangzhou recorded almost one million turtles and tortoises on sale, representing 157 species including 13 species on CITES Appendix I; 77 species were being sold for food or as medicine, and 81 were offered only as pets. Among them were more than 210,000 Southeast Asian Box Turtles (*Cuora amboinensis*) and over 15,000 Indochinese Box Turtles (*Cuora galbinifrons*). In recent years, the pet trade has increased dramatically in China; a series of seven visits to the Yuehe Pet Market in Guangzhou, the largest pet market in China, between 2006 and 2008 revealed more than 39,000 turtles on sale, representing 61 species.

The result of this unrelenting pressure, coupled with increased domestic trade in many Southeast Asian countries, has been a grave threat to the world's largest and most diverse turtle fauna. A 2010 analysis of the Asian turtle trade, prepared for CITES by the IUCN Tortoise and Freshwater Turtle Specialist Group (TFTSG) based on information collected between 2002 and 2008, showed sharp declines (sometimes after an initial rise) in the numbers of heavily traded species in commerce. Some smaller species, primarily exported for the pet trade, appeared to show steady trade levels, but these probably reflected a pattern of repeated "boom and bust" collecting that effectively exterminated the turtles in one area before the hunters moved on to the next. Even trade in the relatively common Southeast Asian Box Turtle showed a decline by an order of magnitude.

With China's own supply of turtles nearing exhaustion, the trade moved outward, first to the turtles of neighboring countries such as Bangladesh, Myanmar, Vietnam, and the Philippines where there is a sizable domestic market for turtle meat. In 2001 and 2002 Steven Platt and his colleagues found that hunters were taking large and, in their view, unsustainable numbers of turtles from the Tonle Sap Biosphere Reserve in Cambodia for sale to urban markets and, presumably, export to Vietnam and China. From nearby countries the trade shifted outward to Indonesia, Papua New Guinea, and beyond. Arthur Georges and his colleagues have reported increasing pressure to enter the Asian turtle trade among the peoples of Papua New Guinea's TransFly Region, impeded only by the difficulty of getting the turtles to market.

The trade has already had a drastic effect on distant turtle populations and on Critically Endangered species such as the Philippine Forest Turtle (*Siebenrockiella crassicollis*). The natural range of the Sulawesi Forest Turtle (*Leucocephalon yuwonoi*) is further from China than that of almost any other geoemydid. Sulawesi Forest Turtles appeared in Chinese markets even before their "official" discovery in 1995, and in great numbers shortly afterward, though the species is very difficult to maintain in captivity. In 1998, 2,000 to 3,000 turtles were exported to China, but only a year later the number had fallen to about 100, probably because its numbers were so depleted that it was no longer worth collecting commercially. A survey in 2005–06 failed to find the species in the wild, but recorded a modest but increasing turtle trade in Central Sulawesi

These Malaysian Giant Turtles (*Orlitia borneensis*) were among a cargo of 10,000 turtles, bound from Southeast Asia to markets in mainland China, confiscated by Hong Kong customs officials on December 11, 2002.

aimed at local ethnic Chinese customers and international markets. At least 50 Sulawesi Forest Turtles were traded per month. Indonesia established an export quota of 100 animals per year in 2003, but exceeded it in 2007. Poor enforcement has meant that the numbers actually traded, legally and illegally, are probably considerably higher.

As the trade spread, turtle faunas of country after country collapsed in its wake. In Vietnam and Laos, turtles became almost impossible to find, even for professional collectors. Ross Keister, who visited Vietnam in 1997 as a member of of the Global Biodiversity Team for the United States Forest Service, reported that things had gotten so bad that "wherever we looked there was what we called a reverse pet shop. A storefront with signs advertising that they will buy any kind of turtle. We've been recently told that these stores are closing since there are no more turtles left to buy."

How, then, was the Asian turtle crisis to be solved? The delegates to the 1999 Cambodia Workshop called for stronger and better-enforced laws, guidelines to help authorities dealing with confiscated turtles, studies on the natural history of Asian turtles and the effect trade is having on them, expanded conservation breeding programs both in Asia and abroad, regulation and monitoring of turtle farming, a search for substitutes for turtle products in traditional medicine, and public education, particularly among local communities. A subsequent Technical Workshop on Conservation of and Trade in Tortoises and Freshwater Turtles, held in Kunming, China, in March 2002, built on the Cambodia recommendations (as well as signaling China's willingness to admit, after some initial reluctance, its central role in the trade). A CITES resolution, *Conservation of and trade in tortoises and freshwater turtles*, adopted in 2000 and revised in 2008, calls for better enforcement, national and international cooperation, scientifically based quotas for species in trade, enactment of appropriate legislation, and enhanced programs of research and public education.

Some of these recommendations have been met. Myanmar has begun a reintroduction program for the Burmese Star Tortoise (*Geochelone platynota*), and is breeding the extremely rare Burmese Roofed Turtle (*Batagur trivittata*) at the Yadanobon Zoo in Mandalay. China has placed restrictions on import and export of tortoises and freshwater turtles. Peninsular Malaysia imposed a zero quota for the export of live freshwater turtles in 2008. In 2009, Cambodia declared almost all of its native species of freshwater turtles as endangered, prohibiting their capture and export.

Public education measures have included posters, identification guides, and local workshops. In 1998, Fauna and Flora International helped set up a Turtle Conservation and Ecology Project in Vietnam's Cuc Phuong National Park, now incorporated into a larger Cuc Phuong Conservation Project. Its objective is "to initiate immediate and urgent action in response to the threat to Vietnam's native turtle populations resulting from the illegal wildlife trade." The project promotes public awareness and education, trains local authorities, performs research on captive breeding, translocates confiscated turtles into protected areas, carries out population surveys, and monitors the trade. Among its efforts has been a children's book, *The Adventures of Lucky Turtle*, that tells the story of "a forest turtle that is caught by hunters and sold to an evil trader, only to escape while being shipped to China with a truck full of other animals." The Turtle Conservation Center at Cuc Phuong houses rescued and confiscated turtles, and in 2010 it opened its Chelonian Visitor Center, devoted entirely to turtle conservation.

There have been repeated calls, including recommendations from both the Cambodia and Kunming workshops, for increased CITES coverage, including if possible the listing of all remaining Asian turtles. In a 2009 analysis of the turtle trade in China Zhihua Zhou and Zhigang Jiang recommended the listing of all Chinese species except the Chinese Softshell on Appendices I or II. This would automatically give them status as national key protected species under Chinese law. The TFTSG has suggested that CITES Parties ban all mass trade in turtles within their jurisdiction. Listing, though, means little without enforcement. In many Asian countries, CITES listings are flouted or ignored, and there have been accusations of complicity between dealers and corrupt officials. Enforcement budgets are often so low that even the most committed customs officers cannot make a serious dent in the trade. The borders between China and many of its neighbors to the south are sieves as far as smuggling of endangered species is concerned, and it is highly unlikely that any national or international regulation will stop the trade by itself.

As yet there are no comprehensive management strategies in place for any Asian freshwater turtle, though a Southeast Asian Regional Action Plan for the conservation of large riverine turtles (*Batagur* spp.) is currently being developed. According to the TFTSG, "dedicated management of collection and trade of wild-collected tortoises and freshwater turtles appears nearly nonexistent in Asia." The only Asian species for which the biology, status, and exploitation have been studied in detail is the Southeast Asian Box Turtle. The study, by Sabine Schoppe, revealed that the species is still exported from peninsular Malaysia in large numbers despite a zero quota established in 2005. In Indonesia, Schoppe estimated that illegal exports from Indonesia amounted to between 10 and 100 times the legal trade of 18,000 live animals per year.

Protected turtles and tortoises from around the world, including species on CITES Appendix I, can be found openly on sale in pet shops and animal markets throughout Southeast Asia. In 2010, TRAFFIC SE Asia found 139 specimens of seven species listed on Appendix I in animal markets in Jakarta, Indonesia, more than on a similar survey in 2004 despite strengthened laws and increased enforcement effort. They included

Filipino veterinary medicine students watch caged Southeast Asian Box Turtles (*Cuora amboinensis*) at the Wildlife Rescue Center in Quezon City, Philippines.

Ploughshare, Radiated, and Spider Tortoises from Madagascar, as well as species supposedly protected under Indonesian law including Pig-nose Turtles, New Guinea Snapping Turtles (*Elseya novaeguinae*) and Malaysian Giant Turtles.

The status of almost all Indonesian freshwater turtles and tortoises remains unknown, but we do have some idea what the trade may be doing to some species. An Indonesian shipment of 10,000 whole and broken turtle plastra, confiscated in Hong Kong in January 2006, largely consisted of the remains of Southeast Asian Box Turtles and Black Marsh Turtles (*Siebenrockiella crassicollis*), but also contained the plastra of 33 Malaysian Giant Turtles. Roger Kendrick and Gary Ades, who analyzed the remains, found that although the smaller turtles included individuals of a variety of size and age classes, all of the Malaysian Giant Turtle remains came from younger animals. ...may mean that large adults have already been ...ated, and, if so, that the trade in this protected ...is unsustainable.

Illegal trade and confiscations continue. In January 2009, the Special Task Force of the of Uttar Pradesh police in India seized more than 5 tonnes (5.5 tons) of turtles, amounting to some 3,000 animals. They included Indian Flapshell Turtles (*Lissemys punctata*) and two species on CITES Appendix I, the Indian Softshell (*Aspideretes gangenticus*) and the Spotted Pond Turtle (*Geoclemys hamiltonii*). The turtles were released, under court order, on the banks of the Yamuna River, and three smugglers were sent to jail. Only a few weeks later, a car carrying 3 tonnes (3.3 tons) of live tortoises, also coming from Uttar Pradesh, was seized at a forest checkpoint. In the same year, Cambodian authorities confiscated 2 tonnes (2.2. tons) of tortoises and snakes near a border crossing. Recent seizures have included 1,490 kg (3,285 lbs) of turtles, mostly Giant Asian Pond Turtles (*Heosemys annandalii*), confiscated in Vietnam in April 2011 en route to the Chinese border. 451 turtles and tortoises, including narrow-headed softshells (*Chitra* spp.), Assam Roofed Turtles (*Pangshura sylhetensis*), Spotted Pond Turtles and 35 Indian Star Tortoises, found at Bangkok Airport in June 2011 inside four suitcases (along with seven Gharials [*Gavialis gangenticus*], a unique and endangered crocodilian).

Some have said that there is in nothing we can do to save Asian turtles in the wild, and that the only solution is to establish "assurance colonies" of animals in captivity. The need to develop coordinated, properly managed breeding programs for at least some Asian turtles led in 2001 to the founding of the Turtle Survival Alliance (TSA), a coalition involving zoos, private breeders and conservation organizations. Assurance colonies in foreign countries cannot preserve the roles turtles play in their native ecosystems, and they rob the people who live with wild turtles of any role in their conservation. The TSA has realized this (as well as facing up to the impracticalities of maintaining such colonies in perpetuity) and has greatly expanded its mandate. Today, though its focus is still on captive breeding and related activities such as headstarting programs and turtle rescue

Large numbers of Giant Asian Pond Turtles (*Heosemys annandalii*) were confiscated in Vietnam in April 2011, en route to the Chinese border.

facilities, it has shifted its centers of activity to the turtles' native countries, with an emphasis on local training and capacity building. It retains the same goal: zero turtle extinctions in the 21st century.

Turtles have a value to humanity unrelated to the pot or the pet shop. Freshwater turtles in Asia eat snails that are intermediate hosts of *Schistosoma*, the deadly human blood fluke. In 1983, as part of India's Ganga Action Plan to clean up the Ganges river, Indian Softshells (*Nilssonia gangenticus*) and Indian Peacock Softshells (*Nilssonia hurum*) were recruited as a natural cleanup crew. Collectors gathered soft-

shell eggs and transferred them to hatcheries at Lucknow and Varanasi. Here, the babies were hatched and reared to a size that would protect them from many of the predators that attack hatchlings. The headstarted turtles were released in large numbers into the Ganges, to feed on the carcasses of humans and livestock commonly dumped into the river.

We must get the message out that wild species in their natural environments are resources to be husbanded and protected, not mines to be pillaged. If we can only do that, we may save at least some of Asia's wild turtles after all.

Since 2006, the National Chambal Centre has protected hatchlings from hundreds of nests of Red-crowned and Three-striped Roofed Turtles (*Batagur kachuga* and *B. dhongoka*) along the Chambal River in Uttar Pradesh, India.

CHAPTER TEN

Peril at Sea

HUMANS HAVE exploited sea turtles for millennia. Bones that have come from Green Sea Turtles (*Chelonia mydas*) have been found among the leavings of early humans in the Niah Caves of Borneo. Traditional sea turtle hunts and egg harvests are still an important part of the lives of indigenous peoples from Central America to New Guinea. Leatherbacks (*Dermochelys coriacea*) are occasionally eaten on Malakula Island in Vanuatu, though on nearby Akhamb Island they are (or were) avoided because of their unusual appearance and a belief that they are bad spirits.

People in the Caribbean have used sea turtles for at least 4,000 years, and thousands of turtles are still taken there every year for human consumption. Communities on the Caribbean coast of Nicaragua have relied on Green Sea Turtle meat for over 400 years, and a commercial fishery operated there in the 1960s and 1970s. The turtle fishery in the Turks and Caicos Islands can be traced back to 700 CE, though in recent years the taste for turtle meat is giving way to a preference for American-style fried chicken and pork ribs. Nonetheless, there is evidence that the

BELOW, RIGHT

On Satawal Island a man distributes the meat of two slaughtered sea turtles, the spoils of a hunting and fishing trip to Pigailoe, or West Fayu Atoll, in the central Caroline Islands.

OPPOSITE

The shells of sea turtles killed by poachers lie on the beach at San Valentin, in the western Mexican state of Guerrero, in 2004.

hunt may be harming nesting populations of Green and Hawksbill Sea Turtles (*Eretmochelys imbricata*) in the region and perhaps beyond.

Ritual and subsistence hunts may not have jeopardized turtle populations in ages past, but our relationship with sea turtles in recent centuries has been far from benign, and certainly far from sustainable.

In 1492, the *Santa Maria* carried Christopher Columbus into seas teeming with turtles. During the 17th and 18th centuries European fishermen hunted the turtles relentlessly, for eggs, meat, shell, and the delicacies known as *calipash*, the gelatinous greenish cartilage lying under the carapace that gives the Green Sea Turtle its name, and *calipee*, its yellowish equivalent cut from between the bones of the plastron. Calipee and calipash are prime ingredients in turtle soup, and whole turtles were killed simply to extract a few handfuls of the stuff. Archie Carr, in *The Sea Turtle: So Excellent a Fishe*, described finding turtles that had not even been killed before the plastron was cut off for its calipee.

The turtles could not withstand such an intense commercial trade. Green sea turtle populations on Bermuda were so depleted by 1620 that the Bermuda Assembly passed laws to protect them— to no avail. Bermuda's turtles were gone by the 18th century, making them probably the first well-documented rookery to be exterminated at our hands.

Rookeries in the Bahamas followed them, and then those on Caribbean coasts and islands. Since Columbus's time, Green Sea Turtle populations in the Caribbean—once totaling some 91 million adults, according to a 2006 estimate—have probably declined by at least 99 percent. The disappearance of that many large animals has probably had serious effects on the Caribbean marine ecosystem. Greens once grazed some 86 percent of sea-grass blades, for example, giving parasites little chance to take hold. Their decline has allowed the blades to ____back, and may be responsible for the spread ____grass wasting disease. The immense nest-____onies in the Caymans, with an estimated

population of 6.5 million adults in the 17th century, collapsed in the 18th. So did the fishery based on them. By 1802, Cayman Islanders had to travel to Cuba, and then to Honduras and Nicaragua, to find turtles. Today, only a few scattered Loggerheads (*Caretta caretta*) and Greens still nest in the islands. Nesting Hawksbills have not been seen since 1999, though the islands remain an important foraging ground for juveniles and adults from elsewhere in the Caribbean. Hawksbills, once numbering some 1.6 million in the Caribbean with a 19th century level of 936,600 in the Bahamas alone, have been reduced to fewer than 30,000 today. Only in recent years has the status of Caribbean sea turtles begun, slowly, to improve.

A similar story can be told for other sea turtle species, and other populations, in many parts of the world. Sea turtles, like other turtles, are victims of poaching and illegal trade in eastern Asia. In northwestern Mexico, sea turtles and their eggs are still eaten despite legal protection in place since 1990 with potentially severe, but rarely imposed, penalties, including up to nine years in jail. Turtles provide Catholics with a sanctioned substitute for red meat at Easter, and are frequently consumed at weddings, Christmas, Mother's Day, and Sundays. Turtle meat, once primarily a food of the poor, is increasingly popular with people who are well-educated and financially secure. According to a 2002 estimate, some 35,000 turtles a year are deliberately killed or taken as bycatch along the Baja California and Sonora coasts. A 2006–2008 survey found a black market for turtle meat in the state of Baja California Sur that killed at least 500 turtles, mostly East Pacific Greens, per year.

According to Jesse Senko and his colleagues, "Sea turtle blood is thought to cure anemia and asthma, oil is extracted to aid childhood respiratory problems, and internal organs are sometimes used in soups." This is despite numerous health problems that eating sea turtles, especially the often-toxic Hawksbills (see page 321, Chapter 8), are

Turtles are exploited in many countries worldwide, for use as meals, souvenirs, and "health products", among other uses.

known to cause. These include contamination by toxins such as those causing ciguatera, accumulated mercury, organochlorone or other pollutants, and the risk of parasites or disease organisms including chlamydia. Senko found that although local physicians in northwestern Mexico knew of these problems, other residents, by and large, did not.

Huge numbers of sea turtle eggs have been, and still are, taken on both sides of the Pacific. Before the 1950s, collectors in China took an estimated 60,000 to 200,000 eggs per year from a single site, Gankou beach in Guangdong Province. Sea turtles were given official protection in China in 1988, and the beach is now the Gangkou Sea Turtle National Nature Reserve.

Decades of egg poaching have destroyed the nesting population at Terengganu, Malaysia, once the largest Leatherback nesting ground in the world. Computer simulations have shown that a 90 percent poaching rate in the Las Baulas Marine Park, Costa Rica (a rate actually recorded at Las Baulas from 1975 to 1991, when the Park was established) would exterminate its Leatherback Sea Turtle nesting population within 45 years (including an initial 11-year period before numbers start to drop).

Greens and Hawksbills (*Eretmochelys imbricata*) have been exploited along the coasts of East Africa for at least 2,000 years; the tortoiseshell trade spread from the Red Sea, the source of tortoiseshell in antiquity, to Madagascar, where exports began as early as 1613. In the Seychelles, concern was expressed for the survival of turtle populations as early as the 18th century.

A commercial Hawksbill fishery that began off the coast of Queensland, Australia, in 1879 had exported at least 39,000 kg (86,020 lbs) of tortoisehell by 1938. A Green Sea Turtle meat industry operated intermittently in the same area between 1867 and 1962. By 1924–1925, a canning factory on North West Island in the Capricorn Group was producing 36,000 tins of turtle soup per year. It had closed by 1932. The hunt was finally outlawed in 1968, but traditional sea turtle

hunts continued. In September 2011 Australian environment minister Tony Burke refused to investigate an alleged black market in sea turtle meat in North Queensland, on the grounds that it would be "patronizing" to indigenous communities for the federal government to impose a ban. Instead, the government intends to consult on how to manage the problem with traditional owners, who have agreed with the Queensland state government to limit their take of Green Sea Turtles to 20 per year after 649 turtle deaths were recorded in the first seven months of 2011.

Between 1961 and 1972, the Philippines shipped tortoiseshell from approximately 45,000 Hawksbills to Japan. At the same time, a large sea turtle leather industry sprang up in Mexico and Ecuador, using skin from the animal's front flippers, the underside of the neck and a rear piece encompassing the hind limbs. The leather, mostly from Olive Ridleys (*Lepidochelys olivacea*) but also from Green Sea Turtles, was exported to Japan, Europe and the United States.

Much of the legal international trade in sea turtles and their products ended after 1981, when all remaining species were added to Appendix I of CITES (see page 415). Even traditional hunts, however, are harming turtle populations today. In the Kai Islands of eastern Indonesia, Leatherbacks were once hunted only for ritual and subsistence use, protected from commerce by a tradition called *adat*. In recent years, as the human population in the islands has grown and changed, *adat* has been forgotten and Leatherbacks and other sea turtles have been killed for food, traditional feasts, and the market. Unfortunately, this shift in the hunt happened at the same time as the nesting colonies of the Kai Island Leatherbacks, 1,000 km (620 mi) away in Irian Jaya, suffered extensive losses from beach erosion, egg poaching, and nest raiding by feral pigs. According to Alexis Suárez, who visited the islands in the mid-1990s, sea turtles are captured with harpoons and hooks, and drown in gill and shark nets throughout the archipelago. Islanders told her that the turtles had declined over the previous few decades.

For many on the island of Bali in Indonesia, turtle meat is *de rigeur* for feasts and religious ceremonies. It has become increasingly popular in general among the Hindu population. Commercial hunting and trade to supply the meat grew rapidly from the late 1960s onward, even after the trade was declared illegal by Indonesian authorities. The largest turtle slaughterhouse in the world may be the Balinese market at Tanjung Benoa. In 2007 an estimated 500 to 1,000 turtles, mostly Greens and Hawksbills, were being illegally imported into Bali each month. Fishermen depleted Bali's own turtle stocks, and now hunt farther afield within Indonesian waters. In 1998, they took an estimated 5,000 turtles in the Aru Islands, a harvest large enough in itself to cover the Balinese quota at the time. This quota was later rescinded after pressure from conservationists, but the government recently reinstated a lower quota of 1,000 turtles per year.

The Indonesian government has prosecuted the most flagrant of the Balinese turtle dealers. In May 2001, the chief among them, Widji Zakaria or Wewe, was sentenced to a year in prison for illegal activities including poaching, transporting and selling Green Sea Turtles. In 2006 a Turtle Conservation and Education Center was established on nearby Pulau Serangan (Turtle Island), one of the centers of the turtle fishery, where it has become a tourist attraction and a boost to the local economy. Among other activities the center raises a small number of hatchling turtles for eventual sale to holders of permits for religious rituals, with the aim of undercutting the illegal trade in wild-caught animals.

A Sea of Problems

Archie Carr wrote, prophetically, in 1967:

> It is now clear that people are so abundant, and the life cycle of a sea turtle is so complicated, that nobody really knows what he is doing to a population when he kills a turtle or takes the eggs from a nest. The capacity of people to consume and their ability to destroy are growing beyond the

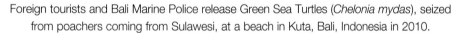

Foreign tourists and Bali Marine Police release Green Sea Turtles (*Chelonia mydas*), seized from poachers coming from Sulawesi, at a beach in Kuta, Bali, Indonesia in 2010.

tolerance of the small populations in which sea turtles live.

Today sea turtles bear the brunt, not just of direct exploitation, but of a host of other pressures including long-term climate fluctuations that may drive their distribution in different parts of the ocean. Thousands drown accidentally every year, entangled or hooked in fishing gear. In March 2011 about 154 Olive Ridley carcasses washed ashore on a beach on the east coast of Andhra Pradesh, India. Locals blamed the death on large trawl nets used by fishing vessels from a nearby harbor. In the Gulf of Mannar in southern India, Green Sea Turtles, and smaller numbers of Olive Ridleys, become entangled in multifilament fishing nets. Those that survive are taken for food; those that drown are thrown back into the sea.

Turtle nesting grounds are degraded, or lost altogether, as we develop beaches and construct seawalls. On Margarita Island, Venezuela, the beach areas with the most suitable natural conditions for nesting Leatherbacks are also the ones most heavily disturbed by human activities, driving the turtles to lest optimal sites.

Artificial lighting draws many hatchling turtles to their deaths (see page 308, Chapter 8), and has been identified as one of the two main threats to turtle nesting grounds in South Asia (the other being habitat loss). The Florida Power and Light Company tried to solve this problem by installing hundreds of "turtle-friendly" orange acrylic filters on streetlights bordering the coast. Unfortunately, hatchling turtles were still attracted to them. Shielding the lights, or turning them off altogether if possible, appears a better solution.

Leatherbacks and other sea turtles searching for jellyfish on the high seas choke on floating garbage, including plastic bags and deflated helium balloons, which they apparently mistake for prey. In 2009 Virginie Plot and Jean-Yves Georges removed 2.6 kg (5.7 lbs) of plastic waste blocking the cloaca of a Leatherback nesting on a beach in French Guiana.

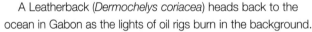

A Leatherback (*Dermochelys coriacea*) heads back to the ocean in Gabon as the lights of oil rigs burn in the background.

A choking hazard in the making: a Green Sea Turtle (*Chelonia mydas*) swims towards a plastic bag in the Comoros.

Plastic bags, nylon cord, and similar debris are common in Green Sea Turtle stomachs in the Gulf of California. An emaciated Green found floating off the Florida Coast later defecated, according to Andrew Stamper and his colleagues, "74 foreign objects... including four types of latex balloons, one piece of mylar balloon, five different types of string, nine different types of soft plastic, four different types of hard plastic, two pieces of nylon line, three pieces of monofilament line (not fishing line), a piece of carpet-like material, and two 2–4 mm tar balls."

Sea turtle bodies have accumulated oil, tar, heavy metals, organochlorone residues, and assorted debris. Pollution and disturbance or damage by boat traffic, fouls feeding grounds on coral reefs or sea grass beds and may spread disease. In the Spratly Islands off Taiwan, in the Philippines and elsewhere, reefs are

Destruction of coral reefs threatens the habitat of Hawksbill Sea Turtles (*Eretmochelys imbricata*) such as these at Layang Layang Atoll, Malaysia.

further damaged by illegal fishing with dynamite and cyanide. All sea turtles exhibit temperature-dependent sex determination (TSD), and global climate change may pose the same threat to their reproduction as it does for TSD turtles on land or in fresh water (see page 289, Chapter 7).

The Marine Turtle Specialist Group of IUCN has classified five of the seven sea turtle species as Endangered or, in the case of the Leatherback, the Hawksbill, Kemp's Ridley (*Lepidochelys kempi*), and the Mediterranean population of the Green Sea Turtle, Critically Endangered (though Kemp's Ridley is now recovering pretty well). Only the Olive Ridley and the Flatback Sea Turtle (*Natator depressus*), with most of its population in protected waters off Australia, are listed in the lower category of Vulnerable. These listings may seem overdramatic, especially for the ridleys, whose populations may be cyclic and whose status is particularly difficult to assess. After all, sea turtles still number in the thousands, despite appallingly heavy egg harvests and continuing environmental stresses. We may, however, be blind to the effect that sea turtle longevity has on our perceptions. As Karen Bjorndal has pointed out:

> Delayed sexual maturity and the corresponding large number of immature age classes mask the effects of intense harvests, so that over-exploitation can be mistaken for sustainable utilization for years, with eventual disastrous results. Year after year for decades, every nesting female and every nest can be killed on a nesting beach, and still, against any reasonable expectation, hawksbills will continue to crawl out on the nesting beach. What appears to be astonishing resilience to total exploitation is in fact not resilience at all, but merely the harvesting of 20 to 40 years' worth of subadults as they become sexually mature and venture onto the nesting beach for the first time.

There are places in the world where sea turtles are holding their own, or even improving their status, in almost every case after years of careful and intensive conservation and management. Leatherback turtles in the Caribbean and South Africa, and Kemp's Ridleys in the Gulf of Mexico, have proven that sea turtles do not have to be doomed if we take the proper actions. After an aggressive 20-year program to protect their nesting beaches and relocate eggs to safe sites, nesting female Leatherbacks at Sandy Point, on St. Croix in the U.S. Virgin Islands, had increased from fewer than 30 in the 1980s to 186 in 2001. The number of hatchlings rose from roughly 2,000 to more than 49,000. Olive Ridley nesting beaches in Oaxaca, Mexico, are now well protected, hosting about a million nests per season.

The protection of nesting beaches has been vital to the conservation of such populations as the Leatherbacks of Tongaland in South Africa, the Green Sea Turtles of Tortuguero National Park in Costa Rica, or the nesting Loggerheads of Florida. Since we started protecting their nesting beaches in the early 1990s, Olive Ridleys in the eastern tropical Pacific have increased their numbers. On the Leatherback nesting grounds of Gandoca Beach, on Costa Rica's Caribbean border with Panama, increased enforcement, beach patrols and changing local attitudes reduced egg poaching from nearly 100 percent before 1990 to only 1–3 percent by 2004. Hawksbills are rebounding after more than 25 years of conservation efforts by the Brazilian Sea Turtle Conservation Program (Projeto TAMAR) in northern Brazil, with the number of nests increasing sevenfold between 1991 and 2006 in the states of Bahia and Sergipe. In Barbados, nesting numbers have increased eightfold since 1992 after years of effort by Barbados Sea Turtle Project (BSTP) and a 1998 moratorium on the taking of sea turtles. The island is now the home of one of the largest rookeries in the Wider Caribbean Region. In the eastern Pacific, Hawksbills had become so rare that they were thought to be locally extinct. Careful surveys have now revealed a small but surviving, and perhaps recovering, population.

Elsewhere, though, the story is often grim. Not all populations rebound after protection; the nesting populations in the Caymans have not, and it is not clear why. The number of Leatherbacks nesting on the Pacific coast of Mexico has crashed despite more than 20 years of protection including coordinated conservation efforts initiated in 1995 under Proyecto Laúd (Leatherback Project). Efforts to protect nests and hatchlings onshore have not been able, it appears, to keep up with the effects of adult and juvenile mortality, from fishing gear and other causes, at sea.

Colin Limpus, in a 1998 survey of turtle populations in the Indo-Pacific, reported declines in population after population, and in species after species. Even the relatively secure Flatback was threatened by near-total predation of its eggs by pigs on its major nesting beaches in the Torres Strait Islands between Australia and New Guinea, and by the death of hundreds of turtles annually in the northern prawn fishery. Limpus concluded:

> It appears that all marine turtle populations in the Indo-Pacific region outside Australia are severely depleted and/or are subjected to overharvest and/or to excessive incidental mortality. Where census data exist, most populations show clear evidence of decline. At the present time, all available data indicate that the general conservation outlook for marine turtles in Southeast Asia is dismal.

The problem, then, is clear; deciding what should be done about it is not.

The traditional approach to sea turtle conservation has been either to focus on protecting nesting beaches, or to collect and raise eggs in turtle hatcheries and release the young into the sea either as soon as they hatch, or after they have grown past their initial and, presumably, most vulnerable size—a controversial procedure called headstarting. These techniques are appealing. They provide the opportunity for hands-on work with turtles themselves, can generate a lot of favorable interest and publicity, and do not usually require one to go up against the fishing industry, beach-front developers, or other powerful interests.

On the Pacific coast of Mexico relocating eggs to hatcheries, as Proyecto Laúd is doing, may be the only way to keep them out of the hands of poachers and introduced predators. Hatchery releases and beach protection have undoubtedly been of great importance to sea turtle conservation, but they have their drawbacks. Incubating eggs in hatcheries may produce large numbers of hatchlings, but this may not always translate into a real increase in the breeding population. Where hatchlings are held too long prior to release, or when large numbers of hatchlings are released at the same time and place (see pages 312-313, Chapter 8), mortality from predation may be particularly high. There have been controversies over such things as incubation temperature; is it better to pick a temperature that produces an equal mix of males and females, or should the sex ratio be shifted one way or the other? The fact that we cannot answer these questions satisfactorily suggests that we may be further, in our attempts at management, from understanding what sea turtles really need than we like to admit.

Using hatcheries to incubate eggs that would otherwise die on the beach, and releasing the young immediately on hatching is still an important and valuable technique for sea turtle conservation. In recent years, however, headstarting has come under severe scrutiny. The most well-known headstarting program was begun in 1978, in an attempt to establish a second nesting colony of Kemp's Ridleys on the Texas coast. The hope was that turtles headstarted from Texas would return there to breed, instead of traveling to the main nesting beach in Mexico. The project became highly controversial;

Newly emerged Green Turtle (*Chelonia mydas*) hatchlings are collected in the João Vieira / Poilão Marine National Park, Guinea-Bissau, site of the largest turtle rookery in West Africa.

Beach patrols, important as they are, have not been enough to protect Leatherbacks in the eastern Pacific, either in northwestern Mexico or at Las Baulas in Costa Rica. For that, only a combined strategy of nest protection and, somehow, reducing the mortality of adults and juveniles at sea will do.

Beach protection and hatchery releases may do little good if the chief problem is the killing of breeding adults, or large subadults, at sea, though it may be responsible for the steady increase in nesting Green Sea Turtles at Tortuguero, Costa Rica, despite a continuing heavy take of subadults and adults off Nicaragua and in other nearby waters. The demonstration that Western Atlantic Leatherbacks spend more time in heavily fished coastal waters than had been appreciated (see page 329, Chapter 8) has shown how important accurate knowledge of turtle movements at sea can be to any useful strategy to conserve them. Since saving the life of a single breeding adult of a long-lived species like a sea turtle may have a far greater conservation impact than releasing hatchlings, biologists have recommended that the adults, not the young, should be the chief focus of sea turtle management. On the important sea turtle nesting islands in the Bolama-Bijagós Biosphere Reserve off Guinea-Bissau, a chief protective measure was the removal of foreign fishing camps involved in the killing of adults. (Illegal fishing still remains a common practice in the area.)

Ideally, of course, conservation should focus on all of a sea turtle's life stages, from egg to breeding adult. If we are to have a real chance of success in sea turtle conservation, we will need the cooperation of the many countries through whose waters they pass in the course of their long lives. This has been the philosophy behind a growing number of sea turtle networks and cooperative strategies in many parts of the world.

The Wider Caribbean Sea Turtle Conservation Network (WIDECAST) founded by Milton Kaufman in 1981, includes "volunteer Country Coordinators (mainly sea turtle experts, natural resource professionals, and community-based conservationists),

questions were raised about whether headstarted turtles could survive in the wild after a year of being fed in captivity. In 1993, the project was abruptly terminated, and arguments about its merits still continue. Kemp's Ridleys, though, have increased exponentially on the Texas Gulf Coast; 911 Kemp's Ridley nests, mostly dug by turtles apparently hatched in the wild, were documented in Texas between 2002 and 2010—more than eleven times the 81 nests recorded in the previous 54 years.

an international Board of Scientific Advisors, and Partner Organizations in 43 Wider Caribbean nations and territories." WIDECAST advises the UNEP Caribbean Environment Programme on sea turtle and related coastal zone issues and oversees a number of regional programs. A Marine Turtle Tagging Centre (MTTC), established in Barbados in 2001 collects and coordinates tagging data from throughout the Caribbean as part of a collaborative effort to manage sea turtles among the many countries they visit on their migrations. In 2011 the MTTC published a combined study of returns from 2,261 female Hawksbills tagged in 12 countries.

WIDECAST has adopted a broad, coordinated approach to sea turtle conservation. According to its website,

> A sustainably managed sea turtle population might be defined as one that meets the needs— ecological, economic, socio-cultural, political, aesthetic, spiritual—of the present without compromising the ability of the population to fulfill these roles in the future. To this end, WIDECAST seeks to bring the best available science to legislation and policy; to education, training and outreach; to conservation and advocacy; and to in situ research and population monitoring.

This integrated approach is defined, at the national level, through Sea Turtle Recovery Action Plans (STRAPs) that discuss everything from legislation and the establishment of Marine Protected Areas (MPAs) to research and awareness raising. The UNEP Caribbean Environment Programme has partnered with WIDECAST to assist governments in developing STRAPs, which to date have been published for nearly two dozen Wider Caribbean nations.

As Jack Frazier has pointed out, "these are shared resources, not owned by any one country, not the unique right of any single nation, nor the sole responsibility of any single state." Though single actions by individual countries can be of great value, no one program can save sea turtles by itself. Sea turtle conservation must be an international concern, and an international effort. In 1996, Malaysia and the Philippines signed a Memorandum of Agreement establishing a jointly managed Turtle Islands Heritage Protected Area (TIHPA), the world's first trans-frontier protected area for sea turtles. In 2004, the United States passed the Marine Turtle Conservation Act (MTCA), which provides thousands of dollars in funding to sea turtle conservation projects around the world.

There is no one way to conserve sea turtles. We need specific measures to protect them, their eggs and their nesting beaches. We need whole-ecosystem approaches: marine protected areas and sanctuaries, and broad solutions to climate change and the pollution and littering of the seas. We need to cooperate with all who value sea turtles, for whatever reason. Sea turtles, more than any other reptile, have become flagship species—international symbols of wildlife conservation, almost as well known, at least in the West, as such "charismatic megafauna" as the giant panda and the African elephant. That gives international initiatives to protect them, and the ecosystems where they live from the beach to the open sea, a valuable, and perhaps vital, head start.

Tumors, Pollution and Disease

In recent decades, growing numbers of sea turtles in many parts of the world have been infected with a mysterious disease, known as *fibropapillomatosis* (FP). FP has become widespread in populations from Indonesia, Australia and the United States, including Puerto Rico and, particularly, Hawaii. It has been found as far afield as Madagascar. Diseased turtles are disfigured with bulbous, fibrous tumors, or *fibropapillomas*, that may swell to 30 cm (12 in) across. Tumors usually grow on their skin, particularly around the eyes and on the soft skin of the

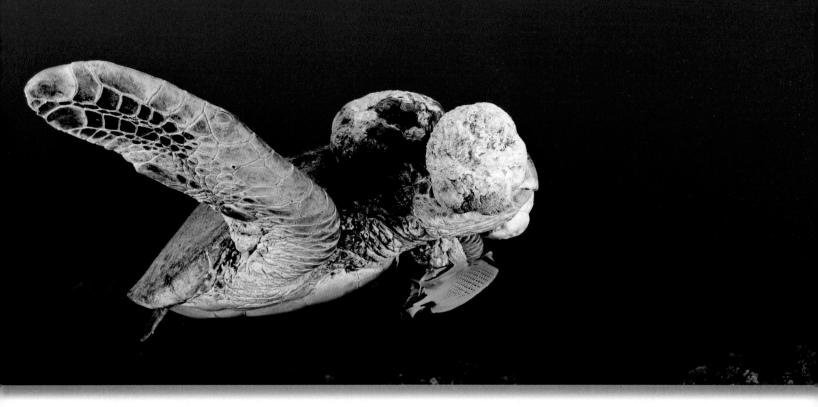

A Hawaiian Green Sea Turtle (*Chelonia mydas*) with fibropapillomatosis (FP); large tumors cover its head and eyes.

neck and flippers. Roughly a quarter of the infected turtles have internal tumors as well, growing in their lungs, heart, liver, kidneys, or gastrointestinal tract. Forty percent of infected Green Sea Turtles studied by George Balazs and his co-workers on Oahu in the Hawaiian Islands had tumors in their mouths. FP most commonly infects Green Sea Turtles, but it is also known in Kemp's and Olive Ridleys, Flatbacks, Loggerheads, and, occasionally, in Hawksbills.

Though the tumors are not cancerous, turtles with the disease are often weak, emaciated and anemic, with imbalanced body chemistry. Internal tumors can cause a variety of problems including bowel obstruction, kidney failure, and flotation difficulties. FP has been a major cause of turtle strandings. In Hawaii, where Green Sea Turtles haul out on certain beaches to bask, Yonat Swimmer found that all of the basking turtles she examined had the disease, probably contracted in polluted lagoons off Oahu. Basking raises the turtles' body temperature, but whether this helps the turtle to combat the disease we do not know. The disease is frequently, but not invariably, fatal, particularly in juveniles, or at

least it weakens its victims to such an extent that they die from other causes.

FP has been known for decades; the first reported case was apparently a Green Sea Turtle, brought to the Key West Aquarium in Florida in 1934, that developed tumors in 1936. Since the 1980s, the disease has spread to other areas, and infected higher and higher proportions of sea turtles within infected populations. Sea turtles in Florida and Hawaii have been particularly hard hit, with FP infecting one-half to three-quarters of the turtles at some sites. Of 418 individual Green Sea Turtles identified on Maui by Peter Bennett and Ursula Kueper-Bennett between 1988 and 2000, 245 showed evidence of the disease. However, though FP in Hawaii reached a peak in the 1990s, it has been declining steadily, at least in some areas, ever since.

Many Green Sea Turtles in Hawaii have completely recovered, and have lost their tumors altogether. In 21 of the 91 turtles the Bennetts found in more than one summer up to 1998, their subsequent sightings showed that the tumors had regressed. Of the recovering animals, only one was a juvenile, and among adults, males seemed three times as likely to regress as females (though in more recent years more females may be regressing). In Florida, however, the FP-infection rate appears to have stabilized, though turtles in both Florida and Australia have recovered from the disease.

We still do not know exactly what effect FP is having on sea turtle populations, though the population of Greens on Hawaii has steadily increased in spite of the disease. Nor do we have a clear understanding of its cause, or, perhaps more accurately, its causes. FP tumors appear to be associated with a number of viruses; more than 95 percent of the tumors studied in Florida carried a herpes virus. Turtles may be growing more vulnerable to the disease, though, because something is weakening their immune systems; Hawaiian turtles in advanced stages of FP have suppressed immune responses. On the other hand, laboratory research suggests that even turtles without suppressed immune systems can contract FP.

There appears to be an environmental component to the spread of FP. Green sea turtles do not appear to contract the disease until they take up life near shore. FP outbreaks may be linked to toxins produced by a number of different algae, whose growth in turn has been linked to marine pollution. In Hawaii, blooms of exotic algae have spread widely, apparently nourished by high nitrogen levels from sewage and agricultural runoff, and many of the Green Sea Turtles in the islands now rely on them for their diet (see page 319, Chapter 8). Green algae sequester nitrogen in the amino acid arginine, which is known to regulate immune activity, promote the growth of herpes viruses, and contribute to the formation of tumors. High algal blooms tend to be commonest in enclosed bays that do not flush out easily, where pollution levels, and nitrogen levels, are often higher than in the open sea. Turtles that eat such algae may be increasing their risks of contracting the disease.

In Australia, blooms of *Lyngbya*, a cyanobacterium (blue-green alga), occasionally smother the sea grass beds in Moreton Bay. The blooms produce a toxin, known to promote tumor growth, which has been detected in turtle meat. Eating such meat has been blamed for at least one human fatality. In Florida, blooms of the dinoflagellate *Prorocentrum*, a single-celled alga, produce biotoxins including okadaic acid, a chemical that produces tumors in mice. Green sea turtles pick up these poisons when they eat sea grass covered with the algal growth. One study suggested that the incidence of FP in Florida was highest in places where the turtles were eating more *Prorocentrum*-covered sea grass. The researchers found almost no FP at a Trident submarine base where only about 3 percent of the sea grass was covered with *Prorocentrum*, while at Mosquito Lagoon, where 79 percent of the sea grass was infested, the FP rate among Green Sea Turtles was 72 percent—a figure that had grown from 29 percent in 1985.

There is much we do not know about FP. We do know, however, that it is spreading, that it is contagious, and that it is most severe in areas where humans pollute the sea. FP has consequences for headstarting. If workers at a headstarting facility are not extremely careful, they may be providing, by keeping unnaturally large numbers of turtles together, a golden opportunity for the disease to spread further.

Hook, Line and Net

Bycatch—the unnecessary and wasteful destruction of animals the fishing industry does not even want—has become a growing conservation concern, and sea turtles have become some of its more high-profile victims.

After the international bans on driftnet fishing in the late 1980s, many fishing fleets turned to longlining (driftnets, or at least some of them, are still out there; discarded "ghost nets" could last up to 600 years). Longline fishing vessels set out great lengths of monofilament line, trailing hook-studded branches baited for valuable catches like Swordfish (*Xiphias gladius*), various tuna species, and Dolphin

(Mahimahi) (*Coryphaena hippurus*). A single pelagic, or high-seas, longline may carry 3,500 hooks and trail out for over 100 km (62 mi). There may be thousands of them being drawn through the ocean at any given time, particularly from the huge offshore fleets of Japan, Korea, and Taiwan.

Though longlines are not the indiscriminate "curtains of death" that driftnets are, they can be deadly all the same. Around the Azores in the Atlantic, where Loggerheads fall victim to swordfish longliners, data from 1998 suggests that the fishing fleets were hooking almost 4,200 turtles in the course of a single May–December season. In 2000 alone, pelagic longline fisheries sailed from 40 nations, set an estimated 1.4 billion hooks, and may have caught an astonishing 200,000 Loggerheads and 50,000 Leatherbacks. The figure is shocking even if many of these were only lightly hooked and survived.

Vessels from Costa Rica, Ecuador, and Chile hunt Mahimahi, tuna, and Swordfish. The longlines

they set for Mahimahi and tuna lie near the surface, where a hooked turtle can snatch a breath and may survive its ordeal. The lines for Swordfish, however, are set deeper, and a turtle caught in them will almost certainly drown. Off the Pacific coast of Costa Rica, coastal fishing vessels tow 24–32 km (15–20 mi) lines bearing 400 to 700 hooks each. By the late 1990s turtles had become the second-largest component of their catch. Between August 1999 and January 2000, Randall Arauz monitored nine such longline trips for the Sea Turtle Restoration Project. The boats caught 253 turtles, almost all of them Olive Ridleys.

Perhaps the most critical longlining victim is the Pacific Leatherback. In June 2000, five well-known sea turtle biologists concluded that Leatherbacks were on the verge of extinction in the Pacific, and placed the blame directly on the fishing industry. They noted that, by a conservative estimate, "longline and gill-net fisheries killed at least 1,500 female Leatherbacks per year in the Pacific during

A female Leatherback (*Dermochelys coriacea*) is trapped in a fishing net off São Tome in West Africa.

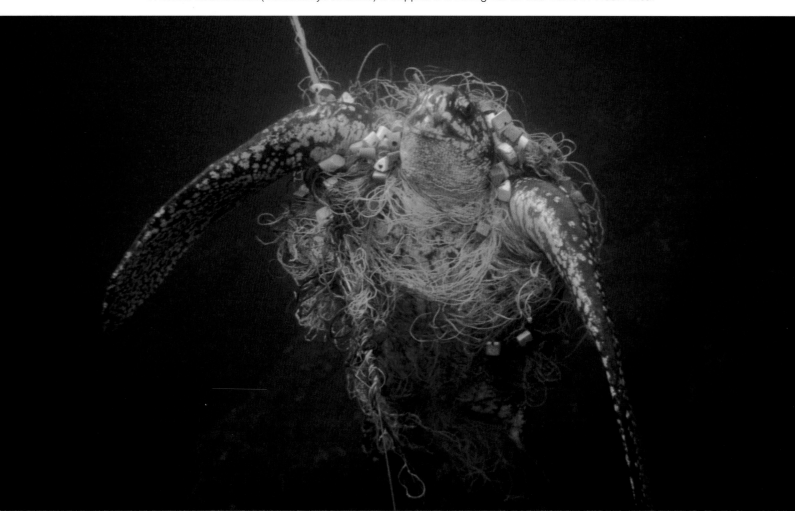

the 1990s. These included Asian trawl, longline and drift-net, Central and South American longline and gill-net, and Hawaiian longline fisheries." The scientists called for reduction of the annual mortality rate (then 23 percent per year) to 1 percent, or fewer than 50 adult females per year in the whole of the Pacific.

Concerns about the effects of longline fisheries on Leatherbacks in particular have led to calls for a total ban, and have resulted in closures of large areas of the ocean. In 2000, a Hawaiian court closed a vast stretch of the central Pacific—as large as the North Atlantic—to longlining for swordfish. The ban stayed in place for four years. In part of the region, the number of lines that can be set out was restricted; in another, longlining was banned altogether. Over the rest of the area, which includes the seas around the main Hawaiian Islands, longlining was only permitted for tuna. Sea turtle biologists and environmentalists applauded the decision (though longliners, as might be expected, bitterly attacked it), but they were concerned that it did not go far enough. The market for swordfish remained, and was met (without import restrictions from the United States) by longline fleets from Mexico, Panama, Costa Rica, South Africa, and other countries that were catching considerably more turtles per weight of Swordfish than the American fleet had been doing.

In 2001, the U.S pelagic longline fleet was barred from over 7.7 million sq km (2. 9 million sq mi) of the northwestern Atlantic, including the Grand Banks, because of high turtle bycatch levels. The ban was only lifted, in 2004, with the proviso that fishing vessels had to use a number of tested techniques to reduce bycatch.

A number of environmental organizations sued the U.S. federal government in 2007 to force it to declare a large area of the Pacific coast as critical habitat for Leatherbacks under the Endangered Species Act. After years of wrangling the suit was settled in July 2011. 108,568 sq km (41,914 sq mi) of ocean was declared a Leatherback safe zone in January 2012. This will not affect fishing fleets as there are already regulations governing their behavior (for example, drift gillnet fishing is banned from mid-August to mid-November, when the turtles are on their foraging grounds. It will affect coastal developments that discharge into the sea including energy projects and water-cooling facilities.

In recent years several multinational conferences have considered what to do about sea turtle bycatch. Scientists have studied the differences between the ways sea turtles and fishes see and smell things in the hope of finding ways to keep turtles, but not fish, away from lines and nets. Researchers, often working with the fishing fleets, have developed measures—some now required by law—to minimize the threats longlining poses for turtles. Fleets are being encouraged to use hooks that, instead of taking a traditional "fishhook" shape, are bent into a wide circle. Large-circle hooks seem to make little difference to the fish catch, but are more difficult for sea turtles to swallow and, since the point on the hook faces inward, do the turtles less damage should they succeed. One set of tests showed that circle hooks reduced the number of turtles hooked by 74 percent in Loggerheads and 75 percent in Leatherbacks. Circle hooks are now being used in a number of countries, but, frustratingly, not all fishing fleets have been quick to adopt them—discouraged, in some cases, by import duties on eco-friendly fishing gear.

In 2005, the World Wildlife Fund held the first International Smart Gear Competition, with a $25,000 grand prize (now up to $30,000, with runner-up prizes of $10,000 each) for the best innovation for reducing bycatch. The first Grand Prize Winner, Steve Beverley, a fisherman from New Caledonia in the southwest Pacific, devised a simple method of weighting longlines set for tuna to keep them below 100 m (330 ft). Tuna fleets catch far fewer turtles if they set their lines below 100 m (330 ft) during the day than they do if they set shallower lines at night, when the tuna come closer to the surface. Not only did his invention reduce the loss of turtles, but it increased the catch of tuna by up to

42 percent. Setting the lines deeper, using fish instead of squid as bait, and retrieving gear during the daytime have all reduced the chances of a turtle being hooked.

Loggerhead Sea Turtles have been frequent victims of a Hawaii-based shallow-depth longline fishery for swordfish. The fishery was closed between 2002 and 2004, and only reopened with requirements that fishing vessels take specific steps to avoid catching the turtles including the use of large-circle hooks. As an additional protection, the fishery was to be closed for the remainder of the year once 17 Loggerheads were taken. In 2006, the fishery reached this limit as early as March, alerting the industry that there was a great deal yet to do if it was to operate safely.

One of the outcomes of this was TurtleWatch, a sea-temperature and ocean-current mapping system that allowed fishing vessels to avoid warmer waters (with surface temperatures above 18.5°C [65.5°F]) where foraging Loggerheads were likely to concentrate. The maps, first used in 2007, not only reduced bycatch, but 65 percent of the bycatch that did occur happened in areas that the maps had recommended that fishing vessels avoid. Thanks to TurtleWatch and other measures, in the 2008 season there was not a single reported case of a Loggerhead caught by the Hawaiian longline fishery.

As serious as the pelagic longline issue is (especially for Leatherbacks), the greatest threat to some sea turtle populations may lie closer to shore. Hundreds of sea turtles are caught every year in bottom-trawling gear in the mid-Atlantic fisheries. Small-scale and artisanal fisheries operate in coastal waters, using a variety of techniques from longlines to gill nets and trawls. Large-mesh gill nets catch an estimated 350 Loggerheads a year of the mid-Atlantic coasts of the United States. Peruvian gill-net fisheries and coastal longliners caught 133 Pacific Leatherbacks in the 2002–2003 season; 55 were released alive, but the others were kept and eaten. In the Mediterranean, probably more than 44,000 sea turtles die per year in fishing gear (not counting those caught deliberately), mostly on longlines or in nets set by smaller vessels. Recent surveys have found numbers of sea turtles entangled in nets or hooked by small-scale longlining vessels in Mexico, Japan, Malaysia, and the Atlantic seaboard of the United States.

Keeping turtles out of gill nets may be as simple as using stiffer net fabric, or, for surface netting, nets short enough for turtles to dive beneath. Gill nets attached to the bottom are frequently tied down at intervals, creating pouches of netting that can become unintentional turtle traps. Setting the nets so that they hang vertically makes them less likely to snare a turtle. Keeping turtles away may be even easier. Experiments in Baja California reduced turtle capture by 54 percent by tying silhouettes of sharks at 10 m (33 ft) intervals along the nets. Each fishery may require its own technological fix, and its own campaign to involve fishers in its design, use and, perhaps most importantly, its acceptance.

TED Wars

No issue has better demonstrated the sociological, economic, legal, and political ramifications of sea turtle conservation than the controversy over Turtle Excluder Devices (TEDs) in the 1980s and 1990s. What started out as a straightforward technological fix, intended to keep sea turtles from drowning in shrimp trawls, became a political nightmare of lawsuits, regulatory battles, protests, massive demonstrations at sea, and, eventually, international legal battles before the tribunals of the World Trade Organization (WTO).

The issue of turtle mortality in shrimp trawls first came to public notice during the 1960s and 1970s. By the 1980s, the U.S. government had identified the drownings as the major factor causing the deaths of Loggerheads and Kemp's Ridleys, in particular, along its Atlantic and Gulf coasts.

In 1980, the U.S. National Marine Fisheries Service (NMFS) presented their solution: the Turtle

Excluder Device or TED. This was a metal cage, or, in later versions, a grid, installed in the trawl. It allowed shrimp to pass through and be caught, but forced turtles out to safety through a trapdoor at the top or bottom. Trials by NMFS showed that TEDs reduced sea turtle mortality by 97 percent. NMFS later approved a number of modified TED designs developed by the industry itself. At first, the industry agreed to adopt TEDs voluntarily. Supporters of TEDs pointed out that shrimpers stood to benefit from the devices. By excluding not only turtles but also unwanted larger fish, TEDs would make the trawls easier to pull, require less fuel to operate, and reduce damage to shrimp that would otherwise be crushed by the larger animals in the net.

Shrimpers, by and large, saw TEDs not as a boon but as a threat, and were reluctant to cooperate with the government. Finally, in 1987, threatened with a lawsuit by the Center for Marine Conservation, Greenpeace and the Environmental Defense Fund under the provisions of the Endangered Species Act, NMFS brought in regulations requiring the seasonal use of TEDs on shrimp trawls in offshore waters from North Carolina to Texas.

The industry, which had never before faced across-the-board federal regulation, reacted in fury. Louisiana challenged the order in court and passed a law prohibiting the enforcement of the federal regulations in the state. Louisiana Governor Edwin W. Edwards told thousands of cheering shrimpers, "Perhaps some species were just meant to disappear. If it comes to a question of whether it's shrimpers or the turtles... bye-bye turtles." In July 1989, as the regulations were about to be reimposed following a court order, hundreds of shrimp vessels staged a 36-hour blockade of Gulf ports in Texas and Louisiana. Despite the protests, in 1991 further regulations made TED use mandatory year-round in most parts of the southeastern United States.

Shrimpers and conservationists remained far apart. The shrimpers saw TEDs as the ruin of their industry. They claimed that the heavy metal grates could be dangerous when the net was hauled back on board. They argued that TEDs allowed many shrimp to escape, and could become tangled with bottom debris, causing fishing gear to be ruined or lost. TED supporters argued that there was little evidence supporting these claims. A 1992 report from the Center for Marine Conservation, the World Wildlife Fund, and the National Wildlife Federation pointed out that shrimp catches actually went up in the first two years following the imposition of TEDs, claims for gear loss and damage went down, and there was not a single report of a TED-related injury.

The shrimpers denied that they were a major cause of turtle deaths. In 1987, however, NMFS estimated that 47,973 turtles were captured annually in commercial shrimp trawls, of which 11,179 drowned. In 1990, the National Academy of Sciences estimated that up to 55,000 turtles drowned per year in U.S. coastal waters in trawls not equipped with TEDs—not including trapped turtles, mostly juveniles, released back into the sea that often died shortly after, probably from shock and oxygen deprivation. In 1991, Charles Caillouet and his colleagues published a study showing that dead turtles washed up on the beaches of southwestern Louisiana and Texas in significantly higher numbers where shrimping boats were most active offshore.

By 1989, shrimpers had moved the TED issue onto the world stage. Faced with mandatory TED use themselves, they persuaded Congress that other countries exporting shrimp to the United States should be forced to play by the same rules. In November 1989, Congress passed a law, which became Section 609 of the 1989 U.S. Endangered Species Act, banning imports of shrimp unless exporting countries met certain conditions relating to sea turtle conservation. Any country seeking to export trawler-harvested shrimp to the United States had to be certified; in effect, it had to prove that its sea turtle protection measures were up to U.S. standards.

Originally, the law was applied only to 14 countries in Central and South America, giving them three years to phase in the use of TEDs in shrimp fisheries. By and large, the countries cooperated, assisted by training missions from NMFS. Only French Guiana, and, for a time, Surinam, failed to achieve certification. In 1996, however, Earth Island Institute challenged the interpretation of the law in court, arguing that it should apply to all nations whose shrimp fisheries could harm sea turtles. In 1996 the U.S. Court of International Trade expanded the number of countries affected by the U.S. law from 14 to about 70.

NMFS and the U.S. State Department immediately began training missions in Asia and Africa. Some Asian countries, including Thailand, instituted laws of their own requiring TED use. A number of Asian countries, however, saw the U.S. law as both an egregious case of eco-imperialism and an attempt to discriminate unfairly against their shrimp fisheries.

In 1997, Thailand, Malaysia, India, and Pakistan lodged formal complaints against the United States with the World Trade Organization (WTO); Thailand, which already used TEDs and had been certified by the U.S. in 1996, claimed to be joining the action as a matter of principle. In March 1998, the WTO ruled against the United States. Pressed by environmental groups, the United States appealed, but on October 12, 1998, the Appellate Body of the WTO ruled against it again. One of the Appellate Body's chief objections was that the U.S. law "*requires* other WTO Members to adopt a regulatory program that is not merely *comparable*, but rather *essentially the same*, as that applied to the United States shrimp trawl vessels." In other words, the law was objectionable because it required exporting countries to use TEDs, not some other technology that worked as well (for example, the "beam trawls" used by some Chinese shrimpers).

The Appellate Body tried hard to avoid the appearance that it was opposed either to environmental protection or to sea turtles:

We have *not* decided that the protection and preservation of the environment is of no significance to the Members of the WTO. Clearly, it is. We have *not* decided that the sovereign nations that are Members of the WTO cannot adopt effective measures to protect endangered species, such as sea turtles. Clearly, they can and should.

This sort of language allowed both the United States and the complainant countries to claim a measure of victory. Nonetheless, environmental organizations, particularly in the West, excoriated the WTO, accusing it of placing trade concerns above the needs of the environment. The decision made sea turtles flagship symbols, not just of the environment, but of the victims of globalization. Some of the protesters agitating against the WTO during the "Battle for Seattle" in 2000 showed up at the barricades dressed in sea turtle costumes.

Meanwhile evidence that TEDs really do make a difference has continued to grow. Maurice Renaud and his colleagues reported in 1997 that the number of sea turtles taken in shrimp nets around the southeastern United States had fallen by an order of magnitude since TED use became mandatory. In 1999, after federal and state enforcement officers in the state of Georgia began boarding shrimp trawlers to check compliance with TED regulations, the numbers of sea turtles stranding on Georgia beaches dropped precipitously. The adoption of TEDs, along with protection of the nesting beaches at Rancho Nuevo, has probably been a major contributor to the greatly improved fortunes of Kemp's Ridley, once the most endangered all sea turtles.

The United States adopted a compromise policy to meet WTO requirements. In June 2001, a WTO dispute-settlement panel, rejecting a further complaint from Malaysia, found that U.S. policy was no longer discriminatory. By 2003, 38 countries (and Hong Kong) had become eligible to export shrimp to the United States, either because they had adopted

TEDs or because, for other reasons, sea turtles were not threatened by their shrimp fisheries.

In February 2003, the National Marine Fisheries Service issued a new set of TED regulations addressing a flaw in the original design. The opening that permitted turtles to escape was simply not big enough for a really large adult, or in particular for an animal the size of a Leatherback. The new regulation required US shrimp trawling fleet to install TEDs with larger openings. This time, the push for these regulations received wide support.

TEDs are now widely used in fisheries in the United States, but acceptance and enforcement problems still exist. Mississippi has strengthened its TED regulations, but Louisiana has banned its wildlife and fisheries inspectors from enforcing federal TED regulations. An attempt to overturn the ban was vetoed by Governor Bobby Jindal in June 2011 in the midst of a rash of sea turtle deaths that have been blamed on everything from shrimpers to the recent oil spill.

TEDs were widely adopted in Australia's Northern Prawn Fishery (NPF) even before the devices were made mandatory in 2000. In Sabah, Malaysia, the Marine Research foundation, in collaboration with the Sabah Department of Fisheries, has been attempting since 2006 to encourage fishers to use TEDS, on the grounds that they reduce fuel costs and lower damage to nets. The best way to get TEDs widely adopted is through cooperation with the fishers themselves. Once they have adopted TEDs, and see that they work, they rarely want to do without them.

Turtle Treaties

During the 1990s, fear of fisheries sanctions like the U.S. TED law helped drive the development of international agreements for the cooperative management and conservation of sea turtles. In the Eastern Hemisphere, some of these agreements have been concluded under the auspices of the Convention on the Conservation of Migratory Species of Wild Animals (CMS), often called the Bonn Convention.

The CMS applies to sea turtles in two ways. All species, except the Flatback, are listed on CMS Appendix I (not to be confused with Appendix I of CITES) and are supposed to receive strict protection on a country-by-country basis from the 116 (as of July 1, 2011) CMS Parties. This protection can include local projects approved by the CMS Scientific Council, funded through the treaty itself. Sea turtles are also listed on the much larger Appendix II, in order to stimulate countries to conclude specialized *Agreements* (in effect, mini-treaties created under CMS auspices) or Memoranda of Understanding (MoUs) for their conservation.

Twenty-six African countries are now Parties to a CMS-brokered Memorandum of Understanding Concerning Conservation Measures for Marine Turtles of the Atlantic Coast of Africa, signed in 1999. Another CMS-brokered MoU, the Memorandum of Understanding on the Conservation and Management of Marine Turtles and their Habitats of the Indian Ocean and South-East Asia (IOSEA MoU), entered into force on September 1, 2001, and by December 2010, 32 countries had signed. Though China, Malaysia, Japan, and a few other states in the region have yet to join, on its 10th anniversary IOSEA could claim "the widest geographic coverage and governmental membership of any instrument for marine turtle conservation in the world."

The Convention on the Conservation and Management of Highly Migratory Fish Stocks in the Western and Central Pacific Ocean (WCPF), which entered into force in June 2004, established a Commission with the power to make binding decisions about, among other things, the conservation of sea turtles. In 2006 the WCPF adopted a Sea Turtle Data Collection and Research Program. The Commission's sea turtle measures, which entered into force in February 2009, include requiring the use of circle hooks and fish, rather than squid, bait the swordfish longline fleets setting lines less than 100 m (330 ft) deep.

The Protocol concerning Specially Protected Areas and Wildlife (known as the SPAW Protocol) entered into force (i.e. became legally binding) on May 25, 2000. SPAW, which has so far been ratified by 12 countries and signed by 5 others, is an addendum to the Convention for the Protection and Development of the Marine Environment of the Wider Caribbean Region (Cartagena Convention). It is designed to protect both species and their habitats. Member countries are required to take some strict measures to protect endangered species (including sea turtles), including prohibiting the "taking, possession or killing" and "commercial trade in such species, their eggs, parts or products."

The first independent treaty exclusively devoted to sea turtles, the Inter-American Convention for the Protection and Conservation of Sea Turtles (IAC), entered into force on May 2, 2001. The IAC has won the support not only of WIDECAST but of fisheries organizations including the Latin American Association for Fisheries Development (OLDEPESCA), which has been involved in the IAC process from the first, though much of OLDEPESCA's support was because they saw the IAC as a preferable alternative to U.S. embargos on Latin American shrimp exports. As of September 2011, the IAC has 15 Parties, with two others currently in the process of ratification.

Parties to the IAC are required to take measures "for the protection, conservation and recovery of sea turtle populations and their habitats," including "the prohibition of the intentional capture, retention or killing of, and domestic trade in, sea turtles, their eggs, parts or products." Other required measures include protection of sea turtle habitats in nesting areas, promotion of research and environmental education, and the reduction, "to the greatest extent practicable, of the incidental capture, retention, harm or mortality of sea turtles in the course of fishing activities" through regulation and the use of appropriate gear, specifically including TEDs. The prohibition against killing sea turtles is not quite as draconian as the one in the SPAW protocol, because

CITES parties defeated Cuban proposals, now abandoned, to trade in tortoiseshell on the grounds that they threatened Hawksbills (*Eretmochelys imbricata*) elsewhere, such as this one off Tuamotu in Polynesia.

it allows for exemptions "to satisfy economic subsistence needs of traditional communities." The IAC has hosted many regional meetings and workshops, and can point to a wide range of accomplishments by its participating countries including research, monitoring and management initiatives and improved regulations protecting sea turtles. The IAC Secretariat, in its 10th anniversary report, celebrates the success of the treaty as "a testament to the extraordinary regional efforts taken to preserve these ancient animals [that] inspires all of us to continue this good work and address the many challenges that sea turtles still face."

The Battle for the Hawksbill

During the late 1990s, CITES became the arena for a bitter and divisive battle over a single species, the Hawksbill. Hawksbills (and Leatherbacks) have been listed on Appendix I of CITES since 1977, making all commercial trade in Hawksbill shell illegal under the treaty (the other sea turtles were transferred to Appendix I in 1981). When Japan joined CITES in 1980, it took advantage of a provision of the treaty allowing new members to declare themselves exempt from the consequences of certain CITES listings. Japan entered these declarations, called reservations, against a number of species, including the Hawksbill. Other CITES Parties remained bound by the listing (except for France, which held a reservation on behalf of its overseas territories until 1984) and therefore could not export tortoiseshell to Japan. Non-Parties, however, were perfectly free to ship Japan all the *bekko* (the Japanese name for tortoiseshell) they liked.

In the 1980s and early 1990s, the Japanese Bekko Association, the professional organization of the Japanese tortoiseshell workers, became the world's largest importer of Hawksbill shell. Among its chief suppliers were Cuba and Mexico, which did not join CITES until 1990 and 1991, respectively. Cuba entered a reservation against the Hawksbill listing on joining, as had St. Vincent and the Grenadines when they joined in 1989, but Mexico did not. That meant that Mexico could no longer trade with Japan, but Cuba could continue to export tortoiseshell as long as Japan maintained its reservation.

In the early 1990s, though, the United States certified Japan under the Pelly Amendment, a law that allows it to bring sanctions against any country that compromises the effectiveness of a wildlife conservation treaty. Faced with potential penalties, Japan withdrew its reservation against the Hawksbill listing in 1994. Overnight, the *bekko* trade became illegal. Even though Cuba still held a reservation against the Hawksbill, it could no longer export tortoiseshell to Japan.

Japan and Cuba were not prepared to let the matter rest. Since a reservation, once dropped, cannot be taken up again, their only option was to get the Hawksbill transferred from CITES Appendix I, which bars legal trade, to Appendix II, which allows it. The Marine Turtle Specialist Group of IUCN, however, had recently classified the Hawksbill as Critically Endangered throughout its range, a step that made transfer to Appendix II for the entire species a political impossibility.

At the 1997 CITES conference in Zimbabwe, Cuba—strongly supported by Japan—introduced a proposal to transfer its population alone to Appendix II. Shell was not to be sold under the terms of the transfer unless it came either from government-registered stockpiles, or from a traditional harvest or experimental ranching program. Only a single trading partner—obviously Japan—was to be allowed, providing that it had agreed not to re-export the shell. This arrangement was in order to prevent laundering of tortoiseshell in other countries.

The Cubans vigorously defended their Hawksbill program. They argued that Cuba's domestic harvest provided a valuable economic incentive for the conservation of its turtles, and created revenue that funds scientific research necessary for their conservation. They asked the CITES community to give them a chance to make an expanded commercial harvest work in the interest of conservation.

Neighboring countries like the Bahamas and Mexico argued that the Cuban "population" included turtles hatched elsewhere in the Caribbean. Tagging and molecular data have since confirmed that Hawksbills from nesting beaches in a number of Caribbean countries mix together on their foraging grounds. Mexico pointed to the improvement in the status of its own Hawksbill population after Cuba stopped exporting tortoiseshell to Japan, suggesting that Cuba had actually been harvesting Mexican turtles. Hawksbill range states outside the Caribbean were concerned that reopening any legal trade would provide laundering opportunities that could stimulate tortoiseshell poaching in their countries. Many sea turtle biologists agreed. According to Colin Limpus, active harvest of Hawksbills continued in Indonesia as of 1996, with tortoiseshell jewelry and ornaments still on sale in shops. Limpus concluded that Hawksbills could only recover in the long term if Japan abandoned its attempts to reopen legal international trade.

The proposal was defeated. In 2000, Cuba tried again, submitting two proposals: one, co-sponsored by Dominica, essentially the same as the 1997 proposal, and a second that would have restricted exports to stockpiled shells only. The proponents and their supporters hoped that if the first proposal was unpalatable, the second might succeed. After intensive lobbying on both sides, the proposals failed. Cuba submitted a further proposal in 2002, but—to the surprise of many—withdrew it before the meeting. Cuba has not brought the matter forward since. It maintains its reservation (as do St. Vincent and the Grenadines and Palau, which took out a reservation when it joined CITES in 2004). Japan still seems committed to reopening the trade; in 2007 it announced that it would continue to support its *bekko* industry for another five years.

In 2008, to the applause of conservationists, Cuba issued a ministerial resolution ending all harvesting of marine turtles. In the words of Dr. Elisa Garcia, Director of Fishing Regulations at the Ministry of Fisheries of Cuba, "This decision reflects the political will of the Cuban government to join the call of the international community to adopt measures that guarantee the conservation of marine turtles." Cuba has phased out turtle fishing, provided compensation and sustainable alternatives to its two remaining turtle fishing communities, and declared itself a regional hub for sea turtle conservation and research.

Must Sea Turtles Pay Their Way?

The argument at CITES that wildlife in developing countries will not survive unless it has economic value has not been widely accepted by sea turtle biologists. To some, this has acted to the detriment of sea turtle conservation. Supporters of the Cayman Turtle Farm, a commercial operation that has repeatedly failed to gain international permission to market its products, called a book on its history *Last Chance Lost*. The farm now operates primarily as a tourist attraction and a headstarting center for Green Sea Turtle hatchlings, and as a source of turtle meat and other products within the Cayman Islands.

Supporters of commercial use of sea turtles argue that denying local people revenue from wildlife in their territory deals them out of the conservation equation. The problem, though, is the same as it is for land and freshwater turtles (see page 369, Chapter 9): even if a sustainable harvest is desirable, the characteristics of turtle life history, and the demography of turtle exploitation, may make it impossible.

One modern sea turtle harvest that might reasonably claim to be sustainable is the egg-collecting program at Ostional, on the Pacific coast of Costa Rica. Ostional is a major *arribada* site for the Olive Ridley, with a long history of human exploitation. During the 1980s, scientists noticed that egg mortality during the Ostional *arribada* was unusually high. The nests on the beach were so densely packed that successive waves of turtles crawling ashore often destroyed the eggs laid by their predecessors. The rotting eggs, in their turn,

Villagers from Ostional, Costa Rica, carry bags of legally collected turtle eggs for delivery to market.

Villagers from Ostional, Costa Rica, collect Olive Ridley (*Lepidochelys olivacea*) eggs during an arribada.

provided sources for infections that could affect other, healthy clutches.

Under these circumstances, there seemed to be no harm in allowing villagers to collect eggs laid during the first hours of the arribada; such eggs were highly unlikely to survive anyway. A legal harvest might undercut egg poaching on other beaches, because the eggs from Ostional could be sold at a lower price. The money earned from legal egg sales could also provide a valuable source of income for villagers who had little opportunity to make money in other ways.

In 1987, the Costa Rican government legalized egg collecting on the beach, provided that it took place only during the first 24 (later 36) hours of the *arribada*. The harvest was to be controlled by a locally established cooperative, the Asociación de Desarollo Integral de Ostional (ADIO). Eighty percent of the revenue from the harvest originally went to the cooperative. This was later reduced to 60 percent, with the rest going to the government.

The Ostional project does appear to have reduced egg poaching. It has certainly put money in the pockets of Ostional villagers. Revenues from the harvest have been used, among other things, to improve the local school, build a community center, and bring electricity to the village. Harvesting actually seems to improve the hatching rate. The eggs that survive are laid on a relatively clean beach, not one saturated with the crushed, rotting eggs laid by the first arrivals. The biggest problem Ostional poses, though, is that it provides a cover for illegal egg collecting elsewhere in Costa Rica. Eggs from both legal and illegal harvests show up in Costa Rican markets, and many poachers see no difference between what they do and what happens at Ostional. For that reason alone, some conservationists argue, the Ostional harvest should be stopped.

The peculiar circumstances at Ostional, where the eggs that are harvested would otherwise be destroyed in the course of the *arribada*, may make similar projects difficult to establish elsewhere. Except in a few special cases, it is probably impossible to exploit sea turtles without causing their decline. As Colin Limpus has written, "the basic problem facing those who want to retain traditional uses of turtles by coastal peoples is that there are increasing numbers of people and a diminishing turtle resource. To continue managing turtles as we have in recent decades is a recipe for their eventual demise."

It is quite possible to make money from sea turtles without killing them or collecting their eggs. Sea turtle nesting beaches are highly popular tourist attractions in a number of countries. According to a WWF review, the average gross revenue per site from sea turtle tourism is almost three times higher than revenue from meat, shell, leather, eggs, or bone. Non-consumptive use that leaves turtles and their eggs where they are "generates more revenue, has greater economic multiplying effects, greater potential for economic growth, creates more support for management, and generates proportionately more jobs, social development and employment opportunities for women than consumptive use."

Ecotourism, though, cannot be the answer for every nesting beach, and the same turtles ecotourists watch at places like Tortuguero may still end up being slaughtered in nearby waters. A number of programs, including three in coastal Kenya, pay people directly for monitoring nesting beaches, identifying and protecting nests, or translocating eggs to a hatchery. The problem is that the money may not always be there. A program in Congo that reimburses fishers who rescue entangled turtles for damage to their nets has fallen short of funding in some years, driving some fishers to sell the meat from trapped turtles instead. Even in the poorest countries, people may need to cherish their sea turtles, or learn to cherish them, without expecting any economic return (as children around the world already do). In several places around the world, local organizations, village cooperatives, and dedicated individuals are proving that this can, indeed, happen.

We have an affinity for sea turtles that has made them icons of conservation—and a delight for children, including this boy watching a basking Green Sea Turtle (*Chelonia mydas*) on the island of Hawaii.

Hope

Surendra Babu was a young auto rickshaw driver in the fishing village of Kolavipalam in North Kerala, India. In 1992, he read a story in *The Hindu*, a national newspaper, about the plight of the Olive Ridley. Poachers had been stealing the turtles and eggs to sell in local markets. With 11 other young men, Babu started his own community organization, Theeram Prakariti Samrakshana Samiti (Coastal Ecosystem Protection Committee), to protect the turtles nesting near his village. Though his group soon had help from the government's Forest Department, the stimulus for its efforts to protect the nesting beaches came entirely from the community. Youths in the group tried to fence

off nest sites, replanted mangrove seedlings in the local estuary, and even built their own hatchery out of local materials. They soon faced a bigger threat than poachers. Illegal sand mining on nearby river estuaries caused the nesting beaches to erode, wearing them away until, in 2001, erosion even claimed the original hatchery. Theeram initiated a number of lawsuits against the mining company, with limited success.

Theeram, now the Theeram Nature Conservation Society, nonetheless continues to this day. Its volunteers have released more than 50,000 hatchling ridleys, and their efforts have made the village into a tourist attraction. The nesting turtles themselves, unfortunately, come in smaller numbers as more of the beach erodes away, but the villagers who supported the group have been recognized by the machinery of the state, have won its respect, and have gained attention that is helping them to improve such things as the water lines supplying their village. By protecting the turtles, they have achieved a level of empowerment that has helped them to better their own lives. Surendra Babu himself has said, "Everybody calls us the turtle people. But it is not we who are preserving the turtles, it is the turtles who have provided us a platform to voice our protest, the turtles who will preserve us."

Theeram is just one many sea turtle projects started by, or deeply involving, ordinary people in local communities. Partnerships between villagers, fishermen, scientists, wildlife officers, and governments have sprung up, and been sustained, in country after country. The Guyana Marine Turtle Conservation Society (GMTCS) works to protect the sea turtle nesting grounds at Shell Beach, Guyana, through direct actions such as beach monitoring and through outreach programs to local communities. Projeto TAMAR in Brazil, started in 1980 as a project of the federal environment department (IBAMA), has become a broad-based conservation organization engaged in a huge range of projects, including field research, community development and public education. The Karumbé Project in southern Brazil, Grupo Tortuguero in northwest Mexico and the Nova Scotia Leatherback Turtle Working Group (NSLTWG) all count fishers among their active members. Jesse Senko and his colleagues found in a series of surveys in Bahia Magdalena, a region in southern Baja California, that local people were overwhelmingly interested in participating in sea turtle conservation, despite some peer pressure against it, and saw it as a positive development for their community.

On the Caribbean coast of Costa Rica, the Sea Turtle Conservancy (formerly the Caribbean Conservation Corporation) operates a Sea Turtle Migration-Tracking Education Program designed to involve the people around Tortuguero National Park in conservation. Its satellite-tagging operations have become a village event. In 2000, the program tagged six Green Sea Turtles and two Hawksbills. The local schools held contests to name the turtles; Elder Esposito, a student in the third grade, named one of the Greens Mariposita del Mar (Little Butterfly of the Sea). Tourists in the nearby ecolodges came to watch the festivities, and local and international press arrived to broadcast the details.

In the Indian Ocean, satellite-tracking data from the Seychelles has helped conservationists there make a political point. As Jeanne Mortimer explained in 1999:

> In the past, some Seychellois complained that it was unfair and futile to expect the people of Seychelles to protect turtles that would only be slaughtered when they migrated from Seychelles to the national waters of other countries. Data from the tracking study, however, indicate that adult Hawksbills nesting in Seychelles may remain within the territorial waters of Seychelles throughout their adult lives. As such, they are a resource belonging to the people of Seychelles, whose responsibility it is to ensure their long-term survival.

The government of the Seychelles banned trade in Hawksbill shell products in 1994, and purchased and locked away 2.27 tonnes (2.5 tons) of raw shell. In November 1998, it took the extraordinary step of burning the entire stockpile—as part of a Miss World Pageant being held in the islands!

In 1996, the community of Lababia in Papua New Guinea established the 47,000 ha (116,140 ac) Kamiali Wildlife Management Area at the site of one of the country's largest Leatherback nesting colonies. Within it, the community has established guidelines banning hunting and fishing except by traditional methods, and has entered into an agreement to ban the harvest and sale of Leatherback eggs. In return for its efforts the community is paid cash equivalent to their market value (about $2,500), and has received benefits including a guest lodge and training center, access to dinghies with coolers to transport fish to the nearest market (a two-hour commute), a small portable sawmill, improvements in local schools, and a water distribution system. Neighbouring communities are trying to follow their example.

Between 1979 and 1999, poachers robbed every single nest along the south coast of Sri Lanka. In 1993, a Turtle Conservation Project began in Sri Lanka, focusing on Rekawa, a small village on the south coast whose beach is a major rookery for Loggerheads, Olive Ridleys, Hawksbills, Greens and, at least formerly, Leatherbacks. Following a series of workshops in local schools, more than 450 pupils and teachers volunteered to help with beach surveys. Former egg poachers are now working with the project, and with government officials, to gather biological data and to protect turtle nests on the beaches. Project director Thushan Kapurusinghe told an international conference in 1999 that, where once not a single turtle egg survived, 98,198 hatchlings reached the sea under the watchful eyes of the project and its volunteers. Nighttime turtle watches for paying visitors help support a loan scheme for members of the community. The project has been providing English classes since 1994, and in 1998 it established a rural medical clinic.

The project has survived a series of disasters that would have destroyed a less committed group. The 2004 tsunami damaged the nesting beaches and swept away project facilities. The tsunami, and the civil war that broke out in 2006, drove off tourists that had once come for the turtle watches. Fortunately both the turtles and the project have survived. Even the year after the tsunami, female turtles returned to the nesting beaches in undiminished numbers.

One of the most successful sea turtle conservation efforts began as a village initiative on the east coast of Trinidad. Nature Seekers Inc. started out in 1990 as a volunteer beach patrol initiative (to reduce the killing of nesting Leatherback turtles). It grew into a guide service for visitors to the nesting beach near the village of Matura. Nature Seekers has become a model for local conservation organizations, winning numerous ecotourism and conservation awards, including inclusion of one it its members as a founding member in the UNEP Global 500 Award Roll of Honor. Nature Seekers has converted poachers, educated other villagers, developed a locally run tourist industry and craft market, and today is one of the village's largest employers. In short, the group has made conservation a way of life in Matura. As an active member of WIDECAST, the group also plays an important role in the broader management of Wider Caribbean sea turtles. In October 2011, after years of efforts by community organizations including Nature Seekers, the government of Trinidad and Tobago banned all sea turtle hunting in the country.

On the Pacific coast of Mexico, local villagers, once hostile to turtle biologists, have begun to take an interest in conserving their nesting Leatherbacks. Some communities have organized themselves into protection committees that have become a matter of local pride. Local initiatives can bring not only pride in their turtles, but some degree of political clout. When one of the most important Loggerhead and Green Sea Turtle nesting beaches in Mexico, at Xcacel in Quintana Roo, was sold to hotel developers in 1997, members of the local community joined international organizations and sea turtle biologists to fight the Mexican government. In April 2001, the Mexican Environment Ministry succumbed to the pressure, annulled the hotel project, and agreed to a public review.

Enthusiasm for sea turtles, and an interest in their conservation, crosses cultures and bridges economic gulfs. It is felt in the developed countries of the north, on the shores of the Indian Ocean, and on islands in the Caribbean. Surely we can derive some hope from that.

A guide observes a nesting Leatherback Turtle (*Dermochelys coriacea*), Trinidad.

Children watch a nesting Leatherback (*Dermochelys coriacea*) at Rémire-Montjoly in French Guiana.

Image Credits

AGE FOTOSTOCK

cover © Martin Woike / Age Fotostock

BIOSPHOTO

17 top © Biosphoto / Cyril Ruoso
17 bottom © Biosphoto / David Santiago Garcia
18 top right © Biosphoto / Michel Gunther
18 bottom left © Biosphoto / Claude Balcaen
18 bottom right © Biosphoto / Sylvain Cordier
25 top © Biosphoto / Thierry Montford
27 © Biosphoto / Régis Cavignaux
30 © Biosphoto / Thierry Montford
34 © Biosphoto / Andrey Nekasov / Visual and Written
37 top © Biosphoto / Sylvain Cordier
37 bottom © Biosphoto / Jean-Jacques Alcalay
39 © Biosphoto / David Massemin
40 © Biosphoto / Martin Harvey
43 © Biosphoto / Gregory Guida
79 bottom © Biosphoto / Philippe Henry
88 top © Biosphoto / Gérard Soury
88 bottom © Biosphoto / Pierre Vernay
90 © Biosphoto / Régis Cavignaux
91 © Biosphoto / J.-L. Klein & M.-L. Hubert
93 © Biosphoto / Paul Starosta
94 © Biosphoto / Oliver Gerhard / Imagebroker
96 © Biosphoto / Andre Seale / Visual and Written
97 © Biosphoto / David Massemin
98 © Biosphoto / Brandon Cole
102 © Biosphoto / Juan-Carlos Muñoz
105 © Biosphoto / Nicolas Cégalerba
112 © Biosphoto / Michel Gunther
115 © Biosphoto / Régis Cavignaux
116 bottom © Biosphoto / Pierre Huguet
117 © Biosphoto / Mark Boulton
132 top © Biosphoto / David Massemin
132 bottom © Biosphoto / John Cancalosi
136 © Biosphoto / David Massemin
141 © Biosphoto / Didier Brandelet
143 © Biosphoto / Kike Calvo / Visual and Written
144 © Biosphoto / Reinhard Dirscherl
145 © Biosphoto / Gérard Soury
148 © Biosphoto / Kike Calvo / Visual and Written
151 © Biosphoto / Régis Cavignaux
152 top © Biosphoto / Michel Gunther
152 bottom © Biosphoto / Olivier Born
156 © Biosphoto / Fabien Michenet
160 © Biosphoto / Alain Mafart-Renodier
161 © Biosphoto / David Massemin
163 © Biosphoto / David Massemin
164 © Biosphoto / Thierry Montford
166 top © Biosphoto / Michel Gunther
167 © Biosphoto / Michel Gunther
170 top © Biosphoto / Jean-Yves Grospas
170 bottom © Biosphoto / Philippe Henry
172 © Biosphoto / Cyril Ruoso
174 © Biosphoto / Daniel Heuclin
176 © Biosphoto / Martin Harvey
177 © Biosphoto / David Massemin
179 © Biosphoto / J.-M. Labat & P. Rocher
186 top © Biosphoto / Kike Calvo / Visual and Written
189 © Biosphoto / Gregory Guida
190 © Biosphoto / Juan Manuel Borrero
191 top © Biosphoto / Régis Cavignaux
195 © Biosphoto / Roger Le Guen
203 © Biosphoto / Michel Gunther
208 © Biosphoto / Régis Cavignaux
213 © Biosphoto / Daniel Heuclin
222 © Biosphoto / Paul Starosta
228 © Biosphoto / Martin Nicoll
235 © Biosphoto / Thierry Montford
236 © Biosphoto / Pierre Huguet
237 © Biosphoto / Robert Henno
247 top © Biosphoto / Roger Le Guen
247 bottom © Biosphoto / Michel Gunther
250 © Biosphoto / Kike Calvo / Visual and Written
251 © Biosphoto / Masa Ushioda / WaterFrame
252 © Biosphoto / Thierry Montford
254 © Biosphoto / Michel Gunther
257 © Biosphoto / Régis Cavignaux
258 © Biosphoto / Gérard Soury
261 © Biosphoto / Malcolm Schuyl / Still Pictures

262 © Biosphoto / Daniel Heuclin
264 © Biosphoto / Olivier Born
268 © Biosphoto / Thomas Vinke / Imagebroker
275 bottom © Biosphoto / Olivier Born
285 © Biosphoto / Paul Starosta
315 © Biosphoto / Michel Gunther
320 © Biosphoto / Daniel Heuclin
322 bottom © Biosphoto / Dominique Halleux
324 © Biosphoto / David Massemin
328 © Biosphoto / Pierre Huguet
330 © Biosphoto / Gérard Soury
331 © Biosphoto / Michel Gunther
326 © Biosphoto / Michel Gunther
334 © Biosphoto / Thierry Montford
346 © Biosphoto / Albert Montanier
347 © Biosphoto / Nicolas Cégalerba
348 © Biosphoto / Olivier Born
349 © Biosphoto / Thierry Montford
351 © Biosphoto / Kike Calvo / Visual and Written
352 © Biosphoto / Gérard Soury
354 © Biosphoto / Jean-Jacques Alcalay
355 © Biosphoto / Pascal Pittorino
357 top © Biosphoto / Pascal Pittorino
360 © Biosphoto / Philippe Henry
362 © Biosphoto / Philippe Henry
366 bottom © Biosphoto / Cyril Ruoso
368 © Biosphoto / Juan Manuel Borrero
370 © Biosphoto / Michel Gunther
372 © Biosphoto / John Cancalosi
376 © Biosphoto / Michel Gunther
381 © Biosphoto / Olivier Born
384 © Biosphoto / Martin Nicoll
393 top © Biosphoto / Régis Cavignaux
393 bottom © Biosphoto / Michel Gunther
397 top left © Biosphoto / Kike Calvo / Visual and Written
397 top right © Biosphoto / Gérard Soury
397 middle left © Biosphoto / Nicolas Cégalerba
397 middle right © Biosphoto / Didier Brandelet
397 bottom left © Biosphoto / Nicolas Cégalerba
397 bottom right © Biosphoto / Mark Boulton
401 top © Biosphoto / Pierre Huguet
404 © Biosphoto / David Santiago Garcia
408 © Biosphoto / Michel Gunther
414 © Biosphoto / Yann Hubert
417 top © Biosphoto / Kike Calvo / Visual and Written
417 bottom © Biosphoto / Kike Calvo / Visual and Written
419 © Biosphoto / Andre Seale / Visual and Written
422 bottom © Biosphoto / Thierry Montford

JOHN CANN

14 © John Cann
35 © John Cann
76 © John Cann
79 top © John Cann
81 © John Cann
83 top © John Cann
83 bottom © John Cann
84 © John Cann
85 © John Cann
86 © John Cann
87 © John Cann
120 top © John Cann
120 bottom © John Cann
122 © John Cann
185 © John Cann
209 © John Cann
227 © John Cann
230 © John Cann
233 © John Cann
265 © John Cann
278 top © John Cann
278 bottom © John Cann
288 © John Cann
299 © John Cann
303 © John Cann
363 © John Cann
365 © John Cann
371 © John Cann
377 © John Cann

CORBIS

19 © Mary Ann McDonald/Corbis
24 © Jim Merli/Visuals Unlimited/Corbis
32 bottom © David A. Northcott/Corbis
59 © DK Limited/Corbis
65 © Jonathan Blair/Corbis
73 © Â KIKE CALVO / Retna/Retna Ltd./Corbis
89 © Hervé Collart/Sygma/Corbis
107 © Jim Merli/Visuals Unlimited/Corbis
125 © Reuters/Corbis
126 © Wayne Lynch/All Canada Photos/Corbis
128 top © Michael Kern/Visuals Unlimited/Corbis
128 bottom © David A. Northcott/Corbis
129 © David A. Northcott/Corbis
137 © Stephen Frink/Corbis
138 © Lynda Richardson/Corbis
139 © Ocean/Corbis
154 © David A. Northcott/Corbis
165 © Joe McDonald/Corbis
186 bottom © Michael & Patricia Fogden/Corbis
201 bottom © David A. Northcott/Corbis
214 © David Muench/Corbis
217 © David A. Northcott/Corbis
220 © Bruce Corbett/All Canada Photos/Corbis
234 © David A. Northcott/Corbis
241 © David A. Northcott/Corbis
244 © David A. Northcott/Corbis
283 © Hervé Collart/Sygma/Corbis
300 © Wayne Lynch/All Canada Photos/Corbis
304 © Frans Lanting/Corbis
308 © Kennan Ward/Corbis
309 © Martin Harvey/Corbis
311 © Jeffrey L. Rotman/Corbis
336 © Kent Kobersteen/National Geographic Society/Corbis
341 © Kent Kobersteen/National Geographic Society/Corbis
357 bottom © Patrick Bennett/Corbis
366 top © CHOR SOKUNTHEA/Reuters/Corbis
369 left © JORGE SILVA/Reuters/Corbis
369 right © Hervé Collart/Sygma/Corbis
378 © Michael Kern/Visuals Unlimited/Corbis
379 © David Ebener/epa/Corbis
382 bottom © David A. Northcott/Corbis
388 © David A. Northcott/Corbis
390 © Reuters/Corbis
392 © ALANAH M. TORRALBA/epa/Corbis
394 © HENRY ROMERO/Reuters/Corbis
395 © Anders Ryman/Corbis
399 © MADE NAGI/epa/Corbis
406 © David Fleetham/Visuals Unlimited/Corbis
422 top © Brian J. Skerry/National Geographic Society/Corbis

INDRANEIL DAS

29 © Indraneil Das
31 © Indraneil Das
32 top © Indraneil Das
116 top © Indraneil Das
118 © Indraneil Das
142 © Indraneil Das
146 © Indraneil Das
147 © Indraneil Das
150 top © Indraneil Das
150 bottom © Indraneil Das
166 bottom © Indraneil Das
242 © Indraneil Das
267 © Indraneil Das
382 top © Indraneil Das
387 © Indraneil Das
389 © Indraneil Das

DRK PHOTO

2-3 © Doug Perrine/DRK PHOTO
13 © Doug Perrine/DRK PHOTO
22 © James P. Rowan/DRK PHOTO
25 © bottom William P. Leonard/DRK PHOTO
28 © Joe McDonald/DRK PHOTO
63 © Stephen J. Krasemann/DRK PHOTO
64 © Stephen J. Krasemann/DRK PHOTO
69 © John Cancalosi/DRK PHOTO
101 top © John Cancalosi/DRK PHOTO

101 bottom © Pete Oxford & Renee Bish/DRK PHOTO
103 © C.C. Lockwood/DRK PHOTO
109 © Doug Perrine/DRK PHOTO
111 © Doug Perrine/DRK PHOTO
130 © John R. Hicks/DRK PHOTO
133 © Lynn M. Stone/DRK PHOTO
134 © Lynn M. Stone/DRK PHOTO
159 © Martin Harvey/DRK PHOTO
162 © Pete Oxford & Renee Bish/DRK PHOTO
180 © Doug Perrine/DRK PHOTO
184 © Joe McDonald/DRK PHOTO
191 bottom © James P. Rowan/DRK PHOTO
193 © Wayne Lankinen/DRK PHOTO
196 © William P. Leonard/DRK PHOTO
198 © David A. Northcott/DRK PHOTO
201 top © John Cancalosi/DRK PHOTO
202 © Doug Perrine/DRK PHOTO
205 © Doug Perrine/DRK PHOTO
210 © Joe McDonald/DRK PHOTO
212 © Doug Perrine/DRK PHOTO
225 © John R. Hicks/DRK PHOTO
231 © C.C. Lockwood/DRK PHOTO
245 © Stephen J. Krasemann/DRK PHOTO
256 © Stephen J. Krasemann/DRK PHOTO
271 top © Joe McDonald/DRK PHOTO
271 bottom © Joe McDonald/DRK PHOTO
275 top © William P. Leonard/DRK PHOTO
280 © Wayne Lankinen/DRK PHOTO
281 © Joe McDonald/DRK PHOTO
282 © Bob Gurr/DRK PHOTO
290 © William P. Leonard/DRK PHOTO
295 © William P. Leonard/DRK PHOTO
305 © Doug Perrine/DRK PHOTO
313 © Doug Perrine/DRK PHOTO
314 © Doug Perrine/DRK PHOTO
317 © Doug Perrine/DRK PHOTO
318 © Doug Perrine/DRK PHOTO
321 © Doug Perrine/DRK PHOTO
322 top © Doug Perrine/DRK PHOTO
323 Doug Perrine/DRK PHOTO
343 Doug Perrine/DRK PHOTO
361 © Jeff Foolt 1 Discovery Comm/DRK PHOTO
383 © Pete Oxford & Renee Bish/DRK PHOTO
385 © Pete Oxford & Renee Bish/DRK PHOTO
401 bottom © Doug Perrine/DRK PHOTO

REBECCA GORDON

329 © Rebecca Gordon

RICHARD HERMANN

338 top © Richard Hermann
338 upper middle © Richard Hermann
338 lower middle © Richard Hermann
338 bottom © Richard Hermann

SARA MAXWELL

188 © Sara Maxwell
327 © Sara Maxwell
400 © Sara Maxwell

RONALD ORENSTEIN

158 © Ronald Orenstein
199 © Ronald Orenstein
269 © Ronald Orenstein
325 © Ronald Orenstein
344 © Ronald Orenstein

DAVID PETERS

52 © David Peters
71 © David Peters

XIAO-CHUN WU

44 © Xiao-Chun Wu
48 © Xiao-Chun Wu
49 © Xiao-Chun Wu

Bibliography

Books About Turtles and Other General References

Cites Identification Guide - Turtles and Tortoises. Ottawa: Minister of Supply and Services, 1999.

Alderton, D. (1997). *Turtles & Tortoises of the World.* New York: Facts on File,.

Bartlett, R. D., and P. Bartlett (1999). *A Field Guide to Florida Reptiles and Amphibians.* Houston: Gulf Publishing.

Bjorndal, K. A., ed. (1995) *Biology and Conservation of Sea Turtles.* Revised Edition. Washington, DC: Smithsonian.

Bolten, A. B. and B. E. Witherington (2003). *Loggerhead Sea Turtles.* Washington, D.C., Smithsonian Books.

Bonin, F., B. Devaux, et al. (2006). *Turtles of the World.* Baltimore, Johns Hopkins University Press.

Boycott, R. C., and O. Bourquin (2000). *The South African Tortoise Book: a Guide to South African Tortoises, Terrapins and Turtles.* 2nd ed. Hilton, South Africa: O. Borquin.

Branch, B. (1998). *Field Guide to Snakes and Other Reptiles of Southern Africa.* 3rd rev. ed. Sanibel Island, Fla.: Ralph Curtis Books.

Buhlmann, K., T. Tuberville, et al. (2008). *Turtles of the Southeast.* Athens, University of Georgia Press.

Campbell, J. A. (1998) *Amphibians and Reptiles of Northern Guatemala, the Yucatán, and Belize.* Animal Natural History Series; V. 4. Norman: University of Oklahoma Press,.

Cann, J. (1998). *Australian Freshwater Turtles.* Singapore: Beaumont

Carr, A. F. (1984). *So Excellent a Fishe: a Natural History of Sea Turtles.* New York: Scribner's.

Carr, A. F. (1995). *Handbook of Turtles: the Turtles of the United States, Canada, and Baja California. Comstock Classic Handbooks.* Ithaca: Comstock Pub. Associates

Chambers, P. (2006). *A sheltered life : the unexpected history of the giant tortoise.* Oxford; New York, Oxford University Press.

Conant, R., J. T. Collins, et al. (1998). a *Field Guide to Reptiles and Amphibians: Eastern and Central North America.* 4th ed. Boston: Houghton Mifflin

Davidson, O. G. (2001*). Fire in the Turtle House : The Green Sea Turtle and the Fate of the Ocean.* New York, Public Affairs.

Devaux, B. and B. De Wetter (2000). *On the Trail of Sea Turtles.* Hauppauge, NY, Barron's Educational Series.

Dodd, C. K. (2001). *North American Box Turtles : A Natural History.* Norman, University of Oklahoma Press.

Dutton, P., D. Squires, et al., eds. (2011). *Conservation of Pacific Sea Turtles.* Honolulu: U of Hawaii Press.

Endangered Species Import and Export Management Office of the People's Republic of China (2002). *Identification manual for turtles and tortoises,* China Forestry Publishing House.

Ernst, C. H., and R. W. Barbour (1989). *Turtles of the World.* Wahington, D.C.: Smithsonian Institution Press.

Ernst, C. H., J. E. Lovich, et al. (1994 (2000)). *Turtles of the United States and Canada.* Washington, D.C.: Smithsonian Institution.

Ferri, V. (2002). *Turtles and Tortoises.* Toronto: Firefly Books.

Franklin, C. J. (2007). *Turtles: An Extraordinary Natural History 245 Million Years in the Making.* McGregor, MN: Voyageur Press.

Froom, B. (1976). *The Turtles of Canada.* Toronto: McClelland and Stewart.

Gibbons, J. W. (1990 (2000)). *Life History and Ecology of the Slider Turtle.* Washington, D.C.: Smithsonian Institution.

Glaw, F., and M. Vences (1994). *A Fieldguide to the Amphibians and Reptiles of Madagascar.* 2nd ed. Bonn: Zoologisches Forschunginstitut und Museum Alexander Koenig,.

Gurley, R. (2003). *Keeping and Breeding Freshwater Turtles.* Ada, Oklahoma, Living Art Publishing.

Harding, James H. (1997) *Amphibians and Reptiles of the Great Lakes Region.* Great Lakes Environment. Ann Arbor: University of Michigan Press,.

Harless, M., and H. Morlock (1989). *Turtles: Perspectives and Research.* Malabar, Florida: Krieger Publishing,.

Hickman, P. M. (2005). *Turtle Rescue.* Buffalo, N.Y., Firefly Books.

Jackson, D. C. (2010). *Life in a shell : a physiologist's view of a turtle.* Cambridge, Mass., Harvard University Press.

Klemens, M. W., ed. (2000) *Turtle Conservation.* Washington, DC: Smithsonian.

LeBuff, C. R. (1990) *The Loggerhead Turtle in the Eastern Gulf of Mexico.* Sanibel, Fla.: Caretta Research.

Liat, L. B. and I. Das (1999 (2000)). *Turtles of Borneo and Peninsular Malaysia.* Kota Kinabalu: Natural History Publications (Borneo).

Lindsay, C. (1995). *Turtle Islands: Balinese Ritual and the Green Turtle.* New York: Takarajima Books.

Lutz, P. L., and J.A. Musick, eds. (1996). *The Biology of Sea Turtles.* Boca Raton, FL: CRC Press.

McNamee, G., and L. A. Urrea (1997). *A World of Turtles: a Literary Celebration.* Boulder, CO: Johnson Books.

Mitchell, J. C. (1994). *The Reptiles of Virginia.* Washington, DC: Smithsonian Institution Press.

Moll, D. and E. O. Moll (2004). *The Ecology, Exploitation, and Conservation of River Turtles.* New York, N.Y., Oxford University Press.

Nabhan, G. P. (2003). *Singing the Turtles to Sea : the Comcáac (Seri) Art and Science of Reptiles.* Berkeley, University of California Press.

National Research Council, ed. (1990). *Decline of the Sea Turtles: Causes and Prevention.* Washington, DC: National Academy Press.

Nicholls, H. (2006). *Lonesome George : the life and loves of a conservation icon.* London; New York, Macmillan.

O'Keefe, M. T. (1995). *Sea Turtles: the Watcher's Guide.* Lakeland, FL: Larsen's Outdoor Pub.

Pedrono, M. (2008). *The Tortoises and Turtles of Madagascar.* Kota Kinabalu, Natural History Publications (Borneo).

Perrine, D. (2003). *Sea Turtles of the World.* Stillwater, MN, Voyageur Press.

Pilcher, Nicolas, and Ghazally Ismail, eds. (2000). *Sea Turtles of the Indo-Pacific: Research, Management and Conservation.* London: ASEAN Academic Press.

Pough, F. H., et al. (2001). *Herpetology.* 2nd ed. Upper Saddle River, N.J.: Prentice Hall, 2001.

Powell, R., J. T. Collins, et al. (1998). a *Key to Amphibians and Reptiles of the Continental United States and Canada.* Lawrence: University Press of Kansas.

Pritchard, P. C. H. (1979). *Encyclopedia of Turtles.* Neptune, N.J.: T.F.H.,.

Pritchard, P. C. H. and P. Trebbau. (1984). *the Turtles of Venezuela.* SSAR Contrib. Herpetol. 2.

Rhodin, A.G.J., Pritchard, P.C.H., van Dijk, P.P., Saumure, R.A., Buhlmann, K.A., Iverson, J.B., and Mittermeier, R.A. (Eds.). *Conservation Biology of Freshwater Turtles and Tortoises: A Compilation Project of the IUCN/SSC Tortoise and Freshwater Turtle Specialist Group.* Chelonian Research Monographs No. 5.

Ripple, J. (1996). *Sea Turtles.* Stillwater, MN: Voyageur Press.

Ruckdeschel, C. and C. R. Shoop (2006). *Sea turtles of the Atlantic and Gulf Coasts of the United States.* Athens, University of Georgia Press.

Rudloe, J. (1989). *Time of the Turtle.* New York: E.P. Dutton.

Rudloe, J. (1995). *Search for the Great Turtle Mother.* 1st ed. Sarasota, Fla.: Pineapple Press.

Safina, C. (2006). *Voyage of the Turtle : In Pursuit of the Earth's Last Dinosaur.* New York, Holt.

Spotila, J. R. (2004). *Sea Turtles: A Complete Guide to their Biology, Behavior, and Conservation.* Baltimore, Johns Hopkins University Press.

Spotila, J. R. (2011). *Saving Sea Turtles: Extraordinary Stories from the Battle Against Extinction.* Baltimore: Johns Hopkins U. Press.

Stanford, C. B. (2010). *The last tortoise : a tale of extinction in our lifetime.* Cambridge, Mass., Belknap Press of Harvard University Press.

Steyermark, A. C., M. S. Finkler, et al. (2008). *Biology of the Snapping Turtle* (Chelydra serpentina). Baltimore: Johns Hopkins U. Press.

Stuart, B. L., P. P. van Dijk, et al. (2001*). Photographic Guide to the Turtles of Thailand, Laos, Vietnam and Cambodia* (English/Vietnamese). New York, Wildlife Conservation Society.

Talib, Z., A. Ali, et al. (2004). *Conservation and Enhancement of Sea Turtles in the Southeast Asian Region.* Kuala Lumpur, Marine Fishery Resources Development and Management Department, Southeast Asian Fisheries Development Centre (SEAFDEC-MFRDMD).

Van Abbema, J. ed. (1997). *Proceedings: Conservation, Restoration, and Management of Tortoises and Turtles - an International Conference.* State University of New York, Purchase: New York Turtle and Tortoise Society.

Van Devender, T. R. (2002). *The Sonoran Desert tortoise : natural history, biology, and conservation.* Tucson, The University of Arizona Press : Arizona-Sonora Desert Museum.

Walls, Jerry G. *Tortoises: Natural History, Care and Breeding in Captivity.* Neptune City, NJ: TFH Publications.

Wyneken, J., V. L. Bels, et al. (eds.) (2008). *Biology of turtles.* Boca Raton, CRC Press.

Young, P. (2003). *Tortoise.* London, Reaktion Books.

Zug, George R., L. J. Vitt et al. (2008). *Herpetology: an Introductory Biology of Amphibians and Reptiles.* 3rd ed. San Diego: Academic Press.

A Word About Words

Turtle Taxonomy Working Group (2011). "Turtles of the world, 2011 update: annotated checklist of taxonomy, synonymy, distribution, and conservation status". In: Rhodin, A.G.J., Pritchard, P.C.H., et al. (eds*.). Conservation Biology of Freshwater Turtles and Tortoises: A Compilation Project of the IUCN/SSC Tortoise and Freshwater Turtle Specialist Group.* Chelonian Research Monographs No. 5, pp. 000.165–000.242, doi:10.3854/crm.5.000.checklist.v4.2011, http://www.iucn–tftsg.org/cbftt/.

Chapter 1: The Essential Turtle

Abdala, V., A. S. Manzano, et al. (2008). "The Distal Forelimb Musculature in Aquatic and Terrestrial Turtles: Phylogeny or Environmental Constraints?" J Anat 213(2): 159-172.

Alibardi, L. (2005). "Proliferation in the Epidermis of Chelonians and Growth of the Horny Scutes." J Morphol 265(1): 52-69.

Angielczyk, K. D., C. R. Feldman, et al. (2011). "Adaptive Evolution of Plastron Shape in Emydine Turtles." Evolution 65(2): 377-394.

Bartol, S. M., J. A. Musick, et al. (2001). "Morphology and Topographical Organization of the Retina of Juvenile Loggerhead Sea Turtles (*Caretta caretta*)." Copeia 2001(3): 718-725.

Bever, G. S. (2009). "Postnatal Ontogeny of the Skull in the Extant North American Turtle *Sternotherus odoratus* (Cryptodira: Kinosternidae)." B Am Mus Nat Hist 330: 1-97.

Bever, G. S. (2009). "The Postnatal Skull of the Extant North American turtle *Pseudemys texana* (Cryptodira: Emydidae), with Comments on the Study of Discrete Intraspecific Variation." J Morphol 270(1): 97-128.

Bonnet, X., F. Lagarde, et al. (2001). "Sexual Dimorphism in Steppe Tortoises (*Testudo horsfieldii*): Influence of the Environment and Sexual Selection on Body Shape and Mobility." Biol J Linn Soc 72(3): 357-372.

Broadley, Donald G. (1997). "Osteological Characters of the Shell and Humerus in Hinged Tortoises of the African Genus *Kinixys*." Chelonian Cons Biol 2(4): 526-31.

Caro, T. and H. B. Shaffer (2010). "Chelonian Antipredator Strategies: Preliminary and Comparative Data from Tanzanian *Pelusios*." Chelonian Cons Biol 9(2): 302-305.

Cebra-Thomas, J., F. Tan, et al. (2005). "How the Turtle Forms Its Shell: a Paracrine Hypothesis af Carapace Formation." J Exp Zool B Mol Dev Evol 304(6): 558-569.

Chansa, W. and P. Wagner (2006). "On the Status of *Malacochersus tornieri* (Siebenrock, 1903) in Zambia." Salamandra 42(2/3): 187-190.

Claude, J., E. Paradis, et al. (2003). "A Geometric Morphometric Assessment of the Effects of Environment and Cladogenesis on the Evolution of the Turtle Shell." Biol J Linn Soc 79(3): 485-501.

Crumly, C. R. and M. R. Sánchez-Villagra (2004). "Patterns of Variation in the Phalangeal Formulae of Land Tortoises (Testudinidae): Developmental Constraint, Size, and Phylogenetic History." J Exp Zool B 302B(2): 134-146.

Davit-Béal, T., A. S. Tucker, et al. (2009). "Loss of Teeth and Enamel in Tetrapods: Fossil Record, Genetic Data and Morphological Adaptations." J Anat 214(4): 477-501.

Delfino, M., T. M. Scheyer, et al. (2010). "An Integrative Approach to Examining a Homology Question: Shell Structures in Soft-Shell Turtles." Biol J Linn Soc 99(2): 462-476.

Depecker, M., C. Berge, et al. (2006). "Geometric Morphometrics of the Shoulder Girdle in Extant Turtles (Chelonii)." J Anat 208(1): 35-45.

Domokos, G. and P. L. Varkonyi (2008). "Geometry and Self-righting of Turtles." Proc Biol Sci 275(1630): 11-17.

Ernst, Carl H., et al. (1997) "A Comparison of Plastral Scute Lengths among Members of the Box Turtle Genera *Cuora* and *Terrapene*." Chelonian Cons Biol 2(4): 603-07.

Esque, T. C., C. R. Schwalbe, et al. (2003). "Effects of Desert Wildfires on Desert Tortoise (*Gopherus agassizii*) and Other Small Vertebrates." Southwest Nat 48(1): 103-111.

Gaffney, E. S. (1979). "Comparative Cranial Morphology of Recent and Fossil Turtles." Bull Amer Mus Nat Hist 164: 65-376.

Galeotti, P., R. Sacchi, et al. (2007). "Olfactory Discrimination of Species, Sex, and Sexual Maturity by the Hermann's Tortoise *Testudo hermanni*." Copeia 2007(4): 980-985.

Gerlach, Justin. (1999). "Feeding Behavior and the Saddleback Shell of *Dipsochelys arnoldi*." Chelonian Cons Biol 3(3): 496-500.

Germano, David J., and R. Bruce Bury (1998). "Age Determination in Turtles: Evidence of Annual Deposition of Scute Rings." Chelonian Cons Biol 3(1): 123-32.

Giles, J. C., J. A. Davis, et al. (2009). "Voice of the Turtle: the Underwater Acoustic Repertoire of the Long-Necked Freshwater Turtle, *Chelodina oblonga*." J Acoust Soc Am 126(1): 434-443.

Gronke, W. K., S. R. Chipps, et al. (2006). "Reticulate Melanism in Western Painted Turtles (*Chrysemys picta bellii*): Exploring Linkages with Habitat and Heating Rates." Am Midl Nat 156(2): 289-298.

Hans-Volker, K. and T. Gottfried (2005). "About the Structure of the Axial Elements of Turtle Shell." Stud Geol Salmanticensia 41: 29-37.

Hays, K. A. and K. McBee (2009). "Ontogenetic Melanism in Three Populations of Red-Eared Slider Turtles (*Trachemys scripta*) in Oklahoma." Southwest Nat 54(1): 82-85.

Herrel, A., J. C. O'Reilly, et al. (2002). "Evolution of Bite Performance in Turtles." J Evolution Biol 15(6): 1083-1094.

Kabigumila, J. (2000). "Growth and Carapacial Colour Variation of the Leopard Tortoise, *Geochelone pardalis babcocki*, in Northern Tanzania." Afr J Ecol 38(3): 217-223.

Kaddour, K. B., E. H. E. Mouden, et al. (2008). "Sexual Dimorphism in the Greek Tortoise: a Test of the Body Shape Hypothesis." Chelonian Cons Biol 7(1): 21-27.

Kinneary, Joseph J. (1996). "The Origin of Marine Turtles: a Pluralistic View of Evolution." Chelonian Cons Biol 2(1,2): 73-78.

Kuchling, Gerald. (1997) "Restoration of Epidermal Scute Patterns During Regeneration of the Chelonian Carapace." Chelonian Cons Biol 2(4): 500-06.

Kuratani, S. and H. Nagashima (2011 (ms)). Developmental Bases For Innovative Evolution of the Turtle Shell.

Kuratani, S., S. Kuraku, et al. (2011). "Evolutionary Developmental Perspective For the Origin of Turtles: the Folding Theory For the Shell Based on the Developmental Nature of the Carapacial Ridge." Evol Dev 13(1): 1-14.

Lambert, Michael R. K. (1995). "on Geographical Size Variation, Growth, and Sexual Dimorphism of the Leopard Tortoise, *Geochelone pardalis*, in Somaliland." Chelonian Cons Biol 1(4): 269-78.

Lambert, Michael R. K., K. L. I. Campbell, et al. (1998). "on Growth and Morphometrics of Leopard Tortoises, *Geochelone pardalis*, in Serengeti National Park, Tanzania, with Observation on Effects of Bushfires and Latitudinal Variation in Populations of Eastern Africa." Chelonian Cons Biol 3(1): 46-57.

Levenson, D. H., S. A. Eckert, et al. (2004). "Photopic Spectral Sensitivity of Green and Loggerhead Sea Turtles." Copeia 2004(4): 908-914.

Lewis, C. H., S. F. Molloy, et al. (2007). "Response of Common Musk Turtles (*Sternotherus odoratus*) to Intraspecific Chemical Cues." J Herpetol 41(3): 349-353.

Lintner, M. (2010). Funktionsmorphologische Untersuchungen der Nahrungsaufnahme von *Heosemys grandis*, Gray 1860 (Chelonia,

Geoemydidae) mit Berücksichtigung der Ontogenie (Thesis). Mag. Rer. Nat., University of Vienna.

Loehr, V. J. T., B. T. Henen, et al. (2006). "Shell Characteristics and Sexual Dimorphism in the Namaqualand Speckled Padloper, *Homopus signatus signatus*." African J Herpetol 55(1): 1-11.

Loew, E. R. and V. I. Govardovskii (2001). "Photoreceptors and Visual Pigments in the Red-Eared Turtle, *Trachemys scripta elegans*." Visual Neurosci 18(05): 753-757.

Lubcke, G. M. and D. S. Wilson (2007). "Variation in Shell Morphology of the Western Pond Turtle (*Actinemys marmorata* Baird and Girard) from Three Aquatic Habitats in Northern California." J Herpetol 41(1): 107-114.

Lyson, T. and W. G. Joyce (2008). "How Did the Turtle Get Its Shoulder Girdle Inside Its Ribcage, or Did It?" J Vertebr Paleontol 28(supplement to issue 3): 109A.

McGaugh, S. E. (2008). "Color Variation Among Habitat Types in the Spiny Softshell Turtles (Trionychidae: *Apalone*) of Cuatrociénegas, Coahuila, Mexico." J Herpetol 42(2): 347-353.

Miller, K. and G. F. Birchard (2005). "Influence of Body Size on Shell Mass in the Ornate Box Turtle, Terrapene ornata." J Herpetol 39(1): 158-161.

Moll, Don, and M. W. Klemens (1996). "Ecological Characteristics of the Pancake Tortoise, *Malacochersus tornieri*, in Tanzania." Chelonian Cons Biol 2(1): 26-35.

Nagashima, H., F. Sugahara, et al. (2009). "Evolution of the Turtle Body Plan By the Folding and Creation of New Muscle Connections." Science 325(5937): 193-196.

Okamoto, C. L. (2002 (2003)). "An Experimental Assessment of Color, Calcium, and Insect Dietary Preferences of Captive Juvenile Desert Tortoises (*Gopherus agassizii*)." Chelonian Cons Biol 4(2): 359-365.

Platt, S. G., H. Liu, et al. (2010). "Fire Ecology of the Florida box turtle (*Terrapene carolina bauri* Taylor) in Pine Rockland Forests of the Lower Florida Keys." Nat Area J 30(3): 254-260.

Pritchard, P.C.H. (1993). "Carapacial Pankinesis in the Malayan Softshell Turtle, *Dogania subplana*." Chelonian Cons Biol 1(1): 31-36.

Rieppel, O. (2001). "Turtles as Hopeful Monsters." BioEssays 23: 987-991.

Rieppel, O. (2009). "How Did the Turtle Get its Shell?" Science 325(5937): 154-155.

Rose, F. L., and F. W. Judd (1991). "Egg Size vs. Carapace-Xiphiplastron Aperture Size in *Gopherus berlandieri*." J Herpetol 25(2): 248-50.

Rowe, J. W., D. L. Clark, et al. (2006). "Effect of Substrate Color on Pigmentation in Midland Painted Turtles (*Chrysemys picta marginata*) and Red-eared Slider Turtles (*Trachemys scripta elegans*)." J Herpetol 40(3): 358-364.

Rowe, J. W., D. L. Clark, et al. (2009). "Reversible Melanization Following Substrate Color Reversal in Midland Painted Turtles (*Chrysemys picta marginata*) and Red-Eared Sliders (*Trachemys scripta elegans*)." J Herpetol 43(3): 402-408.

Sánchez-Villagra, M. R., C. Mitgutsch, et al. (2007). "Autopodial Development in the Sea Turtles *Chelonia mydas* and *Caretta caretta*." Zool Sci 24: 257-263.

Schneider, L., C. Ferrara, et al. (2010). "Description of Behavioral Patterns of *Podocnemis erythrocephala* (Spix, 1824) (Testudines: Podocnemididae) (Red-headed River Turtle) in Captivity, Manaus, Amazonas, Brazil." Acta Amazonica 40(4): 763-770.

Simang, A., P. L. Cunningham, et al. (2010). "Color Selection by Juvenile Leopard Tortoises (*Stigmochelys pardalis*) in Namibia." J Herpetol 44(2): 327-331.

Tokita, M. and S. Kuratani (2001). "Normal Embryonic Stages of the Chinese Softshelled Turtle *Pelodiscus sinensis* (Trionychidae)." Zool Sci 18(5): 705-715.

Trembath, D. F. (2009). "Kyphosis of *Emydura macquarii krefftii* (Testudines: Chelidae) from Townsville, Queensland, Australia." Chelonian Cons Biol 8(1): 94-95.

Vickaryous, M. K. and B. K. Hall (2006). "Homology of the Reptilian Coracoid and a Reappraisal of the Evolution and Development of the Amniote Pectoral Apparatus." J Anat 208(3): 263-285.

Vickaryous, M. K. and J.-Y. Sire (2009). "The Integumentary Skeleton of Tetrapods: Origin, Evolution, and Development." J Anat 214(4): 441-464.

Vieira, L. G., A. L. Q. Santos, et al. (2009). "Ontogeny of the Plastron of the Giant Amazon River Turtle, *Podocnemis expansa* (Schweigger, 1812) (Testudines, Podocnemididae)." Zool Sci 26(7): 491-495.

Werneburg, I., J. Hugi, et al. (2009). "Embryogenesis and Ossification of *Emydura subglobosa* (Testudines, Pleurodira, Chelidae) and Patterns of Turtle Development." Dev Dynam 238(11): 2770-2786.

Wiesner, C. S. and C. Iben (2003). "Influence of Environmental Humidity and Dietary Protein on Pyramidal Growth of Carapaces in African Spurred Tortoises (*Geochelone sulcata*)." J Anim Physiol An N 87(1-2): 66-74.

Wilson, D. S., C. R. Tracy, et al. (2003). "Estimating Age of Turtles From Growth Rings: a Critical Evaluation of the Technique." Herpetologica 59(2): 178-194.

Winokur, R. M. (1982). "Integumentary Appendages of Chelonians." J Morphol 172: 59-94.

Wood, S.C. and C. Lenfant (1976). "Respiration: Mechanics, Control, and Gas Exchange." Biology of the Reptilia. Ed. C. Gans and W.R. Dawson. Vol. 5. New York: Academic Press, pp. 225-274.

Wyneken, J., et al. (1999). "Size Differences in Hind Limbs and Carapaces of Hatchling Green Turtles (*Chelonia mydas*) from Hawaii and Florida, USA." Chelonian Cons Biol 3(3): 491-495.

Zangerl, R. (1969). "The Turtle Shell." The Biology of the Reptilia. Ed. C. Gans and A. d'A. Bellairs. Vol. 1. New York: Academic Press, pp. 311-319.

Chapter 2: Turtles In Time

Albright III, L. B., M. O. Woodburne, et al. (2003). "A Leatherback Sea Turtle From the Eocene of Antarctica: Implications For Antiquity of Gigantothermy in Dermochelyidae." J Vertebr Paleontol 23(4): 945-949.

Anquetin, J. (2011). "Evolution and palaeoecology of early turtles: a review based on recent discoveries in the Middle Jurassic." B Soc Geol Fr 182(3): 231-240.

Anquetin, J., P. M. Barrett, et al. (2009). "A new stem turtle from the Middle Jurassic of Scotland: new insights into the evolution and palaeoecology of basal turtles." Proc Biol Sci 276(1658): 879-886.

Bauer, A. M., and R. A. Sadlier (2000). The Herpetofauna of New Caledonia. Contributions in Herpetology. Ed. Kraig Adler. Ithaca, NY: SSAR.

Benton, M. J. (2004). Vertebrate Paleontology. 3rd ed. Hoboken: Wiley-Blackwell.

Bhullar, B.-A. S. and G. S. Bever (2009). "An Archosaur-Like Laterosphenoid in Early Turtles (Reptilia: Pantestudines)." Breviora 518.

Bocquentin, J. and J. Melo (2006). "*Stupendemys souzai* sp. nov. (Pleurodira, Podocnemididae) From the Miocene-Pliocene of the Solimões Formation, Brazil." Rev Bras Paleontol 9(2): 187-192.

Cadena Rueda, E. A. and E. S. Gaffney (2005). "*Notoemys zapatocaensis*, a New Side-Necked Turtle (Pleurodira: Platychelyidae) from the Early Cretaceous of Colombia." American Museum Novitates 3470: 1-19.

Callaway, J. M., and E. L. Nicholls (1997). Ancient Marine Reptiles. San Diego: Academic Press.

Dalla Valle, L., A. Nardi, et al. (2009). "Beta-keratins of Turtle Shell Are Glycine-Proline-Tyrosine Rich Proteins Similar to Those of Crocodilians and Birds." J Anat 214(2): 284-300.

Danilov, I. G. and J. F. Parham (2006). "A Redescription of '*Plesiochelys*' *tatsuensis* From the Late Jurassic of China, with Comments on the Antiquity of the Crown Clade Cryptodira." J Vertebr Paleontol 26(3): 573–580.

Danilov, I. G. and J. F. Parham (2008). "A Reassessment of Some Poorly Known Turtles From the Middle Jurassic of China, with Comments on the Antiquity of Extant Turtles." J Vertebr Paleontol 28(2): 306-318.

Danilov, I. G., A. O. Averianov, et al. (2006). "*Kirgizemys* (Testudines, 'Macrobaenidae'): New Material From the Lower Cretaceous of Buryatia (Russia) and Taxonomic Revision." Fossil Turtle Research 1: 46-62.

Davit-Béal, T., A. S. Tucker, et al. (2009). "Loss of Teeth and Enamel in Tetrapods: Fossil Record, Genetic Data and Morphological Adaptations." J Anat 214(4): 477-501.

De La Fuente, M. S. and M. Iturralde-Vinent (2001). "A New Pleurodiran Turtle From the Jagua Formation (Oxfordian) of Western Cuba." J Paleontol 75(4): 860-869.

De La Fuente, M. S. and M. S. Fernández (2010). "An Unusual Pattern of Limb Morphology in the Tithonian Marine Turtle *Neusticemys neuquina* from the Vaca Muerta Formation, Neuquén Basin, Argentina." Lethaia: 15-25.

Diedrich, C. G. (2011). "The Shallow Marine Placodont *Cyamodus* of the Central European Germanic Basin - its Evolution, Paleobiogeography and Paleoecology." Historical Biology 23(4): 391-409.

Gaffney, E. S. (1996). "The Postcranial Morphology of *Meiolania platyceps* and a Review of the Meiolaniidae." Bulletin AMNH 229: 1-165.

Gaffney, E. S and F. A. Jenkins (2010). "The Cranial Morphology of *Kayentachelys*, an Early Jurassic Cryptodire, and the Early History of Turtles." Acta Zoologica 91(3): 335-368.

Gaffney, E. S., and P. A. Meylan (1988). "A Phylogeny of Turtles." the Phylogeny and Classification of the Tetrapods, Volume 1: Amphibians, Reptiles, Birds. Ed. M. J. Benton. Oxford: Clarendon. pp. 157-219.

Gaffney, E. S., D. De Almeida Campos, et al. (2001). "*Cearachelys*, a New Side-Necked Turtle (Pelomedusoides: Bothremydidae) from the Early Cretaceous of Brazil." American Museum Novitates 3319: 1-20.

Gaffney, E. S., D. W. Krause, et al. (2009). "*Kinkonychelys*, a New Side-Necked Turtle (Pelomedusoides: Bothremydidae) from the Late Cretaceous of Madagascar." American Museum Novitates 3662: 1-25.

Gaffney, E. S., H. Tong, et al. (2006). "Evolution of the Side-Necked Turtles: the Families Bothremydidae, Euraxemydidae, and Araripemydidae." B Am Mus Nat Hist 300: 1-698.

Gaffney, E. S., K. E. Campbell, et al. (1998). "Pelomedusoid Side-Necked Turtles from Late Miocene Sediments in Southwestern Amazonia." American Museum Novitates 3245: 1-12.

Gaffney, E. S., P. A. Meylan, et al. (2011). "Evolution of the Side-necked Turtles : the Family Podocnemididae." B Am Mus Nat Hist 350: 1-237.

Gaffney, E. S., T. H. Rich, et al. (2007). "*Chubutemys*, a New Eucryptodiran Turtle from the Early Cretaceous of Argentina, and the Relationships of the Meiolaniidae." American Museum Novitates 3599: 1-35.

Gaffney, E.S. (1990). "The Comparative Osteology of the Triassic Turtle *Proganochelys*." Bull Am Mus Nat Hist 194: 1-263.

Gaffney, E.S., and J.W. Kitching (1994). "The Most Ancient African Turtle." Nature 369(6475): 55-58.

Gaffney, E. S. (1992). "*Ninjemys*, a New Name for "*Meiolania*" *oweni* (Woodward), a Horned Turtle from the Pleistocene of Queensland." American Museum Novitates 3049: 1-10.

Gaffney, E. S., and J. W. Kitching (1995). "The Morphology and Relationships of *Australochelys*, an Early Jurassic Turtle from South Africa." American Museum Novitates 3130: 1-29.

Gaffney, E. S., et al. (1987). "Modern Turtle Origins: the Oldest Known Cryptodire." Science 237: 289-91.

Gaffney, E. S., M. Archer, and A. White (1992). "*Warkalania*, a New Meiolaniid Turtle from the Tertiary Riversleigh Deposits of Queensland, Australia." The Beagle, Records of Northern Territory Museum of Arts and Sciences 9(1): 35-48.

Gaillard, C., P. Bernier, et al. (2003). "A Giant Upper Jurassic turtle Revealed by its Trackways." Lethaia 36(4): 315-322.

Geer, A. v. d., M. Dermitzakis, et al. (2008). "Fossil Folklore from India: the Siwalik Hills and the Mahabharata." Folklore 119(1): 71-92.

Head, J. J., S. M. Raza, et al. (1999). "*Drazinderetes tethyensis*, a new large trionychid (Reptilia: Testudines) from the Marine Eocene Drazinda Formation of the Sulaiman Range, Punjab (Pakistan)." Contr Mus Paleontol U Michigan 30(7): 199-214.

Hedges, S. B., and L. L. Poling (1999). "A Molecular Phylogeny of Reptiles." Science 283: 998-1001.

Hill, R. V. (2005). "Integration of Morphological Data Sets for Phylogenetic Analysis of Amniota: The Importance of Integumentary Characters and Increased Taxonomic Sampling." Syst Biol 54 (4): 530-547.

Hirayama, R. (1998). "Oldest Known Sea Turtle." Nature 392: 705-08.

Hooks, G. E. (1998). "Systematic Revision of the Protostegidae, with a Redescription of *Calcarichelys gemima* Zangerl, 1953." J Vertebr Paleontol 18(1): 85-98.

Joyce, W. G. (2007). "Phylogenetic Relationships of Mesozoic Turtles." Bull Peabody Mus Nat Hist 48(1): 3-102.

Joyce, W. G. and J. A. Gauthier (2004). "Palaeoecology of Triassic Stem Turtles Sheds New Light on Turtle Origins." Proc Biol Sci. 271(1534): 1-5.

Joyce, W. G. and J. Sterli (2010). "Congruence, non-homology, and the phylogeny of basal turtles." Acta Zoologica [online preview]: doi:10.1111/j.1463-6395.2010.00491.x.

Joyce, W. G. and M. A. Norell (2005). "*Zangerlia ukhaachelys*, New Species, a Nanhsiungchelyid Turtle from the Late Cretaceous of Ukhaa Tolgod, Mongolia." American Museum Novitates 3481: 1-20.

Joyce, W., S. Lucas, et al. (2009). "A Thin-Shelled Reptile From the Late Triassic of North America and the Origin of the Turtle Shell." Proc Biol Sci. 276(1656): 507-513.

Kear, B. P. (2003). "Cretaceous marine reptiles of Australia: a review of taxonomy and distribution." Cretaceous Research 24(3): 277-303.

Kear, B. P. (2006). "Reassessment of *Cratochelone berneyi* Longman, 1915, a Giant Sea Turtle From the Early Cretaceous of Australia." J Vertebr Paleontol 26(3): 779-783.

Kear, B. P. and M. S. Y. Lee (2006). "A Primitive Protostegid From Australia and Early Sea Turtle Evolution." Biol Lett. 2: 116-119.

Kordikova, E. G. (2002). "Comparative Morphology of the Palate Dentition in *Proganochelys quenstedti* Baur 1887 from the Upper Triassic of Germany and Chelonian Ancestry." N. Jb. Geol. Paläont. Abh. 225(2): 195-249.

Kuratani, S., S. Kuraku, et al. (2011). "Evolutionary Developmental Perspective For the Origin of Turtles: the Folding Theory For the Shell Based on the Developmental Nature of the Carapacial Ridge." Evol Dev 13(1): 1-14.

Lapparent de Broin, F. d. (2000). "The oldest pre-Podocnemidid turtle (Chelonii, Pleurodira), from the early Cretaceous, Ceará state, Brasil, and its environment." Treb. Mus. Geol. Barcelona 9: 43-45.

Lehman, T. M. and S. L. Tomlinson (2004). "*Terlinguachelys fischbecki*, a New Genus and Species of Sea Turtle (Chelonioidea: Protostegidae) From the Upper Cretaceous of Texas." J Paleontol 78(6): 1163-1178.

Lehman, T. M. and S. L. Wick (2010). "*Chupacabrachelys complexus*, n. gen. n. sp. (Testudines: Bothremydidae), from the Aguja Formation (Campanian) of West Texas." J Vertebr Paleontol 30(6): 1709-1725.

Li, C., X.-C. Wu, et al. (2008). "An ancestral turtle from the Late Triassic of southwestern China." Nature 456(7221): 497-501.

Li, C., X.-C. Wu, et al. (2008). "An ancestral turtle from the Late Triassic of southwestern China (supplementary information)." Nature 456(7221): 497-501.

Lipka, T. R., F. á. Therrien, et al. (2006). "A New Turtle From the Arundel Clay Facies (Potomac Formation, Early Cretaceous) of Maryland, U.S.A." J Vertebr Paleontol 26(2): 300-307.

Liu, Y.-x., J. Wang, et al. (2009). "Ethogram of *Sacalia quadriocellata* (Reptilia: Testudines: Geoemydidae) in Captivity." J Herpetol 43(2): 318-325.

Lyson, T. and S. F. Gilbert (2009). "Turtles All the Way Down: Loggerheads At the Root of the Chelonian Tree." Evol Dev 11(2): 133-135.

Lyson, T. R. and W. G. Joyce (2010). "A New Baenid Turtle from the Upper Cretaceous (Maastrichtian) Hell Creek Formation of North Dakota and a Preliminary Taxonomic Review of Cretaceous Baenidae." J Vertebr Paleontol 30(2): 394-402.

Lyson, T. R. and W. G. Joyce (2011). "Cranial Anatomy and Phylogenetic Placement of the Enigmatic Turtle *Compsemys victa* Leidy, 1856." J Paleontol 85(4): 789-801.

Lyson, T. R., E. A. Sperling, et al. (2011). "MicroRNAs Support a Turtle + Lizard Clade." Biol. Lett. doi: 10.1098/rsbl.2011.0477

Lyson, T. R., G. S. Bever, et al. (2010). "Transitional Fossils and the Origin of Turtles." Biol Lett. 6(6): 830-833.

Lyson, T. R., W. G. Joyce, et al. (2011). "*Boremys* (Testudines, Baenidae) from the Latest Cretaceous and early Paleocene of North Dakota: an 11-million-year Range Extension and an Additional K/T Survivor." J Vertebr Paleontol 31(4): 729-737.

Mateus, O. v., L. Jacobs, et al. (2009). "The Oldest African Eucryptodiran Turtle from the Cretaceous of Angola." Acta Palaeontol Pol 54(4): 581-588.

Meylan, P. A., E. S. Gaffney, et al. (2009). "*Caninemys*, a New Side-Necked Turtle (Pelomedusoides: Podocnemididae) from the Miocene of Brazil." American Museum Novitates: 1-26.

Meylan, P. A. (1996). "Skeletal Morphology and Relationships of the Early Cretaceous Side-Necked Turtle, *Araripemys barretoi* (Testudines: Pelomedusoides: Araripemydidae), from the Santana Formation of Brazil." J Vertebr Paleontol 16(1): 20-33.

Meylan, P. A., et al. (2000). "*Sandownia harrisi*, a Highly Derived Trionychoid Turtle (Testudines: Cryptodira) from the Early Cretaceous of the Isle of Wight, England." J Vertebr Paleontol 20(3): 522-32.

Modesto, S. P. (2000). "*Eunotosaurus africanus* and the Gondwanan Ancestry of Anapsid Reptiles." Palaeont. Afr. 36: 15-20.

Naish, D. (2000). "Placodonts: the Bizarre 'Walrus-Turtles' of the Triassic." www.oceansofkansas.com/placodnt.html

Parham, J. F. and J. H. Hutchison (2003). "A New Eucryptodiran Turtle From the Late Cretaceous of North America (Dinosaur Provincial Park, Alberta, Canada)." J Vertebr Paleontol 23(4): 783-798.

Parham, J. F. and N. D. Pyenson (2010). "New Sea Turtle from the Miocene of Peru and the Iterative Evolution of Feeding Ecomorphologies since the Cretaceous." J Paleontol 84(2): 231-247.

Reisz, R. R. and D. Scott (2002). "*Owenetta kitchingorum*, sp. nov., a Small Parareptile (Procolophonia: Owenettidae) From the Lower Triassic of South Africa." J Vertebr Paleontol 22(2): 244-256.

Reisz, R. R. and J. J. Head (2008). "Turtle Origins Out to Sea." Nature 456: 450-451.

Reisz, R. R., and M. Laurin (1991). "*Owenetta* and the Origin of Turtles." Nature 349.6307: 324-26.

Rieppel, O. (2000). "Turtles as Diapsid Reptiles." Zoologica Scripta 29(3): 199-212.

Rieppel, O. (2002). "The Dermal Armor of the Cyamodontoid Placodonts (Reptilia, Sauropterygia): Morphology and Systematic Value." Fieldiana: Geol, New Series 46(1-41).

Rieppel, O., and R. R. Reisz (1999). "The Origin and Early Evolution of Turtles." Ann. Rev. Ecol. Syst. 30: 1-22.

Rougier, G. W., M. S. de la Fuente, et al. (1995). "Late Triassic Turtles from South America." Science 268: 855-58.

Sánchez-Villagra, M. R. and T. M. Scheyer (2010). Fossil Turtles From the Northern Neotropics: the Urumaco Sequence and Finds From Other Localities in Venezuela and Colombia. Urumaco and Venezuelan Paleontology the Fossil Record of the Northern Neotropics. M. R. Sánchez-Villagra, O. A. Aguilera and A. A. Carlini, eds. Bloomington, Indiana, Indiana University Press. pp. 173-191.

Scheyer, T. and P. Sander (2007). "Shell Bone Histology Indicates Terrestrial Palaeoecology of Basal Turtles." Proc Biol Sci. 274(1620): 1885-1893.

Scheyer, T. M. (2007). "Skeletal Histology of the Dermal Armor of Placodontia: the Occurrence of 'Postcranial Fibro-Cartilaginous Bone' and Its Developmental Implications." J Anat 211(6): 737-753.

Scheyer, T. M. (2007). Comparative Bone Histology of the Turtle Shell (Carapace and Plastron) - Implications For Turtle Systematics, Functional Morphology and Turtle Origins. Ph.D, University of Bonn

Scheyer, T. M. (2009). "Conserved Bone Microstructure in the Shells of Long-Necked and Short-Necked Chelid Turtles (Testudinata, Pleurodira)." Fossil Record 12(1): 47-57.

Scheyer, T. M. and J. Anquetin (2008). "Bone Histology of the Middle Jurassic Turtle Shell Remains From Kirtlington, Oxfordshire, England." Lethaia 41(1): 85-96.

Scheyer, T. M. and M. R. Sánchez–Villagra (2007). "Carapace Bone Histology in the Giant Pleurodiran Turtle *Stupendemys geographicus*: Phylogeny and Function." Acta Palaeontol Pol 52(1): 137-154.

Scheyer, T. M. and P. M. Sander (2009). "Bone Microstructures and Mode of Skeletogenesis in Osteoderms of Three Pareiasaur Taxa From the Permian of South Africa." J Evolution Biol 22(6): 1153-1162.

Shimada, K. and G. E. Hooks (2004). "Shark-Bitten Protostegid Turtles From the Upper Cretaceous Mooreville Chalk, Alabama." J Paleontol 78(1): 205-210.

Sterli, J. (2008). "A New, Nearly Complete Stem Turtle From the Jurassic of South America with Implications For Turtle Evolution." Biol Lett 4: 286-289.

Sterli, J. and M. S. de la Fuente (2010). "Anatomy of *Condorchelys antiqua* Sterli, 2008, and the Origin of the Modern Jaw Closure Mechanism in Turtles." J Vertebr Paleontol 30(2): 351-366.

Sterli, J. and M. S. de la Fuente (2011). "A New Turtle From the La Colonia Formation (Campanian-Maastrichtian), Patagonia, Argentina, with Remarks on the Evolution of the Vertebral Column in Turtles." Palaeontology 54(1): 63-78.

Sterli, J., S. Rafael, et al. (2007). "Anatomy and Relationships of *Palaeochersis talampayensis*, a Late Triassic Turtle From Argentina." Palaeontographica Abteilung a 281(1-3): 1-61.

Takahashi, A., T. Kato, et al. (2007). "A New Species of the Genus *Geoemyda* (Chelonii: Geoemydidae) From the Upper Pleistocene of Tokunoshima Island, the Central Ryukyus, Japan." Current Herpetology 26(1): 1-11.

Tong, H., E. S. Gaffney, et al. (1998). "*Foxemys*, a New Side-Necked Turtle (Bothremydidae: Pelomedusoides) from the Late Cretaceous of France." American Museum Novitates 3251: 1-19.

Vickaryous, M. K. and B. K. Hall (2006). "Homology of the Reptilian Coracoid and a Reappraisal of the Evolution and Development of the Amniote Pectoral Apparatus." J Anat 208(3): 263-285.

Werneburg, I. and M. R. Sánchez-Villagra (2009). "Timing of Organogenesis Support Basal Position of Turtles in the Amniote Tree of Life." BMC Evolutionary Biology 9(1): 82.

White, A. W., T. H. Worthy, et al. (2010). "Megafaunal Meiolaniid Horned Turtles Survived Until Early Human Settlement in Vanuatu, Southwest Pacific." Proc Natl Acad Sci 107(35): 15512-15516.

Wood, R. C. (1976). "*Stupendemys geographicus*, the World's Largest Turtle." Breviora 436: 1-31.

Wood, R. C., et al. (1996) "Evolution and Phylogeny of Leatherback Turtles (Dermochelyidae), with Descriptions of New Fossil Taxa." Chelonian Cons Biol 2(2): 266–86.

Zardoya, R. and A. Meyer (2001). "The Evolutionary Position of Turtles Revised." Naturwissenschaften 88(5): 193-200.

Zardoya, R., and A. Meyer(1998). "Complete Mitochondrial Genome Suggests Diapsid Affinities of Turtles." Proc Natl Acad Sci USA 95: 14226-14231.

Chapter 3: Turtles Round The World I: Side-Necks And Hidden-Necks

Albright III, L. B., M. O. Woodburne, et al. (2003). "A Leatherback Sea Turtle From the Eocene of Antarctica: Implications For Antiquity of Gigantothermy in Dermochelyidae." J Vertebr Paleontol 23(4): 945-949.

Alcalde, L., N. N. Derocco, et al. (2010). "Feeding in Syntopy: Diet of *Hydromedusa tectifera* and *Phrynops hilarii* (Chelidae)." Chelonian Cons Biol 9(1): 33-44.

Alves, R. R. and G. G. Santana (2008). "Use and Commercialization of *Podocnemis expansa* (Schweiger 1812) (Testudines: Podocnemididae) For Medicinal Purposes in Two Communities in North of Brazil." J Ethnobiol Ethnomed 4: 3.

Asian Turtle Program of Cleveland Metroparks Zoo. "The Swinhoe's Softshell Turtle (*Rafetus swinhoei*) Project." Retrieved June 29, 2011, From http://www.asianturtleprogram.org/pages/rafetus/rafetus_project.html.

Bailey, K. A., and C. Guyer (1998). "Demography and Population Status of the Flattened Musk Turtle, *Sternotherus depressus*, in the Black Warrior River Basin of Alabama." Chelonian Cons Biol 3(1): 77-83.

Barley, A. J., P. Q. Spinks, et al. (2010). "Fourteen Nuclear Genes Provide Phylogenetic Resolution For Difficult Nodes in the Turtle Tree of Life." Mol Phylogenet Evol 55(3): 1189-1194.

Bona, P. and M. S. De La Fuente (2005). "Phylogenetic and Paleobiogeographic Implications of *Yaminuechelys maior* (Staesche, 1929) New Comb., a Large Long-Necked Chelid Turtle From the Early Paleocene of Patagonia, Argentina." J Vertebr Paleontol 25(3): 569-582.

Bour, R. and H. Zaher (2005). "A New Species of *Mesoclemmys*, From the Open Formations of Northeastern Brazil (Chelonii, Chelidae)." Papéis Avulsos De Zoologia (São Paulo) 45(24): 295-311.

Bowen, B. W., W. S. Nelson, et al. (1993). "A Molecular Phylogeny for Marine Turtles: Trait Mapping, Rate Assessment and Conservation Relevance." Proc Natl Acad Sci USA 90: 5574-77.

Broderick, A. C., R. Frauenstein, et al. (2006). "Are Green Turtles Globally Endangered?" Global Ecology and Biogeography 15(1): 21-26.

Buhlmann, K. A., T. S. B. Akre, et al. (2009). "A Global Analysis of Tortoise and Freshwater Turtle Distributions with Identification of Priority Conservation Areas." Chelonian Cons Biol 8(2): 116-149.

Cadena, E. A., J. I. Bloch, et al. (2010). "New Podocnemidid Turtle (Testudines: Pleurodira) From the Middle-Upper Paleocene of South America." J Vertebr Paleontol 30(2): 367-382.

Cann, J., and J. M. Legler (1994). "The Mary River Tortoise: a New Genus and Species of Short-Necked Chelid from Queensland, Australia (Testudines: Pleurodira)." Chelonian Cons Biol 1(2): 81-96.

Caro, T. and H. B. Shaffer (2010). "Chelonian Antipredator Strategies: Preliminary and Comparative Data From Tanzanian *Pelusios*." Chelonian Cons Biol 9(2): 302-305.

Carvalho, E. A. R., J. C. B. Pezzuti, et al. (2011). "*Podocnemis erythrocephala* Nests in the Lower Tapajós River, Central Amazonia, Brazil." Chelonian Cons Biol 10(1): 146-148.

Chandler, C. H. and F. J. Janzen (2009). "The Phylogenetic Position of the Snapping Turtles (Chelydridae) Based on Nucleotide Sequence Data." Copeia 2009(2): 209-213.

Cisneros, J. C. (2005). "New Pleistocene Vertebrate Fauna From El Salvador." Revista Brasileira De Paleontologia 8(3): 239-255.

De La Fuente, M. S. (2003). "Two New Pleurodiran Turtles From the Portezuelo Formation (Upper Cretaceous) of Northern Patagonia, Argentina." J Paleontol 77(3): 559-575.

De La Ossa V, J. and R. C. Vogt (2011). "Ecologia Populacional De *Peltocephalus dumerilianus* (Testudines, Podocnemididae) Em Dois Tributários Do Rio Negro, Amazonas, Brasil." Interciencia 36(1): 53-58.

Doody, J. S., R. A. Sims, et al. (2003). "Gregarious Behavior of Nesting Turtles (*Carettochelys insculpta*) Does Not Reduce Nest Predation Risk." Copeia 2003(4): 894-898.

Eisemberg, C. C., M. Rose, et al. (2011). "Demonstrating Decline of an Iconic Species Under Sustained Indigenous Harvest – the Pig-Nosed Turtle (*Carettochelys insculpta*) in Papua New Guinea." Biol Conserv. 144(9): 2282-2288.

Engstrom, T. N., H. B. Shaffer, et al. (2002). "Phylogenetic Diversity of Endangered and Critically Endangered Southeast Asian Softshell Turtles (Trionychidae: *Chitra*)." Biol Conserv 104: 173-179.

Escalona, T., T. N. Engstrom, et al. (2008). "Population Genetics of the Endangered South American Freshwater Turtle, *Podocnemis unifilis*, Inferred From Microsatellite DNA Data." Conservation Genetics 10(6): 1683-1696.

Farkas, B., M. D. Le, et al. (2011). "*Rafetus vietnamensis* Le, Le, Tran, Phan, Phan, Tran, Pham, Nguyen, Nong, Phan, Dinh, Truong and Ha, 2010 — Another Invalid Name For an Invalid Species of Softshell Turtle (Reptilia: Testudines: Trionychidae)." Russian J Herpetol 18(1): 65-72.

Flores-Villela, O. A., and G. R. Zug (1995). "Reproductive Biology of the Chopontil, *Claudius angustatus* (Testudines: Kinosternidae), in Southern Veracruz, México." Chelonian Cons Biol 1(3): 181-86.

Florida Fish and Wildlife Conservation Commission (2011). Biological Status Review For the Alligator Snapping Turtle (*Macrochelys temminckii*). 16 pp.

Fonseca, L. G., G. A. Murillo, et al. (2009). "Downward But Stable Trend in the Abundance of Arribada Olive Ridley Sea Turtles (*Lepidochelys olivacea*) At Nancite Beach, Costa Rica (1971–2007)." Chelonian Cons Biol 8(1): 19-27.

Ford, D. K. and D. Moll (2004). "Sexual and Seasonal Variation in Foraging Patterns in the Stinkpot, *Sternotherus odoratus*, in Southwestern Missouri." J Herpetol 38(2): 296-301.

Forero-Medina, G., O. V. Castaño-Mora, et al. (2007). "Abundance, Population Structure, and Conservation of *Kinosternon scorpioides albogulare* on the Caribbean Island of San Andrés, Colombia." Chelonian Cons Biol 6(2): 163-169.

Fossette, S., L. Kelle, et al. (2008). "The World's Largest Leatherback Rookeries: a Review of Conservation-Oriented Research in French Guiana/Suriname and Gabon." J Exp Mar Biol Ecol 356(1-2): 69-82.

Fretey, J., A. Billes, et al. (2007). "Leatherback, *Dermochelys coriacea*, Nesting Along the Atlantic Coast of Africa." Chelonian Cons Biol 6(1): 126-129.

Fritz, U., W. R. Branch, et al. (2010). "Molecular Phylogeny of African Hinged and Helmeted Terrapins (Testudines: Pelomedusidae: *Pelusios* and *Pelomedusa*)." Zoologica Scripta 40(2): 115-125.

Gaffney, E. S., P. A. Meylan, et al. (2011). "Evolution of the Side-Necked Turtles : the Family Podocnemididae." B Am Mus Nat Hist 350: 1-237.

Gallego-García, N. and O. V. Castaño-Mora (2008). "Ecology and Status of the Magdalena River Turtle, *Podocnemis lewyana*, a Colombian Endemic." Chelonian Cons Biol 7(1): 37-44.

Georges, A. and S. Thomson (2006). Evolution and Zoogeography of Australian Freshwater Turtles. Evolution and Biogeography of Australasian Vertebrates. J. R. Merrick, M. Archer, G. Hickey and M. S. Y. Lee, eds. Sydney, Auscipub (Australian Scientific Publishing) Pty Ltd. pp. 291-308.

Georges, A. and S. Thomson (2010). "Diversity of Australasian Freshwater Turtles, with an Annotated Synonymy and Keys to Species." Zootaxa 2496: 1-37.

Georges, A., J. Birrell, et al. (1999). "A Phylogeny For Side-Necked Turtles (Chelonia: Pleurodira) Based on Mitochondrial and Nuclear Gene Sequence Variation." Biol J Linn Soc 67(2): 213-246.

Georges, A., M. Adams, et al. (2002). "Electrophoretic Delineation of Species Boundaries within the Genus *Chelodina* (Testudines: Chelidae) of Australia, New Guinea and Indonesia." Zool J Linn Soc 134(4): 401-421.

Gerlach, J. (2008). "Fragmentation and Demography As Causes of Population Decline in Seychelles Freshwater Turtles (Genus *Pelusios*)." Chelonian Cons Biol 7(1): 78-87.

Gerlach, J. and L. Canning (2001). "Range Contractions in the Critically Endangered Seychelles Terrapins (*Pelusios* Spp.)." Oryx 35(4): 313-321.

Ghaffari, H., E. Taskavak, et al. (2008). "Conservation Status of the Euphrates Softshell Turtle, *Rafetus euphraticus*, in Iran." Chelonian Cons Biol 7(2): 223-229.

Godfrey, M. and B. Godley (2008). "Seeing Past the Red: Flawed IUCN Global Listings For Sea Turtles." Endangered Species Research 6(2): 155-159.

Güçlü, Ö., C. Ulger, et al. (2009). "First Assessment of Mitochondrial DNA Diversity in the Endangered Nile Softshell Turtle, *Trionyx triunguis*, in the Mediterranean." Chelonian Cons Biol 8(2): 222-226.

Guzmán-Hernández, V., E. A. Cuevas-Flores, et al. (2007). "Occurrence of Kemp's Ridley (*Lepidochelys kempii*) Along the Coast of the Yucatan Peninsula, Mexico." Chelonian Cons Biol 6(2): 274-277.

Harden, L., S. Price, et al. (2009). "Terrestrial Activity and Habitat Selection of Eastern Mud Turtles (Kinosternon subrubrum) in a Fragmented Landscape: Implications For Habitat Management of Golf Courses and Other Suburban Environments." Copeia 2009(1): 78-84.

Hays, G. C. (2004). "Good News For Sea Turtles." Trends Ecol Evol 19(7): 349-351.

Head, J. J., O. A. Aguilera, et al. (2006). "Past Colonization of South America By Trionychid Turtles: Fossil Evidence From the Neogene of Margarita Island, Venezuela." J Herpetol 40(3): 378-381.

Iverson, J. B. (2010). "Reproduction in the Red-Cheeked Mud Turtle (*Kinosternon scorpioides cruentatum*) in Southeastern Mexico and

Belize, with Comparisons Across the Species Range." Chelonian Cons Biol 9(2): 250-261.

James, M. C., C. Andrea Ottensmeyer, et al. (2005). "Identification of High-Use Habitat and Threats to Leatherback Sea Turtles in Northern Waters: New Directions For Conservation." Ecology Letters 8(2): 195-201.

Jamniczky, H. A. (2008). "Turtle Carotid Circulation: a Character Analysis Case Study." Biol J Linn Soc 93(2): 239-256.

Jensen, K. A. and I. Das (2008). "Dietary Observations on the Asian Softshell Turtle (Amyda cartilaginea) From Sarawak, Malaysian Borneo." Chelonian Cons Biol 7(1): 136-141.

Joyce, W. G. and T. R. Lyson (2010). "A Neglected Lineage of North American Turtles Fills a Major Gap in the Fossil Record." Palaeontology 53(2): 241-248.

Joyce, W. G., A. Revan, et al. (2009). "Two New Plastomenine Softshell Turtles From the Paleocene of Montana and Wyoming." Bull Peabody Mus Nat Hist 50(2): 307-325.

Karl, H. V. and G. Tichy (2007). "Maorichelys wiffeni n. gen. n. sp., Una Nueva Tortuga Marina Del Eoceno De Nueva Zelanda (Testudines: Dermochelyidae)." Studia Geologica Salmanticensia 43(1): 11-24.

Kenow, K. P., J. M. Kapfer, et al. (2009). "Predation of Radio-Marked Mallard (Anas platyrhynchos) Ducklings By Eastern Snapping Turtles (Chelydra serpentina serpentina) and Western Fox Snakes (Pantherophis vulpinus) on the Upper Mississippi River." J Herpetol 43(1): 154-158.

Kobayashi, R., M. Hasegawa, et al. (2006). "Home Range and Habitat Use of the Exotic Turtle Chelydra serpentina in the Inbanuma Basin, Chiba Prefecture, Central Japan." Current Herpetology 25(2): 47-55.

Krenz, J. G., G. J. P. Naylor, et al. (2005). "Mol Phylogenet Evol of Turtles." Mol Phylogenet Evol 37: 178-191.

Lovich, J., C. Drost, et al. (2010). "Reptilian Prey of the Sonora Mud Turtle (Kinosternon sonoriense) with Comments on Saurophagy and Ophiophagy in North American Turtles." Southwest Nat 55(1): 135-138.

Lyson, T. and S. F. Gilbert (2009). "Turtles All the Way Down: Loggerheads At the Root of the Chelonian Tree." Evol Dev 11(2): 133-135.

Magnusson, W. E., et al. (1997). "Home Range of the Turtle, Phrynops rufipes, in an Isolated Reserve in Central Amazônia, Brazil." Chelonian Cons Biol 2(4): 494-99.

Martins, F. I., F. L. Souza, et al. (2009). "Demographic Parameters of the Neotropical Freshwater Turtle Hydromedusa maximiliani (Chelidae)." Herpetologica 65(1): 82-91.

McCord, W. P. and P. C. H. Pritchard (2002). "A Review of the Softshell Turtles of the Genus Chitra, with the Description of New Taxa From Myanmar and Indonesia (Java)." Hamadryad 27(1): 11-56.

McCord, W. P. and S. A. Thomson (2002). "A New Species of Chelodina (Testudines: Pleurodira: Chelidae) From Northern Australia." J Herpetol 36(2): 255-267.

McGaugh, S. E. and F. J. Janzen (2008). "The Status of Apalone atra Populations in Cuatro Ciénegas, Coahuila, México: Preliminary Data." Chelonian Cons Biol 7(1): 88-95.

McGowan, A., A. C. Broderick, et al. (2008). "Down But Not Out: Marine Turtles of the British Virgin Islands." Animal Conservation 11(2): 92-103.

Meylan, P. A., E. S. Gaffney, et al. (2009). "Caninemys, a New Side-Necked Turtle (Pelomedusoides: Podocnemididae) From the Miocene of Brazil." American Museum Novitates 3639: 1-26.

Naro-Maciel, E., M. Le, et al. (2008). "Evolutionary Relationships of Marine Turtles: a Molecular Phylogeny Based on Nuclear and Mitochondrial Genes." Mol Phylogenet Evol 49(2): 659-662.

Noonan, B. P. (2000). "Does the Phylogeny of Pelomedusoid Turtles Reflect Vicariance Due to Continental Drift?" J Biogeogr 27: 1245-1249.

Padovani Haller, É. C. and M. T. Rodrigues (2006). "Reproductive Biology of the Six-Tubercled Amazon River Turtle Podocnemis sextuberculata (Testudines: Podocnemididae), in the Biological Reserve of Rio Trombetas, Pará, Brazil." Chelonian Cons Biol 5(2): 280-284.

Parham, J. F., C. R. Feldman, et al. (2006). "The Complete Mitochondrial Genome of the Enigmatic Bigheaded Turtle (Platysternon): Description of Unusual Genomic Features and the Reconciliation of Phylogenetic Hypotheses Based on Mitochondrial and Nuclear DNA." Bmc Evolutionary Biology 6: 11.

Piedra, R., E. Vélez, et al. (2007). "Nesting of the Leatherback Turtle (Dermochelys coriacea) From 1999–2000 Through 2003–2004 At Playa Langosta, Parque Nacional Marino Las Baulas De Guanacaste, Costa Rica." Chelonian Cons Biol 6(1): 111-116.

Praschag, P., A. K. Hundsdörfer, et al. (2007). "Genetic Evidence For Wild-Living Aspideretes nigricans and a Molecular Phylogeny of South Asian Softshell Turtles (Reptilia: Trionychidae: Aspideretes, Nilssonia)." Zoologica Scripta 36(4): 301-310.

Praschag, P., C. Schmidt, et al. (2006). "Geoemyda silvatica, an Enigmatic Turtle of the Geoemydidae (Reptilia: Testudines), Represents a Distinct Genus." Organisms Diversity & Evolution 6(2): 151-162.

Praschag, P., H. Stuckas, et al. (2011). "Mitochondrial DNA Sequences Suggest a Revised Taxonomy of Asian Flapshell Turtles (Lissemys Smith, 1931) and the Validity of Previously Unrecognized Taxa (Testudines: Trionychidae)." Vertebrate Zoology 61(1): 147-160.

Restrepo, A., V. P. Páez, et al. (2008). "Distribution and Status of Podocnemis lewyana in the Magdalena River Drainage of Colombia." Chelonian Cons Biol 7(1): 45-51.

Rhodin, J. A. G., A. G. J. Rhodin, et al. (1996). "Electron Microscopic Analysis of Vascular Cartilage Canals in the Humeral Epiphysis of Hatchling Leatherback Turtles, Dermochelys coriacea." Chelonian Cons Biol 2(2): 250–60.

Riedle, J. D., P. A. Shipman, et al. (2005). "Status and Distribution of the Alligator Snapping Turtle, Macrochelys temminckii, in Oklahoma." Southwest Nat 50(1): 79-84.

Roe, J. H. and A. Georges (2008). "Maintenance of Variable Responses For Coping with Wetland Drying in Freshwater Turtles " Ecology 89(2): 485-494.

Romano, P. S. R. and S. A. K. Azevedo (2006). "Are Extant Podocnemidid Turtles Relicts of a Widespread Cretaceous Ancestor?" South American J Herpetol 1(3): 175-184.

Schaffer, J. and R. G. Doupé (2009). "What For the Future of the Jardine River Painted Turtle? a Report Prepared For the Cape York Peninsula Biodiversity Technical Advisory Group." ACTFR Report No. 09/06.

Scheyer, T. M. (2009). "Conserved Bone Microstructure in the Shells of Long-Necked and Short-Necked Chelid Turtles (Testudinata, Pleurodira)." Fossil Record 12(1): 47-57.

Seminoff, J. A., F. V. Paladino, et al. (2007). "Editorial Introduction Refocusing on Leatherbacks: Conservation Challenges and Signs of Success." Chelonian Cons Biol 6(1): 1-6.

Shaffer, H. B., Arthur Georges, et al. (2007). "Defining Turtle Diversity: Proceedings of a Workshop on Genetics, Ethics, and Taxonomy of Freshwater Turtles and Tortoises, Cambridge, Massachusetts, 8–12 August 2005." Chelonian Research Monographs 4.

Shanker, K., B. Pandav, et al. (2003). "An Assessment of the Olive Ridley Turtle (Lepidochelys olivacea) Nesting Population in Orissa, India." Biol Conserv 115: 149-160.

Shanker, K., J. Ramadevi, et al. (2004). "Phylogeography of Olive Ridley Turtles (Lepidochelys olivacea) on the East Coast of India: Implications For Conservation Theory." Molecular Ecology 13(7): 1899-1909.

Shen, J.-W., D. A. Pike, et al. (2010). "Movements and Microhabitat Use of Translocated Big-Headed Turtles (Platysternon megacephalum) in Southern China." Chelonian Cons Biol 9(2): 154-161.

Shipman, P. A. and J. D. Riedle (2008). "Status and Distribution of the Alligator Snapping Turtle (Macrochelys temminckii) in Southeastern Missouri." Southeastern Naturalist 7(2): 331-338.

Sites, J. W. Jr., et al. (1999). "Conservation of the Giant Amazon River Turtle (Podocnemis expansa; Pelomedusidae) - Inferences from Two Classes of Molecular Markers." Chelonian Cons Biol 3(3): 454-63.

Souza, F. L. and A. S. Abe (2000). "Feeding Ecology, Density and Biomass of the Freshwater Turtle, Phrynops geoffroanus, Inhabiting a Polluted Urban River in South-Eastern Brazil." J Zool 252(4): 437-446.

Souza, F. L., and A. S. Abe (1997). "Population Structure, Activity, and Conservation of the Neotropical Freshwater Turtle, Hydromedusa maximiliani, in Brazil." Chelonian Cons Biol 2(4): 521-25.

Stewart, K., M. Sims, et al. (2011). "Leatherback Nests Increasing Significantly in Florida, Usa; Trends Assessed Over 30 Years Using Multilevel Modeling." Ecological Applications 21(1): 263-273.

Tapilatu, R. F. and M. Tiwari (2007). "Leatherback Turtle, Dermochelys coriacea, Hatching Success At Jamursba-Medi and Wermon Beaches in Papua, Indonesia." Chelonian Cons Biol 6(1): 154-158.

Thomson, R. C. and H. B. Shaffer (2010). "Sparse Supermatrices For Phylogenetic Inference: Taxonomy, Alignment, Rogue Taxa, and the Phylogeny of Living Turtles." Syst. Biol. 59(1): 42–58.

Thomson, R. C., A. M. Shedlock, et al. (2008). "Developing Markers For Multilocus Phylogenetics in Non-Model Organisms: a Test Case with Turtles." Mol Phylogenet Evol 49(2): 514-525.

Thomson, S., A. Georges, et al. (2006). "A New Species of Freshwater Turtle in the Genus Elseya (Testudines: Chelidae) From Central Coastal Queensland, Australia." Chelonian Cons Biol 5(1): 74-86.

Thomson, S., R. Kennett, et al. (2000). "A New Species of Long-Necked Turtle (Testudines: Chelidae) from the Arnhem Land Plateau, Northern Territory, Australia." Chelonian Cons Biol 3(4): 675-85.

Tomás, J., B. J. Godley, et al. (2010). "Bioko: Critically Important Nesting Habitat For Sea Turtles of West Africa." Biodiversity and Conservation 19(9): 2699-2714.

Troëng, S., E. Harrison, et al. (2007). "Leatherback Turtle Nesting Trends and Threats At Tortuguero, Costa Rica." Chelonian Cons Biol 6(1): 117-122.

Tuma, M. W. (2006). "Range, Habitat Use, and Seasonal Activity of the Yellow Mud Turtle (Kinosternon flavescens) in Northwestern Illinois: Implications For Site-Specific Conservation and Management." Chelonian Cons Biol 5(1): 108-120.

Turtle Survival Alliance. (2009). "Second Breeding Attempt For Rafetus swinhoei in China Leads to Cautious Optimism." Retrieved June 29, 2011, From http://www.turtlesurvival.org/blog/1-blog/57-second-breeding-attempt-for-rafetus-swinhoei-in-china-leads-to-cautious-optimism.

Turtle Survival Alliance. (2011). "Central American River Turtle (Dermatemys Mawii)." Retrieved June 29, 2011, From http://www.turtlesurvival.org/component/taxonomy/term/summary/105/37.

Vargas-Ramirez, M., O. Castanomora, et al. (2008). "Molecular Phylogeny and Divergence Times of Ancient South American and Malagasy River Turtles (Testudines: Pleurodira: Podocnemididae)." Organisms Diversity & Evolution 8(5): 388-398.

Vargas-Ramírez, M., Y. Chiari, et al. (2007). "Low Genetic Variability in the Endangered Colombian Endemic Freshwater Turtle Podocnemis lewyana (Testudines, Podocnemididae)." Contributions to Zoology 76(1): 1-7.

Vasudevan, K., B. Pandav, et al. (2010). Ecology of Two Endemic Turtles in the Western Ghats: Final Technical Report. Chandrabani, Dehradun, Wildlife Institute of India: 1-74.

Vitek, N. S. and I. G. Danilov (2010). "New Material and a Reassessment of Soft-Shelled Turtles (Trionychidae) from the Late Cretaceous of Middle Asia and Kazakhstan." J Vertebr Paleontol 30(2): 383-393.

Webb, R. G. (1995). "Redescription and Neotype Designation of Pelochelys bibroni from Southern New Guinea (Testudines: Trionychidae)." Chelonian Cons Biol 1(4): 301-10.

Whitaker, N. and J. Vijaya (2009). "Biology of the Forest Cane Turtle, Vijayachelys silvatica, in South India." Chelonian Cons Biol 8(2): 109-115.

Willey, J. S. and R. W. Blob (2004). "Tail Kinematics of Juvenile Common Snapping Turtles during Aquatic Walking." J Herpetol 38(3): 360-369.

Chapter 4: Turtles Round The World Ii: Terrapins And Tortoises

Anon. (2000). a Survey Report on Zambia As a Range State For Pancake Tortoise. CITES CoP13 Inf. 4: 1-5.

Anon. (2007). "Erratum: "A New Species of the Genus Geoemyda (Chelonii: Geoemydidae) From the Upper Pleistocene of Tokunoshima Island, the Central Ryukyus, Japan", By Akio Takahashi, Takafumi Kato, and Hidetoshi Ota, Current Herpetology 26(1): 1–11, 2007." Current Herpetology 26(2): 139-139.

Ashton, K. G., B. M. Engelhardt, et al. (2008). "Gopher Tortoise (Gopherus polyphemus) Abundance and Distribution After Prescribed Fire Reintroduction to Florida Scrub and Sandhill At Archbold Biological Station." J Herpetol 42(3): 523-529.

Ataev, C. A., B. Farkas, et al. (1997). "Reptiles of the Autonomous Republic of Turkmenistan." Chelonian Cons Biol 2(4): 627-34.

Attum, O., S. B. E. Din, et al. (2007). "An Evaluation of the Taxonomic Validity of Testudo werneri." Amphibia-Reptilia 28 393-401.

Austin, J. J., E. N. Arnold, et al. (2003). "Was There a Second Adaptive Radiation of Giant Tortoises in the Indian Ocean? Using Mitochondrial DNA to Investigate Speciation and Biogeography of Aldabrachelys (Reptilia, Testudinidae)." Molecular Ecology 12(6): 1415-1424.

Austin, J. J., E. Nicholas Arnold, et al. (2002). "The Provenance of Type Specimens of Extinct Mascarene Island Giant Tortoises (Cylindraspis) Revealed By Ancient Mitochondrial DNA Sequences." J Herpetol 36(2): 280-285.

Barth, D., D. Bernhard, et al. (2004). "The Freshwater Turtle Genus Mauremys (Testudines, Geoemydidae) — a Textbook Example of an East–West Disjunction or a Taxonomic Misconcept?" Zoologica Scripta 33(3): 213-221.

Bayoff, N. (1995). "Observations and Morphometric Data on the Namaqualand Speckled Tortoise, Homopus signatus signatus (Gmelin, 1789), in South Africa." Chelonian Cons Biol 1(3): 215-20.

Behler, J. L., et al. (1993). "New Localities for Pyxis planicauda in West-Central Madagascar." Chelonian Cons Biol 1(1): 49-51.

Branch, W. R. (2007). "A New Species of Tortoise of the Genus Homopus (Chelonia: Testudinidae) From Southern Namibia." African J Herpetol 56(1): 1-21.

Brown, P. (2004). Scientists Held Hostage on Darwin's Island. the Guardian.

Burns, C. E., C. Ciofi, et al. (2003). "The Origin of Captive Galápagos Tortoises Based on DNA Analysis: Implications For the Management of Natural Populations." Animal Conservation 6(4): 329-337.

Butler, J. A., et al. (1995). "Movements and Home Range of Hatchling and Yearling Gopher Tortoises, Gopherus polyphemus." Chelonian Cons Biol 1(3): 173-80.

Caccone, A., et al. (1999). "Origin and Evolutionary Relationships of Giant Galápagos Tortoises." Proceedings of the National Academy of Sciences 96.23: 13223-28.

Caccone, A., G. Gentile, et al. (2002). "Phylogeography and History of Giant Galapagos Tortoises." Evolution 56(10): 2052-2066.

Cadi, A. and P. Joly (2003). "Competition For Basking Places Between the Endangered European Pond Turtle (Emys orbicularis galloitalica) and the Introduced Red-Eared Slider (Trachemys scripta elegans)." Canadian J Zool 81(8): 1392-1398.

Cadi, A. and P. Joly (2004). "Impact of the Introduction of the Red-Eared Slider (Trachemys scripta elegans) on Survival Rates of the European Pond Turtle (Emys Orbicularis)." Biodiversity and Conservation 13: 2511-2518.

Cadi, A., V. Delmas, et al. (2004). "Successful Reproduction of the Introduced Slider Turtle(Trachemys scripta elegans) in the South of France." Aquatic Conservation: Marine and Freshwater Ecosystems 14(3): 237-246.

Carr, J. L. (2008). "Terrestrial Foraging By Two Species of Semiaquatic Turtles (Testudines: Emydidae)." Southeastern Naturalist 7(4): 748-752.

Chanard, T., K. Thirakhupt, et al. (1996). "Observations on Manouria impressa at Phu Luang Wildlife Sanctuary, Northeastern Thailand." Chelonian Cons Biol 2(1): 109-13.

Chiari, Y. and J. Claude (2011). "Study of the Carapace Shape and Growth in Two Galápagos Tortoise Lineages." J Morphol 272(3): 379-386.

Ciofi, C., M. C. Milinkovitch, et al. (2002). "Microsatellite Analysis of Genetic Divergence Among Populations of Giant Galápagos Tortoises." Molecular Ecology 11(11): 2265-2283.

Cunningham, P. L. and A. Simang (2008). "Ecology of the Bushmanland Tent Tortoise (*Psammobates tentorius verroxii*) in Southern Namibia." Chelonian Cons Biol 7(1): 119-124.

Dalton, R. (2003). "Mock Turtles." Nature 423: 219-220.

Daniels, S. R., M. D. Hofmeyr, et al. (2010). "Systematics and Phylogeography of a Threatened Tortoise, the Speckled Padloper." Animal Conservation 13(3): 237-246.

Darwin, Charles (2000). *The Voyage of the Beagle*. Great Minds Series. Amherst, NY: Prometheus Books.

Dinerstein, E., G. R. Zug, et al. (1987). "Notes on the Biology of *Melanochelys* (Reptilia, Testudines, Emydidae) in the Terai of Nepal." J. Bombay Nat. Hist. Soc. 84(3): 687-88.

Ennen, J. R., B. R. Kreiser, et al. (2010). "Morphological and Molecular Reassessment of *Graptemys oculifera* and *Graptemys flavimaculata* (Testudines: Emydidae)." J Herpetol 44(4): 544-554.

Ennen, J. R., J. E. Lovich, et al. (2010). "Genetic and Morphological Variation Between Populations of the Pascagoula Map Turtle (*Graptemys gibbonsi*) in the Pearl and Pascagoula Rivers with Description of a New Species." Chelonian Cons Biol 9(1): 98-113.

Fidenci, P. and J. Maran (2009). "Illegal Domestic Trade of the Philippine Forest Turtle (*Siebenrockiella leytensis*) in the Philippines." Turtlelog 3: 1-3.

Frazier, J. (2009). "Case 3463 *Testudo gigantea* Schweigger, 1812 (Currently *Geochelone* (*Aldabrachelys*) *gigantea*; Reptilia, Testudines): Proposed Conservation of Usage of the Specific Name By Maintenance of a Designated Neotype, and Suppression of *Testudo dussumieri* Gray, 1831 (Currently *Dipsochelys dussumieri*)." Bulletin of Zoological Nomenclature 66(1): 34-50.

Fritz, U., D. Guicking, et al. (2008). "Diversity of the Southeast Asian Leaf Turtle Genus *Cyclemys*: How Many Leaves on Its Tree of Life?" Zoologica Scripta 37(4): 367-390.

Fritz, U., M. Auer, et al. (2006). "A Rangewide Phylogeography of Hermann's Tortoise, *Testudo hermanni* (Reptilia: Testudines: Testudinidae): Implications For Taxonomy." Zoologica Scripta 35(5): 531-543.

Fritz, U., M. Barata, et al. (2006). "Impact of Mountain Chains, Sea Straits and Peripheral Populations on Genetic and Taxonomic Structure of a Freshwater Turtle, *Mauremys leprosa* (Reptilia, Testudines, Geoemydidae)." Zoologica Scripta 35(1): 97-108.

Fritz, U., S. R. Daniels, et al. (2010). "Mitochondrial Phylogeography and Subspecies of the Wide-Ranging Sub-Saharan Leopard Tortoise *Stigmochelys pardalis* (Testudines: Testudinidae) – a Case Study For the Pitfalls of Pseudogenes and Genbank Sequences." J Zool Syst Evol Res 48(4): 348-359.

Fritz, U., T. Fattizzo, et al. (2005). "A New Cryptic Species of Pond Turtle From Southern Italy, the Hottest Spot in the Range of the Genus *Emys* (Reptilia, Testudines, Emydidae)." Zoologica Scripta 34(4): 351-371.

Gerlach, J. (2004). "Effects of Diet on the Systematic Utility of the Tortoise Carapace." African J Herpetol 53(1): 77-85.

Gerlach, J. (2008). "Redescription of the Skull of the Extinct Madagascan Giant Tortoise, *Dipsochelys abrupta*." Chelonian Cons Biol 7(2): 251-255.

Gerlach, J., and L. Canning (1998). "Identification of Seychelles Giant Tortoises." Chelonian Cons Biol 3(1): 133-35.

Gerlach, J., and L. Canning (1998). "Taxonomy of Indian Ocean Giant Tortoises (*Dipsochelys*)." Chelonian Cons Biol 3(1): 3-19.

Gerlach, J., C. Muir, et al. (2006). "The First Substantiated Case of Trans-Oceanic Tortoise Dispersal." J Nat Hist 40(41): 2403-2408.

Germano, D. J. (2010). "Ecology of Western Pond Turtles (*Actinemys marmorata*) At Sewage-Treatment Facilities in the San Joaquin Valley, California." Southwest Nat 55(1): 89-97.

Gibbs, J. P., C. Marquez, et al. (2008). "The Role of Endangered Species Reintroduction in Ecosystem Restoration: Tortoise–Cactus Interactions on Española Island, Galápagos." Restoration Ecology 16(1): 88-93.

Greaves, W. F. and J. D. Litzgus (2009). "Variation in Life-History Characteristics Among Populations of North American Wood Turtles: a View From the North." J Zool 279(3): 298-309.

Griffin, D., D. Owens, et al. "Diamondback terrapin *Malaclemys terrapin*." Retrieved 1 July, 2011, from http://www.dnr.sc.gov/cwcs/pdf/diamondbackterrapin.pdf.

Hailey, A. and M. R. K. Lambert (2002). "Comparative Growth Patterns in Afrotropical Giant Tortoises (Reptilia Testudinidae)." Tropical Zoology 15: 121-139.

Harfush-Meléndez, M. and J. R. Buskirk (2008). "New Distributional Data on the Tehuantepec Slider, *Trachemys grayi*, in Oaxaca, Mexico." Chelonian Cons Biol 7(2): 274-276.

Harless, M. L., A. D. Walde, et al. (2009). "Home Range, Spatial Overlap, and Burrow Use of the Desert Tortoise in the West Mojave Desert." Copeia 2009(2): 378-389.

Hart, K. M. and C. C. Mcivor (2008). "Demography and Ecology of Mangrove Diamondback Terrapins in a Wilderness Area of Everglades National Park, Florida, Usa." Copeia 2008(1): 200-208.

Herz, M. (2007). "Observations of Eurasian Terrapins in Iran, with Locality Records of *Mauremys caspica ventrimaculata* Wischuf & Fritz, 1996." Radiata 16(3): 54-59.

Hidalgo-Vila, J., C. Diaz-Paniagua, et al. (2009). "Helminth Communities of the Exotic Introduced Turtle, *Trachemys scripta elegans* in Southwestern Spain: Transmission From Native Turtles." Res Vet Sci 86(3): 463-465.

Hirayama, R., N. Kaneko, et al. (2007). "*Ocadia nipponica*, a New Species of Aquatic Turtle (Testudines: Testudinoidea: Geoemydidae) From the Middle Pleistocene of Chiba Prefecture, Central Japan." Paleontol Res 11: 1-19.

Holroyd, P. A. and J. F. Parham (2003). "The Antiquity of African Tortoises." J Vertebr Paleontol 23(3): 688-690.

Holroyd, P. A., J. F. Parham, et al. (2005). "A Reappraisal of Some Paleogene Turtles From the Southeastern United States." J Vertebr Paleontol 25(4): 979-982.

Honda, M., Y. Yasukawa, et al. (2002). "Phylogenetic Relationships of the Asian Box Turtles of the Genus *Cuora* Sensu Lato (Reptilia: Bataguridae) Inferred From Mitochondrial DNA Sequences." Zool Sci 19(11): 1305-1312.

Horne, B. D., R. J. Brauman, et al. (2003). "Reproductive and Nesting Ecology of the Yellow-Blotched Map Turtle, *Graptemys flavimaculata*: Implications For Conservation and Management." Copeia 2003(4): 729-738.

Howeth, J. G., S. E. Mcgaugh, et al. (2008). "Contrasting Demographic and Genetic Estimates of Dispersal in the Endangered Coahuilan Box Turtle: a Contemporary Approach to Conservation." Molecular Ecology 17(19): 4209-4221.

Invasive Species Specialist Group (undated). "*Trachemys scripta elegans* (Red-Eared Slider) Management Information."

Iverson, J. B., and W. P. McCord (1997). "Redescription of the Arakan Forest Turtle *Geoemyda depressa* Anderson 1875 (Testudines: Bataguridae)." Chelonian Cons Biol 2(3): 384-89.

Jackson, J. T., D. E. Starkey, et al. (2008). "A Mitochondrial DNA Phylogeny of Extant Species of the Genus *Trachemys* with Resulting Taxonomic Implications." Chelonian Cons Biol 7(1): 131-135.

Jones, J. C. and B. Dorr (2004). "Habitat Associations of Gopher Tortoise Burrows on Industrial Timberlands." Wildlife Society Bulletin 32(2): 456-464.

Kazmaier, R. T., E. C. Hellgren, et al. (2001). "Effects of Grazing on the Demography and Growth of the Texas Tortoise." Conservation Biology 15(4): 1091-1101.

Lawson, D. P. (2001). "Morphometrics and Sexual Dimorphism of the Hinge-Back Tortoises *Kinixys erosa* and *Kinixys homeana* (Reptilia: Testudinidae) in Southwestern Cameroon." African J Herpetol 50(1): 1-7.

Lindeman, P. V. (1998). "Of Deadwood and Map Turtles (*Graptemys*): an Analysis of Species Status for Five Species in Three River Drainages Using Replicated Spotting-Scope Counts of Basking Turtles." Chelonian Cons Biol 3(1): 137-41.

Litzgus, J. D. and T. A. Mousseau (2004). "Demography of a Southern Population of the Spotted Turtle (*Clemmys guttata*)." Southeastern Naturalist 3(3): 391-400.

Loehr, V. J. T. (2002). "Population Characteristics and Activity Patterns of the Namaqualand Speckled Padloper (*Homopus signatus signatus*) in the Early Spring." J Herpetol 36(3): 378-389.

Loehr, V. J. T. (2010). "Structure and Dynamics of a Namaqualand Speckled Tortoise (*Homopus signatus signatus*) Population Over 5 Years of Rainfall Variation." Chelonian Cons Biol 9(2): 223-230.

Loehr, V. J. T., M. D. Hofmeyr, et al. (2009). "Small and Sensitive to Drought: Consequences of Aridification to the Conservation of *Homopus signatus signatus*." African J Herpetol 58(2): 116-125.

Lovich, J. and K. Meyer (2002). "The Western Pond Turtle (*Clemmys marmorata*) in the Mojave River, California, Usa: Highly Adapted Survivor or Tenuous Relict?" J Zool 256(4): 537-545.

Luiselli, L., E. Politano, et al. (2006). "Assessment of the Vulnerable Status of *Kinixys homeana* (Testudines: Testudinidae) For the Iucn Red List." Chelonian Cons Biol 5(1): 130-138.

Ly, T., H. D. Hoang, et al. (2011). "Market Turtle Mystery Solved in Vietnam." Biol Conserv.

Malonza, P. K. (2003). "Ecology and Distribution of the Pancake Tortoise, *Malacochersus tornieri* in Kenya." J East African Nat Hist 92(1): 81-96.

Mann, G. K. H., M. J. O'riain, et al. (2006). "Shaping Up to Fight: Sexual Selection Influences Body Shape and Size in the Fighting Tortoise (*Chersina angulata*)." J Zool 269(3): 373-379.

Manzano, A. S., J. I. Noriega, et al. (2009). "The Tropical Tortoise *Chelonoidis denticulata* (Testudines: Testudinidae) From the Late Pleistocene of Argentina and Its Paleoclimatological Implications." J Paleontol 83(6): 975-980.

McCord, W. P. (1997). "*Mauremys pritchardi* a New Batagurid Turtle from Myanmar and Yunnan, China." Chelonian Cons Biol 2(4): 555-62.

McCord, W. P., J. B. Iverson, et al. (1995). "A New Batagurid Turtle from Northern Sulawesi, Indonesia." Chelonian Cons Biol 1(4): 311-16.

McMahon, L., and M. Fraser (1998). *a Fynbos Year*. Cape Town and Johannesburg: David Philip.

Mcmaster, M. K. and C. T. Downs (2006). "Population Structure and Density of Leopard Tortoises (*Geochelone pardalis*) on Farmland in the Nama-Karoo." J Herpetol 40(4): 495-502.

Mcneish, H. (2011, 27 June). "Madagascar's 'Tortoise Mafia' on the Attack." Retrieved 3 July, 2011.

Meylan, P. A. and W. Sterrer (2000). "*Hesperotestudo* (Testudines: Testudinidae) From the Pleistocene of Bermuda, with Comments on the Phylogenetic Position of the Genus." Zool J Linn Soc 128(1): 51-76.

Mitrus, S. (2010). "Is the European Pond Turtle *Emys orbicularis* Strictly Aquatic? - Habitats Where the Turtle Lives in Central Europe." Acta Herpetologica 5(1): 31-35.

Murphy, R., K. Berry, et al. (2011). "The Dazed and Confused Identity of Agassiz's Land Tortoise, *Gopherus agassizii* (Testudines: Testudinidae) with the Description of a New Species and Its Consequences For Conservation." Zookeys 113(2011): 39-71.

Nelson, B. (2007). "Tortoise Genes and Islands Beings: Giant Galápagos Reptiles on Slow Road to Recovery." Science News 172(19): 298-300.

Niederberger, A. J., and M.E. Seidel (1999). "Ecology and Status of a Wood Turtle (*Clemmys insculpta*) Population in West Virginia." Chelonian Cons Biol 3(3): 414-18.

Olson, S. L. and P. A. Meylan (2009). "A Second Specimen of the Pleistocene Bermuda Tortoise, *Hesperotestudo bermudae* Meylan and Sterrer." Chelonian Cons Biol 8(2): 211-212.

Olson, S. L., P. J. Hearty, et al. (2006). "Geological Constraints on Evolution and Survival in Endemic Reptiles on Bermuda." J Herpetol 40(3): 394-398.

Outerbridge, M. E. (2008). "Ecological Notes on Feral Populations of *Trachemys scripta elegans* in Bermuda." Chelonian Cons Biol 7(2): 265-269.

Palkovacs, E. P., M. Marschner, et al. (2003). "Are the Native Giant Tortoises From the Seychelles Really Extinct? a Genetic Perspective Based on Mtdna and Microsatellite Data." Molecular Ecology 12(6): 1403-1413.

Parham, J. F., W. B. Simison, et al. (2001). "New Chinese Turtles: Endangered or Invalid? a Reassessment of Two Species Using Mitochondrial DNA, Allozyme Electrophoresis and Known-Locality Specimens." Animal Conservation 4(4): 357-367.

Perälä, J. (2001). "A New Species of Testudo (Testudines: Testudinidae) From the Middle East, with Implications For Conservation." J Herpetol 35(4): 567-582.

Perez-Santigosa, N., C. Díaz-Paniagua, et al. (2008). "The Reproductive Ecology of Exotic *Trachemys scripta elegans* in an Invaded Area of Southern Europe." Aquatic Conservation: Marine and Freshwater Ecosystems 18(7): 1302-1310.

Pittman, S. E. and M. E. Dorcas (2009). "Movements, Habitat Use, and Thermal Ecology of an Isolated Population of Bog Turtles (*Glyptemys muhlenbergii*)." Copeia 2009(4): 781-790.

Platt, K., S. G. Platt, et al. (2008). "Recent Records and Conservation Status of the Critically Endangered Mangrove Terrapin, *Batagur baska*, in Myanmar." Chelonian Cons Biol 7(2): 261-265.

Platt, S. G., K. M. Myo, et al. (2010). "Field Observations and Conservation of *Heosemys depressa* in the Rakhine Yoma Elephant Range of Western Myanmar." Chelonian Cons Biol 9(1): 114-119.

Polo-Cavia, N., P. López, et al. (2008). "Interspecific Differences in Responses to Predation Risk May Confer Competitive Advantages to Invasive Freshwater Turtle Species." Ethology 114(2): 115-123.

Praschag, P., A. K. Hundsdörfer, et al. (2007). "Phylogeny and Taxonomy of Endangered South and South-East Asian Freshwater Turtles Elucidated By MtDNA Sequence Variation (Testudines: Geoemydidae: *Batagur, Callagur, Hardella, Kachuga, Pangshura*)." Zoologica Scripta 36(5): 429-442.

Prévot-Julliard, A.-C., E. Gousset, et al. (2007). "Pets and Invasion Risks: is the Slider Turtle Strictly Carnivorous?" Amphibia-Reptilia 28(139-143).

Pritchard, P. C. H. (1992) "Tortoise Life." Testudo 3 (4): 9-13.

Pritchard, P. C. H. (1996). "The Galápagos Tortoises: Nomenclatural and Survival Status." Chelonian Research Monographs 1: 1-85.

Ramesh, M. (2008). "Relative Abundance and Morphometrics of the Travancore Tortoise, *Indotestudo travancorica*, in the Indira Gandhi Wildlife Sanctuary, Southern Western Ghats, India." Chelonian Cons Biol 7(1): 108-113.

Reeves, D. J. and J. D. Litzgus (2008). "Demography of an Island Population of Spotted Turtles (*Clemmys guttata*) At the Species' Northern Range Limit." Northeastern Naturalist 15(3): 417-430.

Reynoso, V. Ç.-H. and M. Montellano-Ballesteros (2004). "A New Giant Turtle of the Genus *Gopherus* (Chelonia: Testudinidae) From the Pleistocene of Tamaulipas, México, and a Review of the Phylogeny and Biogeography of Gopher Tortoises." J Vertebr Paleontol 24(4): 822-837.

Riedle, J. D., R. C. Averill-Murray, et al. (2008). "Habitat Use By Desert Tortoises (*Gopherus agassizii*) on Alluvial Fans in the Sonoran Desert, South-Central Arizona." Copeia 2008(2): 414-420.

Riyanto, A. (2006). "Notes on Exploitation, Population Status, Distribution, and Natural History of the Sulawesi Forest Turtle (*Leucocephalon yuwonoi*) in North-Central Sulawesi, Indonesia." Chelonian Cons Biol 5(2): 320-323.

Rosenbaum, P. A. and A. P. Nelson (2010). "Bog Turtle Habitat on the Lake Ontario Coastal Plain of New York State." Northeastern Naturalist 17(3): 415-436.

Sánchez-Villagra, M. R. and T. M. Scheyer (2010). Fossil Turtles From the Northern Neotropics: the Urumaco Sequence and Finds From Other Localities in Venezuela and Colombia. Urumaco and Venezuelan Paleontology the Fossil Record of the Northern Neotropics. M. R. Sánchez-Villagra, O. A. Aguilera and A. A. Carlini. Bloomington, Indiana, Indiana University Press: pp. 173-191.

Sasaki, T., Y. Yasukawa, et al. (2006). "Extensive Morphological Convergence and Rapid Radiation in the Evolutionary History of the Family Geoemydidae (Old World Pond Turtles) Revealed By Sine Insertion Analysis." Systematic Biology 55(6): 912-927.

Schoppe, S. (2009). Status, Trade Dynamics and Management of the Southeast Asian Box Turtle in Indonesia. Petaling Jaya, Selangor, Malaysia, TRAFFIC Southeast Asia.

Schoppe, S., J. Matillano, et al. (2010). "Conservation Needs of the Critically Endangered Philippine Forest Turtle, *Siebenrockiella leytensis*, in Palawan, Philippines." Chelonian Cons Biol 9(2): 145-153.

Seidel, M. E. (2002). "Taxonomic Observations on Extant Species and Subspecies of Slider Turtles, Genus *Trachemys*." J Herpetol 36(2): 285-292.

Selman, W. and C. Qualls (2008). "The Impacts of Hurricane Katrina on a Population of Yellow-Blotched Sawbacks (*Graptemys flavimaculata*) in the Lower Pascagoula River." Herpetological Conservation and Biology 3(2): 224-230.

Selman, W. and C. Qualls (2009). "Distribution and Abundance of Two Imperiled *Graptemys* Species of the Pascagoula River System." Herpetological Conservation and Biology 4(2): 171-184.

Shen, J.-W., D. A. Pike, et al. (2010). "Movements and Microhabitat Use of Translocated Big-Headed Turtles (*Platysternon megacephalum*) in Southern China." Chelonian Cons Biol 9(2): 154-161.

Smith, L. L., et al. (1999). "Home Range and Microhabitat Use in the Angonoka (*Geochelone yniphora*) in Madagascar." Chelonian Cons Biol 3(3): 393-400.

Spinks, P. Q. and H. B. Shaffer (2009). "Conflicting Mitochondrial and Nuclear Phylogenies For the Widely Disjunct *Emys* (Testudines: Emydidae) Species Complex, and What They Tell Us About Biogeography and Hybridization." Syst. Biol. 58(1): 1-20.

Spinks, P. Q., R. C. Thomson, et al. (2009). "Assessing What is Needed to Resolve a Molecular Phylogeny: Simulations and Empirical Data From Emydid Turtles." BMC Evolutionary Biology 9: 56.

Starkey, D. E., H. B. Shaffer, et al. (2003). "Molecular Systematics, Phylogeography, and the Effects of Pleistocene Glaciation in the Painted Turtle (*Chrysemys picta*) Complex." Evolution 57(1): 119-128.

Stephens, P. R. and J. J. Wiens (2003). "Ecological Diversification and Phylogeny of Emydid Turtles." Biol J Linn Soc 79(4): 577-610.

Stuart, B. L. and U. W. E. Fritz (2008). "Historical DNA From Museum Type Specimens Clarifies Diversity of Asian Leaf Turtles (*Cyclemys*)." Biol J Linn Soc 94(1): 131-141.

Styrsky, J. N., C. Guyer, et al. (2010). "The Relationship Between Burrow Abundance and Area As a Predictor of Gopher Tortoise Population Size." Herpetologica 66(4): 403-410.

Suzuki, D. and T. Hikida (2010). "Mitochondrial Phylogeography of the Japanese Pond Turtle, *Mauremys japonica* (Testudines, Geoemydidae)." J Zool Syst Evol Res 49(2): 141-147.

Teillac-Deschamps, P., V. Delmas, et al. (2008). "Case Study 12: Red-Eared Slider Turtles (*Trachemys scripta elegans*) Introduced to French Urban Wetlands: an Integrated Research and Conservation Program." Herpetological Conservation 3: 535-537.

Tesauro, J. and D. Ehrenfeld (2007). "The Effects of Livestock Grazing on the Bog Turtle [*Glyptemys* (= *Clemmys*) *muhlenbergii*]." Herpetologica 63(3): 293-300.

Thomson, R. C., P. Q. Spinks, et al. (2010). "Distribution and Abundance of Invasive Red-Eared Sliders (*Trachemys scripta elegans*) in California's Sacramento River Basin and Possible Impacts on Native Western Pond Turtles (*Emys marmorata*)." Chelonian Cons Biol 9(2): 297-302.

Truett, J. P., Mike (2009). "Beyond Historic Baselines: Restoring Bolson Tortoises to Pleistocene Range." Ecological Restoration 27(2): 144-151.

Vasudevan, K., B. Pandav, et al. (2010). Ecology of Two Endemic Turtles in the Western Ghats: Final Technical Report. Chandrabani, Dehradun, Wildlife Institute of India: 1-74.

Waddle, J. H., F. J. Mazzotti, et al. (2006). "Changes in Abundance of Gopher Tortoise Burrows At Cape Sable, Florida." Southeastern Naturalist 5(2): 277-284.

Whitaker, N. and J. Vijaya (2009). "Biology of the Forest Cane Turtle, *Vijayachelys silvatica*, in South India." Chelonian Cons Biol 8(2): 109-115.

Whitelaw, D. M. and R. N. Zajac (2002). "Assessment of Prey Availability For Diamondback Terrapins in a Connecticut Salt Marsh." Northeastern Naturalist 9(4): 407-418.

Wiens, J. J., C. A. Kuczynski, et al. (2010). "Discordant Mitochondrial and Nuclear Gene Phylogenies in Emydid Turtles: Implications For Speciation and Conservation." Biol J Linn Soc 99(2): 445-461.

Zhang, Y., J.-Y. Zhang, et al. (2010). "Isolation and Characterization of 14 Polymorphic Microsatellite Loci in the Asian Yellow Pond Turtle, *Mauremys mutica* (Cantor, 1842)." Aquaculture Research 41(9): e353-e356.

Zug, G. R. (1997). "Galápagos Tortoise Nomenclature: Still Unresolved." Chelonian Cons Biol 2(4): 618-19.

Zylstra, E. R. and R. J. Steidl (2009). "Habitat Use by Sonoran Desert Tortoises." J Wildlife Manage 73(5): 747-754.

Chapter 5: Under The Hood

Albright III, L. B., M. O. Woodburne, et al. (2003). "A Leatherback Sea Turtle From the Eocene of Antarctica: Implications For Antiquity of Gigantothermy in Dermochelyidae." J Vertebr Paleontol 23(4): 945-949.

Avery, R. A. (1982). "Field Studies of Body Temperatures and Thermoregulation." Biology of the Reptilia: Physiology C. Physiological Ecology. Ed. Carl and Pough Gans, F. Harvey. Vol. 12. New York: Academic Press. pp. 93-166.

Bagatto, B. P., and R. P. Henry (1999). "Aerial and Aquatic Respiration in the Snapping Turtle, *Chelydra serpentina*." J Herpetol 33 (3): 490-92.

Bagatto, B., and R. P. Henry (1999). "Exercise and Forced Submergence in the Pond Slider (*Trachemys scripta*) and Softshell Turtle (*Apalone ferox*): Influence on Bimodal Gas Exchange, Diving Behavior and Blood Acid-Base Status." J Exp Biol 202: 267-78.

Bagatto, B., and R. P. Henry (2000). "Bimodal Respiration and Ventilatory Behavior in Two Species of Central American Turtles: Effects of Forced Emergence." Comparative Biochemistry and Physiology 126: 57-63.

Bagatto, B., et al. (1997) "Bimodal Respiration in Two Species of Central American Turtles." Copeia 1997(4): 834-39.

Bartholomew, G. A. (1982). "Physiological Control of Body Temperature." Biology of the Reptilia: Physiology C. Physiological Ecology. Ed. Carl and Pough Gans, F. Harvey. Vol. 12. New York: Academic Press. pp. 167-211.

Ben-Ezra, E., G. Bulté, et al. (2008). "Are Locomotor Performances Coadapted to Preferred Basking Temperature in the Northern Map Turtle (*Graptemys geographica*)?" J Herpetol 42(2): 322-331.

Bentivegna, F., S. Hochscheid, et al. (2003). "Seasonal Variability in Voluntary Dive Duration of the Mediterranean Loggerhead Turtle, *Caretta caretta*." Scientia Marina 67 (3): 371-375.

Bernstein, N. P. and R. W. Black (2005). "Thermal Environment of Overwintering Ornate Box Turtles, *Terrapene ornata ornata*, in Iowa." Am Midl Nat153(2): 370-377.

Brown, G. P., and R. J. Brooks (1991). "Thermal and Behavioral Responses to Feeding in Free-Ranging Turtles, *Chelydra serpentina*." J Herpetol 25 (3): 273-78.

Bulté, G. and G. Blouin-Demers (2010). "Estimating the Energetic Significance of Basking Behaviour in a Temperate-Zone Turtle." Ecoscience 17(4): 387-393.

Carrière, M.-A., N. Rollinson, et al. (2008). "Thermoregulation When the Growing Season is Short: Sex-Biased Basking Patterns in a Northern Population of Painted Turtles (*Chrysemys picta*)." J Herpetol 42(1): 206-209.

Clark, N. J., M. A. Gordos, et al. (2008). "Diving Behaviour, Aquatic Respiration and Blood Respiratory Properties: a Comparison of Hatchling and Juvenile Australian Turtles." J Zool 275(4): 399-406.

Coleman, J. L. and R. L. Gutberlet (2008). "Seasonal Variation in Basking in Two Syntopic Species of Map Turtles (Emydidae: *Graptemys*)." Chelonian Cons Biol 7(2): 276-281.

Coles, W., J. A. Musick, et al. (2000). "Satellite Sea Surface Temperature Analysis and Correlation with Sea Turtle Distribution Off North Carolina." Copeia 2000(2): 551-554.

Converse, S. J. and J. A. Savidge (2003). "Ambient Temperature, Activity, and Microhabitat Use By Ornate Box Turtles (*Terrapene ornata ornata*)." J Herpetol 37(4): 665-670.

Converse, S. J., J. B. Iverson, et al. (2002). "Activity, Reproduction and Overwintering Behavior of Ornate Box Turtles (*Terrapene ornata ornata*) in the Nebraska Sandhills." Am Midl Nat148(2): 416-422.

Costanzo, J. P., R. E. Lee, et al. (2008). "Physiological Ecology of Overwintering in Hatchling Turtles." J Exp Zool Part A: Ecological Genetics and Physiology 309a(6): 297-379.

Crocker, C. E., et al. (2000). "Physiology of Common Map Turtles (*Graptemys geographica*) Hibernating in the Lamoille River, Vermont." J Exp Zool 286: 143-48.

Delmas, V., E. Baudry, et al. (2007). "The Righting Response As a Fitness Index in Freshwater Turtles." Biol J Linn Soc 91(1): 99-109.

Di Trani, C., and M. A. L. Zuffi (1997). "Thermoregulation of the European Pond Turtle, *Emys orbicularis* in Central Italy." Chelonian Cons Biol 2 (3): 428-30.

Dinkelacker, S. A., J. P. Costanzo, et al. (2005). "Anoxia Tolerance and Freeze Tolerance in Hatchling Turtles." J Comp Physiol B 175: 209-217.

Douglas, R. M. and M. Rall (2006). "Seasonal Shelter Selection By Leopard Tortoises (*Geochelone pardalis*) in the Franklin Nature Reserve, Free State, South Africa." Chelonian Cons Biol 5(1): 121-129.

Dubois, Y., G. Blouin-Demers, et al. (2008). "Temperature Selection in Wood Turtles (*Glyptemys insculpta*) and Its Implications For Energetics." Ecoscience 15(3): 398-406.

Dubois, Y., G. Blouin-Demers, et al. (2009). "Thermoregulation and Habitat Selection in Wood Turtles *Glyptemys insculpta*: Chasing the Sun Slowly." J Animal Ecol 78(5): 1023-1032.

Eckert, S. A., et al. (1996). "Shallow Water Diving by Leatherback Turtles in the South China Sea." Chelonian Cons Biol 2 (2): 237–243.

Fao (2004). Report of the Expert Consultation on Interactions Between Sea Turtles and Fisheries within an Ecosystem Context. Rome, Italy, 9-12 March 2004. Fao Fisheries Report. Rome. No. 738: 37p.

Feltz, J. and J. Tamplin (2007). "Effect of Substrate on Selected Temperature in Juvenile Spiny Softshell Turtles (*Apalone spinifera*)." Chelonian Cons Biol 6(2): 177-184.

Filippi, E., L. Rugiero, et al. (2010). "Population and Thermal Ecology of *Testudo hermanni hermanni* in the Tolfa Mountains of Central Italy." Chelonian Cons Biol 9(1): 54-60.

Glen, F., A. C. Broderick, et al. (2006). "Rhythmic Throat Oscillations in Nesting Green Turtles (*Chelonia mydas*)." Chelonian Cons Biol 5(2): 299-301.

Gordos, M. A., M. Hamann, et al. (2007). "Diving Behaviour of *Elseya albagula* From a Naturally Flowing and Hydrologically Altered Habitat." J Zool 272(4): 458-469.

Gordos, M. and C. E. Franklin (2002). "Diving Behaviour of Two Australian Bimodally Respiring Turtles, *Rheodytes leukops* and *Emydura macquarii*, in a Natural Setting." J Zool 258(3): 335-342.

Graham, T. E., and R. W. Guimond (1995). "Aquatic Oxygen Consumption by Wintering Red-Bellied Turtles." J Herpetol 29 (3): 471-74.

Hall, D. H. and R. J. Steidl (2007). "Movements, Activity, and Spacing of Sonoran Mud Turtles (*Kinosternon sonoriense*) in Interrupted Mountain Streams." Copeia 2007(2): 403-412.

Hays, G. (2008). "Sea Turtles: a Review of Some Key Recent Discoveries and Remaining Questions." J Exp Mar Biol Ecol 356(1-2): 1-7.

Heiss, E., N. Natchev, et al. (2010). "The Fish in the Turtle: on the Functionality of the Oropharynx in the Common Musk Turtle *Sternotherus odoratus* (Chelonia, Kinosternidae) Concerning Feeding and Underwater Respiration." the Anatomical Record: Advances in Integrative Anatomy and Evolutionary Biology 293(8): 1416-1424.

Houghton, J. D., T. K. Doyle, et al. (2008). "The Role of Infrequent and Extraordinary Deep Dives in Leatherback Turtles (*Dermochelys coriacea*)." J Exp Biol 211(Pt 16): 2566-2575.

Huestis, D. L. and P. A. Meylan (2004). "The Turtles of Rainbow Run (Marion County, Florida): Observations on the Genus *Pseudemys*." Southeastern Naturalist 3(4): 595-612.

Inozemtsev, A. A., and S. L. Pereshkolnik (1994). "Status and Conservation Prospects of *Testudo graeca* L. Inhabiting the Black Sea Coast of the Caucasus." Chelonian Cons Biol 1 (2): 151-58.

Jackson, D. C. (2000). "How a Turtle's Shell Helps it Survive Prolonged Anoxic Acidosis." News Physiol. Sci. 15: 181-85.

Jackson, D. C. (2000). "Living without Oxygen: Lessons from the Freshwater Turtle." Comparative Biochemistry and Physiology 125: 299-315.

Jackson, D. C. and G. R. Ultsch (2010). "Physiology of Hibernation Under the Ice By Turtles and Frogs." J Exp Zool a Ecol Genet Physiol 313(6): 311-327.

Jackson, D. C., C. E. Crocker, et al. (2000). "Bone and Shell Contribution to Lactic Acid Buffering of Submerged Turtles *Chrysemys picta bellii* at 3°C." Am. J. Physiol. Regulatory Integrative Comp. Physiol. 278: R1564-R71.

Jackson, D. C., et al. (2000). "Lactic Acid Buffering by Bone and Shell in Anoxic Softshell and Painted Turtles." Physiological and Biochemical Zoology 73 (3): 290-97.

Jackson, D. C., et al. (1999). "Ionic Exchanges of Turtle Shell in Vitro and Their Relevance to Shell Function in the Anoxic Turtle." J Exp Biol 202 (5): 513-20.

James, M. C. and N. Mrosovsky (2004). "Body Temperatures of Leatherback Turtles (*Dermochelys coriacea*) in Temperate Waters Off Nova Scotia, Canada." Canadian J Zool 82(8): 1302-1306.

James, M., J. Davenport, et al. (2006). "Expanded Thermal Niche For a Diving Vertebrate: a Leatherback Turtle Diving Into Near-Freezing Water." J Exp Mar Biol Ecol 335(2): 221-226.

Janzen, F. J., G. L. Paukstis, et al. (1992). "Observations on Basking Behavior of Hatchling Turtles in the Wild." J Herpetol 26 (2): 217-19.

King, P., and H. Heatwole (1999). "Seasonal Comparison of Hemoglobins in Three Species of Turtles." J Herpetol 33 (4): 691-94.

Kinneary, J. J. (1993). "Salinity Relations of *Chelydra serpentina* in a Long Island Estuary." J Herpetol 27 (4): 441-46.

Kinneary, J. J. (2008). "Observations on Terrestrial Feeding Behavior and Growth in Diamondback Terrapin (*Malaclemys*) and Snapping Turtle (*Chelydra*) Hatchlings." Chelonian Cons Biol 7(1): 118-119.

Lee, S. M. L., W. P. Wong, et al. (2006). "Nitrogen Metabolism and Excretion in the Aquatic Chinese Soft-Shelled Turtle, *Pelodiscus sinensis*, Exposed to a Progressive Increase in Ambient Salinity." J Exp Zool A 305a(12): 995-1009.

Lindeman, P. V. (1993) "Aerial Basking by Hatchling Freshwater Turtles." Herpetological Review 24 (3): 84-87.

Lyon, B., J. Seminoff, et al. (2006). Chelonia in and Out of the Jacuzzi: Diel Movements of East Pacific Green Turtles in San Diego Bay, USA. Twenty Sixth Annual Symposium on Sea Turtle Biology and Conservation. M. Frick, A. Panagopoulou, A. F. Rees and K. Williams. Crete, Greece., International Sea Turtle Society: 101.

Mcmahon, C. R., C. J. A. Bradshaw, et al. (2007). "Satellite Tracking Reveals Unusual Diving Characteristics For a Marine Reptile, the Olive Ridley Turtle *Lepidochelys olivacea*." Mar Ecol Prog Ser 329: 239-252.

Mcmaster, M. K. and C. T. Downs (2006). "Do Seasonal and Behavioral Differences in the Use of Refuges By the Leopard Tortoise (*Geochelone pardalis*) Favor Passive Thermoregulation?" Herpetologica 62(1): 37-46.

Muir, T. J., J. P. Costanzo, et al. (2010). "Brief Chilling to Subzero Temperature Increases Cold Hardiness in the Hatchling Painted Turtle (*Chrysemys picta*)." Physiol Biochem Zool 83(1): 174-181.

Nebeker, A. V., and R. B. Bury (2000). "Temperature Selection by Hatchling and Yearling Florida Red-Bellied Turtles (*Pseudemys nelsoni*) in Thermal Gradients." J Herpetol 34 (3): 465-69.

Packard, G. C. and M. J. Packard (2001). "The Overwintering Strategy of Hatchling Painted Turtles, or How to Survive in the Cold without Freezing." Bioscience 51(3): 199-207.

Packard, G. C., et al. (1999). "Tolerance for Freezing in Hatchling Turtles." J Herpetol 33 (4): 536-43.

Packard, G. C., M. J. Packard, et al. (2002). "Cold-Tolerance of Hatchling Painted Turtles (*Chrysemys picta bellii*) From the Southern Limit of Distribution." J Herpetol 36(2): 300-304.

Paladino, F. V., et al. (1996). "Respiratory Physiology of Adult Leatherback Turtles (*Dermochelys coriacea*) While Nesting on Land." Chelonian Cons Biol 2 (2): 223–29.

Peterson, C. C. and D. Greenshields (2001). "Negative Test For Cloacal Drinking in a Semi-Aquatic Turtle (*Trachemys scripta*), with Comments on the Functions of Cloacal Bursae." J Exp Zool 290(3): 247-254.

Peterson, C. C., and P. A. Stone (2000). "Physiological Capacity for Estivation of the Sonoran Mud Turtle, *Kinosternon sonoriense*." Copeia 2000 (3): 684-700.

Plummer, M. V., B. K. Williams, et al. (2003). "Effects of Dehydration on the Critical Thermal Maximum of the Desert Box Turtle (*Terrapene ornata luteola*)." J Herpetol 37(4): 747-750.

Priest, T. E. and C. E. Franklin (2002). "Effect of Water Temperature and Oxygen Levels on the Diving Behavior of Two Freshwater Turtles: *Rheodytes leukops* and *Emydura macquarii*." J Herpetol 36(4): 555-561.

Ramsay, S. L., M. D. Hofmeyr, et al. (2002). "Activity Patterns of the Angulate Tortoise (*Chersina angulata*) on Dassen Island, South Africa." J Herpetol 36(2): 161-169.

Reese, S. A., C. E. Crocker, et al. (2001). "The Physiology of Hibernation in Common Map Turtles (*Graptemys geographica*)." Comparative Biochemistry and Physiology Part a 130: 331-340.

Reina, R. D., T. T. Jones, et al. (2002). "Salt and Water Regulation By the Leatherback Sea Turtle *Dermochelys coriacea*." J Exp Biol 205: 1853-1860.

Rollinson, N., G. J. Tattersall, et al. (2008). "Overwintering Habitats of a Northern Population of Painted Turtles (*Chrysemys picta*): Winter Temperature Selection and Dissolved Oxygen Concentrations." J Herpetol 42(2): 312-321.

Rossell, C. R., I. M. Rossell, et al. (2006). "Microhabitat Selection By Eastern Box Turtles (*Terrapene c. carolina*) in a North Carolina Mountain Wetland." J Herpetol 40(2): 280-284.

Salmon, M., M. Hamann, et al. (2010). "The Development of Early Diving Behavior By Juvenile Flatback Sea Turtles (*Natator depressus*)." Chelonian Cons Biol 9(1): 8-17.

Salmon, M., T. Todd Jones, et al. (2004). "Ontogeny of Diving and Feeding Behavior in Juvenile Seaturtles: Leatherback Seaturtles (*Dermochelys coriacea* L) and Green Seaturtles (*Chelonia mydas* L) in the Florida Current." J Herpetol 38(1): 36-43.

Schofield, G., C. M. Bishop, et al. (2009). "Microhabitat Selection By Sea Turtles in a Dynamic Thermal Marine Environment." J Animal Ecol 78: 14-21.

Seymour, R. S. (1982). "Physiological Adaptations to Aquatic Life." Biology of the Reptilia: Physiology D; Physiological Ecology. Eds. C. Gans and F. H. Pough. Vol. 13. New York: Academic Press. pp. 1-51.

Storey, K.B., and J.M. Storey (1996). "Natural Freezing Survival in Animals." Ann. Rev. Ecol. Syst. 27: 365-86.

Swimmer, J. Y. (2006). "Relationship Between Basking and Fibropapillomatosis in Captive Green Turtles (*Chelonia mydas*)." Chelonian Cons Biol 5(2): 305-309.

Ultsch, G. R. (2006). "The Ecology of Overwintering Among Turtles: Where Turtles Overwinter and Its Consequences." Biological Reviews 81(3): 339-367.

Von Brandis, R. G., J. A. Mortimer, et al. (2010). "In-Water Observations of the Diving Behaviour of Immature Hawksbill Turtles, *Eretmochelys imbricata*, on a Coral Reef At D'arros Island, Republic of Seychelles." Chelonian Cons Biol 9(1): 26-32.

Wallace, B. and T. Jones (2008). "What Makes Marine Turtles Go: a Review of Metabolic Rates and Their Consequences." J Exp Mar Biol Ecol 356: 8-24.

Webb, G. J. W. (1978). "Observations on Basking in Some Australian Turtles (Reptilia: Testudines: Chelidae)." Herpetologica 34 (1): 39-42.

Willard, R., G. C. Packard, et al. (2000). "The Role of the Integument As a Barrier to Penetration of Ice Into Overwintering Hatchlings of the Painted Turtle (*Chrysemys picta*)." J Morphol 246(2): 150-159.

Chapter 6: Life As A Turtle

Adams, R. B., J. C. Pitman, et al. (2006). "Texas Tortoise (*Gopherus berlandieri*) Consumed By a Mountain Lion (Puma Concolor) in Southern Texas." Southwest Nat 51(4): 581-582.

Allan, S. A., L.-A. Simmons, et al. (1998). "Establishment of the Tortoise Tick *Amblyomma marmoreum* (Acari: Ixodidae) on a Reptile-Breeding Facility in Florida." J Medical Entomol 35(5): 621-624.

Allanson, M., and A. Georges (1999). "Diet of *Elseya purvisi* and *Elseya georgesi* (Testudines: Chelidae), a Sibling Species Pair of Freshwater Turtles from Eastern Australia." Chelonian Cons Biol 3 (3): 473-77.

Anon. "Arkive - Southern Ground Hornbill (*Bucorvus cafer*)." Retrieved 5 August, 2011, From Http://Www.Arkive.Org/Southern-Ground-Hornbill/Bucorvus-Cafer/Video-00.Html.

Aresco, M. J. (1999). "Habitat Structures Associated with Juvenile Gopher Tortoise Burrows on Pine Plantations in Alabama." Chelonian Cons Biol 3 (3): 507-09.

Aresco, M. J. (2010). "Competitive Interactions of Two Species of Freshwater Turtles, a Generalist Omnivore and an Herbivore, Under Low Resource Conditions." Herpetologica 66(3): 259-268.

Aresco, M. J. and J. L. Dobie (2000). "Variation in Shell Arching and Sexual Size Dimorphism of River Cooters, *Pseudemys concinna*, From Two River Systems in Alabama." J Herpetol 34(2): 313-317.

Ayres, C., M. Calviño-Cancela, et al. (2010). "Water Lilies, *Nymphaea alba*, in the Summer Diet of *Emys orbicularis* in Northwestern Spain: Use of Emergent Resources." Chelonian Cons Biol 9(1): 128-131.

Balensiefer, D. C. and R. C. Vogt (2006). "Diet of *Podocnemis unifilis* (Testudines, Podocnemididae) During the Dry Season in the Mamirauá Sustainable Development Reserve, Amazonas, Brazil." Chelonian Cons Biol 5(2): 312-317.

Barko, V. A. and J. T. Briggler (2006). "Midland Smooth Softshell (*Apalone mutica*) and Spiny Softshell (*Apalone spinifera*) Turtles in the Middle Mississippi River: Habitat Associations, Population Structure, and Implications For Conservation." Chelonian Cons Biol 5(2): 225-231.

Bauer, A. M. and C. J. Mccarthy (2010). "Darwin's Pet Galápagos Tortoise, *Chelonoidis darwini*, Rediscovered." Chelonian Cons Biol 9(2): 270-276.

Beaudry, F., P. G. Demaynadier, et al. (2009). "Seasonally Dynamic Habitat Use By Spotted (*Clemmys guttata*) and Blanding's Turtles (*Emydoidea blandingii*) in Maine." J Herpetol 43(4): 636-645.

Biggins, R. G., and R. S. Butler (2000). "Bringing Mussels Back in the Southeast." Endangered Species Bulletin 2000: 24-26.

Bjorndal, K. A., et al. (1997). "Dietary Overlap in Three Sympatric Congeneric Freshwater Turtles (*Pseudemys*) in Florida." Chelonian Cons Biol 2 (3): 430-33.

Bouchard, S. S. and K. A. Bjorndal (2005). "Microbial Fermentation in Juvenile and Adult Pond Slider Turtles, *Trachemys scripta*." J Herpetol 39(2): 321-324.

Brasil, M. A., G. De Freitas Horta, et al. (2011). "Feeding Ecology of *Acanthochelys spixii* (Testudines, Chelidae) in the Cerrado of CentralBrazil." Chelonian Cons Biol 10(1): 91-101.

Broderick, A. C., M. S. Coyne, et al. (2007). "Fidelity and Over-Wintering of Sea Turtles." Proceedings. Biological Sciences / the Royal Society 274(1617): 1533-1538.

Buhlmann, K. A. (1995). "Habitat Use, Terrestrial Movements, and Conservation of the Turtle, *Deirochelys reticularia* in Virginia." J Herpetol 29 (2): 173-81.

Burghardt, G. M. (1977). "Learning Processes in Reptiles." Biology of the Reptilia, Volume 7, Ecology and Behaviour A. Ed. C. Gans & DW Tinkle. New York: Academic Press. pp. 555-681.

Burgin, S. and A. Renshaw (2008). "Epizoochory, Algae and the Australian Eastern Long-Necked Turtle *Chelodina longicollis* (Shaw)." Am Midl Nat 160(1): 61-68.

Burgin, S. and M. Ryan (2008). "Comparison of Sympatric Freshwater Turtle Populations From an Urbanized Sydney Catchment." Aquatic Conservation: Marine and Freshwater Ecosystems 18(7): 1277-1284.

Burke, V. J., et al. (1993). "Common Snapping Turtles Associated with Ant Mounds." J Herpetol 27 (1): 114-15.

Bury, R. B., D. J. Germano, et al. (2010). "Population Structure and Growth of the Turtle *Actinemys marmorata* From the Klamath-Siskiyou Ecoregion: Age, Not Size, Matters." Copeia 2010(3): 443-451.

Butler, J. A., and S. Sowell (1996). "Survivorship and Predation of Hatchling and Yearling Gopher Tortoises, *Gopherus polyphemus*." J Herpetol 30(3): 455-58.

Calviño-Cancela, M., C. A. Fernández, et al. (2007). "European Pond Turtles (*Emys orbicularis*) As Alternative Dispersers of a "Water-Dispersed" Waterlily (*Nymphaea alba*)." Ecoscience 14(4): 529-534.

Caro, T. and H. B. Shaffer (2010). "Chelonian Antipredator Strategies: Preliminary and Comparative Data From Tanzanian *Pelusios*." Chelonian Cons Biol 9(2): 302-305.

Carrière, M.-A., G. Bulté, et al. (2009). "Spatial Ecology of Northern Map Turtles (*Graptemys geographica*) in a Lotic and a Lentic Habitat." J Herpetol 43(4): 597-604.

Chelazzi, G., T. Naziridis, et al. (2007). "Use of River-Wetland Habitats in a Declining Population of the Terrapin (*Mauremys rivulata*) Along the Strymon River, Northern Greece." J Zool 271(2): 154-161.

Chen, T.-H., and K.-Y. Lue (1998). "Ecology of the Chinese Stripe-Necked Turtle, *Ocadia sinensis* (Testudines: Emydidae), in the Keelung River, Northern Taiwan." Copeia 1998(4): 944-52.

Congdon, J. D., A. E. Dunham, et al. (1982). "Energy Budgets and Life Histories of Reptiles." Biology of the Reptilia, Volume 13. Ed. C. Gans. New York: Academic Press. pp. 233-71.

Converse, S. J. and J. A. Savidge (2003). "Ambient Temperature, Activity, and Microhabitat Use By Ornate Box Turtles (*Terrapene ornata ornata*)." J Herpetol 37(4): 665-670.

Converse, S. J., J. B. Iverson, et al. (2002). "Activity, Reproduction and Overwintering Behavior of Ornate Box Turtles (*Terrapene ornata ornata*) in the Nebraska Sandhills." Am Midl Nat 148(2): 416-422.

Coulson, I. M. and A. Hailey (2001). "Low Survival Rate and High Predation in the African Hingeback Tortoise *Kinixys spekii*." Afr J Ecol 39(4): 383-392.

De La Ossa V, J. and R. C. Vogt (2011). "Ecologia Populacional De *Peltocephalus dumerilianus* (Testudines, Podocnemididae) Em Dois Tributários Do Rio Negro, Amazonas, Brasil." Interciencia 36(1): 53-58.

Degraaf, J. D. and D. G. Nein (2010). "Predation of Spotted Turtle (*Clemmys guttata*) Hatchling By Green Frog (*Rana clamitans*)." Northeastern Naturalist 17(4): 667-670.

Diemer, J. E. (1992). "Home Range and Movements of the Tortoise *Gopherus polyphemus* in Northern Florida." J Herpetol 26(2): 158-65.

Dodd, C. K., Jr., R. Franz, et al. (1994). "Activity Patterns and Habitat Use of Box Turtles (*Terrapene carolina bauri*) on a Florida Island, with Recommendations for Management." Chelonian Cons Biol 1(2): 97-106.

Donaldson, B. M. and A. C. Echternacht (2005). "Aquatic Habitat Use Relative to Home Range and Seasonal Movement of Eastern Box Turtles (*Terrapene carolina carolina*: Emydidae) in Eastern Tennessee." J Herpetol 39(2): 278-284.

Doody, J. S., C. M. Castellano, et al. (2011). "Aggregated Drinking Behavior of Radiated Tortoises (*Astrochelys radiata*) in Arid Southwestern Madagascar." Chelonian Cons Biol 10(1): 145-146.

Dreslik, M. J., A. R. Kuhns, et al. (2005). "Structure and Composition of a Southern Illinois Freshwater Turtle Assemblage." Northeastern Naturalist 12(2): 173-186.

Durden, L. A., J. E. Keirans, et al. (2002). "*Amblyomma geochelone*, a New Species of Tick (Acari: Ixodidae) From the Madagascan Ploughshare Tortoise." J Medical Entomol 39(2): 398-403.

Edge, C. B., B. D. Steinberg, et al. (2009). "Temperature and Site Selection By Blanding's Turtles (*Emydoidea blandingii*) During Hibernation Near the Species' Northern Range Limit." Canadian J Zool 87(9): 825-834.

Edge, C. B., B. D. Steinberg, et al. (2010). "Habitat Selection By Blanding's Turtles (*Emydoidea blandingii*) in a Relatively Pristine Landscape." Ecoscience 17(1): 90-99.

El Mouden, E., T. Slimani, et al. (2006). "*Testudo graeca graeca* Feeding Ecology in an Arid and Overgrazed Zone in Morocco." J Arid Environments 64(3): 422-435.

Elsey, R. M. (2006). "Food Habits of *Macrochelys temminckii* (Alligator Snapping Turtle) From Arkansas and Louisiana." Southeastern Naturalist 5(3): 443-452.

Ennen, J. R. and A. F. Scott (2008). "Diel Movement Behavior of the Stripe-Necked Musk Turtle (*Sternotherus minor peltifer*) in Middle Tennessee." Am Midl Nat 160(2): 278-288.

Eubanks, J. O., W. K. Michener, et al. (2003). "Patterns of Movement and Burrow Use in a Population of Gopher Tortoises (*Gopherus polyphemus*)." Herpetologica 59(3): 311-321.

Fachin-Teran, A., R. C. Vogt, et al. (1995). "Food Habits of an Assemblage of Five Species of Turtles in the Rio Guapore, Rondonia, Brazil." J Herpetol 29 (4): 536-47.

Fachín-Terán, A., R. C. Vogt, et al. (2006). "Seasonal Movements of *Podocnemis sextuberculata* (Testudines: Podocnemididae) in the Mamirauá Sustainable Development Reserve, Amazonas, Brazil." Chelonian Cons Biol 5(1): 18-24.

Fields, J. R., T. R. Simpson, et al. (2003). "Food Habits and Selective Foraging By the Texas River Cooter (*Pseudemys texana*) in Spring Lake, Hays County, Texas." J Herpetol 37(4): 726-729.

Ford, D. K. and D. Moll (2004). "Sexual and Seasonal Variation in Foraging Patterns in the Stinkpot, *Sternotherus odoratus*, in Southwestern Missouri." J Herpetol 38(2): 296-301.

Fuselier, L., and D. Edds (1994). "Habitat Partitioning among Three Sympatric Species of Map Turtles, Genus *Graptemys*." J Herpetol 28(2): 154-58.

Galois, P., M. Léveillé, et al. (2002). "Movement Patterns, Activity, and Home Range of the Eastern Spiny Softshell Turtle (*Apalone spinifera*) in Northern Lake Champlain, Québec, Vermont." J Herpetol 36(3): 402-411.

Gibbs, J. P., E. J. Sterling, et al. (2010). "Giant Tortoises As Ecological Engineers: a Long-Term Quasi-Experiment in the Galápagos Islands." Biotropica 42(2): 208-214.

Gosnell, J. S., G. Rivera, et al. (2009). "A Phylogenetic Analysis of Sexual Size Dimorphism in Turtles." Herpetologica 65(1): 70-81.

Graham, T. E. (1995). "Habitat Use and Population Parameters of the Spotted Turtle, *Clemmys guttata*, a Species of Special Concern in Massachusetts." Chelonian Cons Biol 1(3): 207-14.

Graham, T. E. (1997). "Orientation by the Australian Eastern Long-Necked Turtle, *Chelodina longicollis*. Linnaeus Fund Research Report." Chelonian Cons Biol 2(3): 450-51.

Graham, T. E., A. Georges, et al. (1996). "Terrestrial Orientation by the Eastern Long-Necked Turtle, *Chelodina longicollis*, from Australia." J Herpetol 30(4): 467-77.

Graham, T. E., R. A. Saumure, et al. (1997). "Map Turtle Winter Leech Loads." J. Parasitol. 83(6): 1185-86.

Greaves, W. F. and J. D. Litzgus (2007). "Overwintering Ecology of Wood Turtles (*Glyptemys insculpta*) At the Species' Northern Range Limit." J Herpetol 41(1): 32-40.

Greene, H. W. (1998). "Antipredator Mechanisms in Reptiles." Biology of the Reptilia, Vol. 16, Ecology B, Defense and Life History. Ed. C. Gans and R. B. Huey. New York: Academic Press. pp. 1-152.

Griffiths, C. J., C. G. Jones, et al. (2010). "The Use of Extant Non-Indigenous Tortoises As a Restoration Tool to Replace Extinct Ecosystem Engineers." Restoration Ecology 18(1): 1-7.

Griffiths, Christine J., Dennis M. Hansen, et al. (2011). "Resurrecting Extinct Interactions with Extant Substitutes." Current Biology 21(9): 762-765.

Grosse, A. M., S. C. Sterrett, et al. (2010). "Effects of Turbidity on the Foraging Success of the Eastern Painted Turtle." Copeia 2010(3): 463-467.

Guyer, C., and S. M. Hermann (1997). "Patterns of Size and Longevity of Gopher Tortoise (*Gopherus polyphemus*) Burrows: Implications for the Longleaf Pine Ecosystem." Chelonian Cons Biol 2(4): 507-13.

Hailey, A., I. M. Coulson, et al. (2001). "Invertebrate Prey and Predatory Behaviour of the Omnivorous African Tortoise *Kinixys spekii*." Afr J Ecol 39(1): 10-17.

Hailman, Jack P., J. N. Layne, et al. (1991). "Notes on Aggressive Behavior of the Gopher Tortoise." Herpetological Review 22(3): 87-88.

Hansen, D. M., C. J. Donlan, et al. (2010). "Ecological History and Latent Conservation Potential: Large and Giant Tortoises As a Model For Taxon Substitutions." Ecography 33(2): 272-284.

Hatt, J.-M., M. Clauss, et al. (2005). "Fiber Digestibility in Juvenile Galapagos Tortoises (*Geochelone nigra*) and Implications For the Development of Captive Animals." Zoo Biology 24(2): 185-191.

Hazard, L. C., D. R. Shemanski, et al. (2009). "Nutritional Quality of Natural Foods of Juvenile Desert Tortoises (*Gopherus agassizii*): Energy, Nitrogen, and Fiber Digestibility." J Herpetol 43(1): 38-48.

Hazard, L. C., D. R. Shemanski, et al. (2010). "Nutritional Quality of Natural Foods of Juvenile and Adult Desert Tortoises (*Gopherus agassizii*): Calcium, Phosphorus, and Magnesium Digestibility." J Herpetol 44(1): 135-147.

Hochscheid, S., F. Bentivegna, et al. (2007). "Overwintering Behaviour in Sea Turtles: Dormancy is Optional." Marine Ecology Progress Series 340: 287-298.

Holmstrom, W. F. (1991). "Further Observations on Matamata Prey Herding." J Herpetol 25(3): 363-64.

Hossain, Md. L., and Md. S. U. Sarker. (1995). "Reproductive Biology of the Indian Roofed Turtle, *Kachuga tecta*, in Bangladesh." Chelonian Cons Biol 1(3): 226-27.

Iglay, R. B., J. L. Bowman, et al. (2007). "Eastern Box Turtle (*Terrapene carolina carolina*) Movements in a Fragmented Landscape." J Herpetol 41(1): 102-106.

Innes, R. J., K. J. Babbitt, et al. (2008). "Home Range and Movement of Blanding's Turtles (*Emydoidea blandingii*) in New Hampshire." Northeastern Naturalist 15(3): 431-444.

Inozemtsev, A. A. (1997). "Ecological Distribution and Population Dynamics of the Mediterranean Tortoise, *Testudo graeca nikolskii*, in Xerophytic Forests of the Western Caucasus, Southern Russia." Chelonian Cons Biol (4): 567-72.

Jackson, D. R. (1996). "Meat on the Move: Diet of a Predatory Turtle, *Deirochelys reticularia* (Testudines: Emydidae)." Chelonian Cons Biol 2(1): 105-08.

Jennings, A. H. (2007). "Use of Habitats and Microenvironments By Juvenile Florida Box Turtles, *Terrapene carolina bauri*, on Egmont Key." Herpetologica 63(1): 1-10.

Jones, S. C., W. J. Jordan, et al. (2007). "Fungal Spore Dispersal By the Eastern Box Turtle (*Terrapene carolina carolina*)." Am Midl Nat157(1): 121-126.

Joshua, Q. I., M. D. Hofmeyr, et al. (2010). "Seasonal and Site Variation in Angulate Tortoise Diet and Activity." J Herpetol 44(1): 124-134.

Kabigumila, J. (2001). "Sighting Frequency and Food Habits of the Leopard Tortoise, *Geochelone pardalis*, in Northern Tanzania." Afr J Ecol 39(3): 276-285.

Kaufmann, J. H. (1992). "Habitat Use by Wood Turtles in Central Pennsylvania." J Herpetol 26(3): 315-21.

Kennett, R. (1996). "Growth Models for Two Species of Freshwater Turtle, *Chelodina rugosa* and *Elseya dentata*, from the Wet-Dry Tropics of Northern Australia." J Herpetol 52(3): 383-95.

Keswick, T., B. T. Henen, et al. (2006). "Sexual Disparity in Activity Patterns and Time Budgets of Angulate Tortoises (*Chersina angulata*) on Dassen Island, South Africa." African Zoology 41(2): 224-233.

Kimmons, J. B. and D. Moll (2010). "Seed Dispersal By Red-Eared Sliders (*Trachemys scripta elegans*) and Common Snapping Turtles (*Chelydra serpentina*)." Chelonian Cons Biol 9(2): 289-294.

Kornilev, Y. V., C. K. Dodd, et al. (2010). "Linear Home Range, Movement, and Spatial Distribution of the Suwannee Cooter (*Pseudemys concinna suwanniensis*) in a Blackwater River." Chelonian Cons Biol 9(2): 196-204.

Lagarde, F., X. Bonnet, et al. (2003). "Foraging Behaviour and Diet of an Ectothermic Herbivore: *Testudo horsfieldi*." Ecography 26: 236-242.

Lawson, D. P. (2006). "Habitat Use, Home Range, and Activity Patterns of Hingeback Tortoises, *Kinixys erosa* and *K. homeana*, in Southwestern Cameroon." Chelonian Cons Biol 5(1): 48-56.

Lemell, P., C. J. Beisser, et al. (2000). "Morphology and Function of the Feeding Apparatus of *Pelusios castaneus* (Chelonia; Pleurodira)." J Morphol 244(2): 127-135.

Lemell, P., C. Lemell, et al. (2002). "Feeding Patterns of *Chelus fimbriatus* (Pleurodira: Chelidae)." J Exp Biol 205(10): 1495-1506.

Leuteritz, T. E. J. (2003). "Observations on Diet and Drinking Behaviour of Radiated Tortoises (*Geochelone radiata*) in Southwest Madagascar." African J Herpetol 52(2): 127-130.

Lewis, T. L., and C. A. Faulhaber (1999). "Home Ranges of Spotted Turtles (*Clemmys guttata*) in Southwestern Ohio." Chelonian Cons Biol 3(3): 430-34.

Lewis, T. L., and J. Ritzenthaler (1997). "Characteristics of Hibernacula Use by Spotted Turtles, *Clemmys guttata*, in Ohio." Chelonian Cons Biol 2(4): 611-15.

Ligon, D. B. and J. Reasor (2007). "Predation on Alligator Snapping Turtles (*Macrochelys temminckii*) By Northern River Otters (*Lontra canadensis*)." Southwest Nat 52(4): 608-610.

Ligon, D. B. and P. A. Stone (2003). "Radiotelemetry Reveals Terrestrial Estivation in Sonoran Mud Turtles (*Kinosternon sonoriense*)." J Herpetol 37(4): 750-754.

Lindeman, P. V. (1999) "Aggressive Interactions During Basking among Four Species of Emydid Turtles." J Herpetol 33(2): 214-19.

Lindeman, P. V. (2000). "Evolution of the Relative Width of the Head and Alveolar Surfaces in Map Turtles (Testudines: Emydidae: *Graptemys*)." Biol J Linn Soc 69(4): 549-576.

Lindeman, P. V. (2006). "Diet of the Texas Map Turtle (*Graptemys versa*): Relationship to Sexually Dimorphic Trophic Morphology and Changes Over Five Decades As Influenced By an Invasive Mollusk." Chelonian Cons Biol 5(1): 25-31.

Lindeman, P. V. (2006). "Zebra and Quagga Mussels (*Dreissena* Spp.) and Other Prey of a Lake Erie Population of Common Map Turtles (Emydidae: *Graptemys geographica*)." Copeia 2006(2): 268-273.

Lindeman, P. V. (2008). "Evolution of Body Size in the Map Turtles and Sawbacks (Emydidae: Deirochelyinae: *Graptemys*)." Herpetologica 64(1): 32-46.

Lips, K. R. (1991) "Vertebrates Associated with Tortoise (*Gopherus polyphemus*) Burrows in Four Habitats in South-Central Florida." J Herpetol 25(4): 477-81.

Litzgus, J. D. (2006). "Sex Differences in Longevity in the Spotted Turtle (*Clemmys guttata*)." Copeia 2006(2): 281-288.

Litzgus, J. D., T. A. Mousseau, et al. (2004). "Home Range and Seasonal Activity of Southern Spotted Turtles (*Clemmys guttata*): Implications For Management." Copeia 2004(4): 804-817.

Liu, H., S. G. Platt, et al. (2004). "Seed Dispersal By the Florida Box Turtle (*Terrapene carolina bauri*) in Pine Rockland Forests of the Lower Florida Keys, United States." Oecologia 138(4): 539-546.

Loehr, V. J. T. (2002). "Diet of the Namaqualand Speckled Padloper, *Homopus signatus signatus*, in Early Spring." African J Herpetol 51(1): 47-55.

Loehr, V. J. T. (2006). "Natural Diet of the Namaqualand Speckled Padloper (*Homopus signatus signatus*)." Chelonian Cons Biol 5(1): 149-152.

Longshore, K. M., J. R. Jaeger, et al. (2003). "Desert Tortoise (*Gopherus agassizii*) Survival At Two Eastern Mojave Desert Sites: Death By Short-Term Drought?" J Herpetol 37(1): 169-177.

Lovich, J., C. Drost, et al. (2010). "Reptilian Prey of the Sonora Mud Turtle (*Kinosternon sonoriense*) with Comments on Saurophagy and Ophiophagy in North American Turtles." Southwest Nat 55(1): 135-138.

Lue, K.-Y., and T.-H. Chen (1999). "Activity, Movement Patterns, and Home Range of the Yellow-Margined Boxed Turtle (*Cuora flavomarginata*) in Northern Taiwan." J Herpetol 33(4): 590-600.

Luiselli, L. (1998). "Food Habits of the Pelomedusid Turtle *Pelusios castaneus castaneus* in Southeastern Nigeria." Chelonian Cons Biol 3(1): 106-07.

Luiselli, L. (2006). "Resource Partitioning in the Communities of Terrestrial Turtles: a Review of the Evidences." Rev. Écol. (Terre Vie) 61: 353-365.

Luiselli, L., F. M. Angelici, et al. (2008). "Negative Density Dependence of Sympatric Hinge-Back Tortoises (*Kinixys erosa* and *K. homeana*) in West Africa." Acta Herpetologica 3(1): 19-33.

Luiselli, L., G. C. Akani, et al. (2011). "Food Habits of a Pelomedusid Turtle, *Pelomedusa subrufa*, in Tropical Africa (Nigeria): the Effects of Sex, Body Size, Season, and Site." Chelonian Cons Biol 10(1): 138-144.

Macip-Ríos, R., V. H. Sustaita-Rodríguez, et al. (2010). "Alimentary Habits of the Mexican Mud Turtle (*Kinosternon integrum*) in Tonatico, Estado De México." Chelonian Cons Biol 9(1): 90-97.

Malonza, P. K. (2003). "Ecology and Distribution of the Pancake Tortoise, *Malacochersus tornieri* in Kenya." J East African Nat Hist 92(1): 81-96.

Marten, G. G. (2007). "Turtles." J Amer Mosquito Control Assn 23(Sp2): 221-224.

Martins, F. I. and F. L. Souza (2008). "Estimates of Growth of the Atlantic Rain Forest Freshwater Turtle *Hydromedusa maximiliani* (Chelidae)." J Herpetol 42(1): 54-60.

Mason, M. C., et al. (1999). "Leopard Tortoises (*Geochelone pardalis*) in Valley Bushveld, Eastern Cape, South Africa: Specialist or Generalist Herbivores?" Chelonian Cons Biol 3(3): 435-40.

Mccoy, J. C., E. L. Failey, et al. (2007). "An Assessment of Leech Parasitism on Semi-Aquatic Turtles in the Western Piedmont of North Carolina." Southeastern Naturalist 6(2): 191-202.

McCurdy, D. G., and T. B. Herman (1997). "Putative Anting Behavior in Wood Turtles." Herpetological Review 28 (3): 127-28.

Mcmaster, M. K. and C. T. Downs (2009). "Home Range and Daily Movement of Leopard Tortoises (*Stigmochelys pardalis*) in the Nama-Karoo, South Africa." J Herpetol 43(4): 561-569.

Mitchell, J. C., and A. G. J. Rhodin (1996). "Observations on the Natural History and Exploitation of the Turtles of Nepal, with Life History Notes on *Melanochelys trijuga*." Chelonian Cons Biol 2(1): 66-72.

Moll, D. (1990). "Population Sizes and Forging Ecology in a Tropical Freshwater Stream Turtle Community." J Herpetol 24(1): 48-53.

Morrow, J. L., J. H. Howard, et al. (2001). "Home Range and Movements of the Bog Turtle (*Clemmys muhlenbergii*) in Maryland." J Herpetol 35(1): 68-73.

Murray, R. A., N. O. Dronen, et al. (2004). "Endohelminths From the Black Marsh Turtle, *Siebenrockiella crassicollis*, Confiscated By International Authorities in Hong Kong, People's Republic of China." Comparative Parasitology 71(2): 255-257.

Mushinsky, H. R., T. A. Stilson, et al. (2003). "Diet and Dietary Preference of the Juvenile Gopher Tortoise (*Gopherus polyphemus*)." Herpetologica 59(4): 475-483.

Nagy, K. A., Da. J. Morafka, et al. (1997). "Young Desert Tortoise Survival: Energy, Water, and Food Requirements in the Field." Chelonian Cons Biol 2(3): 396-404.

Natchev, N., E. Heiss, et al. (2011). "Structure and Function of the Feeding Apparatus in the Common Musk Turtle *Sternotherus odoratus* (Chelonia, Kinosternidae)." Contributions to Zoology 80(2): 143-156.

Natchev, N., P. Lemell, et al. (2010). "Aquatic Feeding in a Terrestrial Turtle: a Functional-Morphological Study of the Feeding Apparatus in the Indochinese Box Turtle *Cuora galbinifrons* (Testudines, Geoemydidae)." Zoomorphology 129(2): 111-119.

Nussear, K. E., T. C. Esque, et al. (2007). "Desert Tortoise Hibernation: Temperatures, Timing, and Environment." Copeia 2007(2): 378-386.

Ossa-Velásquez, J. D. L., R. C. Vogt, et al. (2011). "Alimentación De *Peltocephalus dumerilianus* (Testudines: Podocnemididae) En Condiciones Naturales / Feeding of *Peltocephalus dumerilianus* (Testudines: Podocnemididae) in a Natural Environment." Actual Biol 33(94): 85-92.

Ossa, J. D. L., R. C. Vogt, et al. (2009). "The Influence of Temperature on the Feeding Behavior of *Peltocephalus dumerilianus* (Testudines Podocnemidae)." Rev.Mvz Córdoba 14(1): 1587-1593.

Padgett, D. J., J. J. Carboni, et al. (2010). "The Dietary Composition of *Chrysemys picta picta* (Eastern Painted Turtles) with Special Reference to the Seeds of Aquatic Macrophytes." Northeastern Naturalist 17(2): 305-312.

Parker, W. S. (1996). "Age and Survivorship of the Slider (*Trachemys scripta*) and the Mud Turtle (*Kinosternon subrubrum*) in a Mississippi Farm Pond." J Herpetol 30(2): 266-68.

Perez-Emán, J. L., and A. Paolillo (1997). "Diet of the Pelomedusid Turtle *Peltocephalus dumerilianus* in the Venezuelan Amazon." J Herpetol 31(2): 173-79.

Perillo, K. M. (1997). "Seasonal Movments and Habitat Preferences of Spotted Turtles (*Clemmys guttata*) in North Central Connecticut. Linnaeus Fund Research Report." Chelonian Cons Biol 2(3): 445-47.

Pfaller, J. B. (2009). Bite Force Generation and Feeding Biomechanics in the Loggerhead Musk Turtle *Sternotherus minor*: Implications For the Ontogeny of Performance. Msc Thesis, Florida State University.

Pittman, S. E. and M. E. Dorcas (2009). "Movements, Habitat Use, and Thermal Ecology of an Isolated Population of Bog Turtles (*Glyptemys muhlenbergii*)." Copeia 2009(4): 781-790.

Platt, S. G., C. Hall, et al. (2009). "Wet-Season Food Habits and Intersexual Dietary Overlap of Florida Box Turtles (*Terrapene carolina bauri*) on National Key Deer Wildlife Refuge, Florida." Southeastern Naturalist 8(2): 335-346.

Plummer, M. V. (2004). "Seasonal Inactivity of the Desert Box Turtle, *Terrapene ornata luteola*, At the Species' Southwestern Range Limit in Arizona." J Herpetol 38(4): 589-593.

Plummer, M. V., and J. C. Burnley (1997). "Behavior, Hibernacula, and Thermal Relations of Shoftshell Turtles (*Trionyx spiniferus*) Overwintering in a Small Stream." Chelonian Cons Biol 2(4): 489-93.

Plummer, M. V., N. E. Mills, et al. (1997). "Activity, Habitat, and Movement Patterns of Softshell Turtles (*Trionyx spiniferus*) in a Small Stream." Chelonian Cons Biol 2(4): 514-20.

Pritchard, P. C. H. (1984). "Piscivory in Turtles, and Evolution of the Long-Necked Chelidae." Symp. Zool. Soc. Lond. 52: 87-110.

Quinn, N. W. S., and D. P. Tate (1991). "Seasonal Movements and Habitat of Wood Turtles (*Clemmys insculpta*) in Algonquin Park, Canada." J Herpetol 25 (2): 217-20.

Ramsay, S. L., M. D. Hofmeyr, et al. (2002). "Activity Patterns of the Angulate Tortoise (*Chersina angulata*) on Dassen Island, South Africa." J Herpetol 36(2): 161-169.

Readel, A. M., C. A. Phillips, et al. (2008). "Leech Parasitism in a Turtle Assemblage: Effects of Host and Environmental Characteristics." Copeia 2008(1): 227-233.

Remsberg, A. J., T. L. Lewis, et al. (2006). "Home Ranges of Wood Turtles (*Glyptemys insculpta*) in Northern Michigan." Chelonian Cons Biol 5(1): 42-47.

Rhodin, A. G. J., F. Medem, et al. (1981). "The Occurrence of Neustophagia among Podocnemine Turtles." British J Herpetol 6: 175-76.

Riedle, J. D., R. C. Averill-Murray, et al. (2010). "Seasonal Variation in Survivorship and Mortality of Desert Tortoises in the Sonoran Desert, Arizona." J Herpetol 44(1): 164-167.

Rittenhouse, C. D., J. J. Millspaugh, et al. (2007). "Movements of Translocated and Resident Three-Toed Box Turtles." J Herpetol 41(1): 115-121.

Rivera, G. (2008). "Ecomorphological Variation in Shell Shape of the Freshwater Turtle *Pseudemys concinna* Inhabiting Different Aquatic Flow Regimes." Integr. Comp. Biol. 48(6): 769-787.

Rödel, M.-O. (1999). "Predation on Tadpoles by Hatchlings of the Freshwater Turtle *Pelomedusa subrufa*." Amphibia-Reptilia 20: 173-83.

Roe, J. H. and A. Georges (2008). "Maintenance of Variable Responses For Coping with Wetland Drying in Freshwater Turtles " Ecology 89(2): 485-494.

Roe, J. H. and A. Georges (2008). "Terrestrial Activity, Movements and Spatial Ecology of an Australian Freshwater Turtle, *Chelodina longicollis*, in a Temporally Dynamic Wetland System." Austral Ecology 33(8): 1045-1056.

Roe, J. H., A. C. Brinton, et al. (2009). "Temporal and Spatial Variation in Landscape Connectivity For a Freshwater Turtle in a Temporally Dynamic Wetland System." Ecological Applications 19(5): 1288-1299.

Roosenburg, W. M., K. L. Haley, et al. (1999). "Habitat Selection and Movements of Diamondback Terrapins, *Malaclemys terrapin*, in a Maryland Estuary." Chelonian Cons Biol 3(3): 425-29.

Rossell, C. R., I. M. Rossell, et al. (2006). "Microhabitat Selection By Eastern Box Turtles (*Terrapene c. carolina*) in a North Carolina Mountain Wetland." J Herpetol 40(2): 280-284.

Rouag, R., C. Ferrah, et al. (2008). "Food Choice of an Algerian Population of the Spur-Thighed Tortoise, *Testudo graeca*." African J Herpetol 57(2): 103-113.

Rowe, J. and S. Dalgarn (2009). "Effects of Sex and Microhabitat Use on Diel Body Temperature Variation in Midland Painted Turtles (*Chrysemys picta marginata*)." Copeia 2009(1): 85-92.

Rowe, J. W. (1992). "Dietary Habits of the Blanding's Turtle (*Emydoidea blandingi*) in Northeastern Illinois." J Herpetol 26 (1): 111-14.

Rowe, J. W., G. C. Lehr, et al. (2009). "Activity, Movements and Activity Area Size in Stinkpot Turtles (*Sternotherus odoratus*) in a Southwestern Michigan Lake." Am Midl Nat162(2): 266-275.

Schneider, L., C. Ferrara, et al. (2010). "Description of Behavioral Patterns of *Podocnemis erythrocephala* (Spix, 1824) (Testudines: Podocnemididae) (Red-Headed River Turtle) in Captivity, Manaus, Amazonas, Brazil." Acta Amazonica 40(4): 763-770.

Secor, S. M., and J. Diamond (1999). "Maintenance of Digestive Performance in the Turtles *Chelydra serpentina, Sternotherus odoratus,* and *Trachemys scripta.*" Copeia 1999(1): 75-84.

Sharma, R.S.K., D. S.K. Sharma, et al. (1999). "*Amblyomma geoemydae* (Acari: Ixodidae) Collected Off the Asian Brown Tortoise, *Manouria emys* from Terangganu, Malaysia." Tropical Biomedicine 16: 43-47.

Simmons, L.-A. and M. J. Burridge (2002). "Introduction of the Exotic Tick *Amblyomma chabaudi* Rageau (Acari: Ixodidae) Into Florida on Imported Tortoises." Florida Entomologist 85(1): 288-289.

Smar, C. M. and R. M. Chambers (2005). "Homing Behavior of Musk Turtles in a Virginia Lake." Southeastern Naturalist 4(3): 527-532.

Smith, G. R. and J. B. Iverson (2004). "Diel Activity Patterns of the Turtle Assemblage of a Northern Indiana Lake." Am Midl Nat152(1): 156-164.

Smith, R. B., D. R. Breininger, et al. (1997). "Home Range Characteristics of Radiotagged Gopher Tortoises on Kennedy Space Center, Florida." Chelonian Cons Biol 2(3): 358-62.

Souza, F. L., and A. S. Abe (1995). "Observations on Feeding Habits of *Hydromedusa maximiliani* (Testudines: Chelidae) in Southeastern Brazil." Chelonian Cons Biol 1(4): 320-22.

Souza, F. L., and A. Shinya (1998). "Resource Partitioning by the Neotropical Freshwater Turtle, *Hydromedusa maximiliani.*" J Herpetol 32(1): 106-12.

Souza, F. L., J. Raizer, et al. (2008). "Dispersal of *Phrynops geoffroanus* (Chelidae) in an Urban River in Central Brazil." Chelonian Cons Biol 7(2): 257-261.

Steen, D. A., S. C. Sterrett, et al. (2007). "Terrestrial Movements and Microhabitat Selection of Overwintering Subadult Eastern Mud Turtles (*Kinosternon subrubrum*) in Southwest Georgia." J Herpetol 41(3): 532-535.

Stephens, P. R. and J. J. Wiens (2009). "Evolution of Sexual Size Dimorphisms in Emydid Turtles: Ecological Dimorphism, Rensch's Rule, and Sympatric Divergence." Evolution 63(4): 910-925.

Stone, P. A., M. E. B. Stone, et al. (2011). "Terrestrial Flight Response: a New Context For Terrestrial Activity in Sonoran Mud Turtles." Am Midl Nat165(1): 128-136.

Strong, J. N. and J. M. V. Fragoso (2006). "Seed Dispersal By *Geochelone carbonaria* and *Geochelone denticulata* in Northwestern Brazil." Biotropica 38(5): 683-686.

Thiel, R. P. and T. Wilder (2010). "Over-Wintering Characteristics of West-Central Wisconsin Blanding's Turtles, *Emydoidea blandingii.*" Canadian Field-Naturalist 124(2): 134-138.

Tracy, C. R., L. C. Zimmerman, et al. (2006). "Rates of Food Passage in the Digestive Tract of Young Desert Tortoises: Effects of Body Size and Diet Quality." Chelonian Cons Biol 5(2): 269-273.

Tucker, J. K. and J. T. Lamer (2008). "Homing in the Red-Eared Slider (*Trachemys scripta elegans*) in Illinois." Chelonian Cons Biol 7(1): 145-149.

Tuma, M. W. (2006). "Range, Habitat Use, and Seasonal Activity of the Yellow Mud Turtle (*Kinosternon flavescens*) in Northwestern Illinois: Implications For Site-Specific Conservation and Management." Chelonian Cons Biol 5(1): 108-120.

Tuttle, S. E., and D. M. Carroll (1997). "Ecology and Natural History of the Wood Turtle (*Clemmys insculpta*) in Southern New Hampshire. Linnaeus Fund Research Report." Chelonian Cons Biol 2(3): 447-49.

Ultsch, G. R. (2006). "The Ecology of Overwintering Among Turtles: Where Turtles Overwinter and Its Consequences." Biological Reviews 81(3): 339-367.

Vander Haegen, W. M., S. L. Clark, et al. (2009). "Survival and Causes of Mortality of Head-Started Western Pond Turtles on Pierce National Wildlife Refuge, Washington." J Wildlife Manage 73(8): 1402-1406.

Varela, R. O. and E. H. Bucher (2002). "Seed Dispersal By *Chelonoidis chilensis* in the Chaco Dry Woodland of Argentina." J Herpetol 36(1): 137-140.

Vecchio, S. D., R. L. Burke, et al. (2011). "The Turtle is in the Details: Microhabitat Choice By *Testudo hermanni* is Based on Microscale Plant Distribution." Animal Biology 61: 249-261.

Walde, A. D., A. M. Walde, et al. (2009). "Burrows of Desert Tortoises (*Gopherus agassizii*) as Thermal Refugia for Horned Larks (*Eremophila alpestris*) in the Mojave Desert." Southwest Nat 54(4): 375-381.

Walde, A. D., D. K. Delaney, et al. (2007). "Osteophagy By the Desert Tortoise (*Gopherus agassizii*)." Southwest Nat 52(1): 147-149.

Walker, D., and J. C. Avise (1998). "Principles of Phylogeography as Illustrated by Freshwater and Terrestrial Turtles in the Southeastern United States." Ann. Rev. Ecol. Syst. 29: 23-58.

Wilson, D. S. (1991). "Estimates of Survival for Juvenile Gopher Tortoises, *Gopherus polyphemus.*" J Herpetol 25(3): 376-79.

Wilson, D. S., et al. (1999). "Physical and Microhabitat Characteristics of Burrows Used by Juvenile Desert Tortoise (*Gopherus agassizii*)." Chelonian Cons Biol 3(3): 448-53.

Chapter 7: 'Twixt Plated Decks

Anderson, N. J. and B. D. Horne (2009). "Observations on the Nesting Ecology of the Mississippi Mud Turtle, *Kinosternon subrubrum hippocrepis* Gray." Southeastern Naturalist 8(3): 563-565.

Aresco, M. J. (2004). "Reproductive Ecology of *Pseudemys floridana* and *Trachemys scripta* (Testudines: Emydidae) in Northwestern Florida." J Herpetol 38(2): 249-256.

Ashton, K. G., R. L. Burke, et al. (2007). "Geographic Variation in Body and Clutch Size of Gopher Tortoises." Copeia 2007(2): 355-363.

Bager, A. and J. L. O. Rosado (2010). "Estimation of Core Terrestrial Habitats for Freshwater Turtles in Southern Brazil Based on Nesting Areas." J Herpetol 44(4): 658-662.

Baldwin, E. A., M. N. Marchand, et al. (2004). "Terrestrial Habitat Use By Nesting Painted Turtles in Landscapes with Different Levels of Fragmentation." Northeastern Naturalist 11(1): 41-48.

Barzyk, J. E. (1994). "Husbandry and Captive Breeding of the Parrot-Beaked Tortoise, *Homopus areolatus.*" Chelonian Cons Biol 1(2): 138-41.

Baxter, P. C., D. S. Wilson, et al. (2008). "The Effects of Nest Date and Placement of Eggs in Burrows on Sex Ratios and Potential Survival of Hatchling Desert Tortoises, *Gopherus agassizii.*" Chelonian Cons Biol 7(1): 52-59.

Berry, J. F., M. E. Seidel, et al. (1997). "A New Species of Mud Turtle (Genus *Kinosternon*) from Jalisco and Colima, Mexico, with Notes on Its Natural History." Chelonian Cons Biol 2(3): 329-37.

Bjurlin, C. D. and J. A. Bissonette (2004). "Survival During Early Life Stages of the Desert Tortoise (*Gopherus agassizii*) in the South-Central Mojave Desert." J Herpetol 38(4): 527-535.

Bodie, J. R., and R. D. Semlitsch (2000). "Size-Specific Mortality and Natural Selection in Freshwater Turtles." Copeia 2000(3): 732-39.

Bonach, K., C. I. Piña, et al. (2006). "Allometry of Reproduction of *Podocnemis expansa* in Southern Amazon Basin." Amphibia-Reptilia 27: 55-61.

Bonach, K., J. F. Lewinger, et al. (2007). "Physical Characteristics of Giant Amazon Turtle (*Podocnemis expansa*) Nests." Chelonian Cons Biol 6(2): 252-255.

Bonnet, X., F. Lagarde, et al. (2001). "Sexual Dimorphism in Steppe Tortoises (*Testudo horsfieldii*): Influence of the Environment and Sexual Selection on Body Shape and Mobility." Biol J Linn Soc 72(3): 357-372.

Booth, D. T. (1998). "Egg Size, Clutch Size, and Reproductive Effort of the Australian Broad-Shelled River Turtle, *Chelodina expansa.*" J Herpetol 32(4): 592-96.

Booth, D. T. (2002). "The Breaking of Diapause in Embryonic Broad-Shell River Turtles (*Chelodina expansa*)." J Herpetol 36(2): 304-307.

Bowden, R. M., R. T. Paitz, et al. (2011). "The Ontogeny of Postmaturation Resource Allocation in Turtles." Physiol Biochem Zool 84(2): 204-211.

Bowen, K. D., R.-J. Spencer, et al. (2005). "A Comparative Study of Environmental Factors That Affect Nesting in Australian and North American Freshwater Turtles." J Zool 267(4): 397-404.

Britson, C. A. (1998). "Predatory Responses of Largemouth Bass (*Micropterus salmoides*) to Conspicuous and Cryptic Hatchling Turtles: a Comparative Experiment." Copeia 1998(2): 383-90.

Britson, C. A., and W. H. N. Gutzke (1993). "Antipredator Mechanisms of Hatchling Freshwater Turtles." Copeia 1993(2): 435-40.

Brown, G. P., C. A. Bishop, et al. (1994). "Growth Rate, Reproductive Output, and Temperature Selection of Snapping Turtles in Habitats of Different Productivities." J Herpetol 28(4): 405-10.

Buhlmann, K. A., J. D. Congdon, et al. (2009). "Ecology of Chicken Turtles (*Deirochelys reticularia*) in a Seasonal Wetland Ecosystem: Exploiting Resource and Refuge Environments." Herpetologica 65(1): 39-53.

Burke, R. L. and W. Capitano (2011). "Nesting Ecology and Hatching Success of the Eastern Box Turtle, *Terrapene carolina*, on Long Island, New York." Am Midl Nat165(1): 137-142.

Burke, R. L., C. M. Schneider, et al. (2005). "Cues Used By Raccoons to Find Turtle Nests: Effects of Flags, Human Scent, and Diamond-Backed Terrapin Sign." J Herpetol 39(2): 312-315.

Burke, R. L., et al. (1996) "Temperature-Dependent Sex Determination and Hatchling Success in the Gopher Tortoise (*Gopherus polyphemus*)." Chelonian Cons Biol 2(1): 86-88.

Burke, R. L., S. M. Felice, et al. (2009). "Changes in Raccoon (*Procyon lotor*) Predation Behavior Affects Turtle (*Malaclemys terrapin*) Nest Census." Chelonian Cons Biol 8(2): 208-211.

Butler, B. O., and T. E. Graham (1995). "Early Post-Emergent Behavior and Habitat Selection in Hatchling Blanding's Turtles, *Emydoidea blandingii*, in Massachusetts." Chelonian Cons Biol 1(3): 187-96.

Butler, J. A., and T. W. Hull (1996). "Reproduction of the Tortoise, *Gopherus polyphemus*, in Northeastern Florida." J Herpetol 30(1): 14-18.

Butler, J. A., C. Broadhurst, et al. (2004). "Nesting, Nest Predation and Hatchling Emergence of the Carolina Diamondback Terrapin, *Malaclemys terrapin centrata*, in Northeastern Florida." Am Midl Nat152(1): 145-155.

Carroll, D. M. and G. R. Ultsch (2007). "Emergence Season and Survival in the Nest of Hatchling Turtles in Southcentral New Hampshire." Northeastern Naturalist 14(2): 307-310.

Castellano, C. M., J. L. Behler, et al. (2008). "Terrestrial Movements of Hatchling Wood Turtles (*Glyptemys insculpta*) in Agricultural Fields in New Jersey." Chelonian Cons Biol 7(1): 113-118.

Colbert, P. L., R.-J. Spencer, et al. (2010). "Mechanism and Cost of Synchronous Hatching." Functional Ecology 24(1): 112-121.

Congdon, J. D., et al. (2000). "Nesting Ecology and Embryo Mortality: Implications for Hatchling Success and Demography of Blanding;S Turtles (*Emydoidea blandingii*)." Chelonian Cons Biol 3(4): 569-79.

Congdon, J. D., M. Pappas, et al. (2011). "Conservation Implications of Initial Orientation of Naïve Hatchling Snapping Turtles (*Chelydra serpentina*) and Painted Turtles (*Chrysemys picta belli*) Dispersing From Experimental Nests." Chelonian Cons Biol 10(1): 42-53.

Correa-H, J. C., A. M. Cano-Castaño, et al. (2010). "Reproductive Ecology of the Magdalena River Turtle (*Podocnemis lewyana*) in the Mompos Depression, Colombia." Chelonian Cons Biol 9(1): 70-78.

Costanzo, J. P., R. E. Lee, et al. (2008). "Physiological Ecology of Overwintering in Hatchling Turtles." J Exp Zool Part A: Ecological Genetics and Physiology 309a(6): 297-379.

Crews, D., A. Fleming, et al. (2001). "Role of Steroidogenic Factor 1 and Aromatase in Temperature-Dependent Sex Determination in the Red-Eared Slider Turtle." J Exp Zool 290(6): 597-606.

Daza, J. M. and V. P. Páez (2007). "Morphometric Variation and Its Effect on Reproductive Potential in Female Colombian Slider Turtles (*Trachemys callirostris callirostris*)." Herpetologica 63(2): 125-134.

De La Ossa, J., R. C. Vogt, et al. (2009). "Discovery of Cannibalistic Oophagy in *Peltocephalus dumerilianus* (Testudines: Podocnemididae)." Actual Biol 31(90): 81-84.

de Souza, R. R., and R. C. Vogt (1994). "Incubation Temperature Influences Sex and Hatchling Size in the Neotropical Turtle *Podocnemis unifilis.*" J Herpetol 28(4): 453-64.

DePari, J. A. (1996). "Overwintering in the Nest Chamber by Hatchling Painted Turtles, *Chrysemys picta*, in Northern New Jersey." Chelonian Cons Biol 2(1): 5-12.

Díaz-Paniagua, C., C. Keller, et al. (2001). "Long-Term Demographic Fluctuations of the Spur-Thighed Tortoise *Testudo graeca* in Sw Spain." Ecography 24(6): 707-721.

Diffie, S., J. Miller, et al. (2010). "Laboratory Observations of Red Imported Fire Ant (Hymenoptera: Formicidae) Predation on Reptilian and Avian Eggs." J Herpetol 44(2): 294-296.

Dodd, K. L., C. Murdock, et al. (2006). "Interclutch Variation in Sex Ratios Produced At Pivotal Temperature in the Red-Eared Slider, a Turtle with Temperature-Dependent Sex Determination." J Herpetol 40(4): 544-549.

Doody, J. S. (1999). "A Test of the Comparative Influences of Constant and Fluctuating Incubation Temperatures on Phenotypes of Hatchling Turtles." Chelonian Cons Biol 3(3): 529-31.

Doody, J. S., A. Georges, et al. (2003). "Twice Every Second Year: Reproduction in the Pig-Nosed Turtle, *Carettochelys insculpta*, in the Wet–Dry Tropics of Australia." J Zool 259(2): 179-188.

Doody, J. S., A. Georges, et al. (2004). "Determinants of Reproductive Success and Offspring Sex in a Turtle with Environmental Sex Determination." Biol J Linn Soc 81(1): 1-16.

Doody, J. S., M. Pauza, et al. (2009). "Nesting Behavior of the Pig-Nosed Turtle, *Carettochelys insculpta*, in Australia." Chelonian Cons Biol 8(2): 185-191.

Doody, J. S., P. West, et al. (2003). "Beach Selection in Nesting Pig-Nosed Turtles, *Carettochelys insculpta.*" J Herpetol 37(1): 178-182.

Draud, M., M. Bossert, et al. (2004). "Predation on Hatchling and Juvenile Diamondback Terrapins (*Malaclemys terrapin*) By the Norway Rat (Rattus Norvegicus)." J Herpetol 38(3): 467-470.

Du, W.-G., R.-Q. Zheng, et al. (2006). "The Influence of Incubation Temperature on Morphology, Locomotor Performance, and Cold Tolerance of Hatchling Chinese Three-Keeled Pond Turtles, *Chinemys reevesii.*" Chelonian Cons Biol 5(2): 294-299.

Durrell, G. M. (1993). The Aye-Aye and I : a Rescue Mission in Madagascar. 1st U.S. ed. New York: Arcade Pub.: Distributed by Little Brown.

Eendebak, B. T. (1995). "Incubation Period and Sex Ratio of Hermann's Tortoise, *Testudo hermanni boettgeri.*" Chelonian Cons Biol 1(3): 227-31.

Epperson, D. M. and C. D. Heise (2003). "Nesting and Hatchling Ecology of Gopher Tortoises (*Gopherus polyphemus*) in Southern Mississippi." J Herpetol 37(2): 315-324.

Ernst, C H., and G. R. Zug (1994). "Observations on the Reproductive Biology of the Spotted Turtle, *Clemmys guttata*, in Southeastern Pennsylvania." J Herpetol 28(1): 99-102.

Escalona, T., N. Valenzuela, et al. (2009). "Nesting Ecology in the Freshwater Turtle *Podocnemis unifilis*: Spatiotemporal Patterns and Inferred Explanations." Functional Ecology 23(4): 826-835.

Etchberger, C. R., M. A. Ewert, et al. (1992). "Do Low Incubation Temperatures Yield Females in Painted Turtles?" Canadian J Zool 70(2): 391-394.

Ewert, M. A., and D. S. Wilson (1996). "Seasonal Variation of Embryonic Diapause in the Striped Mud Turtle (*Kinosternon baurii*) and General Considerations for Conservation Planning." Chelonian Cons Biol 2(1): 43-54.

Ewert, M. A., R. E. Hatcher, et al. (2004). "Sex Determination and Ontogeny in *Malacochersus tornieri*, the Pancake Tortoise." J Herpetol 38(2): 291-295.

Ewert, M.A., and C.E. Nelson (1991). "Sex Determination in Turtles: Diverse Patterns and Some Possible Adaptive Values." Copeia 1991(1): 50-69.

Ewert, M.A., D.R. Jackson, et al. (1994). "Patterns of Temperature-Dependent Sex Determination in Turtles." J Exp Zool 270(1): 3-15.

Ezaz, T., N. Valenzuela, et al. (2006). "An XX/XY Sex Microchromosome System in a Freshwater Turtle, *Chelodina longicollis* (Testudines: Chelidae) with Genetic Sex Determination." Chromosome Res 14(2): 139-150.

Fantin, C., L. S. Viana, et al. (2008). "Polyandry in *Podocnemis unifilis* (Pleurodira; Podocnemididae), the Vulnerable Yellow-Spotted Amazon River Turtle." Amphibia-Reptilia 29: 479-486.

Fantin, C., P. Farias, et al. (2010). "Polyandry in the Red-Headed River Turtle *Podocnemis erythrocephala* (Testudines, Podocnemididae) in the Brazilian Amazon." Genet. Mol. Res. 9(1): 435-440.

Feinberg, J. A. and R. L. Burke (2003). "Nesting Ecology and Predation of Diamondback Terrapins, *Malaclemys terrapin*, At

Gateway National Recreation Area, New York." J Herpetol 37(3): 517-526.

Ferrara, C. R. and R. C. Vogt (2011). Vocal Communication in Turtles: New Directions For Behavioral Research Program and Abstracts of the Ninth Annual Symposium on the Conservation and Biology of Tortoises and Freshwater Turtles. A. Walde and E. Walton. Orlando, Fl, Turtle Survival Alliance: pp. 25-26.

Ferreira Júnior, P. and P. Castro (2010). "Nesting Ecology of *Podocnemis expansa* (Schweigger, 1812) and *Podocnemis unifilis* (Troschel, 1848) (Testudines, Podocnemididae) in the Javaés River, Brazil." Brazilian J Biol 70(1): 85-94.

Ferreira Júnior, P. D. and P. D. T. A. Castro (2003). "Geological Control of *Podocnemis expansa* and *Podocnemis unifilis* Nesting Areas in Rio Javaés, Bananal Island, Brazil." Acta Amazonica 33(3): 445-468.

Ferreira Júnior, P. D. and P. D. T. A. Castro (2006). "Thermal Environment Characteristics of *Podocnemis expansa* and *Podocnemis unifilis* Nesting Areas on the Javaés River, Tocantins, Brazil." Chelonian Cons Biol 5(1): 102-107.

Ferreira Júnior, P. D. and P. D. Tarso Amorim Castro (2005). "Nest Placement of the Giant Amazon River Turtle, *Podocnemis expansa*, in the Araguaia River, Goias State, Brazil." Ambio 34(3): 212-217.

Ferreira Júnior, P. D., A. Z. Castro, et al. (2007). "The Importance of Nidification Environment in the *Podocnemis expansa* and *Podocnemis unifilis* Phenotypes (Testudines: Podocnemididae)." South American J Herpetol 2(1): 39-46.

Finkler, M. S. 1997). "Impact of Egg Content on Post-Hatchling Size, Body Composition, and Performance in the Common Snapping Turtle (*Chelydra serpentina*). Linnaeus Fund Research Report." Chelonian Cons Biol 2(3): 452-55.

Finkler, M. S. and J. R. E. Gatten (2001). "Rates of Water Loss and Estimates of Survival Time Under Varying Humidity in Juvenile Snapping Turtles (*Chelydra serpentina*)." Copeia 2001(2): 521-525.

Finkler, M. S. and R. Mason (2006). "Does Variation in Soil Water Content Induce Variation in the Size of Hatchling Snapping Turtles (*Chelydra serpentina*)?" Copeia 2006(4): 769-777.

Flitz, B. A. and S. J. Mullin (2006). "Nest-Site Selection in the Eastern Box Turtle, *Terrapene carolina carolina*, in Illinois." Chelonian Cons Biol 5(2): 309-312.

Fordham, D., A. Georges, et al. (2006). "Compensation For Inundation-Induced Embryonic Diapause in a Freshwater Turtle: Achieving Predictability in the Face of Environmental Stochasticity." Functional Ecology 20(4): 670-677.

Freedberg, S., T. J. Greives, et al. (2008). "Incubation Environment Affects Immune System Development in a Turtle with Environmental Sex Determination." J Herpetol 42(3): 536-541.

Georges, A., and S. McInnes (1998). "Temperature Fails to Influence Hatchling Sex in Another Genus and Species of Chelid Turtle, *Elusor macrurus*." J Herpetol 32(4): 596-98.

Georges, A., S. Doody, et al. (2004). Thermal Models of TSD Under Laboratory and Field Conditions. Temperature Dependent Sex Determination in Reptiles. N. Valenzuela and V. Lance. Washington, Smithsonian Institute: pp. 79-89.

Georges, A., T. Ezaz, et al. (2010). "Are Reptiles Predisposed to Temperature-Dependent Sex Determination?" Sex Dev 4(1-2): 7-15.

Gienger, C. M. and C. Richard Tracy (2008). "Ecological Interactions Between Gila Monsters (*Heloderma suspectum*) and Desert Tortoises (*Gopherus agassizii*)." Southwest Nat 53(2): 265-268.

Gist, D. H., S. M. Dawes, et al. (2002). "Sperm Storage in Turtles: a Male Perspective." J Exp Zool 292(2): 180-186.

Goode, J. M. and M. A. Ewert (2006). "Reproductive Trends in Captive *Heosemys grandis* (Geoemydidae)." Chelonian Cons Biol 5(1): 165-169.

Goodman, R. H. Jr. (1997). "Occurrence of Double-Clutching in the Southwestern Pond Turtle, *Clemmys marmorata pallida* in the Los Angeles Basin." Chelonian Cons Biol 2(3): 419-20.

Graham, T. E., and A. A. Graham (1997). "Ecology of the Eastern Spiny Softshell, *Apalone spinifera spinifera*, in the Lamoille River, Vermont." Chelonian Cons Biol 2(3): 363-69.

Hailey, A. and M. R. K. Lambert (2002). "Comparative Growth Patterns in Afrotropical Giant Tortoises (Reptilia Testudinidae)." Tropical Zoology 15: 121-139.

Hailey, A. and R. E. Willemsen (2000). "Population Density and Adult Sex Ratio of the Tortoise *Testudo hermanni* in Greece: Evidence For Intrinsic Population Regulation." J Zool 251(3): 325-338.

Han, X., L. Zhangli, et al. (2008). "Ultrastructure of Anterior Uterus of the Oviduct and the Stored Sperm in Female Soft-Shelled Turtle, *Trionyx sinensis*." the Anatomical Record: Advances in Integrative Anatomy and Evolutionary Biology 291(3): 335-351.

Harrel, J. B., et al. (1996). "Mating Behavior in Captive Alligator Snapping Turtles (*Macroclemys temminckii*)." Chelonian Cons Biol 2(1): 101-05.

Hodsdon, L.A. and Pearson, J.F.W. (1943). "Notes on the discovery and biology of two Bahaman freshwater turtles of the genus *Pseudemys*." Proceedings of the Florida Academy of Sciences 6(2): 17-23.

Hofmeyr, M. D. (2004). "Egg Production in *Chersina angulata*: an Unusual Pattern in a Mediterranean Climate." J Herpetol 38(2): 172-179.

Hughes, G. N., W. F. Greaves, et al. (2009). "Nest-Site Selection By Wood Turtles (*Glyptemys insculpta*) in a Thermally Limited Environment." Northeastern Naturalist 16(3): 321-338.

Iverson, J. B. (1999). "Reproduction in the Mexican Mud Turtle *Kinosternon integrum*." J Herpetol 33(1): 144-48.

Iverson, J. B. (2010). "Reproduction in the Red-Cheeked Mud Turtle (*Kinosternon scorpioides cruentatum*) in Southeastern Mexico and Belize, with Comparisons Across the Species Range." Chelonian Cons Biol 9(2): 250-261.

Iverson, J. B., and P. E. Moler (1997). "The Female Reproductive Cycle of the Florida Softshell Turtle (*Apalone ferox*)." J Herpetol 31(3): 399-409.

Iverson, J. B., R. L. Prosser, et al. (2009). "Orientation in Juveniles of a Semiaquatic Turtle, *Kinosternon flavescens*." Herpetologica 65(3): 237-245.

Jackson, D.R. (1994). "Overwintering of Hatchling Turtles in Northern Florida." J Herpetol 28(3): 401-02.

Jackson, F. D., X. Jin, et al. (2008). "The First in Situ Turtle Clutch From the Cretaceous Tiantai Basin, Zhejiang Province, China." J Vertebr Paleontol 28(2): 319-325.

Janzen, F. J. (1994). "Climate Change and Temperature-Dependent Sex Determination in Reptiles." Proceedings of the National Academy of Science, USA 91: 7487-90.

Janzen, F. J., J. K. Tucker, et al. (2000). "Experimental Analysis of an Early Life-History Stage: Avian Predation Selects For Larger Body Size of Hatchling Turtles." J Evolution Biol 13(6): 947-954.

Johnson, V. M., C. Guyer, et al. (2007). "Phenology of Attempted Matings in Gopher Tortoises." Copeia 2007(2): 490-495.

Johnson, V. M., C. Guyer, et al. (2009). "Patterns of Dispersion and Burrow Use Support Scramble Competition Polygyny in *Gopherus polyphemus*." Herpetologica 65(2): 214-218.

Jones, R. L. (2006). "Reproduction and Nesting of the Endangered Ringed Map Turtle, *Graptemys oculifera*, in Mississippi." Chelonian Cons Biol 5(2): 195-209.

Kabigumila, J. (2001). "Size Composition and Sex Ratio of the Leopard Tortoise (*Geochelone pardalis*) in Northern Tanzania." Afr J Ecol 39(4): 393-395.

Kam, Y.-C. (1994). "Effects of Simulated Flooding on Metabolism and Water Balance of Turtle Eggs and Embryos." J Herpetol 28 (2): 173-78.

Kennett, R. (1999). "Reproduction of Two Species of Freshwater Turtle, *Chelodina rugosa* and *Elseya dentata*, from the Wet-Dry Tropics of Northern Australia." J. Zool. Lond. 247: 457-73.

Kennett, R., A. Georges, et al. (1993). "Early Developmental Arrest During Immersion of Eggs of a Tropical Freshwater Turtle, *Chelodina rugosa* (Testudinata, Chelidae), from Northern Australia." Aust J Zool 41(1): 37-45.

Kennett, R., K. Christian, et al. (1993). "Underwater Nesting by the Tropical Freshwater Turtle, *Chelodina rugosa* (Testudinata, Chelidae)." Australian J Zool 41(1): 47-52.

Kennett, R., K. Christian, et al. (1998). "Underwater Nesting by the Australian Freshwater Turtle *Chelodina rugosa*: Effect of Prolonged Immersion and Eggshell Thickness on Incubation Period, Egg Survivorship, and Hatchling Size." Canadian J Zool - Revue Canadienne de Zoologie 76(6): 1019-23.

Kinney, O. M., R. D. Nagle, et al. (1998). "Water Transport by Nesting Painted Turtles (*Chrysemys picta marginata*) in Michigan." Chelonian Cons Biol 3(1): 71-76.

Kolbe, J. J., F. J. Janzen, et al. (2002). "Experimental Analysis of an Early Life-History Stage: Water Loss and Migrating Hatchling Turtles." Copeia 2002(1): 220-226.

Kostel, F. (1990). "Breeding Behavior and Activity Patterns of the Asian Freshwater Terrapins *Batagur baska* and *Callagur borneoensis*." M.Sc. Thesis. Fordham University.

Lance, V. A. (2009). "is Regulation of Aromatase Expression in Reptiles the Key to Understanding Temperature-Dependent Sex Determination?" J Exp Zool Part A: Ecological Genetics and Physiology 311a(5): 314-322.

Lawniczak, C. J. and M. A. Teece (2005). "Spatial Mobilization of Calcium and Magnesium From the Eggshell of the Snapping Turtle, *Chelydra serpentina*." J Herpetol 39(4): 659-664.

Lee, T. N., M. V. Plummer, et al. (2007). "Use of Posthatching Yolk and External Forage to Maximize Early Growth in *Apalone mutica* Hatchlings." J Herpetol 41(3): 492-500.

Ligon, D. B. and M. B. Lovern (2009). "Temperature Effects During Early Life Stages of the Alligator Snapping Turtle (*Macrochelys temminckii*)." Chelonian Cons Biol 8(1): 74-83.

Litzgus, J. D. and T. A. Mousseau (2003). "Multiple Clutching in Southern Spotted Turtles, *Clemmys guttata*." J Herpetol 37(1): 17-23.

Litzgus, J. D., and R. J. Brooks (1998). "Reproduction in a Northern Population of *Clemmys guttata*." J Herpetol 32(2): 252-59.

Litzgus, J. D., F. Bolton, et al. (2008). "Reproductive Output Depends on Body Condition in Spotted Turtles (*Clemmys guttata*)." Copeia 2008(1): 86-92.

Loehr, V. J. T. (1999). "Husbandry, Behavior, and Captive Breeding of the Namaqualand Speckled Padloper (*Homopus signatus signatus*)." Chelonian Cons Biol 3(3): 468-73.

Loehr, V. J. T., B. T. Henen, et al. (2004). "Reproduction of the Smallest Tortoise, the Namaqualand Speckled Padloper, *Homopus signatus signatus*." Herpetologica 60(4): 444-454.

Lovich, J. E., et al. (1991). "Behavior of Hatchling Diamondback Terrapins (*Malaclemys terrapin*) Released in a South Carolina Salt Marsh." Herpetological Review 22(3): 81-83.

Lovich, J. E., et al. (2000). "Studies of Reproductive Output of the Desert Tortoise at Joshua Tree National Park, the the Mojave National Preserve, and Comparative Sites." Park Science 19(1): 22-24.

Macip-Ríos, R., M. D. L. A. Cisneros, et al. (2009). "Population Ecology and Reproduction of the Mexican Mud Turtle (*Kinosternon integrum*) in Tonatico, Estado De México." Western North American Naturalist 69(4): 501-510.

Martinez, P. A., T. Ezaz, et al. (2008). "An XX/XY Heteromorphic Sex Chromosome System in the Australian Chelid Turtle *Emydura macquarii*: a New Piece in the Puzzle of Sex Chromosome Evolution in Turtles." Chromosome Res 16(6): 815-825.

Mcgaugh, S. E., R. M. Bowden, et al. (2011). "Field-Measured Heritability of the Threshold For Sex Determination in a Turtle with Temperature-Dependent Sex Determination." Evolutionary Ecology Research 13: 75-90.

McMaster, N. L., and T. B. Herman (2000). "Occurrence, Habitat Selection, and Movement Patterns of Juvenile Blanding's Turtles (*Emydoidea blandingii*) in Kejimkujik National Park, Nova Scotia." Chelonian Cons Biol 3(4): 602-10.

Moll, D. (1994). "The Ecology of Sea Beach Nesting in Slider Turtles (*Trachemys scripta venusta*) from Caribbean Costa Rica." Chelonian Cons Biol 1(2): 107-16.

Moll, E. O. (1980). "Natural History of the River Terrapin, *Batagur baska* (Gray) in Malaysia (Testudines: Emydidae)." Malaysian J Sci 6(A): 23-62.

Moll, E. O., K. E. Matson, et al. (1981). "Sexual and Seasonal Dichromatism in the Asian River Turtle *Callagur borneoensis*." Herpetologica 37(4): 181-94.

Moore, J. A., M. Strattan, et al. (2009). "Evidence For Year-Round Reproduction in the Gopher Tortoise (*Gopherus polyphemus*) in Southeastern Florida." Bulletin of the Peabody Museum of Natural History 50(2): 387-392.

Morjan, C. L. and N. Valenzuela (2001). "is Ground-Nuzzling By Female Turtles Associated with Soil Surface Temperatures?" J Herpetol 35(4): 668-672.

Mullins, M. A. and F. J. Janzen (2006). "Phenotypic Effects of Thermal Means and Variances on Smooth Softshell Turtle (*Apalone mutica*) Embryos and Hatchlings." Herpetologica 62(1): 27-36.

Nagle, R. D., M. V. Plummer, et al. (2003). "Parental Investment, Embryo Growth, and Hatchling Lipid Reserves in Softshell Turtles (*Apalone mutica*) From Arkansas." Herpetologica 59(2): 145-154.

Neuwald, J. L. and N. Valenzuela (2011). "The Lesser Known Challenge of Climate Change: Thermal Variance and Sex-Reversal in Vertebrates with Temperature-Dependent Sex Determination." Plos One (): 6(3): E18117. Doi:18110.11371/Journal.Pone.0018117.

Nie, L., C. Guo, et al. (2001). "Sex Determination Mechanism of *Trionyx sinensis*." Chin J Appl Environ Blol. 7: 258–261.

Norris, J. L. (1996) "Male Courtship in the New Guinean Turtle, *Emydura subglobosa* (Pleurodira, Chelidae)." J Herpetol 30(1): 78-80.

Okada, Y., T. Yabe, et al. (2010). "Temperature-Dependent Sex Determination in the Japanese Pond Turtle, *Mauremys japonica* (Reptilia: Geoemydidae)." Current Herpetology 29(1): 1-10.

Onorato, D. (1996). "The Growth Rate and Age Distribution of *Sternotherus minor* at Rainbow Run, Florida." J Herpetol 30(3): 301-06.

Packard, G. C., and M. J. Packard (1988). "The Physiological Ecology of Reptilian Eggs and Embryos." the Biology of the Reptilia. Eds. C. Gans and R.B. Huey. Vol. 16. Seattle: A.R. Liss. pp. 524–605.

Packard, G. C., M. J. Packard, et al. (2000). "Why Hatchling Blanding's Turtles Don't Overwinter inside Their Nest." Herpetologica 56(3): 367-74.

Páez, V. P., and B. C. Bock (1998). "Temperature Effect on Incubation Period in the Yellow-Spotted River Turtle, *Podocnemis unifilis*, in the Colombian Amazon." Chelonian Cons Biol 3(1): 31-36.

Páez, V. P., J. C. Correa, et al. (2009). "A Comparison of Maternal and Temperature Effects on Sex, Size, and Growth of Hatchlings of the Magdalena River Turtle (*Podocnemis lewyana*) Incubated Under Field and Controlled Laboratory Conditions." Copeia 2009(4): 698-704.

Paitz, R. T., S. G. Clairardin, et al. (2010). "Temperature Fluctuations Affect Offspring Sex But Not Morphological, Behavioral, or Immunological Traits in the Northern Painted Turtle (*Chrysemys picta*)." Canadian J Zool 88(5): 479-486.

Palmer, K. S., et al. (1998) "Long-Term Sperm Storage in the Desert Tortoise (*Gopherus agassizii*)." Copeia 1998(3): 702-05.

Pearse, D. E., R. B. Dastrup, et al. (2006). "Paternity in an Orinoco Population of Endangered Arrau River Turtles, *Podocnemis expansa* (Pleurodira; Podocnemididae), From Venezuela." Chelonian Cons Biol 5(2): 232-238.

Pellitteri-Rosa, D., R. Sacchi, et al. (2011). "Courtship Displays Are Condition-Dependent Signals That Reliably Reflect Male Quality in Greek Tortoises, *Testudo graeca*." Chelonian Cons Biol 10(1): 10-17.

Peterson, C. C. and A. Kruegl (2005). "Peaked Temporal Pattern of Embryonic Metabolism in an Emydid Turtle (*Chrysemys picta picta*)." J Herpetol 39(4): 678-681.

Pike, D. A. and R. A. Seigel (2006). "Variation in Hatchling Tortoise Survivorship At Three Geographic Localities." Herpetologica 62(2): 125-131.

Pike, D. A. and T. W. Reeder (2006). "Movement Patterns, Habitat Use, and Growth of Hatchling Tortoises, *Gopherus polyphemus*." Copeia 2006(1): 68-76.

Platt, S. G., H. Sovannara, et al. (2008). "Biodiversity, Exploitation, and Conservation of Turtles in the Tonle Sap Biosphere Reserve, Cambodia, with Notes on Reproductive Ecology of *Malayemys subtrijuga*." Chelonian Cons Biol 7(2): 195-204.

Plummer, M. V., C. E. Shadrin, et al. (1994). "Thermal Limits of Incubation in Embryos of Softshell Turtles (*Apalone mutica*)." Chelonian Cons Biol 1(2): 141-44.

Plummer, M. V., T. N. Lee, et al. (2008). "Effect of a Sand Substrate on the Growth and Condition of *Apalone mutica* Hatchlings." J Herpetol 42(3): 550-554.

Polisar, J. (1996) "Reproductive Biology of a Flood-Season Nesting Freshwater Turtle of the Northern Neotropics: *Dermatemys mawii* in Belize." Chelonian Cons Biol 2(1): 13-25.

Rasmussen, M. L. and J. D. Litzgus (2010). "Patterns of Maternal Investment in Spotted Turtles (*Clemmys guttata*): Implications of Trade-Offs, Scales of Analyses, and Incubation Substrates." Ecoscience 17(1): 47-58.

Refsnider, J. M. (2009). "High Frequency of Multiple Paternity in Blanding's Turtle (*Emys blandingii*)." J Herpetol 43(1): 74-81.

Reina, R. D., P. A. Mayor, et al. (2002). "Nesting Ecology of the Leatherback Turtle, *Dermochelys coriacea*, At Parque Nacional Marino Las Baulas, Costa Rica: 1988-1989 to 1999-2000." Copeia 2002(3): 653-664.

Restrepo, A., V. J. Piñeros, et al. (2006). "Nest Site Selection By Colombian Slider Turtles, *Trachemys callirostris callirostris* (Testudines: Emydidae), in the Mompos Depression, Colombia." Chelonian Cons Biol 5(2): 249-254.

Rollinson, N. and R. J. Brooks (2008). "Sources and Significance of Among-Individual Reproductive Variation in a Northern Population of Painted Turtles (*Chrysemys picta*)." Copeia 2008(3): 533-541.

Roosenburg, W. M., and K. C. Kelley (1996). "The Effect of Egg Size and Incubation Temperature on Growth in the Turtle, *Malaclemys terripin*." J Herpetol 30 (2): 198-204.

Roosenburg, W. M., T. Dennis, et al. (2005). "Egg Component Comparisons within and Among Clutches of the Diamondback Terrapin, *Malaclemys terrapin*." Copeia 2005(2): 417-423.

Roques, S., C. Díaz-Paniagua, et al. (2004). "Microsatellite Markers Reveal Multiple Paternity and Sperm Storage in the Mediterranean Spur-Thighed Tortoise,*Testudo graeca*." Canadian J Zool 82(1): 153-159.

Roques, S., C. Diazpaniagua, et al. (2006). "Sperm Storage and Low Incidence of Multiple Paternity in the European Pond Turtle, *Emys orbicularis*: a Secure But Costly Strategy?" Biol Conserv 129(2): 236-243.

Ross, D A., and R. K. Anderson (1990). "Habitat Use, Movements and Nesting of *Emydoidea blandingi* in Central Wisconsin." J Herpetol 24(1): 6-12.

Rowe, J. W. (1995). "Hatchling Size in the Turtle *Chrysemys picta belli* from Western Nebraska: Relationships to Egg and Maternal Body Size." J Herpetol 29(1): 73-79.

Rowe, J. W., K. A. Coval, et al. (2003). "Reproductive Characteristics of Female Midland Painted Turtles (*Chrysemys picta marginata*) From a Population on Beaver Island, Michigan." Copeia 2003(2): 326-336.

Rowe, J. W., K. A. Coval, et al. (2005). "Nest Placement, Nest-Site Fidelity and Nesting Movements in Midland Painted Turtles (*Chrysemys picta marginata*) on Beaver Island, Michigan." Am Midl Nat154(2): 383-397.

Ruane, S., S. A. Dinkelacker, et al. (2008). "Demographic and Reproductive Traits of Blanding's Turtles, *Emydoidea blandingii*, At the Western Edge of the Species' Range." Copeia 2008(4): 771-779.

Schramm, B G., V. A. Lance, et al. (1999). "Reproductive Cycles of Male and Female Giant Tortoises (*Geochelone nigra*) on the Galápagos Islands by Plasma Steroid Analysis and Ultrasound Scanning." Chelonian Cons Biol 3(3): 523-28.

Seymour, R. S., R. Kennett, et al. (1997). "Osmotic Balance in the Eggs of the Turtle *Chelodina rugosa* During Developmental Arrest under Water." Physiological Zoology 70(3): 301-06.

Sheridan, C. M., J. R. Spotila, et al. (2010). "Sex-Biased Dispersal and Natal Philopatry in the Diamondback Terrapin, *Malaclemys terrapin*." Molecular Ecology 19(24): 5497-5510.

Smith, G. R. and J. B. Iverson (2002). "Sex Ratio of Common Musk Turtles (*Sternotherus odoratus*) in a North-Central Indiana Lake: a Long-Term Study." Am Midl Nat148(1): 185-189.

Smith, K. R., J. A. Hurley, et al. (1997). "Reproductive Biology and Demography of Gopher Tortoises (*Gopherus polyphemus*) from the Western Portion of Their Range." Chelonian Cons Biol 2(4): 596-600.

Smith, L. L., M. Pedrono, et al. (2001). "Morphometrics, Sexual Dimorphism, and Growth in the Angonoka Tortoise (*Geochelone yniphora*) of Western Madagascar." African J Herpetol 50(1): 9-18.

Soares De Almeida, S., J. C. B. Pezzuti, et al. (2005). "Notes on Nesting of *Podocnemis unifilis* (Chelonia: Pelomedusidae) in Small Agricultural Clearings in Eastern Amazonia, Caxiuanã, Pará, Brazil." Bol. Mus. Para. Emílio Goeldi, Sér. Ciências Naturais, Belém 1(1): 243-245.

Spencer, R.-J. and F. J. Janzen (2011). "Hatching Behavior in Turtles." Integrative and Comparative Biology 51(1): 100-110.

Spencer, R.-J. and M. B. Thompson (2003). "The Significance of Predation in Nest Site Selection of Turtles: an Experimental Consideration of Macro- and Microhabitat Preferences." Oikos 102(3): 592-600.

Spencer, R.-J. and M. B. Thompson (2005). "Experimental Analysis of the Impact of Foxes on Freshwater Turtle Populations." Conservation Biology 19(3): 845-854.

Spencer, R.-J., M. B. Thompson, et al. (2001). "Hatch or Wait? a Dilemma in Reptilian Incubation." Oikos 93(3): 401-406.

Steyermark, A. C. and J. R. Spotila (2001). "Effects of Maternal Identity and Incubation Temperature on Snapping Turtle (*Chelydra serpentina*) Growth." Functional Ecology 15(5): 624-632.

Strickland, J., P. Colbert, et al. (2010). "Experimental Analysis of Effects of Markers and Habitat Structure on Predation of Turtle Nests." J Herpetol 44(3): 467-470.

Szerlag-Egger, S. and S. P. Mcrobert (2007). "Northern Diamondback Terrapin Occurrence, Movement, and Nesting Activity Along a Salt Marsh Access Road." Chelonian Cons Biol 6(2): 295-301.

Taskavak, E., and M. K. Atatür (1998). "Distribution and Habitats of the Euphrates Softshell Turtle, *Rafetus euphraticus*, in Southeastern Anatolia, Turkey, with Observations on Biology and Factors Endangering Its Survival." Chelonian Cons Biol 3(1): 20-30.

Thomas, R. B. and R. Altig (2006). "Characteristics of the Foreclaw Display Behaviors of Female *Trachemys scripta* (Slider Turtles)." Southeastern Naturalist 5(2): 227-234.

Thomas, R. B. and W. L. Montgomery (2002). "Conditional Mating Strategy in a Long-Lived Vertebrate: Ontogenetic Shifts in the Mating Tactics of Male Slider Turtles (*Trachemys scripta*)." Copeia 2002(2): 456-461.

Thorbjarnarson, J. B., N. Perez, et al. (1993). "Nesting of *Podocnemis unifilis* in the Capanaparo River, Venezuela." J Herpetol 27 (3): 344-47.

Tucker, J. K. (1999). "Environmental Correlates of Hatchling Emergence in the Red-Eared Turtle, *Trachemys scripta elegans*, in Illinois." Chelonian Cons Biol 3(3): 401-06.

Tucker, J. K. (2000). "Body Size and Migration of Hatchling Turtles: Inter- and Intraspecific Comparisons." J Herpetol 34 (4): 541-46.

Tucker, J. K., and D. A. Warner (1999). "Microgeographic Variation in Response of Red-Eared Slider (*Trachemys scripta elegans*) Embryos to Similar Incubation Environments." J Herpetol 33(4): 549-57.

Tucker, J. K., and G. L. Paukstis (1999). "Post-Hatching Substrate Moisture and Overwintering Hatchling Turtles." J Herpetol 33(4): 608-15.

Tucker, J. K., C. R. Dolan, et al. (2008). "Climatic Warming, Sex Ratios, and Red-Eared Sliders (*Trachemys scripta elegans*) in Illinois." Chelonian Cons Biol 7(1): 60-69.

Tucker, J. K., F. J. Janzen, et al. (1997). "Response of Embryos of the Red-Eared Turtle (*Trachemys scripta elegans*) to Experimental Exposure to Water-Saturated Substrates." Chelonian Cons Biol 2(3): 345-51.

Tuttle, S. E. and D. M. Carroll (2005). "Movements and Behavior of Hatchling Wood Turtles (*Glyptemys insculpta*)." Northeastern Naturalist 12(3): 331-348.

Uller, T. and M. Olsson (2008). "Multiple Paternity in Reptiles: Patterns and Processes." Molecular Ecology 17(11): 2566-2580.

Valenzuela, N. (2004). Temperature-Dependent Sex Determination. Reptilian Incubation: Environment & Behaviour. D. C. Deeming, Nottingham University Press: pp. 211-227.

Valenzuela, N. (2008). "Evolution of the Gene Network Underlying Gonadogenesis in Turtles with Temperature-Dependent and Genotypic Sex Determination." Integr Comp Biol 48(4): 476-485.

Valenzuela, N. (2008). "Relic Thermosensitive Gene Expression in a Turtle with Genotypic Sex Determination." Evolution 62(1): 234-240.

Valenzuela, N. (2010). "Multivariate Expression Analysis of the Gene Network Underlying Sexual Development in Turtle Embryos with Temperature-Dependent and Genotypic Sex Determination." Sex Dev 4(1-2): 39-49.

Valenzuela, N. and D. C. Adams (2011). "Chromosome Number and Sex Determination Coevolve in Turtles." Evolution 65(6): 1808-1813.

Valenzuela, N. and T. Shikano (2007). "Embryological Ontogeny of Aromatase Gene Expression in *Chrysemys picta* and *Apalone mutica* Turtles: Comparative Patterns within and Across Temperature-Dependent and Genotypic Sex-Determining Mechanisms." Dev Genes Evol 217(1): 55-62.

Valenzuela, N., D. C. Adams, et al. (2004). "Geometric Morphometric Sex Estimation For Hatchling Turtles: a Powerful Alternative For Detecting Subtle Sexual Shape Dimorphism." Copeia 2004(4): 735-742.

Vanzolini, P. E. (2003). "on Clutch Size and Hatching Success of the South American Turtles *Podocnemis expansa* (Schweigger, 1812) and P. Unifilis Troschel, 1848 (Testudines, Podocnemididae)." Anais Da Academia Brasileira De Ciências 75(4): 415-430.

Vogt, R. C. (1994). "Temperature Controlled Sex Determination as a Tool for Turtle Conservation." Chelonian Cons Biol 1(2): 159-62.

Vogt, R. C., V. H. Cantarelli, et al. (1994). "Reproduction of the Cabeçudo, *Peltocephalus dumerilianus*, in the Biological Reserve of Rio Trombetas, Pará, Brazil." Chelonian Cons Biol 1(2): 145-48.

Wallis, I. R., B. T. Henen, et al. (1999). "Egg Size and Annual Egg Production by Female Desert Tortoises (*Gopherus agassizii*): the Importance of Food Abundance, Body Size, and Date of Egg Shelling." J Herpetol 33(3): 394-408.

Warner, D. A., J. K. Tucker, et al. (2006). "Claw Function of Hatchling and Adult Red-Eared Slider Turtles (*Trachemys scripta elegans*)." Chelonian Cons Biol 5(2): 317-320.

Whitaker, N. (2006). "Immaculate Conception, Incubation Protocols, and Egg Characteristics of the Ganges Softshell Turtle (*Aspideretes gangeticus*)." Contemporary Herpetology 2006(1): 1-6.

Wilson, D. S. (1998). "Nesting of the Striped Mud Turtle (*Kinosternon baurii*) in Central Florida." Chelonian Cons Biol 3(1): 142-43.

Wilson, Dawn S., H. R. Mushinsky, et al. (1999). "Nesting Behavior of the Striped Mud Turtle, *Kinosternon baurii* (Testudines: Kinosternidae)." Copeia 1999(4): 958-68.

Wilson, G. L. and C. H. Ernst (2005). "Reproductive Ecology of the *Terrapene carolina carolina* (Eastern Box Turtle) in Central Virginia." Southeastern Naturalist 4(4): 689-702.

Zelenitsky, D. K., F. O. Therrien, et al. (2008). "First Fossil Gravid Turtle Provides Insight Into the Evolution of Reproductive Traits in Turtles." Biol Lett 4(6): 715-718.

Zuffi, M. A. L. and A. Plaitano (2007). "Similarities and Differences in Adult Tortoises: a Morphological Approach and Its Implication For Reproduction and Mobility Between Species." Acta Herpetologica 2(2): 79-86.

Chapter 8: The Endless Journey

AlKindi, A. Y. A., I. Y. Mahmoud, et al. (2006). "The Effect of Physical and Human Factors on Beach Selection by Green Turtles (*Chelonia mydas*) at Ras Al-Hadd Reserve, Oman." Chelonian Cons Biol 5(2): 289-294.

Alvarado-Díaz, J., E. Arias-Coyotl, et al. (2003). "Clutch Frequency of the Michoacán Green Seaturtle." J Herpetol 37(1): 183-185.

Anon. (2011). "Proposed TED Rule Would Better Protect Sea Turtles." Sea Turtle Conservancy Newsletter Retrieved 14 September, 2011, from http://www.conserveturtles.org/velador.php?page=velart42a.

Baran, I., and O. Türkozan (1996). "Nesting Activity of the Loggerhead Turtle, *Caretta caretta*, on Fethiye Beach, Turkey, in 1994." Chelonian Cons Biol 2(1): 93-96.

Bass, A. L., and W. N. Witzell (2000). "Demographic Composition of Immature Green Turtles (*Chelonia mydas*) from the East Central Florida Coast: Evidence from Mtdna Markers." Herpetologica 56(3): 357-67.

Benson, S. R., P. H. Dutton, et al. (2007). "Post-Nesting Migrations of Leatherback Turtles (*Dermochelys coriacea*) from Jamursba-Medi, Bird's Head Peninsula, Indonesia." Chelonian Cons Biol 6(1): 150-154.

Benson, S. R., T. Eguchi, et al. (2011). "Large-scale Movements and High-Use Areas of Western Pacific Leatherback Turtles,*Dermochelys coriacea*." Ecosphere 2(7): Art84.

Blamires, S. J. and M. E. Douglas (2004). "Habitat Preferences of Coastal Goannas (*Varanus panoptes*): Are They Exploiters of Sea Turtle Nests At Fog Bay, Australia?" Copeia 2004(2): 370-377.

Blumenthal, J. M., T. J. Austin, et al. (2009). "Ecology of Hawksbill Turtles, *Eretmochelys imbricata*, on a Western Caribbean Foraging Ground." Chelonian Cons Biol 8(1): 1-10.

Bollmer, J. L., et al. (1999). "Multiple Paternity in Loggerhead Turtle Clutches." Copeia 1999(2): 475-78.

Booth, /, and J. A. Peters (1972). "Behavioural Studies on the Green Turtle (*Chelonia mydas*) in the Sea." Animal Behaviour 20(4): 808-12.

Bourjea, J., S. Lapègue, et al. (2007). "Phylogeography of the Green Turtle, *Chelonia mydas*, in the Southwest Indian Ocean." Molecular Ecology 16(1): 175-186.

Bowen, B. W. and S. A. Karl (2007). "Population Genetics and Phylogeography of Sea Turtles." Molecular Ecology 16(23): 4886-4907.

Bowen, B. W., et al. (1995). "Trans-Pacific Migrations of the Loggerhead Turtle (*Caretta caretta*) Demonstrated with Mitochondrial DNA Markers." Proceedings of the National Academy of Science, USA 92: 3731-34.

Bowen, B. W., W. S. Grant, et al. (2007). "Mixed-Stock Analysis Reveals the Migrations of Juvenile Hawksbill Turtles (*Eretmochelys imbricata*) in the Caribbean Sea." Molecular Ecology 16(1): 49-60.

Broderick, A. C., and E. G. Hancock (1997). "Insect Infestation of Mediterranean Marine Turtle Eggs." Herpetological Review 28(4): 190-91.

Brooks, L., J. Harvey, et al. (2008). "Tethered GPS/VHF Transmitters: a High-Tech, Low-Cost Tool For Fine Scale, In-Water Tracks." Noaa Technical Memorandum Nmfs Sefsc [NOAA Tech. Mem. NMFS SEFSC]. No. 567, P. 189.

Brown, C. W. (1990). "The Significance of the South Atlantic Equatorial Countercurrent to the Ecology of the Green Turtle Breeding Population of Ascension Island." J Herpetol 24(1): 81-84.

Cain, S. D., L. C. Boles, et al. (2005). "Magnetic Orientation and Navigation in Marine Turtles, Lobsters, and Molluscs: Concepts and Conundrums." Integrative and Comparative Biology 45(3): 539-546.

Caldwell, R. L. (2005). "An Observation of Inking Behavior Protecting Adult Octopus Bocki From Predation By Green Turtle (*Chelonia mydas*) Hatchlings." Pacific Science 59(1): 69-72.

Campbell, C/ L., C. J. Lagueux, et al. (1996). "Leatherback Turtle, *Dermochelys coriacea*, Nesting at Tortuguero, Costa Rica, in 1995." Chelonian Cons Biol 2(2): 169–72.

Cardona, L., P. Campos, et al. (2010). "Asynchrony Between Dietary and Nutritional Shifts During the Ontogeny of Green Turtles (*Chelonia mydas*) in the Mediterranean." J Exp Mar Biol Ecol 393(1-2): 83-89.

Chaloupka, M., and G. R. Zug (1997). "A Polyphasic Growth Function for the Endangered Kemp's Ridley Sea Turtle, *Lepidochelys kempii*." Fishery Bulletin 95: 849-56.

Chaloupka, M., N. Kamezaki, et al. (2008). "is Climate Change Affecting the Population Dynamics of the Endangered Pacific Loggerhead Sea Turtle?" J Exp Mar Biol Ecol 356(1-2): 136-143.

Champetier De Ribes, G., S. Ramarokoto, et al. (1999). "Intoxications Par Consommation D'animaux Marins À Madagascar." Cahiers Santé 9: 235-241.

Chen, H.-C., I. J. Cheng, et al. (2007). "The Influence of the Beach Environment on the Digging Success and Nest Site Distribution of the Green Turtle, *Chelonia mydas*, on Wan-an Island, Penghu Archipelago, Taiwan." J Coastal Res 23(5): 1277-1286.

Cheng, I. J. (2007). "Nesting Ecology and Postnesting Migration of Sea Turtles on Taipin Tao, Nansha Archipelago, South China Sea." Chelonian Cons Biol 6(2): 277-282.

Christens, E. (1990). "Nest Emergence Lag in Loggerhead Sea Turtles." J Herpetol 24(4): 400-02.

Chung, F. C., N. J. Pilcher, et al. (2009). "Offshore Migratory Activity of Hawksbill Turtle (*Eretmochelys imbricata*) Hatchlings, I. Quantitative Analysis of Activity, with Comparisons to Green Turtles (*Chelonia mydas*)." Chelonian Cons Biol 8(1): 28-34.

Chung, F. C., N. J. Pilcher, et al. (2009). "Offshore Migratory

Activity of Hawksbill Turtle (*Eretmochelys imbricata*) Hatchlings, II. Swimming Gaits, Swimming Speed, and Morphological Comparisons." Chelonian Cons Biol 8(1): 35-42.

Coles, W. C., and J. A. Musick (2000). "Satellite Sea Surface Temperature Analysis and Correlation with Sea Turtle Distribution Off North Carolina." Copeia 2000(2): 551-54.

Collazo, J. A., Boulon, R., Jr., et al. (1992). "Abundance and Growth Patterns of *Chelonia mydas* in Culebra, Puerto Rico." J Herpetol 26(3): 293-300.

Crim, J. L., L. D. Spotila, et al. (2002). "The Leatherback Turtle, *Dermochelys coriacea*, Exhibits Both Polyandry and Polygyny." Molecular Ecology 11: 2097-2106.

Cuevas, E., M. De Los Ángeles Liceaga-Correa, et al. (2010). "Influence of Beach Slope and Width on Hawksbill (*Eretmochelys imbricata*) and Green Turtle (*Chelonia mydas*) Nesting Activity in El Cuyo, Yucatán, Mexico." Chelonian Cons Biol 9(2): 262-267.

Dethmers, K. E. M., D. Broderick, et al. (2006). "The Genetic Structure of Australasian Green Turtles (*Chelonia mydas*): Exploring the Geographical Scale of Genetic Exchange." Molecular Ecology 15(13): 3931-3946.

Diez, C. E. and R. P. Van Dam (2003). "Sex Ratio of an Immature Hawksbill Seaturtle Aggregation At Mona Island, Puerto Rico." J Herpetol 37(3): 533-537.

Eckert, S. A., D. Bagley, et al. (2006). "Internesting and Postnesting Movements and Foraging Habitats of Leatherback Sea Turtles (*Dermochelys coriacea*) Nesting in Florida." Chelonian Cons Biol 5(2): 239-248.

Elshafie, A., S. N. Al-Bahry, et al. (2007). "Mycoflora and Aflatoxins in Soil, Eggshells, and Failed Eggs of *Chelonia mydas* At Ras Al-Jinz, Oman." Chelonian Cons Biol 6(2): 267-270.

Engbring, J., et al. (1992). "Observations on the Defensive and Aggressive Behavior of the Leatherback Turtle (*Dermochelys coriacea*) at Sea." Herpetological Review 23(3): 70-71.

Estabrook, Barry (2001). "Sea Turtle Secrets." Wildlife Conservation 2001: 44-49.

Ferreira, B., M. Garcia, et al. (2006). "Diet of the Green Turtle (*Chelonia mydas*) At Ra's Al Hadd, Sultanate of Oman." Chelonian Cons Biol 5(1): 141-146.

Ficetola, G. F. (2008). "Impacts of Human Activities and Predators on the Nest Success of the Hawksbill Turtle, *Eretmochelys imbricata*, in the Arabian Gulf." Chelonian Cons Biol 7(2): 255-257.

Fitzsimmons, N. N., Limpus, C. J., et al. (1997). "Philopatry of Male Marine Turtles Inferred from Mitochondrial DNA Markers." Proceedings of the National Academy of Sciences of the United States of America 94(16): 8912-8917.

Foley, A. M., S. A. Peck, et al. (2006). "Effects of Sand Characteristics and Inundation on the Hatching Success of Loggerhead Sea Turtle (*Caretta caretta*) Clutches on Low-Relief Mangrove Islands in Southwest Florida." Chelonian Cons Biol 5(1): 32-41.

Fossette, S., C. Girard, et al. (2010). "Atlantic Leatherback Migratory Paths and Temporary Residence Areas." PLOS One 5(11): E13908.

Fossette, S., H. Corbel, et al. (2008). "An Alternative Technique For the Long-Term Satellite Tracking of Leatherback Turtles." Endang Species Res 4: 33–41.

Frick, M. G. and J. D. Zardus (2010). "First Authentic Report of the Turtle Barnacle *Cylindrolepas darwiniana* Since Its Description in 1916." J Crustacean Biol 30(2): 292-295.

Frick, M. G., et al. (2000). "Aerial Observations of Courtship Behavior in Loggerhead Sea Turtles (*Caretta caretta*) from Southeastern Georgia and Northeastern Florida." J Herpetol 34(1): 153-58.

Frick, M. G., J. D. Zardus, et al. (2010). "A New Coronuloid Barnacle Subfamily, Genus and Species From Cheloniid Sea Turtles." Bulletin of the Peabody Museum of Natural History 51(2): 169-177.

Frick, M. G., J. D. Zardus, et al. (2010). "A New *Stomatolepas* Barnacle Species (Cirripedia: Balanomorpha: Coronuloidea) From Leatherback Sea Turtles." Bulletin of the Peabody Museum of Natural History 51(1): 123-136.

Frick, M. G., J. D. Zardus, et al. (2011). "Novel Records and Observations of the Barnacle *Stephanolepas muricata* (Cirripedia: Balanomorpha: Coronuloidea); Including a Case For Chemical Mediation in Turtle and Whale Barnacles." J Nat Hist 45(11-12): 629-640.

Frick, M. G., K. L. Williams, et al. (1998). "Epibionts Associated with Nesting Loggerhead Sea Turtles (*Caretta caretta*) in Georgia, USA." Herpetological Review 29(4): 211-14.

Frick, M. G., K. L. Williams, et al. (2000). "Additional Evidence Supporting a Cleaning Association between Epibiotic Crabs and Sea Turtles: How Will the Harvest of Sargassum Seaweed Impact This Relationship?" Marine Turtle Newsletter 90: 11-13.

Frick, M. G., K. L. Williams, et al. (2004). "Diet and Fecundity of Columbus Crabs, Planes minutus, Associated with Oceanic-Stage Loggerhead Sea Turtles, *Caretta caretta*, and Inanimate Flotsam." J Crustacean Biol 24(2): 350-355.

Frick, M. G., K. L. Williams, et al. (2004). "New Records and Observations of Epibionts From Loggerhead Sea Turtles." Southeastern Naturalist 3(4): 613-620.

Fuller, W. J., A. C. Broderick, et al. (2008). "Utility of Geolocating Light Loggers For Indicating At-Sea Movements in Sea Turtles." Endangered Species Research 4: 139-146.

Fussy, A., P. Pommier, et al. (2007). "Chelonitoxism: New Case Reports in French Polynesia and Review of the Literature." Toxicon 49(6): 827-832.

Garmestani, A. S. and H. F. Percival (2005). "Raccoon Removal Reduces Sea Turtle Nest Depredation in the Ten Thousand Islands of Florida." Southeastern Naturalist 4(3): 469-472.

Garmestani, A. S., et al. (2000). "Nest-Site Selection by the Loggerhead Sea Turtle in Florida's Ten Thousand Islands." J Herpetol 34(4): 504-10.

Geis, A. A., W. J. Barichivich, et al. (2005). "Predicted Sex Ratio of Juvenile Kemp's Ridley Sea Turtles Captured Near Steinhatchee, Florida." Copeia 2005(2): 393-398.

Geis, A., T. Wibbels, et al. (2003). "Predicted Sex Ratio of Juvenile Hawksbill Seaturtles Inhabiting Buck Island Reef National Monument, U.S. Virgin Islands." J Herpetol 37(2): 400-404.

Glen, F., A. C. Broderick, et al. (2006). "Rhythmic Throat Oscillations in Nesting Green Turtles (*Chelonia mydas*)." Chelonian Cons Biol 5(2): 299-301.

Godley, B. J., C. Barbosa, et al. (2010). "Unravelling Migratory Connectivity in Marine Turtles Using Multiple Methods." J Applied Ecol 47(4): 769-778.

Godley, B. J., J. M. Blumenthal, et al. (2008). "Satellite Tracking of Sea Turtles: Where Have We Been and Where Do We Go Next?" Endangered Species Research 4: 3-22.

Green, D. (1993). "Growth Rates of Wild Immature Green Turtles in the Galápagos Islands, Ecuador." J Herpetol 27(3): 338-41.

Grossman, A., C. Sazima, et al. (2006). "Cleaning Symbiosis Between Hawksbill Turtles and Reef Fishes At Fernando De Noronha Archipelago, Off Northeast Brazil." Chelonian Cons Biol 5(2): 284-288.

Hall, S. C. B. and C. J. Parmenter (2008). "Necrotic Egg and Hatchling Remains Are Key Factors Attracting Dipterans to Sea Turtle (*Caretta caretta, Chelonia mydas, Natator depressus*) Nests in Central Queensland, Australia." Copeia 2008(1): 75-81.

Hamann, M., M. H. Godfrey, et al. (2010). "Global Research Priorities For Sea Turtles: Informing Management and Conservation in the 21st Century." Endangered Species Research 11(3): 245-269.

Hatase, H. and K. Tsukamoto (2008). "Smaller Longer, Larger Shorter: Energy Budget Calculations Explain Intrapopulation Variation in Remigration Intervals For Loggerhead Sea Turtles (*Caretta caretta*)." Canadian J Zool 86(7): 595-600.

Hatase, H., K. Omuta, et al. (2007). "Bottom or Midwater: Alternative Foraging Behaviours in Adult Female Loggerhead Sea Turtles." J Zool 273(1): 46-55.

Hatase, H., Y. Matsuzawa, et al. (2004). "Remigration and Growth of Loggerhead Turtles (*Caretta caretta*) Nesting on Senri Beach in Minabe, Japan: Life-History Polymorphism in a Sea Turtle Population." Marine Biology 144(4): 807-811.

Hawkes, L. A., A. C. Broderick, et al. (2007). "Only Some Like it Hot — Quantifying the Environmental Niche of the Loggerhead Sea Turtle." Diversity and Distributions 13(4): 447-457.

Hays, G. (2008). "Sea Turtles: a Review of Some Key Recent Discoveries and Remaining Questions." J Exp Mar Biol Ecol 356(1-2): 1-7.

Hays, G. C., S. Fossette, et al. (2010). "Breeding Periodicity For Male Sea Turtles, Operational Sex Ratios, and Implications in the Face of Climate Change." Conserv Biol 24(6): 1636-1643.

Heithaus, M., A. Frid, et al. (2002). "Shark-Inflicted Injury Frequencies, Escape Ability, and Habitat Use of Green and Loggerhead Turtles." Marine Biology 140(2): 229-236.

Hewavisenthi, S. and C. J. Parmenter (2002). "Egg Components and Utilization of Yolk Lipids During Development of the Flatback Turtle *Natator depressus*." J Herpetol 36(1): 43-50.

Hewavisenthi, S., C. J. Parmenter, et al. (2002). "Incubation Environment and Nest Success of the Flatback Turtle (*Natator depressus*) From a Natural Nesting Beach." Copeia 2002(2): 302-312.

Hilterman, M. L. and E. Goverse (2007). "Nesting and Nest Success of the Leatherback Turtle (*Dermochelys coriacea*) in Suriname, 1999–2005." Chelonian Cons Biol 6(1): 87-100.

Hitipeuw, C., P. H. Dutton, et al. (2007). "Population Status and Internesting Movement of Leatherback Turtles, *Dermochelys coriacea*, Nesting on the Northwest Coast of Papua, Indonesia." Chelonian Cons Biol 6(1): 28-36.

Hodge, R. P., and Wing, B. L. (2000). "Occurrences of Marine Turtles in Alaska Waters: 1960-1998." Herpetological Review 31(3): 148-51.

Huang, W. S., H. W. Greene, et al. (2011). "Territorial Behavior in Taiwanese Kukrisnakes (*Oligodon formosanus*)." Proc National Acad Sci USA 108(18): 7455-7459.

Ireland, J., A. Broderick, et al. (2003). "Multiple Paternity Assessed Using Microsatellite Markers, in Green Turtles *Chelonia mydas* (Linnaeus, 1758) of Ascension Island, South Atlantic." J Exp Mar Biol Ecol. 291(2): 149-160.

James, M. C., C. Andrea Ottensmeyer, et al. (2005). "Identification of High-Use Habitat and Threats to Leatherback Sea Turtles in Northern Waters: New Directions For Conservation." Ecology Letters 8(2): 195-201.

Jensen, M. P., F. A. Abreu-Grobois, et al. (2006). "Microsatellites Provide Insight Into Contrasting Mating Patterns in Arribada Vs. Non-Arribada Olive Ridley Sea Turtle Rookeries." Molecular Ecology 15(9): 2567-2575.

Johnson, S. A., and L. M. Ehrhart (1996). "Reproductive Ecology of the Florida Green Turtle: Clutch Frequency." J Herpetol 30 (3): 407-10.

Kakizoe, Y., M. Fujiwara, et al. (2010). "Cyclical Changes of Plasma Sex Steroids in Captive Breeding Loggerhead Turtles (*Caretta caretta*)." J Zoo Wildlife Med 41(4): 643-648.

Kamel, S. J. and E. Delcroix (2009). "Nesting Ecology of the Hawksbill Turtle, *Eretmochelys imbricata*, in Guadeloupe, French West Indies From 2000–07." J Herpetol 43(3): 367-376.

Kelle, L., N. Gratiot, et al. (2007). "Monitoring of Nesting Leatherback Turtles (*Dermochelys coriacea*): Contribution of Remote Sensing For Real-Time Assessment of Beach Coverage in French Guiana." Chelonian Cons Biol 6(1): 142-147.

Koch, A. U., M. L. Guinea, et al. (2008). "Asynchronous Emergence of Flatback Seaturtles, *Natator depressus*, From a Beach Hatchery in Northern Australia." J Herpetol 42(1): 1-8.

Lagarde, F., M. Le Corre, et al. (2001). "Species and Sex-Biased Predation on Hatchling Green Turtles By Frigatebirds on Europa Island, Western Indian Ocean." the Condor 103(2): 405-408.

Lamont, M. M. and R. R. Carthy (2007). "Response of Nesting Sea Turtles to Barrier Island Dynamics." Chelonian Cons Biol 6(2): 206-212.

Lazar, B., A. Žuljevic, et al. (2010). "Diet Composition of a Green Turtle, *Chelonia mydas*, From the Adriatic Sea." Nat. Croat. 19(1): 263-271.

Lee, P. (2008). "Molecular Ecology of Marine Turtles: New Approaches and Future Directions." J Exp Mar Biol Ecol 356(1-2): 25-42.

Lee, P. L., P. Luschi, et al. (2007). "Detecting Female Precise Natal Philopatry in Green Turtles Using Assignment Methods." Mol Ecol 16(1): 61-74.

Leighton, P. A., J. A. Horrocks, et al. (2011). "Predicting Nest Survival in Sea Turtles: When and Where Are Eggs Most Vulnerable to Predation?" Animal Conservation 14(2): 186-195.

Leslie, A. J., et al. (1996). "Leatherback Turtle, *Dermochelys coriacea*, Nesting and Nest Success at Tortuguero, Costa Rica, in 1990–1991." Chelonian Cons Biol 2(2): 159–68.

Limpus, C., and N. Nichols. (2000) "Enso Regulation of Indo-Pacific Green Turtle Populations." the Australian Experience. Ed. Hammer G.L. et al: Kluwer Academic Publishers, 2000. pp. 399-408.

Lohmann, K., P. Luschi, et al. (2008). "Goal Navigation and Island-Finding in Sea Turtles." J Exp Mar Biol Ecol 356(1-2): 83-95.

Manire, C. A., L. Byrd, et al. (2008). "Mating-Induced Ovulation in Loggerhead Sea Turtles, *Caretta caretta*." Zoo Biology 27(3): 213-225.

Mansfield, K. L., V. S. Saba, et al. (2009). "Satellite Tracking Reveals a Dichotomy in Migration Strategies Among Juvenile Loggerhead Turtles in the Northwest Atlantic." Marine Biology 156(12): 2555-2570.

Maros, A., A. Louveaux, et al. (2005). "Identifying Characteristics of *Scapteriscus* Spp. (Orthoptera: Gryllotalpidae) Apparent Predators of Marine Turtle Eggs." Environmental Entomology 34(5): 1063-1070.

Mazaris, A. D., A. S. Kallimanis, et al. (2009). "Sea Surface Temperature Variations in Core Foraging Grounds Drive Nesting Trends and Phenology of Loggerhead Turtles in the Mediterranean Sea." J Exp Mar Biol Ecol 379(1-2): 23-27.

Mcclellan, C. M., J. Braun-Mcneill, et al. (2010). "Stable Isotopes Confirm a Foraging Dichotomy in Juvenile Loggerhead Sea Turtles." J Exp Mar Biol Ecol 387(1-2): 44-51.

Mcgowan, A., L. V. Rowe, et al. (2001). "Nest Factors Predisposing Loggerhead Sea Turtle (*Caretta caretta*) Clutches to Infestation By Dipteran Larvae on Northern Cyprus." Copeia 2001(3): 808-812.

Mcmahon, C. R., C. J. A. Bradshaw, et al. (2007). "Satellite Tracking Reveals Unusual Diving Characteristics For a Marine Reptile, the Olive Ridley Turtle *Lepidochelys olivacea*." Mar Ecol Prog Ser 329: 239-252.

Meylan, P. A., E. S. Gaffney, et al. (2009). "*Caninemys*, a New Side-Necked Turtle (Pelomedusoides: Podocnemididae) From the Miocene of Brazil." American Museum Novitates 3639: 1-26.

Moncada, F., F. A. Abreu-Grobois, et al. (2006). "Movement Patterns of Green Turtles (*Chelonia mydas*) in Cuba and Adjacent Caribbean Waters Inferred From Flipper Tag Recaptures." J Herpetol 40(1): 22-34.

Moore, M. K. and J. R. M. Ball (2002). "Multiple Paternity in Loggerhead Turtle (*Caretta caretta*) Nests on Melbourne Beach, Florida: a Microsatellite Analysis " Molecular Ecology 11(281-288).

Morreale, S. J., Meylan, A. B., et al. (1992). "Annual Occurrence and Winter Mortality of Marine Turtles in New York Waters." J Herpetol 26(3): 301-08.

Mott, C. R. and M. Salmon (2011). "Sun Compass Orientation By Juvenile Green Sea Turtles (*Chelonia mydas*)." Chelonian Cons Biol 10(1): 73-81.

Moulis, R. A. (1997). "Predation by the Imported Fire Ant (*Scoenopsis invicta*) on Loggerhead Sea Turtle (*Caretta caretta*) Nests on Wassaw National Wildlife Refuge, Georgia." Chelonian Cons Biol 2(3): 433-36.

Nishizawa, H., J. Okuyama, et al. (2010). "Comparative Phylogeny and Historical Perspectives on Population Genetics of the Pacific Hawksbill (*Eretmochelys imbricata*) and Green Turtles (*Chelonia mydas*), Inferred From Feeding Populations in the Yaeyama Islands, Japan." Zool Sci 27(1): 14-18.

Ordoñez, C., S. Troëng, et al. (2007). "Chiriqui Beach, Panama, the Most Important Leatherback Nesting Beach in Central America." Chelonian Cons Biol 6(1): 122-126.

Özdemir, A., Ç. Ilgaz, et al. (2007). "An Assessment of Initial Body Size in Loggerhead Sea Turtle (*Caretta caretta*) Hatchlings in Turkey." Zool Sci 24(4): 376-380.

Parham, J. F., and G. R. Zug (1997). "Age and Growth of Loggerhead Sea Turtles (*Carretta caretta*) of Coastal Georgia: an Assessment of Skeletochronological Age-Estimates." Bulletin of Marine Science 61(2): 287-304.

Parris, L. B., M. M. Lamont, et al. (2002). "Increased Incidence of Red Imported Fire Ant (Hymenoptera: Formicidae) Presence in Loggerhead Sea Turtle (Testudines: Cheloniidae) Nests and Observations of Hatchling Mortality." Florida Entomologist 85(3): 514-517.

Pike, D. A. (2009). "Do Green Turtles Modify Their Nesting Seasons in Response to Environmental Temperatures?" Chelonian Cons Biol 8(1): 43-47.

Pike, D. A., R. L. Antworth, et al. (2006). "Earlier Nesting Contributes to Shorter Nesting Seasons For the Loggerhead Seaturtle, *Caretta caretta*." J Herpetol 40(1): 91-94.

Pilcher, N. (2010). "Population Structure and Growth of Immature Green Turtles At Mantanani, Sabah, Malaysia." J Herpetol 44(1): 168-171.

Pilcher, N. J., and M. Al-Merghani (2000). "Reproductive Biology of Green Turtles at Ras Baridi, Saudi Arabia." Herpetological Review 31(3): 142-47.

Plotkin, P. T. (1996). "Occurrence and Diet of Juvenile Loggerhead Sea Turtles, *Caretta caretta*, in the Northwestern Gulf of Mexico." Chelonian Cons Biol 2(1): 78-80.

Plotkin, P. T. (2010). "Nomadic Behaviour of the Highly Migratory Olive Ridley Sea Turtle *Lepidochelys olivacea* in the Eastern Tropical Pacific Ocean." Endangered Species Research 13(1): 33-40.

Polovina, J. J., G. H. Balazs, et al. (2004). "Forage and Migration Habitat of Loggerhead (*Caretta caretta*) and Olive Ridley (*Lepidochelys olivacea*) Sea Turtles in the Central North Pacific Ocean." Fish. Oceanogr. 13(1): 36-51.

Preen, A. R. (1996). "Infaunal Mining: a Novel Foraging Method of Loggerhead Turtles." J Herpetol 30(1): 94-96.

Price, E. R., B. P. Wallace, et al. (2004). "Size, Growth, and Reproductive Output of Adult Female Leatherback Turtles *Dermochelys coriacea* " Endangered Species Research 5: 1-8.

Putman, N. F., C. S. Endres, et al. (2011). "Longitude Perception and Bicoordinate Magnetic Maps in Sea Turtles." Curr Biol 21(6): 463-466.

Quiñones, J., V. González Carman, et al. (2010). "Effects of El Niño-Driven Environmental Variability on Black Turtle Migration to Peruvian Foraging Grounds." Hydrobiologia 645(1): 69-79.

Rees, A. F., S. Al Saady, et al. (2010). "Behavioural Polymorphism in One of the World's Largest Populations of Loggerhead Sea Turtles *Caretta caretta*." Marine Ecology Progress Series 418: 201-212.

Reina, R. D., P. A. Mayor, et al. (2002). "Nesting Ecology of the Leatherback Turtle, *Dermochelys coriacea*, At Parque Nacional Marino Las Baulas, Costa Rica: 1988-1989 to 1999-2000." Copeia 2002(3): 653-664.

Russell, D. J. and G. H. Balazs (2009). "Dietary Shifts By Green Turtles (*Chelonia mydas*) in the Kāne'ohe Bay Region of the Hawaiian Islands: a 28-Year Study." Pacific Science A63(2): 181-192.

Salmon, M., et al. (1995). "Behavior of Loggerhead Sea Turtles on an Urban Beach. I. Correlates of Nest Placement." J Herpetol 29(4): 560-67.

Salmon, M., et al. (1995). "Behavior of Loggerhead Sea Turtles on an Urban Beach. II. Hatching Orientation." J Herpetol 29(4): 568-76.

Salmon, M., T. Todd Jones, et al. (2004). "Ontogeny of Diving and Feeding Behavior in Juvenile Seaturtles: Leatherback Seaturtles (*Dermochelys coriacea* L) and Green Seaturtles (*Chelonia mydas* L) in the Florida Current." J Herpetol 38(1): 36-43.

Santos, A. J. B., E. M. X. Freire, et al. (2010). "Body Mass and the Energy Budget of Gravid Hawksbill Turtles (*Eretmochelys imbricata*) During the Nesting Season." J Herpetol 44(3): 352-359.

Sasso, C. R. and S. P. Epperly (2007). "Survival of Pelagic Juvenile Loggerhead Turtles in the Open Ocean." J Wildlife Manage 71(6): 1830-1835.

Sasso, C. R., J. Braun-Mcneill, et al. (2007). "Summer Abundance Estimates of *Caretta caretta* (Loggerhead Turtles) in Core Sound, Nc." Southeastern Naturalist 6(2): 365-369.

Schärer, M. T. and J. H. Epler (2007). "Long-Range Dispersal Possibilities Via Sea Turtle - a Case For *Clunio* and *Pontomyia* (Diptera: Chironomidae) in Puerto Rico." Entomological News 118(3): 273-277.

Schäuble, C., R. Kennett, et al. (2006). "Flatback Turtle (*Natator depressus*) Nesting At Field Island, Kakadu National Park, Northern Territory, Australia, 1990–2001." Chelonian Cons Biol 5(2): 188-194.

Schofield, G., C. M. Bishop, et al. (2007). "Novel Gps Tracking of Sea Turtles As a Tool For Conservation Management." J Exp Mar Biol Ecol 347(1-2): 58-68.

Segura, L. N. and R. Cajade (2010). "The Effects of Sand Temperature on Pre-Emergent Green Sea Turtle Hatchlings." Herpetological Conservation and Biology 5(2): 196-206.

Seminoff, J. A., A. Resendiz, et al. (2002). "Diet of East Pacific Green Turtles (*Chelonia mydas*) in the Central Gulf of California, México." J Herpetol 36(3): 447-453.

Seminoff, J. A., A. Resendiz, et al. (2002). "Growth Rates of Wild Green Turtles (*Chelonia mydas*) At a Temperate Foraging Area in the Gulf of California, Mexico." Copeia 2002(3): 610-617.

Seney, E. E. and J. A. Musick (2007). "Historical Diet Analysis of Loggerhead Sea Turtles (*Caretta caretta*) in Virginia." Copeia 2007(2): 478-489.

Senko, J., M. C. López-Castro, et al. (2010). "Immature East Pacific Green Turtles (*Chelonia mydas*) Use Multiple Foraging Areas Off the Pacific Coast of Baja California Sur, Mexico: First Evidence From Mark-Recapture Data." Pacific Science 64(1): 125-130.

Senko, J., V. Koch, et al. (2010). "Fine Scale Daily Movements and Habitat Use of East Pacific Green Turtles At a Shallow Coastal Lagoon in Baja California Sur, Mexico." J Exp Mar Biol Ecol 391(1-2): 92-100.

Sheil, C. A. and D. Portik (2008). "Formation and Ossification of Limb Elements in Trachemys Scripta and a Discussion of Autopodial Elements in Turtles." Zool Sci 25(6): 622-641.

Spring, C. S., and J. Gwyther (1999). "Stomach Contents of an Olive Ridley Turtle (*Lepidochelys olivacea*) from the Gulf of Papua, Papua New Guinea." Chelonian Cons Biol 3(3): 516-17.

Steckenreuter, A., N. Pilcher, et al. (2010). "Male-Biased Primary Sex Ratio of Leatherback Turtles (*Dermochelys coriacea*) At the Huon Coast, Papua New Guinea." Chelonian Cons Biol 9(1): 123-128.

Tiwari, M., and K. A. Bjorndal (2000). "Variation in Morphology and Reproduction in Loggerheads, *Caretta caretta*, Nesting in the United States, Brazil, and Greece." Herpetologica 56(3): 343-56.

Tomillo, P. S., F. V. Paladino, et al. (2010). "Predation of Leatherback Turtle Hatchlings During the Crawl to the Water." Chelonian Cons Biol 9(1): 18-25.

Tucker, A. D., and N. B. Frazer (1994). "Seasonal Variation in Clutch Size of the Turtle, *Dermochelys coriacea*." J Herpetol 28(1): 102-09.

Wallace, B. P., L. Avens, et al. (2009). "The Diet Composition of Immature Loggerheads: Insights on Trophic Niche, Growth Rates, and Fisheries Interactions." J Exp Mar Biol Ecol 373(1): 50-57.

Webster, W. D. and K. A. Cook (2001). "Intraseasonal Nesting Activity of Loggerhead Sea Turtles (*Caretta caretta*) in Southeastern North Carolina." Am Midl Nat145(1): 66-73.

Webster, W.D., and Cook, K.A. (2001). "Interseasonal Nesting Activity of Loggerhead Sea Turtles (*Caretta caretta*) in Southeastern North Carolina." Am Midl Nat 145(1): 66-73.

Weishampel, J. F., D. A. Bagley, et al. (2010). "Nesting Phenologies of Two Sympatric Sea Turtle Species Related to Sea Surface Temperatures." Endangered Species Research 12(1): 41-47.

Wetterer, J. K. and C. D. Lombard (2010). "Fire Ants (Hymenoptera: Formicidae) Along an Important Sea Turtle Nesting Beach on St. Croix, Usvi." Florida Entomologist 93(3): 449-450.

Whiting, S. D., and J. D. Miller (1998). "Short Term Foraging Ranges of Adult Green Turtles (*Chelonia mydas*)." J Herpetol 32(3): 330-37.

Whiting, S. D., J. L. Long, et al. (2007). "Migration Routes and Foraging Behaviour of Olive Ridley Turtles *Lepidochelys olivacea* in Northern Australia." Endang Species Res 3: 1-9.

Wibbels, T., D. Rostal, et al. (1998). "High Pivotal Temperature in the Sex Determination of the Olive Ridley Sea Turtle, *Lepidochelys olivacea*, from Playa Nancite, Costa Rica." Copeia 1998(4): 1086-88.

Wibbels, T., Owens, D. W., et al. (1991). "Soft Plastra of Adult Male Sea Turtles: an Apparent Secondary Sexual Characteristic." Herpetological Review 22(2): 47-49.

Wirsing, A. J., R. Abernethy, et al. (2008). "Speed and Maneuverability of Adult Loggerhead Turtles (*Caretta caretta*) Under Simulated Predatory Attack: Do the Sexes Differ?" J Herpetol 42(2): 411-413.

Witt, M. J., S. Åkesson, et al. (2010). "Assessing Accuracy and Utility of Satellite-Tracking Data Using Argos-Linked Fastloc-Gps." Animal Behaviour 80(3): 571-581.

Witzell, W. N., A. Salgado-Quintero, et al. (2005). "Reproductive Parameters of the Kemp's Ridley Sea Turtle (*Lepidochelys kempii*) At Rancho Nuevo, Tamaulipas, Mexico " Chelonian Cons Biol 4(4): 781-787.

Wood, D. W., and K. A. Bjorndal (2000). "Relation of Temperature, Moisture, Salinity, and Slope to Nest Site Selection in Loggerhead Sea Turtles." Copeia 2000(1): 119-28.

Yalçin-Özdilek, Ş. and M. Aureggi (2006). "Strandings of Juvenile Green Turtles At Samandağ, Turkey." Chelonian Cons Biol 5(1): 152-154.

Yalçin-Özdilek, Ş., H. G. Özdilek, et al. (2007). "Possible Influence of Beach Sand Characteristics on Green Turtle Nesting Activity on Samandağ Beach, Turkey." J Coastal Res 23(6): 1379-1390.

Yasuda, T. and N. Arai (2005). "Fine-Scale Tracking of Marine Turtles Using Gps-Argos Ptts." Zool Sci 22(5): 547-553.

Zug, G. R. (1991). "Estimates of Age and Growth in *Lepidochelys kempii* from Skeletochronological Data." Tenth Annual Workshop on Sea Turtle Biology and Conservation: NOAa Technical Memorandum, 1991. pp. 285-86.

Zug, G. R., H. J. Kalb, et al. (1997). "Age and Growth in Wild Kemp's Ridley Seaturtles *Lepidochelys kempii* from Skeletochronological Data." Biol Conserv 80: 261-68.

Chapter 9: Peril On Land

Altherr, S., and D. Freyer (2000). "Asian Turtles Are Threatened by Extinction." Turtle and Tortoise Newsletter 1: 7-11.

Alves, R. R. and G. G. Santana (2008). "Use and Commercialization of *Podocnemis expansa* (Schweiger 1812) (Testudines: Podocnemididae) For Medicinal Purposes in Two Communities in North of Brazil." J Ethnobiol Ethnomed 4: 3.

Anon. (2000). a Survey Report on Zambia as a Range State for Pancake Tortoise. 4: 1-5.

Anon. (2010). "Comments on the Proposed Conservation of Usage of *Testudo gigantea* Schweigger, 1812(Currently *Geochelone (Aldabrachelys) gigantea*) (Reptilia, Testudines) (Case 3463; See Bzn 66: 34–50, 80–87, 169–186; 274–290; 352–357)." Bulletin of Zoological Nomenclature 67(1).

Anon. (2012). "Wildlife trader Anson Wong freed after court reduces jail term." Star Publications (Malaysia) Bhd. Retreived on 7 May 2012 from thestar.com.my/news/story.asp?file=/2012/2/22/nation/20120222193558&sec=nation.

Aresco, M. J. (2005). "Mitigation Measures to Reduce Highway Mortality of Turtles and Other Herpetofauna At a North Florida Lake." the J Wildlife Manage 69(2): 549-560.

Aresco, M. J. and M. S. Gunzburger (2004). "Effects of Large-Scale Sediment Removal on Herpetofauna in Florida Wetlands." J Herpetol 38(2): 275-279.

Ashton, K. G. and R. L. Burke (2007). "Long-Term Retention of a Relocated Population of Gopher Tortoises." the J Wildlife Manage 71(3): 783-787.

Attum, O., M. Baha El Din, et al. (2007). "Egyptian Tortoise Conservation: a Community-Based, Field Research Program Developed From a Study on a Captive Population." Zoo Biology 26(5): 397-406.

Avissar, N. G. (2006). "Changes in Population Structure of Diamondback Terrapins (*Malaclemys terrapin terrapin*) in a Previously Surveyed Creek in Southern New Jersey." Chelonian Cons Biol 5(1): 154-159.

Baha El Din, S. "*Testudo kleinmanni* in Libya." Retrieved 11 September, 2011, From http://www.tortoisetrust.org/articles/libya.htm.

Barko, V. A., J. T. Briggler, et al. (2004). "Passive Fishing Techniques: a Cause of Turtle Mortality in the Mississippi River." J Wildlife Manage 68(4): 1145-1150.

Beaudry, F., P. G. Demaynadier, et al. (2010). "Identifying Hot Moments in Road-Mortality Risk For Freshwater Turtles." J Wildlife Manage 74(1): 152-159.

Beshkov, V. A., [translated by J. R. Buskirk] (1993 [1984]). "On Distribution, Relative Abundance and Protection of Tortoises in Bulgaria." Chelonian Cons Biol 1(1): 53-62.

Blanvillain, G., J. A. Schwenter, et al. (2007). "Diamondback Terrapins, *Malaclemys terrapin*, As a Sentinel Species For Monitoring Mercury Pollution of Estuarine Systems in South Carolina and Georgia, Usa." Environmental Toxicology and Chemistry 26(7): 1441-1450.

Blasco R, B. H., R. J, et al. (2011). "Earliest Evidence For Human Consumption of Tortoises in the European Early Pleistocene From Sima Del Elefante, Sierra De Atapuerca, Spain." J Hum Evol. 61(4): 503-509.

Bolton, R. M. and R. J. Brooks (2010). "Impact of the Seasonal Invasion of *Phragmites australis* (Common Reed) on Turtle Reproductive Success." Chelonian Cons Biol 9(2): 238-243.

Bombi, P., L. Luiselli, et al. (2011). "When the Method For Mapping Species Matters: Defining Priority Areas For Conservation of African Freshwater Turtles." Diversity and Distributions 2011: 1-12.

Bombi, P., M. D'amen, et al. (2009). "Will Climate Change Affect Terrapin (*Pelusios subniger paritalis* and *P. castanoides intergularis*) Conservation in Seychelles?" Phelsuma 17a(1-12).

Boullay, S. (1995). "Repatriation of Radiated Tortoises, *Geochelone radiata,* from Réunion Island to Madagascar." Chelonian Cons Biol 1(4): 319-20.

Boundy, J. and C. Kennedy (2006). "Trapping Survey Results For the Alligator Snapping Turtle (*Macrochelys temminckii*) in Southeastern Louisiana, with Comments on Exploitation." Chelonian Cons Biol 5(1): 3-9.

Brianti, E., F. Dantas-Torres, et al. (2010). "Risk For the Introduction of Exotic Ticks and Pathogens Into Italy Through the Illegal Importation of Tortoises, *Testudo graeca*." Medical and Veterinary Entomology 24(3): 336-339.

Brown, D. J., V. R. Farallo, et al. (2011). "Freshwater Turtle Conservation in Texas: Harvest Effects and Efficacy of the Current Management Regime." the J Wildlife Manage 75(3): 486-494.

Browne, C. and S. Hecnar (2007). "Species Loss and Shifting Population Structure of Freshwater Turtles Despite Habitat Protection." Biol Conserv 138(3-4): 421-429.

Budischak, S. A., J. M. Hester, et al. (2006). "Natural History of *Terrapene carolina* (Box Turtles) in an Urbanized Landscape." Southeastern Naturalist 5(2): 191-204.

Buhlmann, K. A., T. S. B. Akre, et al. (2009). "A Global Analysis of Tortoise and Freshwater Turtle Distributions with Identification of Priority Conservation Areas." Chelonian Cons Biol 8(2): 116-149.

Buskirk, J. R. (1996). "On the Absence of Spur-Thighed Tortoises, *Testudo graeca*, from Egypt." Chelonian Cons Biol 2(1): 118-20.

Butler, J. A., G. L. Heinrich, et al. (2006). "Third Workshop on the Ecology, Status, and Conservation of Diamondback Terrapins (*Malaclemys terrapin*): Results and Recommendations." Chelonian Cons Biol 5(2): 331-334.

Ceballos, C. P. and L. A. Fitzgerald (2004). "The Trade in Native and Exotic Turtles in Texas." Wildlife Society Bulletin 32(3): 881-891.

Chan, E.-H. and P.-N. Chen (2011). "Nesting Activity and Clutch Size of *Batagur affinis edwardmolli* From the Setiu River, Terengganu, Malaysia." Chelonian Cons Biol 10(1): 129–132.

Chen, T.-H., H.-C. Chang, et al. (2009). "Unregulated Trade in Turtle Shells For Chinese Traditional Medicine in East and Southeast Asia: the Case of Taiwan." Chelonian Cons Biol 8(1): 11-18.

Cheung, S. M. and D. Dudgeon (2006). "Quantifying the Asian Turtle Crisis: Market Surveys in Southern China, 2000–2003." Aquatic Conservation: Marine and Freshwater Ecosystems 16(7): 751-770.

Cites Secretariat (2008). Review of Significant Trade in Specimens of Appendix-II Species: Species Selected Following Cop13. CITES AC23 Doc. 8.4.

Close, L. M., and R. A. Seigel (1997). "Differences in Body Size among Populations of Red-Eared Sliders (*Trachemys scripta elegans*) Subjected to Different Levels of Harvesting." Chelonian Cons Biol 2(4): 563-66.

Conway-Gómez, K. (2007). "Effects of Human Settlements on Abundance of *Podocnemis unifilis* and *P. expansa* Turtles in Northeastern Bolivia." Chelonian Cons Biol 6(2): 199-205.

Daigle, C. and J. Jutras (2005). "Quantitative Evidence of Decline in a Southern Québec Wood Turtle (*Glyptemys insculpta*) Population." J Herpetol 39(1): 130-132.

Damania, R. and E. H. Bulte (2007). "The Economics of Wildlife

Farming and Endangered Species Conservation." Ecological Economics 62(3-4): 461-472.

Decatanzaro, R. and P. Chow-Fraser (2010). "Relationship of Road Density and Marsh Condition to Turtle Assemblage Characteristics in the Laurentian Great Lakes." J Great Lakes Res 36(2): 357-365.

Diemer B., J. E., L. D. Wendland, et al. (2000). "Distribution and Prevalence of Upper Respiratory Tract Disease in Gopher Tortoises in Florida." J Herpetol 34(1): 5-12.

Diesmos, A. C., R. M. Brown, et al. (2008). "Status and Distribution of Nonmarine Turtles of the Philippines." Chelonian Cons Biol 7(2): 157-177.

Dodd, C. K, Jr. (1997). "Clutch Size and Frequency in Florida Box Turtles (*Terrapene carolina bauri*) : Implications for Conservation." Chelonian Cons Biol 2(3): 370-77.

Doupé, R. G., J. Schaffer, et al. (2009). "A Description of Freshwater Turtle Habitat Destruction By Feral Pigs in Tropical North-Eastern Australia." Herpetological Conservation and Biology 4(3): 331-339.

Dreslik, M. J. (1998). "Current Status and Conservation of the River Cooter (*Pseudemys concinna*) in Southern Illinois." Chelonian Cons Biol 3(1): 135-37.

Durrell Wildlife Conservation Trust (2009). "Theft of World's Rarest Tortoises in Madagascar." Durrell News Wednesday 27 May 2009.

Durrell, L. (1994). "A is for Angonoka: the Ploughshare Tortoise Project and the ABC's of Species Conservation." Testudo 4(1).

Education For Nature - Vietnam (2010). Press Release: New Chelonian Visitor Center Promotes Conservation of Vietnam's Tortoises and Freshwater Turtles.

Eisemberg, C. C., M. Rose, et al. (2011). "Demonstrating Decline of an Iconic Species Under Sustained Indigenous Harvest – the Pig-Nosed Turtle (*Carettochelys insculpta*) in Papua New Guinea." Biol Conserv. 144(9): 2282-2288

Ernst, C. H., et al. (1999). "Shell Disease in Turtles in the Rappahannock River, Virginia." Herpetological Review 30(4): 214-15.

Farkas, B. L., L. Sasvári, et al. (1997). "Maximum Size of the Egyptian Tortoise, *Testudo kleinmanni*." Chelonian Cons Biol 2(3): 415.

Feng, H., N. Matsuki, et al. (1996). "Improvement of Fatigue and Acceleration of Recovery From Stress-Induced Deficient Sexual Behavior in Mice Following Oral Administration of Soft-Shelled Turtle Powder." Biol. Pharm. Bull. 19(11): 1447-1450.

Fernández-Chacón, A., A. Bertolero, et al. (2011). "Spatial Heterogeneity in the Effects of Climate Change on the Population Dynamics of a Mediterranean Tortoise." Global Change Biology 17(10): doi10.1111/j.1365-2486.2011.02469.x.

Fidenci, P. and J. Maran (2009). "Illegal Domestic Trade of the Philippine Forest Turtle (*Siebenrockiella leytensis*) in the Philippines." Turtlelog 3: 1-3.

Florida Fish and Wildlife Conservation Commission (2011). Biological Status Review For the Alligator Snapping Turtle (*Macrochelys temminckii*). 16 pp.

Florida Turtle Experts Working Group and IUCN/SSC Tortoise and Freshwater Turtle Specialist Group (2008). Scientific Concerns on Proposed Regulations of Florida's Commercial Softshell Turtle Harvest. Presentation to Governor Charlie Crist , 17 November 2008, Tallahassee, Florida.

Fordham, D. A., A. Georges, et al. (2007). "Demographic Response of Snake-Necked Turtles Correlates with Indigenous Harvest and Feral Pig Predation in Tropical Northern Australia." J Animal Ecol 76(6): 1231-1243.

Fordham, D. A., A. Georges, et al. (2008). "Indigenous Harvest, Exotic Pig Predation and Local Persistence of a Long-Lived Vertebrate: Managing a Tropical Freshwater Turtle For Sustainability and Conservation." J Applied Ecol 45(1): 52-62.

Fordham, D. A., A. Georges, et al. (2009). "Experimental Evidence For Density-Dependent Responses to Mortality of Snake-Necked Turtles." Oecologia 159(2): 271-281.

Fordham, D., A. Georges, et al. (2006). "Feral Pig Predation Threatens the Indigenous Harvest and Local Persistence of Snake-Necked Turtles in Northern Australia." Biol Conserv 133(3): 379-388.

Fratto, Z. W., V. A. Barko, et al. (2008). "Development and Efficacy of a Bycatch Reduction Device For Wisconsin-Type Fyke Nets Deployed in Freshwater Systems." Chelonian Cons Biol 7(2): 205-212.

Fratto, Z. W., V. A. Barko, et al. (2008). "Evaluation of Turtle Exclusion and Escapement Devices For Hoop-Nets." the J Wildlife Manage 72(7): 1628-1633.

Gaertner, J. P., D. Hahn, et al. (2008). "Detection of Salmonellae in Captive and Free-Ranging Turtles Using Enrichment Culture and Polymerase Chain Reaction." J Herpetol 42(2): 223-231.

Galois, P. and M. Ouellet (2007). "Traumatic Injuries in Eastern Spiny Softshell Turtles (*Apalone spinifera*) Due to Recreational Activities in the Northern Lake Champlain Basin." Chelonian Cons Biol 6(2): 288-293.

Gamble, T. and A. M. Simons (2004). "Comparison of Harvested and Nonharvested Painted Turtle Populations." Wildlife Society Bulletin 32(4): 1269-1277.

García, G. (2005). Ecology, Human Impact and Conservation For the Madagascan Side-Necked Turtle (*Erymnochelys madagascariensis* Grandidier, 1867) At Ankarafantsika National Park, Madagascar. Doctor of Philosophy, University of Kent.

Georges, A, and M. Rose (1993). "Conservation Biology of the Pig-nose Turtle, *Carettochelys insculpta*." Chelonian Cons Biol 1(1): 3-12.

Georges, A., F. Guarino, et al. (2006). "Freshwater Turtles of the Transfly Region of Papua New Guinea: Notes on Diversity, Distribution, Reproduction, Harvest and Trade." Wildlife Research 33(5): 373-384.

Gibbons, J. W., et al. (2000). "The Global Decline of Reptiles, Déjà Vu Amphibians." BioScience 50(8): 653-65.

Gibbs, J. P. and D. A. Steen (2005). "Trends in Sex Ratios of Turtles in the United States: Implications of Road Mortality." Conservation Biology 19(2): 552-556.

Gibbs, J. P. and W. G. Shriver (2002). "Estimating the Effects of Road Mortality on Turtle Populations." Conservation Biology 16(6): 1647-1652.

Golder, W., D. Lee, et al. (2000). "Terrapin Conservation Efforts." Turtle and Tortoise Newsletter 2: 7.

Gong, S.-P., A. T. Chow, et al. (2009). "The Chelonian Trade in the Largest Pet Market in China: Scale, Scope and Impact on Turtle Conservation." Oryx 43(2): 213-216.

Gonzalez, J. G. (1993). "Réunion Island - Still a Land of Tortoises." Chelonian Cons Biol 1(1): 51-52.

Gregory, R., and D. S. K. Sharma (1996). "Status of Federal and State Legislation Affecting Chelonian Conservation in Malaysia." Proc. 13th Annual Seminar of the Malaysian Society of Marine Sciences, 1996. pp. 89-97.

Grosse, A. M., J. D. Dijk, et al. (2009). "Diamondback Terrapin Mortality in Crab Pots in a Georgia Tidal Marsh." Chelonian Cons Biol 8(1): 98-100.

Hailey, A. (2000). "Implications of High Intrinsic Growth Rate of a Tortoise Population For Conservation." Animal Conservation 3(3): 185-189.

Haitao, S., J. F. Parham, et al. (2007). "Farming Endangered Turtles to Extinction in China." Conservation Biology 21(1): 5-6.

Haitao, S., J. F. Parham, et al. (2008). "Evidence For the Massive Scale of Turtle Farming in China." Oryx 42(1): 147-150.

Hidalgo-Vila, J., C. Diaz-Paniagua, et al. (2009). "Helminth Communities of the Exotic Introduced Turtle, *Trachemys scripta elegans* in Southwestern Spain: Transmission From Native Turtles." Res Vet Sci 86(3): 463-465.

Holliday, D. K., A. A. Elskus, et al. (2009). "Impacts of Multiple Stressors on Growth and Metabolic Rate of *Malaclemys terrapin*." Environmental Toxicology and Chemistry 28(2): 338-345.

Hong, M., H. Shi, et al. (2008). "Scientific Refutation of Traditional Chinese Medicine Claims About Turtles." Applied Herpetology 5: 173-187.

Hsieh, H.-M., L.-H. Huang, et al. (2006). "Species Identification of *Kachuga tecta* Using the Cytochrome B Gene." J Forensic Sci 51(1): 52-56.

Iskandar, D. T. and W. R. Erdelen (2006). "Conservation of Amphibians and Reptiles in Indonesia: Issues and Problems." Amphibian and Reptile Conservation 4(1): 60-87.

Iucn/Ssc Tortoise & Freshwater Turtle Specialist Group (2011). Implementation of Decision 14.128: a Study of Progress on Conservation of and Trade in CITES-Listed Tortoises and Freshwater Turtles in Asia. CITES SC61 Doc. 47 (Rev. 2) Annex 2.

Ives, I. E., S. G. Platt, et al. (2008). "Field Surveys, Natural History Observations, and Comments on the Exploitation and Conservation of *Indotestudo forstenii*, *Leucocephalon yuwonoi*, and *Cuora amboinensis* in Sulawesi, Indonesia." Chelonian Cons Biol 7(2): 240-248.

Jacobson, E.R., et al. (1995). "Mycoplasmosis and the Desert Tortoise (*Gopherus agassizii*) in Las Vegas Valley, Nevada." Chelonian Cons Biol 1(4): 279-84.

Jaffé, R., C. Peñaloza, et al. (2008). "Monitoring an Endangered Freshwater Turtle Management Program: Effects of Nest Relocation on Growth and Locomotive Performance of the Giant South American Turtle (*Podocnemis expansa*, Podocnemididae)." Chelonian Cons Biol 7(2): 213-222.

Jensen, J. B. and W. S. Birkhead (2003). "Distribution and Status of the Alligator Snapping Turtle (*Macrochelys temminckii*) in Georgia." Southeastern Naturalist 2(1): 25-34.

Jensen, K. A. and I. Das (2008). "Cultural Exploitation of Freshwater Turtles in Sarawak, Malaysian Borneo." Chelonian Cons Biol 7(2): 281-285.

Karlin, M. L. (2008). "Distribution of *Mycoplasma agassizii* in a Gopher Tortoise Population in South Florida." Southeastern Naturalist 7(1): 145-158.

Kemenes, A. and J. C. B. Pezzuti (2007). "Estimate of Trade Traffic of *Podocnemis* (Testudines, Pedocnemididae) From the Middle Purus River, Amazonas, Brazil." Chelonian Cons Biol 6(2): 259-262.

Kendrick, R. and G. Ades (2009). "Taxonomic and Morphometric Analysis of a Trade Confiscation of Turtle Shells From Java, Indonesia." Turtlelog: Online Newsletter of the Iucn/Ssc Tortoise and Freshwater Turtle Specialist Group: 1-4.

Klein, R. G. and K. Cruz-Uribe (2000). "Middle and Later Stone Age Large Mammal and Tortoise Remains From Die Kelders Cave 1, Western Cape Province, South Africa." J Human Evol 38: 169-195.

Klemens, M. W., and D. Moll (1995). "An Assessment of the Effects of Commercial Exploitation on the Pancake Tortoise, *Malacochersus tornieri*, in Tanzania." Chelonian Cons Biol 1(3): 197-206.

Kuchling, G., A. G. J. Rhodin, et al. (2007). "A New Subspecies of the Snakeneck Turtle *Chelodina mccordi* From Timor-Leste (East Timor) (Testudines: Chelidae)." Chelonian Cons Biol 6(2): 213-222.

Kuchling, G., and R. A. Mittermeier (1993). "Status and Exploitation of the Madagascar Big-Head Turtle, *Erymnochelys madagascariensis*." Chelonian Cons Biol 1(1): 13-18.

Lambert, M. R. K. (1993). "On Growth, Sexual Dimorphism, and the General Ecology of the African Spurred Tortoise, *Geochelone sulcata*, in Mali." Chelonian Cons Biol 1(1): 37-46.

Lee, D. S. and K. Smith (2010). "Testudostan: Our Post-Cold War Global Exploitation of a Noble Tortoise." Bull. Chicago Herp. Soc. 45(1): 1-9.

Lo, C.-F., Y.-R. Lin, et al. (2006). "Identification of Turtle Shell and Its Preparations By PCR-DNA Sequencing Method." Gene 14: 153-158.

Lowe, H. (2009). "The Globalization of the Turtle Trade." Tsa Magazine: 48-52.

Lowry, M. B., B. C. Pease, et al. (2005). "Reducing the Mortality of Freshwater Turtles in Commercial Fish Traps." Aquatic Conservation: Marine and Freshwater Ecosystems 15(1): 7-21.

Luiselli, L. (2009). "A Model Assessing the Conservation Threats to Freshwater Turtles of Sub-Saharan Africa Predicts Urgent Need For Continental Conservation Planning." Biodiversity and Conservation 18(5): 1349-1360.

Luiselli, L., et al. (1997) "Problems for Conservation of Pond Turtles (*Emys orbicularis*) in Central Italy: is the Introduced Red-Eared Turtle (*Trachemys scripta*) a Serious Threat?" Chelonian Cons Biol 2(3): 417-19.

Ly, T., H. D. Hoang, et al. (2011). "Market Turtle Mystery Solved in Vietnam." Biol Conserv. 144(5): 1767-1771

Malonza, P. K. (1999). "Status, Ecological Characteristics and Conservation of the Pancake Tortoise, *Malacochersus tornieri*, in Nguni and Nuu Areas, Kenya." M.Sc. Addis Ababa University.

Malonza, P. K. (2003). "Ecology and Distribution of the Pancake Tortoise, *Malacochersus tornieri* in Kenya." J East African Nat Hist 92(1): 81-96.

Marchand, M. N. and J. A. Litvaitis (2004). "Effects of Habitat Features and Landscape Composition on the Population Structure of a Common Aquatic Turtle in a Region Undergoing Rapid Development." Conservation Biology 18(3): 758-767.

Mccoy, E. D., H. R. Mushinsky, et al. (2007). "Conservation Strategies and Emergent Diseases: the Case of Upper Respiratory Tract Disease in the Gopher Tortoise." Chelonian Cons Biol 6(2): 170-176.

Mccoy, E. D., R. D. Moore, et al. (2011). "Effects of Rainfall and the Potential Influence of Climate Change on Two Congeneric Tortoise Species." Chelonian Cons Biol 10(1): 34-41.

Mcneish, H. (2011, 27 June). "Madagascar's 'Tortoise Mafia' on the Attack." Retrieved 3 July, 2011 from http://www.bbc.co.uk/news/world-africa-13799205.

Mogollones, S. C., D. J. Rodríguez, et al. (2010). "A Demographic Study of the Arrau Turtle (*Podocnemis expansa*) in the Middle Orinoco River, Venezuela." Chelonian Cons Biol 9(1): 79-89.

Múnera, M. B., J. M. D. R., et al. (2004). "Ecología Reproductiva y Cacería de la Tortuga *Trachemys scripta* (Testudinata: Emydidae), en el Área de la Depresión Momposina, Norte de Colombia." Rev. Biol. Trop. 52(1): 229-238.

Nazdrowicz, N. H., J. L. Bowman, et al. (2008). "Population Ecology of the Eastern Box Turtle in a Fragmented Landscape." J Wildlife Manage 72(3): 745-753.

Nijman, V. and C. R. Shepherd (2011). "The Role of Thailand in the International Trade in CITES-Listed Live Reptiles and Amphibians." Plos One: 6(3): E17825.

Nussbaum, R A., and C. J. Raxworthy (2000). "Commentary on the Conservation of "Sokatra", the Radiated Tortoise (*Geochelone radiata*) of Madagascar." Amphibian and Reptile Conservation 2(1): 6-14.

Ordorica, A. M., F. H. Pough, et al. (2008). "Seasonal Variations in Microbial Communities in the Nasal Passages of Captive Desert Tortoises." J Arizona-Nevada Acad Sci 40(2): 121-127.

Ozgul, A., M. K. Oli, et al. (2009). "Upper Respiratory Tract Disease, Force of Infection, and Effects on Survival of Gopher Tortoises." Ecological Applications 19(3): 786-798.

Padovani Haller, É. C. and M. T. Rodrigues (2006). "Reproductive Biology of the Six-Tubercled Amazon River Turtle *Podocnemis sextuberculata* (Testudines: Podocnemididae), in the Biological Reserve of Rio Trombetas, Pará, Brazil." Chelonian Cons Biol 5(2): 280-284.

Parham, J. F., W. B. Simison, et al. (2001). "New Chinese Turtles: Endangered or Invalid? a Reassessment of Two Species Using Mitochondrial DNA, Allozyme Electrophoresis and Known-Locality Specimens." Animal Conservation 4(4): 357-367.

Percipalle, M., G. Giardina, et al. (2011). "Salmonella Infection in Illegally Imported Spur-Thighed Tortoises (*Testudo graeca*)." Zoonoses and Public Health 58(4): 262-269.

Petty, A. M., P. A. Werner, et al. (2007). "Savanna Responses to Feral Buffalo in Kakadu National Park, Australia." Ecological Monographs 77(3): 441-463.

Pezuti, J. C. B., and R. C. Vogt (1999). "Nesting Ecology of *Podocnemis sextuberculata* (Testudines, Pelomedusidae) in the Japurá River, Amazonas, Brazil." Chelonian Cons Biol 3(3): 419-24.

Pezzuti, J. C. B., J. P. Lima, et al. (2010). "Uses and Taboos of Turtles and Tortoises Along Rio Negro, Amazon Basin." J Ethnobiol 30(1): 153-168.

Platt, K., S. G. Platt, et al. (2008). "Recent Records and Conservation Status of the Critically Endangered Mangrove Terrapin, *Batagur baska*, in Myanmar." Chelonian Cons Biol 7(2): 261-265.

Platt, S. G. (1994). "*Dermatemys mawei* (Central American River Turtle). Belize: Orange Walk District." Herpetological Review 25(2): 75.

Platt, S. G., H. Sovannara, et al. (2008). "Biodiversity, Exploitation, and Conservation of Turtles in the Tonle Sap Biosphere Reserve, Cambodia, with Notes on Reproductive Ecology of *Malayemys subtrijuga*." Chelonian Cons Biol 7(2): 195-204.

Plummer, M. V., D. G. Krementz, et al. (2008). "Effects of Habitat Disturbance on Survival Rates of Softshell Turtles (*Apalone spinifera*) in an Urban Stream." J Herpetol 42(3): 555-563.

Powell, R., et al. (2000). "Amphibians and Reptiles of the Dominican

Republic: Species of Special Concern." Oryx 34(2): 118-28.

Raxworthy, C. J., and R. A. Nussbaum (2000). "Extinction and Extinction Vulnerability of Amphibians and Reptiles in Madagascar." Amphibian and Reptile Conservation 2(1): 15-23.

Rhodin, A. G. J., R. A. Mittermeier, et al. (1993). "Distribution, Osteology, and Natural History of the Asian Giant Softshell Turtle, *Pelochelys bibroni*, in Papua New Guinea." Chelonian Cons Biol 1(1): 19-30.

Riedle, J. D., D. B. Ligon, et al. (2008). "Distribution and Management of Alligator Snapping Turtles, *Macrochelys temminckii*, in Kansas and Oklahoma." Transactions of the Kansas Academy of Science 111(1 &Amp; 2): 21-28.

Riedle, J. D., P. A. Shipman, et al. (2005). "Status and Distribution of the Alligator Snapping Turtle, *Macrochelys temminckii*, in Oklahoma." Southwest Nat 50(1): 79-84.

Rioux Paquette, S., B. H. Ferguson, et al. (2009). "Conservation Genetics of the Radiated Tortoise (*Astrochelys radiata*) Population From Andohahela National Park, Southeast Madagascar, with a Discussion on the Conservation of This Declining Species." Chelonian Cons Biol 8(1): 84-93.

Riyanto, A. (2006). "Notes on Exploitation, Population Status, Distribution, and Natural History of the Sulawesi Forest Turtle (*Leucocephalon yuwonoi*) in North-Central Sulawesi, Indonesia." Chelonian Cons Biol 5(2): 320-323.

RSPCA (2001). Shell Shock: the Continuing Illegal Trade in Tortoises. Horsham, UK.

Salzberg, A. (1998). "Chelonian Conservation News." Chelonian Cons Biol 3(1): 147-50.

Saumure, R. A., and J. R. Bider (1998). "Impact of Agricultural Development on a Population of Wood Turtles (*Clemmys insculpta*) in Southern Québec, Canada." Chelonian Cons Biol 3(1): 37-45.

Sautner, S. (2000). "A Boost for Brazilian River Turtles." Wildlife Conservation 2000: 17.

Schneider, L., C. R. Ferrara, et al. (2011). "History of Turtle Exploitation and Management Techniques to Conserve Turtles in the Rio Negro Basin of the Brazilian Amazon." Chelonian Cons Biol 10(1): 149-157.

Schoppe, S. (2008). the Southeast Asian Box Turtle *Cuora amboinensis* (Daudin, 1802) in Indonesia. NDF Workshop Case Studies 2. Cancun, Mexico.

Schoppe, S., J. Matillano, et al. (2010). "Conservation Needs of the Critically Endangered Philippine Forest Turtle, *Siebenrockiella leytensis*, in Palawan, Philippines." Chelonian Cons Biol 9(2): 145-153.

Seigel, R. A., and J. W. Gibbons (1995). "Workshop on the Ecology, Status, and Management of the Diamondback Terrapin (*Malaclemys terrapin*), Savannah River Ecology Laboratory, 2 August 1994: Final Results and Recommendations." Chelonian Cons Biol 1(3): 240-43.

Seigel, R. A., R. B. Smith, et al. (2003). "Swine Flu or 1918 Pandemic? Upper Respiratory Tract Disease and the Sudden Mortality of Gopher Tortoises (*Gopherus polyphemus*) on a Protected Habitat in Florida." J Herpetol 37(1): 137-144.

Senneke, D. (2006). "Declared Turtle Trade From the United States." Retrieved 10 September, 2011, From http://www.chelonia.org/articles/us/usmarket_51.htm.

Sharma, D. S. K. (1996). "Conservation of the Painted Terrapin (*Callagur borneoensis*) in Peninsular Malaysia." Conservation and Faunal Biodiversity in Malaysia. Eds. Zainal Abidin Abu Hassan and Zubaid Akbar. pp. 78-92.

Sharma, D. S. K. (1996). "Threats to the Survival of the Painted Terrapin (*Callagur borneoensis*) in Peninsular Malaysia." Proc. 13th Annual Seminar of the Malaysian Society of Marine Sciences. pp. 77-87.

Sharma, D. S. K., I. N. Louis, et al. (1996). "A Review of the Impacts of Coastal, Offshore and Riverine Development on Marine Turtles and Terrapins." National Seminar/Workshop on Marine Turtle and Terrapin Management.

Shepherd, C. R. and B. Ibarrondo (2005). "The Trade of the Roti Island Snake-Necked Turtle *Chelodina mccordi*." TRAFFIC Southeast Asia.

Shi, H., and J. F. Parham (2001). "Preliminary Observations of a Large Turtle Farm in Hainan Province, People's Republic of China." Turtle and Tortoise Newsletter 3: 4-6.

Shipman, P. A. and J. D. Riedle (2008). "Status and Distribution of the Alligator Snapping Turtle (*Macrochelys temminckii*) in Southeastern Missouri." Southeastern Naturalist 7(2): 331-338.

Sloan, K. N., and K. A. Buhlmann (1996). "Stomach Contents of Commercially Harvested Adult Alligator Snapping Turtles, *Macroclemys temminckii*." Chelonian Cons Biol 2(1): 96-99.

Sloan, K., and J. E. Lovich (1995). "Exploitation of the Alligator Snapping Turtle, *Macroclemys temminckii*, in Louisana: a Case Study." Chelonian Cons Biol 1(3): 221-22.

Spencer, R.-J. and F. J. Janzen (2010). "Demographic Consequences of Adaptive Growth and the Ramifications For Conservation of Long-Lived Organisms." Biol Conserv 143(9): 1951-1959.

Steen, D. A. and J. P. Gibbs (2004). "Effects of Roads on the Structure of Freshwater Turtle Populations." Conservation Biology 18(4): 1143-1148.

Steen, D. A., M. J. Aresco, et al. (2006). "Relative Vulnerability of Female Turtles to Road Mortality." Animal Conservation 9(3): 269-273.

Stengel, C. J., C. R. Shepherd, et al. (2011). the Trade in Tortoises and Freshwater Turtles in Jakarta Revisited. Petaling Jaya, Selangor, Malaysia, TRAFFIC Southeast Asia.

Stuart, B. L. and J. F. Parham (2006). "Recent Hybrid Origin of Three Rare Chinese Turtles." Conservation Genetics 8: 169-175.

Timmins, R. J., and K. Khounboline (1999). "Occurrence and Trade of the Golden Turtle, *Cuora trifasciata*, in Laos." Chelonian Cons Biol 3(3): 441-47.

Todd, M. (2011). Trade in Malagasy Reptiles and Amphibians in Thailand. Petaling Jaya, Selangor, Malaysia, TRAFFIC Southeast Asia.

Townsend, W. R., A. Randall Borman, et al. (2005). "Cofán Indians' Monitoring of Freshwater Turtles in Zábalo, Ecuador." Biodiversity and Conservation 14(11): 2743-2755.

Trakimas, G. and J. Sidaravičius (2008). "Road Mortality Threatens Small Northern Populations of the European Pond Turtle, *Emys orbicularis*." Acta Herpetologica 3(2): 161-166.

Trauth, S. E., J. D. Wilhide, et al. (1998). "Population Structure and Movement Patterns of Alligator Snapping Turtles (*Macroclemys temminckii*) in Northeastern Arkansas." Chelonian Cons Biol 3(1): 64-70.

Tuberville, T. D., E. E. Clark, et al. (2005). "Translocation As a Conservation Tool: Site Fidelity and Movement of Repatriated Gopher Tortoises (*Gopherus polyphemus*)." Animal Conservation 8(4): 349-358.

Tucker, J. K., C. R. Dolan, et al. (2008). "Climatic Warming, Sex Ratios, and Red-Eared Sliders (*Trachemys scripta elegans*) in Illinois." Chelonian Cons Biol 7(1): 60-69.

Türkozan, O. and C. Yilmaz (2008). "Loggerhead Turtles, *Caretta caretta*, At Dalyan Beach, Turkey: Nesting Activity (2004–2005) and 19-Year Abundance Trend (1987–2005)." Chelonian Cons Biol 7(2): 178-187.

Türkozan, O., A. Özdemir, et al. (2008). "International Testudo Trade." Chelonian Cons Biol 7(2): 269-274.

Turtle Conservation Centre. (2011). "Setiu River Terrapin Recovery Project." Retrieved 7 September, 2011, from http://www.turtleconservationcentre.org/projects/terrapin-recovery-project/.

Turtle Conservation Coalition [Rhodin, A. G. J., Walde, A.D., Horne, B.D., Van Dijk, P.P., Blanck, T., and Hudson, R. (Eds.)], (2011). Turtles in Trouble: the World's 25+ Most Endangered Tortoises and Freshwater Turtles—2011. Lunenburg, Ma, Iucn/Ssc Tortoise and Freshwater Turtle Specialist Group, Turtle Conservation Fund, Turtle Survival Alliance, Turtle Conservancy, Chelonian Research Foundation, Conservation International, Wildlife Conservation Society, and San Diego Zoo Global.

UNEP-WCMC (2010). Review of Significant Trade: Species Selected By the CITES Animals Committee Following Cop14. CITES AC25 Doc. 9.4 Annex.

Van Dijk, P. P., B. L. Stuart, et al. (2000). "Asian Turtle Trade: Proceedings of a Workshop on Conservation and Trade of Freshwater Turtles and Tortoises in Asia." Chelonian Research Monographs 2: 1-164.

Vasudevan, K. (1998). "Reproductive Ecology of the Indian Softshell Turtle, *Aspideretes gangeticus*, in Northern India." Chelonian Cons Biol 3(1): 96-99.

Walde, A. D., M. L. Harless, et al. (2007). "Anthropogenic Threat to the Desert Tortoise (*Gopherus agassizii*): Litter in the Mojave Desert." Western North American Naturalist 67(1): 147-149.

Walker, R. C. J. (2010). "The Decline of the Critically Endangered Northern Madagascar Spider Tortoise (*Pyxis arachnoides brygooi*)." Herpetologica 66(4): 411-417.

Wimberger, K., A. J. Armstrong, et al. (2009). "Can Rehabilitated Leopard Tortoises, *Stigmochelys pardalis*, Be Successfully Released into the Wild?" Chelonian Cons Biol 8(2): 173-184.

Wolak, M. E., G. W. Gilchrist, et al. (2010). "A Contemporary, Sex-Limited Change in Body Size of an Estuarine Turtle in Response to Commercial Fishing." Conservation Biology 24(5): 1268-1277.

Zhou, T., C. Huang, et al. (2008). "Captive Breeding of Hard-Shelled Chelonians in China." Reptilia (GB) 61: 27-34.

Zhou, Z. and Z. Jiang (2009). "Characteristics and Risk Assessment of International Trade in Tortoises and Freshwater Turtles in China." Chelonian Cons Biol 7(1): 28-36.

Chapter 10: Peril At Sea

Aguirre, A. A. (1998). "Fibropapillomas in Marine Turtles: a Workshop at the 18th Annual Symposium on Biology and Conservation of Sea Turtles." Marine Turtle Newsletter 82: 10-12.

Alfaro-Shigueto, J., P. H. Dutton, et al. (2007). "Interactions Between Leatherback Turtles and Peruvian Artisanal Fisheries." Chelonian Cons Biol 6(1): 129-134.

AlKindi, A. Y. A., I. Y. Mahmoud, et al. (2006). "The Effect of Physical and Human Factors on Beach Selection by Green Turtles (*Chelonia mydas*) at Ras Al-Hadd Reserve, Oman." Chelonian Cons Biol 5(2): 289-294.

Anon. "Indian Ocean - South-East Asian Marine Turtle Memorandum of Understanding." Retrieved 13 September, 2011, from http://www.ioseaturtles.org/index.php.

Anon. (2010). "India: 'Theeram' protects Olive Ridley turtles." Retrieved 13 September, 2011, from http://www.ioseaturtles.org/headline_detail.php?id=2140.

Arthur, K., C. Limpus, et al. (2008). "The Exposure of Green Turtles (*Chelonia mydas*) to Tumour Promoting Compounds Produced By the Cyanobacterium *Lyngbya majuscula* and Their Potential Role in the Aetiology of Fibropapillomatosis." Harmful Algae 7(1): 114-125.

Balazs, G. H., et al. (1998). "Manifestation of Fibropapillomatosis and Rates of Growth of Green Turtles at Kaneohe Bay in the Hawaiian Islands." Proceedings of the Eighteenth International Sea Turtle Symposium, March 3-7, 1998, Mazatlan, Sinaloa, Mexico. Ed. R. Briseno-Duenas F. A. Abreu-Grobois, R. Marquez-Millan, and L. Sarti-Martinez. Vol. U.S. Dep. Commer. NOAa Tech. Memo. NMFS-SEFSC-436. pp. 112-13.

Basheer, M. P. (2003). "Guardians of Sea Turtles." Retrieved 13 September, 2011, From http://www.indiatogether.org/2003/jan/env-turtker.htm.

Bates, H. W. (1864). The Naturalist on the River Amazons. a Record of Adventures, Habits of Animals, Sketches of Brazilian and Indian Life, and Aspects of Nature under the Equator, During Eleven Years of Travel. 2d ed. London: J. Murray.

Beggs, J. A., J. A. Horrocks, et al. (2007). "Increase in Hawksbill Sea Turtle *Eretmochelys imbricata* Nesting in Barbados, West Indies." Endangered Species Research 3: 159-168.

Bell, C. D., J. L. Solomon, et al. (2007). "Monitoring and Conservation of Critically Reduced Marine Turtle Nesting Populations: Lessons From the Cayman Islands." Animal Conservation 10(1): 39-47.

Bell, C. D., J. M. Blumenthal, et al. (2009). "Investigating Potential For Depensation in Marine Turtles: How Low Can You Go?" Conservation Biology 24(1): 226-235.

Bennett, P., U. Keuper-Bennett, et al. (1999). "Remigration and Residency of Hawaiian Green Turtles in Coastal Waters of Honokowai, West Maui, Hawaii." Proceedings of the Nineteenth Annual Symposium on Sea Turtle Biology and Conservation, March 2-6, 1999, South Padre Island, Texas. Pp. 37-39: U.S. Dep. Commer. NOAa Tech. Memo. NMFS-SEFSC-443. pp. 37-39.

Bennett, P., U. Keuper-Bennett, et al. (2001). "The Eyes Have It: Manifestation of Ocular Tumors in the Green Turtle Ohana of Honokowai, West Maui, Hawaii." 21st Annual Sea Turtle Symposium, February 24-28, 2001.

Bhupathy, S. and S. Saravanan (2006). "Status of Marine Turtles in the Gulf of Mannar, India." Chelonian Cons Biol 5(1): 139-141.

Bjorndal, K. A. (1999). "Conservation of Hawksbill Sea Turtles: Perceptions and Realities." Chelonian Cons Biol 3(2): 174-76.

Blumenthal, J. M., T. J. Austin, et al. (2009). "Ecology of Hawksbill Turtles, *Eretmochelys imbricata*, on a Western Caribbean Foraging Ground." Chelonian Cons Biol 8(1): 1-10.

Bogaert, O. V. (2007). "A Second Chance For Bali's Marine Turtles." Retrieved 12 September 2011, 2011, From http://wwf.panda.org/?unewsid=96340.

Bowen, B. W., W. S. Grant, et al. (2007). "Mixed-Stock Analysis Reveals the Migrations of Juvenile Hawksbill Turtles (*Eretmochelys imbricata*) in the Caribbean Sea." Molecular Ecology 16(1): 49-60.

Bräutigam, A. and K. L. Eckert (2006). Turning the Tide: Exploitation, Trade and Management of Marine Turtles in the Lesser Antilles, Central America, Colombia and Venezuela. Cambridge, UK, TRAFFIC International.

Brodie, J., M. Sanjayan, et al. (2008). "Effects of the 2004 Indian Ocean Tsunami on Sea Turtle Populations in Sri Lanka." Chelonian Cons Biol 7(2): 249-251.

Buitrago, J., H. J. Guada, et al. (2008). "Conservation Science in Developing Countries: an Inside Perspective on the Struggles in Sea Turtle Research and Conservation in Venezuela." Environmental Science & Policy 11(6): 562-578.

Caillouet, C. W., Jr, et al. (1995). "Survival of Head-Started Kemp's Ridley Sea Turtles (*Lepidochelys kempii*) Released into the Gulf of Mexico or Ajacent Bays." Chelonian Cons Biol 1(4): 285-92.

Caillouet, C. W., Jr. et al. (1995). "Growth of Head-Started Kemp's Ridley Sea Turtles (*Lepidochelys kempii*) Following Release." Chelonian Cons Biol 1(3): 231-34.

Campbell, L. M. (2002). "Science and Sustainable Use: Views of Marine Turtle Conservation Experts." Ecological Applications 12(4): 1229-1246.

Campbell, L. M. (2007). "Local Conservation Practice and Global Discourse: a Political Ecology of Sea Turtle Conservation." Annals of the Association of American Geographers 97(2): 313-334.

Campbell, L. M., B. J. Haalboom, et al. (2007). "Sustainability of Community-Based Conservation: Sea Turtle Egg Harvesting in Ostional (Costa Rica) Ten Years Later." Environmental Conservation 34: 122-131.

Casale, P. (2011). "Sea Turtle By-Catch in the Mediterranean." Fish and Fisheries 12(3): 299-316.

Catry, P., C. Barbosa, et al. (2009). "Status, Ecology, and Conservation of Sea Turtles in Guinea-Bissau." Chelonian Cons Biol 8(2): 150-160.

Chacón-Chaverri, D. and K. L. Eckert (2007). "Leatherback Sea Turtle Nesting At Gandoca Beach in Caribbean Costa Rica: Management Recommendations From Fifteen Years of Conservation." Chelonian Cons Biol 6(1): 101-110.

Chaloupka, M., G. H. Balazs, et al. (2009). "Rise and Fall Over 26 Years of a Marine Epizootic in Hawaiian Green Sea Turtles." J Wildlife Diseases 45(4): 1138-1142.

Chan, E.-H., and H.-C. Liew (1996). "Decline of the Leatherback Population in Terengganu, Malaysia, 1956–1995." Chelonian Cons Biol 2(2): 196–203.

Chan, S. K.-F., I. J. Cheng, et al. (2007). "A Comprehensive Overview of the Population and Conservation Status of Sea Turtles in China." Chelonian Cons Biol 6(2): 185-198.

Chaves, A., et al. (1996). "Biology and Conservation of Leatherback Turtles, *Dermochelys coriacea*, at Playa Langosta, Costa Rica." Chelonian Cons Biol 2(2): 184–89.

Cray, C., R. Varella, et al. (2001). "Altered In Vitro Immune Responses in Green Turtles (*Chelonia mydas*) with Fibropapillomatosis." J Zoo Wildlife Med 32(4): 436-440.

Crowder, L. (2000). "Leatherback's Survival Will Depend on an International Effort." Nature 405: 881.

Daley, B., P. Griggs, et al. (2008). "Exploiting Marine Wildlife in Queensland: the Commercial Dugong and Marine Turtle Fisheries, 1847–1969." Australian Economic History Review 48(3): 227-265.

Dampier, W. (1698). A New Voyage Round the World. Describing Particularly, the Isthmus of America, Several Coasts and Islands in the West Indies, the Isles of Cape Verd, the Passage by Terra Del Fuego, the South Sea Coasts of Chili, Peru, and Mexico; the Isle of Guam One of the Ladrones, Mindanao, and Other Philippine and East-India Islands near Cambodia, China, Formosa, Luconia, Celebes, &C. New Holland, Sumatra, Nicobar Isles; the Cape of Good Hope, and Santa Hellena. Their Soil, Rivers, Harbours, Plants, Fruits, Animals, and Inhabitants. Their Customs, Religion, Government, Trade, &C. 3d cor. ed. London: Printed for J. Knapton.

Donnelly, M. (2008). "Trade Routes For Tortoiseshell." Swot Report 3: 24-25.

Eckert, K. L. and A. H. Hemphill (2005). "Sea Turtles As Flagships For Protection of the Wider Caribbean Region." MAST 3(2) and 4(1): 119-143.

Eckert, S. A., and L. Sarti (1997). "Distant Fisheries Implicated in the Loss of the World's Largest Leatherback Nesting Population." Marine Turtle Newsletter 78: 2-7.

Eguchi, T., T. Gerrodette, et al. (2007). "At-Sea Density and Abundance Estimates of the Olive Ridley Turtle *Lepidochelys olivacea* in the Eastern Tropical Pacific." Endangered Species Research 3: 191-203.

Fao (2004). Report of the Expert Consultation on Interactions Between Sea Turtles and Fisheries within an Ecosystem Context. Rome, Italy, 9-12 March 2004. Fao Fisheries Report. Rome. No. 738: 37p.

Ferraro, P. J. and H. Gjertsen (2009). "A Global Review of Incentive Payments For Sea Turtle Conservation." Chelonian Cons Biol 8(1): 48-56.

Ferreira, R. L., H. R. Martins, et al. (2001). "Impact of Swordfish Fisheries on Sea Turtles in the Azores." Arquipelago 18a: 75-79.

Fleming, E. H. (2001). Swimming against the Tide: Recent Surveys of Exploitation, Trade, and Management of Marine Turtles in the Northern Caribbean. TRAFFIC North America, Washington, D.C.

Fosdick, P. (1994). Last Chance Lost?: Can and Should Farming Save the Green Sea Turtle? the Story of Mariculture Ltd., Cayman Turtle Farm. York, PA: Irvin S. Naylor.

Frazier, J. (1997). "Guest Editorial: Inter-American Convention for the Protection and Conservation of Sea Turtles." Marine Turtle Newsletter 78: 7-13.

Frazier, J. A. (2005). "Special Issues: Marine Turtles As Flagships." Mast 3(2): 5-38 and 4(1): 213-240.

Garland, K. A. and R. R. Carthy (2010). "Changing Taste Preferences, Market Demands and Traditions in Pearl Lagoon, Nicaragua: a Community Reliant on Green Turtles For Income and Nutrition." Conservation and Society 8(1): 55.

Gilman, E. (2009). Proceedings of the Technical Workshop on Mitigating Sea Turtle Bycatch in Coastal Net Fisheries. 20-22 January 2009, Honolulu, U.S.A. Honolulu; Gland, Switzerland; Bangkok; and Pascagoula, Usa, Western Pacific Regional Fishery Management Council, Iucn, Southeast Asian Fisheries Development Center, Indian Ocean - South-East Asian Marine Turtle Mou, U.S. National Marine Fisheries Service, Southeast Fisheries Science Center.

Gilman, E., E. Zollett, et al. (2006). "Reducing Sea Turtle By-Catch in Pelagic Longline Fisheries." Fish and Fisheries 7(1): 2-23.

Gilman, E., J. Gearhart, et al. (2010). "Mitigating Sea Turtle By-Catch in Coastal Passive Net Fisheries." Fish and Fisheries 11(1): 57-88.

Gjertsen, H. and E. Niesten (2010). "Incentive-Based Approaches in Marine Conservation: Applications For Sea Turtles." Conservation and Society 8(1): 5.

Godley, B., A. Broderick, et al. (2004). an Assessment of the Status and Exploitation of Marine Turtles in the Uk Overseas Territories in the Wider Caribbean. Final Project Report For the Department of Environment, Food and Rural Affairs and the Foreign and Commonwealth Office: 253 pp.

Grayson, J., M. Hamann, et al. (2010). "Options For Managing the Sustainable Use of Green Turtles: Perceptions of Hammond Islanders in Torres Strait." Conservation and Society 8(1): 73.

Greenblatt, R. J., T. M. Work, et al. (2005). "Geographic Variation in Marine Turtle Fibropapillomatosis." J Zoo Wildlife Med 36(3): 527-530.

Gunn, R. and T. Veenstra (2009). "Ghost Nets." SWOT Report 4: 31-33.

Haas, H. L. (2010). "Using Observed Interactions Between Sea Turtles and Commercial Bottom-Trawling Vessels to Evaluate the Conservation Value of Trawl Gear Modifications." Marine and Coastal Fisheries: Dynamics, Management, and Ecosystem Science 2(1): 263-276.

Hamann, M., C. Limpus, et al., Eds. (2006). Assessment of the Conservation Status of the Leatherback Turtle in the Indian Ocean and South-East Asia Iosea Species Assessment: Volume I.

Hernández, R., J. Buitrago, et al. (2007). "Nesting Distribution and Hatching Success of the Leatherback, *Dermochelys coriacea*, in Relation to Human Pressures At Playa Parguito, Margarita Island, Venezuela." Chelonian Cons Biol 6(1): 79-86.

Holloway-Adkins, K., and L. M. Ehrhart (2004). "A Comparison of Habitat Foraging Ecology and the Biotoxin Okadaic Acid in Five Florida Populations of *Chelonia mydas*." Proceedings of the Twenty-first Annual Symposium on Sea Turtle Biology and Conservation, February 24-28, 2001, Philadelphia, Pennsylvania. U.S. Dep. Commer., NOAa Tech. Memo. NMFS-SEFSC.

Horrocks, J. A., B. H. Krueger, et al. (2011). "International Movements of Adult Female Hawksbill Turtles (*Eretmochelys imbricata*): First Results From the Caribbean's Marine Turtle Tagging Centre." Chelonian Cons Biol 10(1): 18-25.

Horrocks, J. A., B. H. Krueger, et al. (2011). "International Movements of Adult Female Hawksbill Turtles (*Eretmochelys imbricata*): First Results From the Caribbean's Marine Turtle Tagging Centre." Chelonian Cons Biol 10(1): 18-25.

Howell, E. A., D. R. Kobayashi, et al. "Turtlewatch." SWOT Report 4: 36-37.

Howell, E. A., D. R. Kobayashi, et al. (2008). "Turtlewatch: a Tool to Aid in the Bycatch Reduction of Loggerhead Turtles *Caretta caretta* in the Hawaii-Based Pelagic Longline Fishery." Endangered Species Research 5: 267-278.

Hughes, G. R. (1996). "Nesting of the Leatherback Turtle (*Dermochelys coriacea*) in Tongaland, Kwazulu-Natal, South Africa, 1963–1995." Chelonian Cons Biol 2(2): 153–58.

Iac Pro Tempore Secretariat (2011). "Cooperating to Conserve Sea Turtles - the Inter- American Convention For the Protection and Conservation of Sea Turtles Celebrates Its 10 Year Anniversary, May 2011."

Innis, C., M. Tlusty, et al. (2008). "Trace Metal and Organochlorine Pesticide Concentrations in Cold-Stunned Juvenile Kemp's Ridley Turtles (*Lepidochelys kempii*) From Cape Cod, Massachusetts." Chelonian Cons Biol 7(2): 230-239.

James, M. C., C. Andrea Ottensmeyer, et al. (2005). "Identification of High-Use Habitat and Threats to Leatherback Sea Turtles in Northern Waters: New Directions For Conservation." Ecology Letters 8(2): 195-201.

Jensen, A. (2009). "Shifting Focus: Redefining the Goals of Sea Turtle Consumption and Protection in Bali." ISP Collection Paper 753.

Khan, M. Z., S. A. Ghalib, et al. (2010). "Status and New Nesting Sites of Sea Turtles in Pakistan." Chelonian Cons Biol 9(1): 119-123.

Landry, M. and C. Taggart (2010). ""Turtle Watching" Conservation Guidelines: Green Turtle (*Chelonia mydas*) Tourism in Nearshore Coastal Environments." Biodiversity and Conservation 19(1): 305-312.

Leroux, G., B. Rakotonirina, et al. (2010). "First Report of *Chelonia mydas* Affected By Cutaneous Fibropapillomatis on the West Coast of Madagascar " Indian Ocean Turtle Newsletter 11: 13-17.

Lewison, R. L., S. A. Freeman, et al. (2004). "Quantifying the Effects of Fisheries on Threatened Species: the Impact of Pelagic Longlines on Loggerhead and Leatherback Sea Turtles." Ecology Letters 7(3): 221-231.

Limpus, C. J. (1997). "Marine Turtle Populations of Southeast Asia and the Western Pacific Region: Distribution and Status." Proceedings of the Workshop on Marine Turtle Research and Management in Indonesia. pp. 37-71.

Long, K. J. and B. A. Schroeder (2004). Proceedings of the International Technical Expert Workshop on Marine Turtle Bycatch in Longline Fisheries. . U.S. Dep. Commerce, Noaa Technical Memorandum Nmfs-F/Opr-26.

Mancini, A. and V. Koch (2009). "Sea Turtle Consumption and Black Market Trade in Baja California Sur, Mexico." Endangered Species Research 7(1): 1-10.

Marcovaldi, M. A., G. G. Lopez, et al. (2007). "Fifteen Years of Hawksbill Sea Turtle (*Eretmochelys imbricata*) Nesting in Northern Brazil." Chelonian Cons Biol 6(2): 223-228.

Martínez, L. S., A. R. Barragán, et al. (2007). "Conservation and Biology of the Leatherback Turtle in the Mexican Pacific." Chelonian Cons Biol 6(1): 70-78.

Mcclenachan, L., J. B. C. Jackson, et al. (2006). "Conservation Implications of Historic Sea Turtle Nesting Beach Loss." Frontiers in Ecology and the Environment 4(6): 290-296.

Moore, J. E., T. M. Cox, et al. (2010). "An Interview-Based Approach to Assess Marine Mammal and Sea Turtle Captures in Artisanal Fisheries." Biol Conserv in Press, Corrected Proof.

Mortimer, J. A. and M. Donnelly (2007). "Marine Turtle Specialist Group 2007 Iucn Red List Status Assessment: Hawksbill Turtle (*Eretmochelys imbricata*)."

Mrosovsky, N. (2000). Sustainable Use of Hawksbill sea turtles: Contemporary Issues in Conservation. Issues in Wildlife Management No. 1. Darwin: Key Centre for Tropical Wildlife Management.

Murray, K. (2009). "Characteristics and Magnitude of Sea Turtle Bycatch in Us Mid-Atlantic Gillnet Gear." Endangered Species Research 8(3): 211-224.

Murthy, K. L. N. and K. V. R. Murthy (2011). "Mass Mortality of *Lepidochelys olivacea* Observed At Kottapeta Beach in Srikakulam Along the East Coast of Andhra Pradesh, India." Indian Ocean Turtle Newsletter 14: 15-17.

Nancarrow, K. and J. Bavas. (September 09, 2011). "Minister Rejects Probe Into Turtle, Dugong Poaching Claims." ABC News, From http://www.abc.net.au/news/2011-09-09/minister-rejects-probe-into-turtle-dugong-poaching-claims/2878450.

Petro, G., F. R. Hickey, et al. (2007). "Leatherback Turtles in Vanuatu." Chelonian Cons Biol 6(1): 135-137.

Pilcher, N. J. and C. Robins (2010). "Trials and Tribulations of Turtle Excluder Devices." Swot Report 4: 18-21.

Pilcher, N. J., E. H. Chan, et al. (2008). "Mass Turtle Poaching: a Case Study From Southeast Asia." SWOT Report 3: 26-27.

Plot, V. and J.-Y. Georges (2010). "Plastic Debris in a Nesting Leatherback Turtle in French Guiana." Chelonian Cons Biol 9(2): 267-270.

Pritchard, P .C. H. (2000). "A Response to Nicholas Mrosovsky's *Sustainable Use of Hawksbill sea turtles: Contemporary Issues in Conservation*." Chelonian Cons Biol 3(4): 761-67.

Pritchard, P. C. H. (1996). "Are Leatherbacks Really Threatened with Extinction?" Chelonian Cons Biol 2(2): 303–06.

Rice, R. (2006). "Understanding the Incentive: How One Community Conserves Turtle, Reef, and Forest." SWOT Report 1: 23.

Richardson, P. (2000). "Obstacles to Objectivity: First Impressions of a Cites COP." Marine Turtle Newsletter 89: 1-4.

Richardson, P. B., A. C. Broderick, et al. (2006). "Marine Turtle Fisheries in the Uk Overseas Territories of the Caribbean: Domestic Legislation and the Requirements of Multilateral Agreements." J Intl Wildlife Law & Policy 9(3): 223-246.

Richardson, P. B., M. W. Bruford, et al. (2009). "Marine Turtles in the Turks and Caicos Islands: Remnant Rookeries, Regionally Significant Foraging Stocks, and a Major Turtle Fishery." Chelonian Cons Biol 8(2): 192-207.

Santidrián Tomillo, P., E. Vélez, et al. (2007). "Reassessment of the Leatherback Turtle (*Dermochelys coriacea*) Nesting Population At Parque Nacional Marino Las Baulas, Costa Rica: Effects of Conservation Efforts." Chelonian Cons Biol 6(1): 54-62.

Santidrián Tomillo, P., V. S. Saba, et al. (2008). "Effects of Illegal Harvest of Eggs on the Population Decline of Leatherback Turtles in Las Baulas Marine National Park, Costa Rica." Conservation Biology 22(5): 1216-1224.

Sea Turtle Restoration Project (2012). "New Leatherback Safe Haven Makes Headlines." Retreived 6 May 2012 from http://www.seaturtles.org/article.php?id=2215.

Sella, K. N., M. Salmon, et al. (2006). "Filtered Streetlights Attract Hatchling Marine Turtles." Chelonian Cons Biol 5(2): 255-261.

Seminoff, J. A., A. Resendiz, et al. (2002). "Diet of East Pacific Green Turtles (*Chelonia mydas*) in the Central Gulf of California, México." J Herpetol 36(3): 447-453.

Senko, J., A. J. Schneller, et al. (2011). "People Helping Turtles, Turtles Helping People: Understanding Resident Attitudes Towards Sea Turtle Conservation and Opportunities For Enhanced Community Participation in Bahia Magdalena, Mexico." Ocean & Coastal Management 54(2): 148-157.

Senko, J., W. J. Nichols, et al. (2009). "to Eat or Not to Eat an Endangered Species: Views of Local Residents and Physicians on the Safety of Sea Turtle Consumption in Northwestern Mexico." Ecohealth 6(4): 584-595.

Simberloff, D., A. F. Rees, et al. (2009). "Filling in the Gaps: New Insights Into Old Questions About Sea Turtle Biology." SWOT Report 4: 14-17.

Spotila, J. R., et al. (1996). "Worldwide Population Declines of *Dermochelys coriacea*: Are Leatherback Turtles Going Extinct?" Chelonian Cons Biol 2(2): 209–22.

Spotila, J. R., Reina, R. D., et al. (2000). "Pacific Leatherback Turtles Face Extinction." Nature 405: 529-30.

Stamper, M. A., C. W. Spicer, et al. (2009). "Morbidity in a Juvenile Green Sea Turtle (*Chelonia mydas*) Due to Ocean-Borne Plastic." J Zoo Wildlife Med 40(1): 196-198.

Steiner, T. M., R. Arauz Vargas, et al. (1998) "First Record of Fibropapilloma on an Olive Ridley Turtle in Nicaragua." Chelonian Cons Biol 3(1): 105.

Stewart, K., M. Sims, et al. (2011). "Leatherback Nests Increasing Significantly in Florida, Usa; Trends Assessed Over 30 Years Using Multilevel Modeling." Ecological Applications 21(1): 263-273.

Suárez, A. (2001). "The Sea Turtle Harvest in the Kai Islands, Indonesia." Asian Review of Biodiversity and Environmental Conservation Arbec July-Sept. 2001.

Suarez, A. and C. H. Starbird (1996). "Subsistence Hunting of Leatherback Turtles, *Dermochelys coriacea*, in the Kai Islands, Indonesia." Chelonian Cons Biol 2(2): 190–95.

Swimmer, J. Y. (2006). "Relationship Between Basking and Fibropapillomatosis in Captive Green Turtles (*Chelonia mydas*)." Chelonian Cons Biol 5(2): 305-309.

Swimmer, J. Y. and E. Gilman (2006). "Fishing Technology Gears Up For Turtle Conservation." SWOT Report 1: 24-25.

Swimmer, Y. and R. Brill (2006). "Sea Turtle and Pelagic Fish Sensory Biology: Developing Techniques to Reduce Sea Turtle Bycatch in Longline Fisheries." NOAA Technical Memorandum NMFS-PIFSC-7.

Sydney Morning Herald. (September 9, 2011). "Aboriginal Clans Agree to Stop Hunting Dugong." Retrieved 12 September, 2011, From http://www.smh.com.au/environment/animals/aboriginal-clans-agree-to-stop-hunting-dugong-20110909-1k0q1.html.

Thomé, J. C. A., C. Baptistotte, et al. (2007). "Nesting Biology and Conservation of the Leatherback Sea Turtle (*Dermochelys coriacea*) in the State of Espírito Santo, Brazil, 1988–1989 to 2003–2004." Chelonian Cons Biol 6(1): 15-27.

Troëng, S. and C. Drews (2004). Money Talks: Economic Aspects of Marine Turtle Use and Conservation. Gland, Switzerland, WWF-International.

Tyning, T. F., ed. (1997). Status and Conservation of Turtles of the Northeastern United States: a Symposium. Lanesboro, MN: Serpent's Tale.

UNEP/CMS, ed. (2000). Conservation Measures for Marine Turtles of the Atlantic Coast of Africa. Cms Technical Series Publication No. 5. Bonn: UNEP/ CMS Secretariat.

van Dijk, P. P., B. L. Stuart, et al., eds. (2000). Asian Turtle Trade: Proceedings of a Workshop on Conservation and Trade of Freshwater Turtles and Tortoises in Asia, Phnom Penh, Cambodia, 1–4 December 1999. Lunenburg, MA: Chelonian Research Foundation.

Van Houtan, K. S. and J. M. Halley (2011). "Long-Term Climate Forcing in Loggerhead Sea Turtle Nesting." PLOS One 6(4): E19043.

Van Houtan, K. S., S. K. Hargrove, et al. (2010). "Land Use, Macroalgae, and a Tumor-Forming Disease in Marine Turtles." PLOS One 5(9): E12900.

Waayers, D. (2006). "Potential For Developing Marine Turtle Tourism As an Alternative to Hunting in Bali, Indonesia." Indian Ocean Turtle Newsletter 4: 12-14.

Wallace, B. P., A. D. Dimatteo, et al. (2010). "Regional Management Units For Marine Turtles: a Novel Framework For Prioritizing Conservation and Research Across Multiple Scales." PLOS One 5(12): E15465.

WWF Global (2011). "Simple Changes in Fishing Gear Can Save Tens of Thousands of Endangered Marine Turtles in the Coral Triangle." Retrieved 14 September, 2011, from http://www.smartgear.org/?199315/simple-changes-in-fishing-gear-can-save-tens-of-thousands-of-endangered-marine-turtles-in-the-Coral-Triangle.

Index